# essentials of marketing THIRD EDITION

## Supporting resources

Visit **www.pearsoned.co.uk/brassington** or register now at
**www.pearsoned.co.uk/mymarketinglab** to find valuable online resources:

### For students

- Self-assessment questions to help you identify your strengths
  and weaknesses.
- Study Plan to help you focus on where to improve.
- Mini-simulations – make marketing decisions and see their impact
  within real business scenarios.
- Podcasts and Newsfeeds to keep you up to date with developments in
  the professional world of marketing.
- E-book version of this textbook for when you're on the go.
- Online gradebook to help you track your progress.
- Video case studies from market-leading organisations and executives.

### For instructors

- Instructor's Manual for the book.
- PowerPoint slides to accompany the book.
- Editable online test banks with automatic grading.
- 'MyResourceBank' – a bank of resources including videos, PowerPoints
  and audio files for you to assign to your students.

For more information please contact your local Pearson Education sales
representative or visit **www.pearsoned.co.uk/brassington**

# essentials of
# marketing

## THIRD EDITION

## Dr Frances Brassington
Principal Lecturer, Oxford Brookes University

## Dr Stephen Pettitt
Former Deputy Vice Chancellor, University of Bedfordshire
and
Marketing Consultant

**PEARSON**

Harlow, England • London • New York • Boston • San Francisco • Toronto • Sydney • Auckland • Singapore • Hong Kong
Tokyo • Seoul • Taipei • New Delhi • Cape Town • São Paulo • Mexico City • Madrid • Amsterdam • Munich • Paris • Milan

Pearson Education Limited
Edinburgh Gate
Harlow
Essex CM20 2JE
England

and Associated Companies throughout the world

*Visit us on the World Wide Web at*:
www.pearson.com/uk

First published 2005
Second edition published 2007
**Third edition published 2013**

ISBN 978-0-273-72764-4

British Library Cataloguing-in-Publication Data
A catalogue record for this book is available from the British Library

Library of Congress Cataloging-in-Publication Data
Brassington, Frances.
  Essentials of marketing / Frances Brassington, Stephen Pettitt. -- 3rd ed.
      p. cm.
  Includes bibliographical references and index.
  ISBN 978-0-273-72764 4 (alk. paper)
 1. Marketing. I. Pettitt, Stephen. II. Title.
  HF5415.B6336 2013
  658.8--dc23
                                2012028708

10 9 8 7 6 5 4 3
16 15 14 13

Typeset in 10/12 minion by 30
Printed and bound by L.E.G.O. S.p.A., Italy

# Brief contents

# Contents

# Guided tour of the book & MyMarketingLab

Snappy **examples** appear in every chapter, illustrating how marketing has been used in a wide range of countries, products and industries.

**Marketing in Action** boxes showcase the application of marketing in the real world, and highlight the importance of an ethical approach to marketing decision-making and practice.

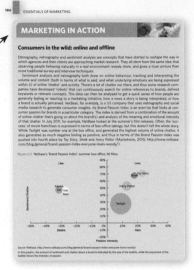

**Questions for Review and Discussion** help you to check your understanding of the topic, stimulate further investigation and encourage debate.

Each chapter ends with a **Case Study** that gives you the opportunity to discuss an organisation's marketing approach.

**References** are included for each chapter, to help you take your studies further in the real world.

# This book is also available with **MyMarketingLab.**

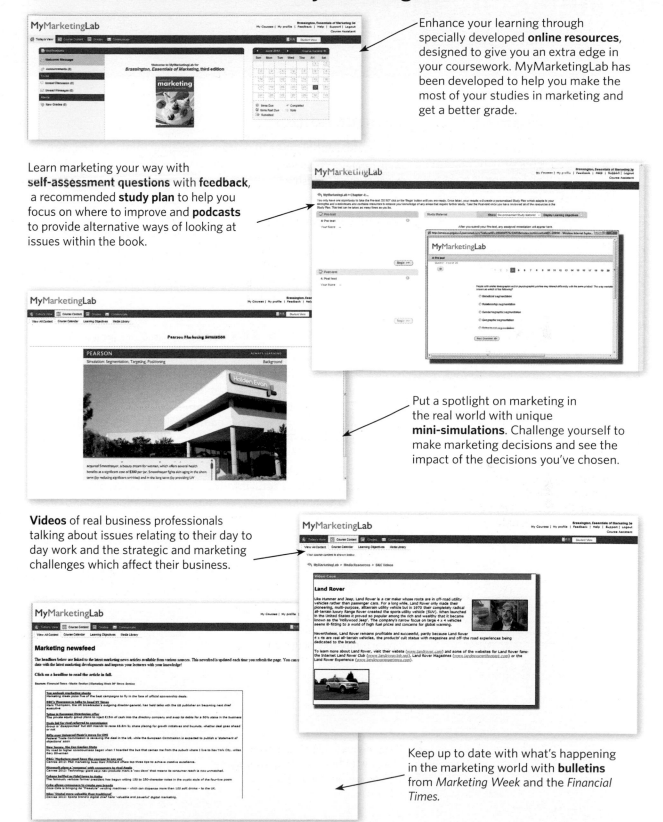

Enhance your learning through specially developed **online resources**, designed to give you an extra edge in your coursework. MyMarketingLab has been developed to help you make the most of your studies in marketing and get a better grade.

Learn marketing your way with **self-assessment questions** with **feedback**, a recommended **study plan** to help you focus on where to improve and **podcasts** to provide alternative ways of looking at issues within the book.

Put a spotlight on marketing in the real world with unique **mini-simulations**. Challenge yourself to make marketing decisions and see the impact of the decisions you've chosen.

**Videos** of real business professionals talking about issues relating to their day to day work and the strategic and marketing challenges which affect their business.

Keep up to date with what's happening in the marketing world with **bulletins** from *Marketing Week* and the *Financial Times*.

**Buy it now at www.pearsoned.co.uk/mymarketinglab**

# Endorsements

## Praise for the previous edition...

*Essentials of Marketing* is the quintessential guide to current marketing thinking. The core concepts of marketing are imaginatively conveyed and reinforced with topical vignettes and cases. An essential read for all marketing students.

*Noel Dennis, Senior Lecturer in Marketing, Teesside University Business School*

The second edition of *Essentials of Marketing* is clearly written, with lots of appropriate examples and illustrations, so the reader can see how the key marketing principles are applied in real life.

*Marianne Hough, Westminster Business School, University of Westminster*

## Praise from Amazon – readers' reviews...

**Very useful for Marketers**. As a second year marketing student this book has come into good use for me. I'm studying various modules at the moment which each come with a recommended book from my tutor; however I am always able to refer to this book additionally, with it sometimes even being better than my more module specific books. Overall a well-written, easy to navigate and very user-friendly book which covers the essential aspects of marketing in sound depth.

**Market this**. This is not a book that you would read from cover to cover; it's more of a detailed reference book providing some very useful information, very easy to navigate through. It is also what I would call thought-provoking. An all-round useful addition to my working and university life.

# Preface

*Essentials of Marketing* is a concise, no-nonsense book, which is designed to contain all the essential information that students need to understand when taking a short introductory course. This book brings together theory and practice. It covers a wide range of applications, industries and markets, exploring the ways in which marketers respond to situations that demand an innovative response. In preparing this new edition, we have particularly focused on understanding how the fast-evolving area of digital marketing is being integrated into marketing thinking and practice. Much that was innovative when we produced the second edition is now mainstream, and since then the emergence of social media and advances in technology that have opened up tools such as m-marketing, s-marketing and f-marketing have made a huge impact on the marketing landscape. Similarly, we have reinforced the emphasis on corporate social responsibility and marketing ethics in this edition, again in line with the increasing importance of these concepts to practising marketers.

We hope that you enjoy working with this textbook and that you find it thought-provoking and stimulating. And of course, we wish you every success in your marketing studies.

## Distinctive features

Written in a lively, elegant style, *Essentials of Marketing* features the following:

- Up-to-date vignettes and examples from a range of industries, organisations and countries.
- End-of-chapter questions to reinforce understanding.
- Real-world case studies designed for discussion drawn from a range of small, medium and large-sized companies.
- Vibrant and fresh text design and imagery offers a wide and provocative range of real-world marketing campaigns.
- A strong focus on CSR and the ethical dilemmas that marketers face.

# About the authors

**Frances Brassington** is a Principal Lecturer in Marketing at Oxford Brookes University Faculty of Business. She graduated from the University of Bradford Management Centre with a BSc (Hons) in business studies and a PhD. She has taught marketing at all levels and on a wide range of undergraduate marketing modules and programmes and has supervised a number of PhD research students. Her own research interests include retail marketing, international marketing and the use of project-based learning in marketing education. She has also designed and delivered marketing programmes for managers and academics in Poland and Bulgaria and has given guest lectures in China and South Africa.

**Stephen Pettitt** is a former Deputy Vice Chancellor of the University of Bedfordshire. He is currently undertaking consultancy projects in marketing and higher education. Previously he was the Pro Vice Chancellor and Dean of Luton Business School, and before that he was Director of Corporate Affairs at the University of Teesside. He has had, therefore, the opportunity to practise and plan marketing as well as being a marketing educator. He also worked at the University of Limerick in Ireland for four years as a Lecturer in Marketing and was the Managing Director of The Marketing Centre for Small Business, a campus company specialising in research and consultancy for the small business sector.

He worked initially in various sales and marketing management posts for Olivetti, Plessey and SKF before taking up a career in higher education. He holds a bachelor's degree in geography and an MBA and PhD from Cranfield. In addition to a wide experience in marketing education at all levels, he has undertaken numerous in-company training, research and consultancy assignments. He has lectured in marketing and entrepreneurship in France, Poland, Bulgaria, Slovakia, South Africa, Switzerland, the USA and Kenya. He has published over 30 papers and articles along with major studies in tourism innovation strategies, large buyer–small firm seller relationships and small firm development.

# Acknowledgements

This is the third edition of *Essentials of Marketing* and there are many people who have helped, directly and indirectly, in its development. Without them it could not have been done.

We would like to offer general thanks to all those individuals and organisations who directly and indirectly have helped to create the examples, case studies and 'Marketing in Action' profiles. In particular, our grateful thanks go to **Hilary Fletcher** and **Vicky Sparks** of ECCO Oxford who so generously provided the material for the Chapter 11 case study.

**Lorna Young's** work on the examples, cases and vignettes for Chapters 5 and 9 has been invaluable for this edition. Her extensive experience as a practitioner and consultant in the market research and advertising industries, as well as her teaching experience, have made a brilliant and insightful contribution. Once again, our most sincere thanks to you, Lorna.

Particular thanks are due to **Alison Prior** for her hard work and resourcefulness in sourcing all the photographs. Her diplomatic skills and patience have been tested to the full, and she's come through with flying colours. Thank you so much for bearing with us, Alison.

We'd also like to thank **Tracy Panther** who provided the basis for the Wrigley's case study in Chapter 2. This case has evolved over the last few years, tracking developments in the marketplace as they happen, and has provided the basis for some fascinating seminar discussions. Thank you Tracy, and thank you also to all the seminar tutors who have worked with this case and given us feedback on it.

The evolution of this book would not have been possible without the support, understanding and constructive feedback that we have received from colleagues. They have offered constructive insights and feedback on various aspects of the book as well as continuing to supply coffee, comradeship and consolation as appropriate. Affectionate and heartfelt thanks, therefore, go to them all.

We would also like to thank all those in the Pearson Education team who have helped to bring this third edition to fruition. In particular, we thank Rachel Gear (Editor in Chief), Amanda McPartlin (Acquisitions Editor), Philippa Fiszzon (Desk Editor) and Maggie Wells (Designer). Their continuous encouragement, support and occasional nagging have been crucial in getting this edition finished. We also thank the unsung heroes behind the scenes: Helene Bellofatto (freelance copy editor), Mavis Collins (freelance permissions editor), Stephen York (freelance proofreader), Doreen Magowan (freelance indexer), Alison Prior (freelance picture researcher) and all of those involved in production, marketing, distribution and sales who have made this book the polished, professional package that it is. They've obviously read it!

We were greatly encouraged by the enthusiasm with which the first two editions were received and thank all of you who adopted and used them. We hope you enjoyed the experience and that you will find this third edition even more stimulating. We have appreciated the reviews and feedback (both formal and informal) that we have had from lecturers and students alike.

# Publisher's acknowledgements

We are grateful to the following for permission to reproduce copyright material:

### Figures

Figure 3.2 from *Change4Life One Year On*, Department of Health (2010) p. 23, © Crown copyright 2010, http://www.dh.gov.uk/prod_consum_dh/groups/dh_digitalassets/@dh/@en /documents/digitalasset/dh_115511.pdf, Crown Copyright material is reproduced with the permission of the Controller, Office of Public Sector Information (OPSI); Figure 6.7 adapted from *Diffusion of Innovations*, 4th ed., The Free Press (Rogers, E.M. 1962) Figure 7–2, p. 262, Copyright © 1995 by Everett M. Rogers, Copyright 1962, 1971, 1983 by The Free Press, all rights reserved, reprinted with the permission of Free Press, a Division of Simon & Schuster, Inc.; Figure 9.2 adapted from *Marketing Communications: From Fundamentals to Strategies*, Txt, 1st ed. (Rothschild, M. 1987) © 1987 South-Western, a part of Cengage Learning, Inc., reproduced by permission, www.cengage.com/permissions; Figure 13.7 from Strategies for Diversification, *Harvard Business Review*, Vol. 25 (5), pp. 113–25 (Ansoff, H.I. 1957), Sept/Oct, Exhibit 1, p. 114. Copyright © 1957 Harvard Business School Publishing Corporation, all rights reserved, reprinted by permission of Harvard Business Review.

### Tables

Tables 2.2 and 2.3 adapted from *Gum in the United Kingdom*, Euromonitor International (2010), used with permission of Euromonitor International; Table 9.2 from *The Marketing Communications Process*, McGraw-Hill (DeLozier, M.W. 1975), Copyright © 1975 The Estate of the late Professor M. Wayne DeLozier.

### Photographs

**Aker Solutions:** Harald Valderhaug 118; **Alamy Images:** AMD Images 423, Art Directors & Trip 514, © David Lee 231, © David R. Frazier Photolibrary, Inc. 468, © Doug Steley C 301, © Hugh Threlfall 210, Jacques Jangoux 72, © Jeff Morgan 14 458, Lana Sundman 360, © Lori Farr 314, © Manor Photography 559, MBI 537, Neils Poulson DK 257, © Queerstock, Inc. 158, © studiomode 142, © Stuwdamdorp 445, Tristar Photos 529; **Brit Insurance:** 485; **© Crown Copyright (2011) Visit Wales:** 553; **Corbis:** Jagadeesh / Reuters 518; **Courtesy of Waitrose Ltd:** 363; **Courtyard Management:** 253; **Dubit Research:** 182; **E M Clements Photography:** 389; **Experian:** 139; **www.eyevine.com:** Doug Healey / NY Times 47; **Getty Images:** Andreas Rentz 15, Bloomberg 112, 506, 531, Boston Globe 477, Jeff Bezos 37, Shaun Botterill - FIFA 268; **Great Ormond Street International Promotions Ltd:** Great Ormond Street Hospital Children's Charity 581; **Greenpeace UK:** 583; **Hi-Tec Sports:** 448; **Highland Spring:** 2; **Image courtesy of The Advertising Archives:** 68, 101, 214, 233, 273, 287, 355, 367, 374, 397, 569; **James Davies:** 107; **James Kirkikis/Photographers Direct:** 329; **Kellogg Group:** 217; **Kista:** 114; **Linn Products Limited:** 501; **Little Dish:** 152; **Lok8u Ltd:** 208; **Lorna Young:** 137; **Mandy Haberman:** 223; **Meet the Bulldog:** 54; **Orange Mobile:** 131; **Press Association Images:** 562, Dave Pratt 34; **Purple PR:** 147; **Rex Features:** Alex Lentati / Evening Standard 498; **Rosina Redwood Photography, Photographersdirect.com:** 471; **Shutterstock.com:** Luis Carlos Jimenez del rio 276, Monkey Business Images 188, Morgan Lane Photography 427, Ryan Rodrick Beiler 353, Valentyn Volkov 298, Valerio D'Ambrogi 42; **Sugro:** 307; **Teuscher Chocolates of Switzerland:** 525; **The Fabulous Bakin' Boys:** 440; **Transport for London:** 345-6; **Wild Pelican:** 228; **Yo-Promotions:** 20; **Cover image:** *Front:* **Zahirah Motala**.

In some instances we have been unable to trace the owners of copyright material, and we would appreciate any information that would enable us to do so.

# CHAPTER 1

# Marketing dynamics

## LEARNING OBJECTIVES

This chapter will help you to:

- define what marketing is;
- trace the development of marketing as a way of doing business and consider the ways in which marketing is changing;
- appreciate the importance and contribution of marketing as both a business function and an interface between the organisation and its customers; and
- understand the scope of tasks undertaken in marketing, and the range of different organisational situations in which marketing is applied.

## INTRODUCTION

**YOU WILL HAVE SOME** sort of idea of what marketing is, since, after all, you are exposed to marketing in some form every day. Every time you buy or use a product, go window shopping, see an advertising hoarding, watch an advertisement, listen to friends telling you about a wonderful new product they've tried, or even when you surf the internet to research a market, company or product for an assignment, you are reaping the benefits (or being a victim) of marketing activities. When marketing's outputs are so familiar, it is easy to take it for granted and to judge and define it too narrowly by what you see of it close to home. It is a mistake, however, to dismiss marketing as 'just advertising' or 'just selling' or 'making people buy things they don't really want'.

What this book wants to show you is that marketing does, in fact, cover a very wide range of absolutely essential business activities that bring you the products you *do* want, when you want them, where you want them, but at prices you can afford, and with all the information you need to make informed and satisfying consumer choices. And that's only what marketing does for you! Widen your thinking to include what marketing can similarly do for organisations purchasing goods and services from other organisations, and you can begin to see why it is a mistake to be too cynical about professionally practised marketing. None of this is easy. The outputs of marketing, such as the packaging, the advertisements, the glossy brochures, the all-singing, all-dancing websites, the presence on Facebook and Twitter, the enticing retail outlets and the incredible bargain-value prices, look slick and polished, but a great deal of management planning, analysis and decision-making has gone on behind the scenes in order to bring all this to you. By the time you have finished this book, you should appreciate the whole range of marketing activities, and the difficulties of managing them.

*eg*

There can surely be no better demonstration of what marketing is about than looking at what has happened to plain, natural water. You might think that branded bottled water is a straight substitute for tap water, but research indicates that 90 per cent of consumers are choosing bottled water over other drinks, not tap water. Highland Spring is a supplier of one such brand of bottled water. It is intent on bringing its brand to life to make it stand out from its competitors, and it is doing so by injecting more personality into the brand. This is necessary because of the difficulty in really distinguishing one brand of water from another in the eyes of the consumer, and because the bottled-water market is growing at a slower rate. According to Mintel (2009a), people are starting to adopt the attitude that bottled water is 'a bit of a con' and to believe that it is no healthier than tap water.

To try to overcome some of this, Highland Spring is using sports personalities to appeal to children or their parents, demonstrating a healthy link between sport and drinking water. It also is tapping into the trend towards a healthier lifestyle, as more and more consumers are switching away from drinks with a high sugar content. An important part of the Highland Spring strategy is to gain distribution, and results are favourable: supermarket penetration has increased over the past year. This is all the more remarkable for having been achieved by offering superior product quality with fewer variants than rivals, and without heavy investment in advertising. But the competition is tough, not only from other European branded water products such as Volvic and Evian, and more locally sourced brands such as Harrogate Spa water, but also from vitamin-enhanced drinks such as V Water and Glaceau (Boakie, 2008; *Just-drinks*, 2010; Mintel, 2009a; www.highland-spring.com/about).

Water is an essential part of a healthy diet

*Source*: Highland Spring, www.highland-spring.com

Before launching further into detailed descriptions, explanations and analyses of the operational tasks that make up the marketing function, however, it is important to lay a few foundations about what marketing really is, and to give you a more detailed overview of why it is so essential and precisely what it involves in practice.

This chapter defines and explores marketing as a philosophy of doing business which puts the customer first and, therefore, casts the marketing department in the role of 'communicator' between the organisation and the outside world. Marketers have to tackle a surprisingly wide range of tasks on a daily basis to fulfil that function and these too are defined. After you have read this chapter, marketing should mean a lot more to you than 'advertising', and you will appreciate that 'making people buy things they don't want' is the one thing that successful marketers do not do.

# Marketing defined

This section is going to explore what marketing is and its evolution. First, we shall look at currently accepted definitions of marketing, then at the history behind those definitions. Linked with that history are the various business orientations outlined on pp. 11–13. These show how marketing is as much a philosophy of doing business as a business function in its own right. It is important to get this concept well established before moving on to the next section where we discuss philosophy and function in the context of the organisation.

## What marketing means

Here are two popular and widely accepted definitions of marketing. The first is the definition preferred by the UK's Chartered Institute of Marketing (CIM), while the second is that offered by the American Marketing Association (AMA):

> **Marketing is the management process responsible for identifying, anticipating, and satisfying customer requirements profitably. (CIM, 2001)**

> **Marketing is the activity, set of institutions, and processes for creating, communicating, delivering, and exchanging offerings that have value for customers, clients, partners, and society at large. (AMA, 2007)**

Both definitions make a good attempt at capturing concisely what is actually a wide and complex subject. Although they have a lot in common, each says something important that the other does not emphasise. Both agree on the following points.

### Marketing is a management process

Marketing has just as much legitimacy as any other business function, and involves just as much management skill. It requires planning and analysis, resource allocation, control and investment in terms of money, appropriately skilled people and physical resources. It also, of course, requires implementation, monitoring and evaluation. As with any other management activity, it can be carried out efficiently and successfully – or it can be done poorly, resulting in failure.

### Marketing is about giving customers what they want

All marketing activities should be geared towards this. It implies a focus towards the customer or end consumer of the product or service. If 'customer requirements' are not satisfactorily fulfilled, or if customers do not obtain what they want and need, then marketing has failed both the customer and the organisation.

## Marketing identifies and anticipates customer requirements

Both definitions accept that marketing is a set of activities that identifies and anticipates customer requirements largely through market research and assessing the information generated. Although communicated more directly in the CIM definition, both definitions do highlight the anticipation and creation of customer requirements as the starting point of marketing. They are saying that the marketer creates some sort of offering only after researching the market and pinpointing exactly what the customer will want.

## Marketing fulfils customer requirements profitably

This pragmatic phrase warns the marketer against getting too carried away with the altruism of satisfying the customer! In the real world, an organisation cannot please all of the people all of the time, and sometimes even marketers have to make compromises. The marketer has to work within the resource capabilities of the organisation, and specifically work within the agreed budgets and performance targets set for the marketing function. Nevertheless, profitability can still be questionable. Marketing practice and, in part, marketing thinking, is now accepted within many non-profit organisations, from schools and universities to hospitals, voluntary organisations and activist groups such as Greenpeace and Friends of the Earth. Each must manage its dealings with its various publics and user groups and manage them efficiently and effectively, but not for profit. That important context aside, most commercial companies exist to make profits, and thus profitability is a legitimate concern. Even so, some organisations would occasionally accept the need to make a loss on a particular product or sector of a market in order to achieve wider strategic objectives. As long as those losses are planned and controlled, and in the longer run provide some other benefit to the organisation, then they are bearable. In general terms, however, if an organisation is consistently failing to make profits, then it will not survive, and thus marketing has a responsibility to sustain and increase profits.

The AMA definition goes a little further.

## Exchanges that have value to customers, clients, partners and society at large

This statement is close to the CIM's 'profitably', but a little more subtle. The idea of marketing as an exchange process to create value is an important one, and was first proposed by Alderson (1957). The basic idea is that I've got something you want, you've got something I want, so let's do a deal. For the most part, the exchange is a simple one. The organisation offers a product or service, and the customer offers a sum of money in return for it. Pepsi offers you a can of cola and you offer payment; you sign a contract to offer your services as an employee and the organisation pays you a salary; the hospital offers to provide healthcare and the individual, through taxes or insurance premiums, offers to fund it. A range of further examples is shown diagramatically in Figure 1.1.

What all these examples have in common is the assumption that both parties value what the other has to offer. If they didn't, they would not be obliged to enter into the bargain. It is up to the marketer to make sure that customers value what the organisation is offering so highly that they are prepared to give the organisation what it wants in return. Whether the marketer is offering a product, a service, or an idea (such as the environmental causes 'sold' by Greenpeace), the essence of the exchange is mutual value. From mutual value can come satisfaction and possible repeat purchases. Of course, the concept of 'value' is difficult to establish; it's an elusive concept, but if consumers determine their notion of 'value' from a comparison of their actual experience compared with their expectations of a particular marketing exchange, then that's what matters to them and that is what will influence their subsequent decision making (Rowley, 2008).

**Figure 1.1**
Exchange
transactions

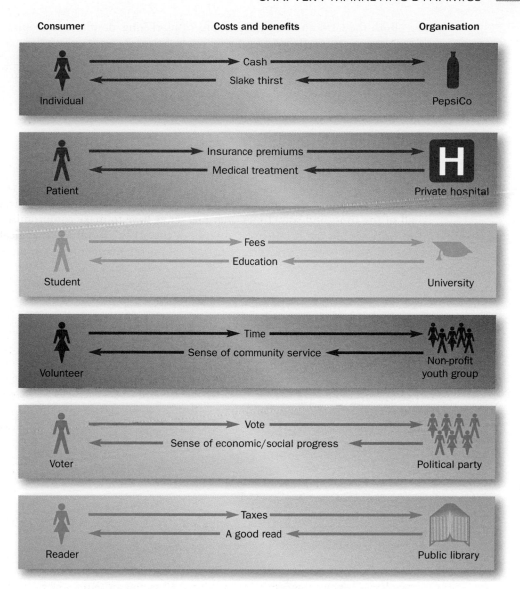

## Pricing, promotion and distribution of ideas, goods and services

In saying that marketing involves the conception, pricing, promotion and distribution of ideas, goods and services, the AMA definition is a little more specific in describing the ways in which marketers can stimulate exchanges. It suggests a proactive seller as well as a willing buyer. By designing products, setting sensible, acceptable and justifiable prices, creating awareness and preferences, and ensuring availability and service, the marketer can influence the volume of exchanges. Marketing can be seen, therefore, as a demand management activity on the part of the selling organisation.

## Society at large

The AMA definition goes much further than the CIM in describing exchanges for society at large. This includes charities, non-profit exchanges and even situations where ideas rather than money are exchanged. It may include funders, volunteers and corporate partners. It allows for a much broader definition of marketing that can encompass far more than traditional profit-making organisations (Andreason *et al.*, 2008).

Both the CIM and AMA definitions of marketing, despite their popular usage, are increasingly being criticised, however, for failing to reflect the realities and difficulties facing marketing in the twenty-first century. This includes not only expanding the social marketing theme but also sustainability issues in a world of shrinking resources. It could also be argued that both definitions could go further in highlighting the drive for customer retention, relationship building and relationship maintenance that now characterises many markets (Grönroos, 2009).

# MARKETING IN ACTION

## All aboard!

The chances are that most of you will not yet be among the target market for cruise holidays. The general perception of cruises tends to be of formal dinners attended by well-off pensioners enjoying their moment of glory at the captain's table. On-board luxury, gluttony and an endless stream of activities appropriate for those of a typical average age of 55 are occasionally interrupted by brief, highly packaged visits ashore with minimal interaction with the local culture. That might be an unduly cynical view; others would see a cruise as the ultimate holiday experience. Typical passengers with Silversea Cruises, for example, are described as an affluent, sophisticated couple who enjoy the club-like atmosphere, exquisite cuisine and polished service. Silversea's six ships operate at the premium end of the market. One of its ships, for example, the *Silver Shadow* offers a holiday that is as 'elegant as a grand hotel experience and as gracious as a long-time friend's home' (www.silversea.com).

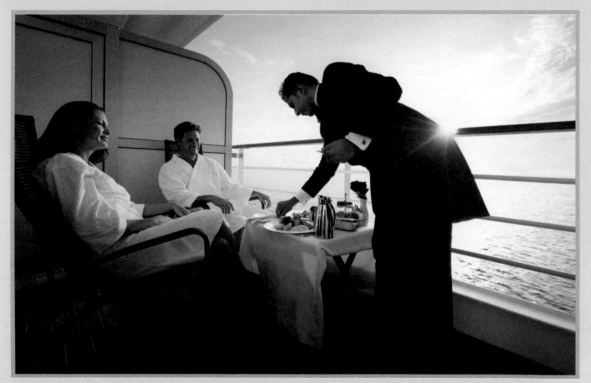

Holiday-makers aboard a Silversea luxury liner

*Source*: Silversea Cruises, www.silversea.com

Although the cruise-ship holiday market occasionally encounters stormy waters associated with international events, especially terrorism and more recently the economic recession, it has still seen significant growth. The number of UK cruise bookings is around one million per annum, and according to Mintel (2010) just 2 per cent of holidaymakers cited a sea cruise as the most recent holiday they took. Interestingly, however, Mintel also noted that the cruise sector has managed to keep its head above the water, despite an overall decline of 14.5 per cent in the number of holidays taken in 2009. This could be a result of a combination of significant discounting of cruise holidays as a short-term tactical measure, and the fact that the typical, older, more affluent target market for cruises was less affected by the recession. Nevertheless, the cruise industry is still looking to broaden its appeal. If it can stretch the age range down to those who are 45 and over, or even 35 and over, it would help to steer cruises out of a narrow niche into a more mainstream holiday package market.

So, here's the major marketing challenge: how do you make new cruise products more appealing to younger people who might well want a little more than tuxedos and ballroom dancing? The answer may lie in the concept of a floating holiday resort with a wider appeal. Now on offer are a wider range of holiday experiences reflected in different and distinctive brands. This has meant new ships designed to offer that experience. For example, a Royal Caribbean Cruises ship is the size of four football fields, has 24 varied restaurants and a multitude of activities for the 8,600 people (including staff) on board.

Island Cruises, now owned by Thomson (itself part of TUI), has targeted the top end of the package-holiday market with cruise holidays starting at £750 per person. Out goes the formality, in come flexible dining times, a choice of restaurants and no fixed table plans. It is sold alongside many other package holidays in the Thomson range and can even be combined with a land stay of seven or 14 days. Overall, it seeks to reflect the elements of a better quality package holiday within a cruise experience. So, sports and salsa classes, live bands and cabaret, kids' club and bars and even an internet café are all definitely in the mix, while tuxedos are definitely out. On shore trips can be booked online before stepping aboard and include such delights as the pyramids and Petra on some trips.

Cruise-ship customers are evolving into three main groups:

- *Mainstream*: First-time cruisers, repeat passengers, young and old alike. Mainstream cruise lines target singles, families and groups – anyone who is looking for a fun and exhilarating holiday.
- *Premium*: First-timers and experienced passengers who enjoy a more upmarket experience in lower-key surroundings. Premium lines attract families, singles and groups. The average age tends to be higher on trips of more than 7–10 days.
- *Luxury*: Well-heeled couples and singles accustomed to the best travel accommodation and service. Travelling in style to far-flung corners of the globe is the dream of luxury-minded passengers. These cruises are full of 'enrichment programmes' with celebrity entertainers, scholarly guest speakers and culinary classes, all augmenting more traditional shipboard activities. Libraries are well stocked with books and films. These adult-oriented luxury cruises are usually inappropriate for children and teens. The lack of organised activities makes them unappealing to young families.

Newer brands might find it easier to position themselves to appeal to different lifestyle and demographic groups, but for operators such as Carnival Corporation owning established brand names such as Cunard, Carnival, Princess Cruises and P&O Cruises, there is a need to balance the interests of their original target market against the demands of the younger, more active customer who needs to be tempted with more than the basic mainstream experience.

The communications appeal has been changed to focus on the experiences and feelings passengers can enjoy during the holiday rather than depicting just the product, the ship, on-board facilities and shore locations. Widening the target group is not without risk, if the more traditional, experienced cruisers have different expectations from the first timers who have been attracted perhaps by the novelty, lower prices and more informal activities.

The marketing offer is evolving but some doubt whether it will really be possible to change the appeal sufficiently to attract a more youthful 35-year-old to cruising. Younger cruisers may make the sector look more appealing, but it is also important to retain customers who value the more

▶ traditional offers. New cruise liners, better facilities, new homeports nearer the customer, interesting on- and off-board activities and new communication strategies may all help, but will the appeal really broaden? As people remain active for longer, perhaps it will only be the late forties and fifties age groups that will appreciate and take full advantage of the potential for self-development through cruising. In that case, the age range appeal may change only a little, but the expectations may change a lot. Either way, many of us will become prime targets in the end, as an ageing population, the desire for more challenging and fulfilling experiences, and increasing affluence put the cruise experience within the reach of many more than just the original small niche. The smart cruise operators will need to understand the needs of the different customer groups and reflect that in what they offer. Carnival is unashamedly offering value, not luxury, and is experimenting with multigenerational ships. Its latest vessel, *Carnival Dream*, provides different facilities in different areas of the ship for different groups. For some, however, this is all too much. Frommer's Travel Guides comment that some of the new generation of cruise ships represent 'a dumbing down of the travel experience' as cruises become much more about the floating resort and less about exploring the places and cultures along the route.

Of course, even the best laid marketing plans can fall victim to unforeseen circumstances. The *Costa Concordia* disaster, in which a cruise liner ran aground and sank off the Italian coast in January 2012, generated a lot of negative publicity for the cruise industry. Potential customers began to question the safety of 'floating resorts' and in the six weeks following the disaster, the peak time for bookings, the two largest cruise operators were reporting a decline in bookings of one-sixth. The industry responded to this with aggressive price cuts (on average 15 per cent) and promotions (such as cabin upgrades), as well as reassuring safety messages. The hope is that these measures will help the industry to weather the immediate storm so that it can emerge into calmer waters and continue working on the longer term focus of developing the cruise experience in line with changing customer needs and expectations.

*Sources*: Johnson (2003); Mintel (2010); Hemphill (2009); Nassauer (2010); Peisley (2009); *Daily Telegraph* (2012); Hendrie (2012); Higgins (2012); www.carnival.com; www.cunard.com, www.silversea.com.

## Relationship marketing

The traditional definitions of marketing tend to reflect a view that the transaction between buyer and seller is primarily seller oriented, that each exchange is totally discrete, and thus lacking any of the personal and emotional overtones that emerge in a long-term relationship made up of a series of exchanges between the same buyer and seller. In B2B markets, in particular, each of these exchanges could involve a complex web of interactions between the staff of both organisations, each seeking to build enduring buyer–seller relationships through which they work together for their mutual benefit against a history of previous exchanges (see for example Dwyer *et al.*, 1987, Fawcett *et al.*, 2010).

In some circumstances, however, the traditional non-relationship view is perfectly appropriate. A traveller on an unknown road passing through a foreign country may stop at a wayside café, never visited before and never to be visited again. The decision to purchase is thus going to be influenced by the ease of parking, the décor and the ambience rather than by any feeling of trust or commitment to the patron. The decision, in short, is based on the immediate and specific marketing offering. Well-lit signs, a menu in your own language and visibly high hygiene standards will all influence the decision to stop. This scenario describes an approach to marketing where the focus is on a single exchange or transaction between the buyer and the seller and that influences the seller to make the menu look good, the parking available and the décor attractive. The chances of your becoming a regular customer in this instance are, of course, unlikely unless you are a frequent traveller on that route.

In contrast, a relationship-focused approach to marketing describes a network of communications and contacts between the buyer and the seller and a series of exchanges over time. Both parties have to be satisfied with the relationship and achieve their respective objectives from it. Marketing, therefore, is part of an interactive process between people, over time, of which relationship creation, building and management are vital cornerstones throughout the supply chain (Grönroos, 2009; Svensson, 2005). Individual exchanges between buyer and seller are important and influenced by previous experiences, good and bad, but any seller that is concerned with the one-off sale and the immediate gain may find that the longer-term interests of both parties are not well served. Companies such as BMW have supplier relationships that go back 50 years or more. Unlike the situation with the single exchange or transaction where profits are expected to follow from today's exchanges, in relationship marketing the time perspective can be very long indeed.

Relationship marketing is not just a B2B phenomenon, however. The internet and direct marketing are creating new opportunities for organisations in mass markets to become much closer to their customers. Consumers often stay loyal to familiar brands, retailers and suppliers for many years and with the enormous power of new technology, individual consumers can be identified and profiles developed, whether through loyalty schemes, monitoring internet shopping behaviour or other ways of capturing detailed information (see Chapter 5). It is now possible to track the purchase behaviour of individual shoppers and to create a database for directly targeted communication (see Chapter 11), and with such power it would be a foolish marketer who did not try to maintain customer loyalty and, hence, improve sales.

Fitness clubs have taken relationship marketing seriously in order to hang on to their customers. Over the past 10 years, membership of fitness clubs has grown significantly and operators such as David Lloyd, Bannatyne's Health Club and Fitness First have all established a share of the market. Mintel (2009b) suggests that around 5.26 million Britons were members of private health and fitness clubs in 2009, and that is forecast to rise to 6.31 million by 2014. However, revenue per member is actually forecast to remain at about £480 over that period, perhaps reflecting market saturation and more competition to keep us in trim. In 2009, the market was worth about £2.5 billion.

Far from being the domain of bodybuilders, fitness is now a popular pastime for the under-thirties, but older age groups see club membership as a 'fashion and lifestyle' statement. For example, David Lloyd entered into cooperation with Saga to attract older members, Recruitment is not enough, however. Clubs have to retain their members too and build relationships with them to try to ensure continued patronage. Key to future success will be the right market positioning, developing a range of brands and a diverse range of services, both sporting and social. This means that clubs will have to keep in touch with their members through newsletters and online media and make sure that usage behaviours are logged so that appropriate messages and services can be targeted to particular groups of members (Mintel, 2009b; *Precision Marketing*, 2004).

## Wider definition of marketing

So, definitions of marketing are moving away from the single exchange, seller-focused perspective adopted by the CIM and AMA definitions towards more socially relevant and relationship-oriented definitions that are considered to reflect the reality of modern marketing far better. Although relationship marketing over time focuses on customers' needs and attitudes as important points of concern, it can also embrace social and ethical concerns as well as issues more directly related to the series of transactions.

A definition that includes the important elements of both the AMA and CIM definitions, but still embraces the evolving relationship orientation, is offered by Grönroos (1999; 2006; 2009):

**Marketing is to establish, maintain and enhance relationships with customers and other partners, at a profit, so that the objectives of the parties involved are met. This is achieved by mutual exchange and fulfillment of promises.**

Such relationships are usually, but not necessarily always, long-term. Some could be little more than a single episode but others could be very enduring. This definition still reflects a managerial orientation towards marketing, but emphasises the mutually active role that both partners in the exchange play. It does not list the activities that marketers undertake, but instead is more concerned with the partnership idea, the concept that marketing is about doing something *with* someone, not doing something *to* them. Of course, not all transactions between buyers and sellers can be considered to be part of a relationship, especially where the purchase does not involve much risk or commitment from the purchaser and thus there is little to gain from entering a relationship (Berry, 1983). This was clearly shown in the wayside café example cited earlier. Overall, however, marketing is increasingly about relationships in both B2B and consumer markets. This makes good business sense, as the cost of retaining a customer is only about one-fifth of finding and acquiring a new one. Thus the philosophy of marketing is moving from a focus on products and services to managing a portfolio of segments and markets (Slater *et al.*, 2009).

The idea of fulfilling promises is also an important one, as marketing is all about making promises to potential buyers. If the buyer decides, after the event, that the seller did not live up to those promises, the chances are that they will never buy again from that seller. If, on the other hand, the buyer decides that the seller has fulfilled their promises, then the seeds of trust are sown, and the buyer may be prepared to begin a long-term relationship with the seller.

Between them, therefore, the three definitions offered say just about everything there is to say about the substance and basic philosophy of marketing. Few would argue with any of that now, but marketing has not always been so readily accepted in that form, as the next two subsections show.

## The development of marketing

The basic idea of marketing as an exchange process has its roots in very ancient history, when people began to produce crops or goods surplus to their own requirements and then to barter them for other things they wanted. Elements of marketing, particularly selling and advertising, have been around as long as trade itself, but it took the industrial revolution, the development of mass production techniques and the separation of buyers and sellers to sow the seeds of what we recognise as marketing today.

In the early days, the late nineteenth and early twentieth centuries, goods were sufficiently scarce and competition sufficiently underdeveloped that producers did not really need marketing. They could easily sell whatever they produced ('the production era' in which a 'production orientation' was adopted). As markets and technology developed, competition became more serious and companies began to produce more than they could easily sell. This led to 'the sales era', lasting into the 1950s and 1960s, in which organisations developed increasingly large and increasingly pushy sales forces, and more aggressive advertising approaches (the 'selling orientation').

It was not really until the 1960s and 1970s that marketing generally moved away from a heavy emphasis on post-production selling and advertising to become a more comprehensive and integrated field, earning its place as a major influence on corporate strategy ('marketing orientation'). This meant that organisations began to move away from a 'sell what we can make' type of thinking, in which 'marketing' was at best a peripheral activity, towards a 'find out what the customer wants and then we'll make it' type of market driven philosophy. Customers took their rightful place at the centre of the organisation's universe. This finally culminated, in the 1980s, in the wide acceptance of marketing as a strategic concept, and yet there is still room for further development of the marketing concept, as new applications and contexts emerge.

Historically, marketing has not developed uniformly across all markets or products. Retailers, along with many consumer goods organisations, have been at the forefront of implementing the marketing concept. Benetton, for instance, developed a strong, unique, international product and retail store image, but within the basic formula is prepared to adapt its merchandising and pricing strategies to suit the demands of different geographic markets. The financial services industry, however, has only very recently truly embraced a marketing orientation, some 10 years or more behind most consumer goods. The focus now is on how a marketing orientation can be developed that creates value for the customer and implemented in a manner that is appropriate for all industries (van Raaij and Stoelhorst, 2008).

## Business orientations

We discuss below the more precise definitions of the alternative approaches to doing business that were outlined above. We then describe the characteristic management thinking behind them, and show how they are used today. Table 1.1 further summarises this information.

**Table 1.1** Marketing history and business orientations – a summary

| Orientation | Focus | Characteristics and aims | Eavesdropping | Main era (generalised) | | |
|---|---|---|---|---|---|---|
| | | | | **USA** | **Western Europe** | **China** |
| **Production** | Manufacturing | ▪ Increase production ▪ Cost reduction and control ▪ Make profit through volume | 'Any colour you want – as long as it's black' | Up to 1940s | Up to 1950s | Up to 1990s |
| **Product** | Goods | ▪ Quality is all that matters ▪ Improve quality levels ▪ Make profit through volume | 'Just look at the quality of the paintwork' | Up to 1940s | Up to 1960s | Largely omitted |
| **Selling** | Selling what's produced – seller's needs | ▪ Aggressive sales and promotion ▪ Profit through quick turnover of high volume | 'You're not keen on the black? What if I throw in a free sun-roof?' | 1940–1950s | 1950–1960s | Early 1990s |
| **Marketing** | Defining what customers want – buyer's needs | ▪ Integrated marketing ▪ Defining needs in advance of production ▪ Profit through customer satisfaction and loyalty | 'Let's find out if they want it in black, and if they would pay a bit more for it' | 1960s onwards | 1970s onwards | Mid-1990s onwards but patchy |
| **Ethical and sustainable marketing** | Serving the needs of the buyer with due respect for the welfare of society and the environment | ▪ Integrated ethical marketing ▪ Defining needs and designing and producing products to minimise harm/damage ▪ Profit through customer satisfaction and loyalty, and through societal acceptance | 'Let's find out if they want it in black, and then produce it as "greenly" as possible and think about what to do when its useful life ends' | Late 1990s onwards | 2000 onwards | Just starting |

## Production orientation

The emphasis with a production orientation is on making products that are affordable and available, and thus the prime task of management is to ensure that the organisation is as efficient as possible in production and distribution techniques. The main assumption is that the market is completely price sensitive, which means that customers are only interested in price as the differentiating factor between competing products and will buy the cheapest. Customers are thus knowledgeable about relative prices, and if the organisation wants to bring prices down, then it must tightly control costs. This is the philosophy of the production era, and was predominant in China in the early stages of economic reform given the scarcity of goods for the masses. Apart from that, it may be a legitimate approach, in the short term, where demand outstrips supply, and companies can put all their effort into improving production and increasing supply and worry about the niceties of marketing later.

A variation on that situation happens when a product is really too expensive for the market, and therefore the means have to be found to bring costs, and thus prices, down. This decision, however, is as likely to be marketing as production driven, and may involve technologically complex, totally new products that neither the producer nor the customer is sure of. Thus DVD players, digital cameras, smart phones, home computers and games consoles were all launched on to unsuspecting markets with limited supply and high prices, but the manufacturers envisaged that with extensive marketing and the benefits gained from progressing along the production and technology learning curve, high-volume markets could be opened up for lower-priced, more reliable products.

## Product orientation

The product orientation assumes that consumers are primarily interested in the product itself, and buy on the basis of quality. Since consumers want the highest level of quality for their money, the organisation must work to increase and improve its quality levels. At first glance, this may seem like a reasonable proposition, but the problem is the assumption that consumers *want this product*. Consumers do not want products, they want solutions to problems, and if the organisation's product does not solve a problem, they will not buy it, however high the quality level is. An organisation may well produce the best ever record player, but most consumers might well rather download their favourite music on to their phone. In short, customer needs rather than the product should be the focus.

In a review of the history of marketing thinking in China, Deng and Dart (1999) considered the market orientation of traditional state enterprises. From 1949 until economic reform began in 1979, Chinese organisations were part of a very rigid, planned economy. During that time denying marketing was a fundamental part of the political belief system and with a low GDP per capita and widespread scarcity of consumer goods, there was little, if any, incentive for the development of marketing activities (Gordon, 1991). The focus was on manufacturing output and all major marketing decisions such as product range, pricing, and selection of distribution channels were controlled by government. The state set production targets for each enterprise, distributed their products, assigned personnel, allocated supplies and equipment, retained all profit, and covered all losses (Zhuang and Whitehill, 1989; Gordon, 1991). The priority was production and virtually any product would do.

Since the reforms and the opening up of the economy, most enterprises, even if state-owned, have to now make marketing decisions as they are no longer allocated production inputs, nor are their outputs assigned to prearranged buyers. Price controls have been relaxed and distribution lists from the state ended. However, the transition process is not yet complete: many state-owned enterprises are being subsidised to retain employment levels and government power is still great. Most Chinese brands still have a long way to go before they can challenge European brands in consumer perception. Much of the growth has been based on Western multinationals benefiting from low-cost labour by contracting out the bulk of manufacturing while marketing is handled elsewhere. However, this may be transitory as once Chinese companies have gained experience of high-specification manufacturing, and learned some marketing and global-branding skills, they may be better able to exploit the low-cost base themselves and create and establish their own seriously competitive brands (Prystay, 2003).

## Sales orientation

The basis for the sales orientation way of thinking is that consumers are inherently reluctant to purchase, and need every encouragement to purchase sufficient quantities to satisfy the organisation's needs. This leads to a heavy emphasis on personal selling and other sales stimulating devices because products 'are sold, not bought', and thus the organisation puts its effort into building strong sales departments, with the focus very much on the needs of the seller, rather than on those of the buyer. Home improvement organisations, selling, for example, double glazing and cavity wall insulation, have tended to operate like this, as has the timeshare industry.

Schultz and Good (2000) proposed that a sales orientation can also emerge from commission-based reward and remuneration packages for sales people, even though the seller might actually want longer-term customer relationships to be established. When the pressure is on to make a sale and to achieve target sales volumes there is a danger that the sales person will focus on the one-off sale rather than the long-term relationship. There is a tension between the need to spend time on relationships and the urge to move on to the next sale.

## Marketing orientation

The organisation that develops and performs its production and marketing activities with the needs of the buyer driving it all, and with the satisfaction of that buyer as the main aim, is marketing oriented. The motivation is to 'find wants and fill them' rather than 'create products and sell them'. The assumption is that customers are not necessarily price driven, but are looking for the total offering that best fits their needs, and therefore the organisation has to define those needs and develop appropriate offerings. This is not just about the core product itself, but also about pricing, access to information, availability and peripheral benefits and services that add value to the product. Not all customers, however, necessarily want exactly the same things. They can be grouped according to common needs and wants, and the organisation can produce a specifically targeted marketing package that best suits the needs of one group, thus increasing the chances of satisfying that group and retaining its loyalty.

A marketing orientation is far more, however, than simply matching products and services to customers. It has to emerge from an organisational philosophy, an approach to doing business that naturally places customers and their needs at the heart of what the organisation does. Henderson (1998) nevertheless urges caution in assuming that a marketing orientation is a guarantee of success in achieving above average performance. There are many internal and external factors at work in determining success, of which effective marketing thinking is but one. If marketing dominates the rest of the organisation it can help to diminish key competencies in other areas such as manufacturing productivity or technological innovation. Furthermore, the marketing department approach to organising the marketing function can isolate marketing from design, production, deliveries, technical service, complaints handling, invoicing and other customer-related activities. As a consequence, the rest of the organisation could be alienated from marketing, making the coordination of customer and market-oriented activities across the organisation more difficult (Piercy, 1992). This underlines the importance of Narver and Slater's (1990) three key factors that help the marketing function to achieve above average performance:

- *interfunctional orientation* enabling cooperation between the management functions to create superior value;
- *competitor orientation* to retain an edge;
- *customer orientation*.

Having established the importance of the marketing concept to an organisation, the chapter now turns to the issue of how it is developing further to meet the changing demands of society.

# Emergent marketing philosophies

The marketing concept and the philosophy of a marketing orientation continue to evolve. In increasingly competitive global markets consisting of increasingly demanding customers, organisations are continually striving to find more effective ways of attracting and retaining customers, and sometimes that could mean refining further exactly what marketing means.

## Corporate social responsibility: societal and ethical marketing

Corporate social responsibility (CSR) suggests that organisations should not only consider their customers and their profitability, but also the good of the wider communities, local and global, within which they exist. As Smith and Higgins (2000) put it, consumers now are not only looking for environmentally sensitive and ethically considerate products, but also for businesses to demonstrate a wider set of ethical commitments to society. The European Commission's definition of CSR is:

> **the voluntary integration of social and environmental concerns in to business operations and in to their interaction with stakeholders. (European Commission, 2010)**

Of course, the problem with that is that there is as yet no widely accepted definition of how such voluntary integration takes place, how it feeds into business operations and how it can be used strategically (Vilanova *et al.*, 2009; Porter and Kramer, 2006). It does, however, place social and environmental concerns at the heart of the business rather than as a bolt-on to core strategy.

Marketing within a CSR context is concerned with ensuring that organisations handle marketing responsibly, and in a way that contributes to the well-being of society. Consumers have become increasingly aware of the social and ethical issues involved in marketing, such as the ethics of marketing to children, fair trade with third-world suppliers, the ecological impact of business, and the extent of good 'corporate citizenship' displayed by companies, for example. Companies looking to establish a reputable and trustworthy image as a foundation for building long-term relationships with their customers thus need to consider the philosophy of CSR seriously if they are to meet their customers' wider expectations, and create and maintain competitive advantage (Balestrini, 2001). Indeed, some companies, such as Body Shop, have adopted a very proactive approach to societal marketing and have made CSR a central pillar of their whole business philosophy (see Hartman and Beck-Dudley, 1999, for a detailed discussion of marketing ethics within Body Shop International).

Of course, its not just about marketing as CSR has a wider impact on the workforce, community relations and the accountability of an organisation (Vilanova *et al.*, 2009). It needs to develop programmes and policies that highlight and measure social and environmental performance, while engaging with various stakeholders during this process (Pearce and Doh, 2005). Perhaps it all boils down to an organisation doing good, not according to its own definition but that of the society in which it operates.

# MARKETING IN ACTION

## Ikea – a CSR strategy that's anything but flat-packed

Ikea is a well respected international retailer operating over 300 stores in 37 countries. Swedish companies, in general, have a very good reputation for high ethical standards and green marketing. Ikea is no exception and has interpreted its corporate values into a series of themes.

### People and the environment

As wood is at the heart of the business, Ikea has taken a particularly strong stand in sourcing wood from responsible suppliers. It doesn't accept illegally cut wood or wood harvested from intact forests, and it works closely with suppliers to trace the origins of the wood used in its products. It still does not source all its wood from Forest Stewardship Council (FSC) (see Chapter 2) accredited suppliers, but that is the long-term goal. Ikea also has its own forest specialists out in the field to share knowledge and trace timber to its source.

Another dimension of caring for the environment is waste, management and the recycling of waste products. That has two dimensions – the company reducing its own waste and getting its customers to recycle. The target is the send no waste at all to landfill. The UK government has stopped developing new landfill sites and the cost of sending waste to existing landfills has increased, so quite apart from the moral dimension, it makes good business sense to improve waste management. In 2008, 11 Ikea stores in the UK spent £900,000 on waste between them, but by 2009 from 19 stores it was just £700,000 (Ellul, 2010). This has been achieved by improving waste collection and then bundling it up for onward disposal, for example, to a paper mill so that each store actually generates revenue from its own waste.

## Products and materials

Ikea insists that all products and materials be adapted to minimise any negative impact on the environment, and that they be safe for customers from a health perspective. This means going back to the design of the original product to ensure safety, quality and environmental aspects and then tracing each step to the end of life cycle.

## Climate change

Ikea takes the impact it has on climate change seriously. This means improving energy efficiency and reducing the effects of greenhouse gases. As part of that initiative, Ikea cooperated with WWF to decrease its ecological footprint through sustainable use of resources. In 2009, around one half of Ikea's stores participated in 'Earth Hour' which meant that for one hour, each store turned off its lights. So, Ikea's commitment to reducing emissions goes far further than the 50 million low energy bulbs it has sold in the past three years.

Ikea products combine stylish design with sound CSR principles

*Source:* Getty Images News/Andreas Rentz

## ▶ Code of conduct

The Ikea code of conduct (IWAY) is intended to guide suppliers and all staff at Ikea on how they should do business. This can be problematic, given that Ikea operates in many different countries. Of particular concern, for example, was Russia where Ikea had to fight corruption when seeking permission to build new stores. Ikea is one of the largest commercial estate owners in Russia and is an obvious target for corruption advances, but its code of conduct strictly prohibits the paying of bribes.

However, it is easy to say that any Western company should play by ethical rules rather than pandering to the most unscrupulous. A scandal broke in February 2010 when accusations were made that through subsidiaries a bribe had been paid to supply power to a new retail development. To get a big shopping centre approved means more than 300 separate permits, but rather than wait for them all to come through, some applications run in parallel with the building work, making it fertile ground for unscrupulous permit approvers. While 'planning gain' is legitimately practised in some countries, for example, requiring a company to invest in local infrastructure projects such as roads as a condition of planning permission, there was an allegation that some of Ikea's money in Russia might have gone further than that (Sagdiyev and Popova, 2010). Ikea had said it was going to pay nothing in terms of bribes when it entered Russia, and it has since been firm on reiterating that position. It has fired two employees, however, for tolerating bribery to get a project completed in St Petersburg. The temptation for managers to 'oil the wheels' through bribery must be great when it is so embedded in local culture – it is slow and difficult to operate ethically under such conditions.

### Working conditions

Ikea products must be manufactured under acceptable working conditions by suppliers who take responsibility for the environment and respect human rights. This means keeping a close watch on suppliers, particularly new ones from developing countries to ensure that the highest ethical standards are upheld. Ikea does not accept child labour among its suppliers or their subcontractors at all. If cases are found, corrective action is essential and if it does not happen, the contract is terminated. Ikea operates a special code of conduct called the 'Ikea way on preventing child labour', which includes unannounced visits by Ikea staff to suppliers.

### Social initiatives

Ikea's 'Social Initiatives' is, again, focused on children, in partnership with UNICEF and Save the Children. Its aim is to provide substantial and lasting change in children's lives. One of its successful campaigns is a scheme whereby Ikea donates 50 per cent of the revenue from sales of soft toys to UNICEF between 1 November and 24 December. The UNICEF partnership goes back to 1988, and Ikea is UNICEF's biggest corporate donor, and so Ikea has a long-term commitment to helping to improve the health, education and the quality of life of children in developing nations. In 2009, Ikea's soft-toys scheme alone generated $10 million.

Information about Ikea's CSR policies appears in brochures, annual reports and its website. It also started publishing annual social and environment responsibility reports in 2003, aiming to tell the world just what it means to be 'doing good'. The latest *The Never Ending Job: Sustainability Report 2009* is published on the web and goes into a lot more detail than is possible here. We hope, however, that this vignette has shown how deeply CSR is integrated into a wide range of Ikea's business functions and strategies.

*Sources*: *The Economist* (2010); Ellul (2010); *Health & Medicine Week* (2010); Ikea (2010); Sagdiyev and Popova (2010); Titova (2010); www.ikea.com.

The Co-operative Bank in the UK has long been a champion of ethical financial-service products and of ethical consumerism in general. Every year, it publishes its *Ethical Consumerism Report* to show how ethical spending is evolving. The spending on ethical products grew threefold over a period of 10 years to a high of £36 billion by 2008. Although most sectors grew at above market rates, the fair trade sector which gives something back to growers and producers (*see* Chapter 2) grew from £22 million in 1999 to £635 million by 2008. Sales also increased significantly for energy efficient electrical appliances and mature financial services, where ethical banking has come to the fore. However, some caution is necessary. Although the average spend per household on ethical products and services was £735 per annum in 2008, that is only a small percentage of household average spend. (Co-operative Bank, 2008).

CSR is rapidly changing from being a 'would like' to a 'must have' feature of business. Although at the time of writing businesses are under no obligation to report on their CSR activities in the UK, many already do and it is likely that pressure for transparency on CSR will only increase. The latest buzzword in corporate accountability is '360 degree reporting' which acknowledges the need to produce annual reports that take a much more holistic view of a company's activities to meet the information needs of pressure groups, those looking for ethical investments, and the wider audience interested in CSR, rather than just shareholders and traditional bankers. Companies in potentially sensitive sectors, such as utilities and transport, have begun to produce separate reports on their CSR performance, for example water company Severn Trent's *Corporate Responsibility Report 2010*. Such documents may not have the most imaginative titles, but they do represent an important step in the evolution of corporate reporting.

## MARKETING IN ACTION

### Consumers behaving badly?

While we are all so busy demanding that organisations take their CSR seriously, it is perhaps easy to forget that responsibilities and obligations of 'good citizenship' extend to us as consumers as well. Don't organisations also have the right to ask just how ethical their customers are? Babakus *et al.* (2004) undertook a survey across six different countries to explore the nature of consumer ethical beliefs and the influences on them. Across the whole sample, respondents tended to regard behaviours such as 'taking towels from hotels and blankets from aircraft as souvenirs' as far less wrong than 'drinking a can of soda in a supermarket and not buying it'. Age and nationality both appeared to be significant influencers. Thus, in general, respondents from Brunei, Hong Kong and the USA were more disapproving of the unethical behaviours than respondents from Austria, France and the UK. Younger consumers (aged under 35) from the USA, France and the UK tended to be more tolerant of unethical consumer behaviour than older people. Young French consumers think that there is nothing wrong with 'cutting in when there is a long line', while young Austrians found this the least acceptable of all the scenarios. Interestingly, the Austrian respondents, regardless of age, were far more tolerant of 'reporting a lost item as stolen to an insurance company to collect the money' than any other nationality.

For marketers, it is perhaps a case of 'caveat vendor' and an indication of the need to make clear to customers what is expected of them and the consequences that will follow unethical behaviour on their part. It is a fine line for organisations to tread, however. Undoubtedly, record companies are well within their legal and ethical rights to take legal action against individuals caught with illegal music downloads, but the publicity given to what are perceived as heavy-handed tactics does not reflect well on corporate reputations. An article in the *Daily Mail* (Poulter, 2005) is a typically emotive report, in that it highlights a couple of individual cases of children as young as 12 receiving demands to pay thousands of pounds in compensation or face legal action. There is an interesting phrase in this article, 'many of those being hit by music industry bosses are ordinary families, rather than criminal gangs', implying that context makes a difference to how behaviour is perceived and judged.

The tone of the media coverage is explained to some extent by academic research into attitudes to illegal downloading and filesharing. Williams *et al.* (2010), for example, in a literature review article suggested that illegal downloading is not generally considered unethical, especially by younger people, and that it is seen as a 'victimless crime' (although 'crime' is not a word that the perpetrators would necessarily use). This is probably reinforced by a distinction between corporate and personal property – people who wouldn't steal from an identifiable individual have fewer qualms about defrauding an organisation. This is also discussed by Shoham *et al.* (2008) whose research found that people didn't take the notion of harm to 'abstract entities' as seriously as harm to individuals, and justified their behaviour in terms of views such as 'no harm is done' and 'businesses deserve it'. Shoham *et al.* (2008) put it nicely: 'many who illegally copy software or knowingly buy counterfeit music CDs consider their acts as taking from the rich (software and music companies) and giving to the poor (themselves).'

Williams *et al.* (2010) also point out that some studies have shown that the anonymity or 'deindividualisation' that is possible through the internet makes it easier for the perpetrator to detach themselves from their actions. Interestingly, consumers who fraudulently return goods to retail stores have said that a certain amount of 'brass neck' and assertive confidence is necessary if you're going to get away with it (Harris, 2010). It's easy to see that a less self-confident person might find the anonymous environment of the internet an easier prospect than a face-to-face confrontation in a public setting! Overriding all this, of course, is the question of cultural and social norms, as suggested in the article by Babakus *et al.* (2004) that we started with. Shoham *et al.* (2008) sum it up as 'everybody does it – so do I; nobody does it – neither do I' which is a particularly strong influence within peer groups. If this sort of illegal activity is considered to be socially acceptable and harmless among certain key groups, does that mean that it is too late for those industries and companies that are the victims to stamp it out? Not necessarily – it has taken some time, but the use of marketing techniques has succeeded in changing attitudes to drink-driving and perhaps by demonstrating a moral dimension by showing that illegal downloading does cause loss and harm to identifiable individuals as well as appealing to self-interest in terms of the consequences of this behaviour (for example, the penalties associated with getting caught or the effect on prices as companies seek to cover their losses) the digital music and software industries can similarly try to turn the tide.

*Sources*: Babakus *et al.* (2004); Harris (2010); Poulter (2005); Shoham *et al.* (2008); Williams *et al.* (2010).

## Towards 'sustainable marketing'

Inextricably tied in with the concept and best practice of CSR in its widest sense is the idea of sustainable development. Sustainability was defined in the Brundtland Report of 1987 as:

> **development that meets the needs of the present without compromising the ability of future generations to meet their own needs. (WCED, 1987)**

Sustainability is not just concerned with environmental and ecological issues, as important as these are, but also with the social, economic and cultural development of society. The wider 'softer agenda' includes, therefore, the fair distribution of economic benefits, human rights, community involvement and product responsibility. This has to be taken seriously by business. As the chairman of BASF said, 'A business cannot be successful in the long term if it does not act responsibly toward the environment and society. That is why sustainability is an integral part of our strategy' (as quoted at www.basf.com/group/sustainability_en/index). Society cannot continue to enjoy economic growth without reference to the consequences for environmental protection and social stability and business ignores that at its peril.

Measuring the 'carbon footprint' of everything we do has become a major issue in responding to global warming. Packaging is an important contributor to that, so Asda, Boots, Tesco and Sainsbury have all voluntarily agreed to reduce the footprint of their in-store packaging by 10 per cent by 2012. This will be achieved by weight reduction, higher recycling rates and higher recycled content. This was part of the 'Courtauld Commitment', which helped to reduce the amount of packaging by 500,000 tons between 2005 and 2009. The Courtauld Commitment is a voluntary agreement aiming to improve resource efficiency and reduce the environmental impact of the grocery sector. Phase 1 ran from 2005 to March 2010 and now in Phase 2, it has the wider aim of improving sustainability over the entire life of products through the supply chain. Twenty-nine retailers have signed the agreement.

Marks and Spencer has suffered particular criticism for its packaging impact, so when it announced that it was also signing the Courtauld Commitment, it was with the aim of at least 50 per cent of its products having at least one one eco or ethical attribute by 2015 and 100 per cent by 2020. The UK government also called on supermarkets, again on a voluntary basis, to show the carbon footprint, country of origin and animal welfare standards on food labels (*Environmental Leader*, 2010; www.wrap.org.uk).

In the light of the whole CSR/sustainability debate, sustainable marketing is likely to become the next stage in the conceptual development of marketing as it focuses on some of the significant long-term challenges facing society in the twenty-first century. The term 'sustainable marketing' came to the fore when Sheth and Parvatiyar (1995) discussed marketing efforts that were both competitively sound and environmentally sustainable. It is now accepted that it is ethically wrong for individuals and firms to pollute and destroy the ecological stability of the planet, reducing the opportunities for tomorrow's consumers (García-Rosell and Moisander, 2008). This means that both individuals and organisations have to make informed and grounded decisions about what is right and fair for society, i.e. get back to 'doing good'! This has now become a key phrase in twenty-first-century marketing thinking (Collier and Wanderley, 2005).

The challenge to marketing thinking therefore is to broaden the concept of exchange to incorporate the longer-term needs of society at large rather than the short-term pursuit of individual gratification and consumption. It is not about marketers revising strategies to exploit new societal opportunities, it is about what society can afford to allow marketers to exploit and over what timescale. This sounds very idealistic: in a competitive world in which the customer is free to choose and, moreover, in which business operates on the principle of meeting customers' needs and wants, it sometimes requires courage for a business to change those principles if those changes precede customer concern and government legislation. Consumers within society will have to travel up a learning curve and that process is only just beginning.

We, therefore, would like to define sustainable marketing as:

**the establishment, maintenance and enhancement of customer relationships so that the objectives of the parties involved are met without compromising the ability of future generations to achieve their own objectives.**

In short, consumers today, whatever the market imperative, cannot be allowed to destroy the opportunities for society tomorrow by taking out more than is being put back in. This not only embraces environmental and ecological issues but also the social and cultural consequences of a consumer society that equates 'more' with 'better'.

How does all this impact on the marketing process? The internalisation of costs (making the polluters pay), green taxes, legislation, support for cleaner technology, redesigned products to minimise resources and waste streams, reverse distribution channels to receive products for recycling and consumer education on sustainability are all an essential part of a new marketing agenda for the twenty-first century. To some it is not a choice, but a mandate that cannot be ignored (Fuller, 1999). Ecological and environmental agendas to date have had an impact on marketing strategy, but it has been patchy. The old adage 'reduce, recycle and reuse', for example, has influenced the type of packaging materials used to ensure recyclability. Clothing manufacturers have produced plastic outdoor clothing that can be recycled; glue manufacturers have reduced the toxic emissions from their products; car manufacturers, in accordance with the EU's End-of-Life Vehicle Directive, now have to consider the recycling or other means of disposal of old cars. However, research often indicates that consumers given a free choice are reluctant to pay more for environmentally friendly products such as organic food and many find it hard to establish the link between their individual buying decision and its global impact. It will require a societal balance and adjustment period, but evidence is mounting that if change does not take place, the negative long-term impact on the environment and society could be irreversible.

# MARKETING IN ACTION

## Sustainability: something to write home about

The greening of marketing has even influenced the make-up of sales promotion items. Eco-initiatives include wooden flashdrives, T-shirts made from fair trade cotton, and pens made from biodegradable or recycled materials, to name but a few! Promotional pens are thrust into our hands by the millions, whether at a student fair, a trade show, with an in-store promotion, or included in a mailshot. As the cost of environmentally friendly alternatives falls and the quality rises, it make sense to switch to green promotional pens. This offers a double bonus – not only a reminder of the company brand name, but also an indirect statement about commitment to sustainability. Green pens are good for the environment, as they can either be made from waste material from standard pens or from plastic recycled from things such as CD covers. Yo-Promotions, for example, offers eco-pens made from recycled paper, plastic, car parts, algae, white goods and even recycled money! Then there are biodegradable pens made of substances such as corn starch.

Procurement International sells many promotional and incentive product lines, including pens. It prominently displays a corporate social responsibility statement, based on the Ten Universal Principles in the UN Global Compact. Procurement International will not knowingly trade with any company that fails to comply with those principles. The UN principles are:

### Human rights

- businesses should support and respect the protection of internationally proclaimed human rights; and
- make sure that they are not complicit in human rights abuses.

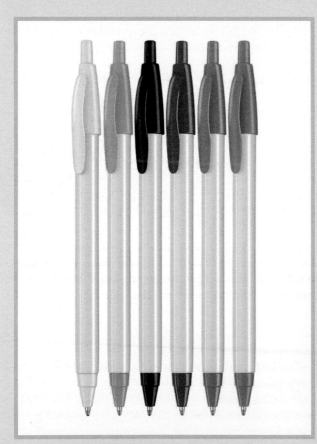

Yo-Promotions' eco-pens

*Source*: Yo-Promotions, www.yo-promotions.co.uk

### Labour standards

- businesses should uphold the freedom of association and the effective recognition of the right to collective bargaining;
- the elimination of all forms of forced and compulsory labour;
- the effective abolition of child labour; and
- the elimination of discrimination in respect of employment and occupation.

### Environment

- businesses should support a precautionary approach to environmental challenges;
- undertake initiatives to promote greater environmental responsibility; and
- encourage the development and diffusion of environmentally friendly technologies.

### Anti-corruption

- businesses should work against all forms of corruption, including extortion and bribery.

Source: www.unglobalcompact.org.

Thus, even with something as ubiquitous as promotional freebies, it would appear that the ethical and environmental revolution has hit home to influence trading behaviour. It could be that the writing is on the wall.

*Sources*: Quilter (2009); www.procurement.ltd.uk; www.yo-promotions.co.uk.

# The marketing concept in the organisation

What does the philosophy of marketing as a way of doing business mean to a real organisation? In this section we explore the practicalities of implementing the marketing concept, showing just how fundamentally marketing can influence the structure and management of the whole organisation. First, we look at the complexity of the organisational environment, and then think about how marketing can help to manage and make sense of the relationship between the organisation and the outside world. Second, we examine the relationship between marketing and the internal world of the organisation, looking, for example, at the potential conflicts between marketing and other business functions. To bring the external and the internal environments together, this section is summarised by looking at marketing as an interface, i.e. as a linking mechanism between the organisation and various external elements.

## The external organisational environment

Figure 1.2 summarises the complexity of the external world in which an organisation has to operate. There are many people, groups, elements and forces that have the power to influence, directly or indirectly, the way in which the organisation conducts its business. The organisational environment includes both the immediate operating environment and the broader issues and trends that affect business in the longer term.

## Current and potential customers

Customers are obviously vital to the continued health of the organisation. It is essential, therefore, that it is able to locate customers, find out what they want and then communicate its promises to them. Those promises have to be delivered (i.e. the right product at the right time at the right price in the right place) and followed up to ensure that customers are satisfied.

## Competitors

Competitors, however, make the organisation's liaison with customer groups a little more difficult, since by definition they are largely pursuing the same set of customers. Customers will make comparisons between different offerings, and will listen to competitors' messages. The organisation, therefore, has not only to monitor what its competitors are actually doing now, but also to try to anticipate what they will do in the future in order to develop counter-measures in advance. European giants Nestlé and Unilever, for example, compete fiercely with each other in several fast moving consumer goods (fmcg) markets.

## Intermediaries

Intermediaries often provide invaluable services in getting goods from manufacturers to the end buyer. Without the cooperation of a network of wholesalers and/or retailers, many manufacturers would have immense problems in getting their goods to the end customer at the right time in the right place. The organisation, therefore, must think carefully about how best to distribute goods, and build appropriate relationships with intermediaries. Again, this is an area in which competition can interfere, and organisations cannot always obtain access to the channels of distribution that they want, or trade on the terms that they want.

## Suppliers

Another crucial link in the chain is the supplier. Losing a key supplier of components or raw materials can mean that production flow is interrupted, or that a lower-quality or more expensive substitution has to be made. This means that there is a danger that the organisation will fail in its promises to the customer, for example by not providing the right product at the right time at the right price. Choice of suppliers, negotiation of terms and relationship building therefore all become important tasks.

**Figure 1.2**
The organisation's environment

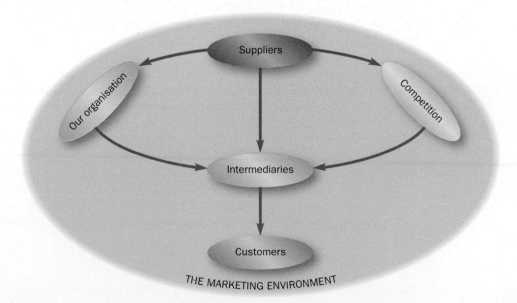

The wider marketing environment, which will be discussed in further detail in Chapter 2, covers all the other influences that might provide opportunities or threats to the organisation. These include technological development, legal and regulatory constraints, the economic environment, and sociocultural changes. It is essential for the organisation to keep track of all these factors, and to incorporate them into decision-making as early as possible if it is to keep ahead of the competition.

This overview of the organisation's world has implied that there are many relationships that matter and that need to be managed if the organisation is to conduct its business successfully. The main responsibility for creating and managing these relationships lies with the marketing function.

# The internal organisational environment

As well as fostering and maintaining relationships with external groups and forces, the marketing function has to interact with other functions within the organisation. Not all organisations have formal marketing departments, and even if they do they can be set up in different ways, but wherever the responsibility for the planning and implementation of marketing lies, close interaction with other areas of the organisation is essential. Not all business functions, however, operate with the same kind of focus, and sometimes there can be potential conflict where perspectives and concerns do not match up. This subsection looks at just a few other functions typically found in all but the smallest organisations and some of the points of conflict between them and the marketers.

## Finance

The finance function, for example, sets budgets, perhaps early in the financial year, and expects other functions to stick to them. It wants hard evidence to justify expenditure, and it usually wants pricing to cover costs and to contribute towards profit. Marketing, on the other hand, tends to want the flexibility to act intuitively, according to fast changing needs. Marketing also takes a longer, strategic view of pricing, and may be prepared to make a short-term financial loss in order to develop the market or to further wider strategic objectives.

In terms of accounting and credit, i.e. where finance comes into contact with customers, the finance function would want pricing and procedures to be as standardised as possible, for administrative ease. An accountant would want to impose tough credit terms and short credit periods, preferably only dealing with customers with proven credit records. Marketing, however, would again want some flexibility to allow credit terms to be used as part of a negotiation procedure, and to use pricing discounts as a marketing tool.

## Purchasing

The purchasing function can also become somewhat bureaucratic, with too high a priority given to price. A focus on economical purchase quantities, standardisation and the price of materials, along with the desire to purchase as infrequently as possible, can all reduce the flexibility and responsiveness of the organisation. Marketing prefers to think of the quality of the components and raw materials rather than the price, and to go for non-standard parts, to increase its ability to differentiate its product from that of the competition. To be fair to purchasing, this is a somewhat traditional view. The rise of relationship marketing (pp. 8–9) and the increasing acceptance of just-in-time (JIT) systems mean that marketing and purchasing are now working more closely than ever in building long-term, flexible, cooperative relationships with suppliers.

## Production

Production has perhaps the greatest potential to clash with marketing. It may be in production's interests to operate long, large production runs with as few variations on the basic product as possible, and with changes to the product as infrequently as possible, at least where mass production is concerned. This also means that production would prefer to deal with standard, rather than customised, orders. If new products are necessary, then the longer the lead time they are given to get production up to speed and running consistently, the better. Marketing has a greater sense of urgency and a greater demand for flexibility. Marketing may look for short production runs of many varied models in order to serve a range of needs in the market. Similarly, changes to the product may be frequent in order to keep the market interested. Marketing, particularly when serving B2B customers, may also be concerned with customisation as a means of better meeting the buyer's needs.

## Research and development and engineering

Like production, research and development (R&D) and engineering prefer long lead times. If they are to develop a new product from scratch, then the longer they have to do it, the better. The problem is, however, that marketing will want the new product available as soon as possible, for fear of the competition launching their versions first. Being first into a market can allow the organisation to establish market share and customer loyalty, and to set prices freely, before the effects of competition make customers harder to gain and lead to downward pressure on prices. There is also the danger that R&D and engineering may become focused on the product for the product's sake, and lose sight of what the eventual customer is looking for. Marketing, in contrast, will be concentrating on the benefits and selling points of the product rather than purely on its functionality.

# Marketing as an integrative business function

The previous subsection took a pretty negative view, highlighting the potential for conflict and clashes of culture between marketing and other internal functions. It need not necessarily be like that, and this subsection will seek to redress the balance a little, by showing how marketing can work with other functions. Many successful organisations such as Sony, Nestlé and Unilever ensure that all functions within their organisation are focused on their customers. These organisations have embraced a marketing philosophy that permeates the whole enterprise and places the customer firmly at the centre of their universe.

What must be remembered is that organisations do not exist for their own sake. They exist primarily to serve the needs of the purchasers and users of their goods and services. If they cannot successfully sell their goods and services, if they cannot create and hold customers (or clients, or passengers, or patients or whoever), then they undermine their reason for existing. All functions within an organisation, whether they have direct contact with customers or not, contribute in some way towards that fundamental purpose. Finance, for example, helps the organisation to be more cost effective; personnel helps to recruit appropriate staff and make sure they are properly trained and remunerated so that they are more productive or serve the customer better; R&D provides better products; and production obviously churns out the product to the required quality and quantity specifications to meet market needs.

All of these functions and tasks are interdependent, i.e. none of them can exist without the others, and none of them has any purpose without customers and markets to serve. Marketing can help to supply all of those functions with the information they need to fulfil their specific tasks better, within a market-oriented framework. Those interdependencies, and the role of marketing in bringing functions together and emphasising the customer focus, are summarised in a simplified example in Figure 1.3.

Although the lists of items in the boxes in Figure 1.3 are far from comprehensive, they do show clearly how marketing can act as a kind of buffer or filter, both collecting information from the outside world then distributing it within the organisation, and presenting the combined efforts of the various internal functions to the external world. Take, for example, two core issues from the 'customers' box: current product needs and future needs.

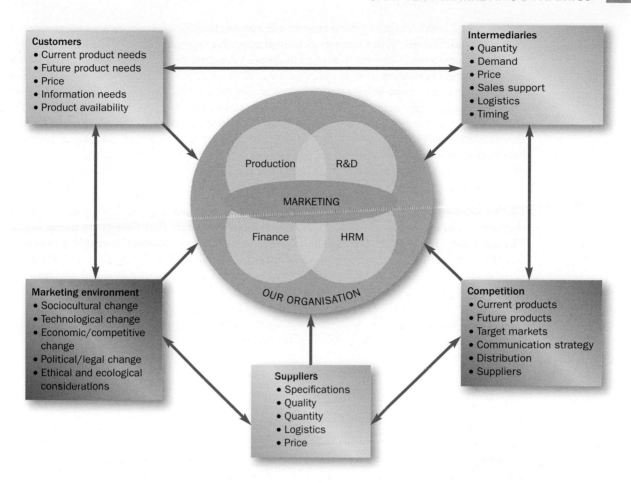

**Figure 1.3** Marketing as an interface

## Current product needs

To satisfy current needs, production has to know how much is required, when and to what quality specification. Production, perhaps with the help of the purchasing function, has to have access to the right raw materials or components at the right price. Keeping current products within an acceptable price band for the customer involves production, purchasing, finance and perhaps even R&D. A sales function might take orders from customers and make sure that the right quantity of goods is dispatched quickly to the right place. Marketing brings in those customers, monitoring their satisfaction levels, and brings any problems to the attention of the relevant functions as soon as possible so that they can be rectified with the minimum of disruption.

## Future needs

Marketing, perhaps with the help of R&D, needs to monitor what is happening now and to try to predict what needs to happen in the future. This can be through talking to customers and finding out how their needs are evolving, or working out how new technology can be commercially exploited, or through monitoring competitors' activities and thinking about how they can be imitated, adapted or improved upon. Inevitably, there is a planning lead time, so marketing needs to bring in ideas early, then work with other functions to turn them into reality at the right time. Finance may have to sanction investment in a new product; R&D might have to refine the product or its technology; production may have to invest in new plant, machinery or manufacturing techniques; purchasing may have to start looking for new suppliers; and personnel may have to recruit new staff to help with the development, manufacture or sales of the new product.

When R&D and marketing do share common goals and objectives, it can be a very powerful combination. Marketing can feed ideas from the market that can stimulate innovation, while R&D can work closely with marketing to find and refine commercial applications for its apparently pointless discoveries.

These examples show briefly how marketing can be the eyes and ears of the organisation, and can provide the inputs and support to help each function to do its job more efficiently. Provided that all employees remember that they are ultimately there to serve customers' needs, the truly marketing-oriented organisation has no problem in accepting marketing as an interface between the internal and external worlds, involving marketing in the day-to-day operation of its functions, and placing marketing insights at the heart of its corporate strategy.

## Marketing management responsibilities

This section outlines specifically what marketing does, and identifies where each of the areas is dealt with in this book.

All of marketing's tasks boil down to one of two things: identifying or satisfying customer needs in such a way as to achieve the organisation's objectives for profitability, survival or growth.

## Identifying customer needs

Implicit in this is the idea of identifying the customer. The development of mass markets, more aggressive international competition and the increasing sophistication of the customer have taught marketers that it is unrealistic to expect to be able to satisfy all of the people all of the time. Customers have become more demanding, largely, it must be said, as a result of marketers' efforts, and want products that not only fulfil a basic functional purpose, but also provide positive benefits, sometimes of a psychological nature.

The basic functional purpose of a product, in fact, is often irrelevant as a choice criterion between competing brands – all fridges keep food cold, all brands of cola slake thirst, all cars move people from A to B, regardless of which organisation supplies them. The crucial questions for the customer are how does it fulfil its function, and what extra does it do for me in the process? Thus the choice of a BMW over a Ford Fiesta may be made because the purchaser feels that the BMW is a better designed and engineered car, gets you from A to B in more comfort and with a lot more style, gives you the power and performance to zip aggressively from A to B if you want, and the BMW name is well respected and its status will reflect on the driver, enhancing self-esteem and standing in other people's eyes. The Fiesta may be preferred by someone who does not want to invest a lot of money in a car, who is happy to potter from A to B steadily without the blaze of glory, who values economy in terms of insurance, running and servicing costs, and who does not feel the need for a car that is an overt status symbol. These profiles of contrasting car buyers point to a mixture of product and psychological benefits, over and above the basic function of the cars, that are influential in the purchasing decision.

This has two enormous implications for the marketer. The first is that if buyers and their motives are so varied, it is important to identify the criteria and variables that distinguish one group of buyers from another. Once that is done, the marketer can then make sure that a product offering is created that matches the needs of one group as closely as possible. If the marketer's organisation does not do this, then someone else's will, and any 'generic' type of product that tries to please most of the people most of the time will sooner or later be pushed out by something better tailored to a narrower group. The second implication is that by grouping customers according to characteristics and benefits sought, the marketer has a better chance of spotting lucrative gaps in the market than if the market is treated as a homogeneous mass.

Identifying customer needs, however, is not just a question of working out what they want now. The marketer has to try to predict what they will want tomorrow, and identify the influences that are changing customer needs. The environmental factors that affect customer needs and wants, as well as the means by which organisations can fulfil them, are discussed further in Chapter 2. The nature of customers, and the motivations and attitudes that affect their buying behaviour, are covered in Chapters 3, while the idea of grouping customers according to common characteristics and/or desired product features and benefits is discussed in Chapter 4. The techniques of market research, as a prime means of discovering what customers are thinking and what they want now and in the future, is the subject of Chapter 5.

## Satisfying customer needs

Understanding the nature of customers and their needs and wants is only the first step, however. The organisation needs to act on that information, in order to develop and implement marketing activities that actually deliver something of value to the customer. The means by which such ideas are turned into reality is the marketing mix. Figure 1.4 summarises the areas of responsibility within each element of the mix.

The concept of the marketing mix as the combination of the major tools of marketing was first developed by Borden in the 1950s (Borden, 1964), and the mnemonic '4Ps' (product, price, promotion and place) describing those tools was coined by McCarthy (1960). The marketing mix creates an offering for the customer. The use of the words *mix* and *combination* are important here, because successful marketing relies as much on interaction and synergy between marketing-mix elements as it does on good decisions within those elements themselves. Häagen Dazs ice cream, for example, is a perfectly good, quality product, but its phenomenal

**Figure 1.4**
The marketing mix

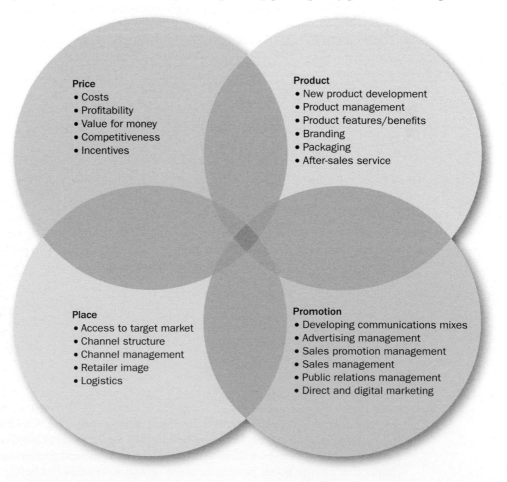

Price
- Costs
- Profitability
- Value for money
- Competitiveness
- Incentives

Product
- New product development
- Product management
- Product features/benefits
- Branding
- Packaging
- After-sales service

Place
- Access to target market
- Channel structure
- Channel management
- Retailer image
- Logistics

Promotion
- Developing communications mixes
- Advertising management
- Sales promotion management
- Sales management
- Public relations management
- Direct and digital marketing

success only came after an innovative and daring advertising campaign that emphasised certain adult-oriented product benefits. A good product with bad communication will not work, and similarly a bad product with the glossiest advertising will not work either. This is because the elements of the marketing mix all depend on each other, and if they are not consistent with each other in what they are saying about the product, then the customer, who is not stupid, will reject it all.

We now look more closely at each element of the marketing mix.

## Product

This area, discussed in Chapter 6, covers everything to do with the creation, development and management of products. It is about not only what to make, but when to make it, how to make it, and how to ensure that it has a long and profitable life.

Furthermore, a product is not just a physical thing. In marketing terms, it includes peripheral but important elements, such as after-sales service, guarantees, installation and fitting – anything that helps to distinguish the product from its competition and make the customer more likely to buy it.

Particularly with fast moving consumer goods (fmcg), part of a product's attractiveness is, of course, its brand imagery and its packaging. Both of these are likely to emphasise the psychological benefits offered by the product. With B2B purchases, however, the emphasis is more likely to be on fitness for functional purpose, quality and peripheral services (technical support, delivery, customisation, etc.). As well as featuring in the product chapter, echoes of these concerns will come through strongly in the chapters on buyer behaviour and segmentation (Chapters 3 and 4).

Although much of the emphasis is on physical products, it must also be remembered that service markets are an increasingly important growth area of many European economies. The product chapters do cover some aspects of services, but the main discussion of the service product is in Chapter 14.

## Price

Price is not perhaps as clear cut as it might seem at first glance, since price is not necessarily a straightforward calculation of costs and profit margins. As Chapter 7 will show, price has to reflect issues of buyer behaviour, because people judge 'value' in terms of their perceptions of what they are getting for their money, what else they could have had for that money and how much that money meant to them in the first place.

Pricing also has a strategic dimension, in that it gives messages to all sorts of people in the market. Customers, for example, may use price as an indicator of quality and desirability for a particular product, and thus price can reinforce or destroy the work of other elements of the marketing mix. Competitors, on the other hand, may see price as a challenge, because if an organisation prices its products very low it may be signalling its intention to start a price war to the death, whereas very high (premium) prices may signal that there are high profits to be made or that there is room for a competitor to undercut and take market share away.

Overall, price is a very flexible element of the marketing mix, being very easy to tinker with. It is also, however, a dangerous element to play around with, because of its very direct link with revenues and profits, unless management think very carefully and clearly about how they are using it. The focus of the pricing chapters, therefore, is on the factors that influence price setting, the short-term tactical uses of pricing in various kinds of market and the strategic implications of a variety of pricing policies.

## Place

Place is a very dynamic and fast moving area of marketing. It covers a wide variety of fascinating topics largely concerned with the movement of goods from A to B and what happens at the point of sale. Chapter 8 therefore looks at the structure of channels of distribution, from e-tailers or mail-order companies that deal direct with the end consumer, to long and complex chains that involve goods passing between several intermediaries before they get to a retailer.

The chapter explores the range of different intermediaries, and the roles they play in getting goods to the right place at the right time for the end buyer, as well as the physical distribution issues involved in making it all happen.

For consumer goods, the most visible player in the channel of distribution is the retailer. Manufacturers and consumers alike have to put a lot of trust in the retailer to do justice to the product, to maintain stocks, and to provide a satisfying purchasing experience. Retailers face many of the same marketing decisions as other types of organisation, and use the same marketing mix tools, but with a slightly different perspective. They also face unique marketing problems, for example store location, layout and the creation of store image and atmosphere. Retailing has therefore been given a strong emphasis in this chapter.

## Promotion

Chapters 9–12 are basically about communication, which is often seen as the most glamorous and sexy end of marketing. This does not mean, however, that marketing communication is purely an 'artistic' endeavour, or that it can be used to wallpaper over cracks in the rest of the marketing mix. Communication, because it is so pervasive and high profile, can certainly make or break a marketing mix, and thus it needs wise and constant analysis, planning and management.

These chapters look at the whole range of marketing communication techniques, not just advertising, but also sales promotions, personal selling, public relations and direct marketing, including the use of electronic media. The activities undertaken within each area, the objectives each can best achieve, their relative strengths and weaknesses, and the kinds of management and planning processes that have to support them are discussed. To put all that into perspective, however, Chapter 9 first looks at the promotional mix as a whole, thinking about the factors that will influence the relative emphasis put on each individual communications area.

It's not just fast moving consumer goods that can benefit from e-marketing through social media and other digital channels. Companies selling family cars can see a lot of potential too. The UK Marketing Director of Hyundai motors said, 'We know that 80 per cent of people research online before they go into dealerships, so we need to generate as much positive content on Google or social networks as possible' (as quoted by *New Media Age*, 2011). To that end, Hyundai invested 25 per cent of its marketing budget in social media in 2011 and used sponsorship of a mum's blogging event (CyberMummy) to generate content for Facebook, Twitter and YouTube. Kia UK has similarly increased its investment in digital media. Kia UK's Database and Digital Marketing Manager said, 'Whereas people used to spend their Sundays driving around dealerships looking at seven different vehicles, they're now looking at seven different websites and going to two different dealers' (as quoted by Smith, 2011), which means that there has to be a strong web presence for the Kia brand and digital linkages with its dealerships. As well as its website, Kia now also uses videos on a YouTube channel, a Facebook page, and pay-per-click advertising to make contact with potential customers and generate interest in its products.

That, then, is the traditional 4Ps approach to marketing that has served very well for many years. More recently, however, it has become apparent that the 4Ps as they stand are not always sufficient. In the services sector in particular, they cannot fully describe the marketing activities that are going on, and so an extended marketing mix, the 7Ps, was proposed by Booms and Bitner (1981), adding people, processes and physical evidence to the traditional 4Ps.

## People

Services often depend on people to perform them, creating and delivering the product as the customer waits. A customer's satisfaction with hairdressing and dentistry services, for example, has as much to do with the quality and nature of the interaction between the customer and the service provider as with the end result. If the customer feels comfortable with a particular service provider, trusts them and has a rapport with them, that is a relationship that a competitor would find hard to break into. Even where the service is not quite so personal, sullen assistance in a shop or a fast-food outlet, for example, does not encourage the customer to come back for more. Thus people add value and a dimension to the marketing package way beyond the basic product offering.

## Processes

Manufacturing processes, once they are set up, are consistent and predictable and can be left to the production management team, and since they go on out of sight of the customer, any mistakes can be weeded out before distribution. Services, however, are 'manufactured' and consumed live, on the spot, and because they do involve people and the performance of their skills, consistency can be rather more difficult than with normal manufacturing. The marketer, therefore, has to think carefully about how the service is delivered, and what quality controls can be built in so that the customer can be confident that they know what to expect each time they consume the service product. This applies, for example, to banks and other retailers of financial services, fast-food outlets, hairdressers and other personal service providers, and even to professionals such as solicitors and management consultants.

Process can also involve queueing mechanisms, preventing waiting customers from getting so impatient that they leave without purchase; processing customer details and payment; as well as ensuring the high professional quality of whatever service they are buying.

## Physical evidence

This final area is of particular relevance to retailers (of any type of product), or those who maintain premises from which a service is sold or delivered. It singles out some of the factors already mentioned when talking about retailers within the place element of the traditional 4Ps approach, such as atmosphere, ambience, image and design of premises. In other service situations, physical evidence would relate to the aircraft in which you fly, the hotel in which you stay, the stadium in which you watch the big match, or the lecture theatre in which you learn.

Other than in the services arena, the 4Ps are still widely accepted as defining the marketing mix. It has never been suggested, however, that the same mix is applicable in all situations or even for the same organisation at different times, so the task of the marketing manager is to review and change the mix to suit emerging circumstances. The marketing mix is simply therefore a set of categories of marketing variables that has become standard in marketing education and is the foundation for the structure of this book. As you read the chapters relating to the four elements of the marketing mix, look to see where aspects of people, process and physical evidence are being incorporated or implied within that traditional structure. Relationship marketing, in any type of market for any type of product, is increasingly throwing the emphasis on adding value to products through service. Inevitably, the extra 3Ps are going to impinge on that, and will be reflected in discussing applications of the original 4Ps.

The particular combination of the 4Ps used by any one organisation needs to give it competitive edge, or differential advantage. This means that the marketer is creating something unique, that the potential customer will recognise and value, that distinguishes one organisation's products from another's. In highly competitive, crowded markets, this is absolutely essential for drawing customers towards your product. The edge or advantage may be created mainly through one element of the mix, or through a combination of them. A product may have a combination of high quality and good value (price and product) that a competitor cannot match; an organisation may have established a 24-hour internet ordering and home delivery service (place) that cannot easily be imitated; an effective and unique communications campaign combined with an excellent product living up to all its promises (promotion and product) can make an organisation's offering stand out above the crowd.

## Strategic vision

It is clear that individual marketing activities must be looked at within the context of a coherent and consistent marketing mix, but achieving that mix has to be an outcome of a wider framework of strategic marketing planning, implementation and control. Chapter 13 looks at these wider issues.

Strategy is concerned with looking into the future and developing and implementing the plans that will drive the organisation in the desired direction. Implicit in that is the need for strategy to inform (and be informed by) marketing. Strategic marketing thinking also needs a certain amount of unblinkered creativity, and can only be really successful if the marketer thinks not in terms of product, but rather in terms of benefits or solutions delivered to the customer. The organisation that answers the question 'What business are you in?' with the reply 'We are in the business of making gloss paint' is in danger of becoming too inwardly focused on the product itself and improving its manufacture (the production orientation). A more correct reply would have been: 'We are in the business of helping people to create beautiful rooms' (the identification of customer needs). The cosmetics executive who said that in the factory they made cosmetics but in the chemist's shop they sold hope, and the power tool manufacturer who said that they did not make drills, they made quarter-inch holes, were both underlining a more creative, outward-looking, problem-solving way of marketing thinking. Products are bought by customers to solve problems, and if the product does not solve the problem, or if something else solves it better, then the customer will turn away.

The organisation that cannot see this and defines itself in product rather than market terms could be said to be suffering from *marketing myopia*, a term coined by Levitt (1960). Such an organisation may well be missing out on significant marketing opportunities, and thus may leave itself open to new or more innovative competitors which more closely match customer needs. A classic example of this is slide-rule manufacturers. Their definition of the business they were in was 'making slide rules'. Perhaps if they had defined their business as 'taking the pain out of calculation' they would still exist today and be manufacturing electronic calculators. Green (1995) discusses how the pharmaceutical companies are thinking about what business they are in. The realisation that patients are buying 'good health' rather than 'drugs' broadened the horizons of companies such as Sandoz in Switzerland, GlaxoSmithKline in the UK and Merck in the USA, all of which have diversified into areas of healthcare other than research and development of drugs. GlaxoSmithKline, in particular, wants to spread its efforts across what it sees as the four core elements of healthcare: prevention, diagnosis, treatment and cure.

Therefore, the distinction between the product and the problem it solves matters, because marketing strategy is about managing the organisation's activities within the real world in which it has to survive. In that turbulent and dynamically changing world, a marketing mix that works today may not work tomorrow. If your organisation is too product focused to remember to monitor how customer needs and wants are changing, then it will get left behind by competitors who do have their fingers on the customer's pulse. If your organisation forgets why it is making a particular product and why the consumer buys it, how can it develop marketing strategies that strike a chord with the customers and defend against the competition?

Think about a drill manufacturer that is product focused and invests vast amounts of time and money in developing a better version of the traditional electric drill. How do you think it would feel if a competitor then launched a hand-held, cordless, laser gun that could instantly zap quarter-inch holes (controllably) through any material with no physical effort on the part of the operator, and with no mess because it vaporises the residue? The laser company was thinking ahead, looking at the consumer's problem, looking at the weaknesses in the currently available solutions, and developing a marketing package that would deliver a better solution.

What we are saying here is that it is not enough to formulate a cosy marketing mix that suits the product and is entirely consistent with itself. That marketing mix is only working properly if it has been thought through with due respect to the external environment within which it is to be implemented. As well as justifying the existence of that marketing mix in the light of current internal and external influences, the strategic marketer has to go further by justifying how that mix helps to achieve wider corporate objectives; explaining how it is helping to propel the organisation in its longer-term desired direction, and finally, how it contributes to achieving competitive edge.

Ultimately, competitive edge is the name of the game. If marketers can create and sustain competitive edge, by thinking creatively and strategically about the internal and external marketing environments, then they are well on the way to implementing the marketing concept and fulfilling all the promise of the definitions of marketing with which this chapter began.

## Marketing scope

Marketing plays a part in a wide range of organisations and applications. Some of these are discussed specifically in Chapter 14, while others are implicit throughout the text.

### Consumer goods

The consumer-goods field, because it involves potentially large and lucrative markets of so many individuals, has embraced marketing wholeheartedly, and indeed has been at the root of the development and testing of many marketing theories and concepts. Consumer goods and markets will be a major focus of this text, but certainly not to the exclusion of anything else. Since we are all consumers, it is easy to relate our own experience to the theories and concepts presented here, but it is equally important to try to understand the wider applications.

### B2B goods

Business-to-business (B2B) goods ultimately end up serving consumers in some way, directly or indirectly. The cleaned wool that the woolcomber sells to the spinner to make into yarn to sell to the weaver to make into cloth eventually ends up in the shops as clothing; the rubber that Dunlop, Goodyear or Firestone buys to make into tyres to sell to car manufacturers ends up being bought by consumers; the girders sold by Tata Steel Europe to a civil engineering contractor for a new bridge end up serving the needs of individuals. If these organisations are going to continue to feed the voracious appetite of consumer markets successfully (the right product in the right place at the right time at the right price – remember?), then they also have to manage their relationships with other organisations, in a marketing-oriented way. A study by Avlonitis *et al.* (1997) found that companies in B2B markets that had developed a marketing orientation were a lot more successful than those that had not. The buying of goods, raw materials and components by organisations is a crucial influence on what can be promised and offered, especially in terms of price, place and product, to the next buyer down the line. If these inter-organisational relationships fail, then ultimately the consumer, who props up the whole chain, loses out, which is not in the interests of any organisation, however far removed from the end consumer. As Chapter 3, in particular, will show, the concerns and emphases in B2B markets are rather different from those of consumer markets, and thus need to be addressed specifically.

### Service goods

Service goods, to be discussed in Chapter 14, include personal services (hairdressing, other beauty treatments or medical services, for example) and professional skills (accountancy, management consultancy or legal advice, for example), and are found in all sorts of markets, whether consumer or B2B. As already mentioned on pp. 29–31, services have differentiated themselves somewhat from the traditional approach to marketing because of their particular characteristics. These require an extended marketing mix, and cause different kinds of management headaches from physical products. Many marketing managers concerned with physical products are finding that service elements are becoming increasingly important to augment their products and to differentiate them further from the competition.

This means that some of the concepts and concerns of services marketing are spreading far wider than their own relatively narrow field, and this is reflected throughout this book. In between the two extremes of a largely service product (a haircut, for instance) and a largely physical product (a machine tool, for instance), are products that have significant elements of both. A fast-food outlet, for example, is selling physical products – burger, fries and a Coke – and that is primarily what the customer is there for. Service elements, such as speed and friendliness of service, atmosphere and ambience, are nevertheless inextricably linked with those physical products to create an overall package of satisfaction (or otherwise) in the customer's mind. This mixture of physical and service products is common throughout the retail trade, and thus services marketing not only features in its own chapter, but also permeates Chapter 8, dealing with distribution.

## Non-profit marketing

Non-profit marketing is an area that increasingly asserted itself in the economic and political climate of the 1980s and 1990s. Hospitals, schools, universities, the arts and charities are all having to compete within their own sectors to obtain, protect and justify their funding and even their existence. The environment within which such organisations exist is increasingly subject to market forces, and altruism is no longer enough. This means that non-profit organisations need to think not only about efficiency and cost effectiveness, but also about their market orientation – defining what their 'customers' need and want and how they can provide it better than their rivals.

Chapter 14 looks in more detail at the particular marketing problems and situations facing non-profit organisations.

eg

The charity, Age UK (born of a merger between Help the Aged and Age Concern in 2009), adopts marketing methods to help serve its core mission: to secure and uphold the rights of disadvantaged older people in the UK and around the world. However high the ideals, in order to deliver the services, it must attract funds to enable it to run campaigns to assist older people. The scale of the challenge is great when it is claimed that 2 million pensioners in the UK live below the poverty line, and at least 20,000 older people die each year as a result of the cold. Funds are needed, therefore, for advice and helplines, lobbying, research publications and direct support for older disadvantaged people.

In order to generate revenue, Age UK must attract donations, gifts and legacies as well as running its network of shops. It organises campaigns to recruit volunteers to collect donations or work in its shops, encourages volunteers to raise funds through entering events such as the Great North Run and the London Marathon or undertaking challenges such as skydiving, cycling from the Andes to the Amazon, or climbing Mount Kilimonjaro, and runs events such as celebrity golf tournaments. Corporate sponsorship and partnerships are especially important and organisations as diverse as Friends Provident, MDS Pharma, Nintendo, Tesco, and Three Valleys Water are pleased to be associated with this worthwhile cause in various capacities.

Skydiving, an Age UK fund-raising event

*Source*: Press Association Images/Dave Pratt

Marketing thinking enables the non-profit-making organisation to fulfil its mission. The exchange offering has to be designed (see Figure 1.1) so that givers feel rewarded, and the messages are communicated in the right way to attract funds, to lobby and to reach older people. The mission may be non-profit-oriented but the marketing methods and culture are as professional and focused as those found in many a commercial organisation (www.ageuk.org.uk).

## Small business marketing

Small business marketing also creates its own perspectives, as discussed in Chapter 13. Many of the marketing theories and concepts laid out in this book have been developed with the larger organisation, relatively rich in management resources, in mind. Many small businesses, however, have only one or two managers who have to carry out a variety of managerial functions and who often have very limited financial resources for investment in researching new markets and developing new products ahead of the rest. These are a few of the many constraints and barriers to the full implementation of the whole range of marketing possibilities. Throughout this book, therefore, we take a closer look at these constraints and consider more pragmatically how marketing theories and practice can be adapted to serve the needs of the small business.

## International marketing

International marketing is a well-established field, and with the opening up of Europe as well as technological improvements that mean it is now easier and cheaper to transfer goods around the world, it has become an increasingly important area of marketing theory and practice. Throughout this book, examples will be found of organisations dealing with issues of market entry strategies, whether to adapt marketing mixes for different markets and how, and the logistics of serving geographically dispersed markets, all providing an interesting perspective on marketing decision-making.

# Chapter summary

- Marketing is about exchange processes, i.e. identifying what potential customers need and want now, or what they are likely to want in the future, and then offering them something that will fulfil those needs and wants. You thus offer them something that they value and, in return, they offer you something that you value, usually money. Most (but not all) organisations are in business to make profits, and so it is important that customers' needs and wants are fulfilled cost effectively, efficiently and profitably. This implies that the marketing function has to be properly planned, managed and controlled.

- Marketing in some shape or form has been around for a very long time, but it was during the course of the twentieth century that it made its most rapid developments and consolidated itself as an important business function and as a philosophy of doing business. By the late 1990s, all types of organisations in the USA and western Europe had adopted a marketing orientation and were looking for ways to become even more customer focused, for example through relationship marketing.

- The marketing orientation has been a necessary response to an increasingly dynamic and difficult world. Externally, the organisation has to take into account the needs, demands and influences of several different groups such as customers, competitors, suppliers and intermediaries, who all exist within a dynamic business environment. Internally, the organisation has to coordinate the efforts of different functions, acting as an interface between them and the customer. When the whole organisation accepts that the customer is absolutely paramount and that all functions within the organisation contribute towards customer satisfaction, then a marketing philosophy has been adopted.

- Marketing's main tasks, therefore, are centred around identifying and satisfying customers' needs and wants, in order to offer something to the market that has a competitive edge or differential advantage, making it more attractive than the competing product(s). These tasks are achieved through the use of the marketing mix, a combination of elements that actually create the offering. For most physical goods, the marketing mix consists of four elements, product, price, place and promotion. For service based products, the mix can be extended to seven elements with the addition of people, processes and physical evidence. The marketer has to ensure that the marketing mix meets the customer's needs and wants, and that all its elements are consistent with each other, otherwise customers will turn away and competitors will exploit the weakness. Additionally, the marketer has to ensure that the marketing mix fits in with the strategic vision of the organisation, that it is contributing to the achievement of longer-term objectives, or that it is helping to drive the organisation in the desired future direction. These marketing principles are generally applicable to any kind of organisation operating in any kind of market. But whatever the application, the basic philosophy remains: if marketers can deliver the right product in the right place at the right time at the right price, then they are making a crucial contribution towards creating satisfied customers and successful, efficient and profitable organisations.

## Questions for review and discussion

**1.1** What is meant by the description of marketing as an *exchange process*?

**1.2** Distinguish between the four main *business orientations*.

**1.3** What is *competitive edge* and why is it so important?

**1.4** Choose a product that you have purchased recently and show how the elements of the marketing mix came together to create the overall offering.

**1.5** Why is the question, 'What business are we in?' so important? How might

(a) a fast-food retailer;

(b) a national airline;

(c) a car manufacturer; and

(d) a hairdresser

answer that question if it was properly *marketing oriented*?

---

## CASE STUDY 1

# DEVICES AND DESIRES

What is a book, and what exactly is the core benefit that the reader derives from it? If it's about engaging with the content, then the emergence of e-reading devices and digital books represents a great development for publishers and readers alike. For the consumer, an e-reader is an immensely convenient way of carrying around a library of hundreds of books that can be accessed whenever and wherever you want – according to Mintel's (2011) survey, 87 per cent of us like to read in bed and 84 per cent of us read while we're on holiday. You can acquire new books cheaply and easily from the comfort of your armchair with instant delivery, without the hassle of having to visit an actual bookshop or waiting for a parcel to be delivered, and of course, once you have an e-book, physical storage space is not an issue. You can annotate the text without permanently marking it, and thus edit your annotations, and you can easily share favourite passages with other readers.

The market for e-books really took off in the UK over Christmas 2010, with 7 per cent of British adults claiming to have been given an e-reader, and then to have paid for and downloaded an average of almost 6 books each in January 2011 (*Telecompaper Europe*, 2011). There are many e-readers on the market, some of which are

dedicated to the one function i.e. downloading and reading books, and some of which are multifunctional, such as the Apple iPad. A pioneer of the dedicated e-reader, however, which perhaps has done the most to stimulate growth in this market, is the Kindle, developed and sold by Amazon, the online retailer.

The e-book revolution started in the USA, but is rolling out across the world, not least because of Amazon's international presence which has given it a ready-made distribution platform and existing customer base in many countries. A Mintel survey undertaken in the UK suggests that 44 per cent of respondents tend to buy most of their books online, buying from sites such as amazon.co.uk. Thus the product launches and marketing activities that Amazon undertakes with the Kindle in the USA follow later in the UK, and then into Germany and beyond. Amazon is thus only now starting to see the same sort of growth take off in the UK and Europe as it has already enjoyed in the USA.

The extensive promotion of Kindle on Amazon's own UK website following its launch into the UK market in 2010 had clearly had an effect in stimulating this growth. It is advertised prominently on the Amazon homepage, and has its own 'department' in which all the Kindle-related hardware, software and accessories are grouped. It is difficult to miss the Kindle on the Amazon website, but rival products (such as the Sony e-reader, for example), are less easy to locate on Amazon, even though they are sold there. The Kindle also features in e-mail direct marketing, particularly in the run-up to major gift-giving occasions such as Christmas, Mother's Day and Father's Day, and this is supported with television advertising to demonstrate both the product's technical features (including its superiority over tablet computers for reading) and the relationship between the device and the user. As a result of all this, the Kindle is now the top-selling item on both amazon.com in the USA and on amazon.co.uk, and it is estimated that over 8 million Kindles were sold in 2010.

In the UK, the Kindle was intially only available through Amazon and currently retails at £111, or £152 including a free global 3G connection allowing the owner to download books from wherever they happen to be. But there is, of course, an important co-dependency in this market – consumers are not going to buy an e-reader unless there are plenty of books to read on it, but e-books are no use unless buyers have invested in the e-reader too. This is perhaps where Amazon's influence as a major global bookseller has been critical, by working with publishers to develop the e-books and co-marketing the Kindle device with those books. For books written in English, the potential market is huge with 600 million native speakers and 1.4 billion worldwide who read English. In contrast, the German market for e-books, for instance, has been slow to take off because of the limited availability of German-language e-books (there are around 95 million native speakers of German and 80 million more non-native speakers worldwide). However, Amazon's launch of the Kindle in Germany in 2011, with 650,000 e-book titles available through its e-bookstore should stimulate more rapid growth (Shahrigian, 2011). In contrast, amazon.co.uk offers around 500,000 titles for purchase, and a further 1 million free titles (classic titles for which the copyright has expired) (Poulter, 2011).

While e-books still only represented 2.5 per cent of the total UK book market in 2010, during April and May 2011, Amazon said it was selling 242 e-books

Is the Kindle the greatest literary innovation since the printing press?
*Source*: Getty Images News/Jeff Bezos

for every 100 hardbacks. In the USA, the ratio is over 200 e-books sold for every 100 'real' books (hardback and paperback combined). One interesting feature of this market that is perhaps part of the reason for this revolution in book-buying habits is that unlike many new electronic devices that appeal largely to younger, tech-savvy customers, the e-readers are finding favour with older consumers as well, and with aficionados of certain literary genres. One publisher suggested that there is a particular niche among '. . . crime or romance readers. They tend to read a lot of books and the cost is a decisive factor: you can get these books cheaper as e-books. If you love crime and you read so much that you can't keep it all, you probably give a lot of books away to charity' (as quoted by Groskop, 2011). Whoever is doing the buying, e-readers are certainly changing purchasing patterns within the publishing industry. Traditionally, book sales peaked in the run-up to Christmas as people bought books as gift. Now, publishers are seeing a further surge in sales in January and February as people who received e-readers as gifts load them up with reading matter.

The pricing of the e-books themselves is also an interesting issue. The publishers are obviously keen to avoid the same sort of piracy problems that are rife within the music industry. It's not easy, however. Consumers' experiences of book buying are based on 'real' books and their price perceptions are rooted more in the perceived value of the physical product than the ideas contained within it. E-books don't incur the costs of printing, distributing and storing 'real' books, but according to the publishers those costs only represent a small proportion of the retail price, on average (Hill, 2011). Consumers can grasp the concept of those specific costs, but they have more trouble, as has been seen in the music industry, with the notion of paying for the intellectual property that they are consuming i.e. the need for the authors to earn a living wage. Research reported by Bradshaw (2011) suggests that 36 per cent of tablet owners (e.g. the iPad) and 29 per cent of e-book readers admitted that they download books without paying for them, and around one-quarter of them are planning to do it even more often in the future. Interestingly, Johnson (2011) makes the point that e-book prices are largely not much cheaper than 'real' books (although there is also a view in some quarters that Amazon is actually pricing e-books very aggressively and making little or no profit margin on them), and while publishers' costs have 'fallen ... dramatically', authors' royalties have not increased, which could tempt more bestselling authors to by-pass the publishers and look towards digital self-publication.

So, what happens next in this marketplace? In 2011, a further development in the USA was the launch of a cut-price Kindle at $114 (£70), a $25 reduction on the price of the standard model, but in return for that discount, the owner has to accept sponsored screen-savers and advertising (euphemistically called 'Kindle with Special Offers'). It is not difficult to imagine how this might evolve into quite sophisticated targeting of individual consumers based on their reading habits (you bought a Jane Austen novel? Here's some adverts for online dating agencies). The 3G model is similarly available for $164 'with Special Offers' compared with $189 for the ad-free version. Some of the first brands to see the potential of this are Olay (cosmetics), Buick (cars) and JP Morgan Chase (promoting Amazon's Visa card). Amazon has, however, promised that the advertisements will not interfere with the reading experience. The 'Special Offers' Kindle has initially been launched in the USA but is expected to be available in the UK in 2012.

And in a further extension of the Kindle brand name, according to Warman (2011), Amazon now has plans to launch a tablet computer to compete with the iPad, which is likely to lead to a price cut for the dedicated e-reader device, but more details of that are yet to emerge.

*Sources*: Bradley (2011); Bradshaw (2011); Edgecliffe Johnson (2011); Groskop (2011); Hill (2011); Johnson (2011); Mintel (2011); Poulter (2011); Shahrigian (2011); *Telecompaper Europe* (2011); Thompson (2011); Warman (2011).

## Questions

1 If a publisher was to ask you, 'What business are we in?', how might you respond?

2 Why do you think the Kindle has been so successful? Discuss this with reference to its marketing mix.

3 Printed books have been around for centuries. It could be argued that they have served their purpose very well and that readers are perfectly satisfied with printed books as a means of knowledge transfer and as a source of personal emotional fulfilment. To what extent, therefore, can you argue that the development of the e-reader and the e-book is a marketing rather than a product oriented business philosophy?

4 Is the traditional, independent bookshop dead?

# References for chapter 1

Alderson, W. (1957) *Marketing Behaviour and Executive Action: A Functionalist Approach to Marketing*, Homewood, IL: Irwin.

AMA (2007) 'Definition of Marketing', accessed via www.marketingpower.com/aboutama/pages/definitionofmarketing.aspx.

Andreasen, A., Lee, N. and Rothschild, M. (2008) 'Further Thoughts on the 2007 AMA Definition of Marketing and its Implications for Social Marketing', *Social Marketing Quarterly*, 14 (2), pp. 101–4.

Avlonitis, G. *et al.* (1997) 'Marketing Orientation and Company Performance: Industrial vs Consumer Goods Companies', *Industrial Marketing Management*, 26 (5), pp. 385–402.

Babakus, E., Cornwell, T., Mitchell, V., and Schlegelmilch, B. (2004) 'Reactions to Unethical Consumer Behaviour Across Six Countries', *Journal of Consumer Marketing*, 21 (4), pp. 254–63.

Balestrini, P. (2001) 'Amidst the Digital Economy, Philanthropy in Business as a Source of Competitive Advantage', *Journal of International Marketing and Marketing Research*, 26 (1), pp. 13–34.

Berry, L.L. (1983) 'Relationship Marketing', in L.L. Berry *et al.* (eds), *Emerging Perspectives of Services Marketing*, Chicago: American Marketing Association.

Boakie, J. (2008) 'Water Brands Begin Fight for Distinction', *Marketing*, 25 June.

Booms, B.H. and Bitner, M.J. (1981) 'Marketing Strategies and Organisation Structures for Service Firms', in J. Donnelly and W.R. George (eds), *Marketing of Services*, Chicago: American Marketing Association.

Borden, N. (1964) 'The Concept of the Marketing Mix', *Journal of Advertising Research*, June, pp. 2–7.

Bradley, J. (2011) 'Put the Kettle on for Kindle Ad Breaks', *Scotland on Sunday*, 17 April.

Bradshaw, T. (2011) 'Women Help Fuel Rise in E-book Piracy', *Financial Times*, 17 May.

CIM (2001) accessed via www.cim.co.uk.

Collier, J. and Wanderley, L. (2005) 'Thinking for the Future: Global Corporate Responsibility in the Twenty-First Century', *Futures*, 37 (2/3), pp. 169–82.

Co-operative Bank (2008) *Ten Years of Ethical Consumerism: 1999–2008*, Co-operative Bank, accessed via www.goodwithmoney.co.uk/assets/Ethical-Consumerism-Report-2009.pdf.

*Daily Telegraph* (2012) 'Cruise Prices Fall', *Daily Telegraph*, 25 February.

Deng, S. and Dart, J. (1999) 'The Market Orientation of Chinese Enterprises During a Time of Transition', *European Journal of Marketing*, 33 (5), pp. 631–54.

Dwyer, F., Shurr, P. and Oh, S. (1987), 'Developing Buyer and Seller Relationships', *Journal of Marketing*, 51 (2), pp. 11–27.

*The Economist* (2010) 'The Corruption Eruption', *The Economist*, 29 April.

Edgecliffe Johnson, A. (2011) 'Amazon's Electronic Book Sales Beat Print', *Financial Times*, 20 May.

Ellul, J. (2010) 'Waste Management – a Cycle of Recycling', 23 April.

*Environmental Leader* (2010) 'Asda, Tesco, Sainsbury's to Cut Packaging Carbon Footprint 10% by 2012', March 5, accessed via www.environmentalleader.com.

European Commission (2010) 'Corporate Social Responsibility', accessed via http://ec.europa.eu/enterprise/policies/sustainable-business/corporate-social-responsibility/index_en.htm.

Fawcett, S., Magnan, G. and Fawcett, A. (2010) 'Mitigating Resisting Forces to Achieve the Collaboration-enabled Supply Chain', *Benchmarking: An International Journal*, 17 (2), pp. 269–93.

Fuller, D. (1999) *Sustainable Marketing: Managerial–Ecological Issues*, Sage Publications.

García-Rosell, J-C. and Moisander, J. (2008) 'Ethical Dimensions of Sustainable Marketing: a Consumer Policy Perspective', *European Advances in Consumer Research*, 8, pp. 210–15.

Gordon, M. (1991) *Market Socialism in China*, Working Paper, University of Toronto.

Green, D. (1995) 'Healthcare Vies with Research', *Financial Times*, 25 April, p. 34.

Grönroos, C. (1999) 'Relationship Marketing: Challenges for the Organization', *Journal of Business Research*, 46 (3), pp. 327–35.

Grönroos, C. (2006) 'On Defining Marketing: Finding a New Roadmap for Marketing', *Marketing Theory*, 6 (4), pp. 395–417.

Grönroos, C. (2009) 'Marketing as Promise Management: Regaining Customer Management for Marketing', *Journal of Business & Industrial Marketing*, 24 (5/6), pp. 351–9.

Groskop, V. (2011) 'Q: What Do Toni Morrison, Cameron Diaz and Karl Lagerfeld Have in Common? A: They are All E-book Converts'. *Daily Telegraph*, 29 January.

Harris, L. (2010) 'Fraudulent Consumer Returns: Exploiting Retailers' Return Policies', *European Journal of Marketing*, 44 (6), pp. 730–47.

Hartman, C. and Beck-Dudley, C. (1999) 'Marketing Strategies and the Search for Virtue: a Case Analysis of the Body Shop International', *Journal of Business Ethics*, 20 (3), pp. 249–63.

*Health & Medicine Week* (2010) 'Ikea: Ikea Raises Over $35 Million Dollars From Soft Toy Campaign', *Health & Medicine Week*, 15 March.

Hemphill, M. (2009) 'Fun Defines the Carnival Cruise Line Brand Philosophy', *International Cruise & Ferry Review*, Spring/Summer.

Henderson, S. (1998) 'No Such Thing as Market Orientation – a Call for No More Papers', *Management Decision*, 36 (9), pp. 598–609.

Hendrie, C. (2012) 'More Overnight Stops Could Lure Passengers Back to Ships', *The Independent on Sunday*, 26 February.

Higgins, M. (2012) 'For Cruise Deals, the Time is Now', *New York Times*, 26 February.

Hill, A. (2011) 'E-books Rewrite an Industry', *Financial Times*, 26 May.

Ikea (2010) 'Ikea: Earth Hour is Coming Up!', Ikea Press Release, 24 March, accessed via www.prweb.com/releases/2010/03/prweb3771114.htm.

Johnson, B. (2003) 'Berth of Success?', *Marketing Week*, 13 November, p. 28.

Johnson, L. (2011) 'Publishers Must Seize the Digital Challenge', *Financial Times*, 11 May.

*Just-drinks* (2010) 'Harrogate Spa Water in Name Switch', *Just-drinks*, 25 February, accessed via www.just-drinks.com/news/.

Levitt, T. (1960) 'Marketing Myopia', *Harvard Business Review*, July/August, pp. 45–56.

McCarthy, E. (1960) *Basic Marketing*, Homewood, IL: Irwin.

Mintel (2009a) 'Bottled Water', October, accessed via http://academic.mintel.com.

Mintel (2009b) 'Health and Fitness Clubs', October, accessed via http://academic.mintel.com.

Mintel (2010) 'Holidays: Attitudes and the Impact of Recession', *Mintel Market Intelligence*, January, accessed via http://academic.mintel.com.

Mintel (2011) 'Books and E-books', *Mintel Market Intelligence*, February, accessed via http://academic.mintel.com.

Narver, J. and Slater, S. (1990) 'The Effect of a Market Orientation on Business Profitability', *Journal of Marketing*, 54 (4), pp. 20–35.

Nassauer, S. (2010) 'What it Takes to Keep a City Afloat', *Wall Street Journal*, 3 March.

*New Media Age* (2011) 'Hyundai to Invest in Digital to Help Boost Market Share', *New Media Age*, 16 June.

Pearce, J. and Doh, J. (2005) 'The High Impact of Collaborative Social Initiatives', *Sloan Management Review*, 46 (3), pp. 30–9.

Peisley, T. (2009) 'Added Value is the Luxury Sector's Answer to the Tough Economy', *International Cruise & Ferry Review*, Spring/Summer.

Piercy, N. (1992) *Marketing-led Strategic Change*, Oxford: Butterworth-Heinemann.

Porter, M. and Kramer, M. (2006) 'Strategy and Society: the link between Competitive Advantage and Corporate Social Responsibility', *Harvard Business Review*, December, pp. 78–92.

Poulter, S. (2005) 'We Had to Pay £2,500 because our Children are Music Pirates', *Daily Mail*, 8 June, p. 7.

Poulter, S. (2011) 'The E-reader Price War', *Daily Mail*, 8 February.

*Precision Marketing* (2004) 'Fitness Clubs Flex their Marketing Muscles', *Precision Marketing*, 16 January, p. 11.

Prystay, C. (2003) 'Made, and Branded, in China: Chinese Manufacturers Move to Market Under Their Own Names', *Wall Street Journal*, 22 August, p. A7.

Quilter, J. (2009) 'Green Pens Pay Their Way', *Marketing*, 20 May, p. 41.

Rowley, J. (2008) 'Understanding Digital Content Marketing', *Journal of Marketing Management*, 24 (5/6), pp. 517–40.

Sagdiyev, R. and Popova, A. (2010) 'Ikea Masters Rules of Russian Business', *The Moscow Times*, 14 May.

Schultz, R. and Good, D. (2000) 'Impact of the Consideration of Future Sales Consequences and Customer-oriented Selling on Long-term Buyer–Seller Relationships', *Journal of Business and Industrial Marketing*, 15 (4), pp. 200–15.

Shahrigian, S. (2011) 'European Consumers Reconsider the Benefits of E-books', *Deutsche Welle*, 10 May.

Sheth, J and Parvatiyar, A. (1995) 'Ecological Imperatives and the Role of Marketing' in M. Polonsky and A. Mintu-Wimsatt (eds), *Environmental Marketing: Strategies, Practice, Theory, and Research*, New York: Haworth Press.

Shoham, A., Ruvio, A. and Davidow, M. (2008) '(Un)ethical Consumer Behavior: Robin Hoods or Plain Hoods?', *Journal of Consumer Marketing*, 25 (4), pp. 200–210.

Slater, S., Mohr, J. and Sengupta, S. (2009) *Marketing of High Technology Products and Innovation*s, 3rd edn. Harlow: Pearson Education.

Smith, N. (2011) 'Digital Strategy: Directing the Online Traffic', *Marketing Week*, 24 March.

Smith, W. and Higgins, M. (2000) 'Cause-related Marketing: Ethics and the Ecstatic', *Business and Society*, 39 (3), pp. 304–22.

Svensson, G. (2005) 'The Spherical Marketing Concept: A Revitalization of the Marketing Concept', *European Journal of Marketing*, 39 (1/2), pp. 5–15.

*Telecompaper Europe* (2011) 'Kindle is top e-book reader for UK consumers – survey', *Telecompaper Europe*, 11 February.

Thompson, J. (2011) 'Bloomsbury Hails the UK's E-book "Revolution"', *The Independent*, 28 May.

Titova, I. (2010) 'Russian Ikea Fires Two Top Managers Over Bribes', *St Petersburg Times*, 16 February.

van Raaij, E. and Stoelhorst, J. (2008) 'The Implementation of a Market Orientation: a Review and Integration of the Contributions to Date', *European Journal of Marketing*, 42 (11/12), pp. 1265–93.

Vilanova, M., Lozano, J. and Arenas, D. (2009) 'Exploring the Nature of the Relationship between CSR and Competitiveness', *Journal of Business Ethics*, 87, pp. 57–69.

Warman, M. (2011) 'Amazon Fires up Kindle to Challenge Might of the iPad', *Daily Telegraph*, 5 May.

WCED (1987), *Our Common Future*, Oxford: Oxford University Press.

Williams, P., Nicholas, D. and Rowlands, I. (2010) 'The Attitudes and Behaviours of Illegal Downloaders', *Aslib Proceedings: New Information Perspectives*, 62 (3), pp. 283–301.

Zhuang, S. and Whitehill, A. (1989) 'Will China Adopt Western Management Practices?', *Business Horizons*, 32 (2), pp. 58–64.

# CHAPTER 2

# The European marketing environment

## LEARNING OBJECTIVES

This chapter will help you to:

- understand the importance of the external environment to marketing decision-making;
- assess the role and importance of scanning the environment as a means of early identification of opportunities and threats;
- appreciate the evolving and diverse nature of the European marketing environment;
- define the broad categories of factors that affect the marketing environment; and
- understand the influences at work within each of those categories and their implications for marketing.

## INTRODUCTION

**MARKETING, BY ITS VERY** nature, is an outward-looking discipline. As the interface between the organisation and the outside world, it has to balance internal capabilities and resources with the opportunities offered externally. Chapter 1 has already shown, however, that the outside world can be a complex and difficult place to understand. Although the definition and understanding of the customer's needs and wants are at the heart of the marketing philosophy, there are many factors influencing how those customer needs evolve, and affecting or constraining the organisation's ability to meet those needs in a competitive environment. Thus, in order to reach an adequate understanding of the customer's future needs and to develop marketing mixes that will satisfy the customer, the marketer has to be able to analyse the external environment and clarify which influences and their implications are most important.

This chapter will dissect the external environment and look closely at the variety of factors and influences that help to shape the direction of marketing thinking. First, the chapter clarifies the nature of the external environment, underlining why it needs to be understood, and what opportunities that understanding offers to the marketer.

Although the environment consists of a wide variety of factors and influences, it is possible to group them under seven broad headings: sociocultural, technological, economic, ethical, political, legal and ecological, thus making the acronym STEEPLE. Each factor will be examined in turn, discussing the various issues they cover and their implications for marketing decision-making.

*eg* Some messages about sustainability do get through to consumers. Take cod, for example. In response to the warning that cod stocks were declining due to over-fishing, consumers switched to haddock. That's good news for cod, but not such good news for haddock. After a while, the Grimsby Fish Merchants' Association thought that the avoidance of cod had gone on long enough and urged consumers to switch back, claiming that cod stocks had recovered. They were supported by some national supermarkets which ran in-store promotions on cod. Critics argued, however, that although cod stocks were recovering, they were still short of sustainable levels. Now it seems that consumers are collectively having to master the art of not over-eating cod from responsibly sourced stocks – work that one out! (Ford, 2010).

There's plenty more fish in the sea?
*Source:* www.shutterstock.com/Valerio D'Ambrogi

# The nature of the European marketing environment

This section will first define the broad groupings of environmental influences, and then go on to look at the technique of environmental scanning as a means of identifying the threats and opportunities that will affect marketing planning and implementation within the organisation.

# Elements of the marketing environment

Figure 2.1 shows the elements of the external environment in relation to the organisation and its immediate surroundings.

As the figure shows, the elements can be divided into six main groupings, known by the acronym **STEEPLE**: Sociocultural, Technological, Economic, Ethical, Political and Legal, and **Ecological** environments.

## Sociocultural environment

The sociocultural environment is of particular concern to marketers as it has a direct effect on their understanding of customers and what drives them. Not only does it address the demographic structure of markets, but it also looks at the way in which attitudes and opinions are being formed and how they are evolving. A general increase in health consciousness, for instance, has stimulated the launch of a wide variety of products with low levels of fat and sugar, fewer artificial ingredients and no additives.

## Technological environment

Technological innovation and technological improvement have had a profound effect in all areas of marketing. Computer technology, for instance, has revolutionised product design, quality control, materials and inventory management, the production of advertising and other promotional materials, and the management and analysis of customer information. The rise in direct marketing as a communication technique and relationship building through brand presence on Facebook, Twitter and in other social media owes a lot to the cheap availability of powerful computerised database management and internet technology.

**Figure 2.1**
Elements of
the external
environment

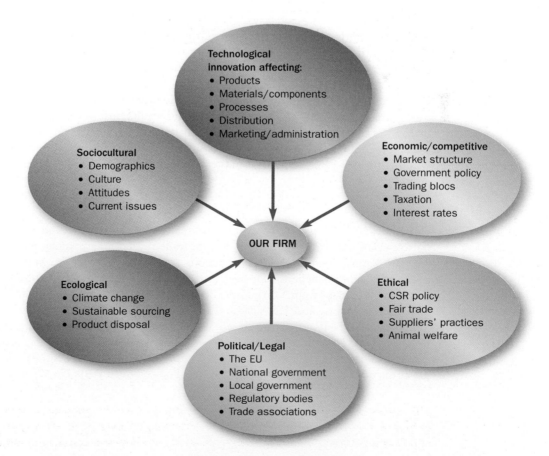

## Economic environment

The economic environment covers both macro- and micro-economic conditions which affect the structure of competition in a market, the cost and availability of money for marketing investment in stock and new products, for example, and the economic conditions affecting a customer's propensity to buy. The global recession of the late 2000s, for instance, caused a significant increase in unemployment at all social levels, and thus affected consumers' willingness and ability to buy many kinds of products.

## Ethical environment

As discussed in Chapter 1, there has been a significant shift over recent years in consumers' and organisations' attitudes to what is acceptable and not acceptable in business. It is interesting to consider whether government regulation leads or follows such a shift. Either way, these increasingly ethical attitudes are having a fundamental influence on everything, from the sourcing and management of raw materials and components right through to the buying decisions that consumers are making at the point of sale.

## Political and legal environments

The political environment covers the external forces at work through the EU, national governments and local authorities and assemblies. The legal environment covers not only the external forces controlled by governments, but also the constraints imposed by other trade or activity oriented regulatory bodies. Some of the rules and regulations developed and implemented by bodies under this heading have the force of law, while others are voluntary, such as advertising codes of practice.

## Ecological environment

Nothing lasts for ever. No resource is infinite, and that message has now permeated the consciousness of consumers and businesses to the extent that sustainability is now high on the agenda. This has been a great achievement for those who have lobbied in recent years, and the shift towards sustainability as a key driver of marketing thinking has really started to accelerate.

Each of the STEEPLE areas will be looked at in more detail on p. 45 *et seq*. There is, of course, much interdependence between them. Rules and regulations concerning 'green' aspects of products, for example, are a result of sociocultural influences pressurising the legislators and regulators. Many issues, therefore, such as international, ethical and green issues, will crop up with slightly different perspectives in the discussion of each STEEPLE element.

*eg*

The international political environment creates all sorts of favoured and banned trade between nations, and any breach of current trade rules can have knock-on effects. Perhaps one of the most famous periods of sanctions was against South Africa in the apartheid era, but more recently sanctions have been imposed on countries such as Iran and North Korea. A shipment of arms from North Korea destined for the Congo was alleged to have transited Chinese territory against UN sanctions imposed in 2009 after a breach of the nuclear test ban. Similarly, Thai authorities seized 35 tonnes of missiles, rockets and grenades bound (probably) for Iran on a Russian plane – which is odd because it was meant to be a shipment of oil-drilling equipment bound for Ukraine! North Korea is banned from exporting any arms under UN Resolution 1874 (Agence France Presse, 2010; Lloyd Parry, 2009).

# Environmental scanning

Even a brief discussion of the STEEPLE factors begins to show just how important the marketing environment is. No organisation exists in a vacuum, and since marketing is all about looking outwards and meeting the customer's needs and wants, the organisation has to take into account what is happening in the real world. The marketing environment will present many opportunities and threats that can fundamentally affect all elements of the marketing mix. In terms of the product, for example, STEEPLE factors help to define exactly what customers want, what it is possible (and legal) to provide them with, and how it should be packaged and presented. Pricing is also influenced by external factors, such as the competition's pricing policies, government taxation and what consumers can afford. STEEPLE factors also affect promotion, constraining it through regulation, but also inspiring the creativity that develops culturally relevant messages to capture the mood of the times and the target audience. Finally, the strength of relationships between manufacturers and retailers or other intermediaries is also affected by the external environment. Competitive pressures at all levels of the distribution channel; technology encouraging joint development and commitment in terms of both products and logistics; shifts in where and how people want to buy: all help to shape the quality and direction of inter-organisational relationships.

Thus the marketing mix is very dependent on the external environment, but the problem is that the environment is very dynamic, changing all the time. The organisation, therefore, has to keep pace with change and even anticipate it. It is not enough to understand what is happening today: by the time the organisation has acted on that information and implemented decisions based on it, it will be too late. The organisation has either to pick up the earliest indicators of change and then act on them very quickly, or try to predict change so that tomorrow's marketing offerings can be appropriately planned.

In order to achieve this successfully, the organisation needs to undertake environmental scanning, which is the collection and evaluation of information from the wider marketing environment that might affect the organisation and its strategic marketing activities. Such information may come from a variety of sources, such as experience, personal contacts, published market research studies, government statistics, trade sources or even through specially commissioned market research.

The approach to scanning can vary from being extremely organised and purposeful to being random and informal. As Aguilar (1967) pointed out, formal scanning can be very expensive and time consuming as it has to cast its net very wide to catch all the possible influences that might affect the organisation. The key is knowing what is important and should be acted upon, and what can wait. Environmental scanning is thus an important task, but often a difficult one, particularly in terms of interpretation and implementation of the information gained.

The following sections look in more detail at each of the STEEPLE factors, and give a further indication of the range and complexity of the influences and information that can affect the marketing activities of the organisation.

# The sociocultural environment

It is absolutely essential for organisations serving consumer markets, directly or indirectly, to understand the sociocultural environment, since these factors fundamentally influence the customer's needs and wants. Many of the factors discussed here will be looked at again in Chapters 3 and 4, and so this is a brief overview of the demographic and sociocultural influences on marketing thinking and activities.

## The demographic environment

Demographics is the study of the measurable aspects of population structures and profiles, including factors such as age, size, gender, race, occupation and location. As the birth rate fluctuates and as life expectancy increases, the breakdown of the population changes, creating challenges and opportunities for marketers, particularly if that information is taken in conjunction with data on family structure and income.

One demographic group of great interest to marketers is what is known as the 'grey market', consisting of the over-fifty age group. The over-fifties represent between 30 and 40 per cent of the population of many EU countries. Their numbers are increasing, and because of better healthcare and financial planning, a significant proportion of them is able to indulge in high levels of leisure-oriented consumption, especially as they are likely to have paid off any mortgage or similar long-term debt, and are not likely to have dependent children. Research into the over-fifties in Germany revealed that rather than thrift and self-denial, the growing emphasis is on enjoyment through consumption. To communicate effectively to this age group, the focus now has to reflect attitude and lifestyle rather than reinforcing an age-based stereotype.

# MARKETING IN ACTION

## Shades of grey

The population of Europe is changing. It is growing and ageing, and within 40 years globally the over-sixties will account for over one-fifth of the population. It has been predicted that half of all babies born in 2000 will live to 100 (Handley, 2010). This is causing marketers to rethink their brand positions and targeting techniques.

In the UK, there are 21 million consumers over the age of 50, i.e. 34 per cent of the population. Also, according to Saga, these consumers hold more than 80 per cent of the country's private wealth, 60 per cent of its savings and 40 per cent of its disposable income. The figures are similar in the USA and the rest of Europe. Herein lies the dilemma. The advertising industry is populated with people in their 20s and 30s who think they know what kind of messages people their 60s and 70s will respond to, but are they right (Clark, 2009)? Can they harness their creativity to communicate as effectively and empathically with older age groups as with their own?

The problem is that the grey market is a not a homogeneous market at all. It is made up of many shades and colours, for example, the outlook, interests and buying motives of a 50-year-old are very different from those of a 75-year-old, and even differ between people in the same narrow age bracket. In short, age is not a defining trait. The rise spending power among those aged between 75 and 100 is almost new ground for marketers and creates new opportunities. Many people in that age group don't want to be reminded of their age and don't want to be patronised in advertising by the stereotypes associated with it. Pitching a brand on age alone is a big turn off for those in the 50–60 age group, and it is only in the 65+ category that consumers start to feel more comfortable with age as a marketing focus and they will accept celebrity endorsement from stars they can identify with, such as Dame Judi Dench, Joanna Lumley, Sean Connery and Terry Wogan! Marketers still need to be careful, however – there are already too many indistinguishable cliché-ridden advertisements out there featuring some ageing actor or ex-newsreader reminding those of us who have hit 50 that we are heading for only one thing, and isn't it time we bought into insurance, medical cover, will writing services, and (heaven help us) pre-paid funeral plans for 'peace of mind for our loved ones'. The market should be handled with sensitivity, especially at the younger end of the over-fifties.

B&Q values the contribution of its older staff members to customer service

*Source*: www.eyevine.com, Eyevine LTD/Doug Healey/NY Times

Even thinking and reasoning change with age. As the consumer gets older, verbal memory declines at a faster rate than visual memory. Therefore, text-heavy copy will not grab an older reader and instead icons need to be used to tell brand stories (Medina, 2009). But even the 75+ age group cannot be considered homogeneous. Lifestyles, locations, life stages, physical and mental capacity will all determine which brands the consumer interacts with (Handley, 2010), and mainstream brands need to adapt if they are going to serve this segment. Some Nintendo Wii games, for example, are pitched at older consumers with golf, fitness and brain training more popular than the chase 'n' shoot type of game; B&Q employs pensioners as store assistants and also offer a discount to pensioners on some days of the week; and Harley Davidson has launched a motor bike with three wheels for the older boy racer, recapturing his 'Easy Rider' years. In some sectors, however, further adaptation is still necessary. The holiday and travel sector, for instance, represents a big market for older people, but travel insurance and single person supplements are bones of contention.

Despite all this it was reported by O'Connell (2010) that just 10 per cent of marketing is aimed at people aged over 50 and even then, it tends to be insulting and irrelevant. Indeed, a survey reported by The *Birmingham Post* (2009) found that 67 per cent of over-fifties feel that advertising does not reflect their life and 62 per cent find advertising patronising. Maybe it is time to shed the sedentary images of the consumer who is more or less finished with life and replace them with someone who has an active social life, enjoys travelling and is an enthusiastic technology user. Let's look a bit deeper and start to appreciate the many shades of grey that exist.

*Sources: Birmingham Post* (2009); Clark (2009); Handley (2010); Medina (2009); O'Connell (2010).

Clearly, the size of a household combined with its income is going to be a fundamental determinant of its needs and wants, and its ability to fulfil them. Many European countries are experiencing a pattern of decline in the average household size and marketers need to be mindful of these changes and to adapt their offerings accordingly. A significant increase in the proportion of single-person households will affect a whole range of marketing offerings, for example solo holidays, smaller apartments, smaller pack sizes, and different advertising approaches with fewer assumptions about family stereotypes.

What is also important is the level of disposable income available (i.e. what is left after taxes have been paid), and the choices the household makes about saving and/or spending it. Table 2.1 shows how the spending of disposable income varies across Europe.

Clearly, housing is a fundamental cost, but the proportion of income it takes varies widely across Europe, with the Bulgarians, Hungarians, Portuguese and Spanish spending the lowest percentage on housing. Looking at the food column, however, it is in the eastern European economies that people are spending relatively more on food as a percentage of their total expenditure. In some of the other categories, the Bulgarians like to communicate, the Finns, Danes, Swedes and Brits like to have a good time, the Portuguese take their health seriously, Italians are possibly Europe's best dressed nation, while the Hungarians seem to enjoy their alcohol! Of course, patterns of expenditure will be dictated to some extent by national income levels and relative prices as well as the marketing environment for the various categories of goods and services in each country.

**Table 2.1** Consumer expenditure by object 2010 (% analysis)

**Selected EU member countries**

| | Food and non-alcoholic beverages | Alcoholic beverages and tobacco | Clothing and footwear | Housing | Household goods and services | Health goods and medical services | Transport | Communications | Leisure and recreation | Education | Hotels and catering | Miscellaneous goods and services |
|---|---|---|---|---|---|---|---|---|---|---|---|---|
| Bulgaria | 21.3 | 3.8 | 3.2 | 19.6 | 4.4 | 3.7 | 20.2 | 5.2 | 5.2 | 0.9 | 8.7 | 3.8 |
| Czech Republic | 16.0 | 7.6 | 4.0 | 21.4 | 5.1 | 2.8 | 11.6 | 3.3 | 10.6 | 0.7 | 7.3 | 9.5 |
| Denmark | 11.5 | 3.2 | 4.6 | 27.2 | 5.5 | 2.6 | 12.0 | 2.1 | 11.1 | 0.8 | 6.7 | 12.8 |
| Finland | 12.5 | 4.8 | 4.6 | 25.2 | 5.3 | 4.6 | 11.4 | 2.7 | 12.0 | 0.4 | 6.6 | 9.8 |
| France | 13.2 | 2.8 | 4.3 | 25.5 | 6.0 | 3.7 | 14.4 | 2.7 | 9.2 | 0.9 | 6.1 | 11.1 |
| Germany | 11.0 | 3.1 | 5.3 | 24.4 | 6.6 | 5.5 | 13.7 | 2.7 | 9.3 | 1.0 | 5.7 | 11.7 |
| Hungary | 17.9 | 10.0 | 3.4 | 20.0 | 5.5 | 3.3 | 15.2 | 3.1 | 7.3 | 1.1 | 5.3 | 8.0 |
| Ireland | 10.2 | 5.1 | 5.2 | 21.2 | 6.3 | 3.5 | 12.2 | 2.8 | 7.0 | 1.3 | 13.7 | 11.5 |
| Italy | 14.8 | 2.7 | 7.6 | 21.0 | 7.4 | 3.0 | 13.0 | 2.5 | 6.9 | 0.9 | 10.2 | 10.0 |
| Netherlands | 11.6 | 2.9 | 5.3 | 23.6 | 6.9 | 0.7 | 12.5 | 4.3 | 10.3 | 0.5 | 5.3 | 16.1 |
| Poland | 20.2 | 6.5 | 4.4 | 24.5 | 4.4 | 4.1 | 8.1 | 3.6 | 7.1 | 1.3 | 2.8 | 13.2 |
| Portugal | 15.6 | 2.8 | 5.5 | 14.6 | 6.4 | 5.6 | 14.3 | 2.8 | 7.6 | 1.2 | 11.3 | 12.4 |
| Slovakia | 17.9 | 4.2 | 3.7 | 26.5 | 5.5 | 4.0 | 8.3 | 3.5 | 8.7 | 1.6 | 6.3 | 9.8 |
| Spain | 13.1 | 3.1 | 4.5 | 17.4 | 4.7 | 3.9 | 11.8 | 3.0 | 9.8 | 1.3 | 19.6 | 7.8 |
| Sweden | 12.6 | 3.2 | 4.9 | 26.9 | 5.4 | 3.3 | 13.1 | 3.3 | 11.3 | 0.4 | 5.4 | 10.3 |
| United Kingdom | 9.7 | 3.6 | 5.5 | 22.3 | 5.0 | 1.5 | 15.5 | 2.2 | 11.2 | 1.5 | 10.0 | 12.0 |

Row totals may not equal 100 due to rounding

*Sources*: compiled from Euromonitor data accessed via https://www.portal.euromonitor.com/Portal/Statistics.aspx
© 2011 Euromonitor International

Such spending patterns are not fixed: they will vary not only because of changes in the demographic and economic structure of the household, but also because of sociocultural influences, discussed in the next subsection. A further factor which cuts across both demographic and sociocultural issues is employment patterns, specifically the number of working women in a community and the rate of unemployment. This influences not only household income, but also shopping and consumption patterns.

# Sociocultural influences

Demographic information only paints a very broad picture of what is happening. If the marketer wants a really three-dimensional feel, then some analysis of sociocultural factors is essential. These factors involve much more qualitative assessment, can be much harder to measure and interpret than the hard facts of demographics and may be subject to unpredictable change, but the effort is worthwhile for a truly marketing oriented organisation.

One thing that does evolve over time is people's lifestyle expectations. Products that at one time were considered upmarket luxuries, such as televisions and fridges, are now considered to be necessities. Turning a luxury into a necessity obviously broadens the potential market, and widens the marketer's scope for creating a variety of products and offerings to suit a spectrum of income levels and usage needs. Televisions, for example, come in a variety of shapes, sizes and prices, from the pocket-sized portable to the cheap, small set that will do for the children's bedroom, to the very large, technically advanced, state-of-the-art status symbol with flat screen, HD and digital connectivity, and even 3D. This variety has the bonus of encouraging households to own more than one set, further fuelling the volume of the market, particularly as improvements in technology and production processes along with economies of scale further reduce prices.

Broadening tastes and demands are another sociocultural influence, partly fuelled by the marketers themselves, and partly emanating from consumers. Marketers, by constant innovation and through their marketing communications, encourage consumers to become bored with the same old standard, familiar products and thus to demand more convenience, variety and variation.

Sociocultural trends have favoured the cooking sauce market over the long term. A desire for more exotic fare in terms of home cooking has seen the rise of Italian, Mexican and other sauces and mixes. The market was worth £557 million by 2009, up 8.6 per cent on the previous year. Other forces have also been at work more recently as consumers move away from restaurants towards home cooking as a response to the recession. Another factor is that families are more prepared to eat together now rather than separately, so that one meal has to satisfy all household members – an oven bake using a cook-in sauce in a large dish is an easy and ideal solution to that. It is true to say, however, that more exotic sauce mixes have also suffered as families switch to 'one meal for all', although Italian sauces are holding up well, particularly lasagne sauces, and represent the largest sector. Nevertheless, there was still growth, for example in Sharwoods' Chinese, Indian and Italian ranges over 2008–9. Sales of pasta bake and potato bake sauces from Homepride have also risen considerably during the recession. The question is whether people will retain these eating and shopping habits as the economy moves out of recession (*The Grocer*, 2010).

Fashions and fads are also linked with consumer boredom and a desire for new stimulation. The clothing market in particular has an interest in making consumers sufficiently discontented with the perfectly serviceable clothes already in the wardrobe that they go out to buy new ones every season. For some consumers, it is important for their social integration and their status to be seen to have the latest products and the latest fashions, whether it be in clothing, music or alcoholic drinks. Nevertheless, linking a product with fashion may create marketing problems. Fashions, by definition, are short lived, and as soon as they become widespread, the fashion leaders are moving on to something new and different. Marketers, therefore, have to reap rewards while they can, or find a means of shifting the product away from its fashionable associations.

More deeply ingrained in society than the fripperies of fashion are underlying attitudes. These change much more slowly than fashion trends and are much more difficult for the marketer to influence. It is more likely, in fact, that the marketer will assess existing or emerging attitudes and then adapt or develop to fit them.

Just taking one example of a major shift in societal attitudes, health consciousness has now started to play a big role in the thinking behind consumer markets. The tobacco market has been particularly hard hit by increased awareness of the risks of smoking, and pressure from health lobbyists and the public has led to increased regulation of that industry. Food products have also been reappraised in the light of health concerns, with more natural ingredients, fewer artificial additives, less salt and less sugar content demanded. Linked with this, the market for low calorie products has also expanded, serving a market that wants to enjoy tasty food in quantity, but lose weight or at least feel that they are eating healthily. Health concerns have also led to a boom in products and services linked with fitness. Health clubs, aerobics classes, exercise videos, sportswear of all kinds and trainers are just some of the things that profited from the fitness boom.

## Consumerism and consumer forces

Changes in consumer attitudes and behaviour might not take hold and become significant quite so quickly without the efforts of organised groups. They themselves often use marketing techniques as well as generating publicity through the media, quickly raising awareness of issues and providing a focal point for public opinion to form around and helping it to gather momentum. In the UK, Which? (formerly the Consumers' Association) has long campaigned for legislation to protect consumers' rights, such as the right to safe products and the right to full and accurate information about the products we buy. As well as lobbying government and organisations about specific issues, Which? also provides independent information to consumers, testing and comparing the features, performance and value for money of competing goods and services in various categories. In a similar vein, specialist websites and magazines, in fields such as computing and hi-fi, also undertake comparative testing of products of interest to their readership.

Newton's third law of motion says that for every action there is an equal and opposite reaction, Marketing isn't physics or even rocket science, but marketers certainly seem to have some regard for Newton's third law: as the market for fattening foods increases, so does the market for slimming aids; arms companies sell increasingly sophisticated weapons, but also the defence systems to counteract them; the market for cigarettes has the market for smoking cessation aids as its opposite. A rise in sales of the major brands of cigarettes in 2009 saw a volume increase in sales for Niquitin and Nicotinell in excess of 15 per cent, suggesting that consumers were appreciating and being influenced by the various government campaigns and warning messages including the national 'No Smoking Day'.

Despite all the anti-smoking messages that are out there, there's a hard core of smokers remaining, and sales of cigarettes in 2009 increased by over 3 per cent to £11.3 billion in the UK. Six of the 10 leading tobacco brands experienced growth in 2009 with 'roll your own' showing the strongest growth. Despite bans on advertising, tighter rules on sponsorship, and the numerous groups promoting anti-smoking messages, the growth in the market continues. This raises the issue of whether the lobbying and existing legislation is enough to deter the hardened smoker or whether more direct control is necessary (Ball, 2010).

Consumer behaviour is also being influenced by the high-profile and sometimes militant pressure being brought to bear on organisations by green groups such as Friends of the Earth and Greenpeace. Although their interest is a wider, altruistic concern with ecology rather than consumer rights, they recognise that corporate practices that are harmful to the environment, wildlife and ecology can be partly discouraged by 'bottom-up' pressure. This means raising awareness, changing attitudes and altering purchasing habits among organisations' core customers.

Consumers have also been encouraged to think about their personal health as well as that of the planet. Sometimes sponsored by government (for example through the UK government's Department of Health) and sometimes through independent groups with a specific interest such as Action on Smoking and Health (ASH) or the British Heart Foundation, the public are urged to change their lifestyles and diets. Once it is generally known and accepted that too much of this, that or the other is unhealthy, food manufacturers are anxious to jump on the bandwagon and provide products to suit the emerging demand.

Pressure groups and consumer bodies are not there just to criticise organisations, of course. They also encourage and endorse good practice, and such an endorsement can be very valuable to the organisation that earns it. A consumer who is inexperienced in buying a particular type of product, or for whom that purchase represents a substantial investment, may well look for independent expert advice, and thus the manufacturer whose product is cited as *Which?* magazine's best buy in that category has a head start over the competition. Organisations may also commission product tests from independent bodies such as Which? or the Good Housekeeping Institute as a means of verifying their product claims and adding the bonus of 'independent expert opinion' to their marketing.

Some have argued that the recession of the late 2000s forced a new realism into consumerism (PWC, 2010). Consumers are behaving more deliberately and purposefully rather than going for conspicuous consumption. This perhaps is prompting retailers to adjust their strategies so that consumers can make more informed decisions. The question is whether consumers will react similarly in the post-recession recovery. PWC (2010) forecasts that around 20 per cent of them will continue that behaviour.

## The technological environment

In an increasingly dynamic world, where the creation, launch and maintenance of a new product are more expensive and difficult than ever, no organisation can afford to ignore the technological environment and its trends.

Even if your organisation does not have the inclination or resources to adopt or adapt new technology, understanding it is important because competitors will exploit it sooner or later, with implications for your product and its marketing.

The costs and the risks involved can be very high, since there is no guarantee that an R&D project will be successful in delivering a solution that can be commercially implemented. Nevertheless, organisations feel the need to invest in R&D, recognising that they will get left behind if they do not, and are optimistic that they will come up with something with an unbeatable differential advantage that will make it all worthwhile.

IBM takes R&D very seriously in its desire to be at the head of the innovation curve and to remain competitive. It has learned that lesson the hard way, though. Originally, the world ran on IBM mainframes and databases but the trend towards smaller networked computers meant that competitors took market share away from IBM. In the 1990s, IBM sought to regain a dominant position in a fast moving, technologically based industry. The search for technological leadership means developing an understanding of how the market is moving and spotting the areas that are likely to offer opportunities. IBM has eight research labs in countries such as Japan and China as well as in the USA, employing around 3,000 researchers. It takes R&D seriously (4,914 patents were awarded in 2009) and has increased investment in this area by 21 per cent since 2002 (www.ibm.com).

IBM's research is high level stuff. Over the years, its labs have developed magnetic storage, the first computer language (Fortran), relational databases and the scanning tunnelling microscope to name but a few. A recent innovation is the creation of a 3D map of the earth so small that 1,000 of them could fit on one grain of salt. This was achieved with a tiny silicon tip 100,000 times smaller than a sharpened pencil, using nanotechnology. It paves the way for more innovation in nanotechnology in electronics, future chip technology, medicine, life sciences, and optoelectronics.

To get the best out of the commercial exploitation of technology, R&D and marketers have to work closely together. R&D can provide the technical know-how, problem-solving skills and creativity, while the marketer can help guide and refine that process through research or knowledge of what the market needs and wants, or through finding ways of creating a market position for a completely innovative product. A lot of this comes back to the question, 'What business are we in?' Any organisations holding the attitude that they exist to solve customers' problems and that they have to strive constantly to find better solutions through higher-quality, lower-cost or more user-friendly product packages will be active participants in, and observers of, the technological environment. A striking example of this is the Italian firm Olivetti, which began by making manual typewriters, then moved into computers as it saw the likely takeover of the word processor as a means of producing business documentation.

The technological environment is a fast-changing one, with far-reaching effects on organisations and their products. Technological advances can affect the materials, components and products, the processes by which products are made, administration and distribution systems, product marketing and the interface between the organisation and the customer. Each of these areas will now be looked at briefly, to give just a flavour of the immense impact that technology has had on marketing practice.

## Materials, components and products

Consumers tend to take products, and the materials and components that go into them, for granted as long as they work and live up to the marketers' promises. Technology does, however, improve and increase the benefits that consumers derive from products, and raise expectations about what a product should be. Some technological applications are invisible to the consumer, affecting raw materials and components hidden within an existing product, while others create completely new products.

One innovation that has revolutionised many product markets is the microchip. Not only are microchips the heart and soul of our home computers, but they also program our washing machines, iPads and mobile phones, among many things. The incorporation of microchips

*eg*

Built-in obsolescence timescales are shortening, and this is increasingly causing tension between manufacturers, governments and environmental groups. Typical of this is the EU's end-of-life vehicle (ELV) directive and its influence on the Chinese automotive industry. It is the third largest car market in the world so the stakes are high. With 43 million cars on the road, a figure that is rapidly growing, it is estimated that between 3 and 6 million of them should have reached the end of their useful life by the end of 2010, yet fewer than 500,000 were brought forward for scrap. Although China does not have to abide by the Directive, it has helped to shape China's own policies and laws and is important to China's growing export industry for cars.

The Chinese automotive industry is still lacking capacity for recycling. There are only 356 qualified ELV dismantlers in China, each approved by the state. The 16,000 people employed in the industry can process 1.2 million vehicles per year, but that is still well short of the 3 million or more estimated by ELV. Recycling produces 200 million tons of scrap steel per annum and the parts from the engine, power transmission, steering, axle and chassis all need to be destroyed and recycled – they cannot not be reused in a refurbished form, according to Chinese law. But the real emphasis needs to be on extending producer responsibility, encouraging manufacturers to think about designing ease of dismantling and recycling into the product; using more environmentally friendly materials; and raising technical specifications. All of that can only benefit China's automotive export trade (Chen and Zhang, 2009; Inness, 2009).

into products has increased their reliability, their efficiency in operation and the range of sophisticated functions that they can perform, all very cost effectively. This in turn has raised consumers' expectations of what products can do, and revised their attitudes towards cost, quality and value for money.

Technology is not just about the physical product itself. It can also affect its packaging. Lightweight plastics and glass, recycled and recyclable materials and cans that incorporate a device to give canned beer the character and quality of draught are examples of packaging innovations that have helped to make products more appealing, enhance their image or keep their cost down.

## Production processes

The fulfilment of marketing promises can be helped or hindered by what happens in the production process. More efficient production can, for instance, increase the volume of product available, thus potentially meeting a bigger demand, or it can reduce the cost of the product, thus giving more scope to the pricing decision. Production can also contribute to better and more consistent product quality, again increasing customer satisfaction. Here are some examples where technology has influenced production processes and indirectly affected marketing activities.

Computer-aided design (CAD) and computer-aided manufacturing (CAM) systems have revolutionised product formulation and testing. In terms of design, technology allows ideas to be visualised, tested and accepted/rejected much more quickly than if paper plans and calculations had to be updated. Similarly, computer-controlled production systems can undertake tasks faster than human operatives, with more consistency and fewer errors. When all this is integrated with sophisticated quality assurance and control techniques, along with online stock management and replenishment systems, the outcome for the customer is that products get to the market more quickly, and in a more refined state, and may be cheaper and more reliable.

Materials handling and waste minimisation are both concerns of efficient, cost-effective production management. Stocks of materials need to be closely monitored; in a large operation, the location of materials needs to be planned so that they can be accessed quickly and spend the minimum amount of time being transported around the site; the packaging and bundling of materials need to be planned to balance out the sometimes conflicting concerns of adequately protecting and identifying the goods, and making sure that they can be unwrapped and put into the production line quickly. Computerised planning models and advances in packaging technology can both help to increase efficiency in these areas.

## Administration and distribution

There is little point in using technology to streamline the production of goods if the support systems are inefficient or if distribution causes a bottleneck between factory and customer. Distribution has benefited from technology, as has materials handling, through systems for locating and tracking goods in and out. Integrated ordering and dispatch functions mean theoretically that as soon as an order is entered into the computer, goods availability can be checked and the warehouse can get on with the job of fulfilling it, while the computer handles all the paperwork, printing off packing slips and invoices, for example, and updating customer records. All of this speeds up the sending of orders to customers and reduces labour involvement, costs and risks of errors.

Telecommunications linking into computer systems can extend the administration efficiencies even further. Large retail chains, for example, are linked with their major suppliers, so that as the retailer's stocks reduce, an order can be sent from computer to computer. Similarly, large organisations with sites and depots spread over a wide geographic area can use such technology to link sites, managing and tracking the flow of goods.

## Marketing and customers

Much of the technology discussed above has implied benefits for the customer, in producing the right product at the right time in the right place at the right price, but technology also plays a part in the marketing processes that form the interface between buyer and seller. Increased and cheaper computer power, which means that large, complex sets of data can be generated, input and analysed quickly and easily, has benefited both market research data collection and analysis, and relationship marketing initiatives, establishing and maintaining a one-to-one dialogue between buyer and seller, is now possible in mass consumer markets. Organisations such as Heinz see this as an exciting development in consumer marketing, and it is only possible because of database technology that permits the storage, retrieval and maintenance of detailed profiles of many thousands, or even hundreds of thousands, of customers. The technology also allows the creation of tailored, personalised marketing offers to be made to subsets of those customers as appropriate.

Advertising media, too, have been improved and proliferated through technology. As well as making use of satellite and cable television channels, marketers can use 'red button' interactive television, text messaging and social networking pages among many other media. These media not only allow them to disseminate information about their products, services, news

*eg*

Social media have become a core element of marketing communications campaigns and an important tool for brands that are trying to develop closer, more interactive relationships with their target customers. Bulldog, with its range of male grooming products ('Man's Best Friend'), has always used social media such as its Facebook page for marketing but in 2011 decided to take it one step further by launching an 'F-commerce' site, i.e. selling its products from its Facebook page rather than just talking about them there. The launch of this was supported by an outdoor media advertising campaign to drive people to the brand's website and Facebook page. The F-commerce trend isn't just an fmcg phemonemon. In June 2011, the band The Kaiser Chiefs also launched an F-commerce site which offered more than just a link through which fans could buy their new album, *The Future is Medieval*. Instead, through this Facebook page, fans could select ten tracks, add their own cover art and then pay to download their customised album. As a further incentive to engage with the site, your unique album was then made available for other customers to buy, earning you £1 commission on each sale. Marsden (2011) declared this a brilliant piece of marketing 'because it uses the three key advocacy activators – experience, involvement and incentives – that drive word of mouth advocacy', which is so important for effective F-commerce (*Marketing Week*, 2011; Marsden, 2011; www.meetthebulldog.com).

Bull Dog wants to be man's best Facebook friend

*Source*: Bull Dog, www.meetthebulldog.com

and corporate philosophy, but also to set up interactive dialogue with customers and potential customers. Company or brand websites, social networking pages or postings on sites such as YouTube can be exciting communications media as they can feature sound and video clips and, if the site is well structured, visitors can select what they want to see and interact with it, and with each other. Also, the information can be updated easily and regularly. In addition, both the internet and interactive digital television allow potential customers to browse through product information, check availability and place an order, all in the comfort of their own armchairs.

Another area that can also be enhanced through computer technology is sales force support. Supplying a sales representative with a laptop or electronic notepad can give access to current information about products, their availability and prices; it can store customer profiles and relevant information; the representative can update records and write reports while the information is still fresh in the mind; and it can store appropriate graphics to enhance a sales presentation. All of this is easily portable and accessible whether the representative is working in Scotland or China.

## The economic environment

The effects of the economic environment are felt by organisations and consumers alike, and it has a profound effect on their behaviour. In the next few pages we look first at the macroeconomic environment, which provides the overall backdrop against which marketing activities take place. As well as issues of national interest, such as the effects of government economic policy on commerce, we cover the influence of international trading blocs and trade agreements. All of these things may provide opportunities or threats for an individual organisation. We then turn to the microeconomic environment. This is rather closer to home for the organisation, looking at the extent to which different market structures constrain or widen the organisation's freedom of action in its marketing activities and its ability to influence the nature of the market.

## The macroeconomic environment

Figure 2.2 shows the basic economic concept of the circular flow of goods and income that makes a market economy go round. Marketing, as an exchange process and indeed as a force that actively encourages more exchanges, is an essential fuel to keep that flow going. The world is not, however, a closed, self-sustaining loop such as that depicted in Figure 2.2. Its operation is severely affected by the macroeconomic influences generated by government economic policy and by membership of international trading blocs and trade agreements.

Governments can develop and implement policies in relation to several macroeconomic influences, which in turn affect markets, organisations and customers. Just a few of these are discussed below.

### Taxation and government spending

Taxes may be direct or indirect. Direct taxation, such as income tax and national insurance contributions, reduces the amount of money, or disposable income, that a household has available to spend on the goods and services that organisations provide. Indirect taxation, such as purchase tax or value added tax (VAT), is collected for the government by the seller, who is obliged to add a percentage to the basic price of the product. Thus a PC sold in the UK may be advertised with two prices: a basic price of £499, then £599 including VAT at 20 per cent.

Some products, such as alcohol, tobacco and petrol, have duty imposed on them, again collected by the seller. Both VAT and duties serve to increase the prices of products for the customer, and marketers need to think about the effect of the tax-inclusive price on the customer's

**Figure 2.2**

Macroeconomic influences on the circular flow of goods and income

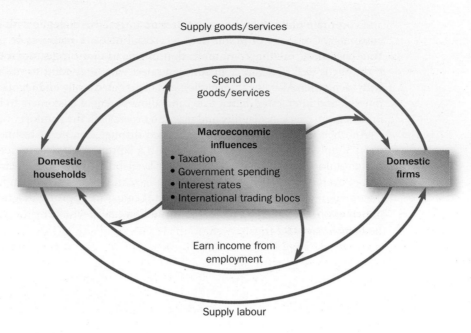

attitude and buying habits. In January 2011, the UK standard VAT rate was rose to 20 per cent, and when rates of duty increase like this, marketers sometimes choose to absorb some of the increase themselves to keep prices competitive, at least in the short term, rather than pass on the entire rise to the buyer.

Rates of VAT and duties vary across Europe and, despite over 30 years of trying, there is still no significant progress in persuading member states to move to a common VAT system based upon harmonised rates and structures. It is compulsory for membership of the EU for VAT rates to be between 15 and 25 per cent, but that still gives a lot of scope for variation (*Wall Street Journal*, 2005). By January 2012, most EU countries had VAT rates of between 20 and 25 per cent, with only Hungary setting it higher at 27 per cent, and Cyprus and Luxembourg both offering the lowest rate of 15 per cent (European Commission, 2012).

Many national governments would regard a centrally imposed VAT rate as further evidence of creeping federalism.

Despite the ending of duty-free allowances within the EU and the low exchange rate of sterling to the euro, the smuggling of cigarettes into the UK is still rife. The traffic in smuggled cigarettes is coming from continental Europe, but the cigarettes themselves originate from further afield, especially China. The good news is that the share of the UK market held by smuggled cigarettes had dropped from 21 per cent in 2001 to 12 per cent by 2008, but the bad news is that this still represents lucrative trade and it is now mainly run by hard-core, organised crime gangs rather than opportunistic smugglers loading up the back of the car after a trip to the continent. The sales of smuggled brands are unregulated, and it can be very difficult to tell whether they are counterfeit. It is estimated that the UK tax authorities lose £2 billion of revenue to the smugglers every year. The EU is also struggling with what to do. It seeks to define just what is meant by 'cigarettes' to avoid manipulation of the laws, to standardise excise duty to around €90 per 1,000 cigarettes, and to harmonise the market. Nevertheless, the smugglers seem to find the profitable loopholes and outlets, whether those are car boot sales or tame retailers (EU, 2010; HMRC, 2010; *Nottingham Evening Post*, 2010).

Using the money they 'earn' from taxes and duties, governments, like any other organisations, are purchasers of goods and services, but on a grand scale. They invest in defence industries, road building and other civil engineering projects, social and health services and many other areas. Such large purchasing power can be used to stimulate or depress economic development, but if a government decides as a matter of policy to cut back on its spending, industry can be very badly hit.

Shipbuilding has long been an area for direct government subsidy or for indirect support by placing government contracts with the yards. The arguments used are linked with preserving jobs or retaining an interest in shipbuilding for strategic defence reasons. So when French government contracts worth €310 million to maintain the operational readiness of the French navy's 22 frigates went to the French company, DCNS, few were surprised (*Dow Jones International News*, 2009). However, dependence on government contracts can be dangerous. Many Italian shipyards are in trouble and are having to lay off workers because government spending has been cut back. This has meant that plans to bring forward contracts to help shipyards out in the short-term have had to be shelved (McLaughlin, 2009).

## Interest rates

Government economic policy affects interest rates, which have an impact on both consumers and business. For many consumers, the most serious effect of a rise in interest rates is on their monthly mortgage repayments. Paying £20 or more per month extra to the mortgage lender means that there is that much less cash available for buying other things, and across the country retail sales can be significantly reduced. Interest rate rises can also affect the attractiveness of credit to the consumer, either when buying large expensive items through instalments, or when using credit cards. A consumer thinking about buying a brand new car, for example, may need a loan, and will look at the repayment levels, determined by interest rates, when deciding how expensive a model can be afforded. To try to reduce this potential barrier to purchasing, many car dealers have entered into arrangements with credit companies to offer 0 per cent financing deals to car buyers.

A country's exchange rate is rather like the price of a share for a company; it is a sign of confidence in the continued prosperity, or otherwise, of an individual nation. Fluctuating exchange rates between different currencies can have a major impact on the prosperity of companies and individual consumers. If a currency is strong, imports become cheaper which is good news for businesses and consumers, but exports become more expensive which is bad news for manufacturers. The strength of sterling in the period after the launch of the euro was blamed by some for precipitating a manufacturing recession in the UK as prices in the prime continental markets become less competitive.

The weak pound in 2009 caused Ford to increase prices by 2.7 per cent in December 2009. Ford argued that the pound had decreased in value by 30 per cent and that it could no longer absorb the increases as it had already lowered costs across the entire UK operation including its dealer network. This was particularly true of the pound to euro conversion which plummeted from €1.40 to the pound to €1.10 over a year or so, demonstrating the impact of declining exchange rates (Press Association, 2009). But what will happen when the pound recovers?

## International trading blocs

Governments also negotiate membership of international trading blocs, and the scope, terms and conditions of international trade agreements. Membership of the EU, for example, and particularly the advent of the single European market (SEM), has had a profound effect on the wider commercial dealings of organisations operating within the EU, as well as on the economic and competitive environment. Organisations which exist in countries outside the EU have found it increasingly difficult to sell into the EU, since there are now many more EU-based potential suppliers for purchasers to turn to, and also the logistics of purchasing within the EU are easier.

The enlargement of the EU to 27 countries in 2007 created a market of over 500 million people. Further expansion is possible, with countries such as Turkey, Iceland, Macedonia and Croatia waiting in the wings, although the pace of change may slow down as the EU constitution is in difficulty; some nations are wary of opening their borders to potential terrorism threats; there are fears that the EU will become unmanageable; and most of the new entrants will need considerable financial support in the short term and may pose a threat to jobs within existing member states. Nevertheless, it is clear that EU enlargement has moved beyond mere considerations of free trade to ensuring peace, preserving democracy, and strengthening liberal values, all well beyond the scope of this book (*The Economist*, 2005; Watson, 2005).

Beyond the confines of formalised trading blocs, business is often affected by the existence of trade agreements. Some of these are protectionist, in that they are trying to cushion domestic producers from the effects of an influx of imports, while others are trying to liberalise trade between nations. For many years, for example, the UK's textile industry benefited from the multifibre arrangement (MFA), which protected jobs and businesses by basically restricting the imports of low-priced clothing from various countries in the Far East. Similarly, Japan agreed to implement voluntary export restraint (VER) with regard to its car industry's sales to western Europe and the USA. This helped to protect domestic car producers and jobs by imposing quotas on Japanese imports. One way of overcoming the restrictions of this VER was international direct investment, i.e. setting up factories within the EU (taking full advantage, by the way, of various EU investment incentives) to produce cars with sufficient local content to be labelled 'European'. Thus those people owning either a Nissan (built in Washington, Tyne and Wear), a Honda (built in Swindon) or a Toyota (built in Derby), for example, are technically driving a British car. From their British manufacturing bases, the companies can legitimately export, without quota constraints, to the rest of the EU under the terms of the SEM.

The protectionist stance of agreements like the MFA however, is, being overshadowed by wider moves towards trade liberalisation, through the General Agreement on Tariffs and Trade (GATT), for example. The broad aim of GATT is to get rid of export subsidies and import tariffs (effectively taxes on imports that push their prices up to make them less competitive compared with the domestically produced equivalent product) to make international trade a great deal fairer. This means that negotiated VERs, which do not depend on tariffs to control imports, are becoming an increasingly important tool.

## The microeconomic environment

The general discussion in Chapter 1 of what marketing is, and its main tools, did not pay particular attention to the structure of markets. It is nevertheless important to think about market structures, because these will influence what sort of competition the organisation is up against, what scope the organisation has to manipulate the 4Ps and how broad an impact the organisation's marketing activities could have on the market as a whole.

Market structures can be defined in four broad categories, based on the number and size of competitors in the market.

## Monopoly

Technically, a monopoly exists where one supplier has sole control over a market, and there is no competition. The lack of competition may be because the monopolist is state owned and/or has a statutory right to be the sole supplier to the market. Traditionally in the EU, this applied to public utilities, such as gas, water, electricity, telephone and postal services, and some key industries such as the railways, steel and coal. Government policy in member states over the past 20 years, however, was to privatise and open up some of these industries to competition, with the idea that if they were exposed to market forces and were answerable to shareholders, they would operate more efficiently and cost effectively. Manufacturing, banking, transportation, energy and public utilities have all been privatised in a significant number of countries.

The EU has taken an interest in some state-owned monopolies. In Sweden, as in other Scandinavian countries, there is a state monopoly for retailing alcohol. The EU rejected the Swedish government's claim that it was better able to control retail sales and thus restrict the potential for Swedes to consume too much liquor. The EU considered that Systembolaget's state monopoly to sell wine, spirits and strong beer was a disproportionate measure for preventing alcohol abuse, and that the protected arrangement contravened the EU ruling on the free flow of goods. At that time, 70 per cent of alcohol sold in Sweden was sold from Systembolaget's stores or through restaurants, and the grocery trade, for example, was not able to sell in competition with Systembolaget. In 1997, however, the European Court of Justice ruled in favour of the Swedish government and thus despite the EU's views, the state monopoly remains. Part of the argument is that the government wants to protect its people from the worst excesses of alcohol by restricting purchases and keeping prices high. There have also been complaints of long queues, poor service and restricted opening times in the state-owned retail alcohol outlets, which further frustrates the consumer.

Systembolaget did improve its service, adding more off-licence outlets, so that by 2009 the customer satisfaction index had risen to 78, a gain of nearly ten points in ten years. It also managed to claw back some losses from cross-border importation from Denmark and Germany so that by 2009, it accounted for 66 per cent of all alcohol sales. In addition, Swedish public opinion had shifted in favour of retaining the state monopoly, so it looks like it's here to stay (Brown-Humes and MacCarthy, 2004; *Dagens Handel*, 2010; EIU, 2010; George, 2004; *Svenska Dagbladet*, 2010; Ward, 2009).

The implication of all this is that a true monopoly is hard to find in a modern market economy, although several near-monopolies are operating. In the UK, a monopoly is deemed to exist where an organisation or a group of collaborating organisations control 25 per cent of a market. Where this occurs, or where a proposed or threatened takeover raises the possibility of its happening, the Competition Commission may undertake an inquiry to establish whether the situation is operating in the public interest and whether there is any unfair competition involved.

This discussion so far has been rather parochial in that it has concentrated on national or regional monopolies. In global markets, however, it is even more difficult, if not impossible, to establish and sustain a monopoly.

As a final thought, the concept of monopoly depends on how 'market' is defined. While it is true that currently SNCF, for example, holds a monopoly on passenger rail travel in France, it does not have a monopoly on moving people from Paris to Lyon. To travellers, rail is only one option, and they might also consider travelling to their destinations by air, by coach or by car. In that sense, the traveller's perception of rail, in terms of its cost, reliability and convenience, is developed in a very competitive context.

## Oligopoly

Well-developed market economies are far more likely to see the emergence of oligopolies than monopolies. In an oligopoly, a small number of firms account for a very large share of the market, and a number of the privatised ex-monopolies discussed above are moving into this category. The oligopoly creates a certain amount of interdependence between the key players, each of which is large enough for its actions to have a big impact on the market and on the behaviour of its competitors. This certainly occurs in large-scale, worldwide industrial markets, such as chemicals, oil and pharmaceuticals, because the amount of capital investment required, the levels of production needed to achieve economies of scale and the geographic dispersion of large customers demanding large quantities make this the most efficient way for these markets to be structured.

Some consumer oligopolies are not necessarily obvious to the casual observer. In the supermarket, the shopper may see a wide variety of brands of laundry products, and thus imagine that there is healthy, widespread competition in that sector. Most brands are owned and managed, however, by either Procter & Gamble (P&G) (Ariel, Bold, Fairy, Lenor, etc.) or Unilever (Persil, Surf and Comfort) and the apparent proliferation of brands is more to do with fragmented demand and the creation of discrete segments (see Chapter 4) than the fragmentation of supply. According to Mintel (2010b), Unilever's Persil held a 25 per cent share of this market with P&G's Ariel close behind, with a 20 per cent share. In a £1.32 billion market, that makes them very valuable and powerful brands.

In total, P&G brands between them had 45 per cent market share in 2010, while Unilever's had 32 per cent. The supermarkets are the biggest threat to this oligopoly, with their own-brands taking 14 per cent of the market, although on that basis it could be argued that they are becoming a part of the oligopoly themselves. That only leaves 9 per cent share for the rest, and Reckitt Benckiser alone takes two-thirds of that with its Vanish stain-remover range and Calgon water softener.

In marketing terms, it is nevertheless still very difficult for a new brand from a new competitor to enter an oligopolistic market, other than in a small niche. This is because the oligopolists have spent many years and vast amounts of marketing money establishing their brands and shares. The threat from a supermarket's own-brand is more serious, however, because of the retailers' inherent control over a major channel of distribution which neither of the oligopolists can afford to lose. All of this really leaves only very small gaps in the market for the smaller competitor, such as that filled by products such as Ecover, a detergent brand that has positioned itself as more environmentally friendly than anything else available, appealing to the 'dark green' consumer.

Oligopolists therefore spend their time watching each other, and developing their marketing strategies and tactics on the basis of what the other main players are doing or are likely to do. If, for example, Unilever launches a new brand, or implements a major new marketing communications strategy, P&G would prefer to anticipate it, thus either pre-empting Unilever or at least having a calculated response ready when needed. From P&G's point of view this is essential, even if it is only to maintain the delicate status quo of the two companies' relative market shares.

## Monopolistic and perfect competition

Good marketing practice and the emphasis on differential advantage have created a market structure that might seem a little paradoxical at first sight: monopolistic competition. The idea is that although there are many competitors in the market (with the emphasis on smaller competitors without enough individual influence to create either an oligopoly or a monopoly, as discussed above), each has a product sufficiently differentiated from the rest to create its own monopoly, because to the customer it is unique, or at least any potential substitutes are considered to be inferior. The concept forms the basis of much of the rest of this book.

Perfect competition is at the opposite end of the spectrum from monopoly, and is about as likely to be found in practice. It involves many small producers, all supplying identical products that can be directly substituted for each other. No producer has the power to influence or determine price, and the market consists of many small buyers, who similarly cannot influence the market individually. There are no barriers to market entry or exit, and all buyers and sellers have complete information about what is happening in the market. All of this is clearly unrealistic. The influence of marketing concepts on even the smallest organisations, along with the development of powerful buyers and sellers in all kinds of markets, consumer and B2B, mean that these conditions cannot hold, and some kind of monopolistic competition or oligopoly soon emerges.

*eg*    Farm produce, such as vegetables, is often cited as an example of near-perfect competition. While it is true that the market does consist of many small suppliers, i.e. individual farms, the nature of the buyer is more complex, ranging from a family buying a few kilos of carrots from a farm shop, to the fruit and vegetable wholesalers and supermarket chains that buy such quantities that they can influence price and other supply variables. Even the product itself can be differentiated, for example organic and non-organic, or class I and class II quality. The farmer can also differentiate the offering through grading and packaging the produce to suit the retail customer. Even carrots, therefore, can be seen to be moving towards monopolistic competition.

# The ethical environment

The ethical environment is concerned with what ought to be done, not just what legally must be done, according to the principles and norms regarding what is right and good at a societal, personal, or organisational level. The benchmarks and standards for ethical behaviour in practice tend to be higher than those enshrined in law, and for some tend to lead rather than follow legislation. Of course, what is right and good for one individual may be wrong for another and that is true in business too. The standards set at individual and societal levels, and the variance between them are important factors in judging the ethical standards of business, and affect all kinds of issues such as product safety, honesty and transparency in communication and the handling of supplier–customer relationships, especially where vulnerable groups of customers are concerned.

Encouraged by various pressure groups and inquisitive media, consumers now want to see greater levels of corporate responsibility, and more transparency in terms of the openness of companies. Bad publicity about employee relations, environmental records, marketing practices or customer care and welfare now has the potential to move consumers to vote with their pockets and shun an organisation and its products. Corporate social responsibility (CSR) is an all embracing term to guide ethical decision-making within an organisation at whatever level, whether it's front line sales staff, the marketing director or the chief executive. CSR policy explicitly states what is and is not appropriate for executives to contemplate, whether internally or externally. Thus ethics has emerged as a powerful influence on the behaviour of buyers and sellers, and as ethical thinking evolves, so must marketing responses.

The growth of 'green' marketing and fair trade initiatives are linked with concerns about the environment and its sustainability, but they are also inextricably linked with ethics and the morality of how people are treated. These issues matter in marketplaces far more than they did a few years ago and represent a significant change in the marketing environment. The problem is, however, that most organisations are keen to establish their green and ethical credentials but it can be difficult to distinguish 'greenwash' from reality. Easyjet, for example, claimed that it is greener to travel by plane rather than car, but that proved to be true only if the calculations were done on a full plane and a car with only one occupant (Randerson, 2009).

In broader terms, society's and thus consumers' attitudes to general issues linked with the environment and animal welfare have become a lot more ethically critical, and this is becoming routinely reflected in the decisions that marketers are making. Similarly, marketers are tackling the ethical issues linked with transparency in the supply chain and fair treatment of suppliers, particularly those from developing economies, as these rise further up the public agenda. The 'right' response isn't always obvious, however. Recent research has suggested, for example, that local and national sourcing and helping local suppliers is more important in consumers' minds than fair trade issues. In an IGD survey (as reported by *Checkout*, 2008), 42 per cent of all European shoppers considered local and national sourcing an issue, 35 per cent animal welfare, and just 15 per cent fair trade. Furthermore, it would appear that consumer ethics are negotiable: the same survey suggested that price is a barrier to switching to 'more ethical' products, especially in a difficult economic environment when household finances are stretched. So the marketer faces the tricky task of implementing their own corporate ethical principles on these issues, but at a price that will keep the consumer on board.

eg

There has long been concern about egg production systems and the cruelty of intensive battery farming. Thanks to the efforts of a number of animal welfare groups, from 2012 there will be an EU ban on 'caged eggs', and thus producers have been switching to alternative methods, while egg packaging has been giving more prominence to the method of production. 'Barn eggs' sound wonderfully rustic, but they are intensively produced and although the birds are not caged and have some room to wander around, they are still kept indoors in dense flocks. 'Free-range eggs' are produced by birds that do have access to an outdoor

Free-range eggs from the Happy Egg Co.
*Source*: Noble Foods, www.thehappyegg.co.uk

area, and the sheds are less densely populated, giving more space per bird. 'Organic eggs' are free range eggs from birds that have been raised on organically approved land and with strict constraints on medication. Obviously, as the welfare standards increase, the retail price of the eggs also increases. Mintel (2010c) suggests that sales of organic eggs fell back from £48 million in 2008 to £30 million in 2010, partly as a result of a more general trend away from organic foods as consumers became more price-conscious during the economic recession, and partly because of a perception that the cheaper free-range eggs provide sufficient standards of welfare to salve most consumers' consciences.

One company that seems to have understood this very well is Noble Foods, which launched The Happy Egg Co. brand early in 2009 with a £1.2 million advertising campaign. Its bright yellow packaging and lighthearted advertising showing happy hens participating in all kinds of outdoor activities against a voice-over that says, 'We create the perfect environment for our free range hens to run, jump and play, because happy hens lay happy eggs and happy eggs are wonderfully tasty' have succeeded in creating a distinctive brand that invokes positive feelings among consumers and has allowed a premium price position to be established and accepted by consumers. Checking egg prices in June 2011, it is interesting to see that the differential between organic eggs and the premium end of the free-range market isn't that great: a pack of Asda six large organic eggs was priced at £1.94, while The Happy Egg Co pack of six free-range eggs was £1.90 (compared with Asda's own-brand pack of six free-range eggs at £1.68) (Mintel 2010a, 2010c; *Packaging News*, 2010; www. asda.co.uk; www.the happyegg.co.uk).

Ultimately, the really ethical consumer is the one who buys fewer goods, buys only through necessity and second-hand where possible, and always asks 'do I really need it and where has it come from?' How many of us can live up to that?

## The political and legal environments

Organisations have to exist in and operate according to the laws of the societies within which they do business, and thus in addition to the more general laws of contract and commerce, products have to conform to safety laws; manufacturing processes are subject to pollution controls; copyright and patents protect innovation; and retailers' opening hours are restricted in Germany, for example, by the *Ladenschlussgesetz,* and in the UK by the Sunday trading laws. We look below at the role and influence of national governments and the European Parliament in making rules that have a direct effect on the marketing mix.

Regulation is not only defined through legislation from national governments or the European Parliament, however. Organisations are also subject to rules passed by regulatory bodies, some of which have statutory powers delegated to them from government, while others are voluntary groupings, such as trade associations, with codes of practice to which the organisation chooses to adhere. We examine the nature and influence of such bodies on p. 67 *et seq.* Inevitably, governments and other regulatory bodies are influenced in their policy making by other sources, such as lobbyists and pressure groups, and on p. 70 we take a wider view of the influences that drive the legislators and rule makers towards their policies.

## National and local government

The obvious responsibility of national governments is to determine and maintain the legislative framework within which organisations do business. This will cover areas such as contract law, consumer protection, financial legislation, competition and trading practices, for example. There are variations in approaches across Europe but increasingly, as European integration proceeds and the internal market is fully liberalised, national governments are working within EU guidelines and directives, with the longer-term aim of achieving consistency across member states.

Within the UK, although Parliament passes legislation and puts it on the statute books, the responsibility for implementing and enforcing it is often delegated to specialist bodies, such as the Office of Fair Trading (OFT), Competition Commission, or Ofcom. The role of such bodies is discussed further on p. 67 *et seq*.

As well as the legislation they pass that affects the day-to-day business practices of organisations, governments can also have profound effects on the competitive environment. The widespread privatisation of publicly owned utilities and other state-controlled national industries in the 1980s and 1990s presented opportunities for new competitors to enter these markets, as well as profoundly changing the culture and business orientation of the newly privatised companies themselves.

Local government also carries some responsibility for implementing and enforcing laws made at a national level. In Germany, local government has responsibility for implementing pollution and noise control legislation. In the UK, local Trading Standards officers may well be the first to investigate claims of shady or illegal business practices. Christmas often heralds a flurry of warnings from Trading Standards officers about dangerous toys, usually cheap imports from the Far East, that do not conform to EU safety standards. Officers can prosecute the retailer and prevent further sales of the offending goods, but by then, significant numbers of the product may already have been sold. Trading Standards offices play an important role in ensuring consumer safety and that fair trading and quality standards are maintained. They are provided by over 200 local authorities in the United Kingdom.

Trading Standards officers investigate many scams and bad practices and bring prosecutions where necessary. In Portsmouth, for example, shops illegally selling cigarettes to under-age children were exposed in a blaze of publicity. The number of offending retailers then dropped from one-quarter of all shops visited to just 10 per cent, vindicating the Trading Standards officers' approach (*The News*, 2010). In addition to this sort of activity and the more traditional case load of dodgy shops selling short measures or rip-off cowboy builders, Trading Standards is also moving in on internet scammers. In Northumberland, for example, organisations were being cold called and told that their computer system had developed faults which could cause problems. Of course, the solution was to grant the caller remote access to fix the problem, which would mean the disclosure of password and other security information. Once inside the system, the scammers have a free hand to do whatever they want (*Northumberland Gazette*, 2010). Trading Standards has a role not only in investigating such scams, but also in damage-limitation by raising people's awareness of what's going on so that they don't fall for it, and are encouraged to report it.

Local authorities in the UK also have responsibility for granting planning permission. For businesses, this means that if they want to build a factory or supermarket, or change the usage of a commercial building, then the local authority has to vet the plans and grant permission before anything can be done. Local authorities are under pressure from small retailers who are worried about the major shift towards out-of-town superstore shopping. The argument is that town centres and small local businesses are dying because people would rather go to the out-of-town retail park or shopping mall. This means that local authorities are increasingly reluctant to grant planning permission for further out-of-town developments, seriously affecting the growth plans of many large retailers.

A proposal to locate a major supermarket in a town is often a controversial decision. In order to mollify local councils, which might be swayed by the vested interests of existing retailers or have concerns about the impact on traffic congestion or parking, the supermarket retailer might offer to take on additional responsibilities such as improving roads or community infrastructure in the area of the proposed development in return for planning permission for the store. This is called 'planning gain'. There is increasing concern about the rise of so-called 'Tesco towns' in which the development of a superstore is part of a much bigger mixed-use development, including homes, other shops, schools and/or leisure facilities funded by the retailer. According to Minton (2010), just nine new schemes on Tesco's drawing boards will provide nearly 4,000 new homes. In Bromley-by-Bow, for example, a Tesco development promises not only a superstore, but also a primary school and hundreds of homes. A Tesco store in Trafford, Manchester was given planning permission once it was linked with the redevelopment of Lancashire County Cricket Club and, similarly, Tesco is building a new stadium for St Helens rugby league club.

Even with such levels of investment and the local regeneration that goes with it, there are many who question the necessity for it as the saturation of towns by supermarkets continues. Sims (2010) claims that nearly 50 per cent of towns have at least five supermarkets within a ten-minute drive, and 42 per cent of towns have five supermarkets to choose from. The retailers don't always get their own way. Sheringham, a quiet town on the north Norfolk coast, faced a direct choice: a brand new Tesco supermarket or an environmentally friendly food store promoted by a local farmer (albeit to be run by Waitrose). Following a vigorous local campaign against the Tesco proposal, but contrary to the advice of local planning officials, the Planning Committee (much to everyone's surprise) voted against Tesco's proposal. That decision is currently facing a legal challenge (Elliott and Pavia, 2010; Glancey 2010).

Although the EU is making considerable progress towards eliminating national regulations that are contrary to fair and free trade, the scale of the task is great. National environmental laws in Germany and Denmark, for example, have been criticised as favouring local rather than international suppliers. The extent to which regulations affect business, therefore, varies between countries and industries. There is a slow move towards standardisation, which generally means that the advanced industrialised northern European nations are tending to deregulate, whereas the southern nations are tending to tighten up controls. Moves towards deregulation have been accompanied by increased self-regulation within industries.

## The European Union

It is unfortunate that the pronouncements from Brussels that make the headlines tend to be the offbeat or trivial ones, such as the proposal to regulate the curve on a cucumber, the redesignation of the carrot as a fruit to allow the Portuguese to carry on their trade in carrot jam, and questions as to whether Cheddar cheese and Swiss rolls can continue to bear those names if they are not made in those places. Despite these delightful eccentricities, the EU works hard towards ensuring free trade and fair competition across member states' boundaries.

The SEM, which officially came into being on 1 January 1993, was the culmination of many years of work in breaking down trade barriers and harmonising legislation across the member states. One area that directly affects marketing is the abolition of frontier controls, so that goods can be transferred from state to state, or carried in transit through states, without lots of paperwork and customs checks. Additionally, road haulage has been freed from restrictions and quotas so that a haulier with a licence to operate in one EU member state can operate in any other. Further European integration is sought through EMU (European monetary union) and the introduction of the euro as a replacement for national currencies. This has made cross-border price comparisons a lot easier for customers and created more transparent pan-European competition. The euro has also eliminated problems caused by fluctuating exchange rates, thus reducing the costs of the cross-border movement of goods and encouraging more imports and exports between the countries of the EU.

In terms of products themselves, a set of European standards have been implemented through a series of directives, ensuring common criteria for safety, public health and environmental protection. Any product adhering to these directives and to the laws of its own country of origin will be acceptable in any member state. Look for the stylised 'CE' symbol on products as the sign that they do conform to European standards.

In other areas of marketing, harmonisation of regulations and codes of practice across member states has not been so easy. The problem with marketing communications, for example, is that the European law makers have to reconcile commercial freedom with consumer protection across 27 different countries, each with its own customs, laws, codes and practices. Sometimes, best practice is followed and harmonisation across all states can be achieved, but in other cases, the law of the country in which a transaction originates applies, by mutual recognition. There are wide variations in best practice across Europe, so finding a common approach will be difficult.

Direct marketing is a relatively new area which has great potential for the marketing of goods across Europe, and yet here too, a variety of national codes are in operation. In the UK,

*eg* Defining just what chocolate actually is or is not has caused controversy in Europe among both politicians and chocolate manufacturers. The argument has been going on for over 30 years, since the UK and Ireland joined the EU with chocolate that included cheaper vegetable fats rather than a higher proportion of cocoa fats. The chocolate wars have been fought between an alliance of France and Belgium and a number of others against the UK, Ireland and five other states. An EU directive favouring one side over the other would create an unfair competitive advantage and would be a far cry from a single European market in chocolate. In 1997, the European Parliament ruled in favour of the France–Belgium alliance, overturning a previous compromise EU directive. This meant that the term 'milk chocolate' could not be used by the UK and the other states on its side and thus products from those states would have to be renamed 'chocolate with milk and non-cocoa vegetable fats' or at least 'milk chocolate with high milk content'. Product labels would also have to show clearly that the product contained vegetable fats.

That was not acceptable to the UK chocolate producers and a further compromise was realised in 2000 with directive 2000/36 which agreed to two definitions of chocolate: 'milk chocolate' and 'family milk chocolate', the latter replacing the 'milk chocolate with high milk content' designation for the UK and Irish markets. Although the terminology was subsequently refined to 'chocolate substitute', it was eventually ruled in 2003 that it infringed EU law on free trade. Common sense at last prevailed, in that the ruling recognised that different chocolate traditions should exist in a marketplace to allow consumers a choice. Despite a rearguard action by Spain and Italy, at least in theory, Cadbury's Dairy Milk should be appearing on Italian supermarket shelves. By insisting on the term 'chocolate substitute', the Italians had effectively created an obstruction for those wishing to enter its market. Effectively, prior to the ruling, the Italians were asking some EU traders to modify their products or presentation and to incur additional packaging costs in the process. There was even the possibility that the consumer might regard a product with the word 'substitute' as inferior. So the 2003 ruling may mean at last that chocolate traditions can be retained and barriers removed for its free movement (Bremner, 1997; Morley, 2003; O'Grady *et al.*, 2010; *The Times*, 2003; Tucker, 1997; www.europa.eu).

for example, 'cold calling' telephone selling (i.e. an organisation phoning a consumer for sales purposes without the consumer's prior permission) is permitted, but in Germany it is almost totally banned. Data protection laws (i.e. what information organisations are permitted to hold on databases and what they are allowed to do with it) and regulations on list broking (i.e. the sale of lists of names and addresses to other organisations) also vary widely across the EU.

## Regulatory bodies

Within the UK, there are many regulatory bodies with greater or lesser powers of regulation over marketing practice. Quasi-governmental bodies, such as the Office of Fair Trading (OFT) and the Competition Commission, have had statutory duties and powers delegated to them directly by government to ensure the maintenance of free and fair commerce.

The OFT in the UK aims to ensure that markets are working effectively. This is achieved by ensuring that competition and consumer protection laws and guidelines are followed in the public interest. It is the OFT that refers mergers to the Competition Commission. Being accountable to parliament, it is able to play a powerful role in shaping an organisation's marketing behaviour. One of its recent activities includes a clampdown on what it perceived as unfair flight pricing. Cheap airline seats offered over the internet sometimes failed to include airport taxes, insurance levies, credit card charges and handling fees, boosting the actual ticket price far beyond the figures advertised. One promotion offered one million seats at 99p, but five screens later, after the addition of taxes, etc., the price was over £60! The Competition Commission ruled that it should be clear to customers what the price of the ticket was going to be before, not after they had purchased. Only then could sensible price comparisons be made.

Slightly more remote from central government, quasi-autonomous non-governmental organisations (quangos) have a specific remit and can act much more quickly than a government department. Quangos such as Ofcom, Ofgem and Ofwat, for instance, exist to regulate the privatised telecommunications, gas and electricity, and water industries respectively in the UK. The prime aim for the quangos is to protect consumer interests by ensuring appropriate levels of competition.

The scope of the work of quangos is clearly extensive and offers necessary protection for the consumer in markets that have been privatised. Suppliers in the industry must also consider the likely public and legislative impact of acting outside the public interest in the development of their marketing strategy and its implementation.

Voluntary codes of practice emerge from associations and trade bodies, with which their members agree to comply. The Advertising Standards Authority (ASA), for example, oversees the implementation and enforcement of the CAP Code (which covers non-broadcast advertising, sales promotion, and direct marketing) and the BCAP Code (for broadcast advertising). The ASA thus regulates television, print, cinema, video, posters, internet, website, SMS text message advertising, and leaflet media and more. The ASA's mission is 'to ensure that advertising in all media is legal, decent, honest and truthful, to the benefit of consumers, business and society' (www.asa.org.uk).

Although Ofcom (Office of Communications) is ultimately responsible for the policing of broadcast television and radio advertising, in November 2004 the day-to-day regulation of both these media was contracted out to the ASA. This means that consumers have a one-stop shop for complaints and that there can be consistency in the decisions made about problematic advertisements in different media. Ofcom is a statutory body, and carries a great deal of weight, since it has the power to issue and control broadcasting licences, and compliance with the advertising codes of practice is effectively part of the licence. The frequency and duration of advertising breaks are restricted and it is Ofcom that ensures that there is a distinct break between programmes and advertisements. Pharmaceuticals, alcohol, tobacco and diet products, to name but a few, are subject to tight restrictions under the code of practice and in addition EU directives specify what is and is not allowed. In 2009, the ASA received nearly 29,000 complaints and each was investigated. As a result, around 2,400 were changed or withdrawn. This does mean, however, that the vast majority were deemed responsible and complied with existing advertising rules.

# MARKETING IN ACTION

## Cruelty, sleaze and blasphemy?

There's nothing like sex, cruelty to animals or religion for getting the British public outraged and complaining to the ASA.

As part of a major marketing campaign running at the time of the 2010 World Cup tournament, the betting company, Paddy Power, ran a television advertisement featuring sight-impaired footballers playing a match using a ball with a bell in it. A cat wearing a collar with a bell on it ran onto the pitch and was accidently kicked into a tree. Over 400 complaints were received, claiming that the advertisement would encourage cruelty to animals. At the time of writing, the ASA was still investigating the issue.

Somewhat fewer complaints (just 33) were received about some magazine and poster advertisements for Diesel jeans. The campaign, entitled 'Be Stupid', featured attractive young women in Diesel jeans doing stupid things – one was flashing her breasts at a CCTV camera, while another appeared to be taking a photo of her genitals. The strapline on all the advertisements was, 'Smart may have the brains, but stupid has the balls. Be stupid. Diesel'. The complainants claimed that the images were offensive, unsuitable to be seen by children and likely to encourage anti-social behaviour. Diesel, however claimed that the images 'did not contain any provocative nudity beyond the usual amounts shown in many swimwear, sportswear or lingerie ads' (www.asa.org.uk). Overall, the complaints were upheld in some respects but not in others. The ASA decided that the print ads which appeared in *Grazia* and *Dazed & Confused* were appropriate, given the readership profiles of those media and the nature of those

A contentious advertisement for Diesel clothing

*Source*: Image courtesy of The Advertising Archives

magazines' editorial content, but that the poster ads should not be allowed to stand as their content was too provocative for such an 'untargeted medium' that might easily be seen by children.

Religion is always a difficult topic for advertisers, and unsurprisingly tends to generate lots of complaints, so the Italian ice-cream company Antonio Federici must have known that it was courting controversy when it developed a print advertisement featuring a pregnant nun eating ice-cream with the strapline 'Immaculately conceived'. At the time of writing, the ASA is still investigating this one, but given that a previous advertisement from the same company showing a priest and a nun kissing was banned, it is quite possible that this will go the same way unless the company can convince the ASA that it is indeed justifiable as an 'intelligent, challenging and iconoclastic piece of advertising' (as quoted by Sweney, 2010b).

*Sources:* ASA (2010); Sweney (2010a; 2010b); www.asa.org.uk.

The ASA is not a statutory body, and can only *request* an advertiser to amend or withdraw an advertisement that is in breach of the code but it also has remedies other than persuasion. It can *request* media owners to refuse to accept or repeat the offending advertisement, generate adverse publicity, and/or *recommend* that the OFT take proceedings to apply for a legal injunction to prevent publication. Most advertisers conform to requests from the ASA to withdraw an advertisement and some avoid any possible problems by voluntarily using the pre-publication vetting service. However, the ASA can now ask for vetting for up to two years if a particular advertiser has proven troublesome in the past. Previously, offending campaigns attracted a lot of publicity because of their sensational nature. Then, when the ASA makes a ruling, further publicity is generated, for instance through opinion articles in newspapers discussing advertising standards which include a picture of an offending advertisement so that the readers know what sort of thing they're talking about. Indirectly, therefore, in some cases, ASA involvement rather defeats its own objectives. There are no hard and fast rules about how far an advertiser can go before running foul of regulatory bodies and this becomes even more complex once you start advertising across European boundaries (see Chapter 10). A naked couple can kiss in a shower in an advertisement for condoms, but a woman's naked buttocks on a poster are 'unnecessarily shocking' in the words of the ASA.

With the development of the SEM and transnational advertising campaigns, marketers not only need to consider national laws, self-regulatory rules and systems across the member states. The European Advertising Standards Alliance (EASA) represents the various advertising regulatory bodies, such as the ASA, across Europe. Although it has no direct powers it can intervene on behalf of complainants by asking the various national regulators to act. For example, when a Luxembourger consumer complained about a French chewing-gum manufacturer's health claims, the case was referred back to the French for investigation and action.

The Institute of Sales Promotion (ISP), the Institute of Practitioners in Advertising (IPA), the Institute of Public Relations (IPR) and the Direct Marketing Association (DMA) are effectively trade associations. All these areas are, of course, subject to prevailing commercial legislation generally, but, in addition, these particular bodies provide detailed voluntary codes of practice setting industry standards for fair dealing with customers. They are not statutory bodies, and only have jurisdiction over their members, with the ultimate sanction of suspending or expelling organisations that breach the code of practice. All of the bodies mentioned here represent organisations with interests in various areas of marketing communications, but trade associations can exist in any industry with similar objectives of regulating the professional practice of their members. There are, for example, the Fencing Contractors Association, the Glass and Glazing Federation, the Association of British Insurers, the British Association of Landscape Industries, and the National House Builders Confederation, to name but a few! As well as regulating business practice, such bodies can also provide other services for members, such as legal indemnities and representation, training and professional development services, and acting as the voice of the industry to government and the media.

## Influences on the political and legal environments

The political and legal environments are clearly influenced by sociocultural factors, and particularly the pressure of public opinion, the media and pressure groups. Greenpeace and Friends of the Earth, for example, have educated consumers to become more aware of the content, origins and after-effects of the products they buy and use, and this led to the phasing out of chlorofluorocarbons (CFCs) as an aerosol propellant and as a refrigerant. The green movement has also spurred the drafting of regulations on the acceptable emissions from car exhausts, which has had a major impact on the product development plans of motor manufacturers for the next few years. Similarly, the consumer movement, through organisations such as Which?, has also played an important role in promoting the rights of the consumer and thus in driving the regulators and legislators towards laws and codes of practice regarding product safety, selling techniques and marketing communications, for instance.

Not all pressure on legislators and regulators originates from pressure groups or consumer-based organisations, of course. Trade associations or groupings lobby the legislators to try to influence regulation in their members' favour. Sometimes, the lobbying is designed to slow the pace of change, influence the nature of any planned legislation, and to delay legislation perceived as potentially harmful to the industry's interests. In the case of tobacco, for instance, government must balance public health concerns against the employment and export potential from manufacturers. It is important, therefore, for the marketer to read the changing political environment, within Europe, in export markets and from international organisations such as the WTO and OECD who are influential in guiding change. Most industries face new legislation that affects them one way or another during the course of a year and an early appreciation gives companies more time to exploit an opportunity or to counter a threat. A failure to get involved early on in lobbying and putting across arguments can have knock-on effects down the line with policies that constrain marketing activity too much without enabling a more open internal market. Some policies could even favour particular member states who have lobbied harder. The directives on online trading and e-commerce, for example, are topical within the EU, so internet marketers cannot afford to miss out on discussions concerning the legislative framework.

With increasing public concern for sustainability, competitiveness of markets, fair trading, product safety and quality and consumer rights, it is a very brave politician that can ignore the pressures for change. However, lobbying and participating in the legislative discussion can help steer outcomes towards those preferred by an organisation. Organisations such as Greenpeace have become very effective at lobbying key decision makers, but tracking the legislative process can be a long and tortuous process. The Commission in Strasbourg frames EU legislation which is then debated and amended by the European parliament before the legislation is endorsed by the Council of Ministers and then implemented though European Directives. Even then it is not over, as individual member states may have to pass legislation to implement at a local level (Simms, 2001). The greater the understanding of the EU and national political processes, the more an organisation can move with change rather than risk being left behind.

## The ecological environment

The ecological environment includes all the earth's resources, including all raw materials or energy sources and their sustainability, needed by or affected by organisations and their marketing activities. This concept was introduced in Chapter 1 as fundamental in considering sustainable marketing and corporate social responsibility. The tourism industry has long recognised that the earth is a finite resource and needs to be protected from over-use.

Climate change is accelerating at a faster rate than many scientists had predicted and thus it is all the more important to reduce personal and organisational carbon footprints. Changing

*eg* Uluru, sometimes known as Ayers Rock, is the massive monolith in Australia's central red desert. As a highlight on the tourism trail, it is the scene of a management battle between cultural preservation and exploitation. The indigenous people regard the rock as a sacred site and want all tourism contact with it stopped. About 100,000 of the 250,000 tourists visiting the site every year want to climb the 348-metre rock, but litter and over-use are starting to deface and degrade the site.

Although the environment minister has refused to impose an outright ban, certain rules are in place limiting the number of tourists climbing the rock, and as the climb is very strenuous, scaling the rock is prevented on really hot days in summer. It's a classic land use clash between the natural environment, aboriginal culture and the tourist experience (*Edmonton Journal*, 2010).

attitudes to consumption and finding better ways of using and managing resources is a necessary part of the solution (Neff *et al.*, 2010). There is no doubt that marketing techniques and planned obsolescence play a role in creating an artificiality in consumption that cuts across ecological issues (Löwy, 2010). Perhaps educating consumers on green consumption offers the best chance of seriously changing what and how we buy. The task will be enormous: how can we, as consumers, be turned off fashion, brands that make statements about who we are, conspicuous consumption and even products we just like when these things are so embedded in our culture and lifestyle?

## MARKETING IN ACTION

### Saving the trees to preserve the woods

The Amazon rainforest is one of the last frontiers on earth. Covering 2.3 million square miles, it has been called the earth's lungs as it absorbs massive amounts of carbon dioxide from the atmosphere each year and converts it back into oxygen. However, land clearance, often by burning, and indiscriminate logging means that 40 per cent of the forest has already been destroyed. It has been estimated that 10,000 square miles of the forest is disappearing each year, despite efforts to restrain deforestation. Deforestation is responsible for 20 per cent of global emissions of carbon dioxide and thus has a direct link to climate change.

Although half the timber that entered the European supply chain in 2009 was responsibly sourced from certified forests, they actually represent only 5 per cent of the world's productive forests. Scientists have estimated that if the rate of illegal logging does not slow down, the tropical rainforest ecosystem will be destroyed by 2030. That's bad news for the lungs of the world. So what has all this to do with marketing and the consumer? It is demand for tropical wood that sets a chain of activities going that can be traced back to the forest. Wood consumption is closely related to per capita income: the higher the income, the higher the wood consumption, and more trees are felled.

Precious Woods Amazon is proud of its record in sustainable logging in tropical regions. The Swiss-owned company was founded in 1994 to show that commercial logging and sustainability could go together. Other loggers have followed, such as Gethal, adopting a planned forest management approach to ensure that rainforest is protected despite commercial interest. Forest management means undertaking proper timber inventories (location, species, measurement), harvesting plans and long harvesting cycles. This is backed up by certification and labelling which clearly communicates to consumers that responsible logging has taken place. The formation of the Forest Stewardship Council (FSC) was regarded even by pressure groups such as Greenpeace as a vital step in making the industry more responsible. Achieving FSC certification means that demanding social, economic and environmental standards have been met. Thus Precious Woods Amazon manages selective logging over a 25-year cycle and always seeks to preserve watercourses and to avoid soil erosion. Part of the deal also includes the principles that 25 per cent of the forest area remains permanently protected and that no pesticides or chemicals should be used.

If consumers were more environmentally oriented, they would read labels to make informed decisions on the best woods to buy. Reputable manufacturers offer wood products from well-managed forests. Although ecofriendly wood may not be a great selling point, it is increasing in popularity as long as it is turned into well-designed and affordable products. This is where the FSC label gives increased reassurance to environmentally aware consumers. Nevertheless, despite all the measures, it has been estimated that 80 per cent of wood exported from Brazil has been cut illegally.

One of the UK's biggest stockists of FSC certified timber products is B&Q. It pioneered the sales of FSC products in the 1990s and yet has still maintained competitive pricing on its wood for the handyman and garden furniture. Other European retailers such as Carrefour, Kingfisher, Marks & Spencer and Ikea launched the Timber Retail Coalition in 2010 to ensure that they meet ethical standards for all timber and wood products sold in the EU. The aim is to try and stop illegal non-certified timber entering the EU supply chain. Thus Carrefour offers more than 70 FSC-labelled products on its garden furniture range, while Marks & Spencer uses FSC or recycled wood materials in store décor, stationery, kitchen rolls and magazines, etc. Ikea will find it more difficult to comply as it buys a lot of timber from China and Russia and only 7 per cent of wood from those countries comes from certified sources (*ENDS Report*, 2009). However, it is worth remembering that the illegal trade is fuelled by the demand for wood in Europe and America. Manage that more responsibly, and the demand for more land from the rainforest recedes.

Hardwood forestry in the tropical rainforest

*Source*: Alamy Images/Jacques Jangoux

In contrast, Ireland continues to buy its wood from non-certified sources (Hilliard, 2010), especially in the construction sector. It is estimated that this figure is around €20 million per year. For example, only 3 per cent of 541 Irish printing companies used certified sources compared with 80 per cent in the UK. All this helps the illegal trade of forest resources and facilitates money laundering, organised crime and human rights abuses. Although there is no legal requirement to buy from certified sources, it would help to end the black market trade.

There are two diametrically opposed views over the future of the rainforest. The FSC scheme, founded in 1993, enabled the environmentalists to negotiate with, rather than protest against, the commercial loggers. Certification and well-managed forests gave the loggers a way of continuing operations with far less pressure from the WWF, Greenpeace and Friends of the Earth. Ecological management, community involvement and good employment practice are all part of the guidelines. In the past, tropical timber markets in Europe and the USA were closed by the boycotting campaigns in the 1990s, but the FSC scheme may allow them to reopen and thus stimulate more cutting in Brazil. The FSC-labelling scheme operates worldwide and enables 'ethical buying' to take place, according to the loggers.

The alternative view, expressed by Laschefski and Freris (2001), questions the whole basis of continued logging before the rainforest has recovered from the ravages of the past thirty years. To them, the FSC has given an unwarranted legitimacy to logging under the ecologically sensitive label that allows commercial loggers to continue. At present, 96 per cent of certified forests are owned by either industrial-scale loggers or governments. However, by shifting the ethical buying responsibility to the consumer, it assumes that the buyer in Germany or the UK is conscious of green products, values the FSC scheme and is prepared to pay a little more rather than buy wood that might have been logged outside FSC guidelines. They argue that the FSC marketing certification legitimises logging when the priority should be preservation and reafforestation. Many of these views are strongly contested by Precious Woods.

The issue really comes back to the consumer in developed and developing countries. Pressure will grow in future years for Brazil to export more. The destruction of forests in SE Asia, the emergence of strong timber demand to fuel growth in China, along with the insatiable appetite for quality wood in Europe and North America, will create increasing pressure on the loggers to consume more forests albeit on a managed basis. So next time you buy wood from a stockist, perhaps you should play your part and ask whether it is FSC certified. You might just be helping to save a small part of one of the last great ecosystems in the world.

*Sources*: Barr (2004); *ENDS Report* (2009); FSC (2010); Hilliard (2010); Laschefski and Freris (2001); Montgomery (2003); Munk (2004); Usborne (2005); www.disasterrelief.org; www.fsc.org; www.preciouswoods.com.

What is clear is that the producer and consumer must work together to adjust to environmental concerns. The impact of protecting the natural environment is fundamental to all areas of marketing, and throughout this book, examples are given of marketers trying to create a greener environment. At its heart, however, its not about increasing consumption but changing the way we consume and what we consume.

## Chapter summary

- This chapter has explored the importance of the external marketing environment as an influence on the way in which organisations do business and make their decisions. Ways in which customers, markets, competitors, technology and regulation are changing are all important pointers to future strategy. Thus failure to understand the environment fully could mean missing out on opportunities or ignoring threats which in turn could lead to lost revenue or, more seriously, loss of competitive advantage.

- Using environmental scanning, a technique for monitoring and evaluating information, organisations can understand their environment more thoroughly, pick up early signs of emerging trends, and thus plan their future activities appropriately. Care must be taken to ensure that all appropriate sources of information are constantly monitored (but avoiding information overload), and that internal mechanisms exist for disseminating information and acting on it.

- The main framework for the chapter is the categorisation of the marketing environment into STEEPLE factors: sociocultural, technological, economic, ethical, political and legal, and ecological.

- The first of the STEEPLE factors is the sociocultural environment. This deals with 'hard' information, such as demographic trends, and with less tangible issues, such as changing tastes, attitudes and cultures. Knowledge of demographic trends gives the marketer a basic feel for how broad market segments are likely to change in the future. To gain the fullest picture, however, the marketer needs to combine demographic information with 'softer' data on how attitudes are changing.

- The second STEEPLE factor is technology. An organisation's technological advances may arise from the exploitation of breakthroughs from other organisations, or may be the result of long-term investment in R&D in-house to solve a specific problem. Either way, technology can present the opportunity to create a clear differential advantage that cannot be easily copied by the competition.

- The economic environment constitutes the third STEEPLE factor, and can be further divided into macro- and microeconomic environments. The macroeconomic environment analyses the effects of the broader economic picture, looking at issues such as taxation, government spending and interest rates. It also takes account of the threats, opportunities and barriers arising from membership of international trading blocs. The microeconomic environment is a little closer to the individual organisation, and is concerned with the structure of the market(s) in which it operates.

- The fourth STEEPLE factor is the ethical environment. This incorporates society's expectations and norms of what is 'moral' and 'right' into the benchmarks and limits that organisations set themselves in what they choose to do. Consumers and investors are increasingly taking 'ethical conduct' into account in assessing their relationships with organisations and their brands.

- The political and legal environments give us the fifth and sixth STEEPLE factors. Laws, regulations and codes of practice emanate from national governments, the EU, local government, statutory bodies and trade associations to affect the way in which organisations do business. Consumer groups and other pressure groups, such as those representing the ecological movement, health issues and animal rights, are active in trying to persuade government to deregulate or legislate, or to influence the scope and content of new legislation.

- The final STEEPLE factor is the ecological environment, reflecting a growing concern about the natural environment and the impact of consumerism upon it. Organisations need to consider, for example, how they can reduce their carbon footprints and continue to satisfy consumer needs and wants more sustainably.

## Questions for review and discussion

**2.1** What is *environmental scanning*, why is it important, and what are the potential problems of implementing it?

**2.2** Differentiate between the *macro-* and *micro-economic environments*.

**2.3** What sources of published demographic data are available via your own university or college library?

**2.4** Find and discuss examples of products that are particularly vulnerable to changing consumer tastes.

**2.5** Find and discuss recent examples of adjudications by the ASA (or the equivalent regulatory body in your own country) of advertisements in a variety of media. Do you agree with its judgement?

**2.6** Using Figure 2.1 as a framework, choose a product and list under each of the *STEEPLE factors* the relevant influences that have helped to make that product what it is.

## CASE STUDY 2

# GOT ANY GUM, CHUM?

Founded in the USA in 1881, Wrigley's has prospered in the gum business for more than a century. Although Wrigley's has been manufacturing gum in the UK since 1927, the chewing of gum, originally an American habit, was made really fashionable in Europe by the American military during the Second World War. Children in the UK were commonly heard calling 'Got any gum, chum?' to American soldiers, who would respond by distributing a share of their rations. Today, gum chewing is one of the world's most common habits.

Manufacturers have long since made claims relating to the oral care and dental hygiene (breath freshening) properties of gum. Gum can remove plaque acids from the mouth and, therefore, it slows the process of tooth decay. A Wrigley's product, Orbit sugar-free gum, was the first gum product to be accredited by the British Dental Association, as a result of its benefits in terms of oral health. In the USA, the Wrigley Science Institute has been conducting extensive research in the search to identify new health benefits of chewing gum, in addition to dental claims. Its claims include that gum chewing helps weight control, reduces stress, and improves memory

(although there is no hard evidence for the latter as yet). Some also argue that chewing gum is a useful displacement activity when trying to give up smoking. Indeed, the introduction of a ban on smoking in public places in Ireland and then in the UK led to increases in gum sales in both countries.

It is argued, however, that gum is an environmentally unfriendly product, and it has been claimed that 80 per cent of all gum ends up somewhere that it shouldn't! Westminster Council estimates that there are 300,000 pieces of gum on the pavement of London's Oxford Street alone. Deposits of gum on the streets represent an ugly, messy and expensive problem for local authorities to deal with and, indeed, it is one of the UK's biggest public cleansing problems. Gum removal is extremely labour intensive and involves the use of costly machinery – a hot-jet pavement blaster costs in the region of £100,000. Some local councils have argued for some time that manufacturers should be responsible for clearing up the mess. The UK government's Department for Environment, Food and Rural Affairs (DEFRA), which is responsible for litter on our streets, commented that it does not wish to penalise a legal product, but it has stated that it wants to see a change in public behaviour regarding the disposal of gum. In recent years the UK litter law has changed to include discarded gum in the official definition of litter. Today, if you drop gum you can be fined up to £80 – theoretically, at least. However, as one of Solihull Council's litter wardens commented, no one has yet been fined for dropping gum because it's so difficult to catch them in the act!

DEFRA has established the Chewing Gum Action Group to tackle the problem of gum on the streets, and whilst gum manufacturers have always claimed that the problem is not their responsibility, they have donated funds of £600,000 to support the Action Group's anti-litter publicity in response to DEFRA's call for further support from manufacturers. It is in the interests of gum manufacturers to cooperate with such initiatives in the hope that this will minimise the potential risk of the introduction of regulation. Such funds are used to support litter wardens and schemes (such as that introduced in Solihull) through which dedicated gum-disposal bins are provided on high-street lamp-posts. Solihull's campaign also involved the use of a blimp carrying the campaign message 'Thanks for binning your gum when you're done' high above the town centre.

Unfortunately, such promotional campaigns do not necessarily have the desired effect, with the Royal Borough of Kensington and Chelsea reporting that, despite a promotional effort designed to reduce gum litter, an *increase* in gum on the high street was evident, leading the council to question whether this was the best way to address the problem. So, what's the solution? A tax on gum? Local-authority lobbying of manufacturers to produce biodegradable gum and/or technologies that facilitate the clean-up exercise?

Wrigley's has recognised this growing problem, and has invested in research over the last 20 years to produce biodegradable gum, with the aim of creating a gum that decomposes completely within a couple of weeks. Indeed, Wrigley's has already registered a patent for a product in this area. It's also worth noting that in 2006 Revolymer Ltd, a spin-off company from the University of Bristol, developed polymers that can be incorporated into gum to prevent it from sticking to pavements, making 'removable gum' a very real possibility. By 2011, the resulting product, 'Rev7' had been approved in the US by the Food & Drug Administration and was about to be launched in that market. It is possible that either or both Wrigley's and Cadbury's could be looking to license that technology to incorporate it into their own products.

Gum is the fastest growing confectionery market in the world, with Euromonitor International forecasting 3.3 per cent annual average value growth in the global gum market between 2007 and 2011, compared with an estimate of just 2.2 per cent for chocolate confectionery. The sugar-free sector of the gum market has done particularly well in recent years, particularly in Europe, where it accounts for the majority of the total gum market in many countries.

This worldwide boom in the gum market had not been reflected in the UK, at least up to 2007. At that time, UK market growth had been relatively static with sales of chewing gum in 2007 hovering around £340 million (that's according to Mintel (2007). Euromonitor (2010) suggests a figure for 2007 sales closer to £370 million). Wrigley's held an 80 per cent share of that market with brands such as Wrigley's Extra, Airwaves, and Orbit, in addition to classic brands such as Spearmint, Doublemint and Juicy Fruit. Wrigley's had dominated the market for decades and looked unassailable.

A few years before 2007, Cadbury's, the world's largest confectionery company, had bought the USA gum company Adams. Adams' portfolio consisted of a range of gum products, including Trident named after three ingredients believed to be good for teeth, and launched in the USA in the 1960s. Adams, however, had never marketed Trident in the UK. Cadbury's, which had never sold gum in the UK before, thus entered the UK gum market in February 2007 with Trident sugar-free gum products, Trident Splash and Trident Soft with the aim of growing the UK market for gum.

This was certainly not the first time that Wrigley had faced competition; there have been other entrants to the UK market over the last 80 years, although it could be said that none of them arrived with Cadbury's brand building expertise, extensive sales force, established distribution channels and substantial experience of the confectionery market. This particular launch must therefore have been seen as representing a real challenge to Wrigley's dominance, although the MD of Wrigley UK claimed that Wrigley welcomed the competition, commenting, 'If you're running a race, running it on your own is actually no fun'. He claimed that the company was well prepared for Cadbury's entry, and indeed went on the say that he fancied Wrigley's chances in the battle for the UK market.

Cadbury's considered the growth potential in the UK market a great opportunity and wanted a slice of the action. This is also perhaps not surprising as, in addition to other environmental factors impacting Cadbury's fortunes, the cost of dairy ingredients had been rising worldwide, increasing by 20 per cent in the first half of 2007.

Cadbury's invested £10 million in the introduction of Trident. Central to the UK campaign was the idea of a 'gum revolution', involving the slogan 'Mastication for the nation' (masticate means to chew, we hasten to add). While analysts commented early on that this was likely to cause confusion and that there existed a real possibility of the slogan being misheard, Cadbury's believed that the phrase summed up the 'pleasure of chewing'. The launch campaign included a range of television and cinema advertisements, and this was where Cadbury's ran into trouble. Two of the four advertisements featured white actors speaking in a Caribbean accent. One of the advertisements, aimed specifically at youngsters, featured a black dub poet enthusing about the product on stage in a club. The advertising resulted in complaints and criticisms from far and wide. Some leading marketing practitioners suggested that this was the worst ad they had ever seen, whilst Ligali, an African British organisation that challenges the misrepresentation of African people in the British media, also objected to it. The organisation was unhappy about the characterisation within the ads, claiming that such cultural stereotyping was offensive, and urged the boycott of products.

The Advertising Standards Authority (ASA) received 518 complaints about the advertising, with criticisms including that it was offensive and racist because it promoted the stereotype of black Caribbean people having particular accents and mannerisms. The ASA upheld these complaints, concluding that the ads had breached advertising codes relating to 'offence' and 'harmful stereotypes' and ruled that the ads should not be shown again. Simon Baldry, MD of Cadbury Trebor Bassett, responded that 'It was never our intention to offend anyone' and denied that the campaign was designed to be controversial. Yet, Cadbury's own pre-advertising research had found that 1 in 5 members of ethnic minorities would find the ad offensive. Despite this, Cadbury's had gone ahead with the ad, based primarily on the positive reactions among young consumers.

Meanwhile, although Wrigley's claimed that it was unaffected by Cadbury's launch, it certainly did not sit back idly watching and waiting. Wrigley's fought back immediately with the launch of a new product, Orbit Complete, accompanied by a television campaign and the use of actors handing out samples of the new product on UK streets. It must, however, be noted that Wrigley's positioning of the new product was quite different from Cadbury's Trident – Wrigley's emphasised 'function' in terms of health and hygiene, and specifically the product's plaque fighting abilities, while Cadbury's positioning of Trident focused primarily on

'flavour and fun'. Closer to the Cadbury's 'flavour and fun' positioning, Wrigley's also launched Extra Fusion in spearmint and melon, and peppermint and berry flavours, and late in 2007 it also launched triple-flavour gums in variants of raspberry, blackcurrant and grapefruit, and orange, pineapple and banana.

Just 10 weeks after its launch, Trident had taken 15 per cent of the UK market for gum, although this figure slipped back slightly to 12.5 per cent. Market share gains exceeded Cadbury's expectations. Yet Wrigley's kept calm, and suggested that this was purely a result of the novelty value of Trident. Overall, in the year following Trident's launch, the total UK market for chewing gum grew by 20 per cent as a result of both companies' investment in their competing brands, and Wrigley's also benefited from this growth with sales up by 5 per cent across the year. Thus Trident evidently stimulated market growth rather than just taking market share from Wrigley's. Nevertheless, Wrigley's still had 86 per cent of the market, and its brands including Juicy Fruit, Spearmint and Doublemint (all more than 100 years old) continued to grow.

By the end of 2010, it appeared that the market had settled down somewhat after the initial stimulus of Trident's launch. Not surprisingly, after all the market activity in 2007, value sales rose sharply and peaked in 2008, as can be seen in Table 2.2. However, from 2009 onwards, they started to fall, and are forecast to continue to fall. This is not so much because of falling *volume* sales, but because of price competition eroding *value* sales. Retailer own brand gums are carving out a value niche for basic spearmint and peppermint gums, for instance, and all the main players are now offering larger economy packs representing more gum for the consumer's money.

**Table 2.2** Chewing gum sales 2006–15

| Year | Value (£m) |
| --- | --- |
| 2006 | £326 |
| 2007 | £370 |
| 2008 | £382 |
| 2009 | £336 |
| 2010 | £307 |
| 2011* | £287 |
| 2012* | £272 |
| --- | --- |
| 2015* | £250 |

\* Forecast.
Source: extracted from Euromonitor (2010), Tables 2 and 10.

**Table 2.3** Chewing gum market shares (by value) 2006–2009

| Company | 2006 | 2007 | 2009 |
|---|---|---|---|
| Wrigley's | 80.43% | 72.13% | 68.44% |
| Cadbury's | 2.42% | 12.77% | 9.10% |
| Own label | 3.96% | 3.70% | 4.43% |
| Others | 13.19% | 11.40% | 18.03% |

*Source*: extracted from Euromonitor (2010), Table 6.

In terms of brand shares, as Table 2.3 shows, although Wrigley's is still predominant its share has fallen back, as has Cadbury's, and as mentioned above, own label is making progress in a value niche. Nevertheless, there is still innovation in the market. In 2009, Wrigley's introduced a new premium brand called '5', while Cadbury's introduced Trebor Extra Strong. However, just when it started to look as though Wrigley's and Cadbury's largely had it sorted out between them, a new contender emerged. Italian company Perfetti Van Melle launched Mentos Pure Fresh Gum featuring antibacterial green tea extract as an aid to oral health. The company's stated aim is for the Mentos gum portfolio to take the number two spot in the market – a clear challenge to Cadbury's. Perhaps more of a niche product is Fairtrade-certified Chicza Rainforest Gum, a Mexican brand manufactured by a farmers' cooperative. It is made from natural gum extract and (unlike other gums) contains no petrochemicals. It also does not stick to clothing or pavements and takes only six weeks to turn to dust.

Chewing all this over then, this is a market with increasing competition and in which neither of the main players can be complacent. There is still room for innovation, and the promise of further twists in a very dynamic marketing environment. For 2011, for example, Wrigley's promised an £11 million marketing budget and was looking to prioritise the UK market because, according to the UK Sales Director, 'on average, Britons use less chewing gum than either Europe or the US'.

*Sources*: Bainbridge (2007); Becket (2010); Bowers (2007); Chomka (2007); Euromonitor (2010); Miller (2007); Mintel (2009, 2007); *The Money Programme* (2007); Reynolds (2010); Riley (2011); www.asa.org.uk; www.bris.ac.uk/research; www.rbkc.gov.uk. Grateful thanks to Tracy Panther for her work on this case.

## Questions

1 Summarise the ways in which STEEPLE factors affected the UK gum market in 2007.

2 Thinking about the microeconomic environment in particular (p. 58 *et seq.*), how would you describe the market structure (a) before Trident's entry, and (b) in 2010? Why do you think the market structure has evolved in that way?

3 Why do you think that Cadbury was initially so successful in competing against the market leader, Wrigley's, with the Trident launch?

4 Which factors should manufacturers pay particular attention to today, in order to achieve a strong and sustainable position in this market? Why?

## References for chapter 2

Agence France Presse (2010) 'China Probes Path of Seized North Korea Arms', Agence France Presse, 25 February, accessed via www.channelnewsasia.com/stories/afp_asiapacific/view/1039896/1/.html.

Aguilar, F.J. (1967) *Scanning the Business Environment*, Macmillan.

ASA (2010) 'Adjudication on Diesel (London) Ltd', accessed via www.asa.org.uk/Complaints-and-ASA-action/Adjudications/2010/6/Diesel-(London)-Ltd/TF_ADJ_48673.aspx.

Bainbridge, J. (2007) 'Sector Insight: Chewing Gum and Mints', *Marketing*, 1 August.

Ball, J. (2010) 'Stop Smoking Kit Sales are up, but so is Tobacco . . .', *The Grocer*, 20 February, p. 25.

Barr, D. (2004) 'A Green Piece of Furniture', *The Times*, 30 April, p. 15.

Becket, A. (2010) 'Wrigley Says it's Got Britain Back in the Gum Habit', *The Grocer*, 10 December.

*Birmingham Post* (2009) 'Marketeers Miss Target When it Comes to Selling to the Over-50s, Study Finds', *Birmingham Post*, 6 July.

Bowers, S. (2007) 'Chewing Gum War Extends Cadbury's Sticky Patch', *The Guardian*, 2 August.

Bremner, C. (1997) 'All Because the Belgians Do Not Like Milk Tray', *The Times*, 24 October, p. 5.

Brown-Humes, C. and MacCarthy, C. (2004), 'EU Calls Time on Nordic Nations' Long Battle Against Alcohol', *Financial Times*, 10 January, p. 6.

*Checkout* (2008) 'Ethical Issues Top of Mind for Shoppers', *Checkout*, June, p. 8.

Chen, M. and Zhang, F. (2009) 'End-of-Life Vehicle Recovery in China: Consideration and Innovation following the EU ELV Directive', *JOM*, 61 (3), pp. 45–52.

Chomka, S. (2007) 'Trident Revives Gum Sales', *The Grocer*, 6 October.

Clark, N. (2009) 'The Many Shades of Grey', *Marketing*, 15 July, pp. 24–5.

*Dagens Handel* (2010) 'Swedes Increasingly Positive to Systembolaget', *Dagens Handel*, 26 March.

*Dow Jones International News* (2009) 'France's DCNS Gets EUR310 Mln French Naval Contract', *Dow Jones International News*, 12 October.

*The Economist* (2005) 'Europe: the End of Enlargement?', *The Economist*, 16 July, p. 38.

*Edmonton Journal* (2010) 'No Ban on Tourists Climbing Uluru', *Edmonton Journal*, 16 January.

EIU (2010) 'Sweden: Competition and Price Regulations', *Economist Intelligence Unit – ViewsWire*, 18 March.

Elliott, V. and Pavia, W. (2010) 'Sheringham Defeats Tesco with Vote for Clive Hay-Smith's Eco-store', *The Times*, 5 March.

*ENDS Report* (2009) 'Supply Chain: Ikea Struggles to Source Sustainable Timber', *ENDS Report*, 31 July.

EU (2010) '52009AE0635; Opinion of the European Economic and Social Committee on the Proposal for a Council directive amending Directives 92/79/EEC, 92/80/EEC and 95/59/EC on the Structure and Rates of Excise Duty Applied on Manufactured Tobacco OJ C 228, 22.9.2009, pp. 130–40', *EUR-Lex*, 4 March.

Euromonitor (2010) 'Gum in the United Kingdom', *Euromonitor International*, accessed via www.portal.euromonitor.com/Portal/Pages/Statistics/Statistics.aspx.

European Commission (2012) *VAT Rates Applied in the Member States of the European Union, European Commission: Taxation and Customs Union*, 1 January, accessed via http://ec.europa.eu/taxation_customs/resources/documents/taxation/vat/how_vat_works/rates/vat_rates_en.pdf.

Ford, R. (2010) 'Consumers Urged to go Back to Cod with a Clear Conscience', *The Grocer*, 28 March.

FSC (2010) 'Timber Retail Coalition Launched to Curb Illegal Logging', FSC, 16 April, accessed via www.fsc.org/fsc-news.html.

George, N. (2004) 'Sweden is Advised to Cut Taxes on Alcohol', *Financial Times*, 10 January, p. 8.

Glancey, J. (2010) 'The Chumps of Norfolk: a Thumping Great Tesco is the Last thing This Seaside Town Needs. But Try Telling the Planners', *The Guardian*, 3 March.

*The Grocer* (2010) 'Baking a Profit?', *The Grocer*, 13 February, pp. 49–52.

Handley, L. (2010) 'The 100-Year-Old Consumer', *Marketing Week*, 22 April.

Hilliard, M. (2010) 'Ireland Logged as Top in EU for Import of Illegal Timber', *Sunday Tribune*, 11 April.

HMRC (2010) 'United Kingdom HM Revenue & Customs Warns Public of Car Boot Criminals', *UK Government News*, 23 March.

Inness, P. (2009) 'Component Obsolescence has Become a Fact of Life', *Electronics Weekly*, 4 March, p. 17.

Laschefski, K. and Freris, N. (2001) 'Saving the Wood', *The Ecologist*, July/August, pp. 40–3.

Lloyd Parry, R. (2009) 'Sanctions-busting Arsenal Found on Pyongyang Plane', *The Times*, 14 December.

Löwy, M. (2010) 'Advertising is a "Serious Health Threat" to the Environment', *Monthly Review*, 1 January.

*Marketing Week* (2011) 'Bulldog Goes Outdoor for F-commerce Launch Drive', *Marketing Week*, 21 April.

Marsden, P. (2011) 'The Kaiser Chiefs and the Future of F-commerce', *Social Commerce Today*, accessed via http://socialcommercetoday.com/the-kaiser-chiefs-and-the-future-of-f-commerce/.

McLaughlin, J. (2009) 'Union Anger Grows at State as Italian Yard Job Cuts Loom', *Lloyd's List*, 27 November.

Medina, K. (2009) 'Understanding Cognitive Processes Enhances Senior Marketing', *Selling to Seniors*, 5 December.

Miller, C. (2007) 'The Chewing Gum War', BBC, accessed via http://news.bbc.co.uk/1/hi/business/6683389.stm.

Mintel (2007) 'Chewing Gum and Mints', *Mintel Market Intelligence*, accessed via http://academic.mintel.com/sinatra/oxygen_academic/search_results/show&/display/id=220151.

Mintel (2009) 'Confectionery UK', *Mintel Market Intelligence*, accessed via http://academic.mintel.com/sinatra/oxygen_academic/search_results/show&/display/id=393958/display/id=461780#hit1.

Mintel (2010a) 'Eggs', *Mintel Market Intelligence*, June, accessed via http://academic.mintel.com/sinatra/oxygen_academic/search_results/show&/display/id=480794/display/id=480794/display/id=480794/display/id=480794/display/id=529881?select_section=480794.

Mintel (2010b) 'Laundry Products UK', *Mintel Market Intelligence*, September, accessed via http://academic.mintel.com/sinatra/oxygen_academic/search_results/show&/display/id=480975/display/id=480975/display/id=547235?select_section=480975.

Mintel (2010c) 'Organic Food UK', *Mintel Market Intelligence*, October, accessed via http://academic.mintel.com/sinatra/oxygen_academic/search_results/display/id=479938/display/id=551459#hit1.

Minton, A. (2010) 'This Town Has Been Sold to Tesco', *The Guardian*, 5 May.

*The Money Programme* (2007) 'The Chewing Gum War', *The Money Programme*, broadcast by the BBC, 25 May.

Montgomery, D. (2003) 'Eco Fashion: Precious Wood', *In Business*, May/June, p. 30.

Morley, C. (2003) 'Choc Horror!', *Evening Mail*, 6 August, p. 13.

Munk, D. (2004) 'Forces of Nature', *The Guardian*, 17 March, p. 12.

Neff, J., Steinberg, B. and Zmuda, N. (2010) 'Marketers Blame the Consumer in New Save-the-planet Pitches', *Advertising Age*, 19 April.

*The News* (2010) 'Under-age Cigarette Sales Fall across Hampshire', *The News*, 9 March.

*Northumberland Gazette* (2010) 'Warning of Password Scammers', *Northumberland Gazette*, 10 March.

*Nottingham Evening Post* (2010) 'Illegal Tobacco in Nottingham', *Nottingham Evening Post*, 29 March.

O'Connell, S. (2010) 'Older, Wiser and More Profitable', *The Sunday Times*, 28 February.

O'Grady, S., Kenber, B., Peck, T. and Morris, S. (2010) 'Did the EU Really Take 15 Years to Define Chocolate?' *The Independent*, 24 April.

*Packaging News* (2010) 'Design: Shelf Review The Happy Egg Co', *Packaging News*, 8 March.

Press Association (2009) '1,000mph Car to be Built in Bristol', *Press Association FeatureFile*, 22 December.

PWC (2010) 'Shopping Behavior to Change as a Result of New Marketplace Realities', PricewaterhouseCoopers and Kantar Retail, 9 March, accessed via www.pwc.com/us/en/press-releases/2010/Shopping-behavior-to-change.jhtml.

Randerson, J. (2009) 'A Practical Guide to Ethical Living: Avoiding Greenwash', *The Guardian*, 28 November.

Reynolds, J. (2010) 'Wrigley and Cadbury Eye Up "Non-stick" Gum', *Marketing*, 13 October.

Riley, L. (2011) 'Mentos Targets Number Two Spot in Gum Market', *The Grocer*, 9 April.

Simms, J. (2001) 'EU Rules, OK?', *Marketing*, 25 January, pp. 23–5.

Sims, P. (2010) '50% of Towns have Five Supermarkets on their Doorsteps', *Daily Mail*, 8 March.

*Svenska Dagbladet* (2010) 'Systembolaget Claims Larger Share of Total Alcohol Sales', *Svenska Dagbladet*, 1 February, p. 6.

Sweney, M. (2010a) 'ASA to Investigate "Offensive" Paddy Power Ad', *The Guardian*, 11 May.

Sweney, M. (2010b) 'Award-winning Ice-cream Ad Featuring Pregnant Nun Stokes Controversy', *The Guardian*, 18 June.

*The Times* (2003) 'Restrictive "Chocolate" Law Breaches EU Free Trade', *The Times*, 21 January, p. 33.

Tucker, E. (1997) 'MEPs Reject Chocolate Compromise', *Financial Times*, 24 October, p. 20.

Usborne, D. (2005) 'Brazil Arrests Civil Servants in Crackdown on Amazonian Logging', *The Independent*, 4 June, p. 26.

*Wall Street Journal* (2005) 'The Tax that France Built', *Wall Street Journal*, 4 March, p. A14.

Ward, A. (2009) 'Fresh Blow to Government's Grip on Monopolies', *Financial Times*, 10 November.

Watson, R. (2005) 'Turkey Faces Fresh Obstacle on Rocky Road to Joining EU', *The Times*, 30 June, p. 40.

# CHAPTER 3

# Buyer behaviour

## LEARNING OBJECTIVES

This chapter will help you to:

- understand the decision-making processes that consumers go through as they make a purchase;
- appreciate how those processes differ between different buying situations;
- understand the influences that affect decision-making, whether environmental, psychological or sociocultural and the implications of those processes and influences for marketing strategies;
- understand the nature and structure of B2B buying and the differences between B2B and consumer buying; and
- analyse the B2B buying process and the factors that influence the outcomes.

## INTRODUCTION

**IN CONTRAST TO CHAPTER** 2, which looked at the broad backdrop against which marketers have to do business, this chapter focuses closely on consumers and B2B customers who are at the centre of many a marketer's universe. While the customer is part of the marketing environment, and is shaped to some extent by the influences already discussed in Chapter 2, it is also very important to understand the more personal and specific influences affecting those customers and the nature of the decision-making processes through which they go.

This chapter, therefore, begins by looking at consumers as buyers and analysing the factors, both internal and external, that determine how and why they make their choices. The later part of the chapter examines B2B buyer behaviour. Having considered some of the differences between consumers and B2B customers in terms of how and why they purchase goods and services, we shall then analyse the B2B buying process and the pressures that shape the decisions that are made within an organisational market.

# The consumer decision-making process

Figure 3.1 offers a deceptively simple model of buyer behaviour presented as a logical flow of activities, working through from problem recognition to purchase to post-purchase evaluation. This section of this chapter deals with this core process.

**Figure 3.1**
The consumer buying decision-making process and its influencing factors

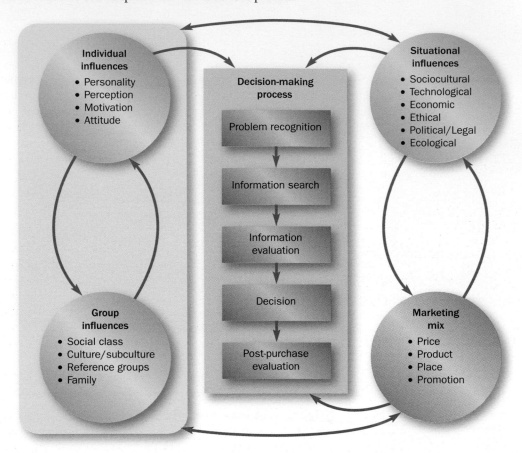

The decision-making process is affected by a number of complex influences, as can be seen in Figure 3.1. Some of these influences relate to the wider marketing environment in which the decision is being made (see pp. 91–93). Others, however, relate to the individual purchaser and therefore pp. 93–102 will consider those influences emanating from within the individual such as personality, attitudes and learning. Similarly, pp. 102–109 will look at how the individual's decisions are affected by their social context, especially family and cultural groupings.

How, why and when we eat is of interest to those supplying the snack-food market, so that they can base their marketing strategies on a sound understanding of consumer behaviour patterns. Around nine out of ten adults snack between meals, over half of them on a daily basis. Hunger and boreedom seem to be the major motivations for snacking, although there is some habitual snacking in front of the telly or the computer and a certain degree of stress or treat snacking going on. Overall, taste and convenience are the most important criteria in selecting a snack, with price and how filling the snack is following close behind. There are, however, subtle differences between different customer groups. Younger, and thus perhaps more cash-strapped consumers gravitate towards price and how filling the snack is, whereas the 35–44-year-olds are more concerned about the fat and calorie content of what they choose. Women tend to go for healthy snacks, while men go for filling snacks. Older age groups favour savoury snacks more than sweet ones (Mintel, 2010b).

Attitudes towards snacking have also changed, with people being more prepared to eat in the street or 'on the go', although that is less prevalent among the over-forty-fives who prefer traditional eating. The preferred snacks for home consumption are fresh fruit, crisps and chocolate bars, while the 'on the go' snacker opts for chocolate bars, crisps and sandwiches. So why isn't fresh fruit as popular for the mobile snacker as it is for ther home-based snacker? Maybe it's about opportunity. If fresh fruit were displayed near the checkout and sold in the same way as confectionery in convenience stores, then perhaps more people would buy it. Fruits such as bananas, apples and satsumas can be priced and sold as single items, and easily eaten 'on the go'. Trials, as reported by Walker (2010a), have suggested that retailers who have adopted this approach have seen fruit sales rise by up to 40 per cent. A snack is often an impulse purchase, and this shows just how powerful the retail environment can be in influencing the decisions that consumers make.

There have been many attempts to create models of consumer decision-making of greater or lesser complexity and detail that try to capture the richness of the experience. The Engel, Blackwell and Miniard (1990) model presented here, although concise and simple in its outline, provides a framework that still allows us to consider, through discussion, many of the more complex elements. It traces the progress of a purchasing event stage by stage from the buyer's point of view, including the definition of likely information needs and consideration of the level of rationality and analytical behaviour leading to the eventual decision.

We now look at each stage in turn.

## Problem recognition

In trying to rationalise the decision-making process, this is a good place to begin. After all, if you are not aware that you have a 'problem', how can you decide to purchase something to solve it? More functional purchases, such as replenishing stocks of washing powder or petrol, may be initiated by a casual glance at current stock levels. Other purchases may be triggered by a definable event. If, for example, the exhaust falls off your car, you will soon become aware of the nature of the problem and the kind of purchase that will provide the remedy.

Where psychological needs are involved, however, the problem recognition may be a slow dawning or may lead to a sudden impulse, when the consumer, realising that the current position or feeling is not the desired one, decides to do something to change it through a purchase (Bruner and Pomazal, 1988). Imagine, for instance, that you are wandering round the supermarket after a tough day at work. You're tired, listless and a bit depressed. You've filled your trolley with the potatoes, bread and milk you intended to buy, but you also slip a bar of chocolate (or worse!) in there on the basis that it will cheer you up as you drive home. The 'problem' here is less definable, based on a vague psychological feeling, and it follows that the solution is also less definable – it could be chocolate, cream buns, wine or clothing, whatever takes the purchaser's fancy.

What the examples given so far do have in common, however, is that the impetus to go into a purchasing decision-making routine comes from the consumer. The consumer identifies or recognises the problem, independently from the marketer, and looks for a solution. As will be seen in the following sections, marketers can then use the marketing mix elements to influence the choice of solution. It is also possible, however, for marketers to trigger the process by using the marketing mix to bring a problem to the consumer's attention.

*eg* Laundry products have a long and venerable history of playing on housewives' fears of being judged inadequate because their family's clothes don't look as white or as clean as their neighbours'. We have thus all become used to assessing these products in terms of their 'cleaning power' and 'stain removal' based not only on what we pick up from their advertising and on-pack messages, but also from our own experience of using them. There is, however, a hitherto ignored menace lurking in our laundry baskets: bacteria. Your washing could look clean and smell fresh, but maybe that's not the whole story – there's an invisible enemy within.

Vanish (www.vanish.co.uk) provides a range of laundry additives that can be used to pre-treat stains before washing, aid stain removal in the wash, and prevent whites from going grey. With its Oxi Action Extra Hygiene product, however, it goes one step further in promising to remove 99.9 per cent of bacteria (although to be honest I'm more worried about the other 0.1 per cent – they must be pretty nasty bacteria to survive all this!). There is a legitimate need being identified here. Perhaps as washing machines and mainstream detergents become more effective at washing at low temperatures, fewer bacteria do get removed during a normal wash cycle. There could also be a response to an emotional need, in that women (and it is primarily women buying such products) want to feel that they are doing all they can to protect their families, especially working mums who might feel some degree of guilt at having less time for home and family.

Despite the pretty pink colour, this brand suggests an uncompromising problem-solving image
*Source*: Reckitt Benckiser Group plc, www.vanish.co.uk

There is, of course, a significant difference between being aware of a need or problem and being able to do something about it. Many needs are latent and remain unfulfilled, either because consumers decide not to do anything about it now, or because they are unable to do anything. We might all feel the need for a three-week holiday in some exotic part of the world, but we must not only be willing, but also financially able, to disappear over the horizon. Problem recognition, if it is to lead anywhere, therefore requires both the willingness and the ability to fulfil the emerging need.

# Information search

Defining the problem is one thing, but defining and implementing the solution is something else. The questions to be answered include what kind of purchase will solve the problem, where and how it can be obtained, what information is needed to arrive at a decision and where that information is available. In some cases, consumers will actively search out relevant information with a view to using it in making a decision, but they can also acquire information passively, storing it away until it is needed. Daily, consumers are exposed to a wide range of media all designed to influence awareness and recall of particular products and services. Thus they 'know' that Vanish Oxi Action Extra Hygiene eliminates bacteria before they get anywhere near a conscious choice of laundry product in the supermarket. When they do get to the point of purchasing, the manufacturers hope that they will recall that knowledge and use it in making the brand choice.

Not all external sources of information are controlled by the marketer – don't forget the power of word of mouth as a marketing tool. Friends, family and colleagues, for example, may all give advice, whether based on experience, knowledge or opinion, to the would-be decision maker in this phase. People are more likely to trust information given through word of mouth, because the source is generally assumed to be unbiased and trustworthy, and the information itself often derives from first-hand experience.

In other situations, the consumer might seek out information from the internet, specialist publications, retailers or even from marketing literature. For example, when buying a car, potential buyers will probably visit competing dealerships to talk to sales staff, look closely at the merchandise and collect brochures. Additionally, they might consult what they consider to be unbiased expert sources of advice such as *What Car?* magazine, and begin to take more notice of car advertisements in all media.

Hauser *et al.* (1993) emphasise the fact that time pressure can interfere with the information search. They found that consumers spend less time searching for different sources as pressure increases. At the other end of the spectrum, however, information overload may cause problems for the potential purchaser. There is evidence to suggest that consumers cannot cope with too much information at product level (Keller and Staelin, 1987). Thus the greater the relevance of the information to consumers, such as the key benefits and applications of the product, the easier it is for them to assimilate and process that information as part of their decision-making. In other words, better and more extensive information may actually lead to poorer buying decisions!

# Information evaluation

On what criteria do you evaluate the information gathered? If you are looking for a new car exhaust system, an online search could generate over 1,000 entries to sift through and even a typical *Yellow Pages* could provide up to ten pages of exhaust system dealerships, featuring over 100 potential outlets within reasonable travelling distance. If you have had no previous experience of any of them, then you have to find a means of differentiating between them. You are unlikely to investigate all of them, since that would take too long, and so you may draw up a shortlist on the basis of those with the biggest feature entries in *Yellow Pages*, those whose names pop up first in an internet search, or those who also advertise prominently in the local press or on television. Such advertising may emphasise the advantages of using a particular outlet, pointing out to the consumer what the appropriate evaluative criteria are (speed, friendliness or price, for example). Location may also be an important factor; some outlets are closer to home or work than others.

In contrast, looking for chocolate in the supermarket, your information evaluation is likely to be less time consuming and less systematic. Faced with a set of brands of chocolate that are known and liked, the evaluation is cursory: 'What do I feel like eating?' The nearest to systematic thinking might be (in desperation) the evaluation of which one really represents the most chocolate for the price. Of course, if a new brand has appeared on the chocolate shelf, then that might break the habitual, unconscious grabbing at the familiar wrapper, and make a consumer stop and look closely to evaluate what the new product has to offer in comparison with the old ones.

What has been happening to varying degrees in the above examples is that the consumer has started to narrow down from a wide list of potential options to an evoked set (Howard and Sheth, 1969), a final shortlist for serious appraisal. Being a part of the consumer's evoked set, and staying there, is clearly important to the marketer, although it is not always easy. To make a choice from within the evoked set, the consumer needs either a formal or an informal means of selecting from the small number of choices available. This, therefore, implies some definition of evaluative or choice criteria.

Again, marketers will be trying to influence this stage. This can be done, for example, through their communications campaigns which may implant images of products in the consumer's mind so that they seem familiar (and therefore less threatening) at the point of sale. They may also stress particular product attributes, both to increase the importance of that attribute in the consumer's mind, i.e. to make sure that the attribute is number one on the list of evaluative criteria, and to ensure that the consumer believes that a particular brand is unsurpassed in terms of that attribute. Point-of-sale material can also reinforce these things, for example through displays, leaflets, the wording on packaging and on-pack promotions.

Generally, therefore, what is happening is that without necessarily being conscious of it, the potential buyer is constructing a list of performance criteria, then assessing each supplier or available brand against it. This assessment can be based on objective criteria, related to the attributes of the product and its use (price, specification, service, etc.) or subjective criteria such as status, fit with self-image or trust of the supplier.

To make the decision easier, the consumer often adopts mental 'rules of thumb' that cut corners and lead to a faster decision. The consumer is especially prepared to compromise on the quality and thoroughness of assessment when the problem-solving situation is less risky and complicated. They may focus on brand, store choice, pricing, promotion or packaging, and will serve to limit the size of the evoked set and to eliminate some of the options.

## Decision

The decision may be a natural outcome of the evaluation stage, if one of the options is noticeably more impressive on all the important criteria than the rest. If the choice is not as clear cut as this, the consumer may have to prioritise the criteria further, perhaps deciding that price or convenience is the one overriding factor. In the car exhaust example, the decision-making is a conscious act, whereas with the impulse purchase of chocolate, the decision may be made almost unconsciously.

In any case, at this stage the consumer must finalise the proposed deal, and this may take place in a retail store, over the telephone, by mail or in the consumer's own home. In the supermarket, finalising the deal may be as simple as putting the bar of chocolate into the trolley with the rest of the shopping and then paying for it at the checkout. With more complex purchases, however, the consumer may have the discretion to negotiate the fine details of cash or credit, any trade-in, order quantity and delivery dates, for example. If the outcome of the negotiation is not satisfactory, then the consumer may regretfully decide not to go ahead with the purchase after all, or rethink the decision in favour of another supplier – you cannot be certain of your customer until they have either handed over their money or signed the contract!

Suppliers, of course, can make it easy or difficult for potential customers to make their purchases. Lack of sales assistants on the shopfloor, long queues or bureaucratic purchasing procedures may all tax the patience of consumers, giving them time either to decide to shop elsewhere or not to bother buying at all. Even if they do persist and make the purchase (eventually), their impression of the supplier's service and efficiency is going to be damaged and this may influence their repeat purchasing behaviour negatively.

Vending machines make it easy for the consumer to make a decision and to take action almost immediately as long as they have some loose change in their pockets. However, vending is often seen as a choice of last resort. Consumers much prefer fresher and healthier options, with more choice and even the personal touch which the vending machine cannot bring. Despite that, vending machine sales in the UK are worth over £1.7 billion, and around 90 per cent of Mintel's survey sample had bought something from a vending machine, mostly hot drinks, soft drinks and confectionery (Mintel, 2009). The demand for good quality coffee on-the-go is such that Whitbread bought Coffee Nation's 900 self-serve vending machines for £59.5 millon in 2011, with a view to branding them as Costa Express and expanding to 3,000 machines in the UK within five years. Whitbread already owns the coffee shop chain Costa Coffee, so the vending machines are a natural extension of that, and the fact that they use freshly ground coffee and fresh milk allows them to maintain a level of quality that is consistent with the Costa brand (BBC, 2011).

The familiarity of brand names and how they are presented is vital to the sale, hence, the growth of glass fronted and chilled cabinets for snack products. But the main limitation is the product range on offer and maybe UK suppliers could learn from the Japanese convenience stores which are fully automated, and offer a wide range of merchandise. However, as Mintel found, outside the core drinks and snacks categories, there are few products that the UK consumer would consider buying from a vending machine. Higher value items, such as electronic goods, electronic games, music and film downloads clothing and footwear are among those that most consumers (70 per cent or more) 'would never buy' from a vending machine, according to Mintel (Mintel, 2009).

These machines give customers fast access to quality coffee in places where time and space are at a premium

*Source*: Whitbread

## Post-purchase evaluation

The consumer's involvement with the product does not finish when cash changes hands, nor should the marketer's involvement with the consumer. Whatever the purchase, there is likely to be some level of post-purchase evaluation to assess whether the product or its supplier lived up to the expectations raised in the earlier stages of the process. Particularly if the decision process has been difficult, or if the consumer has invested a lot of time, effort and money in it, then there may be doubt as to whether the right decision has actually been made. This is what Festinger (1957) labelled cognitive dissonance, meaning that consumers are 'psychologically uncomfortable', trying to balance the choice made against the doubts still held about it. Such dissonance may be aggravated where consumers are exposed to marketing communication that sings the praises of the features and benefits of the rejected alternatives. Generally speaking, the more alternatives that have been rejected, and the more comparatively attractive those alternatives appear to be, the greater the dissonance. Conversely, the more similar to the chosen product the rejected alternatives are, the less the dissonance. It is also likely that dissonance will occur with more significant purchases, such as extended problem-solving items like cars and houses, because the buyer is far more likely to review and assess the decision consciously afterwards.

Clearly, such psychological discomfort is not pleasant and the consumer will work towards reducing it, perhaps by trying to filter out the messages that undermine the choice made (for example advertising for a product that was a rejected alternative) and paying extra attention to supportive messages (for example advertising for the chosen alternative). This all underlines the need for post-purchase reassurance, whether through advertising, after-sales follow-up calls and even the tone of an instruction manual ('Congratulations on choosing the Acme Home Nuclear Reactor Kit, we know it will give you many years' faithful service . . .'). Consumers like to be reminded and reassured that they have made a wise choice, that they have made the best choice for them. From the marketer's point of view, as well as offering post-purchase reassurance, they can minimise the risk of dissonance by making sure that potential buyers have a realistic picture of the product, its capabilities and its characteristics.

Thus the post-purchase evaluation stage is important for a number of reasons. Primarily, it will affect whether the consumer ever buys this product again. If expectations have not been met, then the product may not even make the shortlist next time. If, on the other hand, expectations have been met or even exceeded, then a strong possibility of lasting loyalty has been created. The next shortlist may be a shortlist of one!

Monitoring of post-purchase feelings is an important task of marketing, not only to identify areas in which the product (or its associated marketing mix) falls short of expectations, but also to identify any unexpectedly pleasant surprises the purchaser may have had. The product may, for instance, have strengths that are being undersold. This is a natural part of the cycle of product and service development, improvement and evolution.

There are some points to note about the process as presented here. First, the consumer may choose to end the process at any stage. Perhaps the information search reveals that there is no obvious acceptable solution to the problem, or the information evaluation demonstrates that the cost of solving the problem is too high. It is, of course, the marketer's job to sustain the consumer's interest throughout this process and to prevent them from opting out of it. Second, the process does not necessarily have to run from stage 1 to stage 5 in an unbroken flow. The consumer may backtrack at any point to an earlier stage and reiterate the process. Even on the verge of a decision, it may be felt necessary to go back and get more information, just to make sure. Finally, the time taken over the process may vary enormously, depending on the nature of the purchase and the nature of the purchaser. Many months of agonising may go into making an expensive, important purchase, while only a few seconds may be invested in choosing a bar of chocolate. The next section looks more closely at this issue.

## Buying situations

In the discussion of the decision-making process, it has been made clear that both the flow and the formality of the process, and the emphasis that is put on each stage, will vary from situation to situation. Some of these variations are to do with the particular environment relevant to the transaction (see p. 91 *et seq.*), while others emanate from the consumer (p. 93 *et seq.*) or from the consumer's immediate social surroundings (p. 102 *et seq.*). The current section, however, will look more closely at the effect of the type of purchasing situation on the extent and formality of the decision-making process.

## Routine problem solving

As the heading of this section implies, a routine problem solving purchasing situation is one that the consumer is likely to experience on a regular basis. Most grocery shopping falls into this category, where particular brands are purchased habitually without recourse to any lengthy decision-making process. As with the chocolate-buying example above, there is virtually no information search and evaluation, and the buying decision is made simultaneously with (if not in advance of) the problem recognition stage. This explains why many fmcg manufacturers spend so much time and effort trying to generate such loyalty and why it is so difficult for new products to break into an established market. When the consumer thinks 'We've run out of Colgate' rather than 'We've run out of toothpaste', or when beans really do mean Heinz, then the competition has an uphill marketing task on its hands.

As well as building regular shopping habits, i.e. brand loyalty, the manufacturer is also trying to capitalise on impulse purchasing of many products within this category. While toothpaste and beans can be the objective of a planned shopping trip ('When I go to the supermarket, I need to get . . .'), some other products may be purchased as the result of a sudden impulse. The impulse may be triggered, as mentioned in the previous section, by a realisation of need ('I'm depressed and this chocolate is just what I need to cheer me up'), or by external stimuli, for example eye-catching packaging attracting the shopper's attention. The trigger need not even be inside the store: the smell of coffee or freshly baked bread wafting into the street may draw a customer into a café on impulse, or an attractive shop window display may attract a potential customer into a clothing store that they otherwise had no intention of visiting (even though clothing is not necessarily a routine problem-solving purchase). Whatever the trigger, there is no conscious preplanning or information search, but a sudden surge of desire that can only be fulfilled by a purchase that the shopper may or may not later regret.

*eg*

The retail environment is geared up to encourage unplanned purchases, to make consumers buy on a whim. The Future Foundation found that over the past twenty years the proportion of consumers who admit to buying what they like rather than just what they need has risen from 31 per cent to 45 per cent. Higher disposable incomes, easy access to credit and a trend towards seeing shopping as a leisure pursuit, have all contributed to the increase in impulse buying. The rise of internet shopping is also encouraging impulse buying when casual surfing or a visit to a favourite site may lead to an unplanned purchase. The internet, however, also enables a much greater level of information search and comparison before visiting a retail store. A visit to the Amazon site is a good example of how to stimulate impulse purchases. Most items can be purchased with one click to the shopping basket. A range of 'star choices', 'what's new', special offers and (once the visitor has logged in) tailor-made offers based upon previous visits/purchases all make the final, unplanned click purchase so easy.

Some have argued that shoppers try to counteract their feelings of depression and low self-esteem through the emotional 'lift' and the momentary euphoria provided by 'retail therapy' impulse shopping (for example, O'Guinn and Faber, 1989). Caution and common sense do not enter into it; there is no need to wait, no need to undertake careful assessment of the alternatives, and no need to deliberate over the decision. 'See it, like it, want it, buy it' is for many shoppers a fun part of the retail experience, whether they are looking at food, clothes, books, music or even higher-priced goods.

If impulse buying is a form of lack of self-control, then that's of interest to health watchers and to some fmcg suppliers. If we could control our urges then sugar, carbohydrate and fat consumption would radically reduce – but we're fickle and self-indulgent, so we can't do that very easily! Much promotion is aimed at encouraging buying on impulse, and that's bad news for shoppers whose self-control is very limited (Bamford, 2010).

The items that fall into the routine problem-solving category do tend to be low-risk, low-priced, frequently purchased products. The consumer is happy that a particular brand satisfies their requirements, and there is not enough benefit to be gained from switching brands to make the effort of information search and evaluation of alternatives worthwhile. These so-called low-involvement purchases simply do not carry enough risk, whether measured in terms of financial loss, personal disappointment or damage to social status, for the consumer to get excited about the importance of 'making the right decision'.

## Limited problem solving

Limited problem solving is a little more interesting for the consumer. This is a buying situation that occurs less frequently and probably involves more deliberate decision-making than routine problems do. The goods will be moderately expensive (in the eyes of the individual consumer) and perhaps will be expected to last a long time. Thus, the risks inherent in a 'wrong' decision are that much higher. There will be, therefore, be some element of information search and evaluation, but this is still unlikely to absorb too much time and effort.

An example of this could be a consumer's purchase of a new piece of hi-fi equipment. If it is some years since they last bought one, they might feel that they need to update their knowledge of who makes what, who sells what, and the price brackets in this market. The information search is likely to include talking to any friends with recent hi-fi buying experience, and a trip round locally accessible electrical goods retailers. To this particular consumer, this is an important decision, but not a crucial one. If they make a 'wrong' choice (as defined in the post-purchase evaluation stage), they will be disappointed, but will feel that they have spent too much money to allow them simply to discard the offending product. Having said that, provided that the hi-fi fulfils its primary function of producing music on demand, they can learn to live with it and the damage is limited.

Limited problem solving is also likely to occur in the choice of service products. In purchasing a holiday or choosing a dentist (word-of-mouth recommendation?) the consumer has one chance to make the right choice. Once you are on the plane or in the dentist's chair, it is too late and the wrong choice could turn out to be expensive and painful. The necessity to get it right first time is thus likely to lead to a conscious and detailed information search, perhaps even going as far as extended problem solving, to which we now turn.

## Extended problem solving

Extended problem solving represents a much more serious investment of money, time and effort from the consumer and, consequently, a much higher risk. Purchases of major capital items such as houses or cars fall into this category. These purchases occur extremely infrequently for most people and, given that they often require some kind of a loan, involve a serious long-term commitment. This means that the purchaser is motivated to gather as much information as possible, and to think quite consciously and systematically about what the decision-making criteria should be. That is not to say that the final decision will necessarily be made on purely functional, conscious or rational grounds. If, for example, two different makes of car have similar technical specifications, price, delivery and after-sales service terms, then final differentiation may be in terms of 'which one will most impress the neighbours?'.

## The significance of buying situations

So what? Why categorise purchases in this way? After all, one consumer's limited problem-solving situation may be another's extended problem. This matters because it may add another dimension to help marketers develop more efficient and appropriate marketing strategies. If a significant group of potential buyers can be defined who clearly regard the purchase of a hi-fi as a limited problem-solving situation, then that has implications for the manufacturers in terms of both how and what to communicate, and where and how to distribute. If consumers are thought to regard a product as a limited problem-solving purchase, then perhaps the marketer will prefer to distribute it through specialist outlets, where the potential buyer can get expert advice, and can spend time making detailed product comparisons. Communication may contain a lot of factual information about technical specifications and product features (i.e. what the product can do), as well as selling product benefits (i.e. what all that means to you). In contrast, the same product as a routine problem-solving exercise may be distributed as widely as possible, to ensure availability, regardless of retailer specialism or expertise, and the communication might centre on product image and benefits, ignoring the detailed information.

## Environmental influences

This section is about the wider context in which the decision-making is taking place. All of these environmental influences have already been covered in some depth in Chapter 2, so their treatment here will be brief. What is important is to recognise that decision-making is not completely divorced from the environment in which it is happening, whether the consumer is conscious of it or not.

## Sociocultural influences

There are many pressures in this category and p. 102 *et seq.* looks at them more closely. Individuals are influenced both by current trends in society as a whole and by a need to conform with the norms of the various social groups to which they belong, as well as to enhance their status within those groups.

Examples of social group pressures can be seen in children's markets. Many parents feel unfairly pressured into buying particular goods or brands because the children's friends all have them. There is a fear of the child being marginalised or bullied because they don't possess the 'right' things, whether those are trainers, mountain bikes or computer games.

## Technological influences

Technology affects many aspects of consumer decision-making. Database technology, for example, allows organisations to create (almost) personal relationships with customers. At its extreme, this means that consumers receive better tailored personalised offerings, and thus that their expectations are raised in terms of the quality of the product, communication and service.

In its wider sense, technology applied to product development and innovation has created whole categories of fast evolving, increasingly cheap consumer 'toys' such as tablet computers, smartphones and computer games. Many of these products used to be extended problem-solving goods, but they have moved rapidly towards the limited problem-solving area. As they become cheaper and more widely available, the amount of risk inherent in the purchase reduces for the consumer, who does not, therefore, need to spend quite so much time searching for and evaluating alternative options.

## Economic influences

The late 2000s saw recession and economic hardship across Europe and this inevitably affected consumers' attitudes, as well as their ability and willingness to spend. With uncertainty about employment prospects, many consumers postponed purchasing decisions, adjusted their decision-making criteria or cut out certain types of spending altogether. Price, value for money and a conscious assessment of the need to buy become prevalent influences in such circumstances.

Retailers, in turn, had to respond to the slowdown in trade caused by the economic environment. Money-off sales became prevalent in the high street throughout the year, not just in the traditional post-Christmas period. While this did stimulate sales in the short term, it had one unfortunate effect for retailers. Consumers began to see the lower sale price as 'normal' and resented paying full prices, preferring to wait for the next sale that they were confident would come along soon.

## Ethical influences

Ethical credentials could be a key factor in decision-making, affecting decisions about what to buy, why, using what criteria, where or from whom. Green and Peloza (2011) explored how the incorporation of CSR consideration into consumer decision-making might have changed during the economic recession. Although it was a fairly small-scale qualitative study undertaken in North America, the findings are very interesting. Not surprisingly, perhaps, the recession had had the effect of making consumers become more considered in their buying behaviour. They were thinking more carefully and consciously about whether to buy at all and what to buy; they were budgeting more carefully; and buying less of certain kinds of products, focusing more on 'needs' rather than 'wants'. The kind of CSR activity that carried most weight in decision-making, therefore, was found to be functional, product-oriented CSR, while broader philanthropy was regarded as being expendable in a recession, as consumers become more concerned with price and quality. Thus a product perceived as primarily serving the customer's functional need and additionally demonstrating CSR, perhaps through being 'greener' or supplied under fair trade credentials, would be more likely to be attractive than one focusing more on emotional ('gives me a warm glow of doing the right thing') or social ('makes me look good in the eyes of others') CSR.

## Political and legal influences

Political and legal influences, emanating either from the EU or from national bodies, can also affect the consumer. Legislation on minimum levels of product safety and performance, for example, means that the consumer does not need to spend time getting technical information, worrying about analysing it and comparing competing products on those criteria. Legislation and regulation, whether they relate to product descriptions, consumer rights or advertising, also reduce the inherent risks of making a decision. This takes some of the pressure off the customer, leading to better-informed and easier decisions and less risk of post-purchase dissonance.

## Ecological influences

In wider society, for example, there has been a move in recent years towards demanding more environmentally friendly products, and many consumers who are not necessarily 'deep green' have allowed this to influence their decision-making, looking more favourably on fair trade, CFC-free, recycled or non-animal-tested products.

This discussion of the STEEPLE factors is not exhaustive, but simply acts as a reminder that an individual makes decisions within a wider context, created either by society's own dynamics or by the efforts of the market. Having set that context, it is now appropriate to look more closely at the particular influences, internal and external, that affect the individual's buying behaviour and decision-making.

## Psychological influences: the individual

Although marketers try to define groups of potential customers with common attributes or interests, as a useful unit for the formulation of marketing strategies, it should not be forgotten that such groups or market segments are still made up of individuals who are different from each other. This section, therefore, looks at aspects that will affect an individual's perceptions and handling of the decision-making process, such as personality, perception, learning, motivation and the impact of attitudes.

## Personality

Personality, consisting of all the features, traits, behaviours and experiences that make each of us distinctive and unique, is a very extensive and deep area of study. Our personalities lie at the heart of all our behaviour as consumers, and thus marketers try to define the particular personality traits or characteristics prevalent among a target group of consumers, which can then be reflected in the product itself and the marketing effort around it.

In the mid- to late 1980s, advertising in particular was full of images reflecting the personality traits associated with successful lifestyle stereotypes such as the 'yuppie'. Independent, level-headed, ruthless, ambitious, self-centred, materialistic traits were seen as positive characteristics, and thus marketers were anxious to have them associated with users of their products. The 1990s saw a softening of this approach, featuring images oriented more towards caring, concern, family and sharing as the route to self-fulfilment.

With high-involvement products, where there is a strong emotional and psychological link between the product and the consumer, it is relatively easy to see how personality might affect choice and decision-making. In choosing clothing, for instance, an extrovert self-confident achiever with an extravagant streak might select something deliberately *avant garde*, stylishly daring, vibrantly coloured and expensive, as a personality statement. A quiet, insecure character, with underdeveloped social skills, might prefer to wear something more sober, more conservative, with less attention-seeking potential.

Overall, however, the link between personality and purchasing, and thus the ability to predict purchasing patterns from personality traits, is at best tenuous. Chisnall (1985) takes the somewhat cautious line that personality may influence the decision to buy a certain product type, but not the final brand choice.

## Perception

Perception represents the way in which individuals analyse, interpret and make sense of incoming information, and is affected by personality, experience and mood. No two people will interpret the same stimulus (whether it is a product's packaging, taste, smell, texture or its promotional messages) in exactly the same way. Even the same individual might perceive the stimulus differently at different times. For example, seeing an advertisement for food when you are hungry is more likely to produce a positive response than seeing the same advertisement just after a heavy meal. Immediate needs are affecting the interpretation of the message. Alternatively, relaxing at home on a Sunday afternoon, an individual is more likely to spend time reading a detailed and lengthy print advertisement than they would if they were flicking through the same magazine during a short coffee break in the working day. Naturally, marketers hope that their messages reach target audiences when they are relaxed, at leisure and at ease with the world, because then the individual is more likely to place a positive interpretation on the message and is less likely to be distracted by other pressures and needs.

## Selective attention

Consumers do not pay attention to everything that is going on at once. Attention filters allow the unconscious selection of what incoming information to concentrate on. In daily life we filter out the irrelevant background noise: the hum of the computer, the birds in the garden, the cars in the street, the footsteps in the corridor. As consumers we filter out the irrelevant marketing messages. In reading the newspaper, for instance, a split-second glance spots an advertisement, decides that it is irrelevant and allows the eye to read around it.

This means that marketers have to overcome these filters, either by creating messages that we will decide are relevant or by building attention-grabbing devices into the message. An internet advertisement, for example, might use its position on the page, intense colour, movement or startling images to draw the eye, and more importantly the brain, to it.

## Selective perception

The problems do not stop once the marketer has got the consumer's attention, since people are infinitely creative in interpreting information in ways that suit them. It is less threatening to interpret things so that they fit nicely and consistently with whatever you already think and feel than to cope with the discomfort of clashes and inconsistency.

One way of creating this consistency or harmony is to allow perception to be coloured by previous experience and existing attitudes. A particularly bad experience with an organisation's offering creates a prejudice that may never be overcome. Whatever positive messages that organisation transmits, the consumer will always be thinking 'Yes, but . . .' Similarly, a negative attitude towards a subject will make the consumer interpret messages differently. For example, someone who is deeply opposed to nuclear power will try to read between the lines of the industry's advertising and PR, looking for cover-ups and counter-arguments. This can distort the intended message and even reinforce the negative feelings. Conversely, a good experience makes it a lot easier to form positive perceptions. The good experience from the past creates a solid foundation from which to look for the best in the new experience.

## Selective retention

Not all stimuli that make it through the attention filters and the machinery of perception and understanding are remembered. Many stimuli are only transitory, hence one of the reasons for the repetition of advertising: if you did not notice it or remember it the first time round, you might pick it up on subsequent occasions. Jogging the memory, by repeating messages or by producing familiar stimuli that the consumer can recognise (such as brand names, packaging design, logos or colour schemes), is therefore an important marketing task to reduce the reliance on the consumer's memory.

People have the capacity to remember what they want to remember and to filter out anything else. The reasons for retaining a particular message may be because it touched them emotionally, or it was of immediate relevance, or it was especially entertaining, or it reinforced previously held views. The reasons are many, but the consumer is under no obligation to remember anything.

# MARKETING IN ACTION

## 'Mum, can I have a banana, please?'

Change4Life, with its slogan of 'eat well, move more, live longer', is a £75 million campaign set up by the UK's Department of Health to try to make the British public think about its lifestyle and habits, and change social norms. It is a focal point for messages and information about diet and exercise, and the consequences of neglecting those things. The whole tone of the campaign, however, is fun and upbeat rather than preachy – after all, we've all heard these messages before – with an overarching objective of making people believe that there are small, easy things they can do that will make a positive difference to themselves and their families. The broad thrust of the campaign is shown in Figure 3.2.

**Figure 3.2**  The Change4Life campaign

| Reaching at-risk families | Helping families understand health consequences | Convincing parents that their children are at risk | Teaching behaviours to reduce risk | Inspiring people to believe they can do the behaviours | Creating desire to change | Triggering action | Supporting sustained change |

*Source*: Department of Health (2010), p. 23.

Shaking people out of their habits and complacency isn't easy and the marketing approaches used by Change4Life are multi-layered and complex. The first year of the campaign targeted families with children aged between five and 11 years. Childhood obesity is a growing problem, and making children aware of the importance of good diet and exercise, and getting them to take responsibility for their health in partnership with their parents is one of the aims of Change4Life. The logo and graphics used in communications are very 'cartoony' to appeal to kids and the television advertisements are populated by modelling clay figures in a variety of primary and bright colours to cut across ethnic and age barriers. The tone of the ads (see www.nhs.uk/Change4Life/Pages/watch-change-for-life-tv-adverts.aspx) is playful and funny with a family appeal and a simple message in each one. 'Me sized meals', for example is presented from the perspective of a child who finds himself getting a bit chubby as a result of mum piling the food on his plate at mealtimes. So he has a word with mum who cuts his portions down to a more sensible level. Similarly, 'snack swapper' shows a kid and his mum replacing sweets and other sugary snacks with fresh fruit and other healthier alternatives, while 'activity' depicts a kid realising that sitting in front of the telly or a games console for too long is not very healthy so she persuades her whole family to get up and be more active. Change4Life also sponsored *The Simpsons* on Channel 4 for three months, with a series of idents featuring the Change4Life clay-animation family based on the Simpsons' sofa gags. A lot of this is about raising awareness and opening dialogue within families, partly using 'pester power' as a positive force for change (for once!) and partly giving parents some support in explaining changes that they might want to initiate.

The campaign is not just about advertising, however. The website (www.nhs.uk/Change4Life/Pages/change-for-life.aspx) acts as a portal for all kinds of information packs and supplementary materials that people can request, with ideas about snack swapping and how to persuade kids to be more active, for instance. According to Department of Health (2010, p. 7), 'When families joined Change4Life, they received a questionnaire that asked about a typical day in the life of each of their children. This enabled us to send everyone who completed a questionnaire a tailored action plan with advice for each child. Beyond this, we sent 200,000 of the most at-risk families further support packs, which, through frequent reminders, tips and ideas, aimed to help people keep up good behaviours'. Schools and healthcare professionals were also involved, and there were lots of accessible, local initiatives around the country for families to be involved with.

Change4Life has also recruited partner organisations, from retailers such as Asda, Argos and JJB Sports; food manufacturers such as Kellogg's, Nestlé, Unilever and PepsiCo; sports and activity bodies such as British Cycling, UK Athletics and the Play Providers Association; various government departments and quangos such as the Food Standards Agency, DEFRA and the Department for Transport; and charities such as Diabetes UK, Cancer Research UK and the British Heart Foundation. These partners can then use the Change4Life banner to develop their own interpretation of the campaign and extend its reach. McCain Foods' Corporate Affairs Director, for example, said,

As a responsible food company, we have an important role to play in promoting a healthy balanced lifestyle to our consumers. Our partnership with [UK Athletics] is part of the McCain Foods 'It's All Good' philosophy which aims to encourage consumers to eat healthier foods and to lead healthier lifestyles through leading active lives. McCain is proud to support the government Change4Life initiative by launching Athletics4Life, which aims to help parents and children eat well and lead healthier lifestyles. The programme will encourage consumers, who may not have considered athletics before, to give it a try. (as quoted on www.mccain.co.uk/info/press-releases/olympics.aspx)

The first year of the campaign was declared a success, meeting or exceeding all of its targets. Department of Health (2010) reported that over 400,000 families had joined Change4Life; that 87 per cent of mothers of children under 11 recalled the campaign; and that over 1 million mums had made changes to their children's' diets or activity levels as a result of the campaign.

Despite these achievements, as a result of a change of government and tighter controls over government spending, in July 2010 it was announced that funding for Change4Life was to be withdrawn, with the expectation that business and other interested organisations would bear the cost. Some were not that impressed. The British Heart Foundation's director of policy and communications said, 'We wait with bated breath for the fast food merchants, chocolate bar makers and fizzy drink vendors to beat a path to the public health door. Meanwhile, parents and children continue to be faced with the bewildering kaleidoscope of confusing food labels and pre-watershed junk food ads' (as quoted by Parfitt, 2010). That might be unduly cynical: many of the commercial backers of Change4Life have said that they are prepared to commit more to the campaign, seeing both marketing and social benefits in what it is trying to do. However, by May 2011 it had been announced that the government was going to resume marketing expenditure on the campaign, as a response to an 80 per cent drop in the number of people joining Change4Life; a 90 per cent drop in people phoning the helpline, and a two-thirds reduction in visits to the website (*Marketing Week*, 2011). The government will commit £14 million to the 2011–12 campaign.

*Sources*: Alarcon (2009); Clewes (2011); Department of Health (2010); *Marketing Week* (2011); Parfitt (2010); Sweney (2010), Walker (2010b); www.mccain.co.uk; www.nhs.uk/Change4Life .

## Learning

Perception and memory are closely linked with learning. Marketers want consumers to learn from promotional material, so that they know which product to buy and why, and to learn from experience of the product, so that they will buy it again and pass on the message to others.

Learning has been defined by Hilgard and Marquis (1961) as:

. . . the more or less permanent change in behaviour which occurs as a result of practice.

This implies, from a marketing perspective, that the objective must not only be for the consumer to learn something, but also for them to remember what has been learned and to act on it. Therefore, advertising materials, for instance, are carefully designed to maximise the learning opportunity. A 30-second television advertisement selling car insurance over the phone repeats the number four times and has it written across the bottom of the screen so that the viewer is likely to remember it. Demonstrating a product benefit in an advertisement also helps consumers to learn what they are supposed to notice about the product when they use it. Demonstrating a product in a particular usage context, or associating it with certain types of people or situations, gives the consumer guidelines about what attitudes to develop towards the product.

Humour, and other methods of provoking an emotional response to an advertisement, can also help a message to stick because the recipient immediately becomes more involved in the process. Similarly, associating a product with something familiar that itself evokes certain emotions can allow those feelings to be transferred to the product. Thus the advertisements for Andrex that feature puppies have helped the British public to learn to think of toilet paper as warm, soft, cuddly and harmless rather than embarrassing.

## Motivation

One definition of marketing puts the emphasis on the satisfaction of customers' needs and wants, but what triggers those needs and wants, and what drives consumers towards their fulfilment? Motives for action, the driving forces, are complex and changeable and can be difficult to research, since individuals themselves often cannot define why they act the way they do. An additional problem is that at different times, different motivations might take priority and have more influence over the individual's behaviour.

Maslow's (1954) *hierarchy of needs* has long been used as a framework for classifying basic motivations. Five groups of needs, as shown in Figure 3.3, are stacked one on top of another and form a progression. Having achieved satisfaction on the lowest level, the individual can progress to strive to achieve the goals of the next level up. This model does have a certain logic behind it, and the idea, for instance, that true self-actualisation can only grow from solid foundations of security and social acceptance seems reasonable. However, the model was developed in the context of US capitalist culture, where achievement and self-actualisation are often ends in themselves. It is questionable how far these motives can be extended to other cultural contexts.

Examples of consumer behaviour and marketing activity can be found to fit all five levels.

### Physiological needs

Basic feelings such as hunger and thirst can be potent driving forces. After a strenuous game of squash, the immediate craving for liquid overrides normal considerations of brand preference.

**Figure 3.3**
Maslow's hierarchy of needs

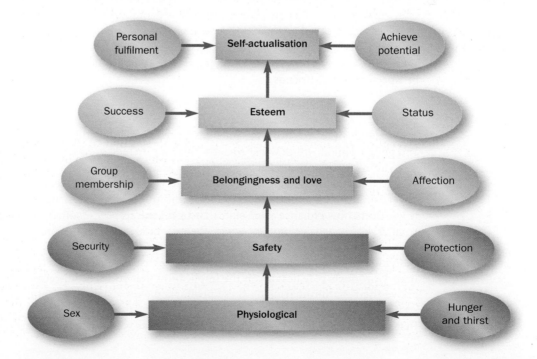

If the sports-centre shop only has one type of soft drink in stock, then it will do. Similarly, seasoned shoppers are well aware of the dangers of visiting a supermarket when they are hungry: so much more seems to go into the trolley.

Marketers can capitalise on such feelings. The soft-drink manufacturer can ensure that the sports centre stocks that brand and that the product image reflects refreshment and thirst-quenching properties. The food manufacturer can advertise at a time of day when the audience is likely to be feeling hungry so that they are more likely to pay attention to the message and remember it.

## Safety needs

Once the individual has taken care of the basic necessities of life, food, drink and warmth, the need for self-protection and long-term survival emerges. In modern Western societies this may be interpreted as the desire for a secure home, protected against intrusion and other dangers (floods and fire, for example). It might also cover the desire for healthcare, insurance services and consumer protection legislation.

The car market in particular has focused on safety needs as a marketing platform. Driving is an inherently dangerous activity, so the manufacturers try to reassure us that their cars are as safe as possible. Various manufacturers have featured side-impact bars, airbags and/or anti-lock braking systems in their advertising, showing how these either protect you or help to prevent accidents.

Safety needs in terms of health protection feature strongly in the marketing strategies of products such as bleaches and toilet cleaners. The kind of approach used often appeals to the mother who takes responsibility for safeguarding the health and well-being of the whole family. The threat from bacteria can be eliminated by choosing the right cleanser.

## Belongingness and love needs

This is about emotional security, wanting to feel accepted and valued by those closest to you. Marketers again play on this need through the portrayal of the family in particular. Over many years, advertising told women that they would be better appreciated and loved as wives and mothers if they did their washing in Persil, cooked with Oxo or fed their husbands cornflakes for breakfast.

Fear of loneliness or personal rejection can be a powerful motivator and features strongly in many marketing campaigns. Toiletries such as deodorants, toothpastes and mouthwashes have all advertised on the basis that you will be more lovable if you use these products, and showing the dire consequences of rejection if you don't. Even anti-smoking campaigns aimed at teenagers have tried this approach, implying that the smell of tobacco on your breath will put off prospective boy/girlfriends.

## Esteem needs

This extends outwards from the previous stage to cover the individual's need for success, status and good opinion within wider society. This may include professional status and respect, standing within social groups, such as sports clubs and societies, or 'what the neighbours think'.

These needs are reflected in a wide variety of product and services marketing. Most car advertising, for example, contains some kind of message implying that if you drive this car it will somehow enhance your status and gain the respect of others. This even applies to the smaller, less expensive models, where the esteem arises from notions of 'wise choice' or 'a car that reflects the positive elements of my character'. More overtly, esteem can derive from the individual's sheer ability to afford the most expensive and exclusive items. Perfumes and other luxury products play heavily on the implication that you are a discerning and élite buyer, a cut above the rest, and that using these products makes a statement about who you are and the status you hold. Brand names such as Rolls-Royce, Gucci and Rolex have acquired such a cachet that simply saying 'she owns a genuine Rolex' speaks volumes about a person's social status.

## Self-actualisation needs

This is the ultimate goal, the achievement of complete satisfaction through successfully fulfilling one's potential. That may mean anything, depending on who you are and what you want out of life. Some will only achieve self-actualisation through becoming the head of a multinational organisation, while others will find it through the successful raising of a happy and healthy family. This is a difficult stage for the marketer to handle, because it is so individual, and thus the hope is that by fulfilling the other needs discussed above, the marketer can help to propel the individual towards self-actualisation. Only the individual can tell, however, when this stage has been reached.

Generally, in Western economies the fulfilment of the very basic needs can be taken for granted, however. Real physiological hunger, thirst and lack of safety do not exist for most people. Manufacturers of food products, for instance, cannot therefore assume that just because their product alleviates hunger it will be purchased and accepted. Any one of hundreds of food brands can do that, and thus the consumer is looking to see how a particular product can fulfil a higher-order need, such as love or esteem. Consequently, foods are often marketed on the basis that your family will enjoy it and love you more for providing it (Oxo, for example) or because your dinner party guests will be pleased (Viennetta or After Eight, for example). The emphasis, therefore, is largely on the higher-order needs (belongingness and love, esteem and self-actualisation).

# Attitudes

As implied at p. 94 above, an attitude is a stance that an individual takes on a subject that pre-disposes them to react in a certain way to that subject. More formally, an attitude has been defined by Hilgard *et al.* (1975) as:

> ... an orientation towards or away from some object, concept or situation and a readiness to respond in a predetermined manner to these related objects, concepts or situations.

Thus in marketing terms, consumers can develop attitudes to any kind of product or service, or indeed to any aspect of the marketing mix, and these attitudes will affect behaviour. All of this implies that attitudes play an important part in influencing consumer judgement, whether through perception, evaluation, information processing or decision-making. Attitudes play a key role in shaping learning and while they are fluid, evolving over time, they are nevertheless often difficult to change.

Williams (1981), in summarising the literature, describes attitudes as having three different components.

## Cognitive

Cognitive attitudes relate to beliefs or disbeliefs, thus: 'I believe that margarine is healthier than butter'. This is a component that the marketer can work on through fairly straightforward advertising. Repeating the message that your product is healthy, or that it represents the best value for money, may well establish an initial belief in those qualities.

## Affective

Affective attitudes relate to feelings of a positive or negative nature, involving some emotional content, thus: 'I *like* this product' or 'This product makes me *feel* . . .'. Again, advertising can help the marketer to signal to the consumer why they should like it, or how they should feel when they use it. For some consumers, of course, affective attitudes can overcome cognitive ones. For example, I may believe that margarine is healthier than butter, but I buy butter because I like the taste better. Similarly, I believe that snacking on chocolate is 'bad', but it cheers me up so I do it anyway.

## Conative

Conative attitudes relate to the link with behaviour, thus attitude x is considered likely to lead to behaviour *y*. This is the hardest one for marketers to predict or control, because so many things can prevent behaviour from taking place, even if the cognitive and affective attitudes are positive: 'I believe that BMWs are excellent quality, reliable cars, and I feel that owning one would enhance my status and provide me with many hours of pleasurable driving, but I simply cannot afford it', or it may even be that 'Audi made me a better offer'.

It is this last link between attitude and behaviour that is of most interest to marketers. Fishbein (1975) developed a model based on the proposition that in order to predict a specific behaviour, such as a brand purchase, it is important to measure the individual's attitude towards performing that behaviour, rather than just the attitude towards the product in question. This fits with the BMW example above, where the most important thing is not the attitude to the car itself, but the attitude towards *purchasing* the car. As long as the attitude to *purchasing* is negative, the marketer still has work to do.

Attitudes can thus involve feelings (positive or negative), knowledge (complete or partial) and beliefs. A particular female consumer might believe that she is overweight. She knows that cream cakes are fattening, but she likes them. All these things come together to form her attitude towards cream cakes (wicked, but seductive) and her behaviour when confronted by one (five minutes wrestling with her conscience before giving in completely and buying two, knowing that she will regret it later). An advertising campaign for cream cakes, centred around the slogan 'naughty but nice', capitalised brilliantly on what is a common attitude, almost legitimising the guilt and establishing an empathy with the hopeless addict. The really admirable thing about that campaign was that the advertiser did not even attempt to overturn the attitude.

It is possible, but very difficult, to change attitudes, particularly when they are well established and deeply ingrained. Companies like Lada and Aeroflot have been trying for years with varying degrees of success. The nuclear industry has also been trying to overcome hostile and suspicious attitudes with an integrated campaign of advertising, PR and site visits (www.sellafieldsites.com). Many people have indeed been responsive to this openness, and have been prepared to revise attitudes to a greater or lesser extent. There will, however, always be a hard core who will remain entrenched and interpret any 'positive' messages in a negative way.

There is a difference between attitudes that relate to an organisation's philosophy, business ethics or market and those that centre around experience of an organisation's specific product or service. An organisation that has a bad reputation for its employment practices, its environmental record or its dealings with suspect foreign regimes will have created negative attitudes that will be extremely difficult to overturn. Similarly, companies operating in certain markets, such as nuclear power, tobacco and alcohol, will never redeem themselves in the eyes of significant groups of the public. People care too much about such things to be easily persuaded to change their outlook. In contrast, negative feelings about a specific product or brand are more amenable to change through skilful marketing.

# MARKETING IN ACTION

## It's a Škoda, honest!

Škoda is a remarkable example of how negative attitudes can be tackled head-on with some success. Surely we all remember a few Škoda jokes from over 10 years ago, for example, 'Why does the Škoda have a heated rear window? To keep your hands warm while you push it.' The communist era in Czechoslovakia meant that the Škoda had become cheap and cheerful but with a terrible reputation matched only by Lada's.

In 1991, VW took over Škoda and after investment in re-tooling, building a quality culture, using components in common with VW brands, and a fresh approach to design, Škoda products improved beyond recognition. The trouble is that consumers were slow to believe it. In the UK, Škoda found that offering a quality product was not enough and sales development was disappointing. Not to be beaten, rather than adopting a eurobland advertising approach for the new Fabia super mini, with a focus on benefits, styling and features, the UK operation decided to tackle the problem by addressing the negative attitudes head-on. The television advertisements featured a car transporter delivery to a Škoda garage. When the unloading was about to begin, the transporter driver changed his mind and drove off – after all, such great cars couldn't be destined for a Škoda dealership (they were!). The self-deprecating humour meant that the advertisement stood out, and in 2001 the campaign was a Marketing Society award winner.

By 2004, and a couple of further advertising campaigns later, Škoda was delighted to come second in a customer satisfaction survey, being beaten to first place by Toyota's prestige Lexus brand. It was not clear, however, despite positive reviews in the motoring press, whether Škoda has quite achieved the mainstream credibility that it hoped for. A review of the Škoda Octavia in a Sunday newspaper in 2004 said that:

> Buying an Octavia is an anti-statement, not just another method of displaying one's aesthetic taste or modernity. Buying a Škoda is like shopping for clothes in your local market, making your own bread, or going out without putting your make-up on – a defiant shrug in the face of the marketing men. (As quoted by Booth, 2004)

There is a kind of post-modern chic implied here: a triumph of functionality over image, and you've got to be a smart consumer to appreciate it. And maybe you need to be an extremely smart marketer to have recognised an emerging weariness with the sleekly marketed 'perfect' images of the major marques such as BMW and Audi, and to occupy the 'anti-statement' niche with confidence.

The campaigns continued with more creative advertising, but this time capitalising on Škoda's customer satisfaction achievements. In 2008, it won the best thirty-second television commercial category for the 'cake' spot which also won three other gold awards. In this advertisement, the Fabia is recreated as a life-size cake. The commercial opens with the cracking of eggs and batter being mixed in a cement-mixer and baked. As the ad unfolds to the soundtrack of Julie Andrews singing 'My Favourite Things', a patisserie car is assembled with every last panel, engine component and tyre tread made from cake, confectionery and other dessert items, even down to a petrol tank full of syrup fuel! The strapline to the advertisement is 'Manufacturer of Happy Drivers'. Instead of directly referring to Škoda's high customer satisfaction scores, the ad actually makes viewers feel happy through the medium of cake and the appreciation of the bakers' skills (Billings, 2008; Iezzi, 2007). 'Cake' was such as successful and memo-

Škoda 'cake' advertisement

*Source*: Image courtesy of The Advertising Archives

rable campaign that in 2010 Škoda decided to re-work the idea to launch a new Fabia to appeal to a cooler, younger audience with the strapline 'All the fun of the Fabia – just a little bit meaner'. This time 'My Favourite Things' was performed by a heavy metal band and the images showed the car being built using swords, crossbows, barbed wire, vultures and snakes by suitably menacing technicians. It was also supported by a website ('made of meaner stuff') and linked in with social media activity. According to Škoda UK's Head of Marketing, 'We have had 1.2 million hits on YouTube, 1,500 tweets, more than 200,000 visits to the microsite and exceptional ad-tracking results, all driving footfall to our showrooms' (as cited by *Marketing*, 2011).

Škoda was also one of the first car manufacturers to advertise on the Nickelodeon kids' television channel. The placement of these advertisements was designed to influence children to influence parental brand choice. This technique has also been used by US manufacturers, for example advertising during the iCarly show to show brand benefits to kids rather than adults.

Škoda also recognises that although its customer satisfaction performance is impressive, it cannot be complacent: Škoda buyers still need reassurance after the sale. Although Škoda still has some way to go to overcome some lingering doubts about the brand, through careful development of the 'anti-statement' concept it still plays on the proposition that dares consumers to be different, but happy, by buying Škoda!

*Sources*: Billings (2008); Bold (2004), Booth (2004), *Campaign* (2010); Hargrave (2004), Iezzi (2007); Kimberley (2001), *Marketing* (2001; 2011), Mudd (2000), *New Media Age* (2011); Simms (2001).

As the cream-cake example quoted above shows, defining attitudes can provide valuable insights into target groups of customers and give a basis for communication with them. Measuring feelings, beliefs and knowledge about an organisation's products and those of its competitors is an essential part of market research (see Chapter 5), leading to a more effective and appealing marketing mix. Identifying changes in wider social or cultural attitudes can also provide the marketer with new opportunities, either for products or marketing approaches.

In summary, the individual is a complex entity, under pressure to take in, analyse and remember many marketing messages in addition to the other burdens of daily life. Marketers need to understand how individuals think and why they respond in particular ways, if they are going to develop marketing offerings that cut through defence mechanisms and create loyal customers. Individuals' behaviour, however, is not only shaped in accordance with their personalities, abilities, analytical skills, etc., as discussed above, but also affected by wider considerations, such as the sociocultural influences that will be discussed next.

## Sociocultural influences: the group

Individuals are influenced, to a greater or lesser extent, by the social and cultural climate in which they live. Individuals have membership of many social groups, whether these are formally recognised social units such as the family, or informal intangible groupings such as reference groups (*see* p. 105 et seq.). Inevitably, purchasing decisions will be affected by group membership, as these sociocultural influences may help the individual to:

- differentiate between essential and non-essential purchases;
- prioritise purchases where resources are limited;
- define the meaning of the product and its benefits in the context of their own lives; and thus to
- foresee the post-purchase implications of this decision.

All of these things imply that the individual's decision has as much to do with 'What other people will think' and 'How I will look if I buy this' as with the intrinsic benefits of the product itself. Marketers have, of course, capitalised on this natural wish to express oneself and gain social acceptance through one's consumption habits, both as a basis for psychographic or lifestyle segmentation (which will be discussed later on p. 140 *et seq.*) and for many years as a basis of fear appeals in advertising.

The following subsections look more closely at some of these sociocultural influences.

# Social class

Social class is a form of stratification that attempts to structure and divide a society. Some argue that egalitarianism has become far more pronounced in the modern Europe, making any attempts at social distinction ill-founded, if not meaningless. Nevertheless, today social class is established largely according to occupation, and for many years, British marketers have used the grading system outlined in Table 3.1. It has been widely used to group consumers, whether for research or for analysing media readership.

**Table 3.1** UK socioeconomic groupings

| % of population | Group | Social status | Occupation of head of household |
|---|---|---|---|
| 3 | A | Upper middle | Higher managerial, administrative or professional |
| 14 | B | Middle | Intermediate managerial, administrative or professional |
| 27 | C1 | Lower middle | Supervisory or clerical, junior managerial, administrative or professional |
| 25 | C2 | Skilled working | Skilled manual workers |
| 19 | D | Working | Semi-skilled and unskilled manual workers |
| 12 | E | Those at lowest level of subsistence | State pensioners or widows, casual or lowest-grade workers |

However, more fundamental problems can be found in attempting to link consumer behaviour with social class. The usefulness of such systems is limited. They rely on the occupation of the head of the household (more correctly called the main income earner), but fail to put that into the context of the rest of the household. Dual income households are now very common, with the second income having a profound effect on the buying behaviour of both parties, yet most of these systems fail to recognise this. They tell very little about the consumption patterns or attitudes that are of such great use to the marketer. The disposable income of a C2 class household may be just as high as that of an A or B household, and they may have certain upmarket tastes in common. Furthermore, two households in the A or B categories could easily behave very differently. One household might consider status symbols to be important and indulge in conspicuous consumption, whereas the other might have rejected materialistic values and be seeking a cleaner, less cluttered lifestyle. These contrasting outlooks on life make an enormous difference to buying behaviour and choices, hence the necessity for psychographic segmentation (see p. 140 *et seq.*) to provide marketers with more meaningful frameworks for grouping customers.

# Culture and subculture

Culture can be described as the personality of the society within which an individual lives. It manifests itself through the built environment, art, language, literature, music and the products that society consumes, as well as through its prevalent beliefs, value systems and government. Rice (1993, p. 242) defines culture as:

> **The values, attitudes, beliefs, ideas, artefacts and other meaningful symbols represented in the pattern of life adopted by people that help them interpret, evaluate and communicate as members of society.**

Breaking that definition down further, Figure 3.4 shows diagrammatically the influences that create culture.

Cultural differences show themselves in very different ways. Although eating, for example, is a basic natural instinct, what we eat and when is heavily influenced by the culture in which we are brought up. Thus in Spain it is normal to begin lunch at 4 p.m. and then have dinner after 10 p.m., while in Poland most restaurants would be closing down at those times. Similarly, lunch in central Europe would almost certainly include sauerkraut, but little fish compared with the wide variety offered on a typical Spanish menu. Even the propensity for eating out may be a cultural factor.

Of course, culture goes much further in prescribing and describing the values and beliefs of a society. It influences shopping hours, with many Mediterranean supermarkets open for far longer hours in the evening than some of their northern European counterparts; the beliefs associated with advertising messages and symbols; the lifestyles of the inhabitants; and the products that are more or less acceptable and available in that culture – for example, try purchasing an electric kettle in Spain or Italy.

Culture is thus very important for the marketer to understand, first because marketing can only exist within a culture that is prepared to allow it and support it, and second, it has to act within boundaries set by society and culture. Over the past 10 years or so, for example, it has become more and more socially unacceptable in Europe for organisations to use animals for testing cosmetics. Society has informally rewritten one of the rules and marketers have had to respond. Changing attitudes to tobacco, alcohol and marketing to children are also examples of areas within which cultural change is altering organisations' approaches to business. In the UK, for instance, food marketers have been criticised for aiming too much advertising of products such as sweets, soft drinks, sugary cereals, crisps and fast foods at children. These kinds of product are thought to be of dubious nutritional value, if consumed in excess, and are also thought to be contributing to an increase in dental decay among children.

Any culture can be divided into a number of subcultures, each with its own specific characteristics, yet existing within the whole. It depends on the onlooker's perspective just how detailed a division is required. An American exporter might say that Europe represents a culture (as distinct from the American culture), with British, French, German and other national subcultures existing within it. Dealing with the home market, however, a German marketer would define Germany, or increasingly the German-speaking territories of Europe, as the dominant culture, with significant subcultures held within it. These subcultures could be based on ethnic origin (Turkish, Polish, Asian or whatever), religious beliefs, or more lifestyle-oriented groupings, defined by the values and attitudes held. Language may also be an important determinant of subculture. In Switzerland, for example, the three main languages reflect different customs, architecture and even external orientations. The Ticino region (Italian speaking) probably identifies itself more closely with Milan than Zurich or Basle as a point of cultural reference.

**Figure 3.4**
Influences on culture

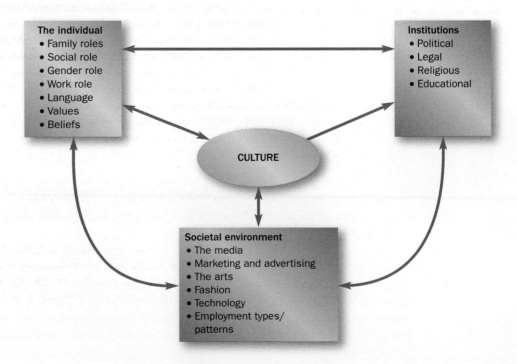

Religion and culture are interdependent influences. In Western markets, marketers are particularly trying to understand how strongly-held beliefs affect the choices that Muslim consumers make. There's a lot at stake here: globally, there are 1.8 billion Muslims, and over half of them are less than 24 years old. In the UK alone, there are over 2 million Muslims and the total across Europe is up to 30 million (Baker, 2010; Kasriel, 2008; Hussain, 2010). Research undertaken by Ogilvy Noor suggests that pasting a superficial veneer of 'Muslim values' on a brand just won't do. Today's young Muslim consumer is very 'aware', questioning, proud of their identity, and looking for goods and services provided by organisations that embrace values compatible with Islam at their heart. 'If you look at some of the values that stem from the Koran, you'll find a list of very emotionally appealing values, such as pure, honourable, honest, consistent, kind, true, trusted, responsible, wise, respectful and intelligent' (Dr Paul Temporal, Said Business School, as quoted by Roberts, 2010). For a mainstream brand, it is simply about reflecting and demonstrating these values and being inclusive of Muslim consumers, without stereotyping them. Ogilvy Noor's research reinforces this, suggesting that 'branding that is empathetic to Islamic values will . . . not only capture the loyalties of the world's Muslim consumers, but also that of the wider population of global consumers everywhere, who are demanding that businesses treat them more fairly, honestly, respectfully, and with their best interests in mind' (Hussain, 2010).

In many ways, the tension within ethnic-based subcultures is between cultural assimilation into the main, dominant culture and the preservation of cultural diversity in language, dress, food, family behaviour, etc. This tension can be seen even on a European scale, where increased emphasis on travel, rapid communication and pan-European marketing is slowly breaking down barriers at the same time as there is a strong movement towards the preservation of distinct national and regional identities.

As far as the immediate future is concerned, even within a united Europe, people are still celebrating and defending their own cultures and subcultures, and marketers need to recognise and empathise with this. One of the reasons (among many) cited for Disneyland Paris's slow start after its opening was that the organisation had underestimated French resistance, in particular, to an undiluted all-American cultural concept in the heart of Europe. Europeans were happy, and indeed eager, to experience Disney on US soil as part of 'the American experience', but could not initially accept it so readily, it would appear, within their own culture.

Subculture need not only be an ethnic phenomenon, however. The existence of a youth subculture, spanning international boundaries, is widely accepted by marketers, and media such as MTV and the internet that reach right across Europe allow marketers to communicate efficiently and cost effectively with that subculture, creating messages that capitalise on the common concerns, interests and attitudes that define this subculture. The core messages strike at something different from, and perhaps deeper than, national or ethnic culture, and thus may have pan-European currency without necessarily becoming bland in the process. That is not to say that all 16–25-year-olds across Europe should be stereotyped as belonging to a homogeneous 'yoof market'. What it does say is that there are certain attitudes and feelings with which this age group are likely to sympathise, and that these can therefore be used as a foundation for more targeted communication that manages to celebrate both commonalities and differences.

## Reference groups

Reference groups are any groups, whether formally or informally constituted, to which an individual either belongs or aspires to belong, for example professional bodies, social or hobby-oriented societies, or informal, vaguely defined lifestyle groups ('I want to be a yuppie'). There are three main types of reference group, each of which affects buying behaviour, and these are discussed in turn below.

## Membership groups

These are the groups to which the individual already belongs. These groups provide parameters within which individuals make purchasing decisions, whether they are conscious of it or not. In buying clothing, for example, the purchaser might think about the occasion for which it is going to be worn and consider whether a particular item is 'suitable'. There is great concern here about what other people will think.

Buying clothes for work is severely limited by the norms and expectations imposed by colleagues (a membership group) and bosses (an aspirant group?), as well as by the practicalities of the workplace. Similarly, choosing clothes for a party will be influenced by the predicted impact on the social group who will be present: whether they will be impressed; whether the wearer will fit in; whether the wearer will seem to be overdressed or underdressed; or whether anyone else is likely to turn up in the same outfit.

Thus the influence of membership groups on buying behaviour is to set standards to which individuals can conform, thus consolidating their position as group members. Of course, some individuals with a strong sense of opinion leadership will seek to extend those standards by exceeding them and challenging the norms with the expectation that others will follow.

## Aspirant groups

These are the groups to which the individual would like to belong, and some of these aspirations are more realistic than others. An amateur athlete or musician might aspire to professional status in their dreams, even if they have little talent. An independent professional single female might aspire to become a full-time housewife with a husband and three children; the housewife might aspire to the career and independent lifestyle. A young, junior manager might aspire to the middle management ranks.

People's desire for change, development and growth in their lives is natural, and marketers frequently exploit this in the positioning of their products and the subtle promises they make. Birds Eye frozen meals will not stop you being a bored housewife, but will give you a little more independence to 'be yourself'; buying Nike, Reebok or Adidas sports gear will not make you into Ronaldo, Messi or Torres, but you can feel a little closer to them.

The existence of aspirant groups, therefore, attracts consumers towards products that are strongly associated with those groups and will either make it appear that the buyer actually belongs to the group or signal the individual's aspirations to the wider world.

The Harley-Davidson brand is all about authority and prestige. It is not a bike for the sports motorcyclist: it seems to attract an awful lot of men in their late thirties and early forties, usually professionals seeking a bit of escapism by cruising the highways. For many of them, ownership of a product that could not be afforded in their dim and distant youth is a symbol of their achievement and success in life. Harley-Davidson, however, is having to appeal to a wider audience to avoid becoming seen as a 'grandad' brand as its traditional middle-aged male market starts to age. Its products and communication strategies are starting to target women and younger riders. They are still thought to be part of the 'dreamer group', wanting to ride and enjoy the Harley experience, and aspiring to join the Harley community. Specifically targeting younger people, for instance, the XL1200N Nightster was launched at an affordable price (a 2011 Nightster starts at about £9,300 in the UK). According to *Bike Trader*, 'Stripped down and gritty, the Nightster reinterprets the Sportster legend with a rugged, minimal neo-retro look. A solo seat adds to the uncluttered feel, as do clipped front and rear fenders that expose chunky tyres' (as quoted on www.autotrader.co.uk/EDITORIAL/BIKES/news/HARLEY-DAVIDSON/50075.html). It's about living the dream on the open road (Bennett, 2008; Devlin, 2007; www.harley-davidson.com/en_GB/Content/Pages/home.html).

Harley-Davidson: an aspirational brand for many bikers

*Source*: James Davies

## Dissociative groups

These are groups to which the individual does not want to belong or to be seen to belong. A supporter of the England soccer team would not wish to be associated with its notorious hooligan element, for example. Someone who had a violent aversion to 'yuppies' and their values might avoid buying products that are closely associated with them, through fear of being thought to belong to that group. An upmarket shopper might prefer not to be seen in a discount store such as Aldi or Lidl just in case anyone thinks they are penny pinching.

Clearly, these dissociations are closely related to the positive influences of both membership and aspirational groups. They are simply the other side of the coin, an attempt to draw closer to the 'desirable' groups, while differentiating oneself from the 'undesirable'.

## Family

The family, whether two parent or single parent, nuclear or extended, with or without dependent children, remains a key influence on the buying behaviour of individuals. The needs of the family affect what can be afforded, where the spending priorities lie and how a purchasing decision is made. All of this evolves as the family matures and moves through the various stages of its lifecycle. Over time, the structure of a family changes, for example as children grow older and eventually leave home, or as events break up families or create new ones. This means that a family's resources and needs also change over time, and that the marketer must understand and respond to these changes.

Traditionally, marketers have looked to the family lifecycle as proposed by Wells and Gubar (1966), and shown in Table 3.2. Over the years, however, this has become less and less appropriate, as it reflects a path through life that is becoming less common in the West. It does not, for example, allow for single parent families, created either voluntarily or through divorce, or for remarriage after divorce which may create new families with children coming together from previous marriages, and/or second families. Other trends too undermine the assumptions of the traditional model of the family lifecycle. According to Whitehead (2009), estimates from the Office for National Statistics in the UK forecast that 20 per cent of women may never have children.

Those who currently do elect to have children are tending to leave childbearing until later in their lives, so that they can establish their careers first. At the other end of the spectrum, the number of single, teenage mothers has increased alarmingly in the UK to 3 per cent of girls aged 15–19, the highest figure in the EU. Overall, however, European birth rates are falling, leading to 'ageing populations' throughout the EU as the proportion of children in the population falls.

**Table 3.2** The family lifecycle

| Stage | Title | Characteristics |
| --- | --- | --- |
| 1 | Bachelor | Young, single, not living at home |
| 2 | Newly married | Young, no children |
| 3 | Full nest I | Youngest child under 6 |
| 4 | Full nest II | Youngest child 6 or over |
| 5 | Full nest III | Older, married with dependent children |
| 6 | Empty nest I | Older married, no children living at home |
| 7 | Empty nest II | Older married, retired, no children living at home |
| 8 | Solitary survivor I | In labour force |
| 9 | Solitary survivor II | Retired |

*Source*: Wells and Gubar (1966).

All of these trends have major implications for consumers' needs and wants at various stages in their lives, as well as for their disposable incomes. The marketer cannot make trite assumptions based on traditional stereotypes of the nuclear family, and something more complex than the Wells and Gubar model is needed to reflect properly the various routes that people's lives can now take. Figure 3.5 offers a revised family lifecycle for the way people live today.

Regardless of the structure of the family unit, members of a household can participate in each other's purchasing decision-making. In some cases, members may be making decisions that affect the whole family, and thus Figure 3.6 shows how a family can act as a decision-making unit where individual members play different roles in reaching the final decision. The

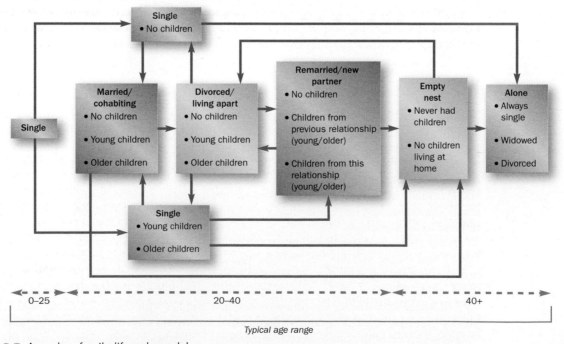

**Figure 3.5** A modern family-lifecycle model

**Figure 3.6**
The family as a decision-making unit

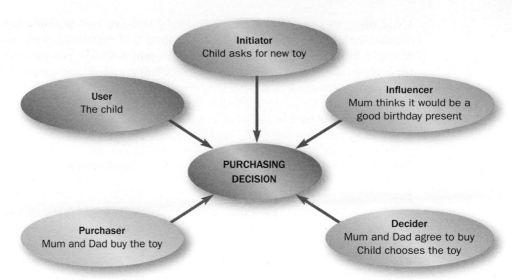

roles that any one member takes on will vary from purchase to purchase, as will the length, complexity and formality of the process. The obvious manifestation of the family decision-making unit is in the ordinary week-to-week grocery shopping. The main shopper is not acting as an individual, pleasing only themselves by their choices, but is reflecting the tastes and requirements of a group of people. In a stereotypical family, Mother may be the ultimate decider and purchaser in the supermarket, but the rest of the family may have acted as initiators ('When you go shopping, will you get me some . . .?' or 'Do you know that we've run out of . . .?' or 'Can we try that new brand of . . .?') or influencers ('If you buy THAT, don't expect ME to eat it'), either before the shopping trip or at the point of sale.

The buying roles may be undertaken by different family members for different purchases at different times. Thus in the example of purchasing a bicycle, a child may well be the user and influencer, but the parents may be the principal deciders and buyers.

Children are an important target group for the marketer, partly because of their ability to pester their parents and influence family purchasing, and partly because of the marketer's desire to create brand loyalty as early as possible in consumers' lives. Not surprisingly, many teachers, parents and consumer groups are concerned that the young and vulnerable may be exposed to unreasonable marketing pressures.

# Defining B2B marketing

So far, this chapter has looked exclusively at consumer buying behaviour. We now turn our attention to organisational buyer behaviour, or B2B marketing. This is the management process responsible for the facilitation of exchange between producers of goods and services and their organisational customers. This might involve, for example, a clothing manufacturer selling uniforms to the army, a component manufacturer selling microchips to IBM, an advertising agency selling its expertise to Kellogg's, Kellogg's selling its breakfast cereals to a large supermarket chain, or a university selling short management training courses to local firms.

B2B marketing and purchasing is a complex and risky business. An organisation may buy many thousands of products and services, costing anything from a few pennies to many millions of pounds per item. The risks are high in these markets where a bad decision, even on a minor component, can bring manufacturing to a halt or cause entire production runs to be scrapped as substandard.

There are several differences between B2B and consumer marketing, as Table 3.3 shows. If a consumer goes to the supermarket and finds that his or her preferred brand of baked beans is not there, then it is disappointing, but not a disaster. The consumer can easily substitute an alternative brand, or go to another supermarket, or the family can have something else for lunch. If, however, a supplier fails to deliver as promised on a component, then the purchasing organisation has a big problem, especially if there are no easily accessible alternative sources of supply, and runs the risk of letting its own customers down with all the commercial damage that implies. Any failure by any link in this chain has a severe impact on the others.

Thus the links have to be forged carefully, and relationships managed over time to minimise the potential problems or to diagnose them early enough for action to be taken.

**Table 3.3** Differences between B2B and consumer marketing

| B2B customers often/usually . . . | Consumer customers often/usually . . . |
| --- | --- |
| ■ purchase goods and services that meet specific business needs | ■ purchase goods and services to meet individual or family needs |
| ■ need emphasis on economic benefits | ■ need emphasis on psychological benefits |
| ■ use formalised, lengthy purchasing policies and processes | ■ buy on impulse or with minimal processes |
| ■ involve large groups in purchasing decisions | ■ purchase as individuals or as a family unit |
| ■ buy large quantities and buy infrequently | ■ buy small quantities and buy frequently |
| ■ want a customised product package | ■ are content with a standardised product package targeted at a specific market segment |
| ■ experience major problems if supply fails | ■ experience minor irritation if supply fails |
| ■ find switching to another supplier difficult | ■ find switching to another supplier easy |
| ■ negotiate on price | ■ accept the stated price |
| ■ purchase direct from suppliers | ■ purchase from intermediaries |
| ■ justify an emphasis on personal selling | ■ justify an emphasis on mass media communication |

# B2B customers

While many B2B buying situations involve a profit-making organisation doing business with other similarly oriented concerns, there are other kinds of organisation that have different philosophies and approaches to purchasing. Overall, there are three main classes: commercial enterprises, government bodies, and institutions, each of which represents a lot of buying power.

Commercial enterprises consist of profit-making organisations that produce and/or re-sell goods and services for a profit. Some are *users* who purchase goods and services to facilitate their own production, although the item purchased does not enter directly into the finished product. Examples of this are CAD/CAM systems, office equipment and management consultancy services. In contrast, *original equipment manufacturers* (OEMs) incorporate their purchases into their own product, as the car manufacturer does with the electrics, fabrics, plastics, paint, tyres, etc. *Re-sellers*, such as retailers, purchase goods for re-sale, usually making no physical changes to them, and thus the value added stems largely from service elements.

Government bodies are also very large, important purchasers of goods and services. This group of B2B buyers includes both local and national government, as well as European Commission purchasing. The range of purchasing is wide, from office supplies to public buildings, from army bootlaces to battleships, from airline tickets to motorways, from refuse collection to management consultancy. Although some purchases may be very large, expensive and high profile, involving international suppliers, as is often seen in defence procurement, others are much more mundane and routine, and involve very little public concern.

Finally, institutions include (largely) non-profit making organisations such as universities, churches and independent schools. These institutions may have an element of government funding, but in purchasing terms they are autonomous. They are likely to follow some of the same procedures as government bodies, but with a greater degree of flexibility of choice.

## Characteristics of B2B markets

The differences between consumer and B2B markets do not lie so much in the products themselves as in the context in which those products are exchanged, that is, the use of the marketing mix and the interaction between buyer and seller. The same model of personal computer, for example, can be bought as a one-off by an individual for private use, or in bulk to equip an entire office. The basic product is identical in specification but the ways in which it is bought and sold will differ.

The following subsections look at some of the characteristics of B2B markets that generate these different approaches.

## The nature of demand

### Derived demand

All demand in B2B markets is derived demand – derived from some kind of consumer demand. So, for example, washing machine manufacturers demand electric motors from an engineering factory, and that is a B2B market. The numbers of electric motors demanded, however, depend on predictions of future consumer demand for washing machines. If, as has happened, there is a recession and consumers stop buying the end product, then demand for the component parts of it will also dry up.

The economic recession has become real to Wagon Automotive. We are buying fewer cars due to the tightening of credit and reduced optimism about future prospects. That means car manufacturers are selling fewer cars which in turn means that those supplying that industry are also having to cut back. Wagon Automotive was a major supplier of panels and car door parts to the manufacturers such as Ford, Honda, General Motors and Nissan but it had to go into administration in December 2008 and close its main UK plant in Walsall. The firm tried to seek commitment from the car manufacturers but understandably in the circumstances that was difficult to give. The knock-on effects don't end there; the myriad of suppliers of materials and parts, such as the steel producers and sub-component manufacturers, to Wagon Automotive have also been affected (BBC, 2008a, 2008b; Essen and Ruddick, 2008).

## MARKETING IN ACTION

### Aircraft orders taking off

When a country or an airline buys aircraft, it is normally highly attractive to the plane manufacturers. No more so than in China, where the planned expansion in the number of commercial jets operating is staggering. In 2010, the 800th Boeing aircraft was delivered to China, and currently Boeing planes account for more than 50 per cent of China's commercial fleet. Over the next 20 years, China is expected to spend $400 billion on nearly 4,000 planes, and this level of demand is of interest not ⊙

Building airliners
*Source*: Getty Images/Bloomberg

just to European (Airbus) and American (Boeing) aircraft manufacturers, but also to their governments as a major source of export revenue and an important bargaining counter in political and trade relations.

Boeing may well currently have the largest share of this market, but it doesn't have it all its own way. First, there is the traditional threat from Airbus as the two industry giants battle it out. The market potential is also attractive to other competitors, but most significantly Airbus is seeking a larger market share. By 2010, Airbus was looking stronger than Boeing, certainly in terms of orders for aircraft from Chinese airlines. Einhorn (2010) reported that Airbus had definite orders for 358 planes compared with Boeing's 244. Einhorn also points out that Airbus has opened an assembly plant in China as a means of transferring knowledge and expertise to help build China's own aviation industry, something that Boeing has not been able to do because of union objections to 'exporting jobs'. Boeing sales, at least in the short term, might also have suffered as a result of a certain coolness between Beijing and Washington over US weapons sales to Taiwan, although Boeing's close partnerships with companies in the Chinese aviation industry mean that the Chinese government would have to weigh up any retaliation carefully to avoid hurting its own businesses. Another threat is China's decision to set up a state-owned company to manufacture passenger jets, which means that the Boeing and Airbus duopoly is likely to be challenged in future. At the moment it is still just about research and development, but eventually it will lead to commercialisation. This is part of a strategy from the Chinese Civil Aviation Authority to import fewer aircraft from overseas. Boeing at least is still upbeat about its prospects, pointing out that even if China's own aircraft builders do develop to become more serious competitors, the sheer scale of the projected demand means that there is still plenty of business potential for both Boeing and Airbus.

It isn't just about the aircraft themselves; there are also the components, electronics, accessories and navigational devices along with the maintenance services. That also includes the many thousands of Chinese employees trained in the US to work on different aircraft. It's very much a two-way relationship: over 30 years or so, Boeing alone has bought $1.5 billion of aviation goods and services from China, and about 5,700 Boeing aircraft in service around the world include Chinese-manufactured parts.

*Sources*: Anderlini (2008); *China Economic Review* (2007); Einhorn (2010); Minder (2007); *People's Daily* (2010); Tita (2010).

### Joint demand

It is also important to note that B2B is often joint demand. That is, it is often closely linked with demand for other B2B products. For example, demand for casings for computers is linked with the availability of disk drives. If there are problems or delays with the supply of disk drives, then the firm assembling the computer might have to stop buying casings temporarily. This emphasises that there is often a need to plan and coordinate production schedules between the buyer and a number of suppliers, not just one.

### Inelastic demand

Elasticity of demand refers to the extent to which the quantity of a product demanded changes when its price changes. Elastic demand, therefore, means that there is a great deal of price sensitivity in the market. A small increase in price will lead to a relatively large decrease in demand. Conversely, inelastic demand means that an increase in price will make no difference to the quantity demanded.

A car battery, for instance, is just one component of a car. A fall in the price of batteries is not going to have an impact on the quantity of cars demanded, and the car manufacturer will demand neither more nor fewer batteries than before the price change. In this context, and indeed in any manufacturing situation where a large number of components are used, demand is inelastic.

## Structure of demand

One of the characteristics of consumer markets is that for the most part they comprise many potential buyers spread over a wide geographic area, that is, they are diffuse, mass markets. Think of the market for fast food, for example, which McDonald's has shown to have worldwide appeal to many millions of customers. B2B markets, in contrast, differ in both respects.

### Industrial concentration

B2B markets tend to have a small number of easily identifiable customers, so that it is relatively easy to define who is or is not a potential customer. McDonald's can persuade non-customers to try its product and become customers; in that sense, the boundaries of the market are fuzzy and malleable, whereas a manufacturer of kilns to the brick and roofing tile industry would have problems in trying to extend its customer base beyond very specific types of customer.

Considerable knowledge, experience and trust can build up between buyers and suppliers. Where there is a finite number of known customers, most organisations in the trade know what the others are doing, and although negotiations may be private, the outcomes are very public.

### Geographic concentration

Some industries have a strong geographic bias. Such geographic concentration might develop because of resource availability (both raw materials and labour), available infrastructure or national and EU government incentives. Traditionally, heavy industry and large mass producers, such as shipbuilders, the coal and steel industries and the motor industry, have acted as catalysts for the development of a range of allied suppliers. More recently, airports and seaports have given impetus to organisations concerned with freight storage, movement, insurance and other related services.

It's not just heavy industry that has tended to concentrate in a few places. Kista Science City, just north of Stockholm in Sweden, has become a leading centre for ICT with particular emphasis on mobile, broadband, multimedia and wireless services. The concept is a result of collaboration between a number of local authorities, business and higher education, leading to a vision of 'a living and growing science city with companies and international level universities, with an attractive supply of housing, service, culture, and recreation to attract a qualified workforce' (as quoted at www.kista.com/adimo4/Site/kista/web/default.aspx?p=1346&t=h401&l=en). The emphasis is on brainpower, with a significant number of locally produced graduates contributing to the research environment. Another attraction is in the established test environments and test markets for multimedia new products. There is a high level of mobile and broadband penetration among the local population, making it a fertile environment for research and test marketing. By 2010, there were over 1,000 ICT companies, both large and small, based in and around Kista, including organisations such as Ericsson, Nokia Siemens Networks, IBM, Cellpoint (mobile applications and systems) and Kiwok (mobile patient monitoring systems). Their presence in Kista has, in turn, attracted many smaller niche suppliers and producers.

A hub of high-tech innovation: Kista Science City, Sweden
*Source*: Kista, www.kista.com

## Buying-process complexity

Consumers purchase primarily for themselves and their families. For the most part, these are relatively low-risk, low-involvement decisions that are made quickly, although there may be some economic and psychological influences affecting or constraining them. In contrast, B2B purchasers are always buying on behalf of other people (i.e. the organisation), which implies certain differences from the consumer situation. These differences give rise to much more complexity in the buying process, and the marketer must appreciate them when designing strategies for encouraging trial and reordering. The various dimensions of complexity are as follows.

## B2B purchasing policy

Certain systems and procedures for purchasing are likely to be imposed on the B2B buyer. There may be guidelines on favoured suppliers, or rules on single/multiple sourcing or on the number of quotes required for comparison before a decision can be sanctioned. Further restraints might also be imposed relating to how much an individual is allowed to spend under particular budget headings on behalf of the organisation before a second or more senior signature is required.

In addition to the formal requirements associated with purchasing, guidelines are often produced on ethical codes of practice. These do not just cover the obvious concerns of remaining within the law and not abusing authority for personal gain, but also address issues such as confidentiality, business gifts and hospitality, fair competition and the declaration of vested interests.

## Professional purchasing

The risk and accountability aspects of B2B purchasing mean that it needs to be done professionally. Much negotiation is required where complex customised technical products are concerned and, even for small components used in manufacturing, defining the terms of supply so that they are consistent and compatible with production requirements (for example, performance specification, delivery schedules and quality standards) is a significant job. Most consumer purchasing does not involve so great a degree of flexibility: the product is standard and on the shop shelf, with clearly defined price, usage and function; take it or leave it.

Peugeot Citroën decided to source more components from companies in developing economies. This was part of a company-wide decision to be a good corporate citizen, but also had a hard-nosed economic edge to it as well, with the aim of lowering the unit cost of components. Peugeot Citroën launched a new global purchasing strategy to obtain up to 5 per cent of its supplies from places such as China, Turkey and Eastern European states. Purchasing offices were opened in Shanghai and some other countries to develop local sourcing knowledge and also to be check that local suppliers could meet the rigorous quality and performance standards demanded by Peugeot Citroën. The real knock-on effect of this policy change, however, is whether European suppliers can compete with these low-cost, increasingly sophisticated components. With Peugeot Citroën's €30 billion annual purchasing spend, every percentage point lost to third world suppliers has implications for European jobs (Griffiths, 2006).

## Group decision-making

The need for full information, adherence to procedures and accountability tends to lead towards groups rather than individuals being responsible for purchasing decisions (Johnson and Bonoma, 1981). While there are group influences in consumer buying, such as the family unit, they are likely to be less formally constituted than in the B2B purchasing situation. It is rare, other than in the smallest organisations or for the most minor purchases, to find individuals given absolute autonomy in organisational spending.

## Purchase significance

The complexity of the process is also dictated by the importance of the purchase and the level of experience the organisation has of that buying situation (Robinson et al., 1967).

For instance, in the case of a *routine re-buy*, the organisation has bought this product before and has already established suppliers. These products may be relatively low-risk, frequently purchased, inexpensive supplies such as office stationery or utilities (water, electricity, gas, etc.). The decision-making process here is likely to involve very few people and be more a matter of paperwork than anything else. Increasingly, these types of purchase form part of computer-based automatic reordering systems from approved suppliers. A blanket contract may cover a specific period and a schedule of deliveries over that time is agreed. The schedule may be regarded as definite and binding for one month ahead, for example, but as provisional for the following three months. Precise dates and quantities can then be adjusted and agreed nearer the time. Increasingly, with JIT systems, schedules may even be day or hour specific.

A *modified re-buy* implies that there is some experience of buying this product, but there is also a need to review current practice. Perhaps there have been significant technological developments since the organisation last purchased this item, or a feeling that the current supplier is not the best, or a desire to renegotiate the parameters of the purchase. An example of this is the purchase of a fleet of cars, where new models and price changes make review necessary, as does the fierce competition between suppliers who, therefore, will be prepared to negotiate hard for the business. The decision-making here will be a longer, more formal and involved process, but with the benefit of drawing on past experience.

*New task purchasing* is the most complex category. The organisation has no previous experience of this kind of purchase, and therefore needs a great deal of information and wide participation in the process, especially where it involves a high-risk or high-cost product. One example of this might be the sourcing of raw materials for a completely new product. This represents a big opportunity for a supplier, as it could lead to regular future business (i.e. routine or modified re-buys). It is a big decision for the purchaser who will want to take the time and effort to make sure it is the right one. Another situation, which happens less frequently in an organisation's life, is the commissioning of new plant or buildings. This too involves a detailed, many-faceted decision-making process with wide involvement from both internal members of staff and external consultants, and high levels of negotiation.

## Laws and regulations

As we saw in Chapter 2, regulations affect all areas of business, but in B2B markets, some regulations specifically influence the sourcing of products and services. An obvious example would be the sourcing of goods from nations under various international trade embargoes. More specifically, governments may seek to regulate sourcing within certain industrial sectors, such as utilities.

## The buying decision-making process

It is just as important for marketers to understand the processes that make up the buying decision in B2B markets as it is in consumer markets. The formulation of marketing strategies that will succeed in implementation depends on this understanding. The processes involved are similar to those presented in the model of consumer decision-making described earlier in that information search, analysis, choice and post-purchase evaluation also exist here, but the interaction of human and organisational elements makes the B2B model more complex.

There are many models of organisational decision-making behaviour, with different levels of detail, for example Sheth (1973), Webster and Wind (1972) and Robinson *et al.* (1967). How the model is formulated depends on the type of organisations and products involved; the level of their experience in purchasing; organisational purchasing policies; the individuals involved; and the formal and informal influences on marketing. Figure 3.7 shows two models of organisational decision-making and, on the basis of these, the following subsections discuss the constituent stages.

## Precipitation

Clearly, the start of the process has to be the realisation that there is a need, a problem that a purchase can solve. The stimulation could be internal and entirely routine: it is the time of year to renew the photocopier maintenance contract. It could be a planned new buy precipitated,

**Figure 3.7**
Models of
organisational
buying decision-
making

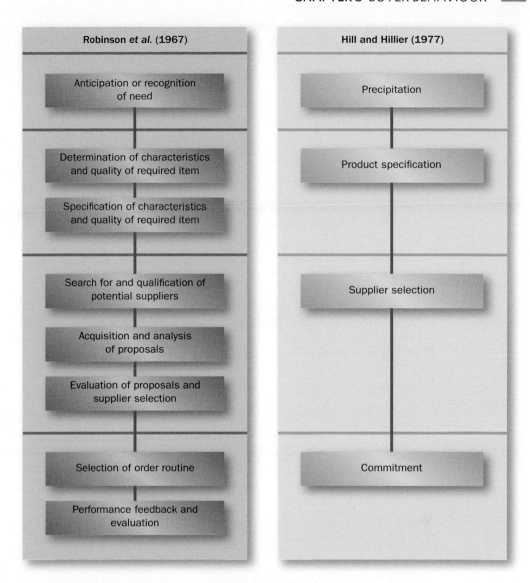

for example, by the implementation of expansion plans or the imminent production of a new product. It could also be something more sudden and dramatic than that, such as the failure of a piece of plant or machinery, or a lack of stock.

External influences can also stimulate a need. If the competition has invested in new technology, then other organisations will have to consider their response. Attending trade exhibitions, talking to visiting sales representatives or reading the trade press might also generate awareness of opportunities, whether based on new technology, cost reduction or quality improvements, which would stimulate the buying process.

Changes in the wider business environment can also trigger a need. The privatisation of electricity supply in the UK created a competitive market for supplying large industrial users. Organisations such as Ford, Tesco and Santander have appointed energy buyers with responsibility for undertaking a modified re-buy review of the electricity supply market. The energy buyers ensure that what was always considered a routine repurchase in the past can now be bought with the most advantageous long-term supply contracts from the most appropriate supplier. Thus changes in the energy environment have precipitated changes in purchasing decisions and processes.

Not all needs can or will be fulfilled and it is possible for the decision-making process to stop here, or be postponed until the organisational or environmental conditions are better. Nevertheless, some opportunities will be followed through and these move on to the next stage, product specification.

## Product specification

Unlike a consumer, for whom half the fun of shopping is often not quite knowing exactly what is wanted, an organisation must determine in some detail precisely what is required, and the greater the strategic significance of the purchase, the more true this is. Think about buying a component to be incorporated into another end product. The physical characteristics of that component must be specified, in terms of its function, its design, expected quality and performance levels, its relationship and compatibility with other components, but there are also the less tangible but no less important considerations of quantity required, delivery schedules and service backup, among others.

These specifications will need the combined expertise of engineers, production managers, purchasing specialists and marketers (representing the interests of the end customer), balancing ideals against cost and practicality. Even external consultants and suppliers could be involved in particularly complex situations. In the first instance, a general specification will be issued to potential suppliers, but a more detailed one would follow later, perhaps after a shortlist of two or three suppliers has been drawn up.

eg

'And the winner of Ship of the Year 2010 is . . . the Skandi Aker'. But what makes her so special? She's been designed to replace the need for oil rigs in certain types of offshore oil exploration that would previously have required a large rig and support vessels. She can operate in depths of up to 3,000 m (compared with similar vessels that can only manage 800 m) with a crew of up to 140, and has been designed to be very environmentally friendly.

She's beautiful! Skandi Aker, Ship of the Year 2010

*Source*: Aker Solutions/Harald Valderhaug, www.akersolutions.com

Overall, she can perform her job far more quickly and cost effectively than a rig, and is very versatile in that she is able to undertake a very wide range of subsea tasks. She took over three years to build, and throughout that time, her builders (STX OSV) and her buyer (DOFCON), continued to work together to refine the specification (www.akersolutions. com; www.shipoftheyear.com; www.stxosv.com).

It is also worthwhile at this stage to define the criteria or priorities for choice. It may not necessarily be cost. If a machine has suddenly broken down, then speed of delivery and installation may be of the essence. In the case of new technology, the choice may hinge on compatibility with existing facilities, the future prospects for upgrading it or the service support offered.

## Supplier selection

The next stage involves the search for a suitable supplier who can best meet all the specified criteria. Sometimes, the inclination to search for potential suppliers can be quite low, and the purchasing department will keep files on who can do what. If existing suppliers can do the job, then they are likely to be favoured. On other occasions, it may be necessary for buyers to be proactive by openly seeking new suppliers and encouraging quotations from those who could meet their requirements. Nevertheless, there is often a bias towards existing suppliers who are known and trusted.

Much depends, of course, on the nature of the purchasing task. A low-risk, frequent purchase might not warrant that kind of search effort, and the existing supplier might simply be asked to tender a price for resupply. One or two other known suppliers might also be requested to quote for the job, just as a checking procedure to make sure that the existing supplier is not taking advantage of the established relationship.

In a high-risk, infrequent purchase (i.e. the new task situation), a more serious, lengthy selection procedure is likely to be implemented. There will be complex discussion, negotiation, revision and reiteration at a high level with a number of potential suppliers before a final decision is made. Additional problems may be caused where different suppliers will be expected to work closely together, such as on the building of a new manufacturing plant, for instance. Their compatibility with each other, their reliability and their ability to complete their part within strict time limits dictated by the overall project schedule may all affect the decision-making.

## Commitment

The decision has been made, the contract signed, the order and delivery schedules set. The process does not, however, end here. The situation has to be monitored as it unfolds, in case there are problems with the supplier. Is the supplier fulfilling promises? Is the purchased item living up to expectations? Are deliveries turning up on time?

Some buyers adopt formal appraisal procedures for their suppliers, covering key elements of performance. The results of this appraisal will be discussed with the supplier concerned in the interests of improving their performance and allowing the existing buyer–seller relationship to be maintained.

In concluding this discussion of the buying process as a whole, we can say that the Hill and Hillier (1977) model has provided a useful framework for discussing the complexities and influences on B2B buying. It is difficult, however, to generalise about such a process, especially where technical and commercial complexity exists. Stages may be compressed or merge into each other, depending on circumstances; the process may end at any stage; there may have to be reiteration: for example if negotiations with a chosen supplier break down at a late stage the search process may have to begin again.

# The buying centre

A potential supplier attempting to gain an order from a purchasing firm needs to know just who is involved in the decision-making process, at what point in the process each person is most influential and how they all interact with each other. Then, the supplier's marketers can deal most effectively with the situation, utilising both the group and individual dynamics to the best of their advantage, for example tailoring specific communication packages to appeal at the right time to the right people, and getting a range of feedback from within the purchasing organisation to allow a comprehensive product offering to be designed.

Clearly, the amount of time and effort the supplier is prepared to devote to this will vary with the importance and complexity of the order. A routine re-buy may consist of a telephone conversation between two individuals to confirm the availability of the product and the fine detail of the transaction in terms of exact price and delivery. A new task situation, however, with the promise of either a large contract or substantial future business, provides much more scope and incentive for the supplier to research and influence the buying decision.

This section, therefore, looks at the different roles that can be played by individuals within the purchasing organisation, and how they interact to form a buying centre or decision-making unit (DMU).

Table 3.4 compares buying centres in consumer and B2B markets, indicating the membership, the roles they play and the functional areas that may be involved.

**Table 3.4** Comparison of DMUs in consumer and B2B markets

| Consumer | Example | B2B | Example |
|---|---|---|---|
| Initiator | Child pesters parents for a new bike. | User | Machine breaks down; the operator reports it, thus initiating the process. May also be asked to help with specs for replacement. |
| Influencer | Mother thinks about it and says, 'Well, perhaps he has grown out of the old one'. | Influencer | User may influence; may also involve R&D staff, accountants, suppliers, sales reps, external consultants. |
| Decider | Father agrees and they all go to Toys 'R' Us where the final decision is the child's, but under restraints imposed by parents' credit card limit. | Decider | May be a senior manager with either an active or a passive role in the whole process. May also be the buyer and/or influencer. |
| Purchaser | Parents pay the bill. | Buyer | Handles the search for and negotiations with suppliers. |
| User | The child. | Gatekeeper | Secretarial staff preventing influencers reaching the decision maker; R&D staff withholding information. |

- *Users*. Users are the people who will use the end product, for example an operator who will use production machinery, or an administrator who will use a computer. These people may trigger the purchasing process through reporting a need, and may also be consulted in setting the specifications for whatever is to be bought.
- *Influencers*. Influencers can affect the outcome of the decision-making process through their influence on others. Influence could stem formally from expertise, for example the advice of an accountant on the return on investment from a piece of capital machinery or that of an engineer on a supplier's technical capability, or it could be an informal, personal influence. Their prime role is in specification, information gathering and assessment.

- *Deciders*. Deciders have the formal or informal authority to make the decision. For routine re-buys, this may be the purchasing officer or someone in a functional role, but organisational structures may dictate that the final decision rests with top management, who are fed information and recommendations from below. The decider's role and level of involvement, therefore, will vary widely, depending on individual circumstances.
- *Buyers*. Buyers have the authority to select and negotiate with suppliers. Buyers with different levels of seniority may exist to handle different types of transaction, for example a routine re-buy could be handled by a relatively junior clerical worker, whereas the high-cost, high-risk new buy might require a senior purchasing manager of many years' experience. Where devolved budgeting exists, the buyer may not belong to a formal purchasing department at all, but be someone who also has a functional role such as R&D or marketing.
- *Gatekeepers*. Gatekeepers have some control over the decision-making process, in that they can control the flow of information by denying access to key members of the buying centre. For example, a PA or purchasing manager may prevent a sales representative from talking directly to an executive, delete e-mails or intercept brochures and mailshots and throw them in the wastepaper basket before they reach the decision maker. Technical staff can also act as gatekeepers in the way in which they choose to gather, present and interpret information to other members of the buying centre.

Bear in mind that the buying centre is not necessarily a fixed entity from transaction to transaction or even within a single transaction. It can be fluid and dynamic, evolving to meet the changing demands of the unfolding situation; it can be either formally constituted (for a major capital project, for instance) or loosely informal (a chance chat over coffee in the canteen between the purchasing manager and an R&D scientist); it can consist of two or three or many people. In other words, it is what it needs to be to do the job in hand.

When analysing the make-up of the buying centre, we should look not only at the allocation of roles between the different functional areas of the organisation, but also at the seniority of the members. Higher expenditure levels or purchases that have a critical impact on the organisation may involve much more senior management. Of course, input from the lower levels of the hierarchy will help to shape the decision, but the eventual authority may rest at board level. Thus, for example, a bank's decision to introduce a new account control system may be taken at a very senior level.

Also, an individual's contribution to it may not be limited to one role. In a small business, the owner/manager may be influencer and buyer as well as decider. Similarly, in a larger organisation, where routine re-buys are concerned, the buyer may also be the decider, with very little call for influencers. Whatever the structure, however fluid the buying centre is, it is still important for the aspiring supplier to attempt to identify the pattern within the target organisation in order to create effective communication links.

Having thus established decision-making structures, the next step is to examine the criteria applied during the process.

## Buying criteria

In the previous sections, the emphasis in terms of decision-making has largely been on rational, functionally oriented criteria. These task-related or economic criteria are certainly important and reinforce the view of the organisation as a rational thinking entity. It is dangerous, however, to fall into the trap of forgetting that behind every job title lurks an individual whose motives and goals are not necessarily geared towards the greater good of the organisation. Such motives and goals may not form a direct, formally recognised part of the decision-making process, but nevertheless, they can certainly cause friction and influence the outcomes of it.

# Economic influences

As has been stressed, it is not always a matter of finding the lowest priced supplier. If the purchasing organisation can make the best use of increased reliability, superior performance, better customer service and other technical or logistical supports from its suppliers, then it can offer a better package to its own customers, with the rewards that brings. This route can also result in lower total costs, since it reduces production delays due to substandard components or delivery failures, and also improves the quality consistency of the purchaser's own end product, thus reducing the costs of handling complaints and replacing goods.

The main criteria are:

- *Appropriate prices.* The appropriate price is not necessarily the lowest, but one representing good value for money taking into account the whole service package on offer.
- *Product specification.* Product specification involves finding the right product to meet the purchaser's specified needs, neither more nor less. There are, of course, various trade-offs between specification and price. The main point is the closeness of the match and the certainty that it will be maintained throughout the order cycle.
- *Quality consistency.* It is important to find a supplier with adequate quality controls to minimise defects so that the purchaser can use the product with confidence. This is especially true for JIT systems, where there is little room for failure.
- *Supply reliability and continuity.* The purchaser needs to be sure that adequate supplies of the product will be available as and when needed.
- *Customer service.* Buyers require reassurance that the supplier is prepared to take responsibility for its product by providing fast and flexible backup service in case of problems.

# Non-economic influences

Powers (1991) summarises non-economic influences under four main headings:

- *Prestige.* Organisations, or more specifically the individuals who make up organisations, hanker after 'status'. They want to be seen to be doing better than their competitors or other divisions within the same organisation. So, for example, they may be prepared to spend a little more when the office accommodation is refurbished on better-quality furnishings, decor and facilities to impress, instil confidence or even intimidate visitors to the site.
- *Career security.* Few people involved in the decision-making process are truly objective about it; at the back of the mind there is always the question, 'What does this mean for my job?' First, there is the risk element. A problem may have two alternative solutions, one which is safe, predictable and unspectacular, and one which is high risk, but promises a high return. If the high-risk decision is made and it all goes wrong, what are the consequences? The individual may not want to be associated with such an outcome and thus will push for the safe route. Second, there is the awareness of how others are judging the individual's behaviour in the decision-making process: 'Am I prepared to go against the main body of opinion on a particular issue that I feel strongly about or will that brand me as a trouble-maker and jeopardise my promotion prospects?'
- *Friendship and social needs.* Needs such as friendship can be dangerous and can sometimes stray very close to ethical boundaries. It is necessary, however, to value trust, confidence and respect built on a personal level between individuals in the buying and selling organisations. It does help to reduce the perceived risk of the buyer–seller relationship.
- *Other personal needs.* The individual's own personality and profile, such as demographic characteristics, attitudes and beliefs, coupled with factors like self-confidence and communication skills, can all shape the extent to which that individual is allowed to participate in and influence the outcome of the decision-making process.

A further dimension of non-economic forces is trust. Trust is the belief that another organisation will act in such a way that the outcomes will be beneficial to both parties and that it will not act in such a way as to bring about negative effects (Anderson and Narus, 1986). Trust can be built at an organisational level, but can also stem from a series of personal relationships between employees.

## Chapter summary

This chapter has centred on consumer and B2B buying behaviour, in terms of both the processes through which potential buyers pass in deciding whether to make a purchase and which product to choose, and the factors that influence the decision-making itself.

- The consumer decision-making process was presented as a number of stages: problem recognition, information search, information evaluation, decision and, finally, post-purchase evaluation.

- The length of time taken over the process as a whole or over individual stages will vary according to the type of product purchased and the particular consumer concerned. An experienced buyer with past knowledge of the market making a low-risk, low-priced routine purchase will pass through the decision-making process very quickly, almost without realising that it has happened. This is a routine problem-solving situation. In contrast, a nervous buyer, lacking knowledge but facing the purchase of a one-off, high-risk, expensive purchase, will prolong the process and consciously seek and analyse information to aid the decision. This is extended problem solving.

- Decision-making is influenced by many factors apart from the type of purchase. Some of these factors are external to the consumer, such as social, economic, legal and technological issues existing within the wider environment. Closer to home, the consumer influences the decision-making process through psychological factors. The type of personality involved; the individual's perceptions of the world and ability to interpret information; the ability to retain and learn from both experience and marketing communication; the driving motivations behind behaviour; and finally the individual's attitudes and beliefs all shape their responses to the marketing offering and ultimately their acceptance or rejection of it. In addition to that, the individual's choices and behaviour are affected by sociocultural influences defined by the groups to which the individual either belongs or wishes to belong. Social class as traditionally defined is of limited help to the marketer, but cultural or subcultural groups provide clearly differentiated groups of potential customers. Other membership groups, formed through work, hobbies and leisure pursuits, provide the individual with norms that act as reference points to aid decision-making. Similarly, aspirations fuel people's needs and wants and marketers can attract customers through reflecting those dreams and promising products that can help fulfil them or at least visibly associate the individual with the aspirant group for a while. One of the strongest group influences comes from the family, affecting decisions on what is purchased, how that decision is made and how the individual feels about that purchase.

- B2B marketing is about exchanges between organisations, whether they are commercial enterprises, government bodies or institutions. B2B markets have a number of distinct characteristics, including the nature of demand (derived, joint and inelastic), the structure of demand (concentrated in size and in geography), the complexity of the buying process and the risks inherent in it.

- The decision-making process that B2B purchasers go through has elements in common with consumer decision-making, but is likely to be formalised, to take longer and to involve more people. B2B buying is likely to involve higher value, less frequently placed orders for products that are more likely to be customised than in consumer markets. Staff with various functional backgrounds, such as purchasing, marketing, finance, engineering, production and R&D, will be involved in the process and form a buying centre. The membership of the buying centre, the roles played and who takes the lead may vary from transaction to transaction or even from stage to stage within a single process.

- The stages in the decision-making process include precipitation, product specification, supplier selection, and commitment to a long-term relationship. The decision-making process is affected not only by rational, measurable economic criteria (price, specification, quality, service, etc.), but also by non-economic influences (prestige, security, social needs, personality) emanating from the individuals involved.

## Questions for review and discussion

**3.1** Why is *post-purchase evaluation* important for:
 (a) the consumer?
 (b) the marketer?

**3.2** How do *perception*, *learning* and *attitudes* affect consumer decision-making, and how can the marketer influence these processes?

**3.3** Define the three main types of *reference group*. Within each type, think of examples that relate to you as a consumer, and analyse how this might affect your own buying behaviour.

**3.4** What are the main differences between *B2B and consumer buying behaviour?*

**3.5** Define the main *economic* and *non-economic* influences on B2B decision-making.

**3.6** How might the *roles* undertaken by various members of a two-parent family vary between the buying decisions for:
 (a) a house?
 (b) something for tonight's dinner?
 (c) a birthday present for a 10-year-old child?
 How would your answer change if it was a one-parent family?

## CASE STUDY 3

# CHOOSE YOUR OWN REMEDY

Have you ever been into a pharmacy to buy a pharmacy-only drug? What was that experience like? Was there a lengthy discussion of the suitability of that drug and discussion of alternatives or was it a cursory, 'Have you used it before? OK then, here it is'? What that represents is the front line of the pharmaceutical industry and manufacturers depend heavily on pharmacists' advice if a drug is not on prescription.

The market for drugs, while heavily regulated, is changing and that is largely due to the way in which consumers are allowed to buy. In most EU countries many drugs are dispensed on prescription only. That means visiting the doctor to get a prescription to take to the pharmacist who provides exactly what the doctor ordered, as required by law along with information about dosage and frequency. There are, however, two other categories of medicine that do not require prescriptions. There are *category P medicines* that can only be sold under the supervision of a pharmacist. P medicines might require a discussion with the pharmacist before dispensing, which could vary from an in-depth exploration of symptoms and other medication that the patient is taking, to a cursory check. Rarely are consumer requests for P medicines refused by pharmacists. The other type is called the *general sales list* (GSL), for the dispensation of which no pharmacy training is required, and staff do not even have to interact with the consumer by asking questions. Typically, these GSL products are widely sold in supermarkets, grocery stores and garages as well as more traditional pharmacy outlets. Examples include painkillers such as paracetamol and ibuprofen. The decision as to which category a drug falls into is taken by each nation's regulatory agency. For P and GSL medicines, no prescription is required and effectively it's the consumer who makes the final decision; a buyer-behaviour situation which the drugs companies are trying to influence. For the purposes of this case study, from now on P and GSL medicines will be referred to collectively as OTC (over the counter) medicines.

In the UK, consumers use pharmacists as information sources more than other Europeans do, but then the British are more prepared to self-medicate in the first place (*Chemist & Druggist*, 2008). Most consumers keep a range of OTC products handy to meet health problems as they arise. Painkillers, indigestion cures and allergy relief (such as hay fever medications) are commonly purchased on a 'just in case' basis and kept at home, and other commonly used OTC medicines include thrush and anti-fungal treatments and back-pain-relief patches, sprays and gels. The market for painkillers alone in the UK was worth £627 million in 2010, and 83 per cent of adults keep a supply of them at home (Mintel, 2010a).

But what happens when the consumer is free to purchase? Most people do not understand what is in a product, what it should be used for and for how long, how to store it, what its side effects and contra-indications are, and when to seek medical advice. All that information is provided with the product, either on the packaging or on a patient information leaflet enclosed in the pack, but most of us don't look far beyond the dosage and certainly don't read the finer detail very carefully, if at all!

Most consumers rely on the brand name and the history of that brand more than anything else, as perhaps they cannot process or handle the information provided. With a prescription drug, the information search and evaluation is effectively taken out of the consumer's hands. The most the consumer has to worry about is taking the right dose at the right time. But with self-medication, it is important for the consumer's health and wellbeing to read the information provided, but how many do? There is of course considerable protection for consumers as drugs must undergo extensive clinical trials before adoption, and there are few examples of drugs, whether OTC or prescription, being subsequently withdrawn due to safety reasons. Occasionally, drugs are switched from prescription to OTC and this actually can increase customer confidence in the product. It is not always a good thing for the consumer to be free to make their own decisions. Sales of eye drops and lotions have grown considerably since the main drug, chloramphenicol, was reclassified as OTC in 2005 (Anekwe, 2008). The trouble, some experts claim, is that it is an antibacterial drug and its widespread indiscriminate use could create resistance – in other words, the more it is used, the less effective it could be. Another potential problem of self-medication is dependency. Widely used drugs, such as painkillers including codeine, can certainly help relieve acute and moderate pain, but overuse can lead to addiction. Around 32,000 people in the UK are thought to be addicted to OTC painkillers (Baker, 2009), largely through lack of understanding of the consequences of prolonged use (because of not reading the information supplied in or on the pack fully?). The restrictions on the open sale of these products are now tighter, for example, the pack size that can be sold OTC is a maximum of 32 tablets and there are now prominent warnings about addiction on the front of the packs: 'Can cause addiction. For three days use only.' Advice about appropriate usage has also been amended to suggest that these drugs should only be used for moderate or acute pain that does not respond to paracetamol, ibuprofen or aspirin alone, rather than as an everyday routine painkiller.

GlaxoSmithKline's weight-loss drug, Alli, is another example of why it is important for consumers to understand drug information thoroughly. The problem with this drug, especially if you don't control your diet carefully while taking it, is that it can have some nasty side-effects relating to sudden and explosive wind and diarrhœa. In the USA, Alli is freely available on supermarket shelves, displayed alongside other slimming aids, but in the UK it can only be purchased with the guidance of the pharmacist, and it is only recommended for adults above a certain body mass. Of course, that doesn't stop consumers buying it if they really want to. GSK's marketing campaign in the UK is based around education and information, presenting the pill as part of a lifestyle change. First, pharmacists were targeted so that they would understand the drug and its limitations. Seven thousand pharmacists have been trained so far. The second strand is consumer targeted, and is based on a combination of online advertising, television and press advertising with advertorial and editorial pieces, all detailing who should use Alli, and how it should be used along with the side effects (*Marketing Week*, 2009). GSK is constantly giving the message that Alli is not a 'magic slimming pill'; it needs to be used as part of a broader weight-loss programme. Alli also sponsors the series *Cook Yourself Thin* on Channel 4, as a way of reinforcing the need to change dietary habits and reduce fat intake as part of the 'Alli programme'.

For OTC medicines generally, over 75 per cent of sales in the UK are made through pharmacies and drug stores and just 13 per cent through supermarkets, but this figure is likely to change as supermarkets become more interested in the sector and develop more extensive ranges of own brand alternatives. Supermarkets have been particularly active in developing own label painkillers, and in 2009, own labels held a 36 per cent share of the painkiller market. Across all OTC products, in 2008 supermarket own brands accounted for 47 per cent of OTC sales in supermarkets, whereas for pharmacies, own brand share was just 32 per cent. OTC products are becoming just another product category for supermarkets which is becoming heavily price-driven. But what the supermarkets are doing is making the products more widely and cheaply available, so consumers are becoming more confident and more familiar with different drugs (and perhaps more complacent about them?). OTC medicines are now as much a part of the regular shopping list as bread and pasta.

The pharmacist, on the other hand, is in a unique position to get people out of the doctor's waiting room and into the pharmacy by not only giving advice but also undertaking health checks. The drive is to encourage the UK public to see the pharmacist as a trusted healthcare advisor, rather than just an OTC retailer to be compared with the supermarkets which offer more competitive prices (Nicholas, 2009). But the implications for staff training are enormous, as most chemists have only one or two pharmacists. Another important development has been the growth of the internet. While there are sites such as NHS Direct which guide consumers towards correct self-diagnosis (or encourage them to seek professional medical help), and others that provide a lot of supportive information, there are also many which are simply selling drugs with few or no questions asked. A quick Google search came up with a large number of suppliers prepared to sell Alli to us in the UK with no checks whatsoever.

*Sources*: Anekwe (2008); Bainbridge (2008); Baker (2009); Business Monitor International (2009a; 2009b; 2009c; 2009d); *Chemist & Druggist* (2008); EMA (2008); Langley and Belcher (2008); *Marketing Week* (2009); Mintel (2010a); Nicholas (2009).

## Questions

1 What kind of influences might affect the problem recognition, information search and information evaluation stages for a consumer buying an OTC medicine?

2 What are the risks of consumers considering OTC drugs, such as painkillers, as routine response purchases, and how can the marketers counteract them?

3 Assess GSK's approach to marketing Alli in the UK. To what extent do you think it is appropriate or sufficient for a category P drug?

4 How might the decision-making process for buying an OTC medicine differ between a pharmacist wanting to re-sell it and a consumer wanting to self-medicate?

# References for chapter 3

Alarcon, C. (2009) 'Simpsons and PepsiCo in Latest Change4Life Push', *Marketing Week*, 5 October.

Anderlini, J. (2008) 'China Waves its Fist in the Face of Competition', *Financial Times*, 11 December.

Anderson, J.C. and Narus, J.A. (1986) 'Towards a Better Understanding of Distribution Channel Working Relationships', in K. Backhaus and D. Wilson (eds) *Industrial Marketing: A German–American Perspective*, Springer-Verlag.

Anekwe, L. (2008) 'OTC Antibiotic Surge Sparks Resistance Fears', *Pulse*, 17 December.

Bainbridge, J. (2008) 'Minor-ailment Remedies – Self-medication Fuels Sales', *Marketing*, 26 November.

Baker, R. (2009) 'Addictive OTC Drugs Forced to Carry Warnings on Packs', *Marketing Week*, 10 September.

Baker, R. (2010) 'Ogilvy Launches Specialist Muslim Division', *Marketing Week*, 21 May.

Bamford, V. (2010) 'Hooked on Meal Deals', *The Grocer*, 16 January, pp. 51–9.

BBC (2008a) 'UK Car Parts Firm Wagon Collapses', BBC, 8 December. Accessed via news.bbc.co.uk/2/hi/business/7770018.stm.

BBC (2008b) 'Wagon Automotive Cutting 292 Jobs', BBC, 19 December. Accessed via http://news.bbc.co.uk/2/hi/business/7791744.stm.

BBC (2011) 'Whitbread Buys Coffee Nation Vending Machines', *BBC News*, 2 March. Accessed via www.bbc.co.uk/news/business-12618232.

Bennett, J. (2008) 'Harley with Youth Appeal', *Bristol Evening Post*, 3 April.

Billings, C. (2008) 'Fallon Sweeps the Board at British Television Ad Awards', *Campaign*, 14 March.

Bold, B. (2004) 'Badge of Honour', *Marketing*, 4 August, p. 24.

Booth, M. (2004) 'Practical But Not a Joke', *The Independent on Sunday*, 14 November, p. 57.

Bruner, G.C. and Pomazal, R.J. (1988) 'Problem Recognition: the Crucial First Stage of the Consumer Decision Process', *Journal of Consumer Marketing*, 5 (1), pp. 53–63.

Business Monitor International (2009a) 'OTC Switches Concern Healthcare Professionals', *BMI Industry Insights – Pharma and Healthcare, Western Europe*, 20 January.

Business Monitor International (2009b) 'OTC Medicines Sales Down, But Prospects Remain Healthy', *BMI Industry Insights – Pharma and Healthcare, Emerging Europe*, 18 June.

Business Monitor International (2009c) 'Government Making Savings Despite Prescription Drug Volumes Increasing', *BMI Industry Insights – Pharma and Healthcare, Western Europe*, 31 July.

Business Monitor International (2009d) 'MHRA Works to Reduce OTC Codeine-Containing Medicines Access', *BMI Industry Insights – Pharma and Healthcare, Western Europe*, 7 September.

*Campaign* (2010) 'Skoda – Made of Meaner Stuff', *Campaign*, 5 November, p. 6.

*Chemist & Druggist* (2008) 'Consumers Rank Usage of OTC Medicines for Minor Ailments', *Chemist & Druggist*, 20 September.

*China Economic Review* (2007) 'Beijing Confirms Challenge to Boeing, Airbus', *China Economic Review*, 20 March.

Chisnall, P.M. (1985) *Marketing: A Behavioural Analysis*, McGraw-Hill.

Clewes, M-L. (2011) 'Government Claim Stats Show Swapathon Success', *Technology Weekly*, 13 May, accessed via http://technologyweekly.mad.co.uk/Main/Secondaryitems/Search/Articles/1108c30835d04a6d8cfb480b9c9f2f37/Government-claim-stats-show-Swapathon-success.html.

Department of Health (2010) *Change4Life One Year On*, HM Government. Accessed via www.dh.gov.uk/prod_consum_dh/groups/dh_digitalassets/@dh/@en/documents/digitalasset/dh_115511.pdf.

Devlin, R. (2007) 'Leaders of the Pack, Now', *Reading Eagle*, 4 September.

Einhorn, B. (2010) 'Airbus May Beat Boeing in China's Aviation Market', *Bloomberg Business Week*, 2 February. Accessed via www.businessweek.com/globalbiz/content/feb2010/gb2010022_703055.htm.

EMA (2008) 'European Medicines Agency Recommends First Switch from Prescription-only to Non-prescription for a Centrally Authorised Medicine', *EMA*, 23 October. Accessed via www.ema.europa.eu.

Engel, J.F., Blackwell, R.D. and Miniard, P.W. (1990) *Consumer Behaviour*, Dryden.

Essen, Y. and Ruddick, G. (2008) 'Wagon Jobs at Risk as Car Parts Group Confirms Administration', *Daily Telegraph*, 7 December.

Festinger, L. (1957) *A Theory of Cognitive Dissonance*, Stanford University Press.

Fishbein, M. (1975) 'Attitude, Attitude Change and Behaviour: a Theoretical Overview', in P. Levine (ed.), *Attitude Research Bridges the Atlantic*, Chicago: American Marketing Association.

Green, T. and Peloza, J. (2011) 'How Does Corporate Social Responsibility Create Value for Consumers?', *Journal of Consumer Marketing*, 28 (1), pp. 48–56.

Griffiths, J. (2006) 'Peugeot Citroën Supply Search Goes Global', *Financial Times*, 2 March.

Hargrave, S. (2004) 'Strategic Play – Skoda: Keeping an Open Mind', *New Media Age*, 26 February, p. 20.

Hauser, J., Urban, G. and Weinberg, B. (1993) 'How Consumers Allocate their Time when Searching for Information', *Journal of Marketing Research*, November, pp. 452–66.

Hilgard, E.R. and Marquis, D.G. (1961) *Conditioning and Learning*, Appleton Century Crofts.

Hilgard, E.R., Atkinson, R.C. and Atkinson R. L. (1975) *Introduction to Psychology*, 6th edn. Harcourt Brace Jovanovich.

Hill, R.W. and Hillier, T.J. (1977) *Organisational Buying Behaviour*, Macmillan.

Howard, J.A. and Sheth, J.N. (1969) *The Theory of Buyer Behaviour*, Wiley.

Hussain, N. (2010) 'Young, Muslim and Ready for Engagement', *Admap*, July/August.

Iezzi, T. (2007) 'Skoda, Fallon Make Striking the Right Tone Look Like a Piece of Cake', *Advertising Age*, 4 June.

Johnson, W.J. and Bonoma, T.V. (1981) 'The Buying Centre: Structure and Interaction Patterns', *Journal of Marketing*, 45 (Summer), pp. 143–56.

Kasriel, D. (2008) 'Spotlighting Europe's Muslim Consumers', *Euromonitor International*, 10 September.

Keller, K.L. and Staelin, R. (1987) 'Effects of Quality and Quantity of Information on Decision Effectiveness', *Journal of Consumer Research*, 14 (September), pp. 200–13.

Kimberley, W. (2001) 'Skoda: an Eastern Europe Success', *Automotive Manufacturing and Production*, June, pp. 26–8.

Langley, C. and Belcher, D. (2008) *Applied Pharmaceutical Practice*, London: Pharmaceutical Press.

*Marketing* (2001) 'Brand Re-vitalisation of the Year', *Supplement to Marketing*, 12 June, p. 12.

*Marketing* (2011) 'Marketing Promotion', *Marketing*, 2 February, p. 13.

*Marketing Week* (2009) 'Building a Brand Rather Than Just Launching a Pill', *Marketing Week*, 23 April.

*Marketing Week* (2011) 'The Call to Action Can't be a Whisper', *Marketing Week*, 19 May.

Maslow, A.H. (1954) *Motivation and Personality*, Harper and Row.

Minder, R. (2007) 'Assembly in China Vital for Sales, Says Airbus', *Financial Times*, 6 September.

Mintel (2009) 'Vending', *Mintel Technology UK*, May. Accessed via http://academic.mintel.com/sinatra/oxygen_academic/search_results/show&/display/id=393968.

Mintel (2010a) 'Analgesics UK', *Mintel Health and Hygiene*, May. Accessed via http://academic.mintel.com/sinatra/oxygen_academic/search_results/show&/display/id=480784/display/id=480784/display/id=480784/display/id=480784/display/id=526638?select_section=480784.

Mintel (2010b) 'Consumer Snacking UK', *Mintel Food UK*, June, accessed via http://academic.mintel.com/sinatra/oxygen_academic/search_results/show&/display/id=480788.

Mudd, T. (2000) 'The Last Laugh', *Industry Week*, 18 September, p. 38–44.

*New Media Age* (2011) 'Skoda Proves that Being a Little Mean isn't Always a Bad Thing', *New Media Age*, 6 January, p. 18.

Nicholas, R. (2009) 'Specialists Feel the Pain', *The Grocer*, 13 June, pp. 49–52.

O'Guinn, T. and Faber, R. (1989) 'Compulsive Buying: a Phenomenological Exploration', *Journal of Consumer Research*, 16 (June), pp. 147–57.

Parfitt, B. (2010) Government Scraps Change4Life Funding', *MCV*, 8 July. Accessed via www.mcvuk.com/news/39914/Government-scraps-Change4Life-funding.

*People's Daily* (2010) 'Boeing Delivers 800th Aircraft to China', *People's Daily*, 21 July. Accessed via http://english.peopledaily.com.cn/90001/90778/90860/7075417.html.

Powers, T.L. (1991) *Modern Business Marketing: A Strategic Planning Approach to Business and Industrial Markets*, St Paul, MN: West.

Rice, C. (1993) *Consumer Behaviour: Behavioural Aspects of Marketing*, Oxford: Butterworth-Heinemann.

Roberts, J. (2010) 'Young, Connected and Muslim', *Marketing Week*, 24 June.

Robinson, P.J. *et al.* (1967) *Industrial Buying and Creative Marketing*, Allyn and Bacon.

Sheth, J. (1973) 'A Model of Industrial Buying Behaviour', *Journal of Marketing*, 37 (October), 50–6.

Simms, J. (2001) 'Think Global, Act Local', *Campaign*, 29 March, pp. 24–5.

Sweney, M. (2010) 'Health Secretary Axes £75m Marketing Budget for Anti-obesity Drive', *The Guardian*, 7 July.

Tita, B. (2010) 'Boeing CEO Sees Plenty of Orders for Company in China', *Wall Street Journal*, 26 May.

Walker, G. (2010a) 'Healthy Snacks Head for the Confectionery Counter', *The Grocer*, 2 July.

Walker, G. (2010b) 'Funding Cuts Force Change4Life Rethink', *The Grocer*, 21 July.

Webster, F.E. and Wind, Y. (1972) *Organisational Buyer Behaviour*, Prentice-Hall.

Wells, W.D. and Gubar, R.G. (1966) 'Life Cycle Concepts in Marketing Research', *Journal of Marketing Research*, 3 (November), pp. 355–63.

Whitehead, T. (2009) 'One in Five Women Stays Childless because of Modern Lifestyle', *Daily Telegraph*, 25 June.

Williams, K.C. (1981) *Behavioural Aspects of Marketing*, Heinemann Professional Publishing.

# CHAPTER 4

# Segmenting markets

## LEARNING OBJECTIVES

This chapter will help you to:

- explain how both B2B and consumer markets can be broken down into smaller, more manageable groups of similar customers;
- understand the effects on the marketing mix of pursuing specific segments;
- understand the potential benefits and risks of segmentation; and
- appreciate the role of segmentation in strategic marketing thinking.

## INTRODUCTION

**BUILDING ON THE UNDERSTANDING** of buyer behaviour and decision-making processes outlined in Chapter 3, this chapter concerns a question that should be very close to any true marketer's heart: 'How do we define and profile our customer?' Until an answer is found, no meaningful marketing decisions of any kind can be made. It is not usually enough to define your customer as 'anyone who wants to buy our product' because this implies a product-oriented approach: the product comes first, the customer second. If marketing is everything we have claimed it to be, then the product is only a small part of a total integrated package offered to a customer. Potential customers must, therefore, be defined in terms of what they want, or will accept, in terms of price, what kind of distribution will be most convenient for them and through what communication channels they can best be reached, as well as what they want from the product itself.

Remember too that in a consumer-based society, possession of 'things' can take on a symbolic meaning. A person's possessions and consumption habits make a statement about the kind of person they are, or the kind of person they want you to think they are. The organisation that takes the trouble to understand this and produces a product that not only serves its functional purpose well, but also appears to reflect those less tangible properties of a product in the purchaser's eyes, will gain that purchaser's custom. Thus sport-shoe manufacturers, such as Reebok and Nike, not only developed shoes for a wide range of specific sports (tennis, soccer, athletics, etc.) but also realised that a significant group of customers would never go near a sports facility and just wanted trainers as fashion statements. This meant that they served three distinctly different groups of customers: the professional/serious sports player, the amateur/casual sports player and the fashion victim. The R&D invested in state-of-the-art quality products, combined with the status connected with the first group and endorsement from leading sports icons, helped these companies to build an upmarket image that allowed them to exploit the fashion market to the full with premium-priced products. This in turn led to the expansion of product ranges to include branded sports and leisure clothing.

*eg*

Nokia decided to investigate whether there are different need-based segments in the mobile phone market. It carried out research among 77,000 people in 21 countries and ran focus groups involving 3,000 people in total. Up to that point, segmentation had been defined only on demographic criteria such as age, but Nokia felt that to get closer to customers it needed to go beyond that. It wanted to understand lifestyle choices and underlying attitudes to mobile purchasing.

By understanding more deeply why people buy phones, how they use them and what brand and product attributes they seek, Nokia was better able to target customers with different offerings. Nokia identified 12 main segments of mobile users and defined four categories for which to make tailored offers:

- *Live.* The essential focus for these users is design and style leadership. Their particular interest is the look, feel and any extra functionality of the phone.
- *Connect.* This group is concerned about ease of use and good looks, but the main focus is how easy it is for them to stay in touch with friends and family through their phone, whether by voice, e-mail or text messaging.
- *Achieve.* This is about the busy business user who wants easy access to e-mail, calendar, contacts and web browsing, as well as voice contact.
- *Explore.* These users are tech-savvy and very excited by the latest gadgets and add-ons. They make extensive use of multimedia to record, browse and share information on the internet.

These groups are global; Nokia found that there are more commonalities across the world than differences. From this research, Nokia was able to design a closer connection between consumers, the product range offered, and the way they were sold. Nevertheless, Nokia cannot be complacent. This is a very dynamic and fast-moving market, which could change the profiles yet again.

Nokia's main concern is mainly on handsets, while Orange has an interesting approach to the segmentation of network access through the various tariffs and plans that it offers. These are grouped around animals, with each one having a different emphasis within the range of plans offered (as at June 2011, http://shop.orange.co.uk):

- *Dolphin.* 'stay social'. This is for sociable people, with an emphasis on keeping in touch through the full range of media, so it offers internet and e-mail access, unlimited texts and between 30 and 1,200 minutes call time per month (depending on how much you choose to pay).

- *Panther.* 'get it all'. This is for heavy users and includes the full multimedia package, including unlimited texts, e-mail, internet, photo messaging and wifi, along with between 300 and 3,000 minutes.
- *Canary.* 'love to talk and text'. This is mainly targets younger users with unlimited texts and between 100 and 900 minutes. This includes the cheapest of all the tariffs at £10 per month (which does, however, limit the use to 500 texts per month), particularly attractive for younger, cash-strapped users.
- *Racoon.* 'keep in touch'. With unlimited landline calls, between 100 and 300 texts, and between 50 and 900 minutes, this is clearly targeting the older user who sees the mobile phone primarily as a phone, making only occasional use of other facilities.

Each animal group contains a range of plans at varying price points and with correspondingly varying services and facilities for 'pay monthly' contracts. For customers who prefer 'pay as you go', there are adapted versions of Dolphin, Canary and Racoon and, additionally, Camel, which offers free international calling minutes as its key selling point. An interesting development is the introduction of the Monkey tariff, aimed at 15–24-year-olds, which offers users free music in return for accepting incoming advertising and other marketing messages on their phones (Harlow, 2007; O'Flaherty, 2009).

Orange's 'Monkey' tariff aimed at users in the age range of 15 to 24

*Source:* Orange Mobile, www.http://shop.orange.co.uk

All this forms the basis of the concept of segmentation, first developed by Smith (1957). Segmentation can be viewed as the art of discerning and defining meaningful differences between groups of customers to form the foundations of a more focused marketing effort. The following section looks at this concept in a little more depth, while the rest of the chapter will examine how the concept can be implemented and its implications for the organisation.

# The concept of segmentation

The introductory section of this chapter has presented the customer-oriented argument for the adoption of the segmentation concept. There is, however, also a practical rationale for adopting it. Mass production, mass communication, increasingly sophisticated technology and increasingly efficient global transportation have all helped in the creation of larger, more temptingly lucrative potential markets. Few organisations, however, have either the resources or the inclination to be a significant force within a loosely defined market. The sensible option, therefore, is to look more closely at the market and find ways of breaking it down into manageable parts, or groups of customers with similar characteristics, and then to concentrate effort on serving the needs of one or two groups really well, rather than trying to be all things to all people. This makes segmentation a proactive part of developing a marketing strategy and involves the application of techniques to identify these segments (Wind, 1978).

It may help you to understand this concept better if you think of an orange. It appears to be a single entity, yet when you peel off the skin you find that it is made up of a number of discrete segments, each of which happily exists within the whole. Eating an orange is much easier (and much less wasteful and messy) if you eat it systematically, segment by segment, rather than by attacking the whole fruit at once. Marketers, being creative folk, have adopted this analogy and thus refer to the separate groups of customers that make up a market as 'market segments'.

The analogy is misleading, however, in that each segment of an orange is more or less identical in size, shape and taste, whereas in a market, segments may be very different from each other in terms of size and character. To determine these things, each segment has its own distinct profile, defined in terms of a number of criteria, referred to as *bases* or *variables*, set by the marketer. The choice of appropriate criteria for subdividing the market is very important (Moriarty and Reibstein, 1986) and thus a significant proportion of this chapter is devoted to thinking about the bases by which segments might be defined in both consumer and B2B markets. Leading on from this, there is also the question of influences that might affect an organisation's choice of segmentation variables. Then, once an organisation has defined its market segments, what is it supposed to do with the information? This too is addressed in this chapter.

B2B and consumer markets, in general, tend to be segmented differently and, therefore, will be discussed separately, beginning with B2B markets.

# Segmenting B2B markets

One major feature of B2B segmentation is that it can focus on both the organisation and the individual buyers within it. Additionally, there is the need to reflect group buying, that is, the involvement of more than one person in the purchasing decision (Abratt, 1993). All of this can be compared with a family buying situation in a consumer market, but operating on a much larger scale, usually within a more formalised process.

Wind and Cardozo (1974) suggest that segmenting a B2B market can involve two stages:

1 *Identify subgroups* within the whole market that share common general characteristics. These are called macro segments and will be discussed further below.
2 *Select target segments* from within the macro segments based on differences in specific buying characteristics. These are called micro segments and are discussed at p. 134.

# Macro segmentation bases

Macro segments are based on the characteristics of organisations and the broader purchasing context within which they operate. Defining a macro segment assumes that the organisations within it will exhibit similar patterns and needs, which will be reflected in similar buying behaviour and responses to marketing stimuli.

The bases used for macro segmentation tend to be observable or readily obtained from secondary information (i.e. published or existing sources) and can be grouped into two main categories, each of which will now be discussed.

## Organisational characteristics

There are three organisational characteristics: size, location and usage rate.

1 *Size.* The size of an organisation will make a difference to the way in which it views its suppliers and goes about its purchasing. A large organisation, for instance, may well have many people involved in decision-making; its decision-making may be very complex and formalised (because of the risks and level of investment involved), and it may require special treatment in terms of service or technical cooperation. In contrast, a small organisation may operate on a more centralised decision-making structure, involving one or two people and with simpler buying routines.

Thomson provides business information to a number of different end-user segments such as lawyers, accountants, investment managers, scientific researchers, and health service professionals. The business has undergone a radical transformation from being essentially paper-based to an internet-based service. Its electronic information products, software and services now provide most of its revenue.

Thomson felt that its existing segmentation model was rather general and thus started to move towards more market-specific profiles of end users in order to find the most practicable market segments. New segments were thus defined within broader market sectors. Within the financial markets sector, for instance, segments such as institutional equity advisers, fixed-income advisers, and investment bankers all emerged. Overall, eight segments of end users were identified and from that, estimates of market size and share were made, and segments were identified in which market share was high or where opportunities existed for expansion.

The process of defining the segments included asking some basic questions, such as what customers do with the information and how it is integrated into their workflow, thus also providing useful inputs to marketing strategy. The next stage was to find out what attributes the information service had to exhibit and how much customers are prepared to pay for it, whether it is real-time data, data for export to spreadsheets or portfolio analysis. This stage had implications for product development, customer service, sales and strategy. Among investment managers, for instance, there were three distinct clusters: basic users, advanced users, and users who all required real-time information. Each group had different needs and valued a different set of attributes and of course differed in how much they were prepared to pay (Harrington and Tjan, 2008).

2 *Location.* Organisations may focus their selling effort according to the geographic concentration of the industries they serve. Such specialisation is, however, slowly breaking down as the old, heavy, geographically based industries, such as shipbuilding, mining and chemical production, become less predominant. Additionally, there is the emergence of smaller more flexible manufacturers, geographically dispersed in new technology parks, industrial estates

and enterprise zones. Nevertheless, there are still examples of geographic segmentation, such as that of computer hardware and software sales, or in the financial sector, which is concentrated in London, Frankfurt, Zurich and the major capitals of the world. Organisations providing certain kinds of services might also look to geographic segments. A haulage company might specialise in certain routes and thus look for customers at specific points to make collection, delivery and capacity utilisation as efficient as possible.

3 *Usage rate.* The quantity of product purchased may be a legitimate means of categorising potential customers. A purchasing organisation defined as a 'heavy user' will have different needs from a 'light user', perhaps demanding (and deserving) different treatment in terms of special delivery or prices, for example. A supplier may define a threshold point, so that when a customer's usage rate rises above it, their status changes. The customer's account may be handed over to a more senior manager and the supplier may become more flexible in terms of cooperation, pricing and relationship building. It is generally a better investment to make concessions in order to cultivate a relationship with a single heavy user than to try to attract a number of light users.

## Product or service application

This second group of segmentation bases acknowledges that the same good can be used in many different ways. This approach looks for customer groupings, either within specific industries as defined by standard industrial classification (SIC) codes, each with its own requirements, or by defining a specific application and grouping customers around that.

The SIC code may help to identify sectors with a greater propensity to use particular products for particular applications. Glass, for example, has many industrial uses, ranging from packaging to architecture to the motor industry. Each of these application sectors behaves differently in terms of price sensitivity, ease of substitution, quality and performance requirements, for instance. Similarly, cash-and-carry wholesalers serve three broad segments: independent grocers, caterers and pubs. Each segment will purchase different types of goods, in different quantities and for different purposes.

The macro level is a useful starting point for defining some broad boundaries to markets and segments, but it is not sufficient in itself, even if such segmentation does happen too often in practice. Further customer-oriented analysis on the micro level is necessary.

## Micro segmentation bases

Within a macro segment, a number of smaller micro segments may exist. To focus on these, the organisation needs to have a detailed understanding of individual members of the macro segment, in terms of their management philosophy, decision-making structures, purchasing policies and strategies, as well as their needs and wants. Such information can come from published sources, past experience of the potential buyer, sales force knowledge and experience, word of mouth within the industry, or at first hand from the potential buyer.

An overview of common bases for micro segmentation is given in Table 4.1.

**Table 4.1** Bases for micro segmentation in B2B markets

- Product
- Applications
- Technology
- Purchasing policies
- DMU structure
- Decision-making process
- Buyer–seller relationships

Gathering, collating and analysing such depth of information is, of course, a time-consuming and sometimes difficult task, and there is always the question of whether it is either feasible or worthwhile. However, there are benefits in defining such small segments (even segments of one!) if it enables fine tuning of the marketing offering to suit specific needs. Given the volumes of goods and levels of financial investment involved in some B2B markets, the effort is not wasted. An organisation that has a small number of very important customers would almost certainly treat each as a segment of one, particularly in a market such as the supply of organisation-wide computer systems where individual customer needs vary so much. In contrast, in a market such as office stationery, where standard products are sold to perhaps thousands of B2B customers, any segmentation is likely to centre around groups aggregating many tens of customers on the macro level.

# Segmenting consumer markets

Segmenting consumer markets does have some similarities with B2B segmentation, as this section indicates. The main difference is that consumer segments are usually very much larger in terms of the number of potential buyers, and it is much more difficult, therefore, to get close to the individual buyer. Consumer segmentation bases also put more emphasis on the buyer's lifestyle and context, because most consumer purchases fulfil higher-order needs (see, for example, Maslow's hierarchy of needs, discussed at p. 97 *et seq.*) rather than simply functional ones. The danger is, however, that the more abstract the segments become, the less easily understood they may become by those designing marketing strategies (Wedel and Kamakura, 1999). Each of the commonly used bases is now discussed in turn.

## Geographic segmentation

Geographic segmentation defines customers according to their location. This can often be a useful starting point. A small business, for example, particularly in the retail or service sector, operating on limited resources, may look initially for custom within its immediate locale. Even multinationals, such as Heinz, often tend to segment geographically by dividing their global organisation into operating units built around specific geographic markets.

In neither case, however, is this the end of the story. For the small business, simply being there on the High Street is not enough. It has to offer something further that a significant group of customers want, whether it is attractively low prices or a high level of customer service. The multinational organisation segments geographically, partly for the sake of creating a manageable organisational structure, and partly in recognition that on a global scale, geographic boundaries herald other, more significant differences in taste, culture, lifestyle and demand. The single European market (SEM) may have created a market of nearly 500 million potential customers, yet the first thing that most organisations are likely to do is to segment the SEM into its constituent nations.

Take the marketing of an instant hot chocolate drink, made with boiling water. In the UK, virtually every household owns a kettle, and hot chocolate is viewed either as a bedtime drink or as a substitute through the day for tea or coffee. In France, however, kettles are not common, and hot chocolate is most often made with milk as a nourishing children's breakfast. Thus the benefits of speed, convenience and versatility that would impress the UK market would be less applicable in the French market. France would require a very different marketing strategy at best or, at worst, a completely different product.

Geographic segments are at least easy to define and measure, and information is often freely available from public sources. This kind of segmentation also has an operational advantage, particularly in developing efficient systems for distribution and customer contact, for example. However, in a marketing-oriented organisation, this is not sufficient. Douglas and Craig (1983), for example, emphasise the dangers of being too geographically focused and making assumptions about what customers in a region might have in common. Even within a small geographic area, there is a wide variety of needs and wants, and this method on its own tells you nothing about them.

Heinz divides its global operation into geographically based subdivisions because it does recognise the effects of cultural diversity and believes in 'local marketing' as the best means of fully understanding and serving its various markets. It is also important to note that any organisation segmenting purely on geographic grounds would be vulnerable to competition coming in with a more customer-focused segmentation strategy.

## Demographic segmentation

Demographic segmentation tells you a little more about the customer and the customer's household on measurable criteria that are largely descriptive, such as age, sex, race, income, occupation, socioeconomic status and family structure.

Demographics might even extend into classifications of body size and shape! It has been suggested that any male with a waist over 102 cm or female with a waist over 88 cm should consider it a warning of obesity. That amounts to an awful lot of people, especially in the UK, Germany and the USA, where the working classes are relatively affluent. Almost 1 in 10 adults in the UK alone are obese and are at risk of weight-related illness (Carter, 2010). That could be good news for some pharmaceutical and diet food manufacturers, but it presents a challenge to some other business sectors. Clothing retailers such as High and Mighty and Evans primarily target larger men and women respectively. Transport operators such as airlines and railways face big problems. Economy-class seats on many aircraft are around 26 inches wide which is pretty cramped, even for those of us who are not built along the lines of a Sumo wrestler! The increasing size of travellers as well as the bad publicity about deep-vein thrombosis being associated with sitting in cramped aircraft on long-haul flights is making airlines rethink their seating arrangements. Train operators are less concerned, however. In a push to cram more passengers into a carriage, modern rolling stock actually offers 6 inches less seat-room for commuters than carriages built in the 1970s (Bale, 2001).

# MARKETING IN ACTION

## An uplifting tale of a developing market

So, how do you segment the bra market? Clearly manufacturers are primarily (but not exclusively) (don't ask!) targeting women, but that is only the beginning. The British bra and lingerie company Gossard has found that a geographic approach to market segmentation can have some validity. The types of product that sell best in various countries are different, partly for the practical reason that women vary in average size across Europe, and partly because of cultural and lifestyle factors. Italian women want to be seductive and thus buy a lot of basques; the Germans are practical and look for support and quality; the French want to be fashionable and impress other women; and the Scandinavians want natural fibres. This is, of course, a grossly generalised survey, but the basic trends are there and give Gossard a basis for developing appropriate new products and strategies for different markets.

You might think that bra size is a useful segmentation variable that cuts across geographic boundaries, and indeed it is: the needs and priorities of larger women perhaps wanting to minimise the impact of their assets are very different from those of smaller women wanting to maximise them. The Wonderbra, for instance, was designed to target younger women, aged between 15 and 25, wanting a fashionable, fun and sexy bra that allows them to make the most of their assets. This appeal was reinforced by advertising slogans such as 'Hello, Boys', 'Mind If I Bring a Couple of Friends?' and 'In Your Dreams' alongside scantily clad, beautiful models. As part of the launch of a new range of D–G cup bras, a poster was created with a mosaic comprising around 8,000 photographs of cleavages forming a larger image of women. In addition, a viral campaign was run featuring Dita Von Teese in sexy underwear and that received 70,000 hits on YouTube within a few days. Even so, the marketers have to take into account more complex lifestyle issues as fashions change. Wonderbra's success is not just about the proportion of smaller-breasted women within the population but also the trend towards more revealing clothes and the desirability of cleavage.

It isn't that innovation in the market has stalled: Playtex, Wonderbra's main competitor in 2007 was the first manufacturer in the UK to launch half-cup-size bras. The MySize line is aimed at women aged over 35 to give a better fit in regular and half-size cups from A to D. This follows on from great success in the USA where the Playtex brand has grown by over 500 per cent since its re-launch in 2003. Wonderbra itself has focused on the Deep Plunge range, which is specifically designed to enhance current clothing fashions. Then there's the Wonderbra '3 Degrees of Hot' bra launched in the USA in 2010 with three push-up levels, 'Hot, Hotter and Sizzlin'. It's a convertible bra, with 100 different ways of wearing it. Aiming at a slightly older, more sophisticated consumer, Gossard launched the Super Smooth which, it claims, gives all the uplift of the Wonderbra but is unique because it has no seams, stitching or elastic. It is designed to be invisible under clothing so that the emphasis is on the effect of the bra rather than on the bra as a garment in its own right.

Lorna and her friends air their customised bras after undertaking the Playtex Moonwalk in London to raise money for breast cancer charities

*Source*: Lorna Young

Marketing managers within this market, however, do need to keep an eye on how the consumer profile is changing. Industry research has indicated that over the last 10 years or so, the average British bust size has increased from 34B to 36C or D, and nearly one-third of British women wear a D cup or larger. This is perhaps less than good news for Wonderbra, but excellent for companies like Bravissimo that specialise in larger sizes.

Nevertheless, underlying (or should that be underwiring?) all this is a remarkable consensus about the core features and benefits that women want from their bras. According to Gossard, 98 per cent want comfort (so what do the other 2 per cent want?!); 83 per cent consider underwear 'as a pleasure and enjoy the fancy and refined side of it'; 78 per cent want silhouette enhancement and 77 per cent want underwear that is invisible under clothing. So whatever you are looking for, whether it's frills, thrills or functionality, the right bra is out there somewhere.

*Sources*: Baker (2004); Bokaie (2007); Broadhead (1995); *Campaign* (2008); *Just-style* (2010); *Marketing Week* (2004a; 2004b); Sweney (2008); Wonderbra (2010); www.gossard.co.uk.

As with the geographic variable, demographics are relatively easy to define and measure, and the necessary information is often freely available from public sources. The main advantage, however, is that demographics offer a clear profile of the customer on criteria that can be worked into marketing strategies. For example, an age profile can provide a foundation for choice of advertising media and creative approach. Magazines, for instance, tend to have readerships that are clearly defined in terms of gender, age bands and socioeconomic groups. The under-thirty-five female reader, for example, is more likely to go for magazines such as *Heat*, *Chat* or *Look* than the over-thirty-fives who are more likely to read *My Weekly*, *Take a Break* or *Woman's Weekly*.

On the negative side, demographics are purely descriptive and, used alone, assume that all people in the same demographic group have similar needs and wants. This is not necessarily true (just think about the variety of people you know within your own age group).

Additionally, as with the geographic method, it is still vulnerable to competition coming in with an even more customer-focused segmentation strategy. It is best used, then, for products that have a clear bias towards a particular demographic group. For instance, cosmetics are initially segmented into male/female; baby products are primarily aimed at females aged between 20 and 35; financial services products to cover school fees appeal to households within a higher income bracket at a particular stage of the family lifecycle. In most of these cases, however, again as with the geographic method, the main use of demographic segmentation is as a foundation for other more customer-focused segmentation methods.

## Geodemographic segmentation

Geodemographics can be defined as 'the analysis of people by where they live' (Sleight, 1997, p. 16) as it combines geographic information with demographic and sometimes even lifestyle data (see below) about neighbourhoods. This helps organisations to understand where their customers are, to develop more detailed profiles of how those customers live, and to locate and target similar potential customers elsewhere. A geodemographic system, therefore, will define types of neighbourhood and types of consumer within a neighbourhood according to their characteristics.

A number of specialist companies, including Experian, offer geodemographic databases. Most of them are generally applicable to a range of consumer markets, although some are specifically designed for specific industries, and others have developed variations on the main database to suit different industries or geographic regions, or are tailored to suit a particular client company's needs.

Such systems are invaluable to the marketer across all aspects of consumer marketing, for example, in planning sampling areas for major market research studies, or assessing locations for new retail outlets, or finding appropriate areas for a direct mail campaign or door-to-door leaflet drop.

Example of a geodemographic profile: Experian™ Mosiac showing 'group' ('liberal opinions') and 'type' ('university fringe') and a list of the key features, rankings and top postal areas

*Source*: Experian™ Mosiac

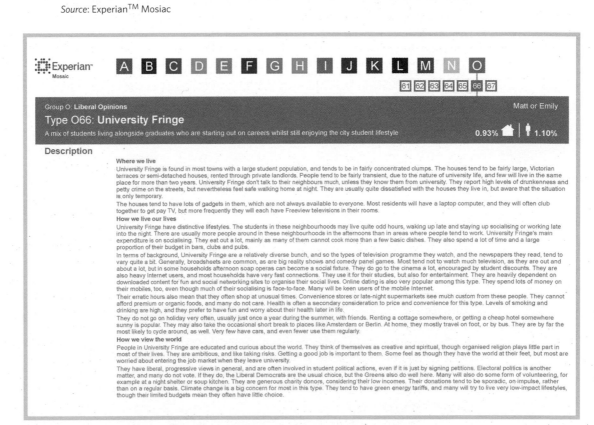

Continuation of the example of a geodemographic profile: Experian™ Mosiac with a detailed 'description' of the type and its 'behaviour'. Do you recognise yourself?

*Source*: Experian™ Mosiac

Door-to-door marketing has evolved still further in its ability to target individual homes. Blanket drops of product samples or sales literature have been used for some time by consumer goods marketers, but the increasing refinement of databases has led to more sophisticated targeting. TNT Post, a leading door-to-door drop company, uses data from Mosaic™ and other market research companies to identify those geodemographic neighbourhoods with a reasonable proportion of households relevant to its client's target audience. Within each neighbourhood postcode there are around 2,500 homes, and there are 8,900 postcodes in the UK. By adopting a micro-targeting system, units as small as 700 households can be identified to reflect differences in housing types even within a neighbourhood. This, matched with mailing lists and databases, enables cost-effective, better targeted door-to-door delivery (www.tntpost.co.uk/Doordrop_Media/index.html).

## Psychographic segmentation

Psychographics, or lifestyle segmentation, is an altogether more difficult area to define, as it involves intangible variables such as the beliefs, attitudes and opinions of the potential customer. It has evolved in answer to some of the shortcomings of the methods described above as a means of getting further under the skin of the customer as a thinking being. The idea is that defining the lifestyle of the consumer allows the marketer to sell the product not on superficial, functional features, but on benefits that can be seen to enhance that lifestyle on a much more emotional level. The term *lifestyle* is used in its widest sense to cover not only demographic characteristics, but also attitudes to life, beliefs and aspirations. Plummer (1974) was an early exponent of lifestyle segmentation, breaking it down into four main categories: activities, interests, opinions and demographics.

### Activities

The activities category includes all the things people do in the course of their lives. It therefore covers work, shopping, holidays and social life. Within that, the marketer will be interested in people's hobbies and their preferred forms of entertainment, as well as sports interests, club memberships and their activities within the community (voluntary work, for instance).

### Interests

Interests refers to what is important to the consumer and where their priorities lie. It may include the things very close to them, such as family, home and work, or their interest and involvement in the wider community. It may also include elements of leisure and recreation, and Plummer particularly mentions areas such as fashion, food and media.

### Opinions

The category of opinions comes very close to the individual's innermost thoughts, by probing attitudes and feelings about such things as themselves, social and cultural issues and politics. Opinion may also be sought about other influences on society, such as education, economics and business. Closer to home for the marketer, this category will also investigate opinions about products and the individual's view of the future, indicating how their needs and wants are likely to change.

### Demographics

Demographic descriptors have already been extensively covered, and this category includes the kinds of demographic elements you would expect, such as age, education, income and occupation, as well as family size, lifecycle stage and geographic location.

The growth of the consumer market in China is creating a challenge for marketers seeking to define segments within potentially the largest consumer groupings in the world. Research has suggested that there are four basic lifestyle orientations in China. Fashion-oriented consumers like to try new brands and products. They prefer fashionability over practicality, and are very sociable. They are strongly influenced by others' opinions and by advertising. They are, however, price-conscious and thus are likely to go for cheaper, fake branded products. Tradition-oriented consumers are also price-aware, but are not fashion-conscious. They are reluctant spenders, preferring cheaper domestic brands to foreign ones and only buying after careful thought. They are family-focused and prefer staying at home to having an active social life outside. Achievement-oriented consumers are the best educated of all the groups. They are self-confident and seek success, challenge and change. They are fashion-conscious but are not particularly price-sensitive, liking high quality brands. They can be impulsive buyers but are not swayed by others' opinions. Finally, moderate-oriented consumers do still have an affinity with traditional Chinese culture, but also embrace elements of modernisation and change without clearly belonging to any of the other three groups (www.sinomonitor.com).

By researching each of these categories thoroughly and carefully, the marketer can build up a very detailed and three-dimensional picture of the consumer. Building such profiles over very large groups of individuals can then allow the marketer to aggregate people with significant similarities in their profiles into named lifestyle segments. As you might expect, because lifestyles are so complex and the number of contributory variables so large, there is no single universally applicable typology of psychographic segments. Indeed, many different typologies have emerged over the years, emphasising different aspects of lifestyle, striving to provide a set of lifestyle segments that are either generally useful or designed for a specific commercial application.

Schoenwald (2001) highlighted some of the dangers in taking psychographic segmentation so far that the relationship between segment characteristics and brand performance becomes lost. Although it may be useful for identifying broad trends, segment boundaries can change as the market changes and some individuals may not fit categories easily or neatly, for example, being conservative on financial issues yet highly progressive when it comes to embracing high technology. Schoenwald reminds us that segmentation is a marketing tool for defining markets better and must, therefore, be actionable and not confusing.

Within the SEM, many organisations have been trying to produce lifestyle-based psychographic segment profiles that categorise the whole of Europe. One such study, carried out by Euro Panel and marketed in the UK by AGB Dialogue, was based on an exhaustive 150-page questionnaire administered across the EU, Switzerland and Scandinavia. The main research areas covered included demographic and economic factors, as well as attitudes, activities and feelings. Analysis of the questionnaire data allowed researchers to identify sixteen lifestyle segments based on two main axes, innovation/conservatism and idealism/materialism. The results also identified twenty or so key questions that were crucial to matching a respondent with an appropriate segment. These key questions were then put to a further 20,000 respondents, which then allowed the definition of 16 segments, including for example Euro-Citizen, Euro-Gentry, Euro-Moralist, Euro-Vigilante, Euro-Romantic and Euro-Business.

Despite the extent and depth of research that has gone into defining typologies such as these, they are still of somewhat limited use. When it comes to applying this material in a commercial marketing context, the marketer still needs to understand the underlying national factors that affect the buying decisions for a particular product.

Nevertheless, there are compelling reasons for such methods of segmentation being worth considering and persevering with, despite their difficulties. Primarily, they can open the door to a better-tailored, more subtle offering to the customer on all aspects of the marketing mix. This in turn can create a strong emotional bond between customer and product, making it more difficult for competitors to steal customers. Euro-segmentation adds a further dimension, in that it has the potential to create much larger and more profitable segments, assuming that the logistics of distribution allow geographically dispersed members of the segment to be reached cost effectively, and may thus create pan-European marketing opportunities.

The main problem, however, as we have seen, is that psychographic segments are very difficult and expensive to define and measure. Relevant information is much less likely to exist already in the public domain. It is also very easy to get the implementation wrong. For example, the organisation that tries to portray lifestyle elements within advertisements is depending on the audience's ability to interpret the symbols used in the desired way and to reach the desired conclusions from them. There are no guarantees of this, especially if the message is a complex one (more of this in Chapter 9). Additionally, the user of Euro-segments has to be very clear about allowing for national and cultural differences when trying to communicate on lifestyle elements.

In summary, psychographic segmentation works well in conjunction with demographic variables to refine further the offering to the customer, increasing its relevance and defendability against competition. It is also valuable for products that lean towards psychological rather than functional benefits for the customer, for instance perfumes, cars, clothing retailers, etc. For such a product to succeed, the marketer needs to create an image that convinces consumers that the product can either enhance their current lifestyle or help them to achieve their aspirations.

## Behaviour segmentation

All the categories of segmentation talked about so far are centred on the customer, leading to as detailed a profile of the individual as possible. Little mention has been made, however, of the individual's relationship with the product. This needs to be addressed, as it is quite possible that people with similar demographic and/or psychographic profiles may yet interact differently with the same product. Segmenting a market in these terms, therefore, is known as behaviour segmentation.

### End use

What is the product to be used for? The answer to this question has great implications for the whole marketing approach. Think about soup, for instance. This is a very versatile product with a range of potential uses, and a wide variety of brands and product lines have been developed, each of which appeals to a different usage segment. A shopper may well buy two or three different brands of soup, simply because the shopper's needs change according to intended use, for example, a dinner party or a snack meal. At this point, demographic and psychographic variables may become irrelevant (or at least secondary) if the practicalities of usage are so important to the customer. Table 4.2 defines some of the possible end uses of soup and gives examples of products available on the UK market to serve them.

Baxters offers a range of high quality soups with more interesting flavours

*Source*: Alamy Images/© studiomode

**Table 4.2** Usage segmentation in the soup market

| Use | Brand examples |
|---|---|
| Dinner-party starter | Baxter's Luxury soups; New Covent Garden soups |
| Warming snack | Heinz soups |
| Meal replacement | Heinz Big Soup |
| Recipe ingredient | Batchelor's condensed soup |
| Easy office lunch | Asda Soup to Go; Batchelor's Cup-a-Soups |

## Benefits sought

This variable can have more of a psychological slant than end usage and can link in very closely with both demographic and psychographic segments. In the case of a car, for example, the benefits sought may range from the practical ('reliable'; 'economic to run'; 'able to accommodate mum, dad, four kids, a granny, a wet dog and the remains of a picnic') to the more psychographically oriented ('environmentally friendly'; 'fast and mean'; 'overt status symbol'). Similarly, the benefits sought from a chilled ready meal might be 'ease of preparation', 'time saving', 'access to dishes I could not make myself', 'a reassuring standby in case I get home late one evening', and for the low-calorie and low-fat versions, 'a tasty and interesting variation on my diet!'. It is not difficult to see how defining some of these *benefit segments* can also indicate the kinds of demographic or lifestyle descriptors that apply to people wanting those benefits.

The business travel segment worldwide has long been a reliable and lucrative target for service providers. As the Chinese economy grows and trade opens up further, some providers are considering how best to serve the needs of business travellers, both domestic and international, visiting Chinese cities. One indigenous new entrant to this market has been particularly successful. Hanting Hotels was founded in Shanghai in 2005, and by the end of 2009 had around 250 hotels, with plans to open between 180 and 200 further outlets per year between 2010 and 2012, some directly operated, some under a franchise arrangement. In the first quarter of 2011 alone, the company opened 35 new hotels, including 16 directly operated ones and 19 franchises.

Hanting Hotels ('Your Home on the Journey') operates under three sub-brands, each targeting a slightly different segment. Hanting Seasons Hotels (priced between RMB 250 and 400 per room per night), Hanting Express Hotels (RMB 150–300) and Hanting Hi Inns (RMB 70–150). Broadly, the Hanting Seasons Hotels are targeting executive travellers; the Hanting Express Hotels target the more cost-conscious regular business traveller; while the Hanting Hi Inns are aiming more for the budget leisure traveller. By 2015, the aim is for the Hanting Express Hotels to be 80 per cent of the portfolio, with the other two sub-brands contributing about 10 per cent each. The regular business traveller can expect a clean, well-appointed room with a desk and internet access, a business centre and (in some hotels) meeting rooms and conference facilities rather than frills and pools! By focusing on specific segments and providing the particular benefits sought under a brand name that is recognisable from city to city, Hanting Hotels is well placed for expansion (*Bloomberg Business Week*, 2010; *China Industry Daily News*, 2011; China Lodging Group, 2010; *The Economist*, 2008).

## Usage rate

Not everyone who buys a particular product consumes it at the same rate. There will be heavy users, medium users and light users. Figure 4.1 shows the hypothetical categorisation of an organisation's customer base according to usage. In this case, 20 per cent of customers account for 60 per cent of the organisation's sales. This clearly raises questions for marketing strategies, for example should we put all our resources into defending our share of heavy users? Alternatives might be to make light users heavier; to target competitors' heavy users aggressively; or even to develop differentiated products for different usage rates (such as frequent-wash shampoo).

Again, this segmentation variable can best be used in conjunction with others to paint a much more three-dimensional picture of the target customer.

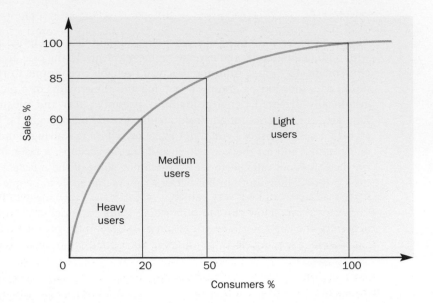

## Loyalty

As with usage rate, loyalty could be a useful mechanism, not only for developing detail in the segment profile, but also for developing a better understanding of which segmentation variables are significant. For instance a carefully thought-out market research exercise might help an organisation to profile 'loyal to us', 'loyal to them' and 'switchers', and then discover what other factors seem to differentiate between each of these groups. More specifically, Wind (1982) identified six loyalty segments as follows:

1  current loyal users who will continue to purchase the brand;
2  current customers who might switch brands or reduce consumption;
3  occasional users who might be persuaded to increase consumption with the right incentives;
4  occasional users who might decrease consumption because of competitors' offers;
5  non-users who might buy the brand if it was modified;
6  non-users with strong negative attitudes that are unlikely to change.

What is certain is that brand loyalty can be a fragile thing, and is under increasing threat. This is partly as a result of the greater number of alternative brands available and incentives or promotions designed by competitors to undermine customer loyalty. The most serious threat in the UK, however, has come from supermarket own-brands, many of which look uncannily like the equivalent manufacturer brands but undercut them on price. Consumers thus believe that the own-brands are just as good, if not identical, and are thus prepared to switch to them and to be more price sensitive.

Assuming that loyalty does exist, even a simple combination of usage rate and loyalty begins to make a difference to the organisation's marketing strategy. If, for example, a large group of heavy users who are also brand switchers was identified, then there is much to be gained from investing resources in a tightly focused marketing mix designed to turn them into heavy users who are loyal to a particular company.

## Attitude

Again, trespassing on the psychographic area, attitude looks at how the potential customer feels about the product (or the organisation). A set of customers who are already enthusiastic about a product, for example, require very different handling from a group that is downright hostile. A hostile group might need an opportunity to sample the product, along with an advertising campaign that addresses and answers the roots of their hostility. Attitude-based segments may be important in marketing charities or causes, or even in health education. Smokers who are hostile to the 'stop smoking' message will need different approaches from those who are amenable to the message and just need reassurance and practical support to put it into practice. Approaches aimed at the 'hostile' smoker have included fear ('look at these diseased lungs'), altruism ('what about your children?') and vanity (warning young women about the effect on their skin), but with little noticeable effect.

### The buyer-readiness stage

Buyer readiness can be a very valuable variable, particularly when one is thinking about the promotional mix. How close to purchasing is the potential customer? For example, at a very early stage the customer may not even be aware that the product exists and, therefore, to get that customer moving closer to purchase, the organisation needs to generate *awareness* of the product. Then there is a need for information to stimulate *interest* in the product. The customer's ability to understand and interpret that information may lead to *desire* for the product, which in turn stimulates *action*: the purchase itself. Figure 4.2 summarises this progression.

Behavioural segmentation, therefore, examines closely the relationship between the potential customer and the product, and there are a number of dimensions on which this can be done. Its main achievement is to bring the relationship between customer and product into sharper focus, thus providing greater understanding of the customer's specific needs and wants, leading to a better defined marketing mix. Another advantage of this kind of segmentation approach is that it provides opportunities for tailored marketing strategies to target brand switchers or to increase usage rates. All these benefits do justify the use of behavioural segmentation, as long as it does not lead to the organisation becoming product centred to the neglect of the customer's needs. The customer must still come first.

## Multivariable segmentation

As has been hinted throughout the previous sections, it is unlikely that any one segmentation variable will be used absolutely on its own. It is more common for marketers to use a multivariable segmentation approach, defining a 'portfolio' of relevant segmentation variables, some of which will be prosaic and descriptive while others will tend towards the psychographic, depending on the product and market in question. The market for adult soft drinks includes

**Figure 4.2**
The AIDA response hierarchy model

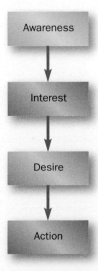

# MARKETING IN ACTION

## Marketing doesn't have to be meaty

You might think that the appropriate segmentation variable for meat-free foods is pretty obvious: it's vegetarians, isn't it? Well, while there is a core market comprising the 6 per cent of the UK population who are vegetarians, there is also a further 60 per cent of the population who eat meat-free meals occasionally and certainly do not see themselves as 'vegetarians'. It might also be reasonable to assume that the meat-free market is driven by ethical (i.e. animal welfare) or environmental (i.e. the resources consumed by meat production and questions around its sustainability) considerations, but actually, these issues motivate only a small proportion of the customer base. The overwhelming drivers are the quest for dietary variety, and health concerns leading to people cutting back on meat consumption and looking for 'lighter' meals.

For marketers, this opens up a range of potential segments within a meat-free market worth about £553 million. Mintel (2010b) has grouped the UK population into four broad segments:

- *Veg-lovers* (20 per cent of the adult population): this includes the 'real' vegetarians, but even so, most of this group enjoys a mixed diet with 40 per cent of them eating meat-free meals at least twice per week. They like cooking from scratch and are confident that they can produce a tasty meat-free meal. However, they are also the most likely to agree that there aren't enough vegetarian options in ready meals, and that if there was greater variety, they would to use them more. Their main motivation for going meat-free is health and a typical veg-lover could be a thirty-something woman from a middle-income household, with children aged between 10 and 15.
- *Gourmets* (25 per cent): these people are adventurous in their cooking, but are the least interested in cutting back on meat. Thirty per cent of them never eat meat-free foods. For those who do, the main motivation is dietary variety, and even then, they would rather cook just with vegetables than use meat substitutes. A typical gourmet could be a 16–24-year-old female student.
- *Traditionalists* (23 per cent): a typical 'traditionalist' might be an affluent male, aged over 50. He sees no need to cut back on meat and regards meat-based foods as better value for money than meat-free ones. About half never eat meat-free foods, and those who do are motivated by 'variety' rather than anything else. They have the most negative attitudes towards meat substitutes.
- *Meat-lovers* (32 per cent): these low-earning men from DE households have no time for meat-free foods, with two-thirds of them never touching the stuff. Those who do are again driven mainly by 'variety'. They don't cook much, and thus use a lot of ready meals but still wouldn't be inclined to try a meat-free version even if it looked tasty.

For the meat-free marketer, there are clear threats and opportunities suggested by these profiles. At one end of the spectrum, the meat-lovers are a lost cause, and at the other end, the veg-lovers represent the greatest opportunity. Those in between seem to have a 'take it or leave it' attitude that they will only engage with a meat-free product if has a strong, distinctive appeal – it needs to clearly communicate an offer of something that a meat-based alternative cannot, whether that's healthiness or variety. Ready meals comprise just under one-quarter of the meat-free market, and the 'variety' message in particular needs to be taken on board by that sector. If the 'gourmet' or the 'traditionalist' consumer is in the supermarket looking at a vegetarian lasagne, then they can make direct comparisons in terms of price with a meat-based equivalent and are likely to conclude that the meat-based version represents better value ('well, it's got more in it, hasn't it?'). This is borne out by research reported by Phillips (2011) which suggests that the meat-free market is losing those marginal consumers as recession bites and value for money becomes more of a priority.

Another issue in this market, according to Bainbridge (2011) is the perception that vegetarian food is bland and needs to be tastier and more exciting, which is consistent with the 'variety' motivation. This

The prize-winning pies

*Source*: Purple PR, www.lindamccartneyfoods.co.uk

insight might be what prompted Linda McCartney Foods to launch a high-profile advertising campaign to find 'the UK's tastiest meat-free dish' by inviting viewers to compete by submitting recipes. The recipe voted as the winner in an online poll was then turned into a product in the Linda McCartney range. With the intensive advertising campaign fronted by national treasure, Sir Paul McCartney, driving viewers to the company website, where there are lots of meat-free ideas, and with the most popular recipes then made available on YouTube (www.youtube.com/user/LindaMcCartneyFoods), there's much to appeal to the 'casual' vegetarian and perhaps to overcome some of the prejudices and barriers.

*Sources*: Bainbridge (2011); Baker (2011); Mintel (2010b); Phillips (2011); www.lindamccartneyfoods.co.uk/.

age segmentation along with some usage considerations (for example as a substitute for wine as a meal accompaniment), some benefit segmentation (healthy, refreshing, relaxing), and lifestyle elements of health consciousness, sophisticated imagery and a desire for exotic ingredients.

The emergence of geodemographics in recent years, as discussed at p. 138 *et seq.* above, is an indicator of the way in which segmentation is moving, that is, towards multivariable systems incorporating psychographics, demographics and geographics. These things are now possible and affordable, as Chapter 5 will show, because of increasingly sophisticated data collection mechanisms, developments in database creation and maintenance (see Chapter 11) and cheaper, more powerful and more accessible computing facilities. A properly managed database allows the marketer to go even further and to incorporate behavioural variables as the purchaser develops a trading history with a supplier. Thus the marketers are creeping ever closer to the individual consumer. The UK supermarkets that have developed and launched store loyalty cards that are swiped through the checkout so that the customer can accumulate points towards discounts, for example, are collecting incredibly detailed information about each individual shopper's profile. It tells them when we shop, how often, which branches of the store we tend to use, how much we spend per visit, the range of goods we buy, and the choices we make between own brands and manufacturer brands. The supermarkets can use this information to help them define meaningful segments for their own customer base, to further develop and improve their overall marketing mix or to make individually tailored offers to specific customers.

# Implementation of segmentation

This chapter so far has very freely used the phrase 'segmenting the market', but before segmentation can take place, there has to be some definition of the boundaries of that market. Any such definition really has to look at the world through the consumer's eyes, because the consumer makes decisions based on the evaluation of alternatives and substitutes. Thus a margarine manufacturer cannot restrict itself to thinking in terms of 'the margarine market', but has to take a wider view of 'the spreading-fats market' which will include butter and vegetable oil based products alongside margarine. This is because, generally speaking, all three of these product groups are contending for the same place on the nation's bread, and the consumer will develop attitudes and feelings towards a selection of brands across all three groups, perhaps through comparing price and product attributes (for example taste, spreadability, cooking versatility and health claims). This opens up a much wider competitive scene, as well as making the margarine manufacturer think more seriously about product positioning and about how and why consumers buy it.

This whole issue of market definition and its implications for segmentation comes back, yet again, to what should now be the familiar question of 'What business are we in?' It is a timely reminder that consumers basically buy solutions to problems, not products, and thus in defining market segments, the marketer should take into account any type of product that will provide a solution. Hence, we are not in 'the margarine market', but in the 'lubricating bread' market, which brings us back full circle to the inclusion of butter and vegetable oil based spreads as direct competitors.

It is still not enough to have gone through the interesting exercise of segmenting a market, however it is defined. How is that information going to be used by the organisation to develop marketing strategies? One decision that must be made is how many segments within the market the organisation intends to target. We look first at targeting.

## Targeting

There are three broad approaches available, summarised in Figure 4.3, and discussed in detail below.

**Figure 4.3**
Segmentation
targeting
strategies

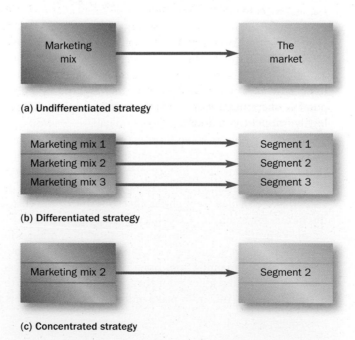

## Concentrated

The concentrated approach is the most focused approach of the three, and involves specialising in serving one specific segment. This can lead to very detailed knowledge of the target segment's needs and wants, with the added benefit that the organisation is seen as a specialist, giving it an advantage over its more mass-market competitors. This, however, carries a risk of complacency, leaving the organisation vulnerable to competitive entry into the segment.

In terms of management, concentration is attractive because costs are kept down, as there is only one marketing mix to manage, and there is still the potential for economies of scale. Strategically, the concentration of resources into one segment may lead to a stronger, more defendable position than that achievable by competitors which are spreading their effort more thinly. However, being a niche specialist may make it more difficult for an organisation to diversify into other segments, whether through lack of experience and knowledge, or through problems of acceptance arising from being identified with the original niche.

The benefits also need to be weighed against the other potential risks. First, all the organisation's eggs are in one basket, and if that segment fails, then there is no fallback position. The second risk is that if competitors see a rival establishing and clearly succeeding in a segment like this, then they may try to take some of it.

## Differentiated

As Figure 4.3 implies, a differentiated strategy involves the development of a number of individual marketing mixes, each of which serves a different segment. For example, Citroën manufactures a range of cars, covering a number of different segments, from the C1 at the bottom end of the price range (around £8,700 on the road), generally intended for the younger female driver, to the C6 in the higher price bracket (around £40,000), intended for the status-seeking executive.

As with the concentrated strategy, this approach does allow the organisation to tailor its offerings to suit the individual segments, thus maintaining satisfaction. It also overcomes one of the problems of concentration by spreading risk across the market, so that if one segment declines, the organisation still has revenue from others.

To be implemented properly, this approach requires a detailed overview of the market and how it is developing, perhaps leading to the early detection of new opportunities or emerging segments. This knowledge is valuable for an organisation with a healthy curiosity about its environment, but is acquired at a cost (in terms of both finance and managerial time). It also leads to increased costs in trying to manage the marketing mixes for a number of products, with possible diseconomies of scale.

Overall, a differentiated strategy dilutes the organisation's efforts through the thin spreading of resources. The organisation must, therefore, be very careful not to overreach itself in the number of segments it attempts to cover. Nevertheless, it can help an organisation to survive in highly competitive markets.

## Undifferentiated

The undifferentiated approach is the least demanding of the three approaches, in that it assumes that the market is one great homogeneous unit, with no significant differences between individuals within that market. Thus a single marketing mix is required that serves the needs of the entire market. The emphasis is likely, therefore, to be on developing mass communication, mass distribution and as wide an appeal as possible.

An undifferentiated approach does have some apparent advantages. It involves relatively low costs, as there is only one marketing mix that does not require the depth of research, fine tuning and updating that a concentrated or differentiated strategy would entail. It could also lead to the possible maximisation of economies of scale, because of having a single product in a potentially large market.

It is naive to hope that you can please everyone. What is likely to happen in reality is that some people will like your product offer more than others, and thus a segment (not of your own definition) will emerge by default. Because your product has not been tailored to that segment, it is unlikely to be exactly what that segment wants, and therefore any competitor who does target the segment more closely will attract those customers.

*eg*

There are very few fmcg markets that are truly undifferentiated, and while milk might at first glance appear to be a commodity, undifferentiated product, in an attempt to improve their margins, milk producers are going out of their way to build additional value into their products in a £3 billion market in the UK. There is organic milk, premium milk (for example filtered milk; low lactose milk; vitamin and omega 3 enriched milks), low fat milk, skimmed milk, etc. Then there is the packaging format, in plastic bottles of between 1 and 6 pints, glass bottles, cartons, and even in bags. If the focus is on the customer rather than the product, there are differences in lifestyle and the benefits sought which have given rise to different groupings. Increasingly, the health aspects have played an important part in consumer choice, for example with diet-conscious adults who perceive milk to be a high fat food but want to retain flavour moving towards 1 per cent fat milk rather than the somewhat bland and watery skimmed milk. Similarly, parents who see milk as an important source of children's nutrition have fuelled significant growth in ready-to-drink flavoured milk (for example, flavoured with chocolate, banana or strawberry, or those branded by and flavoured with chocolate bars such as Mars, Maltesers or Galaxy), which was worth around £160 million in 2010, and forecast to rise to £190 million by 2015. Thus there are numerous ways that different types of milk can be sold in different ways to consumers with different needs. Nevertheless, for every-day liquid milk, there's still some way to go in terms of differentiation through branding – half of consumers believe that supermarket own brand milk is just as good as the branded stuff, still regarding it as a commodity product (*The Grocer*, 2010; Mintel, 2010a; *The Sun*, 2010).

If an undifferentiated approach is possible at all, then it might best be suited for products with little psychological appeal. For example, petrol is essentially a very ordinary product that many of us purchase regularly but never even see (unless we are not very adept with a self-service pump). It makes the car go, regardless of whether it is a Rolls-Royce or a Lada and, traditionally, the only discriminating factor between brands has been price. Petrol retailers have now begun to create market segments, through the petrol itself (as with petrols with extra additives), through the extended product (providing car washes, mini-supermarkets, etc.), and also through strong corporate images that create brands and engender loyalty. All of this is moving the petrol retailers away from undifferentiated strategies.

Quite apart from the advantages and disadvantages connected with each of the alternative approaches above, there are a number of factors influencing the choice of targeting strategy. Marketing theory may well point to a particular strategy as being ideal, but if an organisation's resources cannot support and sustain that strategy, then an alternative must be found. A smaller organisation may, for example, need to adopt a concentrated strategy (perhaps based on a geographic segment in a consumer market, or on a specialist niche in a B2B market) to generate the growth required to allow a wider coverage of the market.

It is also important to make the choice of strategy in the context of the product itself. As has already been indicated, certain types of product lend themselves more readily to certain approaches, for example a product with many potential variations that involve a high level of psychological relationship with the customer (such as clothing or cosmetics) is better suited to a differentiated or concentrated approach. Other products with a more functional bias can be treated in a more undifferentiated way.

It must be reiterated, though, that undifferentiated approaches are becoming increasingly rare. Salt used to be held up to marketing students as the prime example of a commodity product sold in an undifferentiated way. Table 4.3 demonstrates how all that has changed.

**Table 4.3** Differentiation in the salt market

| | |
|---|---|
| ■ Table salt | ■ Iodised salt |
| ■ Cooking salt | ■ Low-sodium salt |
| ■ Sea salt | ■ Garlic salt |
| ■ Rock salt | ■ Celery salt *et cetera!* |
| ■ Alpine rock salt | |

The product's lifecycle stage (*see* Chapter 6 for a full definition of this concept) might also affect the choice of strategy. For example, an innovative new product, of which neither the industry nor the consumer has past experience, may first be marketed with an undifferentiated strategy in order to gain practical knowledge of the market's behaviour and reactions. It is very difficult to undertake meaningful market research in advance of launching such a new product, because the market may have problems conceptualising the product or putting it into context. It will be in the growth and maturity stages of the lifecycle that differentiated strategies will emerge as competitors enter the market and organisations learn from experience.

That last comment is a reminder that strategic decisions cannot be taken in isolation from the activities of the competition. If competitors are clearly implementing differentiated strategies, then it is dangerous for you to adopt a more dilute, undifferentiated approach. It may make more sense to identify the segments within which the competition is strong and then to assess whether it would be possible to attack them head-on in those segments or to find a different niche and make that your own. Thus competition is affecting not only the choice of approach, but the actual choice of segment(s) to target.

# MARKETING IN ACTION

## A little dish of love and goodness

A company that has adopted a concentrated strategy is Little Dish. It has created a new category in the baby/toddler food market: hand-made ready meals. It produces 'fresh, natural meals', such as spaghetti and meatballs, fish pie, and chicken and butternut squash pie, from the sort of ingredients that might be found in any kitchen cupboard, and very importantly, with no additives. Hillary Graves, the founder of the company, didn't like the idea that most ambient baby foods in bottles, jars and pouches have a shelf-life of about 18 months because they have been heat-treated to kill the bacteria. Unfortunately, this process also kills a lot of the natural taste of the food and destroys some of the vitamin content. Little Dish chilled meals have a short shelf-life, but are much more natural in content, appearance and flavour.

The target market appears to be largely middle-class, probably working mums, perhaps short of time or over-stretched, who want the convenience of a ready meal for their toddler, but feel guilty about it, as they are also concerned about their children's nutrition. The fact that the meals are handmade and indeed do not contain anything that a mum wouldn't use if she was making the same meal herself goes a long way to tacking the guilt issue.

The Little Dish website (www.littledish.co.uk) also gives an informal, reassuring family feel to the company, with a lot of quotes from customers that reinforce the targeting and positioning of the brand: 'As a full-time working mum, I find it difficult to cook from scratch, so this is perfect for my little ▶

one'; 'It's such a weight off our minds, if we have had a busy day and just need a quick dinner for Daisy, Little Dish meals are full of good for you yummy stuff and NO junk or hidden bad bits'; 'I just don't have the energy to cook and it makes such a nice change to find a quick and easy meal for my little girl which I trust entirely! . . . The fact that your meals are appealing and with no added nasties has really put my mind at rest'.

Hand-made, ready meals for babies and toddlers from Little Dish

*Source*: Little Dish, www.littledish.co.uk

As well as mainstream television advertising, and good PR coverage in relevant parenting and mother and baby magazines, Little Dish also believes in the effectiveness of face-to-face marketing. It has recruited a team of 'community leaders', all mums with toddlers, around the UK who spend around 10 hours per week organising product tastings and visiting nurseries and toddler groups. Clearly, for a potential customer, the impact of talking directly to a 'mum just like me' and getting to sample the products is very powerful, particularly when it is aligned with a company and a brand that have evolved from a mother's own concern and needs, rather than being the product of a corporate monolith, and is focused first and foremost on the nutritional welfare of toddlers. It obviously works, with Little Dish feeding around 100,000 children per week and generating a turnover of some £7 million in 2010. As Ursell (2010) puts it, 'Clearly, home-cooked food is the gold standard, because rustling up dinner for your children is, after all, an act of love as well as a provision of sustenance and good nutrition, but fresh versions of baby and toddler meals hitting the chill cabinets means that "cheating" no longer needs to come with such a big guilt trip.'

*Sources*: Kuchler (2010); Mintel (2011); Ursell (2010); www.littledish.co.uk.

## Benefits of segmentation

The previous sections of this chapter should at least have served to show that market segmentation is a complex and dangerous activity, in the sense that the process of choosing variables, their measurement and their implementation leaves plenty of scope for poor management and disappointment. Nevertheless, there are few, if any, markets in which segmentation has no role to play, and it is important to remember the potential benefits to be gained, whether looking at the customer, the marketing mix or the competition.

### The customer

The obvious gain to customers is that they can find products that seem to fit more closely with what they want. These needs and wants, remember, are not only related to product function, but also to psychological fulfilment. Customers may feel that a particular supplier is more sympathetic towards them, or is speaking more directly to them, and therefore they will be more responsive and eventually more loyal to that supplier. The organisation that fails to segment deeply enough on significant criteria will lose custom to competitors that do.

## The marketing mix

This is a timely reminder that the marketing mix should itself be a product of understanding the customer. Market segmentation helps the organisation to target its marketing mix more closely on the potential customer, and thus to meet the customer's needs and wants more exactly. Segmentation helps to define shopping habits (in terms of place, frequency and volume), price sensitivity, required product benefits and features, as well as laying the foundations for advertising and promotional decisions. The customer is at the core of all decisions relating to the 4Ps, and those decisions will be both easier to make and more consistent with each other if a clear and detailed definition of the target segments exists.

In the same vein, segmentation can also help the organisation to allocate its resources more efficiently. If a segment is well defined, then the organisation will have sufficient understanding to develop very precise marketing objectives and an accompanying strategy to achieve them, with a minimum of wastage. The organisation is doing neither more nor less than it needs to do in order to satisfy the customer's needs and wants.

This level of understanding of segments that exist in the market also forms a very sound foundation for strategic decisions. The organisation can prioritise across segments in line with its resources, objectives and desired position within the market.

## The competition

Finally, the use of segmentation will help the organisation to achieve a better understanding of itself and the environment within which it exists. By looking outwards, to the customer, the organisation has to ask itself some very difficult questions about its capacity to serve that customer better than the competition. Also, by analysing the competitors' offerings in the context of the customer, the organisation should begin to appreciate the competition's real strengths and weaknesses, as well as identifying gaps in the market.

## The dangers of segmentation

The benefits of segmentation need to be balanced against the dangers inherent in it. Some of these, such as the risks of poor definition and implementation of psychographic segmentation, have already been mentioned.

Jenkins and McDonald (1997) raise more fundamental concerns with market segmentation processes that are not grounded in the capabilities of the organisation. To them, there needs to be more focus on how organisations *should* segment their markets rather than a focus on how to segment using the range of variables mentioned earlier in this chapter. To decide on the 'should' means having an understanding of the organisation, its culture, its operating processes and structure which all influence the view of the market and how it could be segmented (Piercy and Morgan, 1993).

Other dangers are connected with the essence of segmentation: breaking markets down into ever smaller segments. Where should it stop? Catering for the differing needs of a large number of segments can lead to fragmentation of the market, with additional problems arising from the loss of economies of scale (through shorter production runs or loss of bulk purchasing discounts on raw materials, for instance), as mentioned at p. 149 above. Detail needs to be balanced against viability.

Within the market as a whole, if there are a number of organisations in direct competition for a number of segments, then the potential proliferation of brands may simply serve to confuse the customer. Imagine five competitors each trying to compete in five market segments. That gives the customer 25 brands to sort out. Even if customers can find their way through the maze of brands, the administration and marketing difficulties involved in getting those brands on to the supermarket shelves can be very costly.

## Criteria for successful segmentation

Cutting through the detail of how to segment, and regardless of the complexities of segmentation in different types of market, are four absolute requirements for any successful segmentation exercise. Unless these four conditions prevail, the exercise will either look good on paper but be impossible to implement, or fail to deliver any marked strategic advantage.

## Distinctiveness

Any segment defined has to be *distinctive*, that is, significantly different from any other segment. The basis of that difference depends on the type of product or the circumstances prevailing in the market at the time. It may be rooted in any of the segmentation variables discussed above, whether geographic, demographic or psychographic. Note too the use of the word *significant*. The choice of segmentation variables has to be relevant to the product in question.

Without a significant difference, segment boundaries become too blurred, and there is a risk that an organisation's offerings will not be sufficiently well tailored to attract the required customers.

## Tangibility

It must be remembered that distinctiveness can be taken too far. Too much detail in segmentation, without sound commercial reasoning behind it, leads to fragmentation of effort and inefficiency. A defined segment, therefore, must be of a sufficient size to make its pursuit worthwhile. Again, the notion of size here is somewhat vague. For fmcg goods, viable *size* may entail many thousands of customers purchasing many tens of thousands of units, but in a B2B market, it may entail a handful of customers purchasing a handful of units.

Proving that a segment actually exists is also important. Analysis of a market may indicate that there is a gap that existing products do not appear to fill, whether defined in terms of the product itself or the customer profile. The next stage is to ask why that gap is there. Is it because no organisation has yet got round to filling it, or because the segment in that gap is too small to be commercially viable? Does that segment even exist, or are you segmenting in too much detail and creating opportunities on paper that will not work in practice?

## Accessibility

As well as existing, a defined segment has to be *accessible*. The first aspect of this is connected with distribution. An organisation has to be able to find the means of delivering its goods and services to the customer, but this may not be so easy, for example, for a small organisation targeting a geographically spread segment with a low-priced infrequently purchased product. Issues of access may then become an extension of the segment profile, perhaps limiting the segment to those customers within a defined catchment area, or those who are prepared to order direct through particular media. Whatever the solution to problems of access, it does mean that the potential size of the segment has to be reassessed.

The second aspect of access is communication. Certain customers may be very difficult to make contact with, and if the promotional message cannot be communicated, then the chances of capturing those customers are much slimmer. Again, the segment profile may have to be extended to cover the media most likely to access those customers, and again, this will lead to a smaller segment.

## Defendability

In talking about targeting strategies at p. 148 *et seq.* above, one of the recurrent themes was that of the competition. Even with a concentrated strategy, targeting only one segment, there is a risk of competitors poaching customers. In defining and choosing segments, therefore, it is important to consider whether the organisation can develop a sufficiently strong differential advantage to defend its presence in that segment against competitive incursions.

## B2B markets

Most of the above discussion has centred on consumer markets. With specific reference to B2B markets, Hlavacek and Ames (1986) propose a similar set of criteria for good segmentation practice. They suggest, for example, that each segment should be characterised by a common set of customer requirements, and that customer requirements and characteristics should be measurable. Segments should have identifiable competition, but be small enough to allow the supplier to reduce the competitive threat, or to build a defendable position against competition. In strategic terms, Hlavacek and Ames also propose that the members of a segment should have some logistical characteristic in common, for example that they are served by the same kind of distribution channel, or the same kind of sales effort. Finally, the critical success factors for each segment should be defined, and the supplier should ensure that it has the skills, assets and capabilities to meet the segment's needs, and to sustain that in the future.

## Chapter summary

This chapter has focused on the complexities and methods involved in dividing markets into relevant, manageable and targetable segments in order to allow better-tailored offerings to be developed.

- In B2B markets, segmentation techniques are divided into macro and micro variables or bases. Macro variables include both organisational characteristics, such as size, location and purchasing patterns, and product or service applications, defining the ways in which the product or service is used by the buyer. Micro segmentation variables lead to the definition, in some cases, of segments of one customer, and focus on the buyer's management philosophy, decision-making structures, purchasing policies and strategies, as well as needs and wants.

- In consumer markets, five main categories of segmentation are defined: geographic, demographic, geodemographic, psychographic and behaviour based. Between them, they cover a full range of characteristics, whether descriptive, measurable, tangible or intangible, relating to the buyer, the buyer's lifestyle and the buyer's relationship with the product. In practice, a multivariable approach to segmentation is likely to be implemented, defining a portfolio of relevant characteristics from all categories to suit the market under consideration.

- The implications of segmentation are wide reaching. It forms the basis for strategic thinking, in terms of the choice of segment(s) to target in order to achieve internal and competitive objectives. The possibilities range from a niche strategy, specialising in only one segment, to a differentiated strategy, targeting two or more segments with different marketing mixes. The undifferentiated strategy, hoping to cover the whole market with only one marketing mix, is becoming increasingly less appropriate as consumers become more demanding, and although it does appear to ease the managerial burden, it is very vulnerable to focused competition.

- Segmentation offers a number of benefits to both the consumer and the organisation. Consumers get an offering that is better tailored to their specific needs, as well as the satisfaction of feeling that the market is offering them a wider range of products to choose from. The organisation is more likely to engender customer loyalty because of the tailored offering, as well as the benefits of more efficient resource allocation and improved knowledge of the market. The organisation can also use its segmentation as a basis for building a strong competitive edge, by understanding its customers on a deeper psychological level and reflecting that in its marketing mix(es). This forms bonds between organisation/product and customer that are very difficult for competition to break. There are, however, dangers in segmentation, if it is not done well. Poor definition of segments, inappropriate choice of key variables or poor analysis and implementation of the outcomes of a segmentation exercise can all be disastrous. There is also the danger that if competing marketers become too enthusiastic in trying to 'outsegment' each other, the market will fragment to an unviable extent and consumers will become confused by the variety of choice open to them.

- On balance, segmentation is a good and necessary activity in any market, whether it is a mass fmcg market of international proportions, or a select B2B market involving two or three well-known customers. In either case, any segment defined has to be distinctive (i.e. features at least one characteristic pulling it away from the rest that can be used to create a focused marketing mix), tangible (i.e. commercially viable), accessible (i.e. both the product and the promotional mix can reach it) and finally, defendable (i.e. against competition).

# Questions for review and discussion

**4.1** How might the market for personal computers, sold to B2B markets, be segmented?

**4.2** Find examples of products that depend strongly on *demographic segmentation*, making sure that you find at least one example for each of the main demographic variables.

**4.3** What is *psychographic segmentation* and why is it so difficult and so risky to do?

**4.4** In what major way does *behavioural segmentation* differ from the other methods? Outline the variables that can be used in behavioural segmentation.

**4.5** For each *targeting strategy*, find examples of organisations that use it. Discuss why you think they have chosen this strategy and how they implement it.

**4.6** How can *market segmentation* influence decisions about the marketing mix?

# THE COLOUR OF MONEY: IS THE 'PINK POUND' ANY DIFFERENT?

Although gay culture has increasingly become part of the mainstream, with many more openly gay celebrities and gay themes and characters featuring regularly in television dramas and comedies, it is still very difficult to estimate the size of the gay population in the UK. Mintel (2006), for example, suggests that 2–3 per cent of the UK population is gay, while Stonewall (2010) suggests that it is over 6 per cent. As Norman (2010) points out, however, people (particularly those from the lower socioeconomic groups) are still very shy of discussing their sexuality with researchers, which makes it extremely difficult to get an accurate picture.

There is some consensus on the characteristics of the gay market, however. Gay consumers are perceived to have a higher than average income of over £31,000, and are more likely to live in urban areas. Estimates of their spending power also vary, but the 'pink pound' is estimated to be worth over £80 billion (Stonewall, 2010). Those who are cohabiting are likely to be in dual-income households, and are less likely to have dependants. This gives gay consumers more opportunities for lifestyle spending with a strong focus on leisure and socialising, with significant spending on holidays (£3 billion), clothes (£1.9 billion) and CDs/DVDs (£1.6 billion) (*Management Today*, 2008).

There is plenty of opportunity for reaching the gay market. *New Media Age* (2009) reported that 93 per cent of gays use the internet every day, a much higher proportion than the national average. Research has also indicated that they spend up to ten times longer online than the average internet user, are more likely to buy the latest gadgets and are particularly appreciative of those organisations that reach out to communicate with them. The internet is important, in that it allows gay people to build a stronger sense of community and it gives marketers a chance to locate and target the gay market efficiently and discreetly. The average household income of the gay internet user is £38,000 (*New Media Age*, 2009), and there are, of course, many websites set up specifically for online gays, attracting mainstream advertisers, such as British Airways, Vodafone and American Express, as well as companies specifically targeting the gay community.

In the travel market the openly gay segment is only a small proportion of the market. Mintel (2006) found that there were 1.25 million overseas holidays taken by gay people in 2006 but only a small proportion of those were booked with gay-specific travel suppliers or to 'gay destinations'. As society's attitudes continue to become more relaxed, Mintel expects there to be increasingly less demand for gay tourism as a sector in its own right. The preferred holiday activities for gay consumers, and the benefits sought are much the same as anybody else's: relaxation, sightseeing, relaxing on a beach, eating and drinking. Nevertheless, tour operators are still acutely aware of the needs of gay holidaymakers. Thomson holidays, for example, has its Thomson Freedom brochure which features gay-friendly resorts, and accommodation that is GayComfort certified (with a few hotels that are exclusively gay) so that gay couples can be sure that hotel staff have been properly trained in dealing with gay guests and there will be no awkward or embarrassing moments. The brochure also features package holidays to gay festivals and civil ceremony packages (www.thomson.co.uk/brochures/freedom.html).

Thomson has a point here – even if a gay couple is not looking for an explicitly gay holiday, they still want the reassurance that they will be welcome at the resort and the hotel they choose to go to. The tourism authority in Kraków, Poland wanted to target gay tourists, but this caused widespread concern among Catholic associations – a vociferous force to be reckoned with in Poland. One is reported to have said, 'we don't want drunken Britons getting their genitals out in public, but we don't want gays performing public obscenities either' (as quoted by Davies, 2008). Even the word 'gay' had to be dropped from the tourism literature. However, business interests are fighting back with hotels, pub and club owners broadening their offers with special online sections promoting gay tourism and pursuing that lucrative pink pound. Compared with stag-nighters from the UK who 'pack themselves into the car, vomit out of the windows, and run off without paying', according to one taxi driver, the gay community is much more refined (Davies, 2008). For those gay travellers looking for something a little more active, Neilson Adventures is offering a range of adventure holidays, called 'Out', to destinations such as the Himalayas and Peru. All the elements of the trips have been carefully chosen or designed to be gay-friendly (*Travel Trade Gazette*, 2011).

Many mainstream companies have still not realised the potential of the gay market. They say, however, that they target all groups, not just niche markets, and besides that, they can reach the same audience through mainstream media. In their view, many gays' purchasing decisions are made using the same criteria as those of heterosexual consumers. In short, there are no differences in buyer behaviour. Companies, however, could be missing out. Some 60 per cent of gays say that they are more likely to buy products from a company that they perceive to be gay-friendly, and over half are more likely to buy from a company that uses imagery of gay people in its advertising (Stonewall, 2010).

In 2009, Lloyds TSB used an advertisement for financial services which featured a gay couple in the mainstream media. This was very positively received within the gay community, generating a lot of good PR within 'pink' news media. The imagery in the Lloyds TSB advertisement was clear, particularly because it included the statement that 'Lloyds TSB is pleased to help our LGBT [lesbian, gay, bisexual and transgender] customers with their savings needs', but it did not offend the mainstream market nor did it detract from the core message about the product itself.

Not all advertisers are that subtle, however. Heinz produced a television advertisement showing two men kissing as part of a Deli Mayo ad. The trouble was that the vast majority of British parents did not want to their children to see two guys kissing, and did not want the potential embarrassment of having to answer awkward questions about homosexuality because of it. Within a week of it first being broadcast, it was withdrawn after a barrage of complaints to the ASA (Lovell, 2008), although the ASA subsequently ruled that the ad was not offensive. This caused even more controversy for Heinz, as the gay community was then outraged at it being pulled, petitions were submitted and a boycott of Heinz products was called for. Was it naïve of Heinz to approve the advertisement in the first place or was it a cynical device to generate a lot of publicity?

Companies may wish to target the gay segment in their advertising

*Source*: Alamy Images/© Queerstock, Inc.

For organisations looking to target the gay consumer, there is an increasing range of specialist gay online and print media available in addition to the mainstream channels. Gay media offer access to a very attractive and affluent segment, particularly for marketers of upmarket and/or leisure-oriented brands. *Diva*, for example, is a monthly magazine for lesbian and bisexual women. It has a readership of 145,000, 98 per cent of whom are female, and two-thirds of whom are aged between 25 and 44. In socioeconomic terms, it's predominantly an ABC1 readership, with an average full-time income of nearly £25,000 (compared with a national average of £18,500 for women). Similarly, *Gay Times's* core buyer is 'male, aged 25–44, well educated and in a managerial/senior position, with earnings considerably above the national average. He lives in privately owned accommodation alone or with a partner. He is confident, independent, politically aware, brand-loyal, and spends his disposable income on leisure activities, travel, communication and home entertainment' (*Gay Times*, 2010).

While gay media do reach a significant audience, it is still just a subsegment of the total gay population and as the profiles above show, sexual orientation alone is not sufficient for profiling for marketing purposes. Some brands are still wary of societal attitudes and don't want to be to closely associated with what they see as a minority group. Others, however, take a more market-oriented view, arguing that other demographic and attitudinal profiles that gay people share with the non-gay audience are more significant; sexual orientation is just one of the segmentation variables and is probably secondary to income and lifestyle. As one advertising agency put it, 'The suggestion of treating gay men, lesbians, bisexuals and transgender individuals as one group is laughable. Even within gay men, you will find some very clear demographic and attitudinal groups' (as quoted by Murphy, 2008).

Some advertisers, such as Ford cars, will thus see gay media as just another communication channel alongside others, as part of a strategy to reach a lifestyle segment whose sexuality is not their main defining feature. Campaigns by brands such as Armani and Gaultier appeal to a particular lifestyle segment, allowing the audience, whatever its sexual orientation, to associate with the advertising. Some might also use both gay and non-gay media to target a broad market, but tailor their advertising messages in the gay media to resonate more with that particular audience, and then there are those, such as Lloyds TSB (as mentioned above), which use gay imagery in mainstream media.

And for the future? One consultancy firm takes the view that because of the introduction of civil partnerships and the general softening of societal views towards the gay community:

> What you're going to see [in society] is a lot more gay couples settling down to a relatively traditional conservative life of shopping at Sainsbury's and trying to get their kids into the best school. The traditional areas [targeting the gay community] have been entertainment and luxuries, but you're going to see the pink pound diverted into more traditional family commodities; so, for example, family cars as opposed to sports cars. The pink pound is being slightly diverted from the more fun aspects that are traditionally associated with gay culture. (as quoted by Costa, 2010).

This suggests that perhaps many more mainstream marketers are going to have to start being a lot more inclusive in defining their target markets.

*Sources*: Costa (2010); Davies (2008); *Gay Times* (2010); Lovell (2008); *Management Today* (2008); Mintel (2006); Murphy (2008); *New Media Age* (2009); Norman (2010); Stonewall (2010); *Travel Trade Gazette* (2011); www.neilson-adventures.co.uk/.

## Questions

1 To what extent does the gay segment conform to the criteria for successful segmentation?

2 What segmentation bases are relevant to the gay holiday market?

3 What are the risks and rewards for a mainstream company targeting the gay segment?

## References for chapter 4

Abratt, R. (1993) 'Market Segmentation Practices of Industrial Marketers', *Industrial Marketing Management*, 22, pp. 79–84.

Bainbridge (2011) 'Not Just for Veggies', *Marketing*, 2 February.

Baker, L. (2004) 'Size Does Matter', *The Guardian*, 6 August, p. 6.

Baker, R. (2011) 'Linda McCartney to Return to TV after 15 Years', *Marketing Week*, 15 March.

Bale, J. (2001) 'Seats Built for Those that Travel Light', *The Times*, 15 February.

*Bloomberg Business Week* (2010) 'Hanting Inns to Open Up to 600 Hotels by End-2012', 6 April. Accessed via http://investing.businessweek.com/research/stocks/private/snapshot.asp?privcapId=33879031.

Bokaie, J. (2007) 'Playtex Develops Range of Bras in Half-cup Sizes', *Marketing*, 28 February, p. 5.

Broadhead, S. (1995) 'European Cup Winners', *Sunday Express*, 7 May, p. 31.

*Campaign* (2008) 'Wonderbra Unveils Cleavage Collage Poster Campaign', *Campaign*, 15 August, p. 6.

Carter, H. (2010) 'Diabetes and Obesity Rates Soar to "Shocking" Levels', *The Guardian*, 25 October.

*China Industry Daily News* (2011) 'HanTing Hotels Posts RMB 14 Mln in Net Loss in Q1', *China Industry Daily News*, 11 May.

China Lodging Group (2010) *China Lodging Group Ltd. Investor Presentation August 2010*. Accessed via http://ir.htinns.com/corporate_presentation.cfm.

Costa, M-L. (2010) 'Pink Pound's Value Rises in Mainstream Markets', *Marketing Week*, 4 November.

Davies, H. (2008) 'Kraków Caught Between Pink Pound and Boozy Brits', *The Observer*, 17 August.

Douglas, S.P. and Craig, C.S. (1983) *International Marketing Research*, Prentice-Hall.

*The Economist* (2008) 'Room at the Inn', *The Economist*, 26 January, p. 64.

*Gay Times* (2010) 'GT Media Solutions, 2010', pdf file accessed via BRAD at www.bradinsight.com/bradv2/Member/TitlePage.aspx?titleId=4085.

*The Grocer* (2010) 'UK's First 1% Fat Organic Milk', *The Grocer*, 27 February, pp. 34–5.

Harlow, J. (2007) 'Segmenting for Success', *Brand Strategy*, Dec/Jan, p. 11.

Harrington, R. and Tjan, A. (2008) 'Transforming Strategy One Customer at a Time', *Harvard Business Review*, March, pp. 62–72.

Hlavacek, J.D. and Ames, B.C. (1986) 'Segmenting Industrial and High Tech Markets', *Journal of Business Strategy*, 7 (2), pp. 39–50.

Jenkins, M. and McDonald, M. (1997) 'Market Segmentation: Organizational Archetypes and Research Agendas', *European Journal of Marketing*, 31 (1), pp. 17–32.

*Just-style* (2010) 'Wonderbra Launches "Three Degrees" Convertible Bra', *Just-style*, 27 July. Accessed via www.just-style.com/news/wonderbra-launches-three-degrees-convertible-bra_id108430.aspx.

Kuchler, H. (2010) 'Direct Sellers Thrive on Back of Recession', *Financial Times*, 8 May.

Lovell, C. (2008) 'Should Heinz Have Axed "Gay Kiss" Ad?', *Campaign*, 4 July.

*Management Today* (2008) 'Stat of the Month: Gay Abandon', *Management Today*, 1 August.

*Marketing Week* (2004a) 'Can Beattie Bring Subtlety to Gossard?', *Marketing Week*, 22 July, p. 25.

*Marketing Week* (2004b) 'Playtex Reveals Wonderbra Range Designed for Risqué Tops', *Marketing Week*, 5 August, p. 10.

Mintel (2006) 'Gay Travel', *Mintel Market Intelligence*, December, accessed via http://academic.mintel.com/sinatra/oxygen_academic/search_results/show&/display/id=173628/display/id=173628/display/id=249274/display/id=173628/display/id=249286?select_section=173628.

Mintel (2010a) 'Milk and Cream', *Mintel Food UK*, May. Accessed via http://academic.mintel.com/sinatra/oxygen_academic/search_results/show&/display/id=480772/display/id=525930/display/id=525936?select_section=480772.

Mintel (2010b) 'Meat-free Foods', *Mintel Market Intelligence*, December, accessed via http://academic.mintel.com/sinatra/oxygen_academic/search_results/show&/display/id=480957.

Mintel (2011) 'Baby Food and Drink', *Mintel Market Intelligence*, June, accessed via http://academic.mintel.com/sinatra/oxygen_academic/my_reports/display/id=545250&anchor=atom#atom0.

Moriarty, R. and Reibstein, D. (1986) 'Benefit Segmentation in Industrial Markets', *Journal of Business Research*, 14 (6), pp. 463–86.

Murphy, C. (2008) 'The New Demographics: Gay Groups', *Campaign*, 3 October.

*New Media Age* (2009) 'Brands Failing to Seize Online Opportunities to Target the Gay Market', *New Media Age*, 16 April.

Norman, M. (2010) 'Come Out, Come Out, Wherever You Are', *Daily Telegraph*, 25 September.

O'Flaherty, K. (2009) 'Orange Goes Bananas for Mobile Advertising', *Mobile*, 7 August.

Phillips, B. (2011) 'Veggie Brands Feel the Pinch', *The Grocer*, 29 January.

Piercy, N. and Morgan, N. (1993) 'Strategic and Operational Market Segmentation: a Managerial Analysis', *Journal of Strategic Marketing*, 1, pp. 123–40.

Plummer, J.T. (1974) 'The Concept and Application of Lifestyle Segmentation', *Journal of Marketing*, 38 (January), pp. 33–7.

Schoenwald, M. (2001) 'Psychographic Segmentation: Used or Abused', *Brandweek*, 22 January, pp. 34–8.

Sleight, P. (1997) *Targeting Customers: How to Use Geodemographic and Lifestyle Data in Your Business*, 2nd edn, NTC Publications.

Smith, W.R. (1957) 'Product Differentiation and Market Segmentation as Alternative Marketing Strategies', *Journal of Marketing*, 21 (July).

Stonewall (2010) *Marketing: How to Market to Gay Consumers*, Stonewall Workplace Guides, accessed via www.stonewall.org.uk/at_work/research_and_guides/4907.asp.

*The Sun* (2010) 'Bagging a Bargain', *The Sun*, 11 August, p. 13.

Sweney, M. (2008) 'Wonderbra Billboard Ad Features Shots of Thousands of Women', *The Guardian*, 11 August.

*Travel Trade Gazette* (2011) 'Neilson Sets "Out" for Gay Market', *Travel Trade Gazette*, 8 April.

Ursell, A. (2010) 'No Meal Should be Older than Your Baby', *The Times*, 22 June.

Wedel, M. and Kamakura, W. (1999), *Market Segmentation: Conceptual and Methodological Foundations*, Dordrecht: Kluwer.

Wind, Y. (1978) 'Issues and Advances in Segmentation Research', *Journal of Marketing Research*, 15 (3), pp. 317–37.

Wind, Y. (1982) *Product Policy and Concepts*, Methods and Strategy, Addison-Wesley.

Wind, Y. and Cardozo, R. (1974) 'Industrial Marketing Segmentation', *Industrial Marketing Management*, 3 (March), pp. 153–66.

Wonderbra (2010) 'The Wonderbra Brand Turns up the Heat with its 3 Degrees of Hot Ultimate Convertible Bra', Wonderbra Press Release, accessed via www.wonderbrausa.com/thelatest/PressReleases.aspx.

# CHAPTER 5

# Marketing information and research

## LEARNING OBJECTIVES

This chapter will help you to:

- recognise the importance of information to an organisation and the role information plays in effective marketing decision-making;

- understand the role of a marketing information system and a decision support system, and develop an awareness of the various types of information available;

- become familiar with the various steps involved in the marketing research process;

- outline the sources of secondary and primary data, understand their role and the issues involved in their collection and analysis; and

- appreciate some of the ethical concerns surrounding marketing research.

## INTRODUCTION

**THE NATURE AND ROLE** of market research in Europe have seen significant changes in recent years, as organisations increasingly look to do business in a wider range of EU and global markets. Global expenditure on market research was nearly US$29 billion in 2009, 46 per cent of which was spent in Europe and 32 per cent in the USA. Although (after adjustment for inflation) this global expenditure represents a decline compared with 2008, it is interesting to note that expenditure in the Asia Pacific region declined less than other parts of the world. Indeed, expenditure in the emerging markets of India and China actually increased, as companies strive to understand new markets and audiences for their products and services. In established regions, they have to devise ever more competitive strategies to succeed with a highly marketing-literate population, hence, the high proportion of global expenditure that is spent in the USA and Europe (Korczak, 2011; Verrinder, 2010). Whether organisations are concerned with breaking into developing markets, or maintaining or expanding their business within more established markets, the need to have effective information on those markets is essential to inform decisions on the most appropriate market entry and competitive strategies. To support all this, the organisation also needs a properly designed and managed information system to enable timely and appropriate information to be available for the marketing decision-maker (www.esomar.com).

Every aspect of marketing considered in this book, including the definition of markets and market segments, the formulation of an integrated strategy based on the 4Ps and planning and control mechanisms, requires the collection and analysis of information. The better the planning, data collection, information management and analysis, the more reliable and useful the outputs become, and thus marketers are able to make decisions that are more likely to satisfy the needs and wants of selected market segments. The organisation that is prepared to contemplate making a significant change to its marketing effort, without first assessing likely market reaction, is running a very high risk of failure.

In general, gathering information on the actual or potential marketplace not only allows the organisation to monitor trends and issues concerning its current customers, but also helps it to identify and profile potential customers and new markets, and to keep track of its competition, their strategies, tactics and future plans. In this context, market research and information handling offer the organisation a foundation from which it can adjust to the changing environment in which it operates.

*eg*

The mobile phone market is heavily researched now that ownership stands at around 90 per cent, and an increasing volume of transactions are completed using the mobile. The introduction of smartphones has accelerated interest in the market, given the potential to do more with them in terms of consumer buying, and that is of relevance to marketing decision makers. It's a market that is evolving rapidly, so the attitudes and behaviour of users are changing as more people adopt them and get used to the full range of their capabilities.

Exact Target, in a study based on surveys and interviews with smartphone users, found that over 16 per cent of respondents in the USA had made a purchase on their smartphone prompted by a mobile e-mail message. The study indicates how shopping is changing and becoming more dependent on e-mails, text alerts and mobile coupons delivered through smartphones. It shows how consumer interaction with brands and connection to suppliers is evolving in the modern world.

The major findings of the study show that more than two-thirds of users value their smartphone over tablet computers or game systems; 35 per cent of users check their Facebook page each day using their smartphone, and 34 per cent of users have checked their bank balance on their smartphone. Overall, the study indicates that consumers are becoming relaxed about using their smartphone for shopping. Unilever is seriously examining in-store scanning and payment services using smartphones but the app can also be used for advertising and promotion. Facebook has set up deals where coupons are sent by mobile to consumers to redeem at local businesses by its location-based services. Starbucks has an app that drives consumers to its stores and can create prepaid accounts so the customer can 'pay' at the checkout with their phone, and it also allows for an opt-in for marketing messages. All of these examples were well researched to provide an indication of the likely take-up in different industries and buying situations. But as yet, many of the UK's largest retailers are failing to use smartphones to send mobile apps to potential customers, according to a survey from the Internet Advertising Bureau (IAB).

The findings are also of interest to apps producers looking to find new product opportunities. Although they undertake research on their own behalf, the results from secondary research are useful in pinpointing areas requiring closer scrutiny from primary, otherwise known as original research. Again the popularity of particular brands and the operating system used is crucial to the apps' producers and most of this information is tracked through secondary research by independent organisations. Therefore the split for example between Apple's iOS, Blackberry and Windows has important implications for new product development and for retailers seeking to make themselves more accessible for purchases. The number of app downloads is expected to grow from around 11 billion in 2010 to 182.7 billion in 2015, with the number of smartphones sold predicted to more than double to anything between 1.1 billion and 1.8 billion by 2015, depending upon the forecasting organisation. Already the IAB has found that 51 per cent of mobile phone owners, about 23 million people, use their devices to either make a payment, redeem coupons or research products and services. That will grow as more apps are produced and more widespread familiarity with the services on offer is gained, and good market research is essential to monitor the market's evolution and to maximise the opportunities that are emerging (*Business Wire*, 2011; Dredge, 2011; Sweeny, 2011).

This chapter first considers the role of marketing research and discusses the structure of the marketing information system (MkIS) as a means of collecting, analysing and disseminating timely, accurate and relevant data and information throughout the organisation. It then looks at the marketing research planning framework. The stages in designing and implementing a marketing research project are considered, from defining the problem to writing a brief and then executing the project and disseminating the findings. The chapter also looks in detail at sourcing and collecting secondary (or desk) research, from existing or published sources, and primary (or field) research derived from scratch through surveys, observation or experimentation for a specific purpose. The important aspects of designing samples and data collection instruments are explored in some depth, since however well managed the rest of the research process is, asking the wrong questions in the wrong way to the wrong people is a recipe for poor quality marketing information.

Finally, because marketing research is potentially such a complex process, with so much riding on its findings, and because organisations often delegate it to agencies, it is important that it is carried out professionally and ethically. There is, therefore, a section on ethical issues involved in marketing research at p. 198 *et seq*.

Throughout this chapter, the terms *client* and *researchers* have been used. *Client* means the organisation that has commissioned the marketing research, whether from an external agency or from an in-house department. *Researcher* means the individual or the team responsible for actually undertaking the research task, regardless of whether they are internal or external to the client organisation.

# Marketing research: definition and role

Marketing research is at the heart of marketing decision-making and it is important to understand what it involves and its place within the organisation. This section thus discusses the meaning of marketing research and the role that it plays in helping managers to understand new or changing markets, competition, customers' and potential customers' needs and wants.

## Defining marketing research

Marketing research is a critical input into marketing decisions and has been defined by the American Marketing Association (AMA) as follows:

> . . . a function that links the consumer, customer and public to the marketer through information – information used to identify and define marketing opportunities and problems; generate, refine and evaluate marketing actions; monitor marketing performance; and improve the understanding of marketing as a process. Marketing research specifies the information required to address these issues, designs the method for collecting information, manages and implements the data collection process, analyses the results and communicates the findings and their implications. (www.marketingpower.com/AboutAMA/Pages/DefinitionofMarketing.aspx).

Marketing research links the organisation with the environment in which it is operating and involves specifying the problem, gathering data, then analysing and interpreting those data to facilitate the decision-making process. Marketing research is an essential link between the outside world and the marketer through the information used to identify and define marketing opportunities and problems, generate, refine and evaluate marketing actions, monitor marketing performance and improve understanding of marketing as a process. Marketing research thus specifies the information required to address these issues and designs the methods for collecting the necessary data. It implements the research plan and then analyses and interprets the collected data. After that, the findings and their implications can be communicated.

## The role of marketing research

The role of marketing research in consumer markets has become well established across the EU. It is particularly important for manufacturers, because of the way in which retailers and other intermediaries act as a buffer between manufacturers and their end consumers. If the manufacturer is not to become isolated from market trends and changing preferences, it is important that an accurate, reliable flow of information reach the marketing decision maker. It might be very limiting if only feedback from the trade were used in making new product and marketing mix decisions.

Another factor facing the consumer goods marketer is the size of the customer base. With such a potentially large number of users and potential users, the onus is on the organisation to make sure that it generates a backward flow of communication from those customers. The potential size of consumer markets also opens up the prospect of adapting products and the general marketing offering to suit different target groups. Decisions on product range, packaging, pricing and promotion will all arise from a well-understood profile of the different types of need in the market.

Think back to Chapter 4, where the links between market segments and marketing mixes were discussed in more detail. Marketing research is essential for ensuring that segments exist and that they are viable, and for establishing what they want and how to reach them. As markets become increasingly European and global in their scope, marketing research plays an even more crucial role in helping the organisation to Europeanise or globalise its marketing effort, and to decide when to standardise and when to vary its approaches as new markets are opened up.

# MARKETING IN ACTION

## Girls just want to have . . . what?

Girls don't drink beer . . . do they? Girls wouldn't drink beer . . . would they? Molson Coors obviously thinks they would, as in 2011 it launched a female-friendly beer, 'Animée', designed to exploit a £396 million market that is virtually untapped. The beer market generally is in decline with consumers becoming more health conscious and tending not to visit their local pub quite so often. Beer sales have fallen by more than 30 per cent over the past 30 years. The problem for women is that beers are considered all the same and normally are best avoided in favour of wine and spirits. Not surprisingly, 83 per cent of sales of beer are made to men, according to Alcovision.

Molson Coors spent nearly three years researching whether a female-friendly beer represented a real gap in the market, and how to position such a product for market entry. The research cost over £1 million. Over 30,000 women were surveyed to find out why they chose not to drink beer. The attitudes that Molson Coors is facing are very entrenched, as it was not so very long ago that women just didn't buy alcohol at the bar in a pub and it certainly wasn't ladylike to be seen quaffing beer. Those cultural attitudes might have relaxed a bit, but research has indicated that several factors still act as a barrier to women buying beer: a lack of education; too much gas in the beer leading to bloated stomachs (not to mention the beer gut!) and a bitter taste, but perhaps most important of all is the inherent sexism in beer advertising which reinforces stereotype of beer being for blokes. For many years, advertisers have spent money reinforcing the idea that beer is a male drink served by buxom barmaids, so any messages to the contrary have to be very powerful indeed if they are to be believable. Even the sponsorship activity is male-focused, such as Heineken's sponsorship of the UEFA cup, Budweiser's sponsorship of the FA Cup or Greene King's sponsorship of the Rugby Football Union.

Much depends on how the researchers are defining 'beer' or how their respondents are defining it, however. If the definition includes lager as well as the darker beers (ales and stouts) then the picture for female drinkers starts to look less bleak, as lager appears to be a little more female-friendly than the darker beers. According to Mintel (2010), lager is the number one drink for men, with 75 per cent of male drinkers consuming it, while for women, it is only number four, with 42 per cent of female drinkers consuming it on occasion. The top female tipple is white wine, with 60 per cent. Darker beers come fifth in the men's top five (44 per cent), and don't register at all with female drinkers.

What's clear from this is that if you're about to launch a £2 million advertising campaign for a new brand that perhaps will have cost a further million or two to develop, you need to understand what makes a beer female-friendly. If Mintel is right and 42 per cent of female drinkers are already consuming lager (as opposed to the darker beers) then perhaps it is less about the taste and make-up of the product itself and more about developing packaging and marketing communications that will make women more comfortable about buying lager for themselves. It is the task of market research to establish this.

The need for market research extends right through the new product development process, into the launch plan for a product, and beyond, monitoring the product's progress. In this case, the branding, the flavour and level of fizziness, the proposed positioning, and the marketing communications approaches will have to have been tested to ensure that the product and its marketing offering appear to be meeting the market need. The marketing communication could be particularly critical to establishing some credibility for this brand. The industry has done such a good job in making beer and lager extremely bloke-ish over the last twenty years or so that it would be very easy for women to see the launch of something perceived as a pink, watered-down, fluffy girlie product as the ultimate in patronising stereotyping. There is a risk too that women who do already drink lager will reject this because it doesn't look like beer and it doesn't taste like beer, and those who don't already drink beer will see the word 'beer' on the label and be put off, seeing no reason to switch from the multitude of female-oriented non-beer products that they already ▶

Beer brewed for the female palate: Animée from Molson Coors

*Source*: Molson Coors UK

enjoy. After all, a number of so-called female-friendly beers have come and gone over the last few years, and even those that have survived do not appear to be making a huge impact on women's drinking patterns.

*Sources*: Atherton (2011); BBC (2011a); Bamford (2011); Clark (2011); Cole (2011); *Marketing Week* (2011); Mintel (2010); *Relaxnews International* (2011); RFU (2011); Woodard (2011).

In B2B markets, the role of marketing research is still very similar to that in consumer markets, in that it helps the organisation to understand the marketing environment better and to make better informed decisions about marketing strategies. Where the two types of market may differ is in the actual design and implementation of marketing research, because of some of the underlying factors peculiar to B2B markets, such as the smaller number of customers and the closer buyer–seller relationships, as introduced in Chapter 3. Despite any differences, the role of marketing research is still to provide an essential insight into opportunities, markets and customers.

The need for marketing research sometimes arises because the organisation needs specific details about a target market, which is a well-defined, straightforward descriptive research task. Sometimes, though, the research need arises from a much broader question, such as why a new product is not achieving expected market share. The organisation may have a theory about the nature of the problem, but it is up to marketing research to establish whether any assumptions are correct and to check out other possibilities. In practice, most marketing researchers spend a fair proportion of their time on informal projects, undertaken in reaction to specific requests for marketing information. Often these projects lack the scientific rigour associated with the more formal definition of market research. However, problems of a more innovative and complex nature have to be solved through major, formal pieces of market research, simply because of the risks involved in going ahead without the fullest possible insights.

## Types of research

So far, the discussion of marketing research has been very general and has not distinguished between different types of research. There are, however, three main types of research, each suitable as an approach to different kinds of problem.

Exploratory research is often undertaken in order to collect preliminary data to help clarify or identify a problem, rather than for generating problem solutions. Before preparing a major proposal, some exploratory work may be undertaken to establish the critical areas to be highlighted in the main body of the research. Whether primary or secondary sources of data are used, the purpose is to make an initial assessment of the nature of a marketing problem, so that more detailed research work can be planned appropriately.

*eg*

A major credit card company, looking to grow its market share in eastern Europe, recognised from examining secondary data on economic and social trends that its products and the way they were promoted in the mature western European market might not suit this new territory. It commissioned exploratory qualitative research in key countries across eastern Europe to help it to understand attitudes to personal finance within the potential customer base before committing to a large-scale quantitative survey to inform product development. The results of the study pointed up not only the anticipated differences in consumer sophistication between the West and East, but also significant differences in the beliefs and outlook of residents of neighbouring countries. In particular, attitudes to being in debt and using credit were heavily influenced by the heritage and teachings of the Catholic Church in Poland, yet did not feature in feedback from the neighbouring Czech Republic. Once the presumption that there would be a degree of homogeneity in eastern Europe had been dispelled, the company could then go on to design a quantitative questionnaire with sensitivity to local idiosyncrasies within this new geographic target market (with thanks to Fiona Jack, Green Light Research International).

The second type of research, descriptive research, aims to provide the marketer with a better understanding of a particular issue or problem. Descriptive research can range from quite specific briefs, for example profiling the consumers of a particular brand, assessing the actual purchase and repurchase behaviour associated with that brand and the reasons behind the behaviour exhibited. Most research in this category tends to be of a large-scale survey type, designed to provide a means of better understanding of marketing problems through the presentation of both quantitative and qualitative data.

Finally, causal or predictive research is undertaken to test a cause-and-effect relationship so that reasonably accurate predictions about the probable outcome of particular actions can be made. The difficulty with this kind of research for the marketing manager is that to be confident that more of $x$ does cause more of $y$, all the other variables that influence $y$ must be held constant. The real-world laboratory is rarely so obliging, with competitors, retailers and other intermediaries, and the marketing environment generally, all acting independently, doing things that will change the background conditions. Thus researchers trying to establish, for instance, whether or not a promotional 10 per cent price reduction would increase sales volume by 15 per cent during a specified period are faced with the problem of ensuring that all the other variables that might influence sales volume are held constant during the research. Random sampling may help in this process, so that the 10 per cent offer would only be made in a random selection of stores, with the other stores offering normal terms. Any difference in the performance of the product in the two groups of stores is likely to have been caused by the special promotion, since both the 'normal' and the 'promotional' product have been subjected to identical environmental factors, impacting on all the stores, during the same period.

# The origins of research data

There are two main types of data, which are generated by fundamentally different research approaches.

## Qualitative research

Qualitative research involves the collection of data that are open to interpretation, for example people's opinions, where there is no intention of establishing statistical validity. This type of research is especially useful for investigating motivation, attitudes, beliefs and intentions, rather than utilising probability-based samples. It is often based on very small-scale samples and, as a result, cannot be generalised in numerical terms. Although the results are often subjective, tentative and impressionistic, they can reflect the complexity that underlies consumer decision-making, capturing the richness and depth of how and why consumers act in the way they do.

Quantitative techniques, despite their statistical rigour, are rarely able to capture the full complexity and the wealth of interrelationships associated with marketing activity. The real value in qualitative research, therefore, lies in helping marketers to understand not what people say, but what they mean (or think they mean), and a range of techniques have been developed to assist in that task such as:

- survey research/questionnaires
- focus groups
- in-depth interviews
- observational techniques
- experimentation.

All of these are discussed further at p. 180 *et seq.*

## Quantitative research

Quantitative research involves the collection of information that is quantifiable and is not open to the same level of interpretation as qualitative research. It includes data such as sales figures, market share, market size, consumer product returns or complaints, and demographic information (see p. 136 *et seq.*) and can be collected through primary research, such as questionnaire-based surveys and interviews, and through secondary sources, including published data.

Quantitative research usually involves larger-scale surveys or research that enable a factual base to be developed with sufficient strength to allow statistically rigorous analysis. Most of us have been on the receiving end of quantitative research at some time or another, having been collared by an interviewer armed with a clipboard interviewing respondents in the street, or had an invitation to participate in a survey pop up on our computer screens. The success of quantitative research depends in part on establishing a representative sample that is large enough to allow researchers to be confident that the results can be generalised to apply to the wider population. It is then possible to specify that 'Forty-five per cent of the market think that . . . whereas 29 per cent believe . . .'. The research can be undertaken through telephone interviews, face-to-face interviews, or mail or online questionnaires (see p. 180 *et seq.*), and can also utilise secondary data sources (see p. 179 *et seq.*).

The internet is now revolutionising quantitative research. The early emphasis was on gaining cooperation online and structuring questions, but now the techniques used are becoming more sophisticated, interactive, usable over time. and more directly linked to wider information systems to integrate all data sources.

# Continuous research

A large number of research projects are developed specifically to better understand and to overcome marketing problems as they are identified. At p. 175 *et seq.* we trace the development of such projects from inception through to final evaluation. Some research, however, is conducted on a continuous basis. Continuous research is available on an ongoing basis for a subscription or agreement to purchase the updated findings. Usually offered by market research agencies, syndicated research provides much useful data on an ongoing basis. In the UK, retail purchases by consumers are tracked by ACNielsen, while Target Group Index (TGI), produced by Kantar Media, plots the fortunes of some 4,000 brands. Similar services are available in all the main European markets. The quality of such research is very high, but the important advantage is shared cost, since ACNielsen data, for example, are essential to any large multiple retailer or brand manufacturer and they will all buy the data. The price for each organisation is still far, far less than the cost of doing or commissioning the research individually. The big disadvantage, of course, is that competitors also have access to exactly the same information.

There are a number of different approaches to generating continuous data.

## Consumer panels

Market research companies recruit large numbers of households that are prepared to provide information on their actual buying and consumption patterns on a regular basis. The panel may be constituted to provide as wide a coverage of the population as possible, or it may be defined to home in on a particular segment. The make-up of a consumer panel can be quite specific Taylor Nelson Sofres Superpanel is the UK's leading continuous consumer panel and provides purchasing information on all main grocery markets. The panel was launched in 1991 and now consists of 15,000 households which are demographically and regionally balanced to offer a representative picture of the various sub-markets. Data is collected twice weekly through electronic terminals in the home, with purchases being recorded via home-scanning technology. It is highly effective as a market tracking and diagnostics tool (http://superpanel.tns-global.com/superpanel/).

Data can be extracted from consumer panels in two main ways: home audits and omnibus surveys.

**Home audits.** A home audit means monitoring and tracking the purchasing and consumption patterns of individual households. ACNielsen monitors more than 250,000 households in 27 countries via consumer panels. In the UK it has a panel of 15,000 consumers who are given a barcode scanner so that they can scan the groceries they buy and bring home (www.acnielsen.com). Information is then transferred once a week by telephone or online back to ACNeilsen.

Television viewership panels are very similar, in that they involve the recruitment of households and the installation of in-home monitoring equipment. This time, the objective is to use the equipment to enable minute-by-minute recording of audience viewing by channel. From these data, organisations such as AGB and RSMB are able to provide detailed ratings for programmes and viewing patterns during commercial breaks, a critical factor in the sale of advertising time.

**Omnibus surveys.** An omnibus survey, as the term suggests, enables an organisation to participate in an existing research programme whenever it is felt appropriate. When an organisation wants to take part, it can add a few extra questions to the next round of questionnaires sent to the large number of respondents who are regularly contacted. The big advantage is cost, although normally the number of questions that can be asked on behalf of a specific organisation is very small. The speed with which answers are received is also an important factor.

There are three types of omnibus survey: those carried out face-to-face during an interviewer visit to the home, telephone surveys and finally internet surveys. Face-to-face omnibuses tend to offer a larger sample size, often around 2,000 adults, and allow support material to be used. They are also better for exploring more complex or sensitive issues (for example, health or finance-related questioning) than the other two methods. Telephone omnibuses offer a faster turnaround time (about four to five days quicker than a face-to-face survey) but the sample sizes tend to be smaller and the scope of questioning is more limited. Online surveys offer the fastest turnaround, and allow data to be fed through directly to analysis systems. Internet-based surveys also give lots of scope for creativity in data collection – see the item on ChatterBus (below) which not only provides the opportunity for an online focus group style of discussion, but also allows participants to upload photos of themselves using a brand, for example.

Taylor Nelson Sofres (www.tns-ri.co.uk/what-we-do/bmrb-omnibus.aspx) runs a number of regular omnibus surveys as well as specific industry- or issue-based marketing research reports. These include:

- *OnlineBus:* this survey is run online twice a week using between 1,000 and 2,000 adults, and results are turned around within two to three days.
- *24 Hours – NightLine:* this is run Monday to Friday and offers a 24-hour turnaround from surveys of 1,000 adults.
- *CAPI – Face to face Omnibus:* this is the largest UK omnibus survey, run twice a week with between 1,000 and 4,000 adult respondents and a ten-day turnaround of results.
- *PhoneBus:* this survey runs once each weekend, reaching 1,000 adults with a four-day turnaround of results.
- *Ncompass International:* this covers over 80 international markets, with large sample sizes and a weekly run in most of those markets. The results can be turned around in about a week.
- *Kids Omnibus:* this uses online techniques to survey 1,000 children aged between eight and 15 every month, with a one-week turnaround of results. Face-to-face techniques are also used on a continuous basis to survey 500 children aged between seven and 14, and 500 young people aged between 15 and 19, with a four-week turnaround of results.
- *ChatterBus:* this is a live, moderated online discussion that takes place every Wednesday evening. Clients buy time in the discussion in five-minute blocks. A full transcript of the relevant sections of the discussion is available to the client within 24 hours.

There are, of course, other market research agencies offering omnibus survey facilities. Dubit, for example, is an agency that specialises in research among children and teens, and it runs the *Direct to Youth* online omnibus, which surveys 1,000 people aged between 11 and 18 (www.dubitresearch.com).

## Retail audits

The retail audit concept is perhaps the easiest to implement, as it relies on trained auditors visiting selected retail stores and undertaking regular stock checks, although barcode scanning and integration between retailers' systems and those of suppliers is providing even more up-to-date information on what is sold where and when. Changes in stock, both on the shelf and in the warehouse, indicate an accurate figure for actual sales to consumers by pack size. This information is especially useful for assessing brand shares, response to sales promotions and the amount of stock being held within the retail trade. Along with information on price levels, the brand manager has much useful information with which to make revised marketing-mix decisions.

# MARKETING IN ACTION

## Who's in charge? You, gov!

YouGov has emerged in recent years as 'the UK's most quoted research company'. Its stated ambition is, 'to supply a live stream of continuous, accurate data and insight into what people are thinking and doing all over the world, all of the time, so that companies, governments and institutions can better serve the people that sustain them'. Its influence lies in the fact that it has recruited an online panel of over 350,000 people from which it can draw samples for its surveys. As well as surveys, it also runs TellYouGov, which allows panel members to submit opinions on anything via text, e-mail or Twitter at any time. Panel members are incentivised, in that they earn points for participating in surveys or expressing opinions, and then those points can be converted into cash or gifts, or used to enter monthly prize draws. The amount of media exposure that YouGov surveys get is phenomenal, and that isn't just because of its own marketing efforts, or the topical or quirky nature of the work it does. It's as much to do with the fact that its research is underpinned by rigorous methodology and analysis, and it is respected and cited because it is representative and accurate.

YouGov offers both omnibus and bespoke survey services, among other things. It runs a daily (Monday to Friday) omnibus survey, and clients have choice of either a survey of a representative sample of 1,000 adults with results within 24 hours, or a sample of 2,000 with a 48-hour turnaround. It also runs a number of specialist omnibus services, some with a regional focus, such as the Scotland, Wales or London omnibuses, and some with a particular demographic profile, such as parents or children. These tend to run weekly or twice weekly. Interestingly, there is also a weekly Business omnibus, which polls 500 small business decision-makers, and a quarterly MPs omnibus which draws on a representative sample of 100 MPs. Because YouGov has operations all over the world, it can also offer international omnibuses, with the client able to specify which country/countries they want to target with their question(s).

Bespoke research is obviously tailored to a particular client's needs, and can involve anything from a one-off survey to a more complex multi-stage, and possibly even international project involving a wide range of quantitative and/or qualitative methodologies. Clients can also select the level of feedback required, with YouGov offering anything from presentation of basic results through to detailed sophisticated statistical analysis, and, if required, strategic advice based on that analysis. YouGov has done a couple of surveys recently for Bärfrämjandet, a collaboration between Swedish berry growers and the agency that accredits the quality of Swedish produce. Did you know that strawberry jam is the most popular jam in Sweden, followed by raspberry jam and, in third place, raspberry and blueberry jam? Also, 96 per cent of Swedes like strawberries, and 84 per cent want Swedish strawberries. Almost one-quarter of consumers will not buy strawberries unless Swedish-grown ones are available.

YouGov doesn't just undertake the 'normal' range of marketing-related research projects for commercial organisations. It also undertakes opinion polling on political issues and news stories. In the run up to the UK General Election in 2010, for example, the three main party leaders participated in a televised debate and within two hours of that debate ending, YouGov had published feedback on public reaction to it. Four thirty-minute online focus groups took place as soon as the debate ended, with each group comprising eight members selected from YouGov's panel. One of the groups comprised 'undecided' voters, while each of the others comprised voters who identified themselves with one of the three main parties. Because the research took place online, it could be done quickly, and 'The anonymity of the online environment stimulated an open and authentic discussion on an emotionally driven subject providing a rich insight' (www.yougov.co.uk).

The media too commission research from YouGov to inform their journalism. Weight Watchers Magazine, for example, commissioned a survey of a representative sample of 1,200 women to find out how perceptions of weight had changed. The results suggested that women's view of what's 'normal' has indeed shifted, probably as a result of over-exposure in the media of very thin celebrities and models. These results were also reported across the wider media, stimulating a debate on weight issues. Another issue of great public interest, of course, is university tuition fees. The BBC reported a YouGov survey of 4,000 respondents, which reassuringly showed that they were five times as likely to recommend higher education to young people than not to, despite the fact that the words that were most often cited in connection with universities were 'expensive' (with 775 mentions), followed by 'fees' (171 mentions). There were some positive words, however, such as 'important' (116) and 'opportunities' (107), but then 'elitist' (64) and 'waste' (77) also cropped up quite often. Just remember this, though, especially when coursework deadlines, exams and boring lectures are getting you down: when respondents were asked for a single word that best explained why people chose to go into higher education (and let's assume that they are talking about students rather than staff!), 57 per cent said 'fun'.

A final thought. At the time of writing (August 2011), YouGov had just done a survey in which 54 per cent of respondents who support a Premier League team predicted that Manchester United would win the 2011–12 league title. At the other end of the league, 54 per cent also thought that Swansea would be one of the three relegated teams (along with Norwich, 48 per cent and QPR 36 per cent). Were they right? Oh, and apparently 66 per cent of British women prefer the appearance of a man without a beard . . . we could go on for ever with this . . .!

*Sources*: BBC (2011b); *Esmerk* (2011); www.svenskajordgubbar.se/; www.yougov.co.uk.

# Marketing information systems

In order to serve the information needs of the organisation and to support decision-making, marketers need to focus not only on collecting data and information, but also on how to handle and manage issues of storage, access and dissemination (McLuhan, 2001). There is little point in having a highly complex information system that cannot readily deliver what managers want, when they want it and how they want it. Any system must be responsive to the needs of the users.

**Figure 5.1**
The marketing
information
system

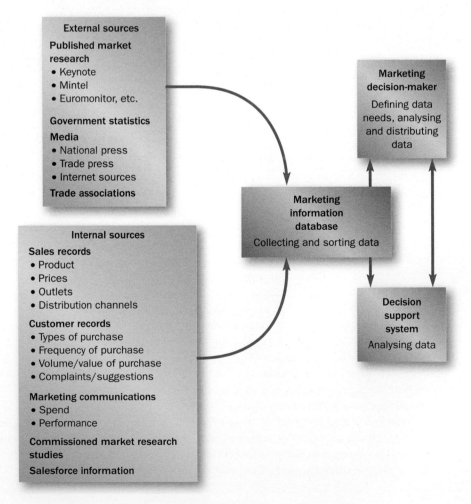

A marketing information system (MkIS) has been defined by the AMA as a:

**set of procedures and methods for the regular, planned collection, analysis, and presentation of information for use in making marketing decisions. (www.marketingpower.com/_layouts/ Dictionary.aspx?dLetter=M)**

Nowadays, most of these systems are computerised and need to coordinate data collection and decision support, as shown in Figure 5.1. The MkIS should be tailored to the specific requirements of the organisation. These will be influenced by the size of the organisation and the resources available as well as the specific needs of decision makers. While these needs are likely to be broadly similar between organisations, they will not be exactly the same and therefore the design of the systems and their sophistication will vary. What is important is that the information is managed in a way that facilitates the decision-making process, rather than just being a collection of data gathering dust.

It can be seen from Figure 5.1 that an MkIS provides a comprehensive framework for managing information. Along with generating huge amounts of data about their day-to-day activities (sales, customer details, incoming and outgoing orders, transactions, service requirements, etc.), organisations are usually in various stages of gathering other data about competitors, new product tests, improved service requirements and changing regulations, for example. Timeliness of information, whether it be for short- or long-term decision-making, is also of importance, as the provision of immediate feedback or projected trend details to decision makers can provide a competitive advantage in the marketplace.

*eg*

Tesco has a sophisticated marketing information system that tracks sales by products and store and that feeds back to suppliers and to management with commercial reports. It provides information to 8,000 people across 2,000 suppliers with data on sales and inventory. Tesco also has over 500 stores internationally and has centralised its key finance, human resources and sales applications across all its sites. By controlling purchasing centrally it ensures productivity is maintained. From a central site in Bangalore it can monitor the performance of each store and manage a store as if in the UK.

At the product level, however, the jewel in Tesco's crown is its Clubcard data. Every time customers use their Clubcard to gain their loyalty points at the checkout, it is adding to the wealth of data that the retailer already has about them. As one retail analyst put it, '[Tesco] can understand where their customers work, where they live, and what happens between those two points. Better than that, they know what you bought, where you bought it, what time of day and what day of week you bought it' (as quoted by McCully, 2008). This allows individual targeting of that customer with offers and information that are relevant to their buying habits, or designed to get them to try different things, based on their lifestyle and family situation. Every three months, Tesco sends out 12 million mailshots to its Clubcard holders, and 97 per cent of them are unique – i.e. tailored to the recipient. And because the data are updated every time the customer shops, it's giving Tesco almost a real-time view of how the shopper's behaviour is changing (or not) and how the shopper is responding to offers and other incentives, so that relevance can be maintained. When all the Clubcard data are aggregated (and around 50 per cent of the UK population holds a Clubcard, so that's a lot of data), the results can be used to create sophisticated profiles of a large number of distinct market segments.

The Clubcard data are analysed by Dunnhumby, a company that has been involved with Tesco since the launch of Clubcard in 1995, and is now almost wholly owned by Tesco, and then passed on to Tesco's Customer Insight department as the basis for sales and marketing activities. Some of the cost of running the Clubcard scheme is covered by selling information on trends and buyer profiles (it's all aggregated data – Tesco doesn't sell data on individuals) to suppliers (*Business Wire*, 2008; *Computer Weekly*, 2008; McCully, 2008).

The other requirement of information is that it should be appropriate to the needs of those using it. Organisations have to manage the information they have, identify what information they need, and present it in the form that the various decision makers require. Not all information that the organisation has is necessarily appropriate for all marketing decision makers. It is therefore important to identify the various needs of those decision makers and to ensure they are supplied with only the information that meets their needs.

## Sources of marketing information

As indicated at the outset of this chapter and in Figure 5.1, there are two main sources of information for an MkIS system, internal and external.

### External sources

External sources are either *ad hoc* studies using secondary and primary research, or continuous data provided by the various syndicated and omnibus studies mentioned earlier. Information comes from sources external to the organisation, such as customers, suppliers, channels of distribution, strategic alliance partners, independent third parties, commercial agencies, industry associations, governmental sources such as Eurostat, etc., and external sources like the internet. The challenge for the marketing manager is to integrate these findings into the organisation to effect change.

### Internal sources

Information also comes from internal sources within the organisation. These include the internal record keeping system (production, accounting, sales records, purchase details, etc.), marketing research, sales representatives' field reports, call details, customer enquiries and complaints, product returns, etc. All of this information, again, must be managed appropriately and distributed in a timely fashion if it is going to be used effectively to assist decision-making.

The development of electronic-point-of-sale (EPOS) technology has revolutionised the flow of information within retail operations, providing a base for fast and reliable information on emerging trends. Either by using a laser barcode scanner or by keying in a six-figure code, retailers can be right up to date in what is moving, where and what the immediate impact will be on stock levels. Retail managers can monitor movement on different product lines on a daily basis and adjust stock, orders and even in-store promotions, based on information either from individual stores or across all the branches. As mentioned earlier, Tesco, with its Clubcard loyalty scheme, can track and record the purchasing and shopping habits of millions of individual customers, and tailor its marketing offerings, both locally and nationally, based on solid, internally generated information.

Clegg (2001) emphasised the importance not just of collecting externally generated marketing data but also of ensuring that there is effective communication within the organisation so that customer contact personnel in particular can contribute fully to building market research knowledge. If the marketing database is seen as being owned by the research department rather than being a knowledge reservoir for the whole organisation, it may not be so well informed of the experiences of customer-facing staff.

Organisations thus get everyday information, often as a matter of course, from a variety of sources that can influence their decision-making, but *intelligence* means developing a perspective on the information that provides a competitive edge, perhaps in new product opportunities or the opening up of a new market segment.

The main difficulty is information overload (Smith and Fletcher, 1999) where there is too much information and not enough intelligence. One study suggested that 49 per cent of managers surveyed cannot cope with the information they receive and another that organisations use as little as 20 per cent of their knowledge (Von Krogh *et al.*, 2000), meaning that a lot of perhaps useful intelligence is locked away or not evident to the decision maker. Collecting marketing information, therefore, should not be an end in itself but should be part of a valuable and usable knowledge management source that can be accessed upon demand in a meaningful and digestible form.

Sometimes environmental scanning can provide useful insights. By deliberately looking at the various influences on product markets, an organisation may spot early warning signs before the competitors are aware of them. This will help in the forward planning process and will be especially useful as an input to strategic development decisions.

## Decision support systems

The availability and use of a range of computer-based decision support systems (DSS) are changing the way information is used and presented to decision makers, and the way in which they interpret it (Duan and Burrell, 1997). While an MkIS organises and presents information, the DSS actually aids decision-making by allowing the marketer to manipulate information and explore 'what if . . .' type questions. A DSS usually comprises a software package, including statistical analysis tools, spreadsheets, databases and other programs that assist in gathering, analysing and interpreting information to facilitate marketing decision-making. By having the DSS connected to the MkIS, marketers further enhance their ability to use the information available. Effectively, this brings the MkIS to the desktop, and even to the personal laptop, with the appropriate connections, servers and modems. This can encourage wide use of information, although there may be some problems about restricting access to more sensitive areas and ensuring that the complexity can be handled from a systems perspective.

The MkIS or DSS will never replace decision makers, only help them. Marketing decisions still need the imagination and flair that can interpret 'hard' information and turn it into implementable tactics and strategies that will maintain competitive edge.

## The marketing research process

When an organisation has decided to undertake a research project, it is important to make sure that it is planned and executed systematically and logically, so that the 'right' objectives are defined and achieved as quickly, efficiently and cost effectively as possible. A general model of the marketing research process is presented here, which can be applied to a wide range of real situations with minor adaptations. Figure 5.2 shows the broad stages, and although it may suggest a logic and neatness that is rarely found in practice, it does at the very least offer a framework that can be tailored to meet different clients, situations and resources. Each stage in the process will now be discussed in turn.

### Problem definition

Problem definition is the first and one of the most important stages in the research process, because it defines exactly what the project is about and as such influences how the subsequent

**Figure 5.2**
The marketing
research process

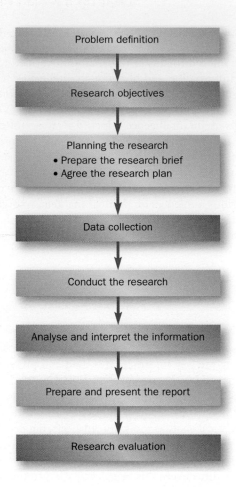

stages are conducted, and ultimately the success of the project itself. The organisation sponsoring the research, whether it intends to use in-house researchers or an agency, needs to define precisely what the problem is and how that translates into research objectives. This may also lead to the identification of other concerns or problems that need to be included in the project. For example, if the fundamental problem has been defined as 'people are not buying our product', the organisation may feel that it should not only explore people's attitudes to the product itself, but also look at how they rate the product on other aspects of the marketing mix in comparison with the competition.

Once the broad nature of the problem has been established, the next stage involves more precise definition of objectives.

## Research objectives

The tight specification of research objectives is important to ensure that the project is developed along the right lines. Usually, primary objectives need to be distinguished from secondary objectives. The primary objective for an electrical components manufacturer seeking to enter the French market, for example, might be to establish the market potential for the products specified and to indicate appropriate market entry strategies. The secondary objectives tend to be more specific and comprehensive. For the components manufacturer they might include:

- defining market trends and competitive structure over the past five years;
- profiling the existing main suppliers in terms of strengths and weaknesses (products, prices, distribution, branding, service, etc.);
- identifying the main buyers of electrical components;

- identifying the main buying criteria when purchasing;
- surveying potential trade and end users for willingness to switch supply source.

The list above is not exhaustive, but the main point is that objectives clearly drive the whole research process, and should provide the necessary foundations for whatever management decisions will have to be taken at the end. In all cases, the research objectives need to be clearly and concisely stated in writing to ensure that the research brief can be adequately prepared.

To be successful at this stage, the project team needs good communication and a solid understanding of the issues involved. This is where exploratory research may be useful, in eliminating some of the possibilities or filling some basic gaps in knowledge and understanding. This could involve some preliminary discussions with distributors, experts or customers. The information collected, including any secondary data, can then be used to prepare the research brief for the formal commissioning of work.

A sportswear brand, originally well known for one core sport, had over time developed ranges for other sports and, in the process, also developed a number of different logos. Research was commissioned with the objective of discovering which single logo could best represent the brand across all sports. Specific outputs required from the research were guidance on the most appropriate and recognisable logo for the brand to adopt, and its optimum positioning on the clothing of sponsored elite athletes in each sport. A worldwide sample of 10,000 sports fans, recruited for their interest in the relevant sports, was questioned on brand awareness and brand image and asked both to nominate their preferred logo from a selection of five shown and to give reasons for their choice. The research company then analysed the most commonly used camera angles from a library of video and press coverage of major sporting events to identify areas of clothing with the highest frequency of exposure. The client gained clear and substantiated recommendations on logo design and siting to achieve maximum exposure on sports apparel (www.sportsmarketingsurveys.com).

## Planning the research

The planning stage falls into two main parts: first, the preparation of the research brief, and second, agreeing the research plan. This applies equally whether the research is conducted in-house or not.

### Prepare the research brief

The research brief originates from the client. Its quality and precision can vary widely. In some cases, the client has a vague idea of what the problem is, but is not sure what the underlying causes or dynamics are. They thus rely heavily on researchers to specify the problem and then decide on the best research design, effectively asking them to undertake the first two stages of the research process. In many ways, the development of this kind of brief is rather like consultancy and may be part of that kind of overall process.

The main points of the research brief (adapted from Hague, 1992) will be:

- a definition of the problem, including its history;
- a description of the product to be researched;
- a description of the market to be researched;
- specific research objectives;
- time and financial budget;
- reporting requirements.

This brief may be the subject of modification and negotiation during the meetings.

## Agree the research plan

On the basis of the brief, a research plan needs to be agreed before the project begins. Not only is this important for cost and timing considerations, but it also ensures that the data generated will enable management decisions to be resolved without the need for further analysis. There is nothing worse than completing a major research project only to find that the results are at best of only partial use to managers!

The details of the research plan will vary according to the project, but ideally it should contain:

- background information for the research;
- research objectives (based on decisions that need to be made and the criteria to be used);
- research methods (secondary and/or primary);
- type of analysis to be employed;
- degree of client involvement;
- data ownership;
- details of subcontractors (if any);
- level and timing of ongoing reporting;
- format of final report;
- timing and cost of research.

An organisation with a major research project may well ask a number of research agencies to tender for the business. Each agency will obviously propose different research plans. These need to be evaluated alongside the organisation's more usual buying criteria. The final decision by the clients should be based on confidence that the chosen agency can best meet its information needs through the research plan proposed, but within any constraints imposed.

# Data collection

The first requirement in preparing the research plan is to identify clearly what additional data are needed and then to establish how they are to be collected. This may involve collecting both primary and secondary data, or just primary data.

## Secondary research

Sometimes also referred to as *desk research*, secondary research consists of data and information that already exist and can be accessed by an organisation. Thus, for example, it would include published government statistics and published market research reports.

Clearly, if secondary research is available that answers the question or solves the problem, then that is the quickest and most efficient way of gathering the necessary data. In many cases, however, secondary data may not be directly applicable, or may only give half the picture.

The pursuit of secondary data should be exhaustive, as secondary data are usually far more cost-effective and quicker to collect than primary data. However, because secondary data were collected for another purpose, they are not always in a form that is useful or appropriate, and thus they often have to be re-analysed to convert them to a form that can be used for a particular project. We will look in detail at secondary research below.

## Primary research

Sometimes also called *field* research, primary research is undertaken or commissioned by an organisation for a specific purpose. The required information does not already exist in any available form and so the research has to be undertaken from scratch.

The advantage of primary research is that it is exactly tailored to the problem in hand, but it can be expensive and time consuming to undertake. We will look in detail at methods of primary research on p. 180 *et seq*.

Once the researchers have recognised that information is needed that is not currently available, they must decide from what source they can most effectively get that information. It is well worth checking secondary data sources first to see what has already been done. Even if secondary data are available, or can be converted, they may still not be sufficient to meet all the researchers' needs, and thus a primary research study may still have to be developed to fill the gaps or further explore the issues. This means that a market research project will often incorporate both primary and secondary research, each complementing the other.

# Secondary research

Secondary data can be either internal or external to the organisation. The former is considered to be part of the normal MkIS (marketing information system), as outlined on p. 172 *et seq*. The advantage of secondary research is that it can be much cheaper and quicker to access, and may provide information that the organisation would not otherwise have the time, resources or inclination to gather. External secondary data offer valuable information to researchers, but of course, the major drawback with secondary data is that the information has been collected for purposes other than this particular research project, and may not be in a suitable or usable form. The organisation also needs to be careful that the secondary data are current, and that they are appropriate and applicable to the problem in hand.

Secondary data can play a variety of roles in the research process. The main role is probably in providing background information on industries and markets, in terms of trends, dynamics and structure. Some of this information may be useful in its own right in informing management decision-making, although it is more likely to provide pointers for further primary research. It can also provide useful information that may assist in sample selection for surveys by indicating the main competitor and customer groups.

## Sources of secondary data

It would be impossible to list all potential sources of data, as the number of sources is so vast and much will depend on the type of research project in question. Whatever the sources used, secondary data vary widely in terms of relevance and quality. Boyd *et al.* (1977) suggest four criteria for evaluating secondary data sources:

1  the pertinence of the data
2  who collects the data and why
3  method of collecting data
4  evidence of careful work.

Although secondary sources of data are widely used, as they tend to be low cost and usually easily obtainable once a source has been identified, the criteria above do suggest some potential problem areas. Often the data fail to get down to the micro level necessary to support management decisions. The focus is often at industry level rather than the sector or segment of particular interest, perhaps within a defined geographical area. Some data may have been collected to promote the well-being of the industry, rather than to provide wholly accurate figures, and sometimes they are not always accurate because of their source, their age or the way they were collected. However, for most surveys the sorting, sifting and analysis of secondary data are useful for purposes ranging from developing sample frames (see p. 189 *et seq*.) to providing comprehensive insights into market size, structure and trends.

## Online databases

Up until the 1990s most secondary data was print-based. Directories, both specialist and general, were essential tools for the market researcher but most have now been supplemented or completely replaced by direct internet access. The key to the internet is offering an effective search engine so that the drudgery can be taken out of searching for and sourcing information. The more sophisticated the search engine, the more powerful the directory in making it easy to search for and access suitable or appropriate data.

It pays, therefore, to explore thoroughly what is currently available before going out and generating more information at a far higher cost. In the case of the eyewear market most of the market data is available so the research focus could shift to understanding detailed buying patterns.

*eg*

Euromonitor market reports are valuable sources of data on markets. They report on categories, channels and also geographic regions. Each year, Euromonitor publishes 17,000 reports on 27 industries and 200 subcategories. A range of techniques is used, including secondary research, store checks, trade interviews and market analysis. For example, the *Eyewear Market in the UK* report was published in 2010 and is available for £1,250. It gives a detailed profile of the structure of the current market and its evolution, and also forecasts for the next five years (www.euromonitor.com/eyewear-in-the-united-kingdom/report).

# Primary research

Once the decision to use primary research has been made, researchers have to define what data need to be collected and how. This section looks specifically at 'how'. First, there is an overview of primary research methods.

Whatever method is chosen as most appropriate to the client's information needs, researchers then have to think about defining a sample of individuals or organisations from the total population of interest (defined as a market segment or an industry, for instance). This topic is covered in some depth on p. 189 *et seq*. Finally, of particular interest to those conducting surveys, p. 191 *et seq*. look specifically at questionnaires.

## Research methods

The three most commonly used methods for collecting primary data are interviews and surveys, observation and experiments.

### Interviews and surveys

Interviews and surveys involve the collection of data directly from individuals. This may be by direct face-to-face personal interview, either individually or in a group, by telephone or by a mail questionnaire. Each of these techniques, considered in turn below, has its own set of advantages and disadvantages, which are summarised in Table 5.1.

**Personal interviews.** A personal interview is a face-to-face meeting between an interviewer and a respondent. It may take place in the home, the office, the street, a shopping mall, or at any prearranged venue. In one extreme case, a holiday company decided to interview respondents who were at leisure on the beach. One can imagine the varied responses!

There are three broad types of personal interview:

■ *The in-depth, largely unstructured interview.* Taking almost a conversational form, this is very useful for exploring attitudinal and motivational issues. It could last for one to two hours and can range fairly freely over a number of relevant issues. There is often scope for the interviewer to explore some topics in more depth if additional unforeseen themes emerge in the interview and thus high-level interviewing skills are needed, along with a sound knowledge of the product-market concept being examined. However, the time taken to complete an interview, and the cost of each interview, make large-scale surveys of this nature prohibitively expensive. In B2B markets, they are often used on a small-scale basis to fill gaps left by other approaches such as mail or telephone surveys.

■ *The structured interview.* This allows the interviewer far less flexibility to explore responses further and results in a more programmed, almost superficial interview. Little use is made of open-ended questions and the questionnaire is carefully designed for ease of recording information and progress through the interview. The use of a standardised questionnaire means that the responses from a large number of individuals can be handled with considerable ease, as there is no need for further interpretation and analysis. The limitations stem mainly from the need to design and pilot the questionnaire very carefully to ensure that it meets the specification expected of it. We look more closely at some of these questionnaire issues at p. 191 *et seq.*

■ *The semi-structured interview.* This is a hybrid of the other two methods and is based around a programmed script, but the inclusion of some open-ended questions gives the interviewer scope to pursue certain issues more flexibly.

**Table 5.1** Comparative performance of interview and survey techniques

|  | Personal interviews | Group interviews | Telephone survey | Mail survey | Online survey |
|---|---|---|---|---|---|
| Cost per response | High | Fairly high | Low | Very low | Very low |
| Speed of data collection | Fast | Fast | Very fast | Slow | Very fast |
| Quantity of data collectable | Large | Large | Moderate | Moderate | Large |
| Ability to reach dispersed population | Low | Low | High | High | High |
| Likely response rate | High | Very high | Fairly high | Low | Fairly high |
| Potential for interviewer bias | High | Very high | Fairly high | None | None |
| Ability to probe | High | High | Fairly high | None | None |
| Ability to use visual aids | High | High | None | Fairly high | High |
| Flexibility of questioning | High | Very high | Fairly high | None | Low |
| Ability to ask complex questions | High | High | Fairly high | Low | Low |
| Ability to get truth on sensitive questions | Fairly low | Fairly high | Fairly high | High | High |
| Respondent anonymity | Possible | Fairly possible | None | None | Possible |
| Likely respondent cooperation | Good | Very good | Good | Poor | Poor |
| Potential for respondent misunderstanding | Low | Low | Fairly low | High | High |

**Group interviews and focus groups.** Group interviews are used to produce qualitative data that are not capable of generalisation to the wider population, but do provide useful insights into underlying attitudes and behaviours relevant to the marketer. A group interview normally involves between six and eight respondents considered to be representative of the target group being examined. The role of the interviewer is to introduce topics, encourage and clarify responses and generally guide proceedings in a manner that is effective without being intrusive (Witthaus, 1999).

In this kind of group situation, individuals can express their views either in response to directed questions or, preferably, in response to general discussion on the themes that have been introduced. Often, the interaction and dialogue between respondents are more revealing of opinions. So that participants will relax enough to open out like this, it is often helpful to select the group concerned to include people of a similar status. For example, a manufacturer of an innovative protective gum shield for sports persons organised different group interviews for sports players (users) and dentists (specifiers). Further subdivision could have been possible by type of sport, or to distinguish the casual player from the professional.

Group interviews are especially useful where budgets are limited or if the research topic is not yet fully understood. If secondary data have clearly indicated in quantitative terms that there is a gap in the market, group interviews may be useful in providing some initial insights into why that gap exists, whether customers are willing to see it filled and with what. This could then provide the basis for more detailed and structured investigation. There are, of course, dangers in generalisation, but if between four and six different discussion groups have been held, some patterns may begin to emerge. For the smaller business with limited funds, group interviews may provide a useful alternative to more costly field techniques.

Online group interviews are also possible, and a good way of quickly bringing together geographically dispersed people. *ChatterBus*, mentioned earlier, is a form of online focus group, and Dubit, the youth research specialist, also provides online focus groups through its 'Clickroom' facility.

**Telephone interviews**. Telephone interviews are primarily used as a means of reaching a large number of respondents relatively quickly and directly. It is far more difficult to ignore a telephone call than a mail survey, although the amount and complexity of information that can be gathered are often limited. In the absence of any visual prompts and with a maximum attention span of probably no more than 10 minutes, the design of the questionnaire needs to be given great care and piloting is essential to ensure that the information required is obtainable.

Dubit: a specialist in youth and family research

*Source*: Dubit Research, www.dubitresearch.com

Mobile phones and particularly smartphones have given telephone research a new lease of life. Unlike the traditional landline, the mobile can provide access to pictures and graphics as a visual aid supporting a survey, and SMS can be used to get a very quick response to one-off questions. Ipsos MORI, for example, has a panel of over 11,000 mobile phone users and used SMS to ask 2,500 of them their views on crime. The survey was done on a Friday, and the results published on Sunday. Surveys conducted via mobiles reach the respondent wherever they happen to be and thus tend to get a quicker response, as they are not dependent on phoning a landline when someone happens to be home. The mobile is also a great way of reaching certain target groups that can otherwise be elusive, such as young people, business people, and those who are generally 'on the go'. A mobile survey can be targeted (i.e. the researchers approach a sample of users) or it can invite anyone to participate by advertising a free text-in number that starts the survey process.

Another survey that Ipsos was involved in used a smartphone app to ask people to share their thoughts, feelings, photos and other information with regard to Prince William's wedding in April 2011. It asked people where they were watching, with whom, and how they felt about the wedding and about the monarchy generally. Participants were asked not only to upload photos of their own celebrations around the event, but also to allow their location to be uploaded via GPS so that the results of the research could be mapped. By using this sort of methodology, the researchers were able to get spontaneous responses as the event was unfolding, and before people had time to revise their feelings in the light of subsequent press coverage and analysis of it (*PR Newswire Europe*, 2011; www.ipsos-mori. com/researchtechniques/datacollection/online/researchviamobilephones.aspx).

The range of applications is wide but the telephone is especially useful for usage and purchase surveys where market size, trends and competitive share are to be assessed. Other applications include assessing advertising and promotional impact, and customer satisfaction studies. Many organisations telephone customers to establish the degree of satisfaction with their recent purchases.

The interviewing process itself is highly demanding, but the use of software packages can enable the interviewer to record the findings more effectively and formally and to steer through the questionnaire, using loops and routing through, depending on the nature of the response. With the demand for such surveys, a number of agencies specialise in telephone research techniques.

Specialist business-to-business research agency B2B International (www.b2binternational. com) describes the main benefits of computer aided telephone interviewing (CATI) to its clients as accuracy and speed. As the questionnaire and routing appear automatically on the screen in front of interviewers, they are left free to concentrate on the interview itself and on recording responses accurately rather than concerning themselves with instructions on paper. There is also less chance of interviewers making a mistake. The nature of the computer-aided approach means that feedback on results can be given in real time, and interviews are generally completed more quickly than with paper equivalents. The approach copes less well with open-ended response questions, however, and although it is time saving in execution, it can be time consuming to set up.

**Mail questionnaires**. This form of research involves sending a questionnaire through the post to the respondent for self-completion and return to the researchers. Questionnaires can, of course, also be handed out at the point of sale, or included in product packaging, for buyers to fill in at their own convenience and then post back to the researchers. Hotels and airlines assess their service provision through this special kind of mail survey, and many electrical goods manufacturers use them to investigate purchasing decisions.

While the mail survey has the advantage of wide coverage, the lack of control over response poses a major problem. Researchers cannot control who responds and when and the level of non-response can create difficulties. Response rates can drop to less than 10 per cent in some surveys, although the more pertinent the research topic to the respondent, and the more 'user friendly' the questionnaire, the higher the response rate. Offering a special incentive can also work (Brennan *et al.*, 1991). In a survey of Irish hotel and guest-house owners, the offer of free tickets to a local entertainment facility proved an attractive incentive. Other larger-scale consumer surveys promise to enter all respondents into a draw for a substantial prize.

**Online questionnaires**. As internet penetration increases, online surveys have, to a large extent taken over from mail surveys, as they are cheaper and quicker to do, and the data input is accurate because it is effectively done directly by the respondent. It is perhaps also easier for a respondent to input answers from a keyboard and upload something rather than going to the trouble of finding a pen, filling in a form and posting it. Consumers are becoming used to being asked to participate in customer experience surveys either when they visit websites or after they have bought something online. The risk, of course, is 'survey fatigue' leading to potential respondents refusing to participate and thus reducing response rates.

Social media are another way of accessing consumer feedback on sites such as Facebook, for example, without going near conventional research. On the Visit Wales website, for example, there is a special section on dog-friendly holidays which was created in response to feedback from consumers on social media. Tetley Tea also used social media research to assess whether bringing back the Tetley Teafolk was a good decision. They used people to pick the characters and to express ideas around merchandising and PR. So using online market research can supplant traditional approaches to research and channel social media activity (Hargrave, 2011; *New Media Age*, 2011).

There is no one best method to select from the group discussed above. Much will depend on the nature of the research brief, especially in the light of the resources available and the quality and quantity of information required for decision-making. The other factor that has become of significant concern is the cost of the research survey. Face-to-face interviews, especially if conducted on an in-depth basis, tend to be the most costly and time consuming, thus making this form of survey less attractive. Other survey techniques, such as group interviews, telephone surveys, mail and online questionnaires, all provide alternative, cheaper ways of gathering data. Each of them, however, also has its own set of limitations. Ultimately, the decision on choice of technique has to put aside absolute cost considerations and think in terms of finding the most cost-effective way of collecting those vital data.

## Observational research

This method involves, as its name implies, the observation by trained observers of particular individuals or groups, whether they are staff, consumers, potential consumers, members of the general public, children or whoever. The intention is to understand some aspect of their behaviour that will provide an insight into the problem that has been identified by the marketing research plan. For example, trials are often conducted with new products in which consumers are asked to use a particular product and are observed while they do so, thus giving information about design, utility, durability and other aspects, such as ease of use by different age groups, and whether people naturally use it in the intended way. This provides an opportunity to test the product and observe how it is used first hand.

Observational research helps to investigate the minute detail of how consumers make decisions or how they use products by observing their behaviour in a natural setting, rather than asking them. Campbells soup, for example, measured the biological signs such as sweat, pulse, breathing, posture and eye gaze of 40 people choosing the product in a store. As a result, the logo on the can was moved to make it clearer for consumers, a need that probably would not have been discovered by normal survey methods. Observing consumer behaviour within a retail store can help to define the most commonly used pathways around a store, the effect of promotional deals at the ends of aisles, the 'hot' and 'cold' zones in terms of customer traffic, and how many shoppers visit and make selections from each aisle, for instance. By using observation as part of a broader research design, richer insights can be gained into behaviour at the point of sale in the supermarket, and that can be coupled with aisle intercepts to probe deeper into motivation with individual shoppers. By being at the point of sale it can assist in determining what promotions are effective and how easy it is for shoppers to find the category (Jung-ho, 2011; *Point of Purchase*, 2011).

Another form of observational research that deliberately seeks feedback on employee performance is mystery shopping (see p. 563). This allows a researcher to go through the same experience as a normal customer, whether in a store, restaurant, plane or showroom. As far as the employees are concerned, they are just dealing with another customer and they are not aware that they are being closely observed. The 'shopper' is trained to ask certain questions and to measure performance on such things as service time, customer handling and question answering. The more objective the measures, the more valuable they are to marketing managers in ensuring that certain benchmark standards are being achieved. Mystery shopping is widely used by the larger retailers and service organisations. When first introduced it was designed to identify sloppy service staff so that they could be retrained or removed when the report was received by management. Now, it is part of a more comprehensive assessment of the service and shopping experience that real consumers enjoy or endure. It supports staff training and helps the organisation to understand the customer–service provider interface (Bromage, 2000).

The potential problems that can be experienced with interviews are also likely with observation where human observers are used. That is, the training and supervision of observers are of great importance and, since it is more subjective, the likelihood of misinterpretation is higher. On the other hand, mechanical observation tools may be used to overcome bias problems, such as supermarket scanners monitoring the purchases of particular consumers or groups of consumers, and the ACNielsen people meters, used to monitor the viewing and listening habits of television watchers and radio listeners.

Other devices can be used to observe or monitor closely the physiological responses of individuals, such as their pupil dilation (using a tachistoscope) when watching advertisements, to indicate degree of interest. A galvanometer, which measures minute changes in perspiration, can also help to gauge a subject's interest in advertisements.

In some ways, observation is a more reliable predictor of behaviour than verbal assertions or intentions. Where interaction is not needed with the respondent, or where the respondent may be unable to recall the minutiae of their own behaviour, direct observation may be a valuable additional tool in the researcher's armoury. It is particularly informative when people are not aware that they are being observed and are thus acting totally naturally, rather than changing their behaviour or framing responses to suit what they think researchers want to see or hear.

Even online shoppers aren't immune from a type of observation. The cookies that websites leave behind record where you've been and what you've looked at, and can be used as a marketing prompt. Browse houses on zoopla.co.uk, or look at goods on the John Lewis website and you'll suddenly find that you're seeing a lot of banner ads relating to that browsing session. Similarly, browsing particular product categories or brands on amazon.co.uk triggers e-mails over the following days prompting you to go back and look again. Not all consumers

# MARKETING IN ACTION

## Consumers in the wild: online and offline

Ethnography, netnography and sentiment analysis are concepts that have started to reshape the way in which agencies and their clients are approaching market research. They all stem from the same idea: that observing people behaving naturally in a real environment reveals more, and gives a truer picture than more traditional survey and interview techniques.

Sentiment analysis and netnography both draw on online behaviour, tracking and interpreting the volume and content (both in terms of what is said, and what underlying emotions are being expressed within it) of online 'chatter' and activity. There's a lot of chatter out there, and thus some research companies have developed 'robots' that can continuously search for online references to brands, defined keywords or relevant concepts. This data can then be analysed to get a quick sense of how people are generally feeling or reacting to a marketing initiative, how a news a story is being interpreted, or how a brand is actually perceived. NetBase, for example, is a US company that uses netnography and social media research to generate consumer insights. Its Brand Passion Index is an exercise that looks at consumer passion for brands in a particular category. The index is derived from a combination of the amount of online chatter that's going on about the brand(s) and analysis of the meaning and emotional intensity of that chatter. In July 2011, for example, NetBase looked at the summer's film releases. Often, the 'success' of movie franchises is expressed in terms of box-office takings, but this doesn't tell the whole story. While *Twilight* was number one at the box office, and generated the highest volume of online chatter, it also generated as much negative feeling as positive, and thus in terms of the Brand Passion Index was pushed into fourth place by *Toy Story*, *Shrek* and *Harry Potter* (Marketwire, 2010; http://www.netbase.com/blog/general/brand-passion-index-everyone-loves-woody/).

**Figure 5.3** Netbase's 'Brand Passion Index': summer box-office, hit films

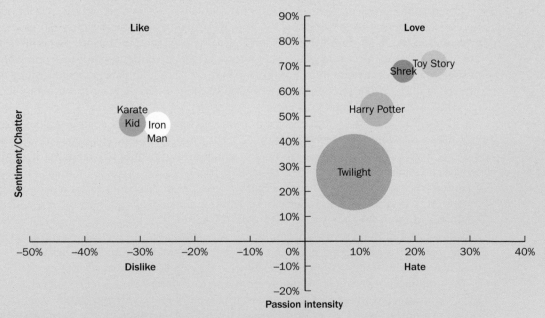

*Source*: Netbase, http://www.netbase.com/blog/general/brand-passion-index-everyone-loves-woody/

In this graphic, the amount of sentiment and chatter about a brand is indicated by the size of the bubble, while the placement of the bubble shows the intensity of passion.

BrainJuicer has developed an 'automated mass ethnography' tool called a DigiVidual. It's a customised avatar, that is given a character and a lifestyle, plus a bank of emotional words related to that lifestyle. The avatar is also programmed with trigger words that would prompt those emotions. The avatar is then let loose for a few days to trawl the net for blogs, tweets, other social media content, and any other websites. Psycho-social analysis is then used to work through the hundreds of 'things' that the avatar has collected to define the recurring themes. The findings can then be presented as stories about the avatar's character and his/her life and feelings, which gives a rich three-dimensional representation of a market segment.

Netnography (or digital anthropology) tends to take a more focused approach, targeting self-defined online communities for in-depth study of their behaviour and interaction. The concept of netnography was developed primarily by Robert Kozinets, who sees it as looking at:

> the entire community as it is, sort of like an ecosystem. That ecosystem has a place for spammers, for trolls, for the people who post obscene messages and photos, and for those who are getting paid to talk about products or services. Everyone in this ecosystem is a 'real' consumer, everyone has a role, and our role as netnographers is to understand how they all work together and interact.
> (as quoted by Pettit, 2010)

Clearly, given the richness and complexity of that 'ecosystem', skilled interpretation of the data generated is required, and that is something that Kozinets also acknowledges:

> Coders need to be highly skilled and to be able to recognize what is unique and powerful about a culture [. . .] A good coder needs to be familiar with the context. If they are coding online data about coffee culture, they need to understand what it is that they are coding. Preferably, they are participants in that culture. If not, then at least they need to be conversant with it, and able to understand it. You wouldn't want someone who didn't understand Japanese culture translating that language – and the same principle applies for a netnographer studying a marketplace culture.
> (as quoted by Pettit, 2010)

Understanding the cultural and historical context within which consumer behaviour takes place is also important in ethnography too, which involves researchers sometimes moving in to live with a family (which is another kind of ecosystem, I suppose) for a while in order to observe the context of the household's relationship with, and usage of a brand or product over time. Some ethnographic research is shorter-term and involves videoing specific interactions or events. The research agency Everyday Lives, for example, specialises in capturing observations of people doing everyday things on video. With so many crowded, mature markets, it is often only by spotting an unconscious consumer need (one that they couldn't tell you about in response to a direct question) or anticipating needs that new products and brands can gain competitive advantage. Everyday Lives has videoed consumers for various client projects doing things like brushing their teeth, shopping in supermarket aisles, preparing food, eating meals, and playing games on their mobile phones. The video footage is watched and analysed with a view to pinpointing new opportunities for product development or improved consumer communication. If new ideas arise from this analysis, the video footage is sometimes used as stimulus in further research with consumers to ask them if the new idea would change or improve their experience in a particular product category. It enables marketing managers to understand the difference between what consumers say and what they do, by uncovering behaviour we didn't know about and understanding consumer brand needs before they can express them. Check out Everyday Lives' website (www.everydaylives.com) and see what they've been watching us do lately.

A situation in which cultural understanding was critical was when VCCP, a UK ad agency, was tasked with developing an anti-binge drinking campaign for the government. The agency team used ethnographic research in Newcastle to get a better insight into how and why binge drinking happens. The team followed and photographed groups of teenaged binge drinkers at each stage of their night out, from the initial 'Tesco trudge' to stock up on drink, through the girly rituals of getting ready for a night out, through to the behaviours associated with the night out itself. It was all found to be very ritualistic and social, and the team were surprised to find that there are 'rules' within the social group. As the agency put it, 'There's kudos in drunkenness, but there's a line you cross when you let the group down and embarrass the people you're with. You go from a hero to a zero among your friends' (as quoted by Clift, 2011). Using these insights, along with analysis of the teens' reactions the morning after when they were shown the photographic evidence of their antics provided the basis for the final campaign advertisements which 'deliberately displace drunken behaviour from the night out to the cold light of day'.

*Sources*: Clift (2011); Kearon (2011); *Marketwire* (2010); Pettit (2010); Tarran (2011); Thorpe (2011); Woodnutt and Owen (2010); www.everydaylives.com; www.netbase.com.

Research can involve videoing consumers doing everyday things like shopping, playing electronic games or preparing food

*Source*: www.shutterstock.com/Monkey Business Images

are comfortable with this. Over 70 per cent of consumers in a recent survey were concerned over how companies collect data on the web though mechanisms such as cookies, although 62 per cent did not have a clear idea what exactly data can be collected when a site is visited (*PR Newswire*, 2011).

## Experimentation

The third method through which primary data can be collected is by conducting an experiment. This may involve the use of a laboratory (or other artificial environment), or the experiment may be set in its real-world situation, for example test marketing a product. In the experimental situation, researchers manipulate the independent variable(s), for example price, promotions or product position on a store shelf, and monitor the impact on the dependent variable, for example sales, to try to determine if any change in the dependent variable occurs. The important aspect of an experiment is to hold most of the independent variables constant (as well as other potentially confounding factors) while manipulating one independent variable and monitoring its impact on the dependent variable. This is usually possible in a laboratory, where control of the environment is within the power of researchers, but far less possible in a real-world situation where a myriad of external complications can occur that can confuse the results.

For example, a manufacturer may want to find out whether new packaging will increase sales of an existing product, before going to the expense of changing over to the new packaging. The manufacturer could conduct an experiment in a laboratory, perhaps by setting up a mock supermarket aisle, inviting consumers in and then observing whether their eyes were drawn to the new packaging, whether they picked it up, how long they looked at it and whether they eventually chose it in preference to the competition. The problem with this, however, is that it is still a very artificial situation, with no guarantees that it can replicate what would have happened in real life. Alternatively, therefore, the manufacturer could set up a field experiment, trialling the new packaging in real stores in one or more geographic regions and/or specific market segments and then monitoring the results.

Not all experimental research designs need to be highly structured, formal or set up for statistical validation purposes. For example, side-by-side experiments where shop A offers a different range or mix from shop B, which in all other respects is identical to shop A, can still reveal interesting insights into marketing problems, even though the rigour of more formal experimental designs is not present.

## Sampling

Particularly in mass consumer markets, time and cost constraints mean that it is impractical to include every single target customer in whatever data gathering method has been chosen. It is not necessary even to begin to try to do this, because a carefully chosen representative sample of the whole population (usually a target market) will be enough to give the researchers confidence that they are getting a true picture that can be generalised. In most cases, researchers are able to draw conclusions about the whole population (i.e. the group or target market) based on the study of a sample.

Figure 5.4, based on Tull and Hawkins (1990), shows the main stages in the sampling process. Each will be considered briefly in turn:

**Figure 5.4**
Stages in the
sampling process

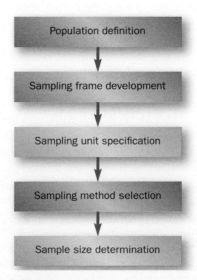

*Source*: adapted from Tull and Hawkins (1990)

## Population definition

The population to be surveyed will derive from the overall research objectives. Often this will be based on a target market or segment, but even then further definition based on markets, products or behaviours is unlikely to be necessary to create a tightly defined population.

## Sampling frame

The sampling frame is the means of access to the population to be surveyed. It is basically a list from which individual names can be drawn. Registers of electors, lists of organisations compiled from directories, or purchased lists are examples of possible sampling frames. Internal customer records may also provide a sampling frame, although researchers need to be very sure that such records give a complete picture, and that there is no doubt that this is the required population for the study, rather than just a cheap, quick and easy way of generating an extensive list of names.

## Sampling unit

The sampling unit is the actual individual from whom researchers want a response. In consumer markets, the sampling unit is usually the name attached to the address in the sampling frame. In B2B markets, however, this stage can be complex because, as we saw in Chapter 3, organisations have a number of individuals concerned with decision-making. It is very important to identify the right individual, as the responses of the purchasing manager in this case may be different from those of the managing director.

## Sampling method selection

The next step in the process is to select the sample method, which is the means by which individual sample units and elements are selected from the larger sampling frame. The main and early decision is whether to use probability or non-probability sampling methods.

**Probability sampling.** Random, or probability sampling, where each member of the population has an equal or known chance of being selected for the sample, offers specified levels of confidence about the limits of accuracy of the results. So if a retailer wanted to do a survey to establish satisfaction levels with checkout services, it might decide to interview every thirtieth customer coming through the checkouts during research sessions held at different times of the week. At the end of the process, the retailer might be able to conclude that the findings were correct to the 95 per cent level of confidence – in other words there was only a one in 20 chance that the sample was biased or unrepresentative.

Stratified sampling is an important method of probability sampling, which involves the division of the sampling frame into defined strata or groups that are mutually exclusive. Random probability samples are then drawn independently from each group. This method is widely used in B2B markets, as they naturally divide into discrete layers or bands, reflecting for example company size, geographic location, market shares or purchase volumes. Researchers could decide, therefore, to take a 100 per cent sample (census) of all the larger firms (defined perhaps by turnover or number of employees) and then use random sampling with the rest. By effectively restructuring the sample frame in a manner best suited to the project, greater confidence can be enjoyed that the sample closely reflects the population in question.

An alternative form of stratified sampling is area sampling. In a survey of German builders' merchants, for example, the first stage would be to divide Germany into regions and then randomly select a small number of those regions as the basis for the sample. Within each chosen region, researchers randomly select the organisations for the sample.

With a random sampling method, it is important for researchers to ensure that the sampling frame used does enable each member to have an equal chance of being selected. Furthermore, actually obtaining responses from the selected sample can be quite difficult. What if the thirtieth customer through the checkout doesn't want to stop? What if there's nobody at home when the interviewer calls round or phones? What if the sampling frame is out of date and the selected consumer has moved house or died? Any of these circumstances violates the ideal of the random sample.

**Non-random sampling.** Non-random samples are much easier to identify than random samples because they are not based on the same strict selection requirements and allow researchers a little more flexibility. The results from these samples are not representative of the population being studied and may lack the statistical rigour generated by random sampling, but they are still often of considerable use to researchers. Two main non-random sampling methods may be used:

1 *Judgemental sampling*. This method is widely used in B2B market research. Sample units are selected deliberately by researchers, because they are felt to represent better sources of the required information. Given the concentrated nature of many industries, if a contracting company for pipework cleaning wanted to enter a new geographical market, for example, it would probably make sense to survey the larger users if that was the target segment of interest, rather than draw at random from all users, large and small. Of course, no inference could be drawn about the wider population from such a sample method.

2 *Quota sampling*. Quota samples are formed when researchers decide that a certain proportion of the total sample should be made up of respondents conforming to certain characteristics. It may be decided, for example, that for a particular study, the sample should consist of 400 non-working women aged between 25 and 35, 250 full-time working and 350 part-time working women in the same age group. This breakdown may reflect the actual structure of the market under consideration. Each interviewer is then told how many completed questionnaires to bring back within each quota category. The choice of respondents is not random, since the interviewer is actively looking for people who fulfil the quota definitions and, once the quota is full, will reject any further respondents in that category.

The advantage of quota sampling is that it is quicker and cheaper to do than a full random sample would be, as no sample frame has to be devised and researchers do not have to worry whether the sampling frame is up to date or not. Furthermore, interviewers are not committed to following up specific respondents. Under a quota sample, if a particular respondent does not want to cooperate, then that's fine – the interviewer will look for another one.

## Sample size

A final yet very important consideration in the sampling process is sample size. While it may be true that the larger the sample, the greater the confidence that it truly represents the population of interest, there is no point in spending more time and money pursuing any bigger sample than you have to. With random sampling based on statistical analysis, researchers can have confidence within prescribed limits that the sample elements are representative of the population being studied.

As one would expect, the higher the levels of confidence required, the greater the size of the sample needed. In Europe, surveys of consumer buying habits are often of around 2000 units, which would typically yield a 95 per cent confidence level that the sample reflects the characteristics of the population. In B2B markets, sample sizes of between 300 and 1,000 can be used to produce high levels of confidence. This would be especially true when suppliers operate within limited geographical areas (such as plumbers, or van hire firms), the value of sales is usually small (motor factors), and the buying organisations are also small.

## Questionnaire design

The questionnaire is a commonly used research instrument for gathering and recording information from interviews, whether face-to-face, mail, internet or telephone surveys. Researchers soon learn that the best-planned surveys soon fall apart if the questionnaire is poorly designed and fails to gather the data originally anticipated. To minimise the risk of disappointment, however, there are several dimensions to consider in questionnaire design.

## Objectives

The aim of a questionnaire is closely linked with the overall purpose of the research. It is tailor-made to meet the information requirements of the study and therefore lies at the heart of the research process. If the questionnaire is to fulfil its role properly as a means of data collection, then there are several areas that need to be analysed, as outlined in Table 5.2.

**Table 5.2** The objectives of a questionnaire

| Objective | Suggestions |
|---|---|
| **To suit the nature of the target population** | Pitch the questions in a way they can understand; ask questions they can be expected to be able to answer given their knowledge and experience. |
| **To suit the research methods** | For example, a telephone survey cannot use the kind of visual aids that a face-to-face interview can; a postal survey is less likely to get responses if it is lengthy or if it is probing feelings and/or attitudes. |
| **To suit the research objectives** | It must be designed appropriately to gather the right information for answering the research questions – no more, no less. |
| **To collect the right kind of data** | The quality and completeness of responses are important for a successful survey. There must also be the right depth of data, whether it is factual or probing attitudes, beliefs, opinions, motivations or feelings. |
| **To aid data analysis** | Ensure that it is as easy as possible to take the raw data from the questionnaires and input them accurately into any analytical framework/software package being used. |
| **To minimise error and bias** | Ensure that the questionnaire is 'tight' enough to allow it to be administered by any interviewer, to any respondent, at any time, in any location with consistency. Also ensure that questions cannot be misinterpreted or misunderstood. |
| **To encourage accurate and full responses** | Avoid leading or judgemental questions; ensure clarity in the way questions are asked; ensure that respondents feel at ease rather than threatened or intimidated by the questions. |

Some thought also needs to be given to ensuring that the questionnaire will retain the interest of the respondent, so that full completion takes place. It is easy with self-administered questionnaires for the respondent to give up if the questionnaire becomes tedious, seems to be poorly explained, or is too long or complex. It is thus important to make sure that the questionnaire takes as little time as possible to complete.

## Types of questions

There are two main types of question that can be asked in a questionnaire: open-ended questions and closed questions. The category of open-ended questions has many significant style variations within it, but they all allow considerable scope for the respondent to express views on the selected theme (and in some cases, on other themes!). Closed questions force the respondent to choose one or more responses from a number of possible replies provided in the questionnaire.

**Open-ended questions.** Questions such as 'In the buying of garden furniture, what factors do you find important?' or 'What do you think of the trend towards out-of-town shopping centres?' are open-ended because they do not give a range of potential answers for the respondent to choose from. In both cases, interviewers could be faced with as many different answers as there are respondents. Using such questions, therefore, can be rewarding, because of the rich insights given in a relatively unrestrained manner. The difficulties, however, emerge in recording and analysing the responses, given their potential length and wide variations. Nevertheless, it has been argued that using open-ended questions can help to build the goodwill of the respondent through allowing an unrestricted response (Chisnall, 1986).

**Closed questions.** Closed questions fall into two broad groups, dichotomous and multiple-choice questions. Dichotomous questions allow only two choices, such as 'yes or no' or 'good or bad'. These questions are easy to ask and easy to answer. With careful pre-coding, it is also relatively easy to analyse responses and to use them for cross-tabulation with another variable, for example to find out whether those who say that they do use a product pay more attention to product-specific advertising than those who say that they do not use it.

Multiple-choice questions are a more sophisticated form of closed question, because they can present a list of possible answers for the respondent to choose from. This could be, for example, a list of alternative factors that might influence a purchasing decision (price, quality, availability, etc.), or it could reflect alternative levels of strength of feeling, degree of importance or other shades of variation in response to the variable under consideration.

These questions need to be designed carefully, to incorporate and group as wide a range of answers as possible, since restraining the amount of choice available creates a potential source of bias. The alternative responses need to reflect the likely range, without overlap or duplication, since this too may create bias. By offering an 'other, please specify' category, these questions provide some opportunity to collect responses that were not originally conceived (but that should have been identified in the pilot stage) or responses that do not fit neatly into the imposed structure. However, the advantage of multiple-choice questions is that again they are relatively straightforward to analyse, if pre-coding has been used.

Multiple choices can also be used to overcome some respondent sensitivities. If asked 'How old are you?' or 'What do you earn?' as open questions, many people may refuse to answer because the questions are too specific and personal. Phrasing the question as 'To which of these age groups do you belong: 17 or under, 18–24, 25–34, 35–44, 45 or over?' allows respondents to feel that they have not given quite so much away. It is unlikely in any case that knowing a respondent's exact age would be of any greater use to researchers. The bands need to be defined to reflect the likely scope of responses from the target respondents, and to be easy for them to relate to. Professionals, for example, will be more likely to relate to bands based on annual salary than manual workers, who are more likely to know what their weekly wage is.

Rating scales are a form of multiple-choice question, widely used in attitude measurement, motivational research and in situations where a number of complex, interacting factors are likely to influence a situation. There are a number of scaling methods, including the following:

1 *Likert summated ratings.* A large number of statements, relevant to the research study, are built up from preliminary research and piloting. These statements are then given to respondents who are asked to respond on a five- or seven-point scale, for example, 'strongly agree', 'agree', 'neither agree nor disagree', 'disagree' and 'strongly disagree'. The responses are scored from 5 (strongly agree) down to 1 (strongly disagree). The average score across all respondents can then be used to establish the general strength of attitude towards the variable under consideration. An examination of the pattern of individual responses may also reveal issues of interest to the marketer.

2 *Semantic differential scales.* These scales were developed to measure differences in the meaning of words or concepts. This method involves a bipolar five- or seven-point rating scale, with each extreme defined by carefully selected adjectives representing opposite extremes of feeling. A study of retail store atmosphere might offer a series of scales including 'warm – cold', 'friendly – unfriendly' or 'fashionable – unfashionable', for example. Once the scales have been defined, the product (or whatever) is rated on each of them to reveal a profile of the respondent's opinion. Such scales can also be used for measuring corporate image or advertising image and for comparing different brands. In the latter case, if two products are plotted at the same time on the same scales, significant differences may emerge, and help the marketer to understand better the relative positioning of products in consumers' minds.

Examples of both types of rating scale can be found in Figure 5.5.

**The wording of questions**. The success or failure of a questionnaire lies as much in the detail as in the grand scheme and design. This includes the detailed wording of questions so that the respondent fully understands what is required and accurate responses are encouraged. The next few paragraphs raise a number of pertinent issues.

It is always important to ensure that the meaning of words and phrases is fully understood by the respondent. Particular effort should be made to avoid the use of jargon and technical language that may be unfamiliar to the respondent.

**Likert scale**

| | Strongly agree | Agree | Neither agree nor disagree | Disagree | Strongly disagree |
|---|---|---|---|---|---|
| Morrisons prices are generally lower than those of other supermarkets | | | | | |
| Morrisons offers the widest range of groceries | | | | | |
| Morrisons staff are always friendly and helpful | | | | | |
| I never have to queue too long at the checkout | | | | | |
| Supermarket own-brands are just as good as manufacturers' brands | | | | | |
| Low prices are important to me in choosing a supermarket | | | | | |
| Supermarkets should provide more personal services | | | | | |

**Semantic differential scale**

| | 1 | 2 | 3 | 4 | 5 | 6 | 7 | |
|---|---|---|---|---|---|---|---|---|
| Modern | | | | | | | | Old-fashioned |
| Friendly | | | | | | | | Unfriendly |
| Attractive | | | | | | | | Unattractive |
| Spacious | | | | | | | | Crowded |
| High-quality goods | | | | | | | | Low-quality goods |
| Wide choice of goods | | | | | | | | Limited choice of goods |
| Convenient opening hours | | | | | | | | Inconvenient opening hours |
| Tidy | | | | | | | | Untidy |
| Short queues | | | | | | | | Long queues |
| Low prices | | | | | | | | High prices |

**Figure 5.5** Examples of rating scales

Ambiguity can lead to misunderstandings and thus poor or inaccurate responses. A question such as 'Do you buy this product frequently, sometimes, seldom or never?' seems to be clear and unambiguous, but think about it for a minute. What does 'frequently' mean? To one respondent it might mean weekly, to another it might mean monthly. Researchers should therefore be as specific as possible.

A further source of ambiguity or confusion occurs when the respondent is asked to cope with too many concepts at once. Two questions should therefore never be piggy backed, i.e. asked in one question, such as: 'How important is price to you, and how do you think we could improve on value for money?'

Leading questions may tempt the respondent to favour a particular answer. This is not, of course, the essence of good research. Thus asking 'Are you, or are you not, in favour of capital punishment?' is more balanced than 'Are you in favour of capital punishment?', which is edging the respondent towards 'Yes' as an answer.

Questions that are too closed are a kind of leading question that may also frustrate researchers. 'Is price an important factor in your purchase?' begs the answer 'Yes', but even if it was a balanced question, the responses tell very little. It does not indicate how important price is to the respondent or what other factors influence the purchase. An open-ended or multiple-choice question might tell much more.

Researchers need to be sympathetic to people's sensitivity. Some areas are highly personal, so building up slowly may be important and 'soft' rather than 'hard' words should be used, for example 'financial difficulties' rather than 'debt'. Of course, the more sensitive the information, the more likely the respondent is to refuse to answer, lie or even terminate the interview.

**Coding and rules**. It is more important to obtain accurate and pertinent information than to design a questionnaire that embraces everything but rarely gets completed. Hague (1992) proposes an ideal length for three different types of questionnaire:

- telephone interviews: five to 30 minutes
- visit interviews: 30 minutes to two hours
- self-completion: four sides of A4 paper, 20–30 questions.

A street interview would need to be very much shorter than 30 minutes to retain interest and prevent irritation.

The layout of the questionnaire is especially important for self-administered questionnaires. A cramped page looks unappealing, as well as making it difficult to respond. Where an interviewer is in control of the questionnaire, the layout should assist the recording and coding of responses and ease of flow through the interview to maintain momentum. Most questionnaires are now designed with data coding and ease of analysis in mind. This means that all responses to closed questions and multiple choices need to be categorised before the questionnaire is released, and that the layout must also be user friendly for whoever has to transfer the data from the completed questionnaire into a database.

The order of the questions is important for respondents, as the more confusing the flow and the more jumping around they have to do, the less likely they are to see it through to completion.

Support materials and explanation can be very important. For a mail survey, a covering letter can be reassuring and persuasive while, at an interview, the interviewer needs to gain the respondent's attention and interest in participation. Visual aids, such as packaging or stills from advertising, can also get respondents more involved, as well as prompting their memories.

## Piloting

Whatever care has been taken in the design of the questionnaire, problems usually emerge as soon as the questionnaire is tried on innocent respondents. Piloting a questionnaire on a small-scale sample can help to iron out any 'bugs', so that it can be refined before the full survey goes ahead. Initially, a fresh eye from colleagues can eliminate the worst howlers, but for most projects, it is best to set aside time for a full field pilot. This would mean testing the questionnaire on a small sub-sample (who will usually not then participate in the main survey) to check its meaning, layout and structure and, furthermore, to check whether it yields the required data and whether it can be analysed in the intended manner.

# Conduct the research

Once the research plan has been developed and the methods of collection and proposed analysis identified, it is necessary to go about conducting the research itself. This stage will vary according to the type of research. The demands of a consumer survey involving perhaps thousands of respondents over a wide geographic area are very different from those of a select number of interviews in depth.

Particularly in primary research, it is this part of the process that often presents the biggest problem, because the collection of the data should not be left to poorly trained or badly briefed field researchers. In recent years, however, considerable progress has been made in professionalising research interviewers, moving away from the rather clichéd image of housewives earning extra cash. Training is now widespread and more male interviewers have been recruited both to enable access to previously no-go areas, such as high-crime housing estates and to handle situations where gender may matter during the interview.

Recruiting market research interviewers is not an easy job. Staff have to be prepared to work afternoons and evenings to make sure that they get representative samples of all kinds of workers. They also have to be well organised and good at managing themselves and their time, especially if they are working out in the field rather than in a telephone interview call centre, for example. All researchers need a strong sense of responsibility and have to be prepared to take an ethical approach to what they do. Field researchers have to be tough, to cope with less cooperative interviewees or to deal with the stranger kinds of people one meets when spending a lot of time hanging around city streets with a clipboard. There are 30,000 interviewers in the UK but the majority work part-time or are contracted for specific projects, with only just over 5,000 working full time. The majority of these are data gatherers rather than data interpreters.

Provided that interviewers read the questions exactly as they are written (an absolute rule in all market research codes of conduct), there is little difference between one interviewer and another on closed questions. There is, however, a huge difference when prompting and probing for open-ended questions. An interviewer who writes down verbatim exactly what the respondent says, encouraging them to clarify and add anything else continually, until the response 'nothing else' is achieved, will improve the quality and richness of data generated. Interviewers who are conscious of taking up too much of the respondent's time, may take less time over the questionnaire and as a consequence sacrifice richness of data for speed of completion.

Increasingly, the bulk of the work is moving away from large scale surveys to internet and observational research, so the nature of the role is changing too. Watching and filming consumers and assessing how they interact with brands requires a different set of skills from interviewing for large scale surveys. In online survey research the interviewer's task is less personal and is required in different locations. It means the researcher's role is more to do with initial screening rather than recording.

There is, however, still a role for field interviewers and well over 50 per cent of research still involves using researchers for face-to-face interviews. Research companies thus take a great deal of care in recruiting and training researchers. Some companies undertake lengthy initial telephone screening, partly to give applicants a better idea of what the job entails and partly to help develop a profile of the candidate. Many companies then insist on a face-to-face interview to check a candidate's appearance (especially for field researchers), their interaction skills and their ability to deal with situations. This is important because staff are effectively representing the research company and its clients and they have to be able to develop a rapport with interviewees quickly, reassure them and hold their attention, often through a fairly long and detailed survey. The pay? £10 to £15 per completed interview or £200–£250 a day for focus group facilitation (Lewis, 2010; www.mrs.org.uk).

There are a number of areas, in any kind of face-to-face research, where careful attention to detail can pay dividends. The greater the need for the interviewer to depart from a carefully prepared script and *modus operandi*, the greater the skill involved and the higher the cost of the interview. This is particularly emphasised in the implementation role of the interviewer who conducts a group discussion or an in-depth interview. The dangers of interview bias are always present where the interviewer records what they think has been said or meant, not what has actually been said in response to a question. This sort of bias can be particularly pronounced where open-ended questions are being used. There are some situations where conducting field research is especially challenging, such as when particular targets or subjects need to be covered. The extremely affluent or poor, ethnic minorities, youth and corporate executives are often harder to reach than many target groups in the UK, although as mentioned earlier, online and mobile phone-based research can often be useful in reaching some of these groups. Community intermediaries are often used, for example, to reach target groups such as older Asian women and the Jamaican community and persuade them to participate in research.

As well as enabling web- and mobile phone-based research methods, technology is also making a big impact in the implementation of field research by assisting in the questioning and recording process. Computer aided telephone interviewing (CATI) and computer aided personal interviewing (CAPI) have revolutionised data collection techniques and are now widely used. CAPI means that each interviewer is provided with a laptop or tablet computer which has the questionnaire displayed on screen. The interviewer can then read out text from the screen and key in the responses. The pre-programmed questionnaire will automatically route the interviewer to different parts of the questionnaire as appropriate (e.g. those who have/have not purchased in the previous three months) and will prompt the interviewer to clarify any illogical answers. It helps quality control by creating greater consistency in interviewer questioning and the recording of answers and furthermore allows the interviewer to concentrate on building a rapport with the respondent to help prevent fatigue and loss of interest in more complex questionnaires. CATI provides similar technology for telephone interviewing and again allows for greater consistency in interviewing and the recording of information. The additional advantage of both methods is the ability to download data quickly for analysis thus offering clients a faster turn-around time on their data requests.

## Analyse and interpret the information

While the quality of the research data is essential, it is the analysis of the data, i.e. turning raw data into useful information, that provides the most value to the organisation. It is on the basis of the reports prepared from the data analysis that significant managerial decisions are likely to be made. The use of sophisticated computer hardware and software packages provides a powerful means of processing large quantities of data relatively easily. CAPI, CATI, scanners that can read completed questionnaires, complex statistical analysis and data manipulation have improved the speed, accuracy and depth of the analysis itself. However, it is still the human element, the researcher's expertise in identifying a trend or relationship or some other nugget hidden within the results, that provides the key component for decision makers and transforms the data and techniques used into valuable information.

Some care needs to be exercised in the interpretation of quantitative data. Outputs of calculations should never overrule sound common sense in assessing the significance and relevance of the data generated. There is sometimes the danger of analysis paralysis, where the use of highly sophisticated techniques almost becomes an end in itself, rather than simply a means of identifying new relationships and providing significant new insights for management. While the old saying that trends, differences or relationships are only meaningful if they are obvious to even the untrained statistical eye may be going too far, it does highlight the danger of misinterpreting cause and effect and the differences between groups of consumers, arising from over-reliance on finely balanced statistics pursued by researchers.

Not all data are quantitative, of course. Qualitative data arising from in-depth interviews or group discussions pose a different kind of challenge to researchers. Whereas quantitative data have to prove their reliability when compared with the wider population, qualitative data can never be claimed to be representative of what a wider sample of respondents might indicate. The main task of qualitative data, therefore, is to present attitudes, feelings and motivations in some depth, whether or not they are representative of the wider population.

To handle qualitative data analysis, great care must be taken in the recording of information. Video or taped interviews are thus helpful in enabling classification and categorisation of the main points to be checked and explored in depth. Similarly, issue or content analysis enables particular themes to be explored across a range of interviews, and the software packages exist to help with this task. For example, if researchers wanted to identify the barriers to exporting in small firms, they might define such themes as market entry, market knowledge, finance or using agents as indicative of the main barriers to be assessed. The data analysis might be supported by a range of quotations from the interviews. Because of the richness and complexity of this kind of data, skilled psychologists are often used to explore and explain much of what is said and, indeed, not said.

So although the risks of bias are great in qualitative analysis, both in data selection and analysis, and although the results can, in untrained hands, be rather subjective and conjectural, the advantage arises from the fresh insights and perspectives that more rigorous statistical techniques would simply not generate.

## Prepare and present the report

The information provided by researchers must be in a form that is useful to decision makers. Too often, research reports are written in highly technical language or research jargon that, to a layperson, is confusing or meaningless. Marketers who want to use these reports to make decisions need them to be easily understandable. A report that is too complex is all but useless. That is why the formal presentation of the report, whether written or verbal (which allows the client to ask questions and seek clarification of points made), should be given as much thought, care and attention as any previous stage in the research process. It also allows the results to be personalised for the receiving organisation which can improve the perceived credibility of the findings and thus increase willingness to take action (Schmalensee, 2001).

Although a verbal presentation can play an important part in sharing understanding, it is the report itself that has the power to influence thinking significantly. Arguments can be carefully presented, with data used appropriately in their support, and the detail surrounding the main findings can be displayed to increase the client's confidence that the research was well executed to plan. There are no standard report formats, as much will depend on the nature of the research task undertaken.

## Research evaluation

Research projects rarely go completely to plan. Although greater care in conducting pilot studies and exploratory research will make it more likely that the actual outcomes will match those planned, problems may still emerge that will require careful consideration in weighing up the value of the project. Thoughtful analysis of the planning, conduct and outcomes of the project will also teach valuable lessons for the future to both clients and researchers.

This stage can involve a review of all aspects of the research plan described above. Any deviations need to be understood, both in terms of the current results and for designing future research. With regard to the research project undertaken, the most important point is whether the research actually provided a sufficient quality and quantity of information to assist management decision-making. Sometimes, the research objectives may have been ambiguous or poorly framed in the context of the marketing problem being addressed. Ultimately, it is the marketing manager who must take responsibility for ensuring that the objectives and research plan were compatible and reflected the requirements, although researchers can help in this task.

## Ethics in marketing research

The ethical concerns surrounding market research have been the subject of an ongoing debate in the industry for a long time. Because much consumer research involves specific groups of consumers, including children and other groups that might be considered vulnerable, it is essential that the researchers' credibility is maintained and that the highest standards of professional practice are demonstrated, and so the industry has established a set of professional ethical guidelines. These guidelines include such matters as protecting the confidentiality of respondents or clients, not distorting or misrepresenting research findings (for example, two major newspapers could both claim to be the market leader by using readership figures gathered over different time spans and failing to mention the time period), using tricks to gain information from respondents, conducting an experiment and not telling those being studied, and using research as a guise for selling and sales lead building.

The European Society for Opinion and Marketing Research (ESOMAR), a leading marketing research association, is actively trying to encourage members to stamp out the practice of 'sugging' (selling under the guise of market research) through an agreed code of practice.

*eg*

When market researchers have to investigate children's behaviour and motivation as consumers, they have to proceed with extreme caution. It is very easy to step over both the legal line and industry codes designed to protect children and young people from predatory practices. Nevertheless, marketers cannot afford to ignore the needs of a segment that has got more disposable income than ever for discretionary purchases, has more influence over household purchases, and is able to persuade guilty, busy parents that a particular purchase will make up for lack of time spent together. Children's views aren't just important to mainstream marketers. Children's charities, such as Barnardos or ChildLine need to know what children think and feel, and even the government admits that 'Real service improvement is only attainable through involving children and young people and listening to their views' (as quoted by Clarke and Nairn, 2011). Little wonder, then, that children are a group that marketers and policy-makers are keen to understand, but they have to balance effective research with 'responsibility'.

Marketers and to some extent policy-makers thus rely on the market research industry to help them understand what makes today's kids tick. The Market Research Society has a firm code of conduct which must be applied when any researcher is dealing with children in a research situation. The objective is 'to protect the rights of children [under-sixteens] and young people [16 and 17-year-olds] physically, mentally, ethically and emotionally and to ensure that they are not exploited.' The rules apply mainly to practicalities: ensuring that parental consent is given; ensuring that children are aware that they can refuse to answer questions or can opt out; and making sure that another adult is present or nearby. The code also requires researchers to ensure that the content is appropriate, i.e. that nothing is discussed that is inappropriate to the age group; that nothing happens that is likely to cause tension between child and parents or peer group; and that there is nothing that is likely to upset or worry a child. Dubit Research, mentioned earlier, that specialises in research with children and young people makes it very clear that all its research is conducted in accordance with MRS guidelines.

As research methods develop to delve deeper into children's commercial motivation and behaviour, with the resulting impact on marketing initiatives, some practitioners have become concerned about the need for the market research industry to face up to its share of social responsibility. The Market Research Society's current position is that the marketing and advertising industries have guidelines they follow on marketing to children, and as long as the market research industry reflects those, it is not up to researchers to lead on the issue. But it is a debate that is likely to continue (Clarke and Nairn, 2011; www.dubitresearch.com; www.mrs.org.uk).

In terms of UK research, all researchers are bound by the legislation covered by the Data Protection Act. There is also the MRS (Market Research Society), a trade association representing the interests of market researchers and market research companies and helping to regulate them. It has its own regulations and codes of conduct for ethical conduct of research by which its members are required to abide. The MRS itself is also a member of the Market Research

Quality Standards Association (MRQSA), an all-industry body that brings together several relevant professional and trade organisations, and part of its work involves accrediting market research companies that comply with international standard ISO20252 for research, data collection and processing. See www.mrs.org.uk/standards/other.htm for a comprehensive set of links to various relevant bodies and codes of practice. Of course, not all providers of market research are committed to compliance and not all bad practice can be eliminated, but considerable progress is being made.

## Chapter summary

- Marketing managers find it impossible to make decisions effectively without a constant flow of information on every aspect of marketing. Everything, from defining target markets to developing marketing mixes to making long-term strategic plans, has to be supported with appropriate information.

- The organisation needs to coordinate its information, collected from a variety of sources, into an MkIS. A formal MkIS brings everything together under one umbrella and provides timely and comprehensive information to aid managers in decision-making. DSS build on the MkIS, also to help decision-making. The DSS uses a variety of computer tools and packages to allow a manager to manipulate information, to explore possible outcomes of courses of action and to experiment in a risk-free environment. There are three different types of market research, exploratory, descriptive and causal, each one serving different purposes. Depending on the nature of the problem under investigation, any of the three types of market research may use qualitative or quantitative data. Rather than individually pursuing a series of marketing research studies, an organisation can participate in continuous research, undertaken by a market research agency on an ongoing basis and usually syndicated.

- There is a general framework for the conduct of a marketing research project that can be applied to almost any kind of market or situation. It consists of eight stages: problem definition, research objectives, planning the research, data collection, research implementation, data analysis, reporting findings and research evaluation.

- *Secondary research* provides a means of sourcing marketing information that already exists in some form, whether internal or external to the organisation. Gaps in secondary data can be filled through *primary research*. The main methods of primary research are interviews and surveys, observation and experiments. *Sampling* is a crucial area for successful market research. There is no need to survey an entire population in order to find answers to questions. As long as a representative sample is drawn, answers can be generalised to apply to the whole population. *Questionnaires* are often used as a means of collecting data from the sample selected, and they must reflect the purpose of the research, collect the appropriate data accurately and efficiently, and facilitate the analysis of data.

- Ethical issues in market research are very important. Researchers have to comply with codes of practice to protect vulnerable groups in society from exploitation. They also have to ensure that respondents recruited for market research studies are fully aware of what they are committing themselves to and that they are not misled at any stage in the research process.

# Questions for review and discussion

**5.1** Why is *market research* an essential tool for the marketing manager?

**5.2** What kinds of marketing problems might be addressed through:

(a) *exploratory*;

(b) *descriptive*; and

(c) *causal* research projects?

**5.3** Define the stages of the *market research process* and outline what each one involves.

**5.4** Discuss the role and content of an *MkIS* and how it might relate to a *DSS*.

**5.5** Evaluate the appropriateness of each of the different *interview and survey-based primary research methods* for:

(a) investigating the buying criteria used by B2B purchasers;

(b) defining the attitudes of a target market towards a brand of breakfast cereal;

(c) profiling purchasers of small electrical goods; and

(d) measuring levels of post-purchase satisfaction among customers.

Clearly define any assumptions you make about each of the situations.

**5.6** Design a questionnaire. It should contain about 20 questions and you should use as many of the different types of question as possible. Pay particular attention to the concerns discussed at pp. 191–195 of the chapter. The objective is to investigate respondents' attitudes to downloading music and their purchasing habits. Pilot your questionnaire on 12 to 15 people (but preferably not people on the same course as you), analyse the results and then make any adjustments. Within your seminar group, be prepared to discuss the rationale behind your questionnaire, the outcome of the pilot and any data analysis problems.

# CASE STUDY 5

# 'AND NOW, HERE ARE THE FOOTBALL RESULTS'

*Lorna Young*

During the 2006/2007 season, revenue in the European Premier Football Leagues totalled €13.6 billion (Deloitte, 2008). The 'big five' – English Premiership, German Bundesliga, Spanish La Liga, Italian Serie A, and French Ligue 1 accounted for €7.1 billion, with the English Premier League representing the highest earner at €2.3 billion. Despite these figures, only 10 clubs in British football are profitable, and the 72 clubs outside of the Premiership, in the British Football League (Championship, League Divisions 1 and 2 collectively), do not have guaranteed access to any of the colossal income stream that broadcast rights to matches paid by the terrestrial and satellite television channels represents. This leaves them almost entirely reliant on the generation of income from matchdays and commercial activities such as sponsorship. Oughton *et al.* (2003) exposed the weakness of the typical football club business model as financially over-reliant on one person or small group of people – witness the pop star Elton John's historical association with Watford FC, the Harrods owner Mohammed Al Fayed's involvement with Fulham FC, and Russian billionaire Roman Abramovich's ownership of Chelsea FC – and proposed that the key to long-term sustainability lay in the wider community. Webster and Clements (2008) went further in declaring that for football clubs to be profitable they need not only to be successful on the pitch, but also to realise the importance of their fans as a revenue stream – particularly those clubs competing in the lower leagues.

So how are football clubs to organise and manage themselves to make decisions with regard to building relationships with their fan base that allow them to improve and become more profitable? With the objective of identifying areas of best practice, highlighting areas for improvement, and to provide the facility to monitor the effectiveness of initiatives taken by clubs over time, in 2006 and 2008 the Football League (the governing body for the 72 clubs outside of the Premiership) enlisted the services of the experienced sports market research company SportsWise to undertake the first Football League Supporters Surveys.

Initially, SportsWise conducted workshops with staff at the League clubs in order to establish factors they considered could be measured, that would reflect success or failure in delivering a positive experience for supporters, and combined findings from this with their previous experience in data-gathering for football and rugby Premiership divisions, to arrive at *key performance indicators* for assessment. In this case, the key performance indicators identified were matchday experience, stadium facilities, ticketing, club products and the club's website. Other areas identified as worthy of investigation were supporter perception of feeling valued by club, contact with club community initiatives, main shirt sponsor feedback, sponsor relationship with supporters, preferred day and kick-off time for non-weekend matches, and time of arrival at stadium on matchdays.

In 2008, the survey used an online methodology. Invitations to participate were emailed to fans on the clubs' databases, click-throughs were placed on The Football League website and individual club websites. An incentive to participate in the survey was offered in the form of the opportunity to win tickets to the 2008 Play-Off Finals at Wembley. A total of 40,319 online questionnaires were completed by supporters across the 72 clubs during December 2007 and January 2008. Screening questions at the outset confirmed club support, match attendance in the last two years, and season ticket holder status, as well as establishing demographics. To ensure that it was representative, overall data was weighted to reflect each club's average match attendance rather than taking the individual club's response rate. In terms of the questionnaire itself, supporters were asked to rate their club's performance on a five-point Likert scale (very good, good, neither good nor poor, poor, very poor) for each of the performance Indicators, which were broken down into key components, for example:

- **Matchday experience** – atmosphere, price of refreshments, standard of refreshments, parking facilities, attitude of staff, matchday programme and pre-match entertainment.

- **Stadium facilities** – fan safety, sightlines, toilet facilities, stadium cleanliness, stewarding, quality and use of PA system.
- **Ticketing** – prices, ease of purchase, ease of obtaining information, attitude of office staff, discounts for children, office opening times.
- **Club products** – price of replica kit, quality of replica kit, design of home kit, value for money, availability of replica kit.
- **Club website** – club news, live match stats, club shop offers, ticket information, hospitality and events, details of community work.

Once the data had been analysed, each club was provided with a report which detailed in tabular form, for each factor rated, the club's 2008 score, the club's 2006 score, the average for the Football League in total, the average for each of the Championship, League 1 and League 2, and the club's ranking within their League for that factor. In addition a table was included detailing the five clubs obtaining the top ranking for each factor within each individual League, and the top five clubs taking the Football League as a whole.

*Sources*: Deloitte (2008); Oughton *et al.* (2003); Webster and Clements (2008); and with thanks to Jon Downer, Research Director of SportsWise Ltd.

## Questions

1 Why do you think a survey of this nature is carried out only every two years rather than more regularly? Why was data deliberately collected during December/January?

2 Why do you think the 'other areas' of investigation, outside of the key performance indicators, were identified as being important? What decisions, made by a football club's management team might be informed by the results of supporters' views?

3 What do you think were the advantages and disadvantages of using an online survey technique for this research? Assuming that the budget was available, what other techniques would you use in addition to the survey described, and why?

4 Think about a company or brand outside the world of sport whose product/service is designed to provide you with an 'experience'. List what you believe would be the key performance indicators if they were to undertake a participants' survey and give reasons why.

# References for chapter 5

Atherton, S. (2011) 'Lager for Ladies. Again', *Guardian Unlimited*, 19 July.

BBC (2011a) 'FA Cup to be Sponsored by Budweiser Beer', BBC News, 16 June, accessed via www.bbc.co.uk/news/business-13792977.

BBC (2011b) '"Costs" and "Fun" Dominate Views of University', *BBC News*, 24 August, accessed via www.bbc.co.uk/news/education-14616788.

Bamford, V. (2011) 'Molson Coors Unveils its Beers for the Girls', *The Grocer*, 16 July.

Boyd, H.W., Westfall, R. and Stasch, S. (1977) *Marketing Research*, 4th edn. Irwin.

Brennan, M., Hoek, J. and Astridge, C. (1991) 'The Effects of Monetary Incentives on the Response Rate and Cost Effectiveness of a Mail Survey', *Journal of the Market Research Society*, 33 (3), pp. 229–41.

Bromage, N. (2000) 'Mystery Shopping', *Management Accounting*, April, p. 30.

*Business Wire* (2008) 'Tesco Reconfirms Commitment to Teradata', *Business Wire*, 11 September.

*Business Wire* (2011) 'New Research Finds Reliance on Smartphones Driving Changes in Consumers' Purchase Habits', *Business Wire*, 29 June.

Chisnall, P.M. (1986) *Marketing Research*, 3rd edn. McGraw-Hill.

Clark, A. (2011) 'A Beer Without the Gut: Could This Appeal to Women Drinkers?', *The Times*, 18 July.

Clarke, B. and Nairn, A. (2011) 'Researching Children: Are We Getting it Right? A Discussion of Ethics', paper presented to the Market Research Society Annual Conference, 2011.

Clegg, A. (2001) 'Talk Among Yourselves', *Marketing Week*, 6 December, pp. 41–2.

Clift, J. (2011) 'VCCP, Google, Yahoo and Wieden + Kennedy – Agencies and tech firms at the MRS Advertising Research Conference', *WARC*, July, accessed via www.warc.com.

Cole, M. (2011) '"Pretty" Beers for Women? A Rather Tasteless Idea', *Guardian Unlimited*, 20 July.

*Computer Weekly* (2008) 'Tesco Plans to Centralise IT Applications Across its Stores Worldwide', *Computer Weekly*, 3 June.

Deloitte (2008) *Deloitte Annual Review of Football Finance*, May, www.deloitte.com.

Dredge, S. (2011) 'Smartphone and Tablet Stats: What's Really Going on in the Mobile Market?', *Guardian Unlimited*, 1 August.

Duan, Y. and Burrell, P. (1997) 'Some Issues in Developing Expert Marketing Systems', *Journal of Business and Industrial Marketing*, 12 (2), pp. 149–62.

*Esmerk* (2011) 'Sweden: Strawberry Jam the Most Popular Jam', *Esmerk*, 21 July.

Hague, P. (1992) *The Industrial Market Research Handbook*, 3rd edn. Kogan Page.

Hargrave, S. (2011) 'Make Trends and Influence People', *Marketing Week*, 24 March.

Jung-ho, L. (2011) 'Observation is Way to Know Consumers', *Joins.com*, 11 April.

Kearon, J. (2011) 'Unlocking the Real Potential of Web-based Market Research', *Admap*, June.

Korczak, D. (2011) 'Looking Back to Market Research in 2010 and Prospects for 2011', ESOMAR, 9 January, accessed via www.esomar.org/index.php?mact=News,cntnt01,detail,0&cntnt01articleid=252&cntnt01returnid=1894.

Lewis, C. (2010) 'Is a Career in Market Research to your Taste?', *The Times*, 19 October.

*Marketwire* (2010) 'Twilight Eclipsed by Toy Story and Shrek: NetBase Brand Passion Index Shows Social Media Movie Fans Love Animated Family Films', *Marketwire*, 13 July.

*Marketing Week* (2011) 'A New Brand to Pull in Women Drinkers', *Marketing Week*, 21 July.

McCully, A. (2008) 'Retailers Play Loyalty Card', *B&T Weekly*, 24 November.

McLuhan, R. (2001) 'How Data Can Help Target Customers', *Marketing*, 27 September, p. 25.

Mintel (2010) 'Consumer Attitudes to Drinking', *Mintel Market Intelligence*, August, accessed via http://academic.mintel.com/sinatra/oxygen_academic/search_results/show&/display/id=479840/display/id=541697?select_section=479840.

*New Media Age* (2011) 'Number Theory', *New Media Age*, 17 March.

Oughton, C., McClean, M., Mills, C. and Hunt, P. (2003) 'Back Home – Returning Football Clubs to their Communities', Football Governance Research Centre, University of London.

Pettit, R. (2010) 'Digital Anthropology: How Ethnography Can Improve Online Research', *Journal of Advertising Research*, 50 (3) pp. 240–2.

*Point of Purchase* (2011) 'How Does One Do Shopper Research?', *Point of Purchase*, 27 June.

*PR Newswire* (2011) 'Valued Opinions Online Survey Shows Concern Over Internet Security', *PR Newswire*, 19 January.

*PR Newswire Europe* (2011) 'IPSOS & Techneos Creating "Citizen Journalism" With Mobile Market Research Tools at the Royal Wedding', *PR Newswire Europe*, 3 May.

*Relaxnews International* (2011) 'Sparkling Pink and Lemon Girlie Beers Launched in the UK', *Relaxnews International*, 22 July.

RFU (2011) 'Greene King IPA Signs England Rugby Sponsorship Extension', RFU, 3 February, accessed via www.rfu.com/News/2011/February/News%20Articles/030211_Greene_King_Renewal.aspx.

Schmalensee, D. (2001) 'Rules of Thumb for B2B Research', *Marketing Research*, 13 (3), pp. 28–33.

Smith, D. and Fletcher, J. (1999) 'Fitting Market and Competitive Intelligence into the Knowledge Management Jigsaw', *Marketing and Research Today*, 28 (3), pp. 128–37.

Sweeny, M. (2011) 'Creating Mobile Content: A Lack of Application', *Guardian Unlimited*, 13 June.

Tarran, B. (2011) 'BrainJuicer banks £141,000 from DigiViduals', *Research*, 24 March.

Thorpe, M. (2011) 'The Blind Ethnographer: Material Ethnography and New Ways of Seeing in the World', paper presented to the Market Research Society: Annual Conference, 2011, accessed via www.warc.com.

Tull, D.S. and Hawkins, D.T. (1990) *Marketing Research: Measurement and Method*, Macmillan.

Verrinder, J. (2010) 'Global Research Turnover Down 4.6%, Says ESOMAR Report', *Research*, 6 September, accessed via www.research-live.com/news/financial/global-research-turnover-down-46-says-esomar-report/4003529.article.

Von Krogh, G., Ichijo, K. and Nonaka, I. (2000) *Enabling Knowledge Creation: How to Unlock the Mystery of Tacit Knowledge and Release the Power of Innovation*, New York: OUP.

Webster, I. and Clements, N. (2008) 'Assessing the Lifetime Value of a Football Fan – Implications for Research and Practice', paper presented to the *Academy of Marketing Conference*, July.

Witthaus, M. (1999) 'Group Therapy', *Marketing Week*, 28 January, pp. 43–7.

Woodard, R. (2011) 'Comment – Spirits – and, for the Lady?', *Just-drinks*, 23 July.

Woodnutt, T. and Owen, R. (2010) 'The Research Industry Needs to Embrace Radical Change in Order to Thrive and Survive in the Digital Era', paper presented to the Market Research Society: Annual Conference, 2010, accessed via www.warc.com.

# CHAPTER 6

# Product

## LEARNING OBJECTIVES

This chapter will help you to:

- define and classify products and the key terms associated with them;
- understand the nature, benefits and implementation of product and brand development;
- understand the product lifecycle concept, its influence on marketing strategies and its limitations;
- appreciate the importance of product positioning and how it both affects and is affected by marketing strategies;
- define the role and responsibilities of the product or brand manager.

## INTRODUCTION

**THE PRODUCT IS AT** the heart of the marketing exchange. Remember that customers buy products to solve problems or to enhance their lives and thus the marketer has to ensure that the product can fully satisfy the customer, not just in functional terms, but also in psychological terms. The product is important, therefore, because it is the ultimate test of whether the organisation has understood its customer's needs.

This chapter raises a number of interesting questions about what makes a product and the importance of brand image and customer perceptions of it. To start the process of thinking about these issues, therefore, this chapter examines some fundamental concepts. The definition of product and ways of classifying products lead to some basic definitions of product ranges. Then, the underlying concepts such as branding, packaging design and quality that give the product its character and essential appeal to the buyer will be examined along with issues relating to brand management.

An important concept linked with product and brand management is that of the product lifecycle. This traces the life story of the product, helping managers to understand the pressures and opportunities affecting products as they mature. To create and sustain long-lived brands, the product range needs to be managed in sympathy with changes in the customer and competitive environment through the concept of product positioning and repositioning. This may involve changes in marketing strategies, including promotion, packaging, design, or even in the target market profile. Every product has to be assessed and managed according to how the consumer perceives it in relation to the competition. This chapter then turns to the practical problems of managing these processes, presenting a brief overview of product management structures. Finally, the issues surrounding the development and management of pan-European brands will be considered.

Eos was a premium airline offering flights from Stansted to New York on its six Boeing 757 planes for around $5,000. It was configured to seat 48 on a plane that normally takes 230 emphasising the luxury and space associated with first class travel. The seats not only extended out to make flat beds, they also had a fold-out table allowing face-to-face meetings, all reinforcing an 'executive' image for the business traveller. It wanted to be known as an upmarket lifestyle brand and thus it used Bose headphones, had a tie-in with top hotels and sought partnerships with other luxury brands to enhance its image as a niche brand appealing to the executive traveller. Eos built a brand personality that carried through to advertising with an emphasis on top-flight service and 'beating the crowds', all designed to serve a small niche better than anyone else.

At its inception in 2005, it had great plans and stated that it would add to the Stansted–New York route in a couple of years, with destinations such as Los Angeles and Washington DC. However, it struggled for survival in a long-haul market dominated by the major airlines who themselves were competing aggressively for the business traveller's custom. Then the decline in business travel associated with the recession and high fuel costs further added to Eos's difficulties. Eventually, Jack Williams, the Eos CEO declared in 2008 that, 'There are times in business when even though you execute your business plan and even though your employees do their jobs beautifully, external forces prevent you from controlling your own destiny' (as quoted by www.edition.cnn.com). Eos ceased operations shortly after (*Marketing Week*, 2008; www.edition.cnn.com; www.eos.com).

## Anatomy of a product

A formal definition of product may be that:

**A product is a physical good, service, idea, person or place that is capable of offering tangible and intangible attributes that individuals or organisations regard as so necessary, worthwhile or satisfying that they are prepared to exchange money, patronage or some other unit of value in order to acquire it.**

A product is, therefore, a powerful and varied thing. The definition includes tangible products (tins of baked beans, aircraft engines), intangible products (services such as hairdressing or management consultancy) and ideas (public health messages, for instance). It even includes trade in people. For example, the creation and hard selling of pop groups and idols are less about music than about the promotion of a personality to which the target audience can relate. Does a Lady Gaga fan buy her latest album for its intrinsic musical qualities or because of the Lady Gaga name on the label? Places are also saleable products. Holiday resorts and capital cities, for example, have long exploited their natural geographic or cultural advantages, building service industries that in some cases become essential to the local economy.

Whatever the product is, whether tangible, intangible or Lady Gaga, it can always be broken down into bundles of benefits that mean different things to different buyers. Figure 6.1 shows the basic anatomy of a product as a series of four concentric rings representing the core product, the tangible product, the augmented product and finally the potential product.

The *core product* represents the heart of the product, the main reason for its existence and purchase. The core benefit of any product may be functional or psychological and its definition must provide something for the marketer to work on to develop a differential advantage. Any make of car will get the purchaser from A to B, but add on to that the required benefits of spaciousness, or fuel economy or status enhancement, and a definition of a core product to which a market segment will relate begins to emerge. The core benefit of a holiday could be to lie in the sun doing absolutely nothing, being pampered for two weeks, at one end of the spectrum or, at the other end, to escape from the world by seeking adventure and danger in unknown terrain. Although it might be argued that a Club 18–30 holiday could satisfy both those core benefit requirements, generally speaking very different packages will emerge to meet those needs.

The definition of the core benefit is important because it influences the next layer, the *tangible product*. The tangible product is essentially the means by which the marketer puts flesh on the core product, making it a real product that clearly represents and communicates the offer of the core benefit. The tools used to create the product include design specification, product features, quality level, branding and packaging. A car that embodies the core benefit of 'fast and mean status symbol', for example, is likely to have a larger engine, sexy design, leather upholstery, lots of electric gadgets, built-in iPod connection, definitely be available in black or red metallic paint (among other choices) and certainly carry a marque such as BMW rather than Lada.

The *augmented product* represents add-on extras that do not themselves form an intrinsic element of the product, but may be used by producers or retailers to increase the product's benefits or attractiveness. A computer manufacturer may offer installation, user training and after-sales service, for instance, to enhance the attractiveness of the product package. None of this affects the actual computer system itself, but will affect the satisfaction and benefits that the buyer gets from the exchange. Retailers also offer augmented products. An electrical retailer selling national and widely available brands such as Hoover, Zanussi, Indesit or

**Figure 6.1**

The anatomy of a product

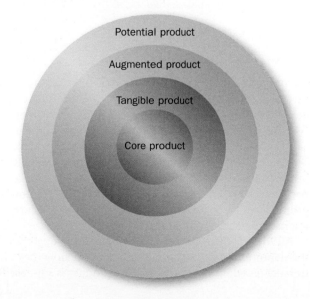

*eg*

Motorists have become very familiar with satellite navigation systems to help them to find their way around (or occasionally get them even more hopelessly lost), and these GPS systems have rapidly become a standard piece of car kit. This is a great success for the various companies that market these systems, but they are nevertheless still thinking about what other commercial opportunities this technology could provide. Other than drivers, who else gets lost occasionally? Kids! Why not tap into deepest parental fear of the trauma of losing a child and by providing a product that helps to avoid it, offer peace of mind? Lok8u, the manufacturer of the 'num8+' are pitching it as 'the world's first GPS locator designed exclusively to locate children. It enables you to find your child, whenever you feel you need to know, at home or abroad. All you need is a mobile phone or computer to find their precise location' (www.lok8u.com/uk/). The child wears a digital watch, in which the GPS device is embedded, and which cannot be removed without triggering an alert to the parent. The system also gives parents some degree of control, in that they can define a safe zone and if the child moves out of that zone, again, an alert is triggered. At any time, a parent can enter a code via a website or mobile phone and get an instant report on exactly where the child is. It will be interesting to see, as the product starts to get established in the marketplace, whether parents will consider £124.99, plus a monthly fee of up to £14.99 depending on usage of the system, a reasonable price to pay for that peace of mind.

A cheaper, less hi-tech solution is the 'Mummy Stay Close' child-distance monitor. It is not GPS-based, and has a very short range, but at £17.99 it probably represents a cost-effective way of keeping tabs on younger children. The child wears a wristwatch-style device and the parent's unit is worn round the neck. The parent can set a 'safe zone' of up to a maximum of 20 metres and if the child strays outside that, an audible alarm is triggered in the parent's unit which only stops when the child is back within range. The child can also press a button on the watch to set off the parent's alarm so that the child can hear where the parent is (*Daily Mail*, 2010; www.amazon.co.uk; www.mummystayclose.co.uk).

The 'num8+' GPS child-distance monitor in the form of a digital watch

*Source:* Lok8u Ltd

Hotpoint needs to make its own mark on each transaction so that the buyer will want to shop there again in the future. Augmenting the product through extra guarantees, cheap financing, delivery and breakdown insurance is more likely to provide memorable, competitively defendable and relatively inexpensive mechanisms for creating a relationship with the consumer than is price competition.

Finally, the *potential product* layer acknowledges the dynamic and strategic nature of the product. The first three layers have described the product as it is now, but the marketer also needs to think about what the product could be and should be in the future. The potential product can be defined in terms of its possible evolution, for example new ways of differentiating itself from the competition.

All four layers of product contribute to the buyer's satisfaction, but the outer two depend on the definition of core product to determine how they are realised. The core itself may be functionally based, in terms of what the product is supposed to do, or it may be benefit or promise based, in terms of how this product will make you feel. It is, however, in the outer layers, the tangible and augmented product, that most of the overt marketing competition takes place (Parasuraman, 1997). The challenge for the marketer is to find out just what customers think is added value, real or subjective (Piercy and Morgan, 1997). Research suggests that it means different things to different people so it is likely to vary across segments (de Chernatony *et al.*, 2000; Wikström and Normann, 1994), across cultures for the international marketer (Assael, 1995) and even for the same customer over time (Jaworski and Kohli, 1993).

## Product classification

To bring order to a wide and complex area of marketing, it is useful to be able to define groups of products that either have similar characteristics or generate similar buying behaviour within a market.

## Product-based classification

A product-based classification groups together products that have similar characteristics, although they may serve very different purposes and markets. There are three main categories: durable products, non-durable products and service products.

- *Durable products.* Durable products last for many uses and over a long period before having to be replaced. Products such as domestic electrical goods, cars and capital machinery fall into this group. A durable is likely to be an infrequently purchased, relatively expensive good. It may require selective distribution through specialist channels and a communications approach that is primarily centred on information and function rather than psychological benefits.
- *Non-durable products.* Non-durable products can only be used once or a few times before they have to be replaced. Food and other fmcg goods fall into this category, as do office consumables such as stationery and computer printer cartridges. A non-durable is likely to be a frequently purchased, relatively low-priced item requiring mass distribution through as wide a variety of outlets as possible and mass communication based on psychological benefits.
- *Service products.* Services represent intangible products comprising activities, benefits or satisfactions that are not embodied in physical products. Items such as financial services, holidays, travel and personal services create problems for marketers, because of their intangibility and inherent perishability. Service providers have to find ways of either bringing the service to the consumer or persuading the consumer to come to the service delivery point. Communication has to develop both functional and psychological benefit themes as well as reassuring the potential customer of the quality and consistency of the service offered.

Although these classifications are ostensibly based on product characteristics, it has proved to be impossible to talk about them without some reference to buyer behaviour, so perhaps it is time to make this dimension more explicit and instead to think about user-based classifications of products.

## User-based classifications: consumer goods and services

The contents of this section are very closely linked with the content of p. 88 *et seq.*, where differences in buyer behaviour were based on whether the purchase was a routine response situation, a limited problem solving situation or an extended problem solving situation. If we begin with these behavioural categories, it is possible to identify parallel groups of goods and services that fit into those situations, giving a very powerful combination of buyer and product characteristics for outlining the basic shape of the marketing mix.

## Convenience goods

Convenience goods correspond to the routine response buying situation. They are relatively inexpensive, frequent purchases. The buyer puts little effort into the purchasing decision and convenience often takes priority over brand loyalty. If the desired brand of breakfast cereal is inexplicably unavailable within the store that the shopper is visiting, they will probably buy an alternative brand or do without rather than take the trouble to go to another shop.

## Shopping goods

Linked with limited problem solving behaviour, shopping goods represent something more of a risk and an adventure to consumers, who are thus more willing to shop around and plan their purchases and even to enjoy the shopping process. Comparison through websites, advertisements and visits to retail outlets may be supplemented by information from easily accessible sources, such as consumer organisations' published reports, word of mouth from family and friends and brochures, as well as advice from sales assistants in the retail setting. A moderately rational assessment of the alternative products based on function, features, service promises and guarantees will lead to a decision. Within the shopping goods classification, there may be brand and/or store loyalty involved, or no loyalty at all. There may also be a pre-existing short list of preferred brands within which the detailed comparison and final choice will be made.

## Speciality goods

Speciality goods equate with the consumer's extensive problem-solving situation. The high-risk, expensive, very infrequently purchased products in this category evoke the most rational

*eg*

Forget the £20 version of a toaster. If you want a Dualit toaster, they start at over £100 and can go up to over £200. Each one is hand-built and they are made in limited quantities, despite increasing demand. The toaster does not pop up; it stops cooking when the timer tells it to and then keeps the toast warm until you throw a lever to get it out. The latest model allows you to specify how many slices you are making, so that you don't waste energy by heating up elements that you don't need. Any Dualit product is designed to last, with cast aluminium ends, stainless steel bodywork and patented heating elements that can produce two, three, four or six variations. Dualit toasters offer superior performance for those who are fussy about their toast. You would have to shop around to find one, however. You have little chance of finding one in Argos, but you might strike lucky in selected stores such as John Lewis, House of Fraser and Debenhams, or through Dualit's own online store. Dualit prides itself in offering a 'shopping good'. The Dualit quality brand name and ethos has been extended into other kitchen appliances, such as kettles, food processors, coffee machines (the latest model, the Espressivo, can take either sealed coffee pods or loose ground coffee) and even a DAB kitchen radio (Norwood, 2011; Watson-Smyth, 2010; www.dualit.com).

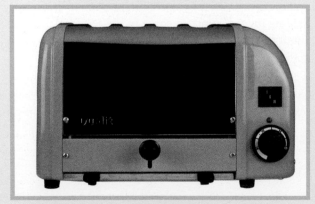

Dualit's quality image is reflected in its design as well as its technical features

*Source*: Alamy Images/© Hugh Threlfall

consumer response that a manufacturer could hope to find. It is not entirely rational, however. The psychological and emotive pull of a brand name like Porsche could still override objective assessment of information, leading to a biased, but happy, decision for the consumer. If you allow the inclusion in this category of products like designer perfumes, those that cost several hundred pounds for 50 ml and would be a once (or never) in a lifetime purchase for most consumers, then rationality goes right out of the window and the purchase is made entirely on the basis of the dream and the imagery woven around the product.

The products in this category need very specialist retailing that will provide a high level of augmented product services, both before and after the sale. Limiting distribution to a small number of exclusive and well-monitored outlets not only protects the product from abuse (for example, inappropriate display or sales advice), but also helps to enhance the product's special image and the status of the buyer.

## Unsought goods

Within the unsought goods category, there are two types of situation. The first is the sudden emergency, such as the burst water pipe or the flat tyre. The organisation's job here is to ensure that the consumer either thinks of its name first or that it is the most accessible provider of the solution to the problem.

The second unsought situation arises with the kinds of products that people would not normally buy without aggressive hard-selling techniques, such as timeshare properties and some home improvements.

# User-based classifications: B2B goods and services

This type of classification of B2B goods and services is linked closely with the discussion at p. 115 *et seq.*, where the spectrum of buying situations from routine re-buy to new task purchasing was discussed. The novelty of the purchase influences the time, effort and human resources put into the purchasing decision. If that is then combined with the role and importance of the purchase within the production environment, it is possible to develop a classification system that is both widely applicable and indicative of particular marketing approaches.

## Capital goods

Capital equipment consists of all the buildings and fixed equipment that have to be in place for production to happen. Such items tend to be infrequently purchased and, given that they are expected to support production over a long lifetime and that they can represent a substantial investment, they are usually regarded as a high-risk decision in the new task category. They thus tend to use extensive decision-making, involving a wide range of personnel from all levels of the organisation and perhaps independent external consultants as well. This category might also include government-funded capital projects such as the building of motorways, bridges, housing and public buildings like hospitals and schools.

## Accessory goods

Accessory goods are items that give peripheral support to the production process without direct involvement. Included in this group, therefore, will be items such as hand tools, fork-lift trucks, storage bins and any other portable or light equipment. Office equipment is also included here, such as PCs, desks, chairs and filing cabinets.

Generally speaking, these items are not quite as expensive or as infrequently purchased as the capital goods. The risk factor is also lower. This suggests that the length of and the degree of involvement in the purchasing process will be scaled down accordingly into something closer to the modified re-buy situation.

### Raw materials

Raw materials arrive more or less in their natural state, having been processed only sufficiently to ensure their safe and economical transport to the factory. Thus iron ore is delivered to Tata Steel; fish arrives at the Findus fish-finger factory; beans and tomatoes are delivered to Heinz; and fleeces arrive at a textile mill. The raw materials then go on to further processing within the purchaser's own production line. The challenge for the supplier of raw materials is how to distinguish its product from the competition's, given that there may be few specification differences between them. Often, the differentiating factors in the purchaser's mind relate to non-product features, such as service, handling convenience, trust and terms of payment, for example.

### Semi-finished goods

Unlike raw materials, semi-finished goods have already been subject to a significant level of processing before arriving at the purchaser's factory. They still, however, need further processing before incorporation into the ultimate product. A clothing manufacturer, therefore, will purchase cloth (i.e. the product of spinning, weaving and dyeing processes), which still needs to be cut and sewn to create the ultimate product.

### Components and parts

Components and parts are finished goods in their own right, which simply have to be incorporated into the assembly of the final product with no further processing. Car manufacturers, for example, buy in headlamp units, alarm systems and microchips as complete components or parts and then fit them to the cars on the assembly line.

If the components are buyer-specified, then the sales representative's main responsibility is to make sure that the right people are talking to each other to clarify the detail of the buyer's precise requirements. Even when the product has been agreed, there is still a need to maintain the relationship. In contrast, supplier-specified products demand clear appreciation of customer needs, carefully designed and priced products and effective selling and promotion to exploit the opportunities identified by market research.

### Supplies and services

Finally, there are several categories of minor consumable items (as distinct from the accessory goods discussed above) and services that facilitate production and the smooth running of the organisation without any direct input. Operating supplies are frequently purchased consumable items that do not end up in the finished product. In the office, this group mainly includes stationery items such as pens, paper and envelopes, as well as computer consumables such as printer toner or ink cartridges and USB memory sticks. Maintenance and repair services ensure that all the capital and accessory goods continue to operate smoothly and efficiently. This category can also include minor consumable items, such as cleaning materials, which assist in providing this service. Business services may well be a major category of purchases for an organisation, involving a great deal of expenditure and decision-making effort, since they involve the purchase of services like management consultancy, accounting and legal advice and advertising agency expertise. This takes the discussion back to new task purchasing and its associated problems of involvement and risk.

## Understanding the product range

Most organisations offer a variety of different products and perhaps a number of variations of each individual product, designed to meet the needs of different market segments. Car companies clearly do this, producing different models of car to suit different price expectations, different power and performance requirements and different usage conditions, from the long-distance sales representative to the family wanting a car largely for short journeys in a busy suburban area.

To understand any product fully, it is essential to appreciate its position in the wider family of the organisation's products. The marketing literature uses a number of terms when talking about the product family that are easy to confuse because of their similarity. Here are some definitions that sort out the confusion and offer some insight into the complexity of the product family.

## Product mix

The product mix is the total sum of all the products and variants offered by an organisation. A small company serving a specialist need may have a very small, tightly focused product mix. Van Dyck Belgian Chocolates, for example, offers boxed chocolates, chocolate bars, liqueur chocolates, fruit-flavoured chocolate, nut chocolates, etc. A large multinational supplier of fmcg products, such as Nestlé, has a very large and varied product mix, from confectionery to coffee to canned goods.

## Product line

To impose some order on to the product mix, it can be divided into a number of product lines. A product line is a group of products that are closely related to each other. This relationship may be production-oriented, in that the products have similar production requirements or problems. Alternatively, the relationship may be market-oriented, in that the products fulfil similar needs, or are sold to the same customer group or have similar product management requirements.

## Product item

A product line consists of a number of product items. These are the individual products or brands, each with its own features, benefits, price, etc. In the fmcg area, therefore, if Heinz had a product line called table sauces, the product items within it might be tomato ketchup, salad cream, mayonnaise, reduced calorie mayonnaise, etc.

## Product line length

The total number of items within the product line is the product line length. Bosch, for example, might have a product line of DIY power tools, as shown in Figure 6.2. Its equivalent industrial range of power tools would probably be even longer.

## Product line depth

The number of different variants of each item within a product line defines its depth. A deep product line has many item variants. A deep line may be indicative of a differentiated market coverage strategy where a number of different segments are being served with tailored products. If we look again at the Bosch example in Figure 6.2, we can break impact drills down into a number of variants, giving a depth of five, each of which has different performance and application capabilities, as well as fitting into different price segments ranging from just under £40 to around £110.

Similarly, in an fmcg market, the Lynx brand (known as Axe outside the UK) produced by Unilever offers great product line depth in male toiletries. Under the Lynx umbrella, aftershave, shaving gel, shower gel, body spray, deodorant (in stick, roll-on and spray forms), shampoo and

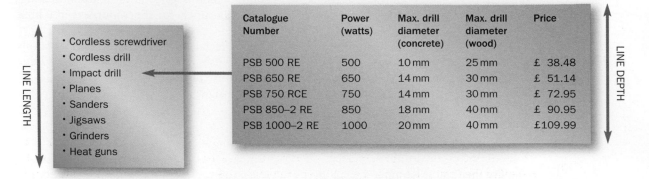

| | Catalogue Number | Power (watts) | Max. drill diameter (concrete) | Max. drill diameter (wood) | Price |
|---|---|---|---|---|---|
| • Cordless screwdriver | PSB 500 RE | 500 | 10 mm | 25 mm | £  38.48 |
| • Cordless drill | PSB 650 RE | 650 | 14 mm | 30 mm | £  51.14 |
| • Impact drill | PSB 750 RCE | 750 | 14 mm | 30 mm | £  72.95 |
| • Planes | PSB 850–2 RE | 850 | 18 mm | 40 mm | £  90.95 |
| • Sanders | PSB 1000–2 RE | 1000 | 20 mm | 40 mm | £109.99 |
| • Jigsaws | | | | | |
| • Grinders | | | | | |
| • Heat guns | | | | | |

**Figure 6.2** Bosch DIY power tools product line
*Source*: www.bosch-do-it.co.uk

conditioner are offered in a variety of fragrances with suitably exotic and macho names such as Dark Temptation, Africa, Fever, Instinct, Excite, and Cool Metal, among many others. This depth does not aim to cover different market segments, but does offer sufficient variation and choice to keep the target segment interested and loyal. The line includes all the basic male toiletry products so that the customer does not need to purchase anything from outside the line, and the variety of fragrances, with a new one introduced every year to keep the line fresh and interesting, allows the customer to experiment and have a change from time to time!

## Product mix width

The width of the product mix is defined by the number of product lines offered. Depending on how broadly or narrowly defined the product lines are, a wide mix might indicate an organisation with a diverse interest in a number of different markets, such as Nestlé.

These definitions will be important for the next chapter's discussion of managing the product mix.

Lynx ads take a humorous approach to communicating the brand's pulling power
*Source*: Image courtesy of The Advertising Archives

# Branding

Branding is an important element of the tangible product and, particularly in consumer markets, is a means of linking items within a product line or emphasising the individuality of product items. This points to the most important function of branding: the creation and communication of a three-dimensional character for a product that is not easily copied or damaged by competitors' efforts. The prosaic definition of brand, accepted by most marketers, is that it consists of any name, design, style, words or symbols, singly or in any combination that distinguish one product from another in the eyes of the customer. Brands are used by people to establish their status far more than religion or political party. We are often judged by the brands we select, the football teams we support, the television programmes we watch, the clothes we buy, the car marque we drive, where we eat and even what we eat. It is, therefore, perhaps of no great surprise that brands are often not about physical attributes but a set of values, a philosophy that can be matched with the consumer's own values and philosophy. Orange represents a bright future, Nike is about achievement ('just do it') and Avantis about life.

## The meaning of branding

The definition of brand provided above offered a variety of mechanisms through which branding could be developed, the most obvious of which are the name and the logo. As with the product mix jargon discussed in the previous section, you are likely to meet a number of terms in the course of your reading and it is important to differentiate between them.

### Brand name

A brand name is any word or illustration that clearly distinguishes one seller's goods from another. It can take the form of words, such as Weetabix and Ferrero Rocher, or initials, such as AA. Numbers can be used to create an effective brand name, such as 7-Up. Brand names can also be enhanced by the use of an associated logo, such as the one used by Apple computers, to reinforce the name, or through the particular style in which the name is presented. The classic example of this is the Coca-Cola brand name, where the visual impact of the written name is so strong that the onlooker recognises the design rather than reads the words. Thus Coca-Cola is instantly identifiable whether the name is written in English, Russian, Chinese or Arabic because it always somehow *looks* the same.

### Trade name

The trade name is the legal name of an organisation, which may or may not relate directly to the branding of its products.

Some companies prefer to let the brands speak for themselves and do not give any prominence to the product's parentage. Laundry product brands produced by either Unilever or Procter & Gamble do not prominently display the company name, although it is shown on the back or side of the pack. Few consumers would realise that Ariel, Bold and Fairy all come from the same stable.

### Trade mark

A trade mark is a brand name, symbol or logo, which is registered and protected for the owner's sole use. To bring the UK into line with EU legislation, the Trades Marks Act, 1994 allowed organisations to register smells, sounds, product shapes and packaging, as well as brand names and logos (Olsen, 2000). This means that the Coca-Cola bottle, the Toblerone bar and Heinz's tomato ketchup bottle are as protectable as their respective brand names. Advertising slogans, jingles and even movements or gestures associated with a brand can also be registered as trade marks. The Act prevents competitors from legally using any of these things in a way that may confuse or mislead buyers, and also makes the registration process and action over infringement much easier.

They do say that imitation is the sincerest form of flattery, but sometime it just isn't seen like that. Ann Summers, the sex accessories retailer, planned to run an advertisement that was a clear parody of Marks & Spencer's meal deal offers and their straplines 'Your M&S' and 'It's not just food, it's M&S food'. The Ann Summers version offered an 'S&M squeal deal' consisting of a 'main' item, a 'side', and a 'dessert' (use your imagination) under the strapline 'It's not just sex, it's Ann Summers sex'. The packaging of the deal and the 'look' of the advertisement were unmistakeably true to the M&S style. M&S didn't take too kindly to this, and its official statement on the subject said, 'Over the last 127 years Marks & Spencer has built up a great reputation for quality and trust in the hearts and minds of the British public. When we believe these values are being infringed, we do whatever we can to protect our brand and our customers. We therefore are taking legal advice with a view to issuing legal proceedings' (as quoted by Baker, 2011). On the basis of this, Ann Summers decided not to run the campaign after all (Baker, 2011; Haslett, 2011).

## Brand mark

The brand mark is specifically the element of the visual brand identity that does not consist of words, but of design and symbols. This would include things like McDonald's golden arches, Apple's computer symbol, or Audi's interlocking circles. These things are also protectable, as discussed under trade marks above.

# The benefits of branding

Branding carries benefits for all parties involved in the exchange process and in theory at least makes it easier to buy or sell products. This section, summarised in Figure 6.3, looks at the benefits of branding from different perspectives, beginning with that of the buyer.

**Figure 6.3**
The benefits of branding

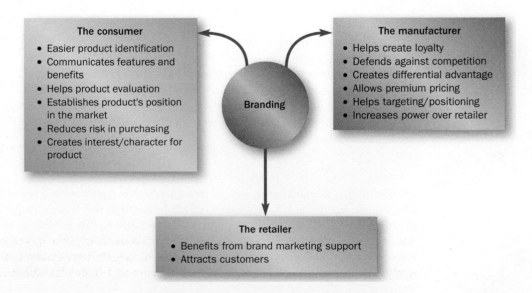

**The consumer**
- Easier product identification
- Communicates features and benefits
- Helps product evaluation
- Establishes product's position in the market
- Reduces risk in purchasing
- Creates interest/character for product

**Branding**

**The manufacturer**
- Helps create loyalty
- Defends against competition
- Creates differential advantage
- Allows premium pricing
- Helps targeting/positioning
- Increases power over retailer

**The retailer**
- Benefits from brand marketing support
- Attracts customers

## Consumer perspective

Branding is of particular value to the buyer in a complex and crowded marketplace. In a super-market, for example, brand names and visual images make it easier to locate and identify required products. Strong branding can speak volumes about the function and character of the product and help consumers to judge whether it is their sort of product, delivering the functional and psychological benefits sought. This is especially true for a new, untried product. The branding can at least help the evaluation of product suitability, and if there is an element of corporate branding it can also offer reassurance about the product's quality pedigree.

This all aids in the shopping process and reduces some of its risks, but it goes further. Giving a product what amounts to a three-dimensional personality makes it easier for consumers to form attitudes and feelings about the product. It gets them sufficiently interested to want to be bothered to do that. This has the double effect of creating brand loyalty (the product as a trusted friend) and of creating something special in the consumer's mind that the competition would find difficult to touch.

This has thus led to brands being regarded as 'packaged meanings' that shoppers can identify with and that organisations are happy to engender. Being able to humanise products with characteristics such as being honest, friendly, trustworthy, fun or *avant garde* all helps to build stronger customer relationships and makes the product attributes almost secondary.

*eg*

Kellogg has been operating in the UK since 1924. During that time it has established a high degree of trust with consumers, although that is not necessarily adequate protection against competition. Weetabix, Nestlé and Alpen have also developed strong bonds of trust with their consumers, so repeat buying cannot be taken for granted. It has also had to move with the times to keep the portfolio fresh. Healthy breakfast cereals have now gone beyond the preserve of a narrow segment into the main-stream mass market, with a trend towards products that include more natural ingredients and less fat and sugar. In 2010, this led Kellogg to reduce the amount of salt in its cereal brands by between 23 per cent (for example, in Frosties and Crunchy Nut) and 33 per cent (for example, in Ricicles and Coco Pops). It's not just about reformulating existing products. Brand variants – such as Coco Pops Rocks, Special K Fruit and Nut Clusters or Special K Yoghurty – help to prevent consumer boredom. New products target new or underdeveloped segments of the market. In 2010, Kellogg spent £4 million on the marketing launch of Krave, a cereal targeting 16–25-year-olds (Charles, 2010; Hook, 2011; Mintel 2010; Reynolds, 2010).

Krave aims to bridge the gap between children's and adults' breakfast cereals

*Source*: Kellogg Group

## Manufacturer perspective

The manufacturer benefits, of course, from the relationship of the buyer with branding. The ease of identification of the product at the point of sale, the connotations of quality and familiarity and the creation of a three-dimensional product personality all help the manufacturer.

The manufacturer's key interest is in the building of defendable brand loyalty to the point where the trust, liking and preference for the brand overcome any lingering price sensitivity, thus allowing a reasonable measure of premium pricing and the prevention of brand switching.

Some of the best known brands that have emerged over the past 50 years have become almost synonymous with the product sector: Kellogg's for cereal, Hoover for vacuum cleaners, and Nike for sports shoes, for example. Achieving such a 'generic brand' position creates considerable strength for the manufacturer in shaping marketing strategy, but it is no guarantee of continued success – ask Levi's or Marks & Spencer.

Other more subtle advantages of branding for the manufacturer are linked with segmentation and competitive positioning strategies. Different brands can be used by one organisation to target different segments. Because the different brands have clearly defined individual characteristics, the consumer does not necessarily link them and thus does not become confused about what the organisation stands for. Even where there is a strong corporate element to the branding, as with Ford cars, the individual models within the range are clearly seen as separate products, serving different market needs, with price differences justified in terms of design and technical specification. Consumers view this wide range of brands positively, as a way of offering as tailored a choice as possible within the confines of a mass market.

It would appear that consumers can't get enough of the UK's top grocery brands. Total sales of the 100 brands in the 2010 Biggest Brands listing amounted to £16.7 billion, a 4.5 per cent increase over the previous year (Nielsen, 2010). Seven out of the top 10 brands in the list had demonstrated growth over the previous year (*The Grocer*, 2010). According to Barnes and Leyland (2010), the brands that maintained their positions or moved up in the top 100 achieved it through recognising and managing consumer needs; investment in effective marketing communications, and adapting to changing market and competitive conditions. One of the highest climbers in 2010 was laundry brand Surf which rose 20 places to number 78 in the list, with a 26.7 per cent rise in sales to £93.1 million. Much of this success is due to adaptation to changing consumer preferences; the launch of the Twilight Sensations range with 'glamour fragrances', such as jasmine and black gardenia or vanilla and black orchid, was designed to deliver the sense of affordable indulgence (or 'cheap pampering') that consumers currently value. Surf is 58 years old, and one of the key characteristics of many of the top brands is age and heritage. This could reflect consumer uncertainty in difficult economic times, encouraging shoppers to take refuge in familiar and well established brands. The top five brands on the list are Coca-Cola (110 years old and worth £1.001 billion), Warburtons (134 years old and worth £706.1 million), Walkers Crisps (62 years old and worth £511.2 million), Hovis (124 years old and worth £458.7 million) and Cadbury's Dairy Milk (105 years old and worth £371.3 million). The oldest brand in the list is Twinings, a venerable 304-year-old tea producer at number 90 in the list and worth £80.8 million. There's a brand whose marketing team have presumably sat down with a nice cup of tea and thought carefully about managing the product mix (for example creating a range of herbal teas and health-oriented teas such as green tea) and the brand's positioning in the marketplace in order to maintain relevance to today's consumers and achieve 11 per cent growth.

This continuous monitoring, adaptation and management of a brand is critical. Being one of the 'top dogs' in your product category guarantees nothing; as Barnes and Leyland (2010) point out, 40 per cent of the biggest brands in 1992 had fallen out of the top 100 completely within 15 years.

Strong branding is also important for providing competitive advantage, not just in terms of generating consumer loyalty, but also as a means of competing head-on, competing generally across the whole market in an almost undifferentiated way or finding a niche in which to dominate. Brand imagery can help to define the extent of competition or exaggerate the differentiating features that pull it away from the competition.

### Retailer perspective

The retailer benefits from branding to a certain extent. Branded products are well supported by advertising and other marketing activities, and so the retailer has some assurance that they will sell. Branded products do draw customers into the store, but the disadvantage is that if a brand is unavailable in one store, then the shopper is likely to patronise another instead. The retailer may prefer the shopper to be less brand loyal and more store loyal! Supermarkets have always recognised the value and necessity of manufacturer-branded goods, but they have also looked for ways of reducing the power that this gives the brand owner. This issue will be looked at in detail later in this chapter.

## Brand valuation

It is clear from the previous section that successful brands are an asset to the brand owner. Successful brands can be long lasting and create a competitive advantage that others find difficult to challenge, as seen for example in the earlier vignette about Britain's 100 biggest grocery brands. Smith (2006) reports that the Institute of Practitioners in Advertisers (IPA) found that a brand contributes between 30 and 70 per cent of a company's value through its intangible assets.

A brand asset has been defined as:

> **A name and/or symbol used to uniquely identify the goods and services of a seller from those of its competitors, with a view to obtaining wealth in excess of that obtainable without a brand. (Tollington, 1998)**

To have a meaningful brand asset requires identification and quantification. Brand valuation emerged through the 1990s as an important measure for brand owners assessing the effectiveness of their brand marketing strategies, their long-term advertising and even the overall worth of the company. Brands represent a financial value to a company reflected through the goodwill component of a balance sheet. The physical assets of a company often now only represent a small part of the value of that company: it is reputation that is worth paying for, as it can bring you loyal customers and committed staff. This reflects the real value of strong brand names. Brands are therefore recognised as assets that give significant long-term competitive advantage when managed carefully (*Marketing Week*, 2007a).

So if brands are the key to the success of a company it makes sense that they are strategically managed by finance and marketing in conjunction with senior management to ensure that the brand portfolio delivers what the company expects and that includes divestment and investment decisions. If used successfully brand valuation is a powerful tool for better decision making and actions (*Marketing Week*, 2007a).

Lest this discussion should seem too enthusiastic about branding, we now turn to some of the disadvantages. Echoing one of the risks of segmentation (discussed in Chapter 4, p. 153), there is the danger of proliferation if brands are created to serve every possible market niche. Retailers are under pressure to stock increasing numbers of lines within a product area, which means in turn that either less shelf space is devoted to each brand or retailers refuse to stock some brands. Both options are unpleasant for the manufacturer. The consumer may also begin to see too much choice and, at some point, there is a risk that the differences between brands become imperceptible to the consumer and confusion sets in.

## Types of brands

The discussion so far has centred on the brands created and marketed by manufacturers and sold through retail outlets. An area of growing importance, however, is the brand created by a wholesaler or retailer for that organisation's sole use. This development has taken place partly because of conflicts and power struggles between manufacturers and retailers, and partly because the retailers also need to generate store loyalty in a highly competitive retail sector.

This section, therefore, distinguishes between the brands emanating from different types of organisation.

## Manufacturer brands

Most manufacturers, particularly in the fmcg sector, are at arm's length from the end buyer and consumer of their product. The retail sector is in between and can make the difference between a product's success and failure through the way the product is displayed or made available to the public. The manufacturer can attempt to impose some control over this through trade promotions, but the manufacturer's best weapon is direct communication with the end buyer. Planting brand names and recognition of brand imagery in the consumer's mind through advertising, sales promotion or digital platforms gives the manufacturer a fighting chance of recognition and selection at the point of sale. Furthermore, the creation of a strong brand that has hard-core loyalty can tip the balance of power back in favour of the manufacturer, because any retailer not stocking that brand runs the risk of losing custom to its competitors.

## Retailer and wholesaler brands

The growth of own-label brands (i.e. those bearing the retailer's name) or own-brands has become a major factor in retailing. Why do it? One possible problem a retailer has is that if a consumer is buying a recognised manufacturer's brand, then the source of that purchase is less relevant. A can of Heinz baked beans represents the same values whether it is purchased from a corner shop or from Harrods. Retailers can differentiate from each other on the basis of price or service, but they are looking for more than that. The existence of a range of exclusive retailer brands that the consumer comes to value creates a physical reason for visiting that retailer and no other. These brands also serve the purpose of giving the consumer 'the retailer in a tin', where the product in the kitchen cupboard is a constant reminder of the retailer and embodies the retailer's values in a more tangible form, reinforcing loyalty and positive attitudes.

Other reasons include the fact that the retailer can earn a better margin on an own-brand and still sell it more cheaply than a manufacturer's brand. This is because it does not face the product development, brand creation and marketing costs that the manufacturers incur. The retailer's own-brand is sold on the back of the retailer's normal marketing activity and not with the massive advertising, promotion and selling costs that each manufacturer's brand has to bear.

The use of own-brand varies across different retailers. Some retailers, such as Aldi, use their own label to create a no-nonsense, no-frills, value-for-money, generic range. Others, such as Marks & Spencer, Sainsbury's and the Albert Heijn chain in the Netherlands have created own-brands that are actually perceived as superior in quality to the manufacturer's offerings.

Given that own-label products seem to put so much power into the hands of the retailers, why do manufacturers cooperate in their production? For a manufacturer of second string brands (i.e. not the biggest names in the market), it might be a good way of developing closer links with a retailer and earning some sort of protection for the manufacturer's brands. In return for the supply, at attractive prices, of own-brand products, the retailer might undertake to display the manufacturer's brands more favourably, or promise not to delist them, for example. The extra volume provides some predictability for the manufacturer and it also could help to achieve economies of scale of benefit to both parties. The danger, of course, is that of the manufacturer becoming too dependent on the retailer's own-brand business.

## Product management and strategy

This chapter has already hinted at a number of important dimensions to be considered in developing and maintaining a branding strategy. Each one will now be treated separately.

## Creating the brand

### New product development

New product development (NPD) is important to organisations for many reasons, including the need to create and maintain competitive advantage through innovation and better serving the customer's changing needs and wants. Whether a product is a totally new innovation, an update of a familiar product or an imitation of a competitor's product, it needs careful planning and development to ensure that it meets customers' needs and wants, that it has a significant competitive advantage and that it is accepted within the marketplace. NPD can be a long and expensive process, with no guarantees that the resulting product will succeed, and therefore to minimise the risks, it needs careful and skilful management to ensure that the best ideas are successfully developed into commercially viable, potentially profitable products with a future.

### Product design, quality and guarantees

**Design**. Design is an integral part of the product itself, affecting not only its overall aesthetic qualities but also its ergonomic properties (i.e. the ease and comfort with which it can be used) and even its components and materials. All of this together can enhance the product's visual appeal, its ability to fulfil its function and its reliability and life span.

The PC has struggled to achieve big design leaps forward. PCs may have become more powerful, smaller and faster, but still the basic designs remain the same and the colour choice is usually limited. In an age in which the computer is an essential part of any home, there has been little progress on PCs designed for particular jobs, for particular rooms, and particular people. There are some attempts to present the PC as an entertainment centre or photographic centre, but generally the efforts have not been convincing. Park (2004) suggested five areas for development and change:

- *Think smaller*: small enough to fit in a pocket but powerful enough to run high-end software, all making the laptop redundant. MS Systems have incorporated a processor into key-sized circuitry, but there is still the issue of plugging into keyboards and monitors.
- *Show it bigger*: flat-screen monitors have taken over from cathode ray tubes, but they tend to go up to only about 17- or 19-inch screen sizes. Microsoft is experimenting with a 44-inch, high-resolution, curve-round screen so that multiple programmes can be viewed at once or the ultimate gaming experience can be realised.
- *Entertain*: the PC should become the command centre for home entertainment. Using high definition video, quality sound processing and wi-fi, a wide range of entertainment applications can be managed from one central point.
- *Make it fit in*: new designs can reduce cable sprawl and save space. IDEO has built an entertainment PC with the computer hidden in the black screen display.
- *Aesthetics*: Apple has led the way in this area with use of colour and interesting designs.

Progress has been made on each front, but most of the effort has gone into the more traditional measures of performance such as processing speed, memory and integration with a wide range of networking and other accessories. For example, screens of 22 inches or more are now becoming more common.

Design is, therefore, increasingly being recognised as being more than just the shape and colour of new products. It also involves the process by which new products and service are produced to meet customer needs and bring creative ideas to reality. Research by the UK Design Council, however, has indicated that smaller companies are often far less design-oriented than larger ones and in some companies, design still plays only a small role in the marketing and product development process. Governments have, however, recognised the importance of design in helping industry to gain a sustainable competitive edge in global markets. Bodies such as the UK's Design Council, the Netherlands Design Institute and the French Agence pour la Promotion de la Création Industrielle promote and support good design practice. The EU also encourages design with initiatives such as the biannual European Community Design Prize aimed at small and medium-sized businesses.

**Quality**. Unlike design, quality is a very well-understood concept among managers. Many organisations now recognise the importance of quality and have adopted the philosophy of total quality management (TQM), which means that all employees take responsibility for building quality into whatever they do. TQM affects all aspects of the organisation's work, from materials handling to the production process, from the product itself to the administrative procedures that provide customer service. Marketers, of course, have a vested interest in all these manifestations of quality, because creating and holding on to customers means not only providing the quality of product that they want (and providing it consistently), but also supporting the product with quality administrative, technical and after-sales service.

In judging the quality of the product itself, a number of dimensions may be considered.

**Performance**. This is about what the product can actually *do*. Thus with the Bosch impact drills mentioned earlier (see Figure 6.2), a customer might perceive the more expensive model with 1,000 watts power as being of 'better quality' than a more basic lower-powered drill. The customer might have more difficulty judging between competing products, however. Black & Decker, for example, produces a range of impact drills that are very similar to the Bosch ones, with minor variations in specification and price levels. If both the Bosch model and the equivalent Black & Decker model offer the same functions, features, benefits and pricing levels, the customer might have problems differentiating between them in terms of performance and will have to judge on other characteristics.

**Durability**. Some products are expected to have a longer life-span than others and some customers are prepared to pay more for what they perceive to be a better-quality, more durable product. Thus the quality level built into the product needs to be suited to its expected life and projected usage. Thus a child's digital watch fitted into a plastic strap featuring a licensed character such as Barbie or Batman, retailing at around £5, is not expected to have the same durability or quality level as a Swiss Tissot retailing at £125. Disposable products in particular, such as razors, biros and cigarette lighters, need to be manufactured to a quality level that is high enough to allow them to perform the required function for the required number of uses or for the required time span, yet low enough to keep the price down to a level where the customer accepts the concept of frequent replacement.

**Reliability and maintenance**. Many customers are concerned about the probability of a product breaking down or otherwise failing, and about the ease and economy of repairs. As with durability, some customers will pay a price premium for what are perceived to be more reliable products or for the peace of mind offered by comprehensive after-sales support. These days most makes of car, for example, are pretty reliable if they are properly maintained and so car buyers may differentiate on the basis of the cost and ease of servicing and the cost and availability of spare parts.

**Design and style**. As mentioned earlier, the visual and ergonomic appeal of a product may influence perceptions of its quality. The sleek, stylish, aerodynamic lines of the Lamborghini contrast sharply with the functional boxiness of the Lada. Packaging design can also enhance quality perceptions.

Marks & Spencer decided it was time to redesign its highly popular handheld travel fan. It decided to go upmarket and produce a premium product showing functionality with high quality styling. It contracted with a design company Smallfry which specialises in taking tired

*eg* The Haberman Anywayup Cup is a prized possession to stop a toddler dripping juice all over you or, worse still, your neighbour's carpet. It used innovation in design, with a slit valve to control the flow of liquid, and yet still matched the alternatives for style. Designed by a mother who had suffered from more traditional cups, the non-spill cup was named as a Design Council Millennium Product; it won the Gold Medal at the Salon International des Inventions in Geneva; and it has won other awards, such as the 'Female Inventor of the Year' for the company's owner. Although there are now many copycat designs which have managed to take market share, about 60 million Anywayup Cups are sold every year, and the company turnover is about £40 million (Appleyard, 2010; Woods, 2009; http://mandyhaberman.com).

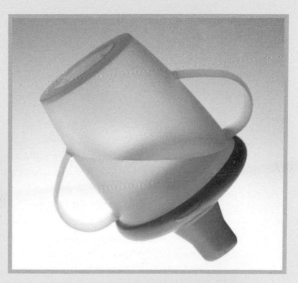

Mandy Haberman's Anyway Up cup for toddlers
*Source*: Mandy Haberman, http://mandyhaberman.com

product designs then adding value through innovative design. The resulting product was a great success and even recouped all its development costs within twelve days of its launch, despite that being in mid-December when the priority is to keep warm, not cool (*Marketing*, 2004)!

**Corporate name and reputation**. If, after all that, customers are still uncertain about the relative quality offerings of the alternative products under consideration, they may fall back on their perceptions of the organisation. Some may feel that Black & Decker is a well-established, familiar name, and if they have had other Black & Decker products that have served well in the past, then that might swing the quality decision in Black & Decker's favour. Others may decide in favour of Bosch because of its associations with high-quality German engineering.

Marketers recognise that quality in the marketplace is a matter of perception rather than technical specification. This is particularly true in consumer markets, where the potential customer may not have the expertise to judge quality objectively and will use all sorts of cues, such as price, packaging or comparison with competitors, to form an opinion about quality level.

**Guarantees.** One way in which an organisation can emphasise its commitment to quality and its confidence in its own products and procedures is through the guarantees it offers. Although customers are protected under national and EU laws against misleading product claims and goods that are not fit for their intended purpose, many organisations choose to extend their responsibility beyond the legal minimum. Some will offer extended warranties. Others are less ambitious and simply offer 'no questions asked' refunds or replacements if the customer is unhappy with a product for any reason at all. Such schemes not only reflect the organisation's confidence in its product and its commitment to customer service, but also reduce the risk to the customer in trying the product.

It may also be possible for the organisation to use its guarantees to create a differential advantage over its competitors. The danger is, however, that promises can be copied and once similar guarantees have become widespread within a particular market or industry, they start to be seen as a normal part of the product package and their impact may be lost as customers look for other differentiating factors.

# MARKETING IN ACTION

## A charitable view of branding

Should branding techniques be used in the non-profit/cause-related sector? Some argue that the whole rationale for non-profit organisations is serving the cause upon which they are focused. Money spent on branding is just another form of administration which should be avoided, it is argued. After all, donors give with a view to helping the cause, not to paying the overheads. So excessive use of slick branding could be counterproductive: what is gained by positive brand messages is lost in concern for the cost of it. In addition, for most non-profit organisations big brand communication exercises are not viable anyway through lack of resources. Often, they have to rely on the website, direct mail, and volunteers.

Branding, however, does have a role to play. The building of a brand personality is central to the creation of strong emotional ties and generates greater trust and loyalty which has a positive impact on the cause itself (Johnson *et al.*, 2000). By developing brand communities, a high degree of impact can be achieved that influence loyalty and relationship. The real way a consumer can identify whether their values are compatible with those of the brand is through brand personality. As the benefits of many cause-related activities are intangible, a well-known brand and a brand personality with meaning can actually help stakeholders' understanding and support for the cause (Sargeant, 1999). For a smaller charity in particular, a clear brand identity is vital and as its scope and activities evolve over time, its brand identity has to change to keep pace. 'Restless Development' started life as 'Students Partnership Worldwide'. Its initial focus was sending gap-year students to teach in India and Zimbabwe, but over the years it evolved to encompass broader social projects on sanitation and HIV, for example and it was felt that the name and image needed to change too. The Deputy Chief Executive said, 'We wanted to capture what we are about now. The old name, look and feel didn't reflect this' (as quoted by Plummer, 2010).

At the opposite end of the size scale, Oxfam too takes the development and management of its brand identity very seriously. Oxfam had 14 affiliates across the world, each with its own brand identity. By bringing them all together under a single unified 'Oxfam International' brand, the charity aims to strengthen and extend its global reach as well as increasing its income from donations. In other words, 'one of the aims will be to communicate that the charity has a 'visionary' personality that works towards a better future' (Roberts, 2011).

By showing people what a charity's resources can do and how donations can make a real difference, brand communication can be very helpful, especially in a crowded non-profit market. All of this can only help to enhance the reputation of the cause and the feeling of goodwill in contributing towards its mission. Thus global non-profit brands such as Greenpeace, the Red Cross, Médecins sans Frontières and the Worldwide Fund for Nature all use branding extensively in furthering their causes.

*Sources*: Aaker (1997); Hassay and Peloza (2009); Johnson *et al.* (2000); Murray (2007); Plummer (2010); Roberts (2011); Sargeant (1999); Stride (2006); von Lindenfels (2009).

## Naming, packaging and labelling the brand

**Selecting a brand name.** A brand name must be memorable, easy to pronounce and meaningful (whether in real or emotional terms). As manufacturers look increasingly towards wider European and international markets, there is a much greater need to check that a proposed name does not lead to unintended ridicule in a foreign language. Neither the French breakfast cereal 'Plopsies' (chocolate-flavoured puffed rice) nor the gloriously evocative Slovakian pasta brand 'Kuk & Fuk' are serious contenders for launch into an English-speaking market. From a linguistic point of view, care must be taken to avoid certain combinations of letters that are difficult to pronounce in some languages.

Language problems apart, the ability of a brand name to communicate something about the product's character or functional benefits could be important. Blackett (1985) suggests that approaches to this can vary, falling within a spectrum ranging from freestanding names, through associative names, to names that are baldly descriptive. This spectrum is shown with examples of actual brand names in Figure 6.4. Names that are totally freestanding are completely abstract and bear no relation to the product or its character. Kodak is a classic example of such a name. *Associative* names suggest some characteristic, image or benefit of the product, but often in an indirect way. Pledge (furniture polish), Elvive (shampoo) and Impulse (body spray) are all names that make some kind of statement about the product's positioning through the consumer's understanding of the word(s) used in the name. The extremely prosaic end of the spectrum is represented by descriptive names. Names such as Chocolate Orange, Shredded Wheat and Cling Film certainly tell you about what the product is, but they are neither imaginative nor easy to protect. Bitter Lemon, for example, began as a brand name and was so apt that it soon became a generic title for any old bottle of lemon-flavoured mixer. Somewhere between associative and descriptive names come a group with names that are descriptive, but with a distinctive twist. Ex-Lax (laxative), Lucozade (fizzy glucose drink) and Bacofoil (aluminium cooking foil) are names that manage to describe without losing the individuality of the brand.

In summary, there are four 'rules' for good brand naming. As far as possible, they need to be:

1 *distinctive*, standing out from the competition while being appealing to the target market and appropriate to the character of the product;

2 *supportive* of the product's positioning with respect to its competitors (p. 242 *et seq.* will discuss positioning in further detail), while remaining consistent with the organisation's overall branding policy;

3 *acceptable*, recognisable, pronounceable and memorisable, in other words, user-friendly to the consumer; and finally,

4 *available*, registerable, protectable (i.e. yours and only yours).

With respect to this last point, it is important to ensure that the suggested brand name is not infringing the rights of existing brands. This is particularly difficult with international brands.

**Packaging.** Packaging is an important part of the product that not only serves a functional purpose, but also acts as a means of communicating product information and brand character (Harrington, 2005). The packaging is often the consumer's first point of contact with the actual product and so it is essential to make it attractive and appropriate for both the product's and the customer's needs.

McVitie's (www.unitedbiscuits.co.uk) has managed to differentiate its Jaffa Cakes (www.jaffacakes.co.uk) brand from supermarket 'look-alike' own brands by producing innovative packaging for mini-Jaffa Cakes. The pack consists of six individually sealed plastic segments, joined by perforations, which can be easily separated. The pack is bright orange, with the texture of orange peel to emphasise the nature of the product. Each segment provides a portion of Jaffa Cakes and can be packed into a lunch box or just used as a convenient snack. Meanwhile, the other five segments remain sealed and therefore stay fresh until required.

**Figure 6.4**
The brand-name spectrum

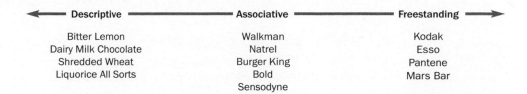

| ← Descriptive | Associative | Freestanding → |
|---|---|---|
| Bitter Lemon | Walkman | Kodak |
| Dairy Milk Chocolate | Natrel | Esso |
| Shredded Wheat | Burger King | Pantene |
| Liquorice All Sorts | Bold | Mars Bar |
| | Sensodyne | |

Packaging is any container or wrapping in which the product is offered for sale and can consist of a variety of materials such as glass, paper, metal or plastic, depending on what is to be contained. The choice of materials and the design of the packaging may have to take account of the texture, appearance and viscosity of the product, as well as its perishability. Dangerous products such as medicines or corrosive household cleaners need special attention. Other design issues might include the role of the packaging in keeping the product ready for use, the means of dispensing the product and the graphic design, presenting the brand imagery and the statutory and desired on-pack information.

# MARKETING IN ACTION

## Cost control? It's in the bag

The humble plastic bag is the centre of some controversy. Marks & Spencer became the first major UK retailer to bring in a 5p charge in for its carrier bags. Its aim was to lower packaging costs by 20 per cent over a three-year period (*Brand Strategy*, 2008). This, of course, is popular with some groups, especially the 'greens' and middle classes concerned with the environment. The important question is whether it actually will cut down the number of bags that are thrown away after single use; certainly the trials suggested a 70 per cent drop in usage. According to the British Retail Consortium (BRC), between 2006 and 2010, the number of single-use bags dropped from 10.6 billion per year to 6.1 billion, so perhaps the message is getting through to consumers (McCarthy, 2010).

Ikea also charges for bags as does Aldi, but it's unclear in some cases whether the motivation is environmental or economic. Others, such as Tesco and Sainsbury's, put the focus on the environmental impact, while the industry as a whole seeks better solutions. Take, for example, the new biodegradable plastic bag has been launched for the grocery sector. It will rot away to water and $CO_2$ in just 90 days, so it can be safely composted at home (*The Grocer*, 2008a). However, these actions still fall a long way short of those implemented in some other European countries. In Ireland, a tax on plastic bags has been levied since 2002, resulting in a 90 per cent drop in consumption, while in France it is the norm to pay for supermarket bags which can be reused and then returned to the store for recycling and replaced free when they wear out. Some UK retailers do offer this as an option to their customers (often alongside a free supply of single-use bags!) and acceptance of that sort of model seems to be growing. Meanwhile, the UK government threatens to legislate, but so far has not delivered. Of particular concern is the single-use bag, and a form of green levy is being considered to reduce further the number of bags consumed each year (Barker and Braithwaite, 2008). The Welsh Assembly went so far as to is announce plans to tax paper and plastic bags by between 5 and 15 per cent from 2010. The Welsh environment minister said, 'I have long said that carrier bags represent a waste of resources and they are an iconic symbol of the throwaway society we now seem to live in' (as quoted by ENDS, 2009). By March 2011, however, the tax still had not been imposed and the packaging industry was fighting back, calling for the tax proposals to be withdrawn, on the basis that the Environment Agency's research had found that a cotton shopping bag has to be re-used at least 131 times to have less environmental impact than a single-use plastic bag (Gyekye, 2011). But despite the protestations of the packaging industry, and the significant progress that has been made in reducing bag use, the EU is still threatening draconian measures in terms of bag taxes or bans, claiming that each European uses 500 bags per year and that this needs to be reduced (Gloger, 2011).

*Sources*: Barker and Braithwaite (2008); Braithwaite (2008); *Brand Strategy* (2008); ENDS (2009); Gloger (2011); *The Grocer* (2008a); Gyekye (2011); McCarthy (2010).

Naturally, there is a cost involved in all of this and thus the organisation needs to be reassured that a particular solution to its packaging needs and problems will either serve a functional purpose or enhance the product's image and competitive standing in the market. Although it can cost £100,000 to create a packaging design for an fmcg product, it seems a very reasonable sum compared with the £3 million or more that will be spent on the advertising to launch that same product. McKenzie (1997) found that the packaging design had become a vital element in developing a brand proposition to the consumer both in advertising and point-of-sale promotion. This could be the case both for a new product launch and for relaunching existing products that might be starting to look tired.

With the rise of the self-service ethos in consumer markets, packaging has indeed grown in importance. It has to communicate product information to help the consumer make a choice, to communicate brand image and positioning and, mostly, to attract attention at the point of sale and invite the consumer to explore the product further (Pieters and Warlops, 1999). Thus packaging is an important part of the overall product offering and has a number of marketing and technical dimensions, some of which are discussed below.

**Functions of packaging**. First among the functions of packaging are the practicalities. Packaging must be functional: it must protect the product in storage, in shipment and often in use. Other packaging functions centre on convenience for the consumer, both in terms of ease of access and ease of use. In the convenience food sector, ease of use has come with the development of packaging that can be placed straight inside a microwave oven and thus serves as a cooking utensil and serving dish. This underlines the necessity for packaging materials, design and technology to develop in parallel with markets and emerging market needs. Consumer pressure for fewer preservatives and additives in food products has also encouraged the development of packaging that better preserves pack content. Products also need to be protected from tampering, and many jars or packages now have at least a visually prominent seal on the outer pack with the verbal warning that the product should not be used if the seal is damaged.

In addition to offering functional information about product identity and use, packaging also serves a promotional purpose. It needs to grab and hold the consumer's attention and involve them with the product.

It has been suggested that packaging may be the biggest medium of communication for three reasons (Peters, 1994):

- its extensive reach to nearly all purchasers of the category;
- its presence at the crucial moment when the purchase decision is made; and
- the high level of involvement of users who will actively scan packaging for information.

This involvement of the user makes the packaging an essential element in branding, both in the communication of brand values and as an essential part of the brand identity (Connolly and Davidson, 1996).

Packaging can also be used as a means of distributing coupons, for advertising other related products, announcing new products, presenting on-pack offers or distributing samples and gifts. A special can was developed for Lucozade Sport, for example, that allowed 'instant win' vouchers to be sealed into the packaging, separate from the liquid. There is more on all of this in Chapter 10.

**Packaging in the marketing mix**. Packaging plays an important part in the marketing mix. This chapter has already outlined its functional importance, its communication possibilities and its crucial role as a first point of physical contact between the buyer and the product. Effective and thoughtful packaging is recognised as a means of increasing sales.

Even the choice of the range of pack sizes to offer the market can reinforce the objectives of the marketing mix. Trial-size packs, clearly labelled as such, help with new product launch (see also Chapter 10) by encouraging low-risk product trial. Small-sized packs of an established product may reinforce a commitment to a market segment comprising single-person households or infrequent users. Larger packs target family usage, heavy users generally or the cost-conscious segment who see the large pack as better value for money. The increase in out-of-town shopping by car means that consumers are far better able than ever before to buy large,

*eg* Wild Pelican from Vinovation offers a South African white wine, a Spanish red and a French rosé. What's unusual about that? They are all packaged in uniform 20 cl aluminium cans with different colours to distinguish each type. The company takes the view that this fits better with certain aspects of modern lifestyles among the 18–40 age group, for example, the growth in more informal drinking occasions such as picnics, barbecues or beach parties, where bottles and glasses can be awkward and cumbersome. There are many other advantages in using cans, such as recycling considerations, and the fact that they chill more quickly and stay cool for longer than bottles. There is also demand from single people for single-serving packs that can be consumed on the sofa in front of the telly with minimum risk of spillage! For those who lack confidence about judging wine, it is an ideal format for trying different wines rather than spending a lot on a 75 cl bottle, all of which then has to be consumed fairly quickly. It is, however, difficult to image a prosaic can of wine replacing the crystal glasses and impressively labelled bottle on the dinner party table, and it would be interesting to see whether the packaging format affects the consumer's assessment of the quality of the wine itself . . . (*The Grocer*, 2008b; www.wildpelican.com; www.rexam.com/winecans/files/pdf/casestudy_wildpelican.pdf).

Wild Pelican: wine sold in cans
*Source*: Wild Pelican

bulky items. This trend has developed further into the demand for multiple packs. Pack sizes may also be closely linked with end-use segmentation (see p. 142). Ice-cream can be packaged as either an individual treat, a family block or a party-sized tub. The consumer selects the appropriate size depending on the end use, but the choice must be there or else the consumer will turn to another brand.

In developing a new product or planning a product relaunch, an organisation thus needs to think carefully about all aspects of packaging and its integration into the overall marketing mix of the product. Although only a small number of brands can be supported by heavy national advertising, for the rest, packaging represents the investment priority for communicating the brand message (Underwood *et al.*, 2001). The technical and design considerations, along with the likely trade and consumer reactions, need to be assessed. Consumers in particular can become very attached to packaging. It can be as recognisable and as cherished as a friend's face and consumers therefore, may not, take kindly to plastic surgery! Sudden packaging changes may lead to a suspicion that other things about the product have also changed for the worse. All of this goes to show that, as with any aspect of marketing, packaging design and concepts need careful research and testing, using where possible one of the growing number of professional consultancies in the field.

**Labelling.** Labelling is a particular area within the packaging field that represents the outermost layer of the product. Labels have a strong functional dimension, in that they include warnings and instructions, as well as information required by law or best industry practice. Labels state, at the very least, the weight or volume of the product (often including a stylised letter 'e', which means that the variation in weight or volume between packs is within certain tolerances laid down by the EU), a barcode and the name and contact address of the producer. Consumer demand has also led to the inclusion of far more product information, such as ingredients, nutritional information and the environmental friendliness of the product.

The prominence and detail of health and safety instructions are also becoming increasingly important, as organisations seek to protect themselves against prosecution or civil liability should the product be misused. These instructions range from general warnings to keep a product out of the reach of children, to prohibitions on inhaling solvent-based products, through to detailed instructions about the use of protective clothing.

# Developing the brand

## Product range brand policy

For most fmcg organisations, the decision on whether to brand the product range or not is an easy one. Branding is essential for most products in these markets. Difficulty arises with some homogeneous products because in theory the customer does not perceive sufficient difference between competing products to make branding feasible. As suggested on p. 149 *et seq.* in the discussion on undifferentiated products, however, there are fewer and fewer truly homogeneous products to be found. Petrol brands, for example, have now been created that differentiate on the basis of service factors and the use of sales promotions as an integral part of the offering, as well as enhanced fuels.

Once the decision to brand has been made, there are still a number of choices, one of which is the degree of independence that the brand is to be given in terms of its relationship with both other brands and the originating organisation.

*Generic brands* represent one extreme, where a single brand image covers a wide range of different products. This is mainly found in supermarkets, where a range of very low-priced, basic staple products are packaged with the minimum of frills and often the minimum permissible information on the packaging, such as Tesco's Everyday Value range. This is still a form of branding, in the sense that it is creating a distinctive character for a set of products.

At the opposite extreme, individual products are given entirely separate individual brand identities. There is thus no obvious relationship between different products produced by the same organisation. This is known as *discreet branding*. It is a useful policy to adopt if the intention is to compete in a number of different segments because it reduces the risk of one product's positioning affecting the consumer's perception of another product. It also means that if one product gets into trouble, perhaps through a product-tampering scare or through production problems causing variable quality, the other products are better insulated against the bad reputation rubbing off onto them too. The big disadvantage of the discreet approach to branding, however, is that each brand has to be set up from scratch, with all the expense and marketing problems associated with it. The new brand cannot benefit from the established reputation of any other brand.

One way of allowing brands to support each other is by using a monolithic approach to branding, which uses a family name (usually linked with the corporate name) with a single brand identity for the whole product range.

A compromise between monolithic and discreet branding is an approach that allows individual brand images, but uses a corporate or family name as a prominent umbrella to endorse the product. Some organisations, such as Ford and Kellogg, use a *fixed endorsed* approach. Here, there is a rigid relationship between the company name and the brand, with a high degree of consistency between the presentation of different brands (but not as extreme as the Heinz approach). A *flexible endorsed* approach, such as that practised by Cadbury's, gives the brand more latitude to express its individuality. The company name may be more or less prominent, depending on how much independence the organisation wants the brand to have. These products seem to enjoy the best of both worlds. The family name gives the products and any new products a measure of credibility, yet the individuality of the products allows variety, imagination and creativity without being too stifled by the 'house style'. Marketing costs are, however, going to be higher because of the need to develop and launch individual identities for products and then to communicate both the family image and the individual brand images.

## Product range and brand extension

A kind of flexible endorsement that does not involve the corporate name is where a brand name is developed to cover a limited number of products within a product line. Consumers may be more favourably inclined towards brands that are associated with known and trusted products (DelVecchio, 2000).

**Extending the brand range**. This example raises the issue of brand extension. Such a policy is cost efficient in that it saves the cost of developing totally new images and promoting and building them up from nothing: for example, easyJet is actively extending its brand name into 'easyEverything'. It has been argued, however, that the introduction of additional products to the brand family can dilute the strength of the brand (John *et al.*, 1998). As the number of products affiliated to a brand name increases, the original brand beliefs may become less focused and start to be fuzzier in consumers' minds. To some extent, Virgin has suffered from this. Extending the brand name from a successful airline to the more problematic rail service could damage the core brand reputation.

Brand extension happens not only 'horizontally', as in the Mars case (see below). Brands can also be extended upwards, downwards or in both directions. An upwards extension might involve introducing a higher-priced, higher-quality, more exclusive product, while a downwards extension might require a basic, no-frills product at a rock-bottom, mass-market price.

In thinking about such an extension, the marketer needs to be sure that the gaps thus filled are worth filling. Will sufficient customers emerge to take up the new product? Will the trade accept it? Is it a significant profit opportunity? Will it simply cannibalise existing products? This last issue is particularly important; there is no point in extending a product range downwards if the main effect is to pull customers away from an existing mid-range product.

*eg* The confectionery sector has been especially active in building brand extension strategies. There are three advantages: it builds awareness and thus the scope for impulse buying, it supports the launch of new products as the consumer is already basically familiar with the core brand and, finally, it can maximise revenue. Mars, for example, pioneered extending chocolate brands into ice-creams. Strategically, this was an interesting move: in summer if chocolate sales drop there is always the opportunity to improve ice-cream sales. The Mars Bar, therefore, has transformed itself into a master brand, even though it still exists as a stand-alone item. Although the Mars organisation is careful about what innovation it encourages, its market share nevertheless has been increasing. This more deliberate approach enables the product to be supported and properly launched, rather than allowing it to be unsupported in the early critical period. This is important when supermarket shelf space is a finite resource and there are many new products competing for it (*Marketing Week*, 2007c).

The Mars ice cream bar is instantly recognisable as a sister brand to the chocolate bar

*Source*: Alamy Images/© David Lee

An upwards extension could create a product with higher margins (see Chapter 7) as well as enhancing the organisation's image. It also helps to build a kind of staircase for the customer to climb. As customers become more affluent or as their needs and wants become more sophisticated, they can trade up to the next product in the range and still maintain their loyalty to one organisation.

A downwards extension can be used to attack competitors operating at the volume end of the market. It can build a larger base of sales if a lower-priced product broadens the number of potential customers. Then, by introducing people to the bottom of the range product and forming some kind of relationship with them, it may be possible to get them to trade up, thus assisting sales of the mid-range product. This would be the ideal situation, but do remember the risks of cannibalisation if the bottom of the range product acts as a magnet to existing mid-range customers. There can be a risk of undermining brand equity by extensions at the bottom of the range. This can cause an overall loss of equity to the whole range that is greater than the incremental sales of the new products (Reibstein *et al.*, 1998).

*eg* What does Bentley Motors, the top of the range luxury car brand, have in common with children's gifts and clothing? Well, Bentley thinks that its brand appeal could have cachet among younger consumers. So, along with the Bentley-branded travel robe for men and women made of cashmere and cotton with silk lining priced at £936.17 (all prices in this example are as cited by www.bentleycollection.com in May 2010 and exclude VAT), the sterling silver model of a vintage Bentley (£29,782.98), other more affordable items of clothing, collectable model cars, and leather accessories, Bentley has branched into children's items. These range from a baby's cashmere hat and scarf set (£59.58) for the smallest member of the family to a 'replica Bentley Le Mans race suit' (£55.28) for the older kids. All the Bentley merchandise has clearly been selected for quality and exclusivity, and is entirely in keeping with the Bentley brand values. You might not be able to afford the dream car itself, but you can afford a little piece of the brand dream (*Marketing Week*, 2007b; www.bentleycollection.com).

At the opposite end of the spectrum, easy4men was a range of men's toiletries developed as part of the easyGroup's brand extension strategy into many different markets, such as car hire, mobile phones and hotels. The price positioning was 40 per cent less than the market leader, offering a no-frills alternative, The colour was orange and the price much lower, but which bloke wants to be told by his girlfriend that he smells cheap (and surely jokes about eau de easyJet were only just over the horizon)? The range comprised nine products but was de-listed by Boots, the sole distributor of the range, after just one year (Bowery, 2006).

**Filling the product range**. The option of filling the product range involves a very close examination of the current range, then creating new products to fill in any gaps between existing products. One way of filling out the range could be to increase the number of variants available. The product remains the same, but it has a range of different presentations. Thus a food product might be available in single-serving packs, family-sized packs or catering-sized freezer packs. Tomato ketchup is available in squeezy bottles as well as in glass ones.

Filling the range can be a useful strategy for keeping the competition out, by offering the consumer some novelty and a more detailed range of products closer to their needs, and to add incrementally to profits at relatively low risk. The danger, however, is the risk of adding to costs, but with no overall increase in sales. This is the risk of cannibalisation, of fragmenting existing market share across too many similar products. There is the added irony that the consumer might well be indifferent to these variants, being perfectly satisfied with the original range.

**Deleting products**. The final stages of a product's life are often the hardest for management to contemplate. The decision to eliminate a poor seller that may be generating low or even negative profits is a tough one to make. The economic rationale for being ruthless is clear. A product making

# MARKETING IN ACTION

## Recipe for a filling breakfast

Kellogg's Corn Flakes has become a tradition for breakfast eating since its introduction in 1906. It virtually invented a style of breakfast upon which other brands have capitalised, creating a market which is worth £1.5 billion in the UK alone. This market is still growing, and while it's good news for Kellogg's that sales of Corn Flakes are also growing, the bad news is that they're growing more slowly than the overall market, and more slowly than key competitors. Corn Flakes, worth £66.9 million in 2009, is only fourth in the market in terms of share behind Weetabix (£113 million), Special K (£110 million) and Crunchy Nut (£74.3 million). Part of the problem is better positioning by competitors (including brands such as Special K and Crunchy Nut owned by Kellogg's itself) to tap into consumer health concerns. Although Kellogg's has responded by cutting by 30 per cent the salt level in its Corn Flakes, the brand has nevertheless lost some of its impetus, especially with younger consumers.

As already implied above, Kellogg's is not a one-product company, and through careful portfolio and brand management it has been able to offset any slowdown or decline in its iconic brand. Special K, number two in the market, focuses on health and slimming and now has nine varieties to prevent consumers getting bored. Both Special K and Crunchy Nut target a more adult consumer, but there are also all the children-oriented brands such as Coco Pops and Rice Krispies. Overall, then, despite stiff competition from the likes of Weetabix, Cereal Partners (with Cheerios, for example) and Quaker, as well as supermarket own brands, Kellogg's has still managed to retain a significant presence on the breakfast table.

*Sources*: Bokaie (2007); Durrani (2010); Mintel (2010).

poor returns absorbs management time and can quickly drain resources if it is being kept alive by aggressive selling and promotion. There is, however, often a reluctance to take action. There are various reasons for this, some of which are purely personal or political. Managers often form emotional attachments to the products they have looked after: 'I introduced this product, I backed it and built my career on it'. If the offending product was launched more recently, then its deletion might be seen as an admission of failure on the part of its managers. They therefore, would, prefer to try just once more to turn the product round and to retain their reputations intact.

Other reasons for being reluctant to delete a product are based on a desire to offer as wide a range as possible, regardless of the additional costs incurred. While there is still some demand (however small) for a particular product, the organisation feels obliged to continue to provide it, as a service to its customers. Suddenly deleting that product might result in negative feelings for some customers. Car owners, in particular, become attached to certain models and react badly when a manufacturer decides to withdraw them from the available range.

All of this means that there is a need for a regular systematic review to identify the more marginal products, to assess their current contribution and to decide how they fit with future plans. If new life can be injected into a product, then all well and good, but if not, then the axe will have to fall and the product be phased out or dropped immediately.

*eg*

Sometimes, a product deletion can be a strategic move. Quaker Oats, the porridge brand owned by PepsiCo in an umbrella for a number of oat-based products. In 2009, Quaker launched Paw Ridge, a quick-cook porridge targeting kids. It ticked all the right boxes: child-friendly branding and graphics; an interactive website with lots of information and activities; and for the mums, the reassurance that the product was 100 per cent natural and provided a very healthy breakfast, especially when compared with some of the more sugary kids' cereals on the market. As PepsiCo itself said, 'The entire range also meets the nutrient profiling model developed by the FSA and OFCOM to ensure only healthy products can be advertised to children' (PepsiCo, 2009). Although the breakfast cereal marketplace as a whole was struggling somewhat at the time, the quick-cook porridge sector was actually showing healthy growth, so all in all, it was a good time to launch Paw Ridge which generated £1.6 million in sales in its first year. The problem, however, was that Quaker has hoped for more from the brand, and in addition, it appears to have been somewhat dwarfed

Paw Ridge: a brand of quick-cook porridge from Quaker Oats

*Source:* www.pepsico.co.uk. Image used courtesy of The Advertising Archives

by Quaker's other quick-cook porridge range, Oat So Simple, a rapidly growing brand turning over more like £40 million and holding over 58 per cent share of the hot cereals market. So, less than two years after its launch, poor old Paw Ridge was deleted, or rather rebranded under the Oat So Simple name as part of a longer-term strategy to strengthen Oat So Simple's positioning. Quaker was quoted as saying, 'At PepsiCo, cereals and juices are squarely focused on the health agenda and so Oat So Simple is still positioned to deliver a healthy breakfast or snack with whole oats. In the long term, we aim to bring in younger consumers in bigger numbers and introduce new occasions for the brand, such as an afternoon snack' (as quoted by *Marketing Week*, 2011). Quaker also admitted that 'Paw Ridge did not perform as hoped. We have moved our children's products under Oat So Simple as mums are already used to buying the brand for themselves' (as quoted by Bamford, 2011). (Bainbridge, 2010; Bamford, 2011; Hook, 2011; *Marketing Week*, 2011; PepsiCo, 2009; Ryan, 2010).

# The product lifecycle

The product lifecycle (PLC) concept reflects the theory that products, like people, live a life. They are born, they grow up, they mature and, eventually, they die. During its life, a product goes through many different experiences, achieving varying levels of success in the market. This naturally means that the product's marketing support needs also vary, depending on what is necessary both to secure the present and to work towards the future. Figure 6.5 shows the theoretical progress of a PLC, indicating the pattern of sales and profits earned. The diagram may be applied either to an individual product or brand (for example Kellogg's Corn Flakes) or to a product class (breakfast cereals).

Figure 6.5 indicates that there are four main stages: introduction, growth, maturity and decline, and these are now discussed in turn along with their implications for marketing strategy.

## Stage 1: introduction

At the very start of the product's life as it enters the market, sales will begin to build slowly and profit may be small (even negative). A slow build-up of sales reflects the lead time required for marketing efforts to take effect and for people to hear about the product and try it. Low profits

**Figure 6.5**
The product lifecycle

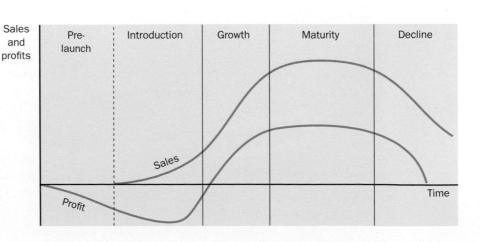

are partly an effect of the low initial sales and partly a reflection of the possible need to recoup development and launch costs.

The marketer's main priority at this stage is to generate widespread awareness of the product among the target segment and to stimulate trial. If the product is truly innovative, there may be no competitors yet and so there is the added problem of building primary demand (i.e. demand for the class of product rather than simply demand for a specific brand) as a background to the actual brand choice.

There is also a need to gain distribution. With new fmcg lines, the retail trade may be hard to convince unless the product has a real USP (unique selling point), because of the pressure on shelf space and the proliferation of available brands. In parallel with that, there is still the task of generating awareness among consumers and moving them through towards a purchase. The decision on the product's price, whether to price high or low or whether to offer an introductory trial price, could be an important element in achieving that first purchase.

*eg*

Microsoft Windows XP exhibited a classic PLC shape. After its introduction in 2001, it went through a rapid growth phase, then achieved stability in line with the dynamics of the PC market, and then went into decline as Vista started to take over in 2006. However, that is not quite the end of the story. Service packs are a way of extending the life of an operating system by incorporating upgrades, security fixes and modifications to a system even though it is currently not available. XP Service Pack 3 was not released until April 2008, some time after the operating system had been replaced by Vista (www.microsoft.com). As a free download, the service pack isn't adding to the sales of XP, but it has helped to extend the life of the XP brand. Microsoft, however, claims that it is the last one, so there will be no SP4.

It didn't all go according to plan, however. Vista was not as welcome or as popular as Microsoft had intended, and consumers were slow to upgrade their systems. Additionally, the base of XP systems is larger than expected. It is estimated that there are 550 million XP users worldwide and many were reluctant to convert to Vista with widely reported software gliches, whether real or imaginary. Even some OEM users continued to use XP, prolonging the life of the product, but for the majority it was Vista or nothing. Sales were planned at 85 per cent to Vista and 15 per cent to XP, but in reality it was closer to being a 75:25 split! So while the PLC did show a decline in operating system terms, there has been a more gradual withdrawal of support to allow users to upgrade, but it still means final termination of XP at an undisclosed date. But that is unlikely to be caused by Vista now, as that too has been superceded by Windows 7, launched in 2009. Presumably, that will be followed at some point by Windows 8 and 9, although given that by May 2011 Windows 7 had sold over 350 million licences and had become the fastest selling operating system ever it might not be any time soon! (Hooper, 2008; Lunarsoft, 2011; Schofield, 2007).

Given the failure rate of new products and the importance of giving a product the best possible start in life, the introduction stage is likely to make heavy demands on marketing resources. This can be especially draining for a smaller organisation, but nevertheless is necessary if the product is to survive into the next stage: growth.

## Stage 2: growth

In the growth stage, there is rapid increase in sales. One reason for this might be that word is getting around about the product and the rate of recruitment of new triers accelerates. Another reason is that the effects of repeat purchases are starting to be seen. There is some urgency at this stage to build as much brand preference and loyalty as possible. Competitors will now have had time to assess the product, its potential and its effect on the overall market, and will thus have decided their response. They may be modifying or improving their existing products or entering a new product of their own to the market. Whatever they do, they will deflect interest and attention away from the product and there is a risk that this will flatten the growth curve prematurely unless the company takes defensive steps.

Figure 6.5 shows that profits start to rise rapidly in this stage. This too might be affected by competitive pressure, if other organisations choose to compete on price, forcing margins down. Again, repeat purchases that build brand loyalty are the best defence in these circumstances.

Even though the product might seem to be still very young and only just starting to deliver its potential, towards the close of the growth stage might be a good time to think about product modifications or improvements, either to reinforce existing segments or to open up new ones. This is about keeping one step ahead of the competition. If the initial novelty of your product has worn off, buyers might be vulnerable to competitors' new products. This might also threaten the security of your distribution channels, as heavy competition for shelf space squeezes out weaker products perceived as heading nowhere. This all reinforces, yet again, the need for constant attention to brand building and the generation of consumer loyalty, as well as the necessity for the cultivation of good relationships with distributors.

Another good reason for considering modifying the product is that by now you have real experience of producing and marketing it. The more innovative the product (whether innovative for your organisation or innovative within the market), the more likely it is that experience will have highlighted unforeseen strengths and weaknesses in the product and its marketing. This is the time to learn from that experience and fine-tune the whole offering or extend the product range to attract new segments.

# MARKETING IN ACTION

## Fizzing into growth

Sales of functional energy drinks and sports drinks are in the growth stage of the PLC compared with more traditional drinks, such as Coke or Pepsi. Sports drinks provide instant energy in the form of carbohydrates and electrolytes (sugar and sodium to the likes of us). It is taken before, during or after exercise to improve performance and to recover fluids and salts lost through exercise. Energy drinks also give a short term energy boost to stimulate the mind and body through ingredients such as caffeine, taurine and glucuronoalactone. They can also be used as a pick-me-up to help sleepy long-distance drivers. The key selling point is the stimulation provided, and indeed one brand does this none too subtly through the name 'Simply Cocaine' (www.simplycocaine.com). Not surprisingly, the brand which contains an awful lot of caffeine but nothing illegal, has come in for some criticism because of the potential associations, especially as it employs a cartoon character called Charlie. The company claims, however, that 'We are targeting people aged between 18 and 35, people with a sense of humour and feel that it is just a fun name' (as quoted by BBC, 2009).

Whether they are positioned as having health and fitness benefits or as an aid to energy/stimulation, these drinks are being bought in record numbers by consumers. Consumption of sports drinks in western Europe, for instance, rose by over 100 per cent between 2001 and 2008, and energy drinks were not far behind. The continued forecast growth of these drinks fits in with a number of key trends across the global market. They add value when marketed with an appeal to those with a busy, energetic lifestyle which demands a boost during the working day. Energy drinks are particularly successful in cultures with long working hours and low annual leave rates. Of course, all of this does not go unnoticed, and the drinks are criticised by motoring associations, for example, as being only good for an hour followed by a corresponding low, while health organisations particularly fear that they encourage wilder behaviour among teenagers (Williams, 2009).

Interestingly, a new category of anti-energy drinks is now emerging in the market. The perfect anti-dote for the highs! 'Slow Cow', is a Canadian product, launched into the UK market in 2010, which claims to provide a relaxing and calming sensation. It apparently wants to be 'the "Red Bull" of relaxing drinks' (Froment, 2010). So . . . let's all open a can, turn the music down low and chill out for the rest of this chapter.

*Sources*: BBC (2009); Froment (2010); *Just-drinks* (2008); Lewis (2007); Williams (2009).

At some point, the growth period comes to an end as the product begins to reach its peak and enters the next stage: maturity.

## Stage 3: maturity

During the maturity stage, the product achieves as much as it is going to. The accelerated growth levels off, as everyone who is likely to be interested in the product should have tried it by now and a stable set of loyal repeat buyers should have emerged. The mobile phone market, for example, had achieved 70 per cent penetration in the UK by the end of 2001 and sales levelled off to upgrading and replacement rather than converting those harder-to-win customers. This is not a cause for complacency, however. There are few new customers available and even the laggards have purchased by now. This means that there is a high degree of customer understanding of the product and possibly of the market. They know what they want, and if your product starts to look dated or becomes unexciting compared with newer offerings from the competition, then they might well switch brands. Certainly, the smaller or more poorly positioned brands are going to be squeezed out. In these circumstances, the best hope is to consolidate the hard-core loyal buyers, encouraging heavier consumption from them. It may also be possible to convert some brand switchers into loyal customers through the use of sales promotions and advertising.

At this stage, there is likely to be heavy price competition and increased marketing expenditure from all competitors in order to retain brand loyalty. Much of this expenditure will be focused on marketing communication, but some may be channelled into minor product improvements to refresh the brand. Distribution channels may also need careful handling at this stage. Unless the product remains a steady seller, the retailer may be looking to delist it to make room on the shelves for younger products.

The sales curve has reached a plateau, as the market is saturated and largely stable. Any short-term gains will be offset by similar losses and profits may start to decline because of price competition pressure. It is thus very important to try, at least, to retain existing buyers. Sooner or later, however, the stability of the maturity phase will break, either through competitive pressure (they are better at poaching your customers than you are at poaching theirs) or through new developments in the market that make your product increasingly inappropriate, pushing the product into the decline stage.

## Stage 4: decline

Once a product goes into decline for market-based reasons, it is almost impossible to stop it. The rate of decline can be controlled to some extent, but inevitably sales and profits will fall regardless of marketing effort.

Decline can often be environment related rather than a result of poor management decisions. Technological developments or changes in consumer tastes, for example, can lead to the demise of the best-managed product. New technologies are increasingly becoming a powerful force that

The disposable nappy market is on a bit of a rollercoaster. Nappy sales are obviously directly related to the birth rate; so a bumper year for new births means a bumper year for nappy sales! The birthrate was falling up to 2004; it increased again until 2008, but it is forecast to decline again between 2010 and 2013. Although this is outside the control of the nappy manufacturers, there are things they can do to try to dampen the effects of there being fewer babies in the marketplace. Competitive price promotions, for example, undermine profit and the value of sales, but do protect market share for individual brands. Innovation has helped, not only through improving nappy design and developing 'greener' nappies, but also by extending brands into wipes and handwash has helped to expand their growth. Similarly the development of pull-ups, encouraging slower and later potty training, and absorbent night-time pyjama pants substitutes for older kids has also arrested some of the potential decline. So, with measures in place to mitigate the effects of any decline in the birthrate through product development and brand stretching; a robust approach to dealing with any threat from reusable nappies; and maybe a willingness to sacrifice value in the interests of volume, long term decline is being held at bay. The only other thing the manufacturers can do is just hope for the return of larger families! (Bainbridge, 2006; Leyland, 2011; Mintel, 2008).

can destroy an established market in a few years. Polaroid built a market around instant photos, but digital cameras offer the same facility with a lot more flexibility. Cravens *et al.* (2000) highlighted the danger of becoming obsessed with improving and extending products in the mature or decline stages and not recognising more fundamental changes to the market.

Faced with a product in decline, the marketer has a difficult decision of whether to try slowing down the decline with some marketing expenditure, or to milk the product by withdrawing support and making as much profit out of it as possible as it heads towards a natural death. In the latter case, the withdrawing of marketing support aimed at distributors in particular is quite likely to speed up the delisting process.

## Facets of the PLC

The PLC is more of a guide to what could happen rather than a prescription of what will happen. At its best, it does provide some useful indications at each stage of some of the marketing problems and issues that could arise. It is, after all, a form of collective wisdom based on the history of many brands. But before applying the concept in practice, it is necessary to dig deeper and think about a number of issues before the PLC becomes a really useful tool.

### Length

It is very difficult to predict how long it will take a product to move through its life. The length of the PLC varies not only from market to market, but also from brand to brand within a market. Some board games, for example, such as Monopoly, Scrabble and, more recently, Trivial Pursuit are well-established, long-term sellers, whereas other games, particularly those linked with television shows (remember Countdown, Blockbusters and Neighbours board games?), have much shorter spans.

The problem is that the length of the PLC is affected by so many things. It is not only the pace of change in the external environment, but also the organisation's handling of the product throughout its life. The organisation's willingness and ability to communicate effectively and efficiently with both the trade and the consumer, its policy of supporting the product in the critical early period and its approach to defending and refreshing its products will all affect how the PLC develops.

## Self-fulfilling prophecy

Linked with the previous point, there is a real danger that the PLC can become a self-fulfilling prophecy (Wood, 1990). A marketing manager might, for example, imagine that a product is about to move from growth into maturity. Theory may suggest appropriate marketing strategies for this transition and, if these are implemented, the product will start to behave as though it is mature, whether it was really ready for it or not.

## Shape

The shape of the PLC offered in Figure 6.5 is necessarily a generalisation. Products that get into marketing problems at any PLC stage will certainly not follow this pattern. Products that spend relatively longer in one stage than another will also have distorted PLC curves. A product that has a long and stable maturity, for instance, will show a long flat plateau in maturity rather than Figure 6.5's gentle hillock. Different market circumstances could also distort this hypothetical curve. Five different scenarios, the innovative product, the imitative product, the fashion product, the product failure and the revitalisation, each with its own PLC shape, are shown in Figure 6.6.

**Innovative product**. The innovative product is breaking totally new ground and cannot really utilise consumers' previous experience as a short cut to acceptance. People feel that they have managed perfectly well without this product in the past, so why do they need it now? Having to educate the market from scratch is neither easy nor cheap. Sony, in introducing the Walkman, had to undertake this task and, of course, it not only laid the foundations for its own product, but also broke the ground for 'me too' subsequent imitative entrants.

**Imitative product**. Imitative products, such as new confectionery brands or the first non-Sony personal stereo, do not require as much spadework as the innovative product. They take advantage of the established market and the buyer's existing knowledge and past experience, and thus will move into the growth stage very quickly. The main considerations for the imitative

**Figure 6.6**

PLC variations on a theme

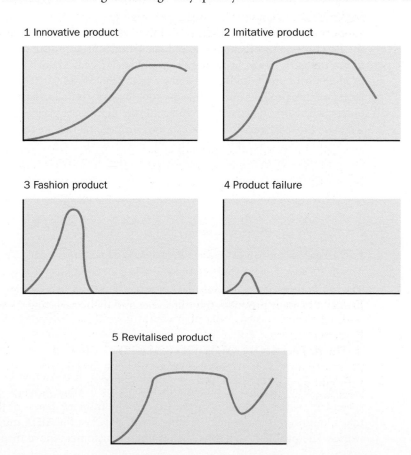

marketer are establishing clear, differentiated positioning of the product against existing brands, encouraging trial and making repeat purchase as easy as possible.

**Fashion product**. Fashion products have a naturally short PLC. Fads are an extreme form of fashion product, accentuating the rapid sales increase followed by the rapid decline. The timing of entry into the market is critical and those who succeed in making a quick return in these markets are those who spot the trend early. There is little opportunity for late entrants. It is interesting to note that some fads retain a hard core of enthusiasts, for example skateboarding.

**Product failure**. Some products never even achieve a growth stage: they fail. This may be because the product itself is badly thought through or because it never gained awareness or distribution. New food products from small manufacturers without the resources to create strong brands may fail because they simply cannot gain mass distribution from retailers unwilling to take risks with unknown producers or brands.

**Revitalisation product**. The revitalisation phase of the PLC shows that marketing effort can indeed influence the course of a lifecycle. By updating a product, either through design or through a fresh marketing approach, new life can be injected to regenerate customer and retailer interest and loyalty. Tango, for example, was a standard, uninteresting fizzy orange drink until some surreal, controversial and imaginative advertising repositioned it as a trendy teenage drink. Hiam (1990) argued that many products can be revitalised and that 'maturity simply reflects saturation of a specific target market with a specific product form'. Changing the form of product and expanding the target market could help new growth creation. Generally, it is argued that 'it is a myth that products have a predetermined life span'.

## Product level, class, form and brand

As said at the beginning of this section, the PLC can operate on a number of different levels. It is important to distinguish between the PLCs of total industries (such as the motor industry), product classes (such as petrol-driven private vehicles), product forms (such as hatchback cars) and individual brands (such as the Renault Megane).

Industries and product classes tend to have the longest PLCs, because they are an aggregate of the efforts of many organisations and many individual products over time. An industry, such as the motor industry, can be in an overall state of fairly steady maturity for many years even as individual product forms and brands come and go. In the motor industry, for example, the hatchback is probably a mature product form, while the people carrier is still in its growth stage. Although a number of hatchback 'brands' have come and gone, the number of people carrier 'brands' is still growing. At the same time, the earliest entrants in the European market are starting to reach maturity.

Despite these weaknesses, the PLC is a well-used concept. Product marketing strategies should, however, take into account other considerations as well as the PLC, as the next section shows.

## Market evolution

The marketing manager needs to understand how markets develop over time, in order better to plan and manage products, their lifecycles and their marketing strategies.

## The diffusion of innovation

The product lifecycle is clearly driven by changes in consumer behaviour as the new product becomes established. The rate at which the growth stage develops is linked in particular to the speed with which customers can be led through from awareness of the product to trial and eventual adoption of the product, in other words how fast the AIDA model (see Figure 4.2 on p. 145) works. The problem is, however, that not all customers move through it with equal speed and

**Figure 6.7**
Diffusion of innovation: adopter categories

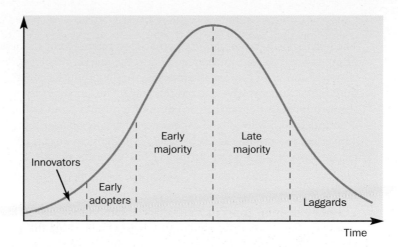

eagerness and some will adopt innovation more quickly than others. This has led to the concept of the diffusion of innovation (Rogers, 1962), which looks at the rate at which innovation spreads across a market as a whole. Effectively, it allows the grouping or classification of customers depending on their speed of adoption into one of five adopter categories, as shown in Figure 6.7.

## Innovators

Innovators are important in the early stages of a product's lifecycle to help get the product off the ground and start the process of gaining acceptance. They form only a small group, but they buy early and are prepared to take a risk. In consumer markets, innovators tend to be younger, better educated, more affluent and confident. In B2B markets, innovators are likely to be profitable and, again, willing to take risks in return for the potential benefits to be gained from being first.

## Early adopters

Early adopters enter the market early, but are content to let the innovators take the real pioneering risks with a new product. They do, however, soon follow the lead of the innovators and are always alert to new developments in markets of interest to them. Once the early adopters begin to enter the market, the growth stage of a PLC can then develop.

Both innovators and early adopters tend to be opinion leaders and thus it is important for the promoter of a new product to target them and win them over. The mass market, however, looks particularly to the early adopters for a lead, as they are more of a mainstream group than the innovators. The early adopters are thus critical for making a product generally acceptable and for spreading word-of-mouth recommendations about the product's value and benefits.

## Early majority

With the early majority the mass market starts to build up, as more and more people enter it. The early majority is more risk averse than previous groups and wants some reassurance that the product is tried and tested before making a commitment themselves to it. This group may be relatively well educated, with above-average incomes, but that may depend on the nature of the product concerned. When a product does reach the early majority, social pressure may begin to build: 'You really must get yourself an ice-cream maker – you can't possibly manage without one.' This begins to move the product towards the late majority.

## Late majority

The late majority customers are perhaps less interested or bothered about the product category, or are content to wait until they see how the market develops. They are a little behind the early majority and want more reassurance about the product's benefits and worth. It could be argued that digital cameras have entered this stage. The late majority may have more choice of alternative products in the market, as competition builds, and will certainly have the benefit of the accumulated knowledge and experience of the previous groups. Once the late majority has been converted, the product is likely to be reaching its mature stage, a steady plateau of repeat purchases, with very few new customers left to enter the market.

## Late adopters or laggards

The last remaining converts are the late adopters or laggards. They may be very averse to change and, have therefore, resisted adopting a new product, or they may have had attitudinal or economic problems coming to terms with it. Alternatively, they may just have been very slow in hearing about the product or in relating its benefits to their own lifestyles. They may be in the lower socioeconomic groups or they may be older consumers.

The benefits of being among the late adopters are that others have taken all the risks, the ephemeral brands or manufacturers are likely to have disappeared, it may thus be easier to identify the best products on the market, and the price may be falling as competitors fight for share among a shrinking market. By the time the late adopters get into the market, however, the innovators and early adopters are likely to have moved on to something else and thus the whole cycle begins again!

As this discussion has implied, diffusion of innovation has strong links with the product lifecycle concept and can be used both as a means of segmenting a market and for suggesting appropriate marketing strategies. In the early stages, for example, it is important to understand the needs and motivations of the innovators and early adopters and then to attract attention and generate trial among these groups. Other than knowing that they have innovative tendencies, however, it can be difficult to profile the groups using more concrete demographic or psychographic variables. In that case, it is important for the marketer to think in product terms. Perhaps hi-fi innovators and early adopters may be reached through specialist magazines that review new products, for example.

# Positioning and repositioning products

A crucial decision, which could affect the length of a product's life and its resilience in a market over time, concerns the product's positioning. Product positioning means thinking about a product in the context of the competitive space it occupies in its market, defined in terms of attributes that matter to the target market. The important criterion is how close to the ideal on each of those attributes, compared with competing products, your product is judged to be by the target market. Harrod's, for example, is positioned as a high-quality, exclusive departmental store. In order to reinforce this positioning with its target market, Harrods (www.harrods.com) makes sure that its product ranges, its staff expertise, its displays and overall store ambience are of equally high quality.

It is the target customer's definition of important attributes and their perception of how your product compares on them that matter. Marketing managers have to stand back from their own feelings and must ensure that the attributes selected are those that are critical to the customer, not those that marketing managers would like to be critical. The range of attributes judged to be important will vary according to the particular market segments under consideration.

The concept of product positioning is clearly focused on a customer-based perspective, but it still has serious implications for product design and development. The decision about positioning is made during the product's development and will be reflected in a whole range of the product's characteristics, including brand image, packaging and quality, as well as in the pricing and communication elements of the marketing mix.

Defining and selecting an appropriate position for a product involves three stages.

**Stage 1**. Detailed market research needs to be carried out during the first stage in order to establish what attributes are important to any given market segment and their order of preference. This background research will centre on a class of products rather than on individual brands within the class. Thus a particular segment, for example, might regard softness, absorbency and a high number of sheets on the roll as the three most important attributes of toilet tissue, in that order of preference.

**Stage 2**. Having identified the important attributes, in the second stage further research now shortlists the existing products that offer those attributes. Brands such as Kleenex Velvet and Andrex might be seen as fulfilling the needs of the toilet tissue segment mentioned above.

**Stage 3**. In the third stage, it is necessary to find out:

(a) what the target market considers to be the ideal level for each of the defined attributes; and

(b) how they rate each brand's attributes in relation to the ideal and to each other.

The conclusions from this hypothetical research may be, for instance, that while Andrex has more sheets per roll than Kleenex (thus apparently achieving a better rating for Andrex on an important attribute), in relation to the ideal Andrex is perceived to have too many (too bulky for the roll holder), whereas Kleenex might be perceived to have too few (runs out too quickly). Both products could thus improve their offering.

Once the positioning process has been completed for all the relevant attributes, it is useful to be able to visualise the complete picture graphically, by creating a perceptual map of the market. Figure 6.8 shows such a hypothetical map of the toilet tissue market, using price and softness as two dimensions that might represent important attributes. This shows that Brand A is serving the bottom end of the market in Segment 1, offering a cheap, purely functional product, whereas Brand B is aimed at the discerning customer in Segment 2 who is prepared to pay a little more for a gentler experience. Brand C seems to be closer to Segment 1 than Segment 2, but is overpriced compared with Brand A for a similar quality of product. Brand D is floating between the two segments, with nothing to offer that is particularly appealing to either.

In some cases, of course, two dimensions are insufficient to represent the complexities of target market opinion. Although this creates a far more difficult mapping task, any number of further dimensions can be included using multidimensional scaling techniques (Green and Carmone, 1970).

Perceptual mapping helps to provide insights into appropriate competitive actions. For instance, a fundamental decision could be whether to try to meet the competition head-on or to

**Figure 6.8**

Perceptual map of the toilet-tissue market

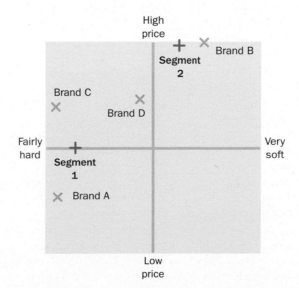

differentiate your product away from them. The map can show just how far away from the competition your product is perceived to be and where its weaknesses lie, leading to an understanding of the marketing tasks involved in improving the product offering. If the intention is to differentiate, the map can indicate whether your product is sufficiently different in terms of attributes that matter and whether market niches exist that your product could be adapted to fill.

All of this implies that assessing and defining meaningful product positioning is an important early step in marketing management. This process can bring to light opportunities, it can highlight potential dangers of cannibalising one's own products and it can help to define competitive pressures, strengths and weaknesses. It is also a step in making the decision to modify a current product range by repositioning selected products.

## Repositioning and modifying products

Positioning might have to be adjusted for many reasons as both the product and its market mature. Developing technology, evolving competition, changing customer needs and wants all mean that products have to be constantly appraised and reviewed. Nevertheless, a major product repositioning exercise can be very costly and risky (alienating or confusing existing buyers and failing to attract new ones, for instance). This means that the marketing manager needs to be sure that the changes will be perceptible and relevant to the target market, that the market is willing to accept change and that the repositioning will produce measurable benefits.

Repositioning has a number of serious implications. It might involve redefining or enlarging segments and it may well involve redesigning an entire marketing strategy. Such a fundamental revamp of a product is most likely to take place in the maturity stage of the PLC, when the product is beginning to fade a little.

There are three main areas for repositioning and product improvement.

**Quality**. As discussed at p. 222 *et seq.*, quality has a number of dimensions. With physical products, quality can be defined in terms of reliability, durability and dependability, which are generally applicable across most products. There are, however, product-specific quality dimensions that the target market could use as indicators of a quality product, such as speed, taste, colour, materials, ingredients and even price and packaging.

Jimmy Choo Ltd, the luxury shoe group, uses Halle Berry, Nicole Kidman and Cate Blanchett along with many other celebrities as part of a deliberate product placement strategy in films and on television. From its launch in 1996, the emphasis has been on exclusivity. The early adopters are considered critical for a fashion brand, and to encourage them, Jimmy Choo deliberately keeps its shoes exclusive through limited distribution. It has 32 stores worldwide in 100 countries and rarely advertises, other than in upmarket magazines. In 2007, after just 10 years, the company was valued at £187 million as it became a global brand.

It needs to be very protective of its upmarket position and rarely contemplates brand extensions or repositioning for any of its merchandise for fear of damaging the quality perception. With prices starting at £300 for its main product – shoes – it carefully selects brand extensions into such areas as handbags and upmarket sunglasses but definitely does not contemplate socks, handkerchiefs and downmarket shoe ranges. Indeed, it was a difficult decision to take out an Oxford Street concession in Selfridges as that suggests 'availability' which is the last thing Jimmy Choo wants for its brand.

However, in 2009 it began to look as though Jimmy Choo was looking to relax its attitude a little and exploit its well cultivated brand positioning with carefully selected partners. For instance, it announced a new licence agreement with Inter Parfums SA for the creation, development and distribution of fragrances under the Jimmy Choo brand, and then late in 2009 H&M launched a one-off range of Jimmy Choo products in 19 of its UK stores. With prices ranging from £50 to £180, the products are relatively expensive for H&M, but much cheaper than Jimmy Choo's mainstream ranges. H&M has had previous experience of entering into partnership with designer clothing brand, thus mitigating some of the risk for Jimmy Choo. While both brands gained a lot of publicity from this venture, presumably Jimmy Choo was also looking to use this more affordable range to give a new generation of fashionistas an experience of the brand and to then tempt them into its own stores. The question remains, however, as to whether there is a risk of Jimmy Choo becoming a 'bubble brand', i.e. one of those brands 'which hop between high street and Bond Street until their stars fade' (Mortishead, 2009). (Clark, 2011; *Daily Mail*, 2009; Grande, 2003; Mortishead, 2009; Saigol, 2004; Sibbles and Pidd, 2009; Whitworth, 2009; www.jimmychoo.com).

Raising the quality of a physical product could be achieved perhaps through better components or refined manufacturing. For a service product, it could mean major refurbishment for the premises or developing the way in which the experience is packaged. Whatever the product or the means employed, raising the quality offers the prospect of charging higher prices and increasing profit margins. It might, however, lead to increased competition from other organisations greedy for a share of that prosperity. The other point to consider carefully is whether the target market will either recognise or value the newly raised quality.

**Design**. Thinking in an aesthetic rather than an engineering context, design affects the impact of the product on the senses. This concept can be difficult to handle, as it covers areas such as the appearance, texture, taste, smell, feel or sound of the product, all of which involve the customer in some very subjective assessments. These areas do, however, provide many combinations of variables that could offer the opportunity for change. If the objective is to reposition a product, just changing its visual appearance or its packaging (probably with 'new improved . . .' splashed across it) could give customers sufficient cues and justification for revising their opinions of it.

It must be stressed that any design changes are a waste of time and resources unless they matter to the market, can be communicated to that market and are implemented to achieve defined objectives.

**Performance**. Like design, performance relies on the customer's initial, rather impressionistic assessment. A more concrete appreciation of performance may only come after product use. The kind of factors under consideration here include convenience, safety, ease of handling, efficiency, effectiveness and adaptability to different situations. A car's performance, for instance, can be measured in terms of its acceleration, braking ability or fuel economy, depending on what is important to the buyer. Improving the fuel economy at the expense of acceleration might change the character of the car, making it less appealing to a 'boy racer' type of segment, but positioning it more firmly and more positively in the 'heavy urban usage' segment. Even the fuel itself has been repositioned in terms of its performance-enhancing capabilities, with some brands promising to be more engine friendly or to improve engine performance.

Quality, design and performance are often inextricably interlinked. Proposed changes under one heading have implications for the others. Improving a car's fuel economy may involve better-quality components under the bonnet as well as a more aerodynamic body design.

It does not really matter whether a proposed change is classified as relating to quality, design or performance, or all three. What does matter is that as part of the product management process, all the relevant options are assessed to make sure that the product continues to achieve its maximum potential, either within its existing segment(s) or through repositioning into a new one. Quality, design and performance all provide possibilities for the major or minor changes that will ensure this.

# Product management and organisation

There is a range of management structures for marketing, depending on the tasks required and the environmental opportunities and threats. Products are extremely important as revenue earners and so they need careful management. Product-centred management structures can help to ensure that they do get the care they deserve. A product or brand manager handles part of a range or even an individual brand if it is very critical. Product managers operate across all functional areas, especially marketing, but also liaise with R&D, production and logistics to ensure the best opportunities and treatment for their product(s). Their job is to manage the product throughout its lifecycle, from launch, through any modifications, to its eventual demise. It can often be a total commitment and may include commissioning research, liaising with distribution and even handling sales with major account negotiations. The product manager will also be involved in planning advertising approaches, media selection and packaging.

In terms of planning, controlling and monitoring product performance, the product manager is likely to have to produce an annual product plan, specifying actions, resources and strategies for the coming trading period. This helps the manager to justify the investment of resources in the product and also allows early recognition of problems with the product and proposed corrective action.

This kind of product management structure is used in larger fmcg organisations in particular, where there is significant emphasis on new product development and major mass-market brands. It may also be applicable in some B2B markets, but as Davis (1984) suggests, the structure and complexity of some B2B markets mean that other options may also have to be considered. If, for example, the same product or component is sold to a range of different end users, then it may be better to divide management responsibility by end user (or segment) rather than by product. A car component, for example, may be sold to car manufacturers, servicing and repair workshops or specialist retailers. Each of these customer groups needs different handling and the component manufacturer may prefer to have specialist marketing managers for each one. A different approach is to divide marketing management responsibility on a geographic basis, particularly where international marketing is the norm. The logic is the same as for the end-user focus: each territory has a unique profile and very different demands and handling needs, requiring a specialist manager. Both of these alternatives, allocating responsibility by end user or geographic area, take account of the day-to-day marketing needs of the organisation's products but potentially leave an unfilled gap for a 'product champion'. The last thing the organisation wants is for managers to develop the attitude that they only sell the product and that its wider strategic development is 'somebody else's problem'.

# Chapter summary

- Product is defined as covering a wide variety of goods, services and ideas that can be the subject of a marketing exchange. The product itself is layered, consisting of the core product, the tangible product and, finally, the augmented product. Using the tangible and augmented product, manufacturers, service providers and retailers can create differential advantage. Products can be classified according to either their own characteristics (durable, non-durable or service) or buyer-oriented characteristics. In consumer markets, these are linked with the frequency of purchase and the length and depth of the information search. In B2B markets, they are more likely to relate to the final use of the product. An organisation's product mix, made up have some common link, either operational or marketing based. Product mix width is established by the number of product lines, while product line depth is defined according to the number of individual items within a line.

● Branding is an important way of creating differentiated tangible products. It helps the manufacturer to establish loyalty through the three-dimensional character imposed on the product, as well as deflecting consumer attention away from price. Branding is carried out not only by manufacturers, but also by retailers who want to create a more tangible character for themselves, as well as wanting consumers consciously to prefer to shop at their outlets. Relevant issues concerning brand owners include the creation and design of products and their brand identities as expressed through the core and tangible product via elements such as naming, quality, packaging and labelling. The strategic management of product and brand ranges is also important.

● The product lifecycle (PLC) concept is the foundation for the idea that products move through stages in their lives and that they may, therefore, have different marketing needs over time. The PLC suggests four stages: introduction, growth, maturity and decline. Inevitably, the PLC is a very general concept, perhaps too general to be of real use, and there are many practical problems in using it. For an organisation, product management is important not only for making sure that existing products live profitable and efficient lives, and that they are deleted at the most appropriate time, but also to enable it to plan for the future and the flow of new products, taking advantage of new technologies and other opportunities. This implies the need for a balanced portfolio of products: some still in development, some in the early stages of their lives, some more mature and some heading for decline.

● One way of ensuring that products get the most out of their lifecycles is to think about how they are positioned. This means defining what attributes or benefits are important to the market, then researching how your product, its competitors and a hypothetical ideal product are rated against those criteria, then analysing each brand's position in relation to the others and to the ideal. Perceptual mapping, using two or more dimensions, can help to visualise the state of the market. All of this can stimulate debate as to whether a product needs to be further differentiated from its competitors or brought closer to the market segment's ideal. Over a product's lifecycle, repositioning may become necessary in response to the changing marketing and competitive environment.

● In fmcg companies in particular, product or brand managers may be given the responsibility of looking after a particular product or group of products. Although a similar product management structure may be found in B2B markets, alternative options may be considered. Management responsibility may be divided by end user or on a geographic basis, again because the needs of different regions may differ. In either case, the organisation can develop managers with depth of expertise relating to a specific group of end users or a particular geographic market.

## Questions for review and discussion

**6.1** Choose three different brands of shampoo that you think incorporate different *core products*.

   (a) Define the *core product* for each brand.

   (b) How does the *tangible product* for each brand reflect the *core product?*

**6.2** What is a *speciality product* and how might its marketing mix and the kind of buying behaviour associated with it differ from those found with other products?

**6.3** Develop a weighted set of five or six criteria for 'good' labelling. Collect a number of competing brands of the same product and rate each of them against your criteria. Which brand comes out best? As a result of this exercise, would you adjust your weightings or change the criteria included?

**6.4** Discuss the relationship between product adopter categories and the stages of the PLC. What are the implications for the marketer?

**6.5** Define *product positioning* and summarise the reasons why it is important.

**6.6** Choose a consumer product area (be very specific – for example, choose shampoo rather than haircare products) and list as many brands available within it as you can.

(a) What stage in the *PLC* has each product reached?

(b) What stage has the *product class* or *form* reached?

(c) Does any one organisation own several of the brands and, if so, how are these brands distributed across the different *PLC stages?*

# CASE STUDY 6

# OPULENCE IN THE ORIENT

If you have an image of China of cloth-capped workers slaving away in state-owned enterprises you had better think again. If the demand for luxury brands is anything to go by, with up to 25 per cent growth per year China is the world's third largest consumer of luxury brands already and is expected to replace Japan by 2015 to become second only to the United States. With a growing number of (dollar) millionaires (320,000 already, worth $1.6 billion between them), China is a huge potential market. It has been estimated that luxury branded goods could reach 200–300 million people in five to 10 years, with 100 million of them being at the top end of the market. By 2009, the Chinese market for luxury goods was worth about $8.6 billion, and according to China Merchants Bank, holders of its unlimited credit card spent an average of $85,000 each in the first eight months after it was launched, mostly on luxury goods.

Although reliable national statistics are often difficult in China, retail sales were estimated at $1.84 trillion in 2009, an increase of 16.9 per cent over the previous year (*People's Daily*, 2010). Per capita income on average is equivalent to only around $2,000, and even for the middle classes it is only

$6,000 compared with $40,000 in the United States (Wiederhecker, 2007a). There are also significant income differences between the first and second tier cities in China and the rest of the country; just 15 Chinese cities between them account for 18 million middle class consumers.

Middle-class consumers like luxury brands as they give status and prestige over many local products. Interestingly, Beijing tends to be more conservative, and buying is about brand heritage and history whereas Shanghai, towards which younger consumers look, is more about fashion trends. The market is not only growing rapidly, however. It is also changing by becoming more mature, more saturated and more segmented as more brands are attracted to this large market. Brand awareness is increasing too with an average of over 63 luxury brands recognised. The main motive is still personal indulgence, connoisseurship and trendsetting to reinforce perceived social status. Furthermore, Chinese consumers have shown themselves prepared to pay a premium for foreign brands, especially from Europe. However, a lot of the richest Chinese customers are first-generation entrepreneurs with a much younger profile and outlook than their Western equivalents, which could cause some targeting problems for some of the more staid and middle-aged luxury brands. The luxury men's clothing brand Ermenegildo Zegna takes an adaptable view: 'You have to constantly fine-tune. We've become much more scientific and analytical. We seek constant feedback from the customer, and monitor how particular items are doing – we take that into account in our store planning, we adjust our marketing efforts accordingly, the look of each store, the product mix' (as quoted by Wassener, 2009).

Chinese millionaires are keen to exhibit their worth through the products they wear and consume, thus highlighting the significance of branding. Thus China has become an attractive market for many luxury goods manufacturers including Bulgari, Louis Vuitton and Giorgio Armani (Wiederhecker, 2007b). The next phase of expansion is the opening of stores outside the three main cities so Shenyang, Chengdu and Jinan are just some of the middle-sized cities now receiving attention. It is this next phase of rollout to cover these second tier cities that will fuel even more demand. There is an added advantage that more stores mean getting more brands in front of Chinese consumers, and as overheads and staffing costs are low not too many sales are needed to make a store profitable. One such store is Ermenegildo Zegna which has 56 boutiques across key Chinese cities such as Beijing, Chengdu, Hangzhou, Shanghai, Shenyang, Shenzhen and Xian, among others. 'Asia has an incredible thirst for fashion and quality; the region is very important for us. Greater China has been our fastest growing market for the past three years', said Gildo Zegna, the Chief Executive (as quoted by Wassener, 2009).

However, it is not all good news. The new Chinese consumers are less loyal to brands, so brand switching is more evident as they align their personal image with a basket of brands. There is also the problem of counterfeit goods. Although this is not an issue with the millionaires (who would want to be seen wearing a fake watch?), maybe as more and more cities are included and more consumers are brought within reach of luxury brands, it could become a problem. There are also issues of whether the distribution channels are sufficient for expansion, with too many luxury brands trying to get a share of space, and finally there are the problems of government economic policy in taxing luxury goods in a punitive way (Michaels, 2007). This is already happening with items such as golf equipment, yachts, large cars and luxury watches. Nevertheless, despite these cautionary comments, the next phase of Western luxury brand expansion is now well underway and it is clear that Chinese consumers are broadly the same as their Western counterparts in terms of what they get out of brands, and their aspirations, expectations and satisfaction.

*Sources*: Dyer (2006); Michaels (2007); *People's Daily* (2010); Socha (2009); Wassener (2009); Wiederhecker (2007a; 2007b); Zhen (2009).

## Questions

1 Why is branding so important for luxury goods?

2 To what extent do you think the packaging considerations are the same for a luxury product and a mainstream fmcg product?

3 What kind of factors might a luxury goods company such as Ermenegildo Zegna take into account when deciding to launch its brand into the Chinese market?

## References for chapter 6

Aaker, J. (1997) 'Dimensions of Brand Personality', *Journal of Marketing Research*, 34 (3), pp. 347–56.

Appleyard, D. (2010) 'We're the Mothers of Invention!', *Daily Mail*, 4 November.

Assael, H. (1995) *Consumer Behavior and Marketing Action*, 5th edn, Cincinnati, OH : South-Western College Publishing.

Bainbridge, J. (2006) 'Slowed to a Crawl', *Marketing*, 5 April, p. 32.

Bainbridge, J. (2010) 'Off to a Healthy Start', *Marketing*, 17 March.

Baker, R. (2011) '"Ann Summers" Squeal Deal Ruffles M&S Feathers', *Marketing Week*, 20 April.

Bamford, V. (2011) 'Oat So Simple Gets Two New Ranges as Paw Ridge is Axed', *The Grocer*, 14 May.

Barker, A. and Braithwaite, T. (2008) 'Brown Warns Retailers on Use of Plastic Bags', *Financial Times*, 1 March, p. 5.

Barnes, R. and Leyland, A. (2010) 'What Keeps Brands in the Charts', in 'Britain's 100 Biggest Brands', supplement to *The Grocer*, 20 March.

BBC (2009) 'Drink Criticised over Drug Name', BBC, 2 September, accessed via www.bbc.co.uk.

Blackett, T. (1985) 'Brand Name Research – Getting it Right', *Marketing and Research Today*, May, pp. 89–93.

Bokaie, J. (2007) 'Kellogg's Corn Flakes', *Marketing*, 12 September, p. 22.

Bowery, J. (2006) 'Boots to Delist easy4men One Year after Launch', *Marketing*, 15 February, p. 3.

Braithwaite, T. (2008) 'M&S Bag Fee Captures Green Mood', *Financial Times*, 29 February, p. 4.

*Brand Strategy* (2008) '5p for Plastic Bags', *Brand Strategy*, March, p. 6

Charles, G. (2010) 'Find a Healthy Balance', *Marketing*, 31 March.

Clark, N. (2011) 'Von Furstenberg, Bottled', *Marketing*, 29 June.

Connolly, A. and Davidson, L. (1996) 'How Does Design Affect Decisions at the Point of Sale?', *Journal of Brand Management*, 4 (2), pp. 100–7.

Cravens, D., Piercy, N. and Prentice, A. (2000) 'Developing Market-driven Product Strategies', *Journal of Product and Brand Management*, 9 (6), pp. 369–88.

*Daily Mail* (2009) 'Hundreds of Shoppers Flock to H&M for Jimmy Choo Launch', *Daily Mail*, 15 November.

*Daily Mail* (2010) 'Worried Parents Can Track Children with GPS Locator Watch', *Daily Mail*, 7 January.

Davis, E.J. (1984) 'Managing Marketing', in N.A. Hart (ed.), *The Marketing of Industrial Products*, McGraw-Hill.

de Chernatony, L., Harris, F. and Dall'Olmo Riley, F. (2000) 'Added Value: Its Nature, Roles and Sustainability', *European Journal of Marketing*, 34 (1/2), pp. 39–56.

DelVecchio, D. (2000) 'Moving Beyond Fit: The Role of Brand Portfolio Characteristics in Consumer Evaluations of Brand Reliability', *Journal of Product and Brand Management*, 9 (7), pp. 457–71.

Durrani, A. (2010) 'Kellogg to Cut Salt in Nation's Favourite Cereals by up to a Third', *Brand Republic*, 29 January.

Dyer, G. (2006) 'China Increases Taxes on Big Cars', *Financial Times*, 23 March, p. 37.

ENDS (2009) 'Wales Goes Ahead with Bag Tax Despite Criticism', ENDS Report, 5 November, accessed via www.endsreport.com/index.cfm?action=bulletin.article&articleid=21409.

Froment, D. (2010) 'Slow Cow Veut Devenir le Red Bull des Boissons Calmantes', *Les Affaires*, 15 April.

Gloger, D. (2011) 'Ban Shopping Bags Says EU', *Daily Express*, 20 May.

Grande, C. (2003) 'Stepping Out, but Oh So Discreetly', *Financial Times*, 29 July, p. 8.

Green, P.E. and Carmone, F.J. (1970) *Multidimensional Scaling and Related Techniques in Marketing Analysis*, Allyn and Bacon.

*The Grocer* (2008a) 'Bags Melt Away on the Compost Heap', *The Grocer*, 9 February, p. 56.

*The Grocer* (2008b) 'Global Tour of Wine, in Cans', *The Grocer*, 29 March, p. 75.

*The Grocer* (2010) 'Britain's 100 Biggest Brands', supplement to *The Grocer*, 20 March.

Gyekye, L. (2011) 'Call for Welsh Environment Minister to Ditch Bag Tax', *Packaging News*, 11 March, accessed via www.packagingnews.co.uk/news/call-for-welsh-environment-minister-to-ditch-bag-tax/.

Harrington, S. (2005) 'Innovation in Packaging', *The Grocer*, 5 February, pp. 38–40.

Hassay, D. and Peloza, J. (2009) 'Building the Charity Brand Community', *Journal of Non-profit and Public Sector Marketing*, 21 (1), pp. 24–55.

Haslett, E. (2011) 'M&S Gets its Knickers in a Twist Over Ann Summers "Your S&M" Ad', *Management Today*, 20 April.

Hiam, A. (1990) 'Exposing Four Myths of Strategic Planning', *Journal of Business Strategy*, September/October, pp. 23–8.

Hook, S. (2011) 'Instant Success', *The Grocer*, 15 January.

Hooper, L. (2008) 'The End of XP is Near', *CRN*, 28 April, p. 14.

Jaworski, B. and Kohli, A. (1993) 'Market Orientation: Antecedents and Consequences', *Journal of Marketing*, 57, pp. 53–70.

John, D., Loken, B. and Joiner, C. (1998) 'The Negative Impact of Extensions: Can Flagship Products be Diluted?', *Journal of Marketing*, 62 (1), pp. 19–32.

Johnson, L., Soutar, G. and Sweeney, J. (2000) 'Moderators of the Brand Image / Perceived Product Quality Relationship', *Journal of Brand Management*, 7 (6), pp. 425–33.

*Just-drinks* (2008) 'The Euromonitor International 2008 Industry Review from just-drinks: Management Briefing: Soft Drinks', *Just-drinks*, January, accessed via www.just-drinks.com/briefings/.

Lewis, H. (2007) 'Global Market Review of Functional Energy and Sports Drinks', *Just-drinks*, June, accessed via www.just-drinks.com/briefings/.

Leyland, J. (2011) 'Widening the Window of Opportunity', *The Grocer*, 22 January.

Lunarsoft (2011) 'Windows 7 Sales Speed Up in 2011', accessed via www.lunarsoft.net/frontpage/windows-7-sales-speed-up-in-2011.

*Marketing* (2004) 'Marketing Design Awards', *Marketing*, November, p. 16.

*Marketing Week* (2007a) 'Top Brands: The Value of World Leadership', *Marketing Week*, 1 February, p. 26.

*Marketing Week* (2007b) 'Bentley Bids to Boost Appeal with Junior Clothing Range', *Marketing Week*, 25 October, p. 8.

*Marketing Week* (2007c) 'Mars Lends its Support to Brand Extensions', *Marketing Week*, 6 December, p. 7.

*Marketing Week* (2008) 'Eos Wants "Lifestyle" Branding to Take Flight', *Marketing Week*, 24 January, p. 4.

*Marketing Week* (2011) 'Quaker Plots Expansion Strategy for Oat So Simple', *Marketing Week*, 19 May.

McCarthy, M. (2010) 'Dramatic Fall in Number of Plastic Bags Given Out by Supermarkets', *The Independent*, 26 August.

McKenzie, S. (1997) 'Package Deal', *Marketing Week*, 11 September, pp. 67–9.

Michaels, A. (2007) 'China's Taste for Luxury Bears Risks', *Financial Times*, 5 June, p. 28.

Mintel (2008) 'Nappies and Baby Wipes', *Mintel Market Intelligence*, April, accessed via http://academic.mintel.com/sinatra.

Mintel (2010) 'Breakfast Cereals', *Mintel Market Intelligence*, February, accessed via http://academic.mintel.com/sinatra/oxygen_academic.

Mortishead, C. (2009) 'Will the High Street Scuff Jimmy Choo's Image?', *The Times*, 19 November.

Murray, S. (2007) 'Getting the Message Across', *Financial Times*, 11 December, p. 4.

Nielsen (2010) 'Time-Tested Companies Top Britain's 100 Biggest Brands', The Nielsen Company, 26 March, accessed via http://blog.nielsen.com/nielsenwire/consumer/time-tested-companies-top-britains-100-biggest-brands/.

Norwood, G. (2011) 'The Next Big Thing at Home', *Sunday Telegraph*, 23 January.

Olsen, J. (2000) 'Disharmony in Europe Puts Brand Owners at Risk', *Managing Intellectual Property*, December/January, pp. 52–63.

Parasuraman, A. (1997) 'Reflections on Gaining Competitive Advantage Through Customer Value', *Journal of the Academy of Marketing Science*, 25 (2), pp. 154–61.

Park, A. (2004) 'PCs Have Barely Changed Styles Since their Birth', *Business Week*, 21 June, p. 86.

PepsiCo (2009) 'Paw Ridge – Quaker Launches New Healthy Breakfast Cereal for Children', 22 September, accessed via www.pepsico.co.uk/our-company/media-centre/news-and-comment/paw-ridge-quaker-launches-new-healthy-breakfast-cereal-for-children.

Peters, M. (1994) 'Good Packaging Gets Through to the Fickle Buyer', *Marketing*, 20 January, p. 10.

*People's Daily* (2010) 'China's Retail Sales up 16.9% in 2009', *People's Daily*, 21 January, accessed via http://english.people.com.cn/90001/90778/90862/6875095.html#.

Piercy, N. and Morgan, N. (1997) 'The Impact of Lean Thinking and the Lean Enterprise on Marketing: Threat or Synergy?', *Journal of Marketing Management*, 13, pp. 679–93.

Pieters, R. and Warlops, L. (1999) 'Visual Attention During Brand Choice: The Impact of Time Pressure and Task Motivation', *International Journal of Research in Marketing*, 16, pp. 1–16.

Plummer, J. (2010) 'At Work: Communications', *Third Sector*, 28 September.

Reibstein, D.J. *et al*. (1998) 'Mastering Marketing. Part Four: Brand Strategy', *Financial Times* Supplement, pp. 7–8.

Reynolds, J. (2010) 'Kellogg Axes Coco Pops Cereal Brand Extensions', *Marketing*, 2 February, accessed via www.marketingmagazine.co.uk.

Roberts, J. (2011) 'Oxfam: Single Bond Binds Hearts and Minds', *Marketing Week*, 17 February.

Rogers, E.M. (1962) *Diffusion of Innovation*, The Free Press.

Ryan, C. (2010) 'Chocs Away!', *The Grocer*, 14 August.

Saigol, L. (2004) 'For Sale Sign on Jimmy Choo', *Financial Times*, 1 November, p. 22.

Sargeant, A. (1999) 'Charitable Giving: Towards a Model of Donor Behaviour', *Journal of Marketing Management*, 15, pp. 215–38.

Schofield, J. (2007) 'Bullish Microsoft Brushed off Industry "Disappointment" over Vista', *The Guardian*, 26 July.

Sibbles, H. and Pidd, E. (2009) 'H&M Braced for Jimmy Choo Queues', *The Guardian*, 13 November.

Smith, C. (2006) 'Intangible Ignorance', *Marketing*, 4 October, p. 25.

Socha, M. (2009) 'Chasing Gold in China: Luxury Brands Step Up Expansion in the East', *Women's Wear Daily*, 11 November.

Stride, H. (2006) 'An Investigation into the Values Dimensions of Branding: Implications for the Charity Sector', *International Journal of Non-profit and Voluntary Sector Marketing*, 11 (2), pp. 115–24.

Tollington, T. (1998) 'Brands: The Asset Definition and Recognition Test', *Journal of Product and Brand Management*, 7 (3), pp. 180–92.

Underwood, R., Klein, N. and Burke, R. (2001) 'Packaging Communication: Attentional Effects of Product Imagery', *Journal of Product and Brand Management*, 10 (7), pp. 403–22.

von Lindenfels, M. (2009) 'How Does a Small Charity on a Tight Budget Create a Successful Brand', *Third Sector*, 23 November, accessed via www.thirdsector.co.uk.

Wassener, B. (2009) 'Younger Buyers Challenge Luxury Retailers in Asia', *New York Times*, 18 November.

Watson-Smyth, K. (2010) 'The Dualit Electric Toaster', *The Independent*, 1 October.

Whitworth, M. (2009) 'I Wanted to Give Something Back', *Daily Telegraph*, 26 October.

Wiederhecker, A. (2007a) 'Chinese Hang onto Opulent Dreams'; *Financial Times*, 14 April, p. 8.

Wiederhecker, A. (2007b) 'Retailers Tap into Hierarchy of the Nouveau Super-riche', *Financial Times*, 4 June, p. 4.

Wikström, S. and Normann, R. (1994) *Knowledge and Value*, London: Routledge.

Williams, H. (2009) 'The Energy Crisis', *The Independent*, 20 October.

Wood, L. (1990) 'The End of the Product Life Cycle? Education Says Goodbye to an Old Friend', *Journal of Marketing Management*, 6 (2), pp. 145–55.

Woods, S. (2009) 'Copycat Trap', *Design Week*, 13 August, p. 17.

Zhen, Y. (2009) 'Luxury Consumers Still Spending Big', *China Daily*, 23 March, p. 4.

# CHAPTER 7

# Price

## LEARNING OBJECTIVES

This chapter will help you to:

- define the meaning of price;
- understand the different roles price can play for buyers and sellers and in different kinds of market;
- appreciate the nature of the external factors that influence pricing decisions;
- explore the internal organisational forces that influence pricing decisions;
- understand the managerial process that leads to price setting and the factors that influence its outcomes.

## INTRODUCTION

**AT FIRST GLANCE, PRICE** might seem to be the least complicated and perhaps the least interesting element of the marketing mix, not having the tangibility of the product, the glamour of advertising or the atmosphere of retailing. It does play a very important role, however, in the lives of both marketers and customers, and deserves as much strategic consideration as any other marketing tool. Price not only directly generates the revenues that allow organisations to create and retain customers at a profit (in accordance with one of the definitions of marketing in Chapter 1), but can also be used as a communicator, as a bargaining tool and as a competitive weapon. The customer can use price as a means of comparing products, judging relative value for money or judging product quality.

Ultimately, the customer is being asked to accept the product offering and (usually) to hand money over in exchange for it. If the product has been carefully thought out with the customer's needs in mind, if the distribution channels chosen are convenient and appropriate to that customer, if the promotional mix has been sufficiently seductive, then there is a good chance that the customer will be willing to hand over some amount of money for the pleasure of owning that product. But even then, the price that is placed on the product is crucial: set too high a price, and the customer will reject the offering and all the good work done with the rest of the marketing mix is wasted; too low, and the customer is suspicious ('too good to be true'). What constitutes 'a high price' or 'a low price' depends on the buyer, and has to be put into the context of their perceptions of themselves, of the entire marketing package and of the competitors' offerings. Pricing has a spurious certainty about it because it involves numbers, but do not be misled by this; it is as emotive and as open to misinterpretation as any other marketing activity.

It is thus important for the marketer to understand the meaning of price from the customer's point of view, and to price products in accordance with the 'value' that the customer places on the benefits offered.

This chapter expands on these initial concepts of price. It will look further at what price is, and what it means to marketers and customers in various contexts. It will also examine more closely the role of price in the marketing mix, and how it interacts with other marketing activities. This sets the scene for a focus on some of the internal factors and external pressures that influence pricing thinking within an organisation. The final section of the chapter then draws all this together to give an overview of the managerial process that leads to decisions on pricing strategies and price setting.

## eg

How would you like it if you were asked to 'name your own price' for a particular good or service? It sounds crazy, but a number of suppliers are doing just that in the USA. In 2007, Radiohead, the rock band, allowed fans to download its latest album 'In Rainbows' with each buyer deciding what they were prepared to pay for it. *Paste*, the US music and arts magazine did something similar, with each customer determining his or her own annual subscription. This ultimate form of buyer power can also apply to services. One World Café, serving organic food in Salt Lake City, asks its customers to pay what they think the meal is worth. People who can't afford to pay are given chores around the restaurant and garden. The belief is that this encourages people to value food, a point often lost with US consumers.

The key question is whether such a pricing approach could ever become mainstream or just remain a gimmicky option for a quirky minority. Could it work in Europe or Scandinavia? Tony Cram from Ashridge Business School doubts it, suggesting that people may feel uncomfortable entering into a transaction where the price is not known; there is higher value placed on a fixed price that is communicated with clarity (*Brand Strategy*, 2007). It could work where there is a strong sense of the brand among potential customers, such as with Disney, but would be a brave marketer that recommended it to the board!

How much would you pay for this album?

*Source*: Courtyard Management

There has to be trust between the supplier and the customer base, as an item that is perceived as free may also be perceived as being of low value. Even Radiohead, with a dedicated fan base, found that only 38 per cent of those who downloaded the album paid anything at all for it – the rest chose to pay nothing (Sherwin, 2008). Furthermore, by 2010, there were reports that the Recording Industry Association of America (RIAA) and the International Federation of the Phonographic Industry (IFPI) were asking ISPs to disable the accounts of bloggers who were passing on the songs for free (*NME*, 2010). Meanwhile, Morrissey has refused to follow Radiohead's example by self-releasing a new album, saying: 'I don't have any need to be innovative in that way. I am still stuck in the dream of an album that sells well not because of marketing, but because people like the songs' (as quoted by *NME*, 2011).

Despite the potential problems, all of this is a reminder that pricing should not be left either to competitors or to finance departments because it is a critical and dynamic element of the marketing mix. Allowing customers to give a brand a stiff kick in the bottom line by determining their own price could be a great way of reminding marketers that their role is constantly to delight their customers – the higher the delight, the more revenue your product or service generates (*Brand Strategy*, 2007; *NME*, 2010, 2011; Sherwin, 2008).

# The role and perception of price

Price is the value that is placed on something. What is someone prepared to give in order to gain something else? Usually, price is measured in money, as a convenient medium of exchange that allows prices to be set quite precisely. This is not necessarily always the case, however. Goods and services may be bartered ('I will help you with the marketing plan for your car repair business if you service my car for me'), or there may be circumstances where monetary exchange is not appropriate, for example at election time when politicians make promises in return for your vote. Any such transactions, even if they do not directly involve money, are exchange processes and thus can use marketing principles (see Chapter 1 for the discussion of marketing as an exchange process). Price is any common currency of value to both buyer and seller.

Even money-based pricing comes under many names, depending on the circumstances of its use: solicitors charge fees; landlords charge rent; bankers charge interest; railways charge fares; hotels charge a room rate; consultants charge retainers; agents charge commission; insurance companies charge premiums; and over bridges or through tunnels, tolls may be charged. Whatever the label, it is still a price for a good or a service, and the same principles apply.

Price does not necessarily mean the same things to different people, just because it is usually expressed as a number. You have to look beyond the price, at what it represents to both the buyer and the seller if you want to grasp its significance in any transaction. Buyer and seller may well have different perspectives on what price means. We now turn to that of the buyer.

## The customer's perspective

From the buyer's perspective, price represents the value they attach to whatever is being exchanged. Up to the point of purchase, the marketer has been making promises to the potential buyer about what this product is and what it can do for that customer. The customer is going to weigh up those promises against the price and decide whether it is worth paying (Zeithaml, 1988).

In assessing price, the customer is looking specifically at the expected benefits of the product, as shown in Figure 7.1.

**Figure 7.1**
Factors
influencing
customers' price
assessments

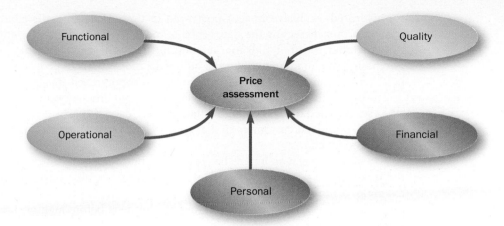

## Functional

Functional benefits relate to the design of the product and its ability to fulfil its desired function. For example, a washing machine's price might be judged on whether or not it can handle different washing temperatures, operate economically and dry as well as wash.

## Quality

The customer may expect price to reflect the quality level of the product (Erickson and Johansson, 1985). Thus a customer may be prepared to pay more for leather upholstery in a car, or for solid wood furniture rather than veneer, or for hand-made Belgian chocolates rather than mass produced. Quality perceptions may be to do with the materials or components used in the product, as in these examples, or with the labour involved in making it. Quality may also, however, be a less tangible judgement made on the basis of corporate image. BMW, Heinz and Cadbury's are perceived as quality companies, and therefore they are perceived as producing quality products. The consumer can thus accept that those organisations might charge higher prices.

## Operational

In B2B markets, price may be judged in relation to the product's ability to influence the production process. For example, a new piece of machinery might be assessed on its ability to increase productivity, make the production line more efficient or reduce the labour content of the finished goods. Even in a consumer market, operational issues might be considered. For instance, the purchase of a microwave oven increases the operational efficiency of the kitchen, both making it easier to cater for the staggered mealtimes resulting from the modern family's fragmented lifestyle, and giving the chief cook more time to pursue other interests.

## Financial

Particularly in B2B markets, many purchases are seen as investments, and therefore the expected return on that investment is important in judging whether the price is worthwhile or not. New machinery, for example, is expected to pay for itself over time in terms of increased efficiency, output, labour saving, etc. Note that this judgement is made not only in terms of production outputs, but also in terms of long-term cost savings, efficiency gains and productivity improvements.

## Personal

Personal benefit is a difficult category for the marketer to gauge, as it attempts to measure price against intangible, individual, psychological benefits such as status, comfort, self-image (Chapter 3 reminded you about these benefits), etc. Some high-involvement products, such as perfumes, use high pricing deliberately as a means of amplifying the upmarket, with sophisticated, exclusive images portrayed in their packaging, distribution and advertising strategies, thus increasing the status enhancement and 'feel good' factor of the purchase.

Remember too that B2B markets are not immune from the effects of personal factors. Purchasing can be influenced by the individual motivations of people involved (as discussed at p. 122 *et seq.*), and even by a desire to enhance a corporate self-image.

The problem is, of course, that different buyers put different values on different benefits. This endorses the need for market segmentation (see Chapter 4), which can begin to sort out groupings of like-minded customers so that appropriately tailored marketing mixes (including price) can be developed.

So far, it has been assumed that price perception and judgements of value are constant in the mind of the potential buyer. They are, however, variable according to circumstances. For example, a householder thinking of replacing water pipes would probably be very price sensitive and get quotes from a number of plumbers before making a decision. A burst pipe in the winter, however, would have that same householder paying almost any price to get a plumber round immediately. In any such distress purchase, the value placed on immediate problem solution justifies paying a premium price.

Another factor influencing price perception is scarcity. Where supply is severely limited and demand is high, prices can take on a life of their own and begin to spiral.

## The seller's perspective

Price is a distinctive element of the marketing mix for the seller, because it is the only one that generates revenue. All the other elements represent outgoing costs. Price is also important, therefore, because it provides the basis of both recovering those costs and creating profit:

**Profit = Total revenue − Total cost**

where total revenue is the quantity sold multiplied by the unit price, and total cost represents the costs of producing, marketing and selling the product. Quantity sold is itself dependent on price as well as on the other marketing mix elements. The motor industry has suggested that although a car dealership selling a large number of cars every year could well generate 80 per cent of its turnover from car sales, it is generating only just over one-third of its total profits from those sales. In comparison, the workshop might generate only 5 per cent of turnover, but 25 per cent of profit. This reflects the fact that for some products, competitive pressures may keep margins tight. To increase profit in such areas, therefore, the organisation may have to find a way of either reducing the costs involved, or justifying higher prices.

The seller, however, must always take care to think about price from the perspective of the customer. In pure economic terms, it would be assumed that reducing a price would lead to higher sales because more people could then afford and want the product. As the introduction to this chapter suggested, however, a low price may be interpreted as making a negative statement about the product's quality, and a sudden reduction in price of an established product may be taken to mean that the product's quality has been compromised in some way.

Similarly, a high price may not always be a bad thing for a seller. If buyers equate price with quality (and in the absence of information or knowledge of the market, it may be the only indicator they pick up), then a higher price might actually attract customers. Part of the psychological benefit of the purchase for the customer might well be derived from its expense, for example in purchasing gifts where one feels obliged to spend a certain amount on the recipient either to fulfil social expectations or to signal affection. The higher the price, the more exclusive the market segment able to afford the product or service. Many more rail travellers, for example, choose to travel second class than in the higher-priced first-class accommodation.

The seller also needs to remember that sometimes the cost to the customer of purchasing a product can be much greater than its price. These broader considerations might have an inhibiting effect on purchase. When consumers were buying DVD players for the first time, for example, they did not only look at the ticket price of the machine, but also weighed up the costs of replacing favourite video cassettes with discs. A business buying a new computer system has to consider the costs of transferring records, staff training and the initial decrease in productivity as they learn to find their way around the new system and the costs of installation (and of removing the old equipment). The whole marketing strategy for a product has to recognise the real cost to the customer of accepting the offering and work to overcome such objections, whether through pricing, a better-tailored product offering or effective communication and persuasion.

Whatever type of market an organisation is in, whatever market segments it seeks to serve, it must always be aware that price can never stand apart from the other elements of the marketing mix. It interacts with those elements and must, therefore, give out signals consistent with those given by the product itself, place and promotion. Price is often quoted as a reason for not purchasing a product, but this reflects a tendency to use price as a scapegoat for other failings in the marketing mix. Price is a highly visible factor and at the point of purchase it hits the buyer where it hurts – in the pocket. As has been said before in this chapter, if the rest of the marketing mix has worked well up to the point of sale, then the price should not be too great an issue, because the buyer will have been convinced that the benefits supplied are commensurate with the price asked. Price is seen here as a natural, integrated element in harmony with the rest of the offering. It could be argued that a buyer who is wavering and uses price as the ultimate determinant of whether to purchase is either shopping in the wrong market segment or being ill-served by sloppy marketing.

*eg*

The Sony PlayStation 3 (PS3) has always been a bit of a problem child – it promised a lot but never quite fulfilled it. The vision is clear from Sony's point of view: the PS3 fits in to living room hardware alongside a Sony LCD TV, with a Blueray disc drive to watch films and so on, and it's all interconnected. The trouble is that consumers didn't necessarily share that vision. In part, that reflected concern over the high price tag of the PS3. Consequently, the Nintendo Wii was outselling PS3 in most markets, despite heavy marketing investment in the PS3 especially in the run up to Christmas 2007. Only by introducing a 40 gigabyte model and cutting prices by as much as $100 on older models was Sony able to recover sales in the run up to Christmas. The problem is that some analysts believe it took Sony too long to lower prices, as it tried to recoup the high investment costs. Even with lower prices on PS3, many consumers still preferred the more expensive Wii (at over $100 more) and some were even prepared to wait for one if there were local supply shortages. Nevertheless, the PS3 price cut did help to boost sales in the short term for Christmas, but in the longer term, analysts were estimating that it would be 2011 before PS3 regained a lead over the Wii.

So, what's happened since 2007? By 2011, the biggest threat to PS3 was the Xbox 360 and its Kinect technology. As one industry analyst pointed out, while Xbox has the novelty of Kinect driving console sales, PS3 only has the promise of new games, and 'I doubt that many hard core gamers have held off purchasing a PS3 while they waited for Killzone 3 to come out. At this point in the cycle, the only people who have waited are those who planned to buy a console at a price point under $200, and while I think that there are a lot

In the console price wars, the Wii is currently winning

*Source*: Alamy Images/Neils Poulson DK

of those people, [PS3] pricing remains stubbornly high' (as quoted by Brightman, 2011). In June 2011, in the UK Argos was selling a PS3 bundle for £279.99; an Xbox Kinect bundle for £249.99 and a Wii bundle for £129.99. In terms of global sales over the whole lifecycle of the current generation of consoles, the Wii is well in the lead with 84.6 million consoles sold, while PS3 and Xbox are pretty evenly matched at 47.9 million and 50 million consoles sold respectively. Of course, different geographic regions are at different stages of their lifecycles, so price competition is more pronounced in some more mature markets than others and each console thus has some geographic areas in which it performs more strongly than in others (Brightman, 2011; Burns, 2008; Purchese, 2011; Sanchanta, 2007a, 2007b; Williams, 2008).

# External influences on the pricing decision

The previous sections of this chapter have shown that there is more to pricing than meets the eye. It is not a precise science because of the complexities of the marketing environment and the human perceptions of the parties involved in the marketing exchange. There will always be some uncertainty over the effect of a pricing decision, whether on distribution channels, competitors or the customer. Nevertheless, to reduce that uncertainty, it is important to analyse the range of issues affecting pricing decisions. Some of these are internal to the selling organisation, and are thus perhaps more predictable, but others arise from external pressures, and are therefore more difficult to define precisely. There is also some variation in the extent to which the organisation can control or influence these issues. Figure 7.2 summarises the main areas of external influence, while this section of the chapter defines them and gives an overview of their impact on the pricing decision, in preparation for the more detailed scrutiny of price setting and strategies towards the end of this chapter.

## Customers and consumers

As p. 254 *et seq.* showed, pricing cannot be considered without taking into account the feelings and sensitivities of the end buyer. Different market segments react to price levels and price changes differently depending on the nature of the product, its desirability and the level of product loyalty established.

**Figure 7.2**
External influences on the pricing decision

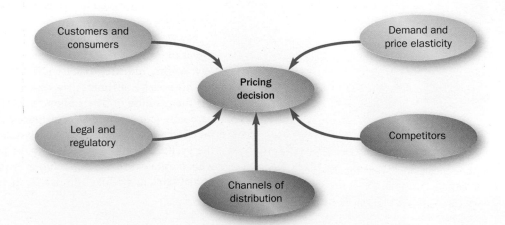

For all the glamorous hair-swishing fantasies that get woven into shampoo advertising, consumers are actually quite practical in their approach to shopping for this product and treat it as something of a commodity. Price is a big influence for more than half of buyers, and special offers (for example, bulk discounts such as buy 3 bottles for £3) influence the choices of over 70 per cent of shampoo shoppers, and the brands don't seem to be able to change this. This means that brand switching is rife, price-based competition has escalated with profit margins cut right back, and thus over a five-year period, volume sales have outpaced value sales. It is also interesting to note that because the owners of the major brands in the market (Procter & Gamble, L'Oréal and Unilever) are so focused on price competition, the supermarket own-label products have made very little impact – for the shopper, if you can get a 'trusted brand' for the same price as an own-brand equivalent, it's a no-brainer! There isn't really a distinct and separate price-sensitive segment to target as there is in other fmcg sectors where a wider range of price points can be sustained and the major brands come at the premium end of the price range (Bainbridge, 2011a; Mintel, 2011c).

The marketer has to be careful to set prices within an area bounded at the bottom end by costs and at the top end by what the market will tolerate. The bigger that area, the more discretion the marketer has in setting price. The organisation can increase its pricing discretion either by reducing costs (thereby lowering the bottom boundary) or by raising the consumers' threshold (by better targeted communication or by improving the product offering).

The consumers' upper threshold is difficult to define as it is linked closely with perceptions of the product and its competitive standing. A product perceived as better than the competition will have a higher upper threshold than one perceived as poor value. In the latter case, the upper limit on price may be very close to cost. Similarly, a product with strong brand loyalty attached to it can push its upper limit higher because the product's desirability blunts any price sensitivity, enabling a price premium to be achieved. By basing a price on the perceived value of the offer, a close match can be found with what the customer is prepared to pay (Nimer, 1975; Thompson and Coe, 1997).

## Demand and price elasticity

Customers' attitudes towards price and their responsiveness to it are reflected to some extent in economic theories of demand. Marketers' pricing objectives and the estimation of demand are thus very closely linked (Montgomery, 1988). As pricing objectives change, for example if there is a decision to move upmarket into a premium-priced segment, the nature and size of potential demand will also change. Similarly, it is important for the marketer to be able to estimate demand for new product. The definition of demand is flexible here; it may mean demand across an entire product market, or demand within a specific market segment, or be organisation specific.

When the congestion charge was introduced in central London in 2003, part of the rationale was to reduce the amount of traffic, and it does seem that the thought of paying £8 per day just to drive into London has made many motorists think about whether their journeys are necessary or whether public transport is a better option. A negative knock-on effect of this, however, has been a significant fall in demand for car parking space. According to Hamilton (2008), Westminster Council had seen a 13 per cent drop in occupancy of its public car parks since the congestion charging scheme was introduced. In response to this, the Council trialled a demand-led 'real time' method of setting parking charges at its 250-bay Queensway car park. Thus at times when there were between 200 and 250 cars parked, drivers were charged £2 per hour for parking. If, however, the car park had fewer than 50 cars parked, the rate droped to 20p per hour. This meant that motorists could potentially pay only £4.80 for a whole day's parking, compared with an average of £20 in other car parks in central London (Westminster Council, 2008). However, until they arrived at the entrance to the car park, drivers didn't know what the applicable charge would be. The trial was a success in terms of improving occupancy and the scheme continued. However, in 2011, with a view to saving £3 million per year, Westminster Council awarded a 25-year lease for running 14 car parks, including Queensway, to Q-Park, a specialist parking contractor (*Hampstead & Highgate Express*, 2011). Queensway now appears to have reverted to a standard, flat, hourly charge for parking.

## Demand determinants

For most products, it seems logical that if the price goes up, then demand falls and, conversely, if the price falls, then demand rises. This is the basic premise behind the standard demand curve shown in Figure 7.3, which shows the number of units sold (Q1) at a given price (P1). As price increases from P1 to P2, demand is expected to fall from Q1 to Q2. This classic demand curve may relate either to a market or to an individual product. As an example, if the dollar is weak against other currencies, Americans generally find foreign holidays more expensive and thus do not travel.

The shape of the demand curve, however, will be influenced by a range of factors other than price. Changing consumer tastes and needs, for example, might make a product more or less desirable regardless of the price. The economic ability to pay is still there, but the willingness to buy is not. Fluctuations in real disposable income could similarly affect demand, particularly for what could be considered luxury items. In a recession, for instance, consumers may cut back on demand for foreign holidays or new cars. In this case, the willingness exists, but the means to pay do not. The availability and pricing of close substitute products will also change the responsiveness of demand. For example, the introduction of the DVD player into the mass market had a disastrous effect on demand for video players.

All of these factors are demand determinants that the marketer must understand in order to inject meaning into the demand curve. As Diamantopoulos and Mathews (1995) emphasise, however, demand curves are very subjective in nature. They depend very much on managerial judgements of the likely impact of price changes on demand, since most organisations do not have the kind of sophisticated information systems that would allow a more objective calculation. In reality, then, it is a *perceived* demand curve that drives managerial decisions rather than a 'real' one.

Not all products conform to the classic demand curve shown in Figure 7.3. Some products with a deep psychological relationship with the consumer, perhaps with a high status dimension, can show a reverse price–demand curve where the higher the price is the higher the

**Figure 7.3**
The classic demand curve

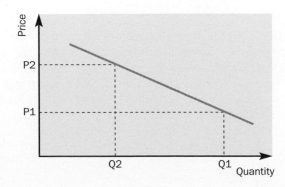

demand. As Figure 7.4 shows, as the price goes down from P1 to P2 and demand falls from Q1 to Q2, the product loses its mystique and demand falls. There is, however, still an upper threshold beyond which the good becomes too expensive for even a status-conscious market. Then as the price rises higher, beyond P3, a more normal relationship holds true in which higher price leads to lower demand. This creates a boomerang-shaped demand curve. Knowing at what point the curve begins to turn back on itself could be useful for a marketer wishing to skim the market. Price too high and you could have turned the corner, becoming too exclusive.

Another dimension of the demand curve is that marketers can themselves seek to influence its shape. Figure 7.5 shows how the demand curve can be shifted upwards through marketing efforts. If the marketer can offer better value to the customer or change the customer's perceptions of the product, then a higher quantity will be demanded without any reduction in the price. It is valuable for the marketer to be able to find ways of using non-price-based mechanisms of responding to a competitor's price cut or seeking to improve demand, to avoid the kind of mutually damaging price wars that erode margins and profits. This may create a new demand curve, parallel to the old one, so that demand can be increased from Q1 to Q2 while retaining the price at P1.

## Price elasticity of demand

It is also important for the marketer to have some understanding of the sensitivity of demand to price changes. This is shown by the steepness of the demand curve. A very steep demand curve shows a great deal of price sensitivity, in that a small change in price, all other things remaining equal, leads to a big change in demand. For some essential products, such as electricity, the demand curve is much more shallow; changes in price do not lead to big changes in demand. In this case, demand is said to be inelastic because it does not stretch a lot if pulled either way by price. The term price elasticity of demand thus refers to the ratio of percentage change in quantity over percentage change in price:

$$\text{Price elasticity} = \frac{\text{\% change in quantity demanded}}{\text{\& change in price}}$$

**Figure 7.4**
The boomerang demand curve

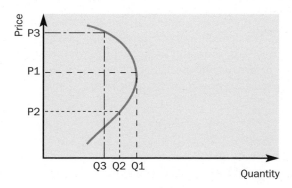

**Figure 7.5**
The parallel demand curve

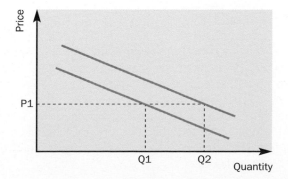

Thus the higher the price elasticity of demand, the more sensitive the market. Goods like electricity have a price elasticity much closer to zero than do goods like convenience foods. For most goods, as the quantity demanded usually falls if the price rises, price elasticity is often negative, but by convention the minus sign is usually ignored.

Fine fragrances, especially those with designer names, might fall into this category of demand curve. The fragrance houses have been careful to price them sufficiently highly to position them well away from ordinary toiletries. This means that fine fragrances appeal not only to a well-to-do segment who can easily afford this sort of product on a regular basis, but also to those who aspire to be part of this elite and are prepared to splash out what seems to them to be a large sum of money occasionally to bring themselves closer to a world of luxury and sophistication. In either case, the high price is part of the appeal and the excitement of the product. The higher the price, the bigger the thrill. If the price became too high, however, the aspiring segment would probably fall away and live out their fantasies with something more affordable. They might find £30 to £80 acceptable, but £70 to £120 might be perceived as too extravagant. Even the elite segment might have its upper threshold. If the price of designer-label fine fragrances becomes too high, then they might as well buy the designer's clothes instead if they want to flaunt their wealth and status!

It is important for the marketer to understand price elasticity and its causes, whether for an organisation's brand or within the market as a whole, as a basis for marketing mix decisions. There are a number of factors that will influence the price sensitivity (i.e. the price elasticity of demand) of customers. According to economic theory, the emergence of more, or closer, substitutes for a product will increase its price elasticity as buyers have the option of switching to the substitute as the price of the original product rises. From a marketing perspective, however, it does not seem quite so simple. The emergence of vegetable-based spreadable fats, for example, has offered consumers an alternative to butter and thus something with which to compare the price of butter. Further than that, however, it has completely changed the character of butter's demand curve from that of a necessity (a fairly flat straight line) to that of a luxury (more of a boomerang shape). Those who now choose to buy butter because of its superior taste or because of the status it bestows on the contents of the buyer's fridge will be no more price sensitive now than they ever were and, indeed, may even be less so.

# MARKETING IN ACTION

## Not a barrel of laughs

The price of a barrel of oil on the commodities market might not seem to be a particularly interesting topic at first glance, but its impact is far-reaching for all of us. In 2005, oil was $55 per barrel, but by June 2011 it had hit $112. The most obvious and immediate effect felt by consumers is on petrol prices. According to the AA (2011), mid-June 2011, the UK had the twelfth highest unleaded petrol price in Europe, at 136.1 pence per litre, and the second highest diesel price. The Netherlands had the highest unleaded petrol price, equivalent to 150.33 per litre, with Estonia enjoying the cheapest European petrol at 106.6 pence per litre. Historically, we have tended to think of petrol as a relatively inelastic product, i.e.

changes in price do not lead to changes in consumption, but there is now evidence that faced with rising petrol price, families are starting to think more carefully about their motoring habits. A survey reported by Hawkes (2008) suggested that 29 per cent had cut visits to out-of-town retail parks, and far more people were choosing to walk to local shops rather than drive. Similarly, an RAC survey reported by King (2011) suggested that 48 per cent of drivers were cutting back on journeys for financial reasons. Tesco claimed that sales volumes were down in its largest stores because shoppers were less willing to drive to them, while Sainsbury's similarly said that sales at its local convenience stores were growing far faster than at its out of town sites.

The rising price of oil has also had an effect on consumers through increased food prices. This has happened partly because of increased airfreight and road transport fuel costs, and partly because of increased production and packaging costs. Farmers and food processors have to pay for fuel for their equipment and machinery, and plastic packaging costs have risen because plastic is a derivative of oil.

Other businesses badly affected are airlines. Many airlines, including British Airways, easyJet and Ryanair, have cut routes altogether, shed jobs and grounded older, less fuel-efficient aircraft. Fuel surcharges are also a way of recouping at least some of those rising costs directly from passengers. From September 2011, for example, Flybe imposed a £3 per passenger fuel surcharge. Flybe operates short-haul domestic and European services, but the fuel surcharges on long-haul travel are, of course, much higher. As at May 2011, BA's fuel surcharge was £85 per flight (so that's £170 for a return trip) on journeys of between five and nine hours, and £98 on longer flights (between 20 and 40 per cent of the ticket cost). First class passengers faced a fuel surcharge of £145 per journey. With fuel now comprising over one-third of BA's costs, a rise in surcharges was perhaps inevitable. Similarly, Qantas announced in April 2011 that it was increasing fuel surcharges on all its services. The surcharge would rise from A$190 for a one-way journey from Australia to the UK to A$290, for example. This is perhaps not surprising, given that Qantas faces an annual fuel bill of nearly A$3 billion and the airline claimed that, 'The revised fuel surcharges cover less than half of the increase in fuel cost for the Qantas International business for next year' (as quoted by Heasley and Wen, 2011). For smaller airlines, the situation is even more critical. One of the reasons that Silverjet, the business-class-only transatlantic airline went bust was spiralling costs. In November 2007, it cost about £28,600 in fuel for a return flight to New York, but by the end of May 2008, that had risen to £44,000. There are limits to how much can be passed on to passengers via ticket prices, especially for those airlines whose USP is 'low prices' and within a recessionary economic environment, but perhaps there is more that can be done in terms of fuel efficiency. China Southern Airline calculated that one flush at 30,000 ft burns one litre of oil . . . so if you have 300 or more passengers having a good time with the drinks trolley on a long-haul flight, that's a significant amount of fuel being indirectly flushed down the loo. Perhaps this is an opportunity for yet another surcharge, and the era of pay-as-you-go flights is just around the corner.

*Sources*: The AA (2011); Buckley and Lindsay (2008); Clark (2011); Hawkes (2008); Heasley and Wen (2011); Hutchison and Ruddick (2008); King (2011); Leroux and Fildes (2011); Macefield (2011); O'Doherty (2008); Odell and Wembridge (2011); www.petrolprices.com; www.roadtransport.com.

As well as looking at the influence of substitutes on the shape and steepness of demand curves, it is also interesting to consider the relative importance of the purchase to the buyer. A purchase involving a relatively large cash outlay compared with the buyer's income will make that buyer more price sensitive. As discussed in Chapter 3, the more risky and infrequent the purchase, the more rational the buyer becomes, and more important the value for money aspects of the offering become. A rise in the price of cars, for example, might deter a potential buyer from replacing an old car.

## Channels of distribution

An organisation's approach to pricing has also to take into account the needs and expectations of the other members of the distribution chain. Each of them will have a desired level of profit margin and a requirement to cover the costs associated with handling and reselling the product, such as transport, warehousing, insurance and retail display, for example. Even with a service product, such as insurance or a holiday, distributing through agents who claim commission on sales to cover premises, staffing, administration and profit has an impact on the price of the service.

All of this tends to erode the manufacturer's pricing discretion, because effectively it adds to the producer's costs and takes the total much nearer to the consumer's upper limit. How much erosion there is will depend on the balance of power between manufacturer and intermediaries.

## MARKETING IN ACTION

### Clothing kids with a clear conscience

Barely has the summer term finished at the end of July and the shops are starting to display their 'back to school' clothing ranges. For a harassed parent, despairing of how quickly the little one grows out of his clothes, and the wear and tear resulting from playground football scuffles and other activities that mum would rather not know about, the aggressive price competition between retailers must seem like a godsend. According to Mintel (2010b), the UK schoolwear market is worth around £959 million and as a necessity purchase, it is a relatively safe, if competitive, market for retailers. Asda leads the market as a whole, with 15 per cent market share (by value), closely followed by Tesco with 14 per cent and M&S with 11 per cent. Over the last few years, supermarkets have taken an increasingly large share of this market, capitalising on the role that convenience plays in purchase decisions, and indeed 49 per cent of schoolwear buyers agreed that they 'tend to buy schoolwear from supermarkets nowadays' (Mintel, 2010b). This could reflect the low involvement nature of many schoolwear purchases – a white polo shirt is a white polo shirt in the eyes of the shopper. If that is what is specified by your child's school and the supermarket is offering a multipack of three for less than £3, then why hesitate?

It's all great news for parents, but how many of them stop to think about how the retailers can offer such ridiculously low prices? Undoubtedly, some of them are using schoolwear as a loss leader to attract customers into the store and are prepared to absorb any losses, but as retail prices get driven ever lower, it is possible that pressure is being put on suppliers to reduce their prices. Much of this cheap clothing is manufactured in countries such as Bangladesh, Sri Lanka, China, Vietnam and Turkey, in factories offering poor working conditions, minimal wages (less than a living wage in some places) and minimal rights for workers. War on Want found workers in Bangladesh earning 7p per hour and working 70 hours per week (as reported by Rosselson, 2008). Most retailers, of course, claim that they source ethically, and point to their membership of the Ethical Trading Initiative (ETI), but some agencies such as War on Want and Labour Behind the Label say that under-pay and over-work are often found in factories used by ETI members and want retailers to be a lot more transparent in publishing details about the factories they use. Labour Behind the Label's Sam Maher said, 'Unless companies can prove to us that workers are working in decent conditions, then it's unlikely that just because they are ETI members workers are being treated fairly and being paid enough' (as quoted by Rosselson, 2008).

Rosselson (2008) makes a very interesting point:

> **School uniforms offer companies an opportunity to really show that they can source responsibly. Unlike fashion ranges, which are subject to fast moving trends and seasonal changes, school uniforms are standard clothing items. This means that some purchasing practices which lead to ethical principles being compromised could be tackled. The time between order and delivery could be longer, taking off the pressure for factories to push their workers into working such long hours.**

Perhaps parents too need to take a more thoughtful approach to their purchasing and start demanding more information on the origins and sourcing of what they buy.

Mintel (2010b) suggests that as yet only 9 per cent of schoolwear buyers said that they 'prefer ethical brands and would like to be able to buy schoolwear that has not been made using child labour', but at least it's a start. In 2010, Tesco was the only major retailer offering a complete fairtrade cotton school uniform, but there are niche suppliers and retailers specialising in ethical schoolwear. It comes at a price, however, but at least in paying a little more, the buyer can be confident that they are not exploiting a worker. Let's face it, many parents wouldn't think twice about paying more than £13 for a child's branded tee-shirt, so why shouldn't they also pay a fairer price for schoolwear?

*Sources:* Hook (2011); Mintel (2010b); Rosselson (2008).

## Competitors

The point has been made several times during the course of this chapter that pricing decisions have to be made in a competitive context. The level and intensity of competition and the pricing decisions that other organisations make in the market will influence any producer's own pricing. It is not just about relative positioning ('If the budget version is £10 and the premium quality version is £70, then if we want to signal a mid-range product we have to charge £45'). It also concerns strategic decisions about the extent to which the organisation wishes to use price as an aggressive competitive weapon. Price and non-price competition will be discussed later in this chapter.

The influence of competition on price will depend on the nature of the product and the number and size of competitors within the market.

### Monopoly

Few monopoly situations, where there is only one supplier serving the whole market, exist. Traditionally, monopolies have been large state-owned enterprises providing public services such as utilities, telecommunications and mail, or operating economically crucial industries such as steel and coal. Legislation protected the monopoly from competition. In theory, monopolists have no competitive framework for pricing and can, therefore, set whatever prices they like as the customer has no choice but to source from them. In practice, however, governments and independent watchdog bodies have imposed regulations and pressurised monopolists into keeping prices within socially acceptable limits. Even if that was not enough, the growth of international competition and the availability of alternatives also have an impact. The price and availability of fuel, oil, gas or nuclear power, for instance, all affect the price and demand for coal.

### Oligopoly

The UK's deregulated telecommunications market is an oligopoly, where a small number of powerful providers dominate the market between them. Each player in the market is very conscious of the rest and makes no move without due consideration of the likely competitive response. Pricing is a particularly sensitive issue in such markets and, where oligopolists choose to price very closely with each other, accusations of collusion are bound to arise. Sudden changes in price by one organisation might be construed as a threat by the rest, but prior and public notification of price rises can be used to defuse suspicion.

These developments are not surprising, as a price war between oligopolists is something that all parties involved would prefer to avoid. Since oligopolists are likely to be fairly evenly matched, it is difficult for any one of them to be sure that it can win. While the war goes on, the consumer may be happy, but the oligopolists are simply eroding their profit margins to dangerously thin levels, not gaining any competitive ground, and causing themselves much stress about the eventual outcome.

## Monopolistic competition

Most markets fall into the category of monopolistic competition where there are many competitors, but each has a product differentiated from the rest. Price is not necessarily a key factor in these markets, as product features and benefits serve to differentiate a product and diffuse the competitive effect. The emphasis in these markets is on branding or adding value so that the customer is prepared to accept a different price from its competitors. Miele, a German manufacturer of kitchen and laundry appliances, for example, has developed a reputation for selling very high-quality goods at a price premium. It can thus price its products substantially higher than those of its competitors, because Miele's customers believe that they are getting good value for money in terms of quality, durability and service.

## Perfect competition

As with its direct opposite, the monopoly, perfect competition is hard to find. It implies that there are very many sellers in the market with products that are indistinguishable from each other in the eyes of the buyer. There is, therefore, little flexibility on price, because no one seller has either enough power to lead the rest or the ability to differentiate the product sufficiently to justify a different price. If one seller increases the price, either the rest will follow suit or customers will change suppliers, bringing the aberrant supplier back into line. One supplier's reduction in price will attract custom until such time as other suppliers follow suit.

To avoid this kind of powerless stalemate, most markets have evolved into offering differentiated products, even with the most uninteresting commodities (see the example at p. 151 on salt, for instance). Nor does the equality of suppliers last for long in most markets. One or two more astute or powerful suppliers usually emerge to lead the market into monopolistic competition.

# Legal and regulatory framework

European marketers increasingly need to understand the national and European legal and regulatory framework when setting and adjusting prices. Aspects of this were discussed at p. 63 *et seq*. Some organisations, such as public utilities, tend to have their pricing policies carefully scrutinised by the government to make sure that they are in the public interest, especially where a near-monopoly is operating. Even after privatisation, such organisations are not entirely free to price as they wish. As mentioned in Chapter 2, for example, the privatised water, gas, telephone and electricity companies in the UK are answerable to quasi non-governmental organisations (QUANGOs), watchdog bodies set up by the government.

In the UK, resale price maintenance, that is, the power of manufacturers to determine what the retail price of their products should be, was abolished in the early 1960s. Although it was retained in a few selected product areas, over the years it has been gradually dropped. Achieving very much the same effect, however, within the EU, some industries have negotiated selective distribution agreements that effectively allow them to control prices by having the right to decide who should or should not be allowed to sell their products.

Finally, at a more mundane level, manufacturers and retailers may be obliged by law to include duty or tax as part of their pricing. Alcohol and tobacco in particular are targeted by many governments for high rates of duty, partly as a public health measure (keep the prices high to discourage over-consumption), and partly as an excellent revenue earner. In the UK, petrol is also subject to high rates of duty (with a higher rate on leaded petrol than on unleaded or diesel). Excise duties and VAT account for over two-thirds of the cost of a litre of unleaded petrol and the actual cost of the fuel is only around one-quarter of the price per litre that the motorist pays.

# Internal influences on the pricing decision

Pricing is, of course, also influenced by various internal factors. Pricing needs to reflect both corporate and marketing objectives, for example, as well as being consistent with the rest of the marketing mix. It is also important to remember, however, that pricing may also be related to costs, if the organisation is looking to generate an acceptable margin of profit. Figure 7.6 summarises the internal influences on price, and the rest of this section discusses each of them in further detail.

## Organisational objectives

The area of organisational objectives is an internal influence, linked with corporate strategy. Marketing plans and objectives have to be set not only best to satisfy the customer's needs and wants, but also to reflect the aspirations of the organisation. These two aims should not be incompatible! Organisational objectives such as target volume sales, target value sales, target growth in various market segments and target profit figures can all be made more or less attainable through the deployment of the marketing mix and particularly through price.

Corporate strategy is not concerned simply with quantifiable target setting. It is also concerned with the organisation's relative position in the market compared with the competition. Pricing may be used to help either to signal a desire for leadership (whether in terms of lowest cost or price, or superior quality) or to establish a clearly differentiated niche, which can then be emphasised and consolidated through the other elements of the marketing mix.

At the other end of the pricing spectrum, discount supermarket chains, such as Netto, Aldi, and Lidl, are trying to achieve objectives relating to price leadership in the market. Obviously, low pricing within their stores is their primary tool, but this can only be achieved through cost reduction (hence the minimalist retail environment and low levels of customer service) and accepting lower profit margins (1 per cent, compared with the industry average of between 5 per cent and 8 per cent). Achieving all of this is also dependent on attracting many more customers through the doors to generate the higher volume of sales needed to make a reasonable profit. The higher volumes also give the discount retailer scope for negotiating more favourable terms with the manufacturers for bulk buying.

Organisational objectives can change over time as the organisation and its markets evolve. A new business, or a new entrant into a market, faces initial problems of survival. There is a need to generate orders to use excess capacity and to establish a foothold in the market. Relatively low pricing (at the sacrifice of profit margins rather than quality) is just one possible way of doing that. Once established, the organisation can begin to think in terms of target profits and building a competitive position, which may involve a revised approach to pricing. Using price as part of an integrated marketing mix, the organisation can aim to achieve market leadership in terms of whatever criteria are important. Once leadership is achieved, objectives have to be redefined to maintain and defend that leadership, thus keeping competition at arm's length.

**Figure 7.6**
Internal influences on the pricing decision

Corporate objectives can also have both short- and long-term dimensions to them. In the short term, for example, a small business on the verge of collapse might use low price as a survival tactic to keep it afloat, even if its longer-term ambitions include quality leadership at a higher price.

## Marketing objectives

As the previous subsection has implied, marketing and organisational objectives are very closely interrelated and influence each other to a great extent. The distinction, though, is that while organisational objectives relate primarily to the operation, the well-being and the personality of the organisation as a whole, marketing objectives are more closely focused on specific target markets and the position desired within them.

*eg*

English Premiership season tickets are some of the most expensive in Europe, and early indications were that some fans would be facing big price increases for the 2011/12 season. Both Arsenal and Liverpool announced 6.5 per cent price rises, which meant that adult season tickets at Liverpool would range from £725 to £802, while the cheapest season ticket at Arsenal would be £985.

It's not just about season ticket costs, however. Virgin Money's Football Fans' Inflation Index shows that since January 2006, rising ticket costs have contributed to an increase in a fan's match day costs from £77.95 to £101.04 (as at May, 2011), taking into account a basket of relevant goods including a gallon of petrol, a pint of lager, a bacon roll, a train fare, sandwiches, a match ticket, a replica shirt, pay-per-view cost and a match programme (that's certainly my idea of a good afternoon out). Against a backdrop of economic hardship putting pressure on disposable income, and season tickets at top clubs costing around £1,000, it's not surprising that some fans are thinking twice about whether to renew their season tickets. Virgin Money's survey of premiership football fans suggested that 15 per

'We're not spending any more ...'
*Source*: FIFA via Getty Images/Shaun Botterill – FIFA

cent of them would not be renewing season tickets for the 2011/12 season, and 31 per cent of regular match attendees would be cutting back on the number of matches they go to. The survey indicated that West Ham would be worst affected with 30 per cent of fans not renewing (but that could be as much to do with fans' disgust at the club's relegation to the Championship); Aston Villa would lose 27 per cent of season ticket holders (but again, Aston Villa hadn't exactly covered itself in glory in 2010/11), and even Manchester United stood to lose 28 per cent. In contrast, Liverpool looked like losing only 4 per cent of its season ticket holders, and that's consistent with findings from an ING Direct survey (ING Direct, 2011) that indicated that Liverpool fans were among the most willing to spend whatever it takes to follow their club.

Generally, though, fans are not happy, and a spokesman for the Football Supporters Federation expressed the view that '… the football industry still has huge sums of money coming into it at the top of the game, mostly through media rights. But too much of it stays at the top and too much of it is used on ridiculously high player wages, rather than on helping its loyal customers through these difficult times' (as quoted by Virgin Money, 2011). In recognition of this, eight premiership clubs announced price freezes on season ticket prices for 2011/12.

Newly promoted clubs are taking contrasting approaches to this. Swansea City took the view that it wanted to keep its season ticket price rises as low as possible as a reward to its loyal supporters, and thus the increase was less than 15 per cent, despite the promotion to the Premiership and the resulting increase in demand for season tickets. Fellow-promotees QPR, however, seemed to have decided to capitalise on the Premiership premium with rises closer to 40 per cent (Brown, 2011; ING Direct, 2011; Rej, 2011; Veysey, 2011; Virgin Money, 2011).

Marketing objectives are achieved through the use of the whole marketing mix, not just the price element, emphasising again the need for an integrated and harmonious marketing mix. An organisation may have a portfolio of products serving different segments, each of which requires a different approach to pricing. Such a differentiated strategy can be seen in telecommunications, with BT developing a range of tariffs for both domestic and business users to suit different needs and priorities.

In that sense, it is no different from a car manufacturer making a cheap and cheerful £8,000 run-about model at one end of the range and a sleek, executive £40,000 status machine at the other. The key is to use the other elements of the marketing mix to support the price or to provide a rationale for it. The concept of the product portfolio and the management issues surrounding it are fully covered in Chapter 13.

Another product concept that might influence the pricing of a particular product over a period of time is the product lifecycle (see p. 234 *et seq.*). In the introductory stage, a lower price might be necessary as part of a marketing strategy to encourage trial. Advertising this as 'an introductory trial price' would be one way of preventing 'low price = low quality' judgements. As the product becomes established through the growth and early maturity stages, and gains loyal buyers, the organisation may feel confident enough to raise the price. As indicated earlier, this has to be done with due reference to the competitive situation and the desired positioning for both product and organisation. In late maturity and decline, it is possible that price reductions could be used to squeeze the last breath out of the dying product.

## Costs

From a marketing perspective, price is primarily related to what the customer will be prepared to pay for a particular product offering. The actual cost of providing that offering cannot,

difficult to estimate costs in advance. The percentage will be agreed between buyer and seller in advance, and then just before, or after, the project's completion, buyer and seller agree the admissible costs and calculate the final price. It sounds straightforward enough, but in large, complex construction projects, it is not so easy to pin down precise costs. Problems arise where the seller is inflating prices, and it can take some time for buyer and seller to negotiate a final settlement.

An industry operating on this kind of pricing method, using a standard percentage, is oriented less towards price competition, and more towards achieving competitiveness through cost efficiency.

**Experience curve pricing.** Over time, and as an organisation produces more units, its experience and learning lead to more efficiency. This can also apply in service situations (Chambers and Johnston, 2000). Cost savings of 10–30 per cent per unit can be achieved each time the organisation doubles its experience.

Some organisations use this learning curve, essentially predicting how costs are going to change over time, as part of the price-planning process. Such planning means not only that the organisation is under pressure to build the volume in order to gain the experience benefits, but also that if it can gain a high market share early on in the product's life, it can achieve a strong competitive position because it gains the cost savings from learning sooner (Schmenner, 1990). It can thus withstand price competition.

The problem with cost-based methods is that they are too internally focused. The price determined has to survive in a marketplace where customers and competitors have their own views of what pricing should be. An organisation's price may thus make perfect sense in cost terms and generate a respectable profit contribution, but be perceived as far too high or far too low by customers in comparison with the features and benefits offered. The price may also be way out of line compared with a competitor with a different kind of cost base.

## Demand-based pricing

Demand-based pricing looks outwards from the production line and focuses on customers and their responsiveness to different price levels. Even this approach may not be enough on its own, but when it is linked with an appreciation of competition-based pricing, it provides a powerful market-oriented perspective that cost-based methods just do not provide.

At its simplest, demand-based pricing indicates that when demand is strong, the price goes up, and when it is weak, the price goes down. This can be seen in some service industries, for example, where demand fluctuates depending on time. Package holidays taken during school holidays at Christmas, Easter or in the summer when demand is high are more expensive than those taken at other times of the year when it is more difficult for families to get away. Similarly, holidays taken when weather conditions at the destination are less predictable or less pleasant are cheaper because there is less demand. Even within the course of a single day, travel prices can vary according to demand. Tickets on shuttle flights between Heathrow and UK regional airports vary in price depending on when the peak times for business travellers occur.

There is an underlying assumption that an organisation operating such a flexible pricing policy has a good understanding of the nature and elasticity of demand in its market, as already outlined at p. 259 *et seq*.

One form of demand-based pricing is psychological pricing. This is very much a customer-based pricing method, relying as it does on the consumer's emotive responses, subjective assessments and feelings towards specific purchases. Clearly, this is particularly applicable to products with a higher involvement focus, i.e. those that appeal more to psychological than to practical motives for purchase. Thus, for example, high prices for prestige goods help to reinforce the psychological sense of self-indulgence and pampering that is such an important part of the buying experience. At the other end of the scale, lots of big splashy '10% off' or 'buy one get one free' offers scattered round a retail store on key items helps to create and reinforce a value-for-money image and the sense of getting a bargain.

## Competition-based pricing

This chapter has frequently warned of the danger of setting prices without knowing what is happening in the market, particularly with respect to one's competitors. According to Lambin (1993), there are two aspects of competition that influence an organisation's pricing. The first is the structure of the market. Generally speaking, the greater the number of competitors, i.e. the closer to perfect competition the market comes, the less autonomy the organisation has in price setting. The second competitive factor is the product's perceived value in the market. In other words, the more differentiated an organisation's product is from the competition, the more autonomy the organisation has in pricing it, because buyers come to value its unique benefits.

The UK toy market was worth around £2.2 billion in 2010, but had been through a couple of years of turmoil. At the end of 2008, Woolworths went out of business. Woolworths had been the UK's number three toy retailer, and as its stores started to close, stock was being heavily discounted to get rid of it, and other retailers also started to discount, partly as a means of remaining competitive and partly as a means of trying to take some of Woolworths' market share. All of this was happening around Christmas time, the key period in what is a very seasonal market. Even after all the fuss about Woolworths had died down, price remained a key competitive weapon as economic recession made consumers more price-sensitive. According to Mintel (2010c), 29 per cent of toy buyers compare prices online before they buy, and 28 per cent make the most of special offers at the point of sale. Additionally, the market is dominated by large multiple retailers who can source goods cost effectively, and can afford to discount heavily. The grocery multiples in particular can source cheap own-brand products made in the Far East, and if they choose, use toys as a loss-leader to get customers into their stores in the run up to Christmas.

It's probably fair to say, though, that the supermarkets are quite selective in what they choose to stock in their stores. Something like 88 per cent of the toys they sell are priced at £5 or less, and consist of small, fast-turnaround items (ideal for impulse purchases) rather than the big bulky expensive boxed toys that sell more slowly. Across all toy retailers, the average price paid for a toy is £10.20, while in the supermarkets, it is only £3.79 (Bamford, 2011). Although, as yet the supermarkets' collective share of the toy market is only 15 per cent (with Tesco taking over half of this) compared with Argos's 24 per cent and Toys R Us's 17 per cent, as supermarkets seek to expand their non-food offerings, this is an obvious area for expansion, and if that happens, it's hard to imagine that the focus will continue to be on anything other than price competition (Bamford, 2011; Mintel, 2010c).

Most markets are becoming increasingly competitive, and a focus on competitive strategy in business planning emphasises the importance of understanding the role of price as a means of competing. An organisation that decides to become a cost leader in its market and to take a price-oriented approach to maintaining its position needs an especially efficient intelligence system to monitor its competitors. Levy (1994) looked at organisations that offer price guarantees in B2B markets. Any supplier promising to match the lowest price offered by any of its rivals needs to know as much as possible about those rivals and their cost and pricing structures in order to assess the likely cost of such a promise.

In consumer markets, market research can certainly help to provide intelligence, whether this means shopping audits to monitor the comparative retail prices of goods, or consumer surveys or focus groups to monitor price perceptions and evolving sensitivity relative to the rest of the marketing mix. Data gathering and analysis can be more difficult in B2B markets, because of the flexibility of pricing and the degree of customisation of marketing packages to an individual customer's needs in these markets. There is a heavy reliance on sales representatives' reports, information gained through informal networks within the industry and qualitative assessment of all those data.

Competitive analysis can focus on a number of levels, at one end of the spectrum involving a general overview of the market, and at the other end focusing on individual product lines or items. Whatever the market, whatever the focus of competitive analysis, the same decision has to be made: whether to price at the same level as the competition, or above or below them.

An organisation that has decided to be a price follower must, by definition, look to the market for guidance. The decision to position at the same level as the competition, or above or below them, requires information about what is happening in the market. This is pricing based on the 'going rate' for the product. Conventional pricing behaviour in the market is used as a reference point for comparing what is offered, and the price is varied from that. Each supplier to the market is thus acting as a marker for the others, taking into account relative positioning and relative offering.

Effectively, pricing is based on collective wisdom, and certainly for the smaller business it is easier to do what everyone else does rather than pay for market research to prove what the price ought to be, and run the risk of getting it wrong. In a seaside resort, for example, a small bed and breakfast hotel is unlikely to price itself differently from the one next door, unless it can justify doing so by offering significantly better services. Within an accepted price range, however, any one organisation's move may not be seen as either significant or threatening by the rest.

The dangers of excessive price competition, in terms of both the cost to the competitors and the risk to a product's reputation, thus attracting the 'wrong' kind of customer, have already been indicated. But if neither the organisation nor the product has a particularly high reputation, or if the product has few differentiating features, then price competition may be the only avenue open unless there is a commitment to working on the product and the marketing mix as a whole.

## Pricing tactics and adjustments

Pricing tactics and adjustments are concerned with the last steps towards arriving at the final price. There is no such thing as a fixed price; price can be varied to reflect specific customer needs, the market position within the channel of distribution or the economic aspects of the deal.

Particularly in B2B markets, price structures give guidelines to the sales representative to help in negotiating a final price with the customer. The concern is not only to avoid overcharging or inconsistent charging, but to set up a framework for pricing discretion that is linked with the significance of the customer or the purchase situation.

At one extreme, price structure may involve a take it or leave it, single-price policy, such as IKEA operates. It offers no trade discount for organisational purchasers, seeing itself largely as a consumer-oriented retailer. Compare this with some industrial distributorships, which offer different levels of discount to different customers. Most try to find a middle ground, between consistent pricing and flexibility for certain key customers.

A variation on price structures, special adjustments to list or quoted prices can be made either for short-term promotional purposes or as part of a regular deal to reward a trade customer for services rendered.

Discounts consist of reductions from the normal or list price as a reward for bulk purchases or the range of distribution services offered. The level and frequency of discounts will vary according to individual circumstances. Blois (1994) points out that most organisations offer discounts from list prices and that these discounts form an important part of pricing strategies. There are many examples of discounts in consumer and B2B markets. The promotional technique of 'buy two and get the third free' is effectively a bulk discount and is found on many products in many supermarkets. Similarly, a promotion that enables a consumer to collect loyalty points and then swop them for money-off vouchers is a form of cumulative discount. In B2B markets, a retailer may be offered a twelfth case of a product free if eleven are initially purchased (quantity discount), or a rebate on the number of cases of a product sold by the end of the trading period (cumulative discount).

Allowances are similar to discounts, but usually require the buyer to perform some additional service. Trade-in, for example, makes a transaction more complicated because it involves the exchange of a good as well as money for whatever is being purchased. It is a common practice in the car market, where consumers trade in their old cars as part exchange for a new one. The qualitative judgement of the value of the trade-in disguises the discount offered, and it is further complicated by the attitudes of the respective parties. A car that is an unreliable liability to the owner may have potential to a dealer with a particular customer in mind or a good eye for scrap. The owner thinks they are getting a good deal on the old car, while the dealer thinks they can actually recoup the trade-in value and make a bit more besides.

Finally, geographic adjustments are those made, especially in B2B markets, to reflect the costs of transport and insurance involved in getting the goods from buyer to seller. In consumer markets, they can be seen in the case of goods ordered online or by mail-order, which often carry an extra charge for postage and packing. Zoned pricing relates price to the geographic distance between buyer and seller. A DIY warehouse, for example, might add a £5 delivery charge to any destination within five miles, £7.50 for up to 10 miles, £10 for up to 15 miles and so on, reflecting the extra time and petrol involved in delivering to more distant locations. Operating a single zone means that the delivery price is the same regardless of distance, as is the case with the domestic postal service, which charges on the weight of letters rather than the destination. The international mail service does, however, operate on a multiple-zone basis, dividing the world up into areas and pricing to reflect different transport costs.

## Chapter summary

- Pricing is a broad area, defined as covering anything of value that is given in exchange for something else. 'Price' is a blanket term to cover a variety of labels and is a key element in the marketing exchange. Price is usually measured in money, but can also involve the bartering of goods and services.

- Price serves a number of purposes. It is a measure against which buyers can assess the product's promised features and benefits and then decide whether the functional, operational, financial or personal advantages of purchase are worthwhile or not. The seller faces the difficult job of setting the price in the context of the buyers' price perceptions and sensitivities. In a price-sensitive market, finding exactly the right price is essential if customers are to be attracted and retained. The seller also needs to remember that price may involve the buyer in more than the handing over of a sum of money. Associated costs of installation, training and disposal of old equipment, for example, are taken into account in assessing the price of a B2B purchase.

- The external influences influencing the pricing decision include customers, channels of distribution, competition and legal and regulatory constraints.

- Corporate and marketing objectives set the internal agenda in terms of what pricing is expected to achieve, both for the organisation as a whole and for the specific product.

The organisation's costs relating to the development, manufacture and marketing of the product will also affect price.

● The process of price setting involves a great deal of research and managerial skill. The five stages of the process are setting price objectives; estimating demand; setting pricing policies and strategies; determining the price range; and finally, defining any pricing tactics and adjustments that might be necessary.

## Questions for review and discussion

**7.1** Define *price elasticity*. Why is this an important concept for the marketer?

**7.2** To what extent and why do you think that *costs* should influence pricing?

**7.3** Define the various stages involved in *setting prices*.

**7.4** Find an example of a *price-sensitive* consumer market. Why do you think this market is price sensitive and is there anything that the

manufacturers or retailers could do to make it less so?

**7.5** Choose a consumer product and explain the role that pricing plays in its marketing mix and *market positioning*.

**7.6** To what extent and why do you think that a marketing manager's pricing decision should be influenced by the competition's pricing?

## CASE STUDY 7

# YOU WANT TO GO COMPARE? SIMPLES

One of the more interesting side-effects of the internet is that it has made it a lot easier to be price sensitive by taking the time, cost and physical effort out of 'shopping around' for goods and services. In the pre-internet days, if consumers wanted to shop around for a good deal on a new fridge-freezer, they might have to spend a couple of weekends doing a tour of local stores comparing specifications and prices, and perhaps travel a bit further afield to a bigger city or out of town shopping centre where there might be more choice or more competitive prices to be found. It was a similar story with services such as car insurance: an annual ritual of setting aside time to compile a list of brokers and insurance providers from the *Yellow Pages*, then phoning round them all, going through the same basic information set with all of them, writing down all the quotes and

details of what is or isn't included in the cover offered, and finally making a decision and phoning one of them back. It would be hard to blame a shopper who decided that for the sake of saving a few pounds it wasn't worth the effort, thus effectively placing speed, convenience and lack of hassle higher up the decision-making-criteria list than price.

Once the shopper goes online, of course, it's a different story. Detailed comparison of product or service specifications, price and even availability across hundreds of geographically dispersed providers is just a few clicks away, and once a buying decision has been made, it's equally easy to complete the deal online. The advent of price-comparison websites has made it all even easier, by effectively providing a one-stop marketplace for the shopper so that they can enter their requirements/details just once and receive a structured comparison of a wide range of competing offers.

A survey conducted by *New Media Age* (2011) found that many respondents thought that the internet was the cheapest place to buy things (ranging from 82 per cent finding it the cheapest place to buy CDs/DVDs to 20 per cent for groceries), and that 76 per cent used online prices as a reference point to negotiate prices for the same items in shops. So, for the shopper, at first glance this might seem like a fantastic idea. The price-comparison website looks like the shopper's best friend, a neutral third party that does all the hard work and gives you a list of the best deals for you, in order of appropriateness. Unfortunately, it's often not that transparent or simple, however. Few shoppers pause to think about how the price-comparison websites make their money, for instance. The fact is that they generate revenue from commission earned from 'click throughs', i.e. if you find a deal you like the look of on the price-comparison website and click through to follow it up on the supplier's own site, then the price-comparison site gets paid. In financial services, for example, this, on average, might be £40 commission on an insurance policy or up to £150 for a loan application (Wallop, 2009). This sort of arrangement gives the price-comparison websites an incentive to feature those suppliers paying the most commission more prominently and, of course, there is no incentive at all to 'push' the products of those suppliers who are not prepared to pay commission at all. A YouGov survey (reported by *Marketwire*, 2011) suggested that, on average each shopper on price-comparison websites generates £64.59 in commission, which amounts to £652.5 million per year for the industry. And then there's the revenue they earn on top of that from selling on your personal details to other marketers.

The shopper might also imagine that the price-comparison website has full coverage of the market, but this is not necessarily the case. In the financial-services market, for instance, neither Aviva not Direct Line, both prominent brands in the marketplace, have their products listed on price-comparison sites, and both make a virtue of this in their marketing and advertising campaigns. A further issue is that there might also be an assumption that because it's all online, the prices quoted are 'real time' prices. Again, this is not necessarily the case. Many of these websites rely on the supplier of the goods to update the pricing information, which means that prices could be several days out of date so that the consumer clicks through for what seems like a good deal only to find that the product is no longer available at that price.

This could be particularly disadvantageous for the consumer if online retailers are frequently adjusting their prices in response to competitive conditions, demand patterns or other environmental pressures. If the price-comparison websites are not reflecting this, then it's questionable whether they are actually serving the shopper's needs as well as they could.

There is also a risk, particularly thinking about financial services such as car insurance, that the focus on price diverts the consumer's attention away from the detail of what they are actually getting for their money. The car-insurance market is potentially very lucrative for the price comparison sites as Mintel (2011b) reports that three-quarters of motorists look for a better deal when they renew their policies. But because of this focus on price, in order to make policies look like great deals, some price-comparison websites set a very high default level of 'voluntary excess' (i.e. the amount that the policyholder will pay towards the cost of any claim - if you agree to pay the first £1,000 of a claim, your insurance premium will be lower than if you are only prepared to pay the first £250, for instance). On top of this, some policies also have a 'compulsory excess' hidden in the detail, which again keeps the premium down, but will result in a nasty surprise when you make a claim if you haven't read the small print. Car insurance can be complex, and it is difficult sometimes to tell whether you are actually comparing like with like when you are faced with a page of search results - it pays to engage with the fine detail before you buy!

Consumers aren't completely oblivious to all this, of course. A *Which?* survey reported by Cumbo (2009) suggested that there is a healthy level of cynicism out there: just one-third of respondents said they trusted the website to find the best price available, and two-thirds thought that they would be presented with the products that would earn the most commission for the website. However, the YouGov survey mentioned earlier suggested that consumers seriously underestimate the amount of commission that they are paying, with over 40 per cent of respondents guessing that it would be up to 10 per cent, when in fact that actual level is around 24 per cent. Despite the mistrust, consumers seem to have embraced the involvement of price-comparison websites, not least because of the proactive marketing strategies of some of the providers who are fighting for market share. A 'big four' group of price-comparison sites has emerged in the UK, comprising comparethemarket.com, confused.com, gocompare.com and moneysupermarket.com all of whom spend very heavily on television advertising campaigns, making it very difficult for any other new entrant to be noticed.

A kind of advertising war kicked off when comparethemarket.com captured the public imagination with Aleksandr Orlov, the meerkat character ('compare the meerkat dot com, compare the market dot com. Simples') and then gocompare.com responded with a series of advertisements featuring portly opera singer, Gio Compario, (memorable but voted the most annoying ads on TV). In 2010, gocompare.com spent £28.15 million on advertising, and similarly, moneysupermarket.com spent £24 million and confused.com £22.5 million. Comparethemarket.com only spent £16.4 million, but that could be because the meerkat character had already become established. These are big spends, but in creative terms, both moneysupermarket.com and confused.com have as yet struggled to find a formula as appealing as the meerkat, and when confused.com took a brave decision to reduce its advertising expenditure, it quickly lost market share to the others. It came back with Cara, its own animated character who stages big song and dance numbers to demonstrate the reach and diversity of confused.com's customer base, or as the company itself out it, 'Price-comparison sites have tended to try to succeed by irritating. We want to produce advertisements people like' (as quoted by Parsons, 2010).

A big problem is, though, that there appears to be no brand loyalty as such in this marketplace. According to Mintel (2010a), among those using price comparison sites for financial services, the most important factors are 'accurate quotations', 'lowest price' and 'clear and transparent comparisons'. 'A well-known/reputable brand' came a long way down the list. Nevertheless, the branding and advertising has to generate a basic level of trust and drive people to the website, but once they are there, it's the competitiveness of the deals on offer that matters – the customer is directly comparing the price-comparison sites! Mintel (2010a) found that nearly 90 per cent of people who have used a price-comparison site for financial services have used 'the big four' and 80 per cent have used more than one. One of Mintel's respondents sums up a typical view: 'I usually check out a few different sites just to get an idea of what price range they come up with, normally stick [*sic*] to what I think are the four main ones, gocompare.com, moneysupermarket.com, confused.com and comparethemarket.com'. Only 14 per cent of those using price-comparison sites have just one favourite site that they always use.

The situation is further complicated by what happens once the customer has located a deal that they like. Datamonitor research reports that 55 per cent of car insurance policies were 'instigated via online price-comparison sites' in 2010 (as reported by *Reactions*, 2011) and forecasts that this will rise to 63 per cent by 2012. There is, however, a difference between 'instigation' and 'purchasing'. Around

Aleksandr's engaging personality has made him a celebrity in his own right.

*Source*: http://meerkat.comparethemarket.com. Image used courtesy of The Advertising Archives

one-quarter of price-comparison website users use the website to narrow the choices and then pick up the phone and contact the insurer direct. In some cases this is about the reassurance and security of human contact, and the ability to probe further what they are getting for their money, but for others there is a perception that a further discount can be negotiated, using the internet price as a bargaining tool.

Finally, here's a closing thought from the MD of an advertising agency:

> The simple truth is [that a price-comparison website] means a greater variety of products, more incentives, such as discount vouchers, softer benefits, such as consumer advice, and a sense of community. This all leads to referred brand satisfaction. So, again, why cut out the middleman?' (as quoted by *Marketing*, 2010)

*Sources*: Cumbo (2009); *M2 Presswire* (2009); *Marketwire* (2011); *Marketing* (2010); Mintel (2010a, 2011b); *New Media Age* (2011); Parsons (2010); *Reactions* (2011); Wall (2011); Wallop (2009).

## Questions

1 What do you think are the key factors influencing the price of car insurance? Use Figures 7.2 and 7.6 to help you structure your answer.

2 What are the advantages and disadvantages of opting out of allowing your products or services to feature on price-comparison websites, as Direct Line and others have done?

3 Are there any types of goods or services for which price-comparison websites might be inappropriate? Why?

4 In general, to what extent do you think that the easy online availability of price information and comparison is a good thing for marketing?

## References for chapter 7

The AA (2011) 'Fuel Price Report, June 2011', accessed via http://www.theaa.com/motoring_advice/fuel/index.html.

Bainbridge, J. (2011a) 'Treatment Has its Rewards', *Marketing*, 29 June.

Bainbridge, J. (2011b) 'Value Proves Hard to Find', *Marketing*, 6 July.

Bamford, V. (2011) 'It's All to Play For', *The Grocer*, 18 June.

Baumol, W.J. (1965) *Economic Theory and Operations Analysis*, Prentice Hall.

Blakely, R. (2007) 'Apple Cuts Third Off Price of its iPhone 68 Days After Launch', *The Times*, 7 September.

Blois, K. (1994) 'Discounts in Business Marketing Management', *Industrial Marketing Management*, 23(2), pp. 93–100.

*Brand Strategy* (2007) 'The Price is Right', *Brand Strategy*, 10 December, p. 14.

Brightman, J. (2011) 'Xbox 360 to Remain Ahead of PS3 in 2011, Says Pachter', *Industry Gamers*, 21 March, accessed via www.industrygamers.com/news/xbox-360-to-remain-ahead-of-ps3-in-2011-says-pachter/.

Brown, A. (2011) 'Season Ticket Frenzy Grows as Swans Join the Big Time', *South Wales Evening Post*, 3 June.

Buckley, C. and Lindsay, R. (2008) 'Silverjet Left Grounded as Sky-high Fuel Costs Bring End to Golden Age of Flying', *The Times*, 31 May, p. 48.

Burns, S. (2008) 'Wii Sales Beating Xbox 360 and PS3', *Personal Computer World*, 18 February, accessed via www.pcw.co.uk/2209876.

Chambers, S. and Johnston, R. (2000) 'Experience Curves in Services: Macro and Micro Level Approaches', *International Journal of Operations and Production Management*, 20(7), pp. 842–59.

Clark, P. (2011) 'BA Lifts Fuel Surcharge to Seven-year High', *Financial Times*, 6 April.

Cooper, L. (2011) 'Promotions Switch Focus to Added Value', *Marketing Week*, 30 June.

Costa, M. (2010) 'Brand Promises at Centre of Product Innovation', *Marketing Week*, 9 December.

Cumbo, J. (2009) 'Consumers Not Satisfied with Comparison Sites', *Financial Times*, 18 November.

Cuthbertson, R. (2006) 'Price Promotions Aren't the Villain of the Piece', *Promotions & Incentives*, April.

Dean, J. (1950) 'Pricing Policies for New Products', *Harvard Business Review*, 28 (November), pp. 45–53.

Diamantopoulos, A. and Mathews, B. (1995) *Making Pricing Decisions: A Study of Managerial Practice*, Chapman & Hall.

Erickson, G.M. and Johansson, J.K. (1985) 'The Role of Price in Multi-attribute Product Evaluations', *Journal of Consumer Research*, 12, pp. 195–9.

*The Grocer* (2010) 'Paper Products', *The Grocer*, 18 December.

Hamilton, F. (2008) 'Congestion Charge Brings an Unlikely Benefit – Parking in Central London at 20p an Hour', *The Times*, 16 June, p. 9.

*Hampstead & Highgate Express* (2011) 'A Number of Westminster Council's Car Parks are to be Leased Out', *Hampstead & Highgate Express*, 3 February.

Hawkes, S. (2008) 'Surging Petrol Price Sparks Big Drop in Car Journeys', *The Times*, 25 June, p. 41.

Heasley, A. and Wen, P. (2011) 'Qantas Hikes US, UK Airfares', *Canberra Times*, 20 April.

Hook, S. (2011) 'The Kids Smarten Up', *The Grocer*, 7 May.

Hutchison, P. and Ruddick, G. (2008) 'Milk, Beer, Soap: Why Oil Affects Everything We Take for Granted', *Daily Telegraph*, 18 June, p. 7.

ING Direct (2011) 'Man City Tops Value League', *ING Direct*, accessed via www.ingdirect.co.uk/valueleague.

Karlgaard, R. (2007) 'The Cheap Revolution', *Wall Street Journal*, 3 October.

King, M. (2011) 'Rising Petrol Prices Will Cause Drivers to Reduce Family Trips', *The Guardian*, 21 June.

Kunz, B. (2010) 'How Apple Plays the Pricing Game', *Bloomberg Businessweek*, 6 September, accessed via www.msnbc. msn.com/id/38980367/ns/business-us_business/t/ how-apple-plays-pricing-game/.

Lambin, J.J. (1993) *Strategic Marketing: A European Approach*, McGraw-Hill.

Leroux, M. and Fildes, N. (2011) 'Sainsbury's Urges Oil Giants to Join Petrol Price', *The Times*, 16 June.

Levy, D.T. (1994) 'Guaranteed Pricing in Industrial Purchases: Making Use of Markets in Contractual Relations', *Industrial Marketing Management*, 23(4), pp. 307–13.

*M2 Presswire* (2009) 'Christmas Bargain Hunters', *M2 Presswire*, 15 December.

Macefield, S. (2011) 'Oil Prices Fall – Yet Holiday Surcharges Stay', *Daily Telegraph*, 14 May.

*Marketwire* (2011) 'Price Comparison Websites Take Over £650m in Commission Each Year from Consumers', *Marketwire*, 17 May.

*Marketing* (2010) 'Can Brands Afford Not to be Shown on Price-comparison Websites?', *Marketing*, 13 January.

Mintel (2009) 'Edible Oils', *Mintel Market Intelligence*, August, accessed via http://academic.mintel.com/sinatra/oxygen_ academic/search_results/show&/display/id=394591/ display/id=477821?select_section=394591.

Mintel (2010a) 'Web Aggregators', *Mintel Finance Intelligence*, November, accessed via http:// academic.mintel.com/sinatra/oxygen_academic/ my_reports/display/id=479949&anchor=atom/display/ id=555371?select_section=479949.

Mintel (2010b) 'Schoolwear', *Mintel Market Intelligence*, November, accessed via http://academic.mintel.com/ sinatra/oxygen_academic//display/&id=479952/display/ id=479952/display/id=479952/display/id=479952/ display/id=554462.

Mintel (2010c) 'Toy Retailing', *Mintel Retail Intelligence*, December, accessed via http://academic.mintel.com/ sinatra/oxygen_academic/search_results/show&/display/ id=480969/display/id=559106?select_section=559109.

Mintel (2011a) 'Household Paper Products', *Mintel Market Intelligence*, February, accessed via http://academic.mintel. com/sinatra/oxygen_academic/search_results/show&/ display/id=545442.

Mintel (2011b) 'Motor Insurance', *Mintel Finance Intelligence*, March, accessed via http://academic.mintel.com/sinatra/ oxygen_academic/search_results/show&/display/ id=545182.

Mintel (2011c) 'Shampoo, Conditioners and Treatments', *Mintel Market Intelligence*, April, accessed via http://academic. mintel.com/sinatra/oxygen_academic/search_results/sho w&&type=RCItem&sort=relevant&access=accessible&a rchive=hide&source=non_snapshot&list=search_results/ display/id=545521.

Monroe, K. and Cox, J. (2001) 'Pricing Practices that Endanger Profits', *Marketing Management*, September/ October, pp. 42–6.

Monroe, K. and Della Bitta, A. (1978) 'Models for Pricing Decisions', *Journal of Marketing Research*, 15 (August), pp. 413–28.

Montgomery, S.L. (1988) *Profitable Pricing Strategies*, McGraw-Hill.

Moore, E. (2011) 'Airlines Oppose Ruling on Cards', *Financial Times*, 1 July.

Nagle, T. (1987) *The Strategy and Tactics of Pricing*, Prentice Hall.

*New Media Age* (2011) 'Consumers are Increasingly Turning to the Web for Bargains', *New Media Age*, 12 May.

Nimer, D. (1975) 'Pricing the Profitable Sale Has a Lot to Do with Perception', *Sales Management*, 114(19), pp. 13–14.

*NME* (2010) 'Bloggers Sharing Radiohead's "In Rainbows" Told to Take Files Down', *New Musical Express*, 3 August, accessed via www.nme.com/news/radiohead/52343.

*NME* (2011) 'Morrissey Refuses to Self-release New Album Like Radiohead's "In Rainbows"', *New Musical Express*, 28 June, accessed via www.nme.com/news/morrissey/57629.

O'Doherty, G. (2008) 'Cross Your Legs . . . It's the New Loo-fare Airline', *Irish Independent*, 21 June, p. 36.

Odell, M. and Wembridge, M. (2011) 'Bad Weather Causes Flybe to Nosedive into Red', *Financial Times*, 1 July.

Parsons, R. (2010) 'Confused.com Uses Ad to Make Emotional Connection', *Marketing Week*, 11 November.

Perks, R. (1993) 'How to Win a Price War', *Investor's Chronicle*, 22 October, pp. 14–15.

Porter, J. (2011) 'Extending the Olive Branch', *The Grocer*, 28 May.

Purchese, R. (2011) 'Xbox 360 Play Station 3', *Eurogamer*, accessed via www.eurogamer.net/ articles/2011-02-09-analysed-lifetime-ps3-and-360-sales.

*Reactions* (2011) 'Price Comparison Sites Dominate UK Motor', *Reactions*, 3 January.

Rej, A. (2011) 'Liverpool Increase Ticket Prices', *BBC*, 17 May, accessed via http://news.bbc.co.uk/go/pr/fr/-/sport1/hi/ football/teams/l/liverpool/9489260.stm.

Robertson, D. and Milner, L. (2011) 'OFT Calls for Law Change to End Unfair Debit Card Charges', *The Times*, 29 June.

Rosselson, R. (2008) 'Back to School', accessed via http:// dnn.ethicalconsumer.org/FreeBuyersGuides/clothing/ schooluniforms.aspx.

Sanchanta, M. (2007a) 'Stakes High for Sony in its War of Perception', *Financial Times*, 25 July, p. 20.

Sanchanta, M. (2007b) 'A Price Cut Too Late for PlayStation 3', *Financial Times*, 6 December, p. 25.

Schmenner, R. (1990) *Production/Operations Management*, New York: Macmillan.

Sherwin, A. (2008) 'Radiohead Say OK Computer to iTunes', *The Times*, 4 January.

Thompson, K. and Coe, B. (1997) 'Gaining Sustainable Competitive Advantage through Strategic Pricing: Selecting a Perceived Value Price', *Pricing Strategy and Practice*, 5 (2), pp. 70–9.

Veysey, W. (2011) ' Arsenal hike season ticket prices by four per cent for executive fans, sparking fears of stadium-wide increase', *Goal.com*, 15 March, accessed via www.goal.com/en-gb/news/2896/premier-league/2011/03/15/2395360/arsenal-hike-season-ticket-prices-by-four-per-cent-for-executive-fans.

Vincent, M. (2011) 'Investors are Like Passengers on Managers' Flights of Fancy', *Financial Times*, 1 July.

Virgin Money (2011) 'Nearly One in Seven Season Ticket Holders Not Renewing', *Virgin Money*, accessed via http://uk.virginmoney.com/virgin/news-centre/press-releases/2011/nearly-one-in-seven-season-ticket-holders.jsp.

Wall, E. (2011) 'Getting the Best out of Comparison Websites', *Sunday Telegraph*, 12 June.

Wallop, H. (2009) 'Consumers "Miss Out" By Relying on Comparison Sites', *Daily Telegraph*, 5 December.

Westminster Council (2008) 'Park from 20p per hour at Queensway Car Park', accessed via www.westminster.gov.uk/carparks/queensway_trial.cfm.

Williams, I. (2008) 'UK PlayStation 3 Sales Reach One Million', *Personal Computer World*, 14 February, accessed via http://www.pcw.co.uk/2209707.

Zeithaml, V.A. (1988) 'Consumer Perceptions of Price, Quality and Value', *Journal of Marketing*, 52 (July), pp. 2–22.

Zimbardo, P. (2010) 'What's Behind Apple's iPhone Pricing Strategy?', *Seeking Alpha*, 21 June, accessed via http://seekingalpha.com/article/211063-what-s-behind-apple-s-iphone-pricing-strategy.

# CHAPTER 8

# Place

## LEARNING OBJECTIVES

This chapter will help you to:

- define what a channel of distribution is and understand the forms it can take in both consumer and B2B markets;
- discuss the rationale for using intermediaries and their contribution to efficient and effective marketing efforts;
- differentiate between types of intermediary and their roles; and
- appreciate the factors influencing channel design, structure and strategy and the effect of conflict and cooperation within channels.

## INTRODUCTION

Shopaholics of the world unite! Retailing is one of the highest-profile areas of marketing and, like advertising, has had a tremendous impact on society, culture and lifestyles. To some, shopping is an essential social and leisure activity, while to others, it is a chore. It offers some a chance to dream and, for most of us, an opportunity at some time or other to indulge ourselves. We often take for granted the availability of wide ranges of goods and know that if we search hard enough, we will find just what we are looking for. Some people, indeed, find that half the fun is in the searching rather than the ultimate purchase.

Although to us as consumers retailing means fun, excitement and the opportunity to splash out vast quantities of cash (thanks to plastic cards!), it is a very serious business for the managers and organisations that make it happen. It is often the last stage in the channel of distribution before consumption, the final link in fulfilling the responsibility of a marketing-oriented supply chain to get the product to the customer in the right place at the right time. The retail store is thus at the end of an extremely efficient and sophisticated distribution system designed to move goods down the distribution channel from manufacturer to consumer. A retailer can be just one of the intermediaries whose role is to facilitate that movement of goods and to offer them at a time and place (and at a price) that is convenient and attractive to the end consumer.

In considering how and why goods get to consumers, the chapter begins with a definition of channels of distribution, highlighting the roles played by different types of intermediaries, and looks at the relative merits of using intermediaries compared with direct selling. Attention then turns to the strategic decision-making necessary to design and implement a channel strategy. Although channels of distribution are important economic structures, they are also social systems involving individuals and organisations. This chapter, therefore, also considers issues associated with the general conduct of the relationship.

*eg*

WH Smith is a leading high street retailer of news, books and stationery. It has over 580 high street stores and over 500 outlets at airports, railway stations, bus stations, hospitals and motorway service areas. The internet branch operates 24 hours a day service. Every year around 320 million customers visit its stores, buying over 30 million books per year and over 1.1 million magazines every week. Despite its size, however, WH Smith has struggled to achieve dominance in the market and sales have been declining.

The problem is that WH Smith has yet to redefine its core merchandise proposition in a retail environment that has changed dramatically from the days when it dominated the high street for books, cards, music and stationery supplies. Specialist competitors, such as Staples for stationery and Waterstones for books, had become slicker and more aggressive, while online retailers, such as Amazon, were competing on breadth of range and price, and supermarkets, such as Tesco, had also started nibbling at the other end, offering wide ranges of magazines and cards, and unbeatable deals on a small number of the very best sellers in CDs/DVDs and books. WH Smith was longer regarded as the automatic specialist destination store for anything in particular and responded by introducing higher shelving units to increase turnover per foot$^2$, undertaking product line rationalisation, and selling off space within its stores to Post Office counters.

Although this has improved profitability, sales are still at best static and WH Smith has thus tried some other ideas, even experimenting with some stores offering only books, magazines and newspapers. In 2011, and perhaps as a natural extension to inviting the Post Office into its stores to provide goods and services, WH Smith announced a partnership with QualitySolicitors [*sic*] to provide legal services access points, initally in 150 stores. Another diversification is workplace shops. In the first stage, eight were opened, with plans for a further forty. These shops are located in companies such as Axa with big offices and in business centres such as Manchester's Spinningfields. WH Smith suggests that stores can be sustainable in workplaces with a minimum of 2,000 employees. This format has a lot in common with WH Smith's hospital outlets, where there is also a captive market, but some have been critical of the workplace venture, as confectionery, snacks, sandwiches and drinks would have to feature a lot more prominently and these are not traditionally areas of strength for WH Smith. One product area that is a traditional strength for WH Smith is greetings cards. Having successfully translated this into an online provider of personalised greetings cards, funkypigeon.com, WH Smith has now decided to open three Funky Pigeon stores, located in busy railway stations in and around London. Customers can use in-store tablet computers to personalise and print their cards. It will be very interesting to see just how well an online concept can translate onto the high street.

All of this just goes to show that even the biggest retail names cannot be complacent, and particularly in an era of differentiation, strong competition and price consciousness, there is a constant pressure on retailers to assess just how well their chosen retail formats and strategies meet the needs of a very dynamic marketplace (Baksi, 2011; Harrison, 2011; MacDonald, 2010; www.whsmithplc.co.uk).

# Channel structures

A marketing channel can be defined as the structure linking a group of individuals or organisations through which a product or service is made available to the consumer or industrial user. The degree of formality in the relationships between the channel members can vary significantly, from the highly organised arrangements in the distribution of fmcg products through supermarkets, to the more speculative and transient position of roadside sellers of fruit and vegetables.

*eg*

The prospect of penetrating the Chinese retail market is a daunting challenge for Western retailers, to say the least. Although it is a fast developing and growing retail market, outside the major cities it is a very fragmented market that is geographically vast and consists of over 1 billion people buying at, or close to subsistence levels. It's a huge collective spend, but very low average individual expenditure. However, as the primary cities start to get saturated, retailers are starting to look at secondary and tertiary regions for growth. There are signs that it is worth the investment. The income gap is starting to close, with more wealth (and thus disposable income) starting to be generated outside the primary cities. Chinese consumers are also starting to appreciate western-style retailing, with chain stores, department stores and hypermarkets/supermarkets accounting for about 22 per cent of retail sales. Groceries accounted for around 40 per cent of retail expenditure in 2010, and 60 per cent of that was spent at 'modern' hypermarket/supermarket outlets.

A major problem for retailers in China is poor infrastructure, however. The distribution industry is very fragmented, with over 30,000 distributors, and no carrier has more than 1 per cent of the market. Logistics, shipping and warehousing are still very inefficient. Physical infrastructure is improving, though with a network of roads, railways and bridges being built, but there is still a lot of development to be done. On the supply side too there's a lot of fragmentation. For fresh produce, for instance, there are very few big farms, and direct supply is thus difficult to organise. Then there's local government to be dealt with in operating outside the primary cities. As the Economist Intelligence Unit (2011) puts it, 'The market has a Wild West feel. Huge areas of China are wide open, and it helps if you are chums with the local lawman'. Retailers need a licence from local government to get access to land and property, and prime space tends to go to local operators. Good location is as important a success factor in China as it is elsewhere: Carrefour has already closed four stores which failed to compete effectively against intense competition in secondary and tertiary cities, and all those stores were located on cheaper, inferior sites. Two more closures are likely to follow. Nevertheless, Carrefour has continued to expand as far as Urumqi the far west of China as well as Hohhot in Inner Mongolia. Inner Mongolia is a new, and some might argue, a brave departure for Carrefour. Although the relative lack of competition is an obvious attraction, disposable incomes are lower and there is a lower susceptibility to modern retail formats. Also, in more remote areas, the supply chain is at greater risk making it harder to respond to demand patterns which means carrying increased stock at the branch to cover for erratic supply. After all, any back up supply could be days away. With this in mind, it will be interesting to track this store's progress.

Undoubtedly, the market has been stimulated by the injection of Western retailers' investment and expertise, for example Wal-Mart, Carrefour, Auchan and Tesco in grocery; Ikea and B&Q in home furnishing and DIY; H&M, Gap and Mango in fashion, among many others. In 2011, Whitbread entered into a joint venture with plans to open 300 Costa Coffee outlets in conjunction with a Chinese partner. It's not just about US and European retailers, though. Major retail chains from the Philippines and Thailand, for instance, have invested heavily in shopping malls and stores in China. Sun Art, a company with French retailer Auchan and experienced Thai retailer Ruentex as its controlling shareholders, is the leading hypermarket chain with 12 per cent market share. Wal-Mart holds 11.2 per cent, and Carrefour 8.1 per cent. Both Carrefour and Wal-Mart have been active in China since the mid-1990s and yet they have not been able to establish real dominance, and as both local and international competition intensifies it seems increasingly unlikely that they ever will.

UK retailer Tesco was a relatively late entrant into the market in 2004, and by 2011 had 96 hypermarkets/supermarkets and 12 smaller Express stores. To try to overcome logistical issues, Tesco in 2011 opened a logistics centre in Zhejiang initially to serve the 53 stores in the East of China, but also with a view to serving the regions to the north-east and south, and in central China. Tesco also appears to have decided that the future lies in shopping malls and has entered into a venture to develop 23 'Lifespace' branded malls, each comprising between 40,000 and 60,000 m$^2$, 10,000m$^2$ of which will be a Tesco hypermarket with the rest given over to restaurants, a cinema and around 250 other stores (Best, 2010; BMI Industry Insights, 2011; Business Monitor International, 2011; Economist Intelligence Unit, 2011; *Industry Updates*, 2011; Leng, 2011; Marian, 2011; *Relaxnews International*, 2011; *Thai News Service*, 2011).

The route selected to move a product to market through different intermediaries is known as the channel structure. The chosen route varies according to whether the organisation is dealing with consumer or B2B goods. Even within these broad sectors, different products might require different distribution channels.

## Consumer goods

The four most common channel structures in consumer markets are shown in Figure 8.1. As can be seen, each alternative involves a different number of intermediaries, and each is appropriate to different kinds of markets or selling situations. Each will now be discussed in turn.

### Producer–consumer (direct supply)

In the producer–consumer direct supply channel, the manufacturer and consumer deal directly with each other. There are many variants on this theme. It could be a factory shop or a pick-your-own fruit farm. Door-to-door selling, such as that practised by double-glazing companies, and party-plan selling, such as Tupperware and Ann Summers parties, are all attempts by producers to eliminate intermediaries.

**Figure 8.1**
Channel structures for consumer goods

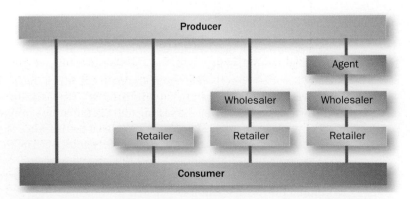

### Producer-retailer-consumer (short channel)

The producer–retailer–consumer route is the most popular with the larger retailers, since they can buy in large quantities, obtaining special prices and often with tailormade stock-handling and delivery arrangements. This route is typically used by large supermarket chains and is most appropriate for large manufacturers and large retailers who deal in such huge quantities that a direct relationship is efficient.

In the car trade, a local dealer usually deals directly with the manufacturer, because, unlike fmcg products, there is a need for significant support in the supply infrastructure and expertise in the sales and service process. This is an example of the grey area between retailing and distributorships.

### Producer-wholesaler-retailer-consumer (long channel)

The advantage of adding a wholesaler level can be significant where small manufacturers and/ or small retailers are involved. A small manufacturing organisation does not necessarily have the skills or resources to reach a wide range of retail customers and, similarly, the small corner shop does not have the resources to source relatively small quantities direct from many manufacturers. The wholesaler can provide a focal point for both sides, by buying in bulk from manufacturers, then splitting that bulk into manageable quantities for small retailers; by bringing a wider assortment of goods together for the retailer under one roof; by providing access to a wider range of retail customers for the small manufacturer; and by similarly providing access to a wider range of manufacturers' goods for the small retailer. Effectively, the wholesaler is marketing on behalf of the manufacturer.

The wholesaler can also act on behalf of relatively large manufacturers trying to sell large volumes of frequently reordered products to a wide retail network. Daily national newspapers, for example, are delivered from the presses to the wholesalers, which can then break bulk and assemble tailormade orders involving many different titles for their own retail customers. This is far more efficient than each newspaper producer trying to deal direct with each small corner shop newsagent.

### Producer-agent-wholesaler-retailer-consumer

This is the longest and most indirect channel. It might be used, for example, where a manufacturer is trying to enter a relatively unknown export market. The agent will be chosen because of local knowledge, contacts and expertise in selling into that country, and will earn commission on sales made. The problem is, however, that the manufacturer is totally dependent on the agent and has to trust the quality of the agent's knowledge, commitment and selling ability. Nevertheless, this method is widely used by smaller organisations trying to develop in remote markets, where their ability to establish a strong presence is constrained by lack of time, resources or knowledge.

## B2B goods

As highlighted in Chapter 3, B2B products often involve close technical and commercial dialogue between buyer and seller, during which the product and its attributes are matched to the customer's specific requirements. The type and frequency of purchase, the quantity purchased and the importance of the product to the buyer all affect the type of channel structure commonly found in B2B markets. Office stationery, for example, is not a crucial purchase from the point of view of keeping production lines going and, as a routine repurchase, it is more likely to be distributed through specialist distributors or retailers such as Staples or Rymans. In contrast, crucial components that have to be integrated into a production line are likely to be delivered direct from supplier to buyer to specific deadlines. The variety of B2B distribution channels can be seen in Figure 8.2. Each type will now be discussed in turn.

**Figure 8.2**
Channel
structures for B2B
goods

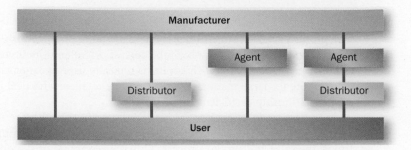

## Manufacturer–user

The direct channel is most appropriate where the goods being sold have a high unit cost and perhaps a high technical content. There is likely to be a small number of buyers who are perhaps confined to clearly defined geographical areas. To operate such a channel, the manufacturer must be prepared to build and manage a sales and distribution force that can negotiate sales, provide service and administer customer needs.

Konstruktions-Bakelit, one of Sweden's largest manufacturers of industrial plastic components, deals directly with customers such as Volvo, Saab and Alfa Laval. This is because of the need for considerable dialogue during the design and development stage to ensure a close fit between the customer's specification and components that are made to order. There would be a very high risk of misunderstanding if a third party were introduced.

Sales branches tend to be situated away from the manufacturer's head office in areas where demand is particularly high. They are a conveniently situated focal point for the area's sales force, providing them with products and support services so that they in turn can better meet their customers' needs more quickly. Sales branches may also sell products themselves directly to small retailers or wholesalers.

Sales offices do not carry stock, so, although they might take orders from local customers, they are only acting as agents and will pass the order on to head office. Again, they provide a locally convenient focus in busy areas.

## Manufacturer–distributor–user

Less direct channels tend to be adopted as the number of customers grows, the size of customers reduces, and the number of intermediary functions also increases. Building materials, for example, are often sold to builders' merchants, who then sell to the building trade based on lower order quantities, and consequently with a greater range of stock availability but greater proximity to local need. The philosophy is similar to that of the short channel of distribution discussed in the consumer context on p. 295.

This less direct type of structure can also apply to software products. Moser GmbH is one of the leading software houses in Germany and specialises in selling to small trade and handicraft organisations. Although it had over 10,000 software installations in Germany and the Netherlands, it decided to seek expansion elsewhere in Europe. This was done by selling through other software and system houses which already had the sales and technical appreciation to generate sales for Moser. Moser's MOS'aik software is now in use in more than 100,000 workplaces (www.moser.de).

## Manufacturer–agent–user

Sometimes an agent is introduced to act on behalf of a group of manufacturers in dealing with users in situations where it would not be economically viable to create a direct selling effort, but where there is a need for selling expertise to generate and complete transactions.

Teijo Pesukoneet from Nakkila in Finland specialises in technically advanced cleaning machines for metal components in enclosed cabinets. Although it has its own sales offices in Sweden and Norway, it operates through agents in other western and eastern European markets such as the UK, Germany, Poland and Latvia, among others. Agents are trained to handle technical queries and sales enquiries but relay orders to Finland for direct delivery.

Generally speaking, agents do not take title to goods, but may buy and sell, usually on a commission basis, on behalf of manufacturers and retailers. They facilitate an exchange process rather than participating fully in it. They tend to specialise in particular markets or product lines and are used because of their knowledge, or their superior purchasing or selling skills, or their well-established contacts within the market. The distinction between an agent and a broker is a fine one. Agents tend to be retained on a long-term basis to act on behalf of a client, and thus build up working rapport. A broker tends to be used on a one-off, temporary basis to fulfil a specific need or deal.

The main problem with agents is the amount of commission that has to be paid, as this can push selling costs up. This cost has to be looked at in context and with a sense of proportion. That commission is buying sales performance, market knowledge and a degree of flexibility that would take a lot of time and money to build for yourself, even if you wanted to do it. The alternative to using agents, therefore, may not be so effective or cost efficient.

# MARKETING IN ACTION

## Oranges: squeezing value from logistics

The next time you tuck into a South African orange, stop to think of the many stages in the distribution channel through which the product has moved, from the South African orange growers to the local supermarket. Each year, 1 million pallets of fruit are exported, with western Europe consuming over 50 per cent of them. The industry is made up of 200 private farmers and 1,200 growers in cooperatives. Many growers and cooperatives pool their output for marketing and distribution purposes under the Capespan International selling operation. Capespan is a giant in the global fruit market. It operates worldwide through a network of subsidiaries, joint ventures and alliance partners, with international assets that include interests in shipping, port handling and cold storage, warehousing, distribution and marketing. It doesn't just supply global markets with fruit from South Africa; it sources produce from 43 other markets as well. The challenge for Capespan has been to align its distribution strategy with increased international competition, greater customer sophistication and the demands of ever powerful supermarket chains. Product freshness, variety, quality and supply must all meet customer demand and the product must move smoothly through the supply chain from grower to buyer.

The process begins with a close working relationship with the independent growers. Capespan provides comprehensive advice, including access to market data, a pre-season marketing plan

▶ per fruit variety, and trading terms by market. Weekly orders are planned, including detail on pricing, delivery, shipping, packing and quality specifications. As the season progresses, there are also regular updates covering actual vs. target sales, market trends and competitor activity. Capespan's work in planning ahead and negotiating price deals five weeks before delivery means that the pricing risk is shifted to the importing country, and that the product will be packed and shipped as required by the retailer.

The oranges move from the growers to the fruit-handling facilities run by Capespan near the major ports such as Durban, Cape Town and Port Elizabeth. Capespan purchases the oranges and then adds handling and transportation costs and a profit margin. The services provided include some initial degreening, environmental control, labelling and packing, all before shipment. It also arranges shipment, increasingly in large bulk bins for ease of handling, from the ports. At this stage, data is collected on the fruit, size, type, quality grade, treatment and origin.

European ports such as Flushing, Sheerness and Tilbury have been selected as destinations. A partnership approach between Capespan and the port authorities has resulted in a specialist infrastructure for handling and storing palletised or binned oranges. In order to ensure that the right oranges arrive at the right EU port, data is sent to Capespan planners in Europe, who then decide which fruit should be unloaded at which port to meet local demand. On arrival, Capespan re-inspects the produce. Where necessary, the cartons are labelled and quality control checks undertaken to ensure that the fruit is consistent with specific buyers' expectations. This all helps to preserve the reputation of the Capespan brand name, Outspan. There are plans to add more valuable services such as pre-packing, size grading and fruit preparation for fresh fruit salad. After processing, the oranges are ready either to enter the UK domestic distribution chain or to go for further storage. Because an electronic data system has been used, fruit that has ripened during transit is ready to leave port quickly in 'table-fresh' condition.

Shipment can be to external pre-packers contracted by the supermarkets or straight to the wholesale and supermarket distribution systems at regional or central warehouse collection points. In the UK, shipments tend to go straight to the supermarkets' regional distribution units to help lower the carbon footprint. These shipments fulfil orders placed either direct by the supermarkets or through selling agents dealing with Capespan in the UK. Some oranges also go into the fruit and vegetable distribution chain and end up being sold in markets and through wholesalers dealing with specialist fruit and vegetable stores.

Capespan relies heavily on timely information produced at every step of the supply chain to manage the procurement, distribution, marketing and sales processes. Customised information systems and pallet tracking systems are used for tracking and stock control. Using data provided by the order and shipments, a decision support infrastructure ensures that information is generated to support Capespan's key decisions, such as destination priorities, and that information is also provided in the most useful form to suppliers.

Oranges require a large network for their marketing and distribution

*Source*: www.shutterstock.com/Valentyn Volkov

The success of Capespan, therefore, has been driven by the provision of specialist technical skills to add value in the distribution chain. This includes:

- ensuring consistent quality and leading brand packaging;
- enabling economies of scale to be achieved in logistics shipping, and packing materials;
- creating access to worldwide markets for growers who would otherwise have difficulty establishing and managing an international distribution chain;
- providing customer-specific packaging services at source, for example punnets and boxes;
- installing an effective IT system, internet and intranet for the benefit of channel members, with web-based stock trading and product flow information that would be cost-prohibitive for an individual grower; and
- globally coordinated marketing.

The value added by Capespan is clear, as independent, sometimes small growers would not have the resources or expertise to undertake all these tasks, and the wholesalers in the buying markets would not have the local knowledge of the African fruit growing industry. That knowledge and expertise is what Capespan's customers are willing to pay for, and generated around £240 million in sales in 2010.

*Sources*: Barker (2009a); *Lloyd's List* (2007); Thomas (2011); van Gass (2008); www.capespan.com; www.networking.ibm.com; www.oracle.com.

### Manufacturer–agent–distributor–user

A model comprising manufacturer–agent–distributor–user links is particularly useful in fast-moving export markets. The sales agent coordinates sales in a specified market, while the distributors provide inventory and fast restocking facilities close to the point of customer need. The comments on the longest channel of distribution in the consumer context (see p. 295) are also applicable here.

Increasingly, using multiple channels of distribution is becoming the rule rather than the exception (Frazier, 1999). Where there is choice, the retailer could have a virtual, web-based store as well as physical retail outlets. In global markets stronger branded manufacturers could adopt different methods to reach customers, depending upon local distribution structures. Using multiple channels enables more market segments to be reached and can increase penetration levels, but this must be weighed against lower levels of support from trade members who find themselves facing high degrees of intrachannel competition.

The type of structure adopted in a particular sector, whether industrial or consumer, will ultimately depend on the product and market characteristics that produce differing cost and servicing profiles. These issues will be further explored in the context of the main justification for using marketing intermediaries, described next.

## Rationale for using intermediaries

Every transaction between a buyer and a seller costs money. There are delivery costs, order picking and packing costs, marketing costs, and almost certainly administrative costs associated with processing an order and receiving or making payment. The role of the intermediary is to increase the efficiency and reduce the costs of individual transactions. This can be clearly seen in Figure 8.3.

If six manufacturers wished to deal with six buyers, a total of 36 links would be necessary. All of these transaction links cost time and money to service, and require a certain level of administrative and marketing expertise. If volumes and profit margins are sufficient, then this may be

**Figure 8.3**
The role of
intermediaries

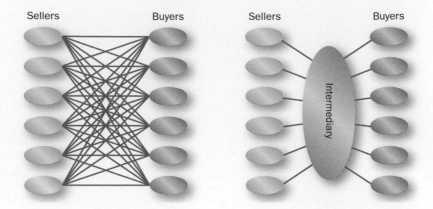

a viable proposition. However, in many situations this would add considerably to the cost of the product. By using an intermediary, the number of links falls to just 12, and each buyer and each seller needs to maintain and service only one link. If this makes sense when considering only six potential buyers, just imagine how much more sensible it is with fmcg goods where there are millions of potential buyers! On economic grounds alone, the rationale for intermediaries in creating transaction efficiency is demonstrated.

However, there are other reasons for using intermediaries, because they add value for the manufacturer and customer alike. These value-added services fall into three main groups (Webster, 1979), as shown in Figure 8.4.

## Transactional value

The role of intermediaries in assisting transaction efficiency has already been highlighted. To perform this role adequately, the intermediary, as an interconnected but separate entity, must decide on its own strategic position in the marketplace, and therefore assemble products that it believes its own desired customers need and then market them effectively. The selection is extremely important, and requires careful purchasing in terms of type, quantity and cost to fit the intermediary's own product strategy.

### Risk

The risks move to the intermediary, who takes title to the goods and, as legal owner, is responsible for their resale. Of course, it is in the manufacturer's interest to see the product moving through the distribution system in order to achieve sales and profit objectives. However, the risk of being lumbered with obsolete, damaged or slow-moving stock rests with the intermediary, not the manufacturer. This is a valuable service to that manufacturer.

**Figure 8.4**
Value-added
services provided
by intermediaries

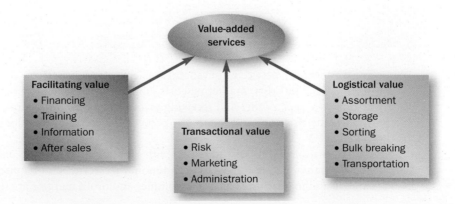

## Marketing

With the transfer of title and risk, the need to market effectively increases. Intermediaries may recruit and train their own sales forces to resell the products that they have assembled. This is another valuable service to the manufacturer, as it means that the product may have a greater chance of being brought to the attention of the prospective customer, especially in B2B markets. In consumer markets, retailers are an important interface between the manufacturer and the consumer. Retailers take responsibility for the pricing, display and control of the products offered, the processing of cash and/or credit transactions, and, if necessary, delivery to the customer. If retailers fail to ensure that adequate stocks of products are available to buy, or if they provide inadequate customer service or an unappealing retail environment, then sales could be lost.

In most retail situations, the consumer enters a carefully planned and controlled environment designed to create a retail environment that helps to establish and reinforce the ambience and image desired. In some, this may be a low-cost minimalist approach that reinforces a no-frills, value-for-money philosophy, with simple picking from racks and pallets or drums. In others, music, decor and display are all subtly developed and designed around themes to create a more upmarket, higher-quality shopping experience.

The retail environment can also include a range of additional services. Convenient parking is a critical issue where customers are buying in bulk, or want fast takeaway services (the 'drive-thru' fast-food operator has found the logical solution to this one!). Additional services in the form of credit, delivery, returns and purchasing assistance can help to differentiate a retailer.

*eg* IKEA, despite having achieved a €23.8 billion turnover in 2010 and nearly 700 million visits to its 316 stores in 35 countries, has often been criticised over the level of customer service and advice it offers. It has achieved high degrees of consistency worldwide in its operations, with self-assembly, self-service, high-design merchandise that is affordable, especially for the first-time homeowner. The problem, however, can be seen (and experienced) by anyone visiting an IKEA store on a busy Saturday. Parking can be difficult, the availability of instore

Ikea furnishings for the home
*Source*: Alamy Images/© Doug Steley C

advice variable, the checkout queues long, and there is an overall impression that the retailer is seemingly reluctant to make the shopper's burden easier.

The service solutions seem pretty straightforward in concept, but are perhaps more difficult to implement. Opening more stores would help, but that raises issues of finding suitable sites and getting planning permission. Within existing stores, it is primarily about staffing levels, so hiring more in-store staff, installing more checkouts, and finding promotional methods to spread shopper visits more evenly over the week could all help. Improving access to online shopping might also ease some of the pressure on stores. In the UK, for example, customers in England and Wales can order furniture online for home delivery but not smaller items and accessories such as rugs, lighting, cookware and pictures. Scottish customers can browse an online catalogue and then e-mail an order to the Edinburgh store, triggering a stream of backwards and forwards dialogue regarding prices, order fulfilment dates, home delivery or collection from the store, and payment methods. In Northern Ireland, there is no online or home shopping service, but it is possible to have your purchases delivered. Other retailers have provided an adequate shopping experience online and few people nowadays want to spend a whole or half day battling for a parking space, searching for trolleys and queueing at checkouts. IKEA's challenge is to improve customer service satisfaction to match the high levels of merchandise satisfaction it achieves and the company is certainly aware of this need to improve the customer experience all round (Davidson, 2009; Hansegard, 2011; www.ikea.com).

# Logistical value

## Assortment

A critical role for the intermediary is the assembly of an assortment of products from different sources that is compatible with the needs of the intermediary's own customers. This assortment can operate at product or brand level. A drinks wholesaler, for example, may offer a full range of merchandise from beer to cognac, but within each category considerable brand choice may also be offered. The benefit to the customer is the wide choice available from one source, supported perhaps by a competitive and comprehensive pre- and post-sales service. However, for other intermediaries the choice may be more limited. If one manufacturer occupies a dominant position, the choice of competing brands may be severely restricted to just complementary products. In many car dealerships, for example, only one manufacturer's new cars can be sold, although there might be more flexibility over second-hand cars.

Assortment strategy is a critical variable in a retailer's marketing strategy. The key is to build an assortment to reflect the needs of the target market.

Within a particular product area or market, variety is ensured, as retailers seek to differentiate their offerings from those of their competitors, although increasingly this is becoming more difficult. In any assortment strategy there are risks in misjudging changes in customer fads or tastes. This is particularly noticeable in high fashion areas where even the sale rails do not move assortments that have been left behind.

Wholesalers can play a major role in providing the wide assortment of goods required. While some retailers deal directly with manufacturers, others, particularly smaller stores, may prefer the convenience and accessibility of the wholesaler, especially where fast, responsive supply is assured. In the book trade, for example, it is difficult for a retailer to offer anything like the total number of titles available. Instead, the retailer acts as an order conduit, so that either the wholesaler or the publisher can service individual orders that have been consolidated into economic shipment sizes. The wholesaler can maintain a much wider range of products than is possible in all but the largest retail groups, and can provide efficient support activities for rapid stock replenishment.

## Storage, sorting and bulk breaking

A further dimension of logistical value is the accumulation and storing of products at locations that are appropriate and convenient to the customer. The small manufacturer can make one large delivery of output to the wholesaler's warehouse, where it can be stored until a retailer wants it, and broken down into smaller lots as necessary. The hassles of transporting small quantities to many different locations, finding storage space and insuring the goods are taken away from the manufacturer.

eg

Freshness and natural foods are in fashion. The healthy alternative to junk food has gained in popularity and the sales of freshly prepared salads has grown disproportionately. Of course, it was so different some time ago before distribution channels had evolved. A walk around a market in any country reveals how it used to be for most people 70 years ago with row upon row of sellers with small units offering piles of undifferentiated home-grown seasonal fruit and vegetables and little else, a far cry from the supermarkets. By using intermediaries, farmers or market gardeners do not need to find their own markets. Supermarkets buy in bulk direct from the growers, or a fruit and vegetable wholesaler can accumulate various types of produce from specialist growers, sort them, and then make larger deliveries of assorted goods to the next point in the chain, thus gaining economies in transport costs.

Some intermediaries, however, add value by processing or packing fresh produce to suit the consumer's or the retailer's needs better. Groupe Florette is one such intermediary which sells pre-packed salads and fresh stir-fry and snack vegetables mostly into the European hypermarket and supermarket trade. It has 11 production sites across five different countries, and produces some 91,000 tonnes of finished product every year. That's an awful lot of salad leaves. Trading under the Florette brand, its turnover in 2010 was €388 million, and its main market is France, accounting for 40 per cent of its turnover, followed by Spain (29 per cent) and the UK (21 per cent). In 2008, its UK turnover on pre-packed salads was just £44 million, representing 7 per cent share of a £615 million market. Since supermarket own brands accounted for 92 per cent of the market, however, this nevertheless means that Florette was the only significant branded product on the shelves. In order to extend its reach into the own brand sector, in 2009 Florette acquired the British company, Salads to Go, giving a combined turnover of £75 million and a 20 per cent market share.

To make its European-wide business a success, Florette had to invest in high levels of quality control, strict temperature control and specialist preparation machinery. It also needs regular supply, and thus has contracted with growers from across Europe.

Florette's heritage and expertise of handling salad leaves has been honed over 11 years and means that the product

It's a big logistical challenge to get fresh produce from the field to the consumer's fridge in tip-top condition

*Source*: Florette

mix and selection is carefully blended with a considered process so that the consumer benefits from superior taste, longer shelf life and fridge life:

- Florette uses dedicated suppliers to grow its lettuce leaves, which are measured by strict criteria with all substandard material rejected on delivery.
- Florette ensures that the harvest to the chill chain is of the shortest possible time – the Florette factory site is in Lichfield in Staffordshire, at the doorstep of the Vale of Evesham, the key leaf-supply region.
- The Florette chill chain starts from harvest and ends on the supermarket shelf to maintain leaf freshness, whereas other manufacturers chill after the raw material leaves have been trimmed.
- Florette mechanically cuts its leaves – this unique trimming system is quicker and less damaging to the raw material, minimising cell damage and leaf deterioration (oxidisation).

Florette knows the field of origin, the variety, the date of harvesting, and the date and place of packaging to ensure that even when distribution lines are extended, freshness of the produce can be guaranteed. All of this enables the consumer to enjoy top quality, fresh produce available locally (Barker, 2009b; Mintel, 2009; www.florette.org.uk).

Sorting is a very basic step in the logistical process, and means grouping many diverse products into more uniform, homogeneous groups. These groups may be based on product class and further subdivided by such factors as size, shape, weight and colour. This process may also add value by grading, which means inspecting, testing or judging products so that they can be placed into more homogeneous quality grades. These standards may be based on intermediary or industry predetermined standards. Large supermarket chains, for example, are particularly demanding about the standardisation of the fruit and vegetables that they retail. If you look at a carton of apples in a supermarket, you will see that they are all of a standard size, colour and quality. Mother Nature hasn't quite worked out how to ensure such uniformity, so the producers and wholesalers have to put effort into sorting out and grading the top quality produce for the high street. The second-class produce ends up in less choosy retail outlets, while the most irregular specimens end up in soup, fruit juices and ready meals.

A further important role for the intermediary, as already implied, is bulk breaking, the division of large units into the smaller, more manageable quantities required by the next step in the chain. Whereas a builder's merchant may purchase sand by the lorry load, the small builder may purchase by the bagged pallet load, and the individual consumer by the individual bag. The value of bulk breaking is clear to the DIY enthusiast, who certainly would not wish to purchase by the pallet load. There is, of course, a price to pay for this convenience, and the consumer would expect to pay a higher price per bag purchased individually than the builder would pay per bag purchased by the pallet load.

## Transportation

A final role is in actually transporting the product to the next point in the chain. Lorry loads may be made up of deliveries to several customers in the same area, thus maximising the payload, and with careful siting of warehouse facilities, minimising the distances the products have to travel. Again, this is more efficient than having each manufacturer sending out delivery vans to every customer throughout the country.

The provision of storage and transportation has become increasingly important with the widening distance, in terms of both geography and the length of distribution channels, between producer and consumer. Purchasing patterns increasingly include products sourced from wherever the best deal can be offered, whether local or international. As production becomes more concentrated into a relatively small number of larger operations, the need to move products over large distances increases. The distance can be even greater in the foodstuffs area, with the demand for exotic and fresh foods from elsewhere in Europe and well beyond. The availability of Chilean grapes in UK supermarkets in winter, for example, is the end point of a long series of distribution decisions including a number of intermediaries.

Retailers and wholesalers, by allowing larger shipments to be made and then breaking bulk, play an important role in establishing economies of scale in channels of physical distribution. Some wholesalers are themselves heavily involved in performing physical distribution roles such as inventory planning, packing, transportation and order processing in line with customer service objectives. This assists the manufacturer as well as the retailer. Often the wholesaler will incur costs in inward-bound transportation, maintain a safety stock buffer and absorb associated inventory and materials handling expenses, all of which represent savings for the manufacturer.

# Facilitating value

## Financing

The intermediary also offers a range of other value-added services either to the manufacturer or to the customer. Not only do intermediaries share the risks, as outlined above, they also provide a valuable financing benefit. The manufacturer has to manage only a small number of accounts (for example with two or three wholesalers rather than with 200 or more individual retailers) and can keep tighter control over credit periods, thus improving cash flow. As part of the service to the consumer, retailers may offer credit or other financial services such as credit card acceptance, easy payment terms and insurance. Manufacturers selling direct would not necessarily be interested in such financial services.

## Information, training and after-sales service

Both retailers and wholesalers are part of the forward information flow that advises customers and persuades them to buy. Although in the supermarket environment the role of personal advice is minimal, many retailers, especially those in product lines such as clothing, hobbies, electrical goods and cars, are expected to assist the consumer directly in making a purchase decision and to advise on subsequent use. These are the kinds of goods that require limited or extended decision-making behaviour, as discussed at p. 90 earlier. Manufacturers might well invest in training wholesale or retail staff in how to sell the benefits of their product ranges and provide after-sales service support.

Wholesalers are also important sources of advice for some retailers and users. The more specialised a wholesaler, the greater the opportunity for developing an in-depth market understanding, tracking new or declining products, analysing competitive actions, defining promotions needed and advising on best buys. This role may be especially valuable to the smaller retailer who has less direct access to quality information on broader trends in a specific market. Similarly, an industrial distributor may be expected to advise customers on applications and to assist in low-level technical problem solving.

Market information and feedback are precious commodities, as we saw in Chapter 5. The intermediary is much closer to the marketplace, and therefore alert to changes in consumer needs and competitive conditions. Passing on this information up the channel of distribution can enable manufacturers to modify their marketing strategies for the benefit of all parties. While there is no replacement for systematic, organised market research, information derived from sales contacts and meetings with intermediaries provides specific, often relevant intelligence. For the small manufacturer, with very limited market research resources, this can be particularly invaluable.

All the above functions need to be performed at some point within the marketing channel. The key decision concerns which member undertakes what role. This decision may be reached by negotiation, where the power in the channel is reasonably balanced, or by imposition, when either manufacturer or retailer dominates. Whatever the outcome, the compensation system in terms of margins needs to be designed to reflect the added value role performed.

## Types of intermediary

As we have already seen, many marketing channels involve the physical movement of goods and the transfer of legal title to the goods to various types of intermediary. This section summarises the key characteristics of each of those types.

### Distributors and dealers

Distributors and dealers are intermediaries who add value through special services associated with stocking or selling inventory, credit and after-sales service. Although these intermediaries are often used in B2B markets, they can also be found in direct dealing with consumers, for example, computer or motor dealers. The term usually signifies a more structured and closer tie between the manufacturer and intermediary in order that the product may be delivered efficiently and with the appropriate level of expertise. Clearly, some retail outlets are also closely associated with dealerships and the distinction between them may be somewhat blurred.

### Agents and brokers

Agents and brokers are intermediaries who have the legal authority to act on behalf of the manufacturer, although they do not take legal title to the goods or indeed handle the product directly in any way. They do, however, make the product more accessible to the customer and in some cases provide appropriate add-on benefits. Their prime function is to bring buyer and seller together. Universities often use agents to recruit students in overseas markets.

### Wholesalers

Wholesalers do not normally deal with the end consumer but with other intermediaries, usually retailers. However, in some situations sales are made directly to the end user, especially in B2B markets, with no further resale taking place. An organisation may purchase its catering or cleaning supplies from a local cash and carry business that serves the retail trade. A wholesaler does take legal title to the goods as well as taking physical possession of them.

Sugro, a UK wholesale group that is part of a German-based parent company, is made up of 51 wholesalers and cash-and-carry operators specialising mainly in confectionery, snacks and soft drinks. From its depots it services 41,000 outlets including CTN (confectionery, tobacco, news) stores, convenience stores, petrol forecourt stores and pubs. It has 350 field and telesales staff and 450 delivery vehicles to keep those outlets supplied. The advantages for small independent retailers sourcing from the group are mainly linked with the group's centralised bulk buying from major manufacturers, the availability of Sugro own-brands on some lines, as well as an efficient and comprehensive stocking and delivery service. As well as these core services, Sugro also supports its retail members by offering them market intelligence, including Nielsen data on top selling product lines, although some suppliers were not happy about this as they had either not wanted this information to be freely shared, or had wanted to provide their own data. Advice on merchandising and display techniques is also available. The retailer can even buy into a store brand image. Nearbuy and Sugro Convenience are both convenience store brands developed by Sugro through which a retailer's store can be converted inside and out to the relevant brand template, and then after that the retailer can continue to get marketing support and access to special deals and promotions.

Sugro doesn't only provide services to smaller retailers; it is also mindful of the needs of smaller wholesalers too. A buying group called Acorn has been launched by Sugro specifically for wholesalers of snacks, soft drinks and confectionery that have an annual turnover of £3 million or less, and are thus too small to negotiate really good deals from suppliers. Sugro believes that such wholesalers need the kind of buying power and experience that a buying and marketing group like Sugro can provide in order to compete with their bigger competitors and to grow (*The Grocer*, 2011; Phillips, 2010; www.sugro.co.uk).

Sugro provides an invaluable service for small retailers

*Source*: Sugro, www.sugro.co.uk

## Franchisees

A franchisee holds a contract to supply and market a product or service to the design or blueprint of the franchisor (the owner or originator of the product or service). The franchise agreement covers not only the precise specification of the product or service, but also the selling and marketing aspects of the business. The uniformity of different branches of McDonald's is an indication of the level of detail covered by a franchise agreement. There are many products and services currently offered through franchise arrangements, especially in the retail and home services sector.

## Retailers

Retailers sell direct to the consumer and may either purchase direct from the manufacturer or deal with a wholesaler, depending on purchasing power and volume. Retailers can be classified on a number of criteria, not all of which are immediately obvious to the average shopper. These are discussed in this section which will also help to shed further light on what retailers actually do and why they are important to both manufacturer and consumer.

### Form of ownership

Retailing was for many years the realm of the small, independent business. Some grew by adding more branches and some grew by acquisition, but it is only since the 1950s that the retail structure of the high street has evolved significantly, favouring the larger organisation. Nevertheless, there are still several predominant forms of ownership to be found.

**Independent**. Still the most common form of ownership in terms of number of retail outlets is independent. Typically, the independent retail outlet is managed by a sole trader or a family business. For the consumer, the main benefits are the personalised attention and flexibility that can be offered. These operations can be highly individualistic in terms of the variety and quality of merchandise stocked, ranging from very upmarket to bargain basement.

Although it may not be possible for the small independent to compete on price and breadth of range offered, the key is to complement the big multiples rather than to try to compete head-on. Howe (1992) is clear about forces that work against the small retailer, such as changing population patterns, the drift towards out-of-town shopping, supply and resource problems, and the sheer scale and professionalism of the large multiple chains. To combat this, the small retailer thus needs to look for niches, specialised merchandise, flexible opening hours and special services and to make more effective use of suppliers. This boils down to sound management and marketing thinking.

# MARKETING IN ACTION

## Shopping for the rural dream

Small village grocery shops are becoming an endangered species. Although there are some 57,000 rural shops in Britain, estimates have suggested that 300 village shops close every year and that around 40 per cent of all villages now have no food store. The village shop is a victim of increased consumer mobility and the attraction of the supermarkets, most of which offer online shopping with home delivery and some of which even run weekly free bus services to their stores. Many village stores have come to depend on a core clientele of largely elderly customers who are not 'into' internet shopping and have limited mobility. Unfortunately, as they die, the village store dies with them. It used to be the case that having a Post Office franchise helped these shops to survive, as it attracts people into the store and generates extra revenue, but even that is now in doubt as many of the services traditionally offered by Post Offices have shifted online (although lack of broadband coverage or slow broadband speeds, along with the number of elderly people who do not have any internet access makes this a further blow for rural communities).

There are individuals and organisations fighting to save the village stores, however. The Rural Shops Alliance represents over 8,000 independent rural shops, campaigning on their behalf, acting as a forum to share good practice and as a source of help and advice. Its Chief Executive feels that there is hope for the village shop:

> Local shops are under considerable pressure at the moment. But people are much more conscious of petrol prices than they used to be. And a lot of people have started to realise that when you go to the supermarket somewhere, you've spent £100 on your basket without really realising it. When you go to local shops three or four times a week, you're buying what you need rather than being tempted by the special offers on supermarket aisles. The supermarkets with their high advertising budgets have got people into a frame of mind that it's a bargain. (as quoted by Stephens, 2011)

The key to it is differentiation, providing things that the big supermarkets do not. That could well be local produce. A shop in the village of Stottesdon, near Bridgnorth, began as a spin-off from the local pub, The Fighting Cocks. Visitors were so impressed with the quality of the food served in the pub, they wanted to be able to buy the same local produce for themselves. The pub's landlady saw an opportunity to open a shop in a converted outbuilding with some funding help from the Countryside Agency. She now has a thriving business, Shop at The Cocks, selling locally sourced fish, meat, fruit and vegetables, as well as pies and ready meals.

It is also becoming increasingly common for communities to take matters into their own hands collectively. The Plunkett Foundation is an organisation that (among other things) advises and supports rural communities to set up and run community-owned shops. There are over 260 such shops trading in England, Wales and Scotland, and around 20 new ones opening every year. According to the Plunkett

Foundation, over 97 per cent of these shops are successful and survive, and there are many reasons for this. Obviously, a key factor is self-interest: a community store is run democratically by the people for the people and thus there should be a good understanding of what people need and want. All of them stock everyday essentials, and virtually all of them also stock local produce. Three-quarters sell newspapers and over half incorporate a Post Office. There is also the knowledge that the profit is being spread among the local community, with an average of 22 per cent being ploughed back into community projects. Running costs can also be kept down by drawing on volunteers – 90 per cent of these stores use volunteers, with an average of 30 volunteers per shop each giving two to four hours of service per week. The volunteers don't just help out in the shop; some can offer professional business and management expertise to help the enterprise too. Premises can also be cheaper. Unlike a commercial enterprise that will need to acquire retail premises, a community-owned shop can be run from a village or church hall. The Plunkett Foundation can provide help with legal structures and access to funding, as well as general information and advice.

It is not just independent entrepreneurs or community-minded people who are striving to protect rural shops, however. It is perhaps ironic that supermarket chains, such as Tesco, are also starting to see some value in smaller local shops, especially as there is now more reluctance to grant planning permission for larger units, and some would argue that there is over-provision of big name supermarkets in most cities and towns. Tesco, for example, thinks that there is an opportunity for acquiring the sites of failed rural shops to operate as Tesco Express convenience stores, and Waitrose too has expanded its convenience store network. Both retailers are conscious of the sensitivities of rural communities and seek to provide stores where there is currently no provision rather than competing directly with existing retailers, and also seek to provide local goods and produce as part of the product mix. It might even be the case that having a big grocery retail name on a village high street might benefit other local retailers by keeping shoppers within the community rather than driving out to shop elsewhere.

*Sources:* Golding (2009); Gray (2010); Plunkett Foundation (2011); *Rural Retailer* (2011); Stephens (2011); www.plunkett.co.uk; www.ruralshops.org.uk).

**Corporate chain**. A corporate chain has multiple outlets under common ownership. The operation of the chain will reflect corporate strategy, and many will centralise decisions where economies of scale can be gained. The most obvious activity to be centralised is purchasing, so that volume discounts and greater power over suppliers can be gained. There are, of course, other benefits to be derived from a regional, national or even international presence in terms of image and brand building. Typical examples include Next and M&S. Some chains do allow a degree of discretion at a local level to reflect different operating environments, in terms of opening hours, merchandise or services provided, but the main strength comes from unity rather than diversity.

**Contractual system**. The linking of members of distribution channels through formal agreements rather than ownership (i.e. a contractual system) is discussed later in this chapter. For retail or wholesale sponsored cooperatives or franchises, the main benefit is the ability to draw from collective strength, whether in management, marketing or operational procedures. In some cases, the collective strength, as with franchises, can provide a valuable tool for promoting customer awareness and familiarity, leading in turn to retail loyalty. The trade-off for the franchisee is some loss of discretion, both operationally and strategically, but this may be countered by the benefits of unity. Franchising might also pass on the retailing risk to the franchisee.

If the independent retailer wants to avoid the risks of franchising, yet wants to benefit from collective power, then affiliation to either a buying group or a voluntary chain might be the answer. Buying groups are usually found in food retailing and their purpose is to centralise the purchasing function and to achieve economies of scale on behalf of their members.

## Level of service

The range and quality of services offered vary considerably from retailer to retailer. Some, such as department stores, offer gift-wrapping services, and some DIY stores offer home delivery, but in others most of the obligation for picking, assessing and taking the product home rests with the customer. The following three types of service level highlight the main options.

**Full service**. Stores such as Harrods provide the full range of customer services. This includes close personal attention on the shopfloor, a full range of account and delivery services, and a clear objective to treat each customer as a valued individual. Such high levels of service are reflected in the premium pricing policy adopted.

**Limited service**. The number of customers handled and the competitive prices that need to be charged prevent the implementation of the full range of services, but the services that are offered make purchasing easier. Credit, no-quibble returns, telephone orders and home delivery may be offered. This is a question of deciding what the target market 'must have' rather than what it 'would like', or defining what is essential for competitive edge. A retailer, such as Next, that claims to sell quality clothing at competitive prices cannot offer too many extra services because that would increase the retailer's costs. They do, however, have to offer a limited range of services in order to remain competitive with similar retailers.

**Self-service**. In self-service stores, the customer performs many of the in-store functions, including picking goods, queueing at the checkout, paying by cash or perhaps credit card, and then struggling to the car park with a loaded trolley. Some food and discount stores operate in this mode, but the trend is towards offering more service to ease bottleneck points that are particularly frustrating to the customer. This could include the provision of more staff at the delicatessen counter, more checkouts to guarantee short queues, and assistance with packing.

## Merchandise lines

Retailers can be distinguished by the merchandise they carry, assessed in terms of the breadth and depth of range.

**Breadth of range**. The breadth of range represents the variety of different product lines stocked. A department store (see p. 312 *et seq.* for a fuller discussion) will carry a wide variety of product lines, perhaps including electrical goods, household goods, designer clothing, hairdressing and even holidays.

A catalogue retail showroom (see p. 318), such as Argos, is not expected to display its whole range of stock 'live' and is thus able to provide much greater breadth and depth of range than its department store rivals. It is limited only by its logistical systems and ability to update and replenish its in-store warehouses quickly. Argos has over 750 stores and in 2010 over £4 billion was generated in sales from the 130 million people who passed through its stores. It has been estimated that 18 million UK housholds have an Argos catalogue at home at any one time. In addition, online shopping and ordering has been introduced that can involve secure payment, home delivery or showroom collection. The main problem for Argos is its image. Although refurbishment is taking place, some of its stores look tired and a little downmarket; many people buy well-known brands from them, but few admit to it, although its shopping catalogue has massive penetration and sales have consistently grown. Argos has remained true to its strengths, providing convenience, availability and choice at low prices and internet sales are growing rapidly. Argos's experience with the catalogue approach to retailing, when the product cannot be seen before purchase, the catalogue's penetration into 70 per cent of UK homes, and the established in-store technology along with an established home delivery operation all mean that it is well placed to build further on its initial success with internet selling (Braithwaite and Killgren, 2007; www.argos.com).

**Depth of range**. The depth of range defines the amount of choice or assortment within a product line, on whatever dimensions are relevant to that kind of product. A clothing store that stocks cashmere jumpers might be said to have a shallow range if the jumpers are available only in one style, or a deep range if they are available in five different styles. Introducing further assortment criteria, such as size range and colour, creates a very complex definition of depth. A speciality or niche retailer, such as Tie Rack, would be expected to provide depth in its product lines on a number of assortment criteria.

*eg*

Swedish retailer Hennes and Mauritz (H&M) is Europe's second largest clothing retailer behind Inditex (owner of the Zara chain). H&M operates over 2,200 stores in 38 countries, and is continuing to expand globally. It owns over a dozen own-labels covering men's, women's and children's clothing, casual and classic wear, and underwear and outerwear. The 'Conscious' collection, launched in 2011, for example, is ethically and sustainably sourced, using organic and recycled materials. All H&M's ranges are targeted at specific segments in the 14–45 age range, but the assortment varies by region to suit local demographics and tastes.

The formula has been a great success: H&M generated revenue of SKr127 billion (about £12 billion) in 2010. Its key to success is flexible supply lines, strong ranges and ability to identify the coming trend, hitting it quickly and then moving on. It shares many of the characteristics that have made IKEA successful: keen prices, good design, and sourcing from low-cost countries. Quality may not always be at the forefront, but is adequate for the life expectancy of a fashion item.

Although it is a speciality retailer, concentrating on fashion, it provides a broad but shallow range, compared with other fashion retailers which specialise in just women's wear or jeans (narrow and deep). H&M is happy to offer low prices, reasonable quality and a wide range of fashionable clothing. To keep customers interested in its stores and to broaden the width of range further, there is a constant stream of new products whether designed by in-house staff or special celebrity collections, such as the David Beckham men's underwear range. H&M has also acquired other retail names, again as a means of broadening its appeal, thus COS (Collection of Style) serves a slightly more upmarket, sophisticated consumer, while Monki, Weekday and Cheap Monday target a younger, more fashion-conscious consumer. All of this means an extensive logistics operation involving regional warehouses, supplied from within Europe and from Asia. However, like all European retailers, H&M has had to face up to a downturn in consumer spending, the rising price of cotton, and rising production costs in Asia. While some retailers have responded by raising prices, H&M has chosen to keep its prices steady. Some analysts, however, think that H&M is in a less favourable position than Inditex, partly because Inditex is less exposed to rising Asian production costs as it sources most of its goods from Spain, Portugal and Morocco; partly because H&M targets a younger, more price-conscious segment that has been badly hit by unemployment; and partly because Inditex has expanded faster in emerging markets such as China (Chesters, 2011; Goldfingle, 2011; *Marketing*, 2011; Ward, 2011; www.hm.com).

## Operating methods

The area of operating methods has seen significant change, with the recent growth of alternatives to the traditional approach. Traditional store retailing, which itself includes a wide number of types of retailer, still predominates. These various types are considered in the next section. Non-store retailing, however, where the customer does not physically travel to visit the retailer, has become increasingly popular. This is partly because of changing customer attitudes, partly because of the drive upmarket made by the mail-order companies in particular, and partly because of technological advances in logistics. The whole area of non-store shopping will be further discussed at p. 318 *et seq.*

## Store types

A walk down any high street or a drive around the outskirts of any large town reveals a wide range of approaches to selling us things. There are retailers of all shapes and sizes, enticing us in with what they hope are clearly differentiated marketing mixes. The following discussion groups retailers according to the type of retail operation that they run. Each type will be defined, and the role it plays within the retail sector will be discussed.

**Department stores**. Department stores usually occupy a prominent prime position within a town centre or a large out-of-town shopping mall. Most towns have one, and some centres, such as London's Oxford Street, support several. Department stores are large and are organised into discrete departments consisting of related product lines, such as sports, ladies' fashions, toys, electrical goods, etc.

To support the concept of providing everything that the customer could possibly want, department stores extend themselves into services as well as physical products, operating hairdressing and beauty parlours, restaurants and travel agencies. In some stores, individual departments are treated as business units in their own right. Taking that concept a little further, it is not surprising that concessions or 'stores within a store' have become common. With these, a manufacturer or another retail name purchases space within a department store, paying either a fixed rental per square metre or a percentage commission on turnover, to set up and operate a distinct trading area of its own. Jaeger, a classic fashion manufacturer and retailer, operates a number of its own stores throughout the UK, but also generates a significant amount of turnover from concessions within department stores such as Sefridges, Harvey Nichols and House of Fraser.

**Variety stores**. Variety stores are smaller than department stores, and they stock a more limited number of ranges in greater depth. Stores such as BhS and Marks & Spencer in the UK, and Monoprix in France, provide a great deal of choice within that limited definition, covering ladies' wear, menswear, children's clothing, sportswear, lingerie, etc. Most, however, carry additional ranges. BhS, for example, offers housewares and lighting, while Marks & Spencer offers shoes, greeting cards, plants, and extensive and successful food halls within its stores.

Like department stores, the major variety stores such as Monoprix in France and Kaufhalle in Germany operate as national chains, maintaining a consistent image across the country, and some also operate internationally. Whatever the geographical coverage of the variety store chain, given the size of the stores, they need volume traffic (i.e. lots of customers), and thus to develop a mass-market appeal they need to offer quality merchandise at no more than mid-range price points. Variety stores tend to offer limited additional services, with a tendency towards self-service, and centralised cashier points. In that sense, they are something between a department store and a supermarket.

**Supermarkets**. Over the last few years, the supermarket has been accused of being the main culprit in changing the face of the high street. The first generation of supermarkets, some 30 years ago, were relatively small, town-centre operations. As they expanded and cut their costs through self-service, bulk buying and heavy merchandising, they began to replace the small, traditional independent grocer. They expanded on to out-of-town sites, with easy free parking, and took the customers with them, thus (allegedly) threatening the health of the high street.

The wheel then turned full circle. As planning regulations in the UK tightened, making it more difficult to develop new out-of-town superstores, retailers began looking at town centre sites again. They developed new formats, such as Tesco Metro and Sainsbury's Local, for small stores carrying ready meals, basic staple grocery goods such as bread and milk, and lunchtime snacks aimed at shoppers and office workers.

The dominance of supermarkets is hardly surprising, because their size and operating structures mean that their labour costs can be 10–20 per cent lower than those of independent grocers, and their buying advantage 15 per cent better. This means that they can offer a significant price advantage. Additionally, they have made efficiency gains and increased their cost effectiveness through their commitment to developing and implementing new technology in the areas of EPOS, shelf allocation models, forecasting and physical distribution management systems. The effective management of retail logistics, therefore, has become a major source of sustainable competitive advantage (Paché, 1998). Most supermarkets, however, work on high turnover and low operating margins.

**Hypermarkets**. The hypermarket is a natural extension of the supermarket. According to the IGD (Institute of Grocery Distribution), a supermarket can be anything between 300 and 2,500 m$^2$, and a superstore is between 2,500 and 6,000 m$^2$. In both formats, food sales predominate. A hypermarket is anything over 6000 m$^2$ in size, and non-food products account for a significant proportion of sales (www.igd.com). A hypermarket provides even more choice and depth of range, but usually centres mainly around groceries. Examples of hypermarket operators are Intermarché and Carrefour in France, Tengelmann in Germany and ASDA in the UK. Because of their size, hypermarkets tend to occupy new sites on out-of-town retail parks. They need easy access and a large amount of space for parking, not only because of the volume of customers they have to attract, but also because their size means that customers will often buy a great deal at a time and will therefore need to be able to bring the car close to the store.

Obtaining planning permission is becoming increasingly difficult for new hypermarket locations anywhere in Europe. Nevertheless, a small number of developments are still taking place as part of new out-of-town shopping centres, with hypermarkets such as Auchan playing a central role. The 'hypermarket for better living' in Val d'Europe, Marne-la-Vallée (Paris region, France), is a further example of continued development. The extended range of services include a beauty salon, a nursery, computers for use by customers, the possibility of watching DVD trailers and listening to the CDs on offer, and an optician. The Irish planning authorities have looked at the effects of hypermarket and superstore developments in other EU countries and concluded that they damage town centres, leading to the closure of small shops, and cause traffic congestion. As a result of this, the Irish government introduced planning guidelines designed to place further restrictions on the development of superstores and hypermarkets.

The impact on the environment and town planning is, therefore, a far more important consideration than in the past in granting planning permission. Arrangements for the recycling of packaging, store architecture which blends in with surroundings, access arrangements, and the impact on retail diversity are now to the fore.

**Out-of-town speciality stores**. An out-of-town speciality store tends to specialise in one broad product group, for example furniture, carpets, DIY or electrical. It tends to operate on an out-of-town site, which is cheaper than a town-centre site and also offers good parking and general accessibility. It concentrates on discounted prices and promotional lines, thus emphasising price and value for money. A product sold in an out-of-town speciality store is likely to be cheaper than the same item sold through a town-centre speciality or department store.

The store itself can be single storey, with no windows. Some care is taken, however, over the attractiveness of the in-store displays and the layout. Depending on the kind of product area involved, the store may be self-service, or it may need to provide knowledgeable staff to help customers with choice and ordering processes. Recent years have seen efforts to improve the ambience of such stores and even greater care over their design.

Toys 'R' Us, in particular, has become known as a 'category killer' because it offers so much choice and such low prices that other specialist toy retailers cannot compete easily. Its large out-of-town sites mean that it is efficient in terms of its operating costs, and its global bulk buying means that it can source extremely cheaply. Shoppers wanting to buy a particular toy know that Toys 'R' Us will probably have it in stock, and shoppers who are unsure about what they want have a wonderful browsing opportunity. Additionally, the out-of-town sites are easily accessible and make transporting bulky items much easier. The small, independent toy retailer, in contrast, cannot match buying power, cost control, accessibility or choice and is likely to be driven out of business.

# MARKETING IN ACTION

## Pampering your pets

There are an awful lot of pets in the UK. According to the Pet Food Manufacturers Association (PFMA), there are about 8 million cats, 8 million dogs, 1 million rabbits, 1 million birds and 1.5 million guinea pigs and hamsters. Pets don't have to be cute and cuddly, of course. There are 40 million pet fish swimming around, and there has also been a big rise in interest in low-maintenance reptiles as pets – there are 9 million of them. They all need grooming and bedding products (well, perhaps not the fish); they all need feeding and healthcare products; they all need accessories and toys. Overall, the pet-care market was worth over £2,600 million in 2010, of which £519 million represented sales of pet accessories and healthcare, capitalising on people's pampering of their pets. About 55 per cent of UK adults own a pet, and their attitude to their pets is summed up by the fact that 87 per cent of pet owners agreed or strongly agreed with Mintel's (2011a) survey statement, 'My pet(s) is/are part of the family'. As members of the family, pets seems to be being treated very well, and spending on pet-care generally does not seem to have fallen victim to recessionary cutbacks in consumer spending. Mintel's survey also showed that only 20 per cent of pet owners had cut back on the amount they spent on their pets in the previous year; 44 per cent claim to be more interested in the nutritional content of pet food than the price; and 35 per cent agreed or strongly agreed that they 'like spoiling [their] pet with treats'.

Because I'm worth it!

*Source*: www.coloribus.com. Image used courtesy of Alamy Images/ © Lori Farr

There's a clear opportunity here for a category killer, and Pets at Home has grasped that opportunity with both hands (or possibly with all four paws), certainly as far as accessories and healthcare are concerned. It is the only nationwide specialist pet store in the UK, with over 280 outlets and an annual turnover of just under £520 million. Although the distribution of petfood, especially dog and cat food is as diverse as that of any other fmcg product and inevitably involves the major grocery chains, competition in retailing other petcare supplies tends to come mainly from small specialist stores and garden centres such as Wyevale, with the supermarkets only carrying a very limited range of the fastest-moving pet supplies.

Pets at Home tends to occupy edge-of-town or out-of-town stores averaging around 9,000 feet$^2$ with the obvious benefits of easy parking and availability of everything the pet owner could possibly need (including the pet itself, if you're looking for a smaller non-dog or non-cat type of pet) under one roof. It's not just about products. Pets at Home recognises that the pet owner is looking for a complete range of goods and services in caring for their animals, and thus 73 of the stores incorporate a veterinary practice, and 43 of the larger stores incorporate grooming salons.

The stores are also used as venues for special events, such as advice sessions on petcare, fundraising events for animal welfare charities, puppy training classes, and adoption events for rehoming cats and dogs again in conjunction with local animal rescue centres. Animal welfare is clearly very important to the company, and it has its own charity Support Adoption for Pets as well as ploughing some of its profits back into other animal welfare charities. As new stores are opened, local newspapers are used to encourage local organisations to make themselves known to the company.

While a lot of thought and investment has been put into the stores themselves, Pets at Home also recognises the importance of a multichannel strategy and substantial investment has also been made in the website, both as a source of information and as a shopping channel. Although live animals can only be bought in the stores, virtually everything else can be bought online either for later collection from the customer's preferred store or for home delivery. The website can also be used to check availability of items in local stores so that customers can avoid a wasted journey if items are out of stock. The provision of online shopping facilities is clearly important, but the company also sees the website as an important means of initiating and strengthening relationships with customers. As the company itself says:

We have a strong starting point offline – we adopt more than 50,000 pets a year and have strong relationships with animal charities. Pets At Home has a unique place in the pet market and we now want to replicate that on the web. We want people to see us as the first point of call when looking for information about their pet. (as quoted by *New Media Age*, 2010)

*Sources*: Bawden (2011); *Birmingham Mail* (2011); *M2 Presswire* (2010); Mintel (2011a); *New Media Age* (2010); www.petsathome.com; www.pfma.org.uk.

**Town-centre speciality stores**. Like out-of-town speciality stores, town-centre speciality stores concentrate on a narrow product group as a means of building a differentiated offering. They are smaller than the out-of-town speciality stores, averaging about 250 m². Within this sector, however, there are retailers such as florists, lingerie retailers, bakeries and confectioners that operate in much smaller premises. Well-known names such as H&M (see p. 311), Superdrug, Thorntons, Next and HMV all fit into this category.

Other examples of products sold through town centre speciality stores are footwear, toys, books and clothing (although often segmented by sex, age, lifestyle or even size). Most are comparison products, for which the fact of being displayed alongside similar items can be an advantage, as the customer wants to be able to examine and deliberate over a wider choice of alternatives before making a purchase decision. Given their central locations, and the need to build consumer traffic with competitive merchandise, the sector has seen the growth of multiple chains, serving clearly defined target market segments with clearly defined product mixes, such as most of the high street fashion stores. To reinforce the concept of specialisation and differentiation, some, especially the clothing multiples, have developed their own-label brands.

A visit to Thorntons may be a delight for those of us who are chocaholics, but it seems that there just aren't enough of us! Following a number of years of disappointing sales figures, the new incoming CEO undertook an in-depth strategy review in the first half of 2011 and announced some major changes. Underpinning these changes was the conclusion that the brand and the stores were not sufficiently differentiated and not sufficiently 'de-seasonalised'. Thorntons is a retailer that people turn to for gift chocolate and confectionery for key events such as Christmas, Easter, Valentine's Day and Mother's Day, but it tends to be somewhat forgotten in between.

To address this, the strategic review assessed all of Thorntons'-owned retail locations and concluded that at least 180 of them should be closed over the course of three years, thus halving the number of company-operated stores. In some of these locations, franchisees might be sought to replace the closed store and in others, Thorntons concessions with a limited product range might be set up in card and gift shops, for example. This last idea in particular helps with the de-seasonalisation to some extent, by associating the brand with more personal every-day and general occasions such as birthdays, anniversaries, thank-yous, congratulations, etc. These occasions will be promoted more heavily in the Thorntons stores and are further reinforced through the development of new products retailing at under £5 as good value little gifts. Alongside revamped merchandising (including point of sale communication; in-store product sampling; better displays and layout etc.) and improved service, it is hoped that these changes will increase the frequency with which each customer visits a Thorntons outlet. The company also wants to capture more customer data in-store to link through to an improved customer relationship management system and online operation which again will help to increase the value of each customer and frequency of purchase.

As well as its online store, high street stores and franchises, Thorntons has 30 factory outlets which sell excess stock and 'misshapes'. In 10 of these outlets, Thorntons has also opened cafés and there are also cafés in 25 other Thorntons stores. The cafés are profitable and non-seasonal, and thus will be maintained. The final channel to the end customer is through what Thorntons calls its 'commercial' sales, i.e. selling its branded products through other retailers such as supermarkets. At the time of the review, commercial sales accounted for 37 per cent of revenue, with in-store sales accounting for around 50 per cent, but the plan appears to be to build the commercial business so that it becomes the main source of revenue. Some have argued that this represents a threat to the Thorntons branded stores and cannibalises the business, but Thorntons' view is that each channel to the end consumer contributes something different and complementary: 'Our own stores play a very important role in bringing our brand to life. The value of that is then played out to the benefit of sales in all our channels' (as quoted by Stodell, 2011). (Barrett, 2011; Clark, 2011; Stodell, 2011; Thorntons, 2011; Wembridge, 2011)

Town-centre speciality stores usually offer a mixture of browsing and self-service, but with personnel available to help if required. The creation of a retail atmosphere or ambience appropriate to the target market is very important, including for instance the use of window display and store layout. This allows the town centre speciality store to feed off consumer traffic generated by larger stores, since passing shoppers are attracted in on impulse by what they see in the window or through the door. The multiples can use uniform formulae to replicate success over a wide area, but because of their buying power and expertise, they have taken a great deal of business away from small independents.

**Convenience stores**. Despite the decline of the small, independent grocer in the UK, there is still a niche that can be filled by convenience stores. Operating mainly in the groceries, drink and CTN sectors, they open long hours, not just 9 a.m. until 6 p.m. The typical CTN is still the small, independent corner shop that serves a local community with basic groceries, newspapers, confectionery and cigarettes, but the range has expanded to include books, stationery, video hire, and greetings cards.

They fill a gap left by the supermarkets, which are fine for the weekly or monthly shopping trip, if the consumer can be bothered to drive out to one. The convenience stores, however, satisfy needs that arise in the meantime. If the consumer has run out of something, forgotten to get something at the supermarket, wants freshness, or finds six unexpected guests on the doorstep who want feeding, the local convenience store is invaluable. If the emergency happens outside normal shopping times, then the advantages of a local, late-night shop become obvious. Such benefits, however, do tend to come at a price premium. To try to become more price competitive, some 'open-all-hours' convenience stores operate as voluntary chains, such as Spar, Londis, Today's and Mace, in which the retailers retain their independence but benefit from bulk purchasing and centralised marketing activities. The priority for many CTNs is to keep trying new services and lines that might sell in the local community. A large number now have off-licences, and the provision of other outsourced services, including dry cleaning and shoe repairs. The National Lottery ticket terminals have provided a boost to income, while even sales of travel cards and phone cards have generated new streams of revenue.

Two more recent developments in convenience retailing are forecourt shops at petrol stations and computerised kiosks. Many petrol retailers, such as Jet and Shell, have developed their non-petrol retailing areas into attractive mini-supermarkets that pull in custom in their own right. In some cases, they are even attracting customers who go in to buy milk or bread and end up purchasing petrol as an afterthought. Sales through forecourts in 2011 were worth around £4.2 billion, representing a 13 per cent share of the convenience market, showing what an important revenue earner forecourt retailing has become (IGD, 2011d). The next stage of development could be more cash dispensers installed at forecourt sites, and eventually internet access. Forecourts could also become pick-up locations for home shopping orders. Offering a diversified portfolio of services can be a critical factor in the survival of some rural petrol stations.

The launch of Tesco Express, stores of up to 3,000 feet$^2$ sited in smaller towns, heralded the start of Tesco's interest in the convenience retail sector. Its later acqusition of the One Stop chain in 2003 followed by the acquisition of 77 stores in 2010 from the Mills Group was a real wake-up call for small urban independent convenience stores. It forced many to think very carefully about the catchment area they were serving and what customers really want from a convenience store. Some independents have moved quickly to join symbol groups such as Spar, Londis and Costcutter to gain the benefits of their buying power and marketing and merchandising expertise, and membership of symbol groups continues to increase year on year with a consequent fall in the number of unaffiliated independent stores. Competition in the convenience sector can only get more intense: Tesco isn't the only grocery multiple that is expanding in this area. Sainsbury's is also well established in the convenience store business, and in 2011, Waitrose announced that it would be opening 20 conveniece stores around London over an eighteen-month period, with a longer-term aim of having 300–400 such stores across the country. Morrison's too has started to open M-local stores.

The multiples might not yet have a huge share of the convenience sector (about 15 per cent) but with their enormous buying power there is plenty of scope to offset costs and maintain margins, and yet compete strongly on price. It is true to say that many consumers expect to pay more in a convenience store, and that they are willing to pay a premium for the convenience provided. But there are limits. According to the IGD, most consumers are content to pay a premium of around 5–10 per cent, and yet prices in many independents are more than 15 per cent higher than in the supermarkets. Tesco Express and Sainsbury's Local typically charge only 5 per cent more than in their superstores, thus presenting a tough challenge to their competitors, although Morrisons has declared that its M-local stores will charge the same as its superstores on main items. Interestingly, and adding to the independents' problems, many consumers perceive that the prices they are paying in convenience stores are higher than they actually are, which is a problem for independents seeking to retain business in areas where consumers have a choice of where to shop (Felsted, 2011b; Hall, 2011; IGD, 2010).

**Discount clubs**. Discount clubs are rather like cash and carries for the general public, where they can buy in bulk at extremely competitive prices. Discount clubs, however, do have membership requirements, related to occupation and income.

*eg*  Costco is a form of discount club for both traders and individual members, with over 550 warehouse outlets across seven countries including 22 UK locations. Over 400 outlets are in the USA, Costco's home country. The format is large warehouses selling high-quality, nationally branded and selected private-label merchandise at low prices to businesses purchasing for commercial use or resale, and also to individuals who are members of selected employment groups. Products are packaged, displayed and sold in bulk quantities in a no-frills, warehouse atmosphere on the original shipping pallets. The warehouses are self-service and the member's purchases are packed into empty product boxes. By stripping out the service and merchandising, the prices can be kept low. Costco has no advertising or investor relations department and comparatively few staff. Overheads must also be kept as low as possible to ensure profitability (www.costco.co.uk).

The discount clubs achieve their low prices and competitive edge through minimal service and the negotiation of keen bulk deals with the major manufacturers, beyond anything offered to the established supermarkets. Added to this, they pare their margins to the bone, relying on volume turnover, and they purchase speculatively. For instance, they may purchase a one-off consignment of a manufacturer's surplus stock at a very low price, or they may buy stock cheaply from a bankrupt company. While this allows them to offer incredible bargains, they cannot guarantee consistency of supply, thus they may have a heap of televisions one week but once these have been sold, that is it, there are no more. The following week the same space in the store may be occupied by fridges. At least such a policy keeps customers coming back to see what new bargains there are.

**Markets**. Most towns have markets, as a last link with an ancient form of retailing. There are now different types of market, not only those selling different kinds of products but street markets, held on certain days only; permanent markets occupying dedicated sites under cover or in the open; and Sunday markets for more specialised products.

**Catalogue showrooms**. Catalogue showrooms try to combine the benefits of a high street presence with the best in logistics technology and physical distribution management. The central focus of the showroom is the catalogue, and many copies are displayed around the store as well as being available for the customer to take home for browsing. Some items are on live display, but this is by no means the whole product range. The consumer selects from the catalogue, then goes to a checkout where an assistant inputs the order into the central computer. If the item is immediately available, the cashier takes payment. The consumer then joins a queue at a collection point, while the purchased product is brought round from the warehouse behind the scenes, usually very quickly.

A prime example of this type of operation is Argos, which carries a very wide range of household, electrical and leisure goods. It offers relatively competitive prices through bulk purchasing, and savings on operating costs, damage and pilfering (because of the limited displays).

## Non-store retailing

A growing amount of selling to individual consumers is now taking place outside the traditional retailing structures. Non-store selling may involve personal selling (to be dealt with in Chapter 12), selling to the consumer at home through television, the internet or telephone links or, most impersonally, selling through vending machines.

**In-home selling**. The longest-established means of selling to the consumer at home is through door-to-door selling, where the representative calls at the house either trying to sell from a suitcase (brushes, for example), or trying to do some preliminary selling to pave the way for a more concerted effort later (with higher-cost items such as double glazing, burglar alarms and other home improvements). Cold calling (i.e. turning up unexpectedly and unannounced) is not a particularly efficient use of the representative's time, nor is it likely to evoke a positive response from the customer.

A more acceptable method of in-home selling that has really taken off is the party plan. Here, the organisation recruits ordinary consumers to act as agents and do the selling for them in a relaxed, sociable atmosphere. The agent, or a willing friend, will host a party at a house and provide light refreshments. Guests are invited to attend and during the course of the evening, when everyone is relaxed, the agent will demonstrate the goods and take orders.

Since the pioneering days of the Tupperware party, many other products have used the same sort of technique. Ann Summers, for instance, is an organisation that sells erotic lingerie and sex aids and toys through parties. The majority of the customers are women who would otherwise never dream of going into 'that kind of shop', let alone buying 'that kind of merchandise'. A party is an ideal way of selling those products to that particular target market, because the atmosphere is relaxed, the customer is among friends, and purchases can be made without embarrassment amidst lots of giggling. One of the best features of party selling is the ability to show and demonstrate the product. This kind of hands-on, interactive approach is a powerful way of involving the potential customer and thus getting them interested and in a mood to buy.

The main problem with party selling, however, is that it can be difficult to recruit agents, and their quality and selling abilities will be variable. Supporting and motivating a pyramid of agents and paying their commission can make selling costs very high.

**Mail order and teleshopping**. Mail order has a long history and traditionally consists of a printed catalogue from which customers select goods that are then delivered to the home, either through the postal service or via couriers. This form of selling has, however, developed and diversified over the years. Offers are now made through magazine or newspaper advertisements, as well as through the traditional catalogue, and database marketing now means that specially tailored offers can be made to individual customers. Orders no longer have to be mailed in by the customer, but can be telephoned, with payment being made immediately by credit card. The strength of mail order varies across Europe, but it is generally stronger in northern Europe than in the south. It is strong in Germany through companies such as Otto Versand, Quelle and Nekermann.

Teleshopping represents a much wider range of activities. It includes shopping by telephone in response to television advertisements, whether on cable, satellite or terrestrial channels. Some cable and satellite operators run home-shopping channels, such as QVC, where the primary objective is to sell goods to viewers.

**Online shopping**. At least for larger retailers, multichannel shopping using both 'bricks and mortar' and virtual stores is fast becoming the norm. As can be seen in many of the examples scattered throughout this chapter and in Case Study 8, an online operation can represent a cost-effective way of expanding a retailer's reach and of adding value to the customer's experience through additional information and content; relationship building through two-way dialogue; and particularly when social networking is taken into account, building horizontal brand communities of like-minded customers. For smaller retailers too, the internet represents a relatively easy and low-cost means of starting a business, unconstrained by the need for premises, and free of geographic constraint. Even the smallest business can now reach a global market and particularly for those selling highly specialised goods, the broad 'reach' of the internet is vital for viability.

Earlier in the chapter, we looked at store-based retailing in China. Internet shopping is also starting to take off there. In 2010, online shopping was worth US$77 billion generated from 148 million online shoppers, representing just 31 per cent of internet users, so there is still a lot of scope for expansion, especially as the number of internet users is expected to rise from 457 million to 750 million by 2015.

Online sales accounted for just 3 per cent of total retail sales in 2010, although it is forecast that this will reach 5 per cent by 2015. That doesn't sound like much of an increase, but considering that total retail sales will quadruple over that period, it's actually a very substantial rise in value. To put it into context, only about 4.5 per cent of US retail sales and about 5.9 per cent of sales in the EU are online.

Although Chinese retailers are committed to expanding their online selling, with 93 per cent of respondents to a survey saying that they are or will soon be involved in e-commerce, they are still very wary of the risk of cannibalising their in-store sales. Foreign retailers seem to be still concentrating on getting their bricks and mortar retailing sorted out and are in less of a hurry to get into the Chinese virtual world. Tesco is currently trialling home delivery of clothing and grocery items, while Wal-Mart has gone further than most by buying a stake in Yihaodian, China's leading online grocery retailer, and the only one with national coverage. Wal-Mart is thus buying into an established infrastructure and a lot of expertise. Yihaodian has grown from having just 3000 SKUs (stock keeping units – effectively product lines) and a few hundred suppliers to having 70,000 SKUs and 2,000 suppliers, so it has clearly had to solve a lot of operational and logistical problems (Business Monitor International, 2011; Marian, 2011; *Shanghai Daily*, 2011).

The growth of Amazon as an online retailer and price comparison sites shows just how much impact the internet can have on a conventional distribution channel. There are several advantages of online distribution:

- The viewer is actively searching for products and services, and so every site hit could gain a potential customer if interest can be maintained. Regular and loyal customers can take short cuts and skip all the general background information; 'shopping baskets' help the customer to keep track of what they have bought on this visit, and 'wish lists' keep a record of things that they might want to buy in the future or request as gifts from friends and family. Books, music, DVDs, groceries, clothing, travel and electrical goods have all become significant contributors to the e-tail economy.

- Print and mailing costs are eliminated because no catalogue has to be produced and distributed each season. Although costs will be incurred in developing and maintaining an interesting website, they still represent a saving, especially because a website increases the seller's flexibility as it can be changed far more easily than the printed page with instant updates on prices, product availability and special offers. Amazon has well over 80 million users, yet the cost of communicating with them is a fraction of the cost that would have been incurred through direct mail or media advertising.

- Order processing and handling costs are reduced with online ordering as everything is already in electronic form and the customer is handling all the order entry without assistance. This means that the organisation has to ensure that all the 'behind the scenes' logistics operations can cope with changes in ordering patterns. Linking back into the organisational systems for stock control and order fulfilment is essential if customer service levels are to be maintained.

- The IT systems have to be able to offer real time information flows between the customer, customer support, distribution and the supply chain. Only then can realistic claims be made for cost efficient and effective customer service, whether a small parcel is delivered to Milan or Middlesbrough. Order tracking reassures customers that their purchases are on their way.

- There is also huge potential for data mining from the vast database of customer information that is built up. This can help with cross- and up-selling to existing customers (i.e. getting them to buy related items or getting them to trade up to more expensive items), as well as enhancing marketing efforts by helping to profile segments, appropriate advertising media, assess the impact of sales promotions, etc.

- Better after-sales service can be provided online, not only because of cheaper and easier communication, but also through feedback links, usage information, news flashes on any product changes and mechanisms for fault reporting.
- The internet, aided by smartphones, has allowed the development and distribution of digital products, in the form of magazines, books music and video and, of course, apps.
- Manufacturers can get closer to the customer and potentially reduce costs through disintermediation, which simply means cutting one or more intermediaries out of the distribution channel. Thus the package holiday company that sells online direct to the consumer rather than through a travel agent is bypassing an intermediary, as is the designer-label clothing manufacturer that sells direct rather than through a trendy Oxford Street retailer. There is a risk attached to this (quite apart from alienating the traditional intermediaries who are losing business), however. As discussed earlier in this chapter, one of the roles of the intermediary is to bring assortments of products together and make them visible to the target market in one place. Online direct selling by a manufacturer loses this advantage and depends heavily on the consumer's ability to find the manufacturer's website; hence the growth of price comparison sites, online directories, online malls and search engines, among others, to help guide the consumer to relevant sites or to sell goods to them as a retailer would.

**Vending**. Vending machines account for a very small percentage of retail sales, less than 1 per cent. They are mainly based in workplaces and public locations, for example offices, factories, staffrooms, bus and rail stations, etc. They are best used for small, standard, low-priced, repeat purchase products, such as hot and cold drinks, cans of drink, chocolate and snacks, bank cash dispensers and postage stamps. They have the advantage of allowing customers to purchase at highly convenient locations, at any time of the day or night. Vending machines can also help to deliver the product in prime condition for consumption, for example, the refrigerated machines that deliver a can of ice-cold Coke. A human retailer cannot always maintain those conditions.

## Channel strategy

With the various added-value roles implicit in the marketing channel, decisions need to be taken about the allocation and performance of these roles, the basis of remuneration within the system, and the effectiveness of alternative configurations in enabling market penetration to be achieved competitively and efficiently. This is channel strategy.

## Channel structures

The basic forms of channel design were outlined in Figures 8.1 and 8.3. These are known as conventional channels, in which the various channel activities are agreed by negotiation and compromise, recognising that both sides need each other. The particular structure adopted should reflect the market and product characteristics, taking into consideration such factors as market coverage, value, quantity sold, margin available, etc. (Sharma and Dominguez, 1992).

Where a manufacturer needs to reach distinct target markets, a dual or multiple distribution approach may be adopted, which means that each target market may be reached by two or more different routes. For example, IBM will sell direct to large users and organisations, but will go through the retail trade to reach the consumer segment. This pattern works well, provided that discreteness is maintained and as long as the arrangement reflects the various buyers' differing pre- and post-purchase servicing needs. However, problems can emerge if the same product is sold to the same target market through different channels. A book publisher, for example, may create some friction with the book trade if it actively encourages direct ordering and other subscription services at lower prices than the retail trade can manage. This potential for conflict may well increase as direct marketing and home shopping gain in popularity.

## Competition in channels

Not all competition in channels comes from traditionally expected direct sources, as we see from Figure 8.5. Sometimes, internal channel competition can reduce the efficiency of the whole channel system. Each of the four types of competition identified by Palamountain (1955) is considered in turn below.

**Horizontal competition**. Horizontal competition, as can be seen in Figure 8.5, is competition between intermediaries of the same type. This type of competition, for example between supermarkets, is readily visible. Each one develops marketing and product range strategies to gain competitive advantage over the others.

Discount grocery retailers are characterised by limited product ranges that generally do not include leading brands, low-cost 'no-frills' stores and low-priced goods. As they rely on selling high volumes of products to generate profit, they have expanded across Europe in search of greater volumes and economies of scale. Netto started in Denmark, and Aldi and Lidl both originated in Germany, which has a strong discount retail culture. Each of them is a powerful force in its home market and the discount retail formula has been transferred successfully to many other European countries. The stores tend to be between 500 and 1,000 m² in size and are situated mainly in highly populated residential areas.

In the early days when the discounters first tried to get established in the UK market, Hogarth-Scott and Parkinson (1994) researched the effect of a discounter opening a store close to an established supermarket in the UK. They found that although 57 per cent of shoppers had tried the discounter once, only 4 per cent of customers had been lost to the discounter, representing 4.7 per cent of turnover. Little has changed since that research was done.

Mintel (2010b) found that while 39 per cent of shoppers use Tesco for their main shop, only 2 per cent use Aldi and 1 per cent Lidl. Looking at secondary shops, 41 per cent use Tesco, and Lidl and Aldi jump to 20 and 16 per cent respectively. This is selective top-up shopping, but during a time of economic hardship, it has helped Aldi and Lidl to increase their market shares to 3.4 per cent and 2.6 per cent respectively. Both discounters have had to adapt their business models to suit the UK consumer. Aldi for instance has increased the number of product lines it offers, and while it doesn't have big name brands, it has introduced some premium lines, and has also introduced some Fairtrade products. Lidl has begun to introduce in-store bakeries and some big brands to tempt shoppers in.

Nevertheless, it is difficult for the discounters to make much progress against the mainstream retailers. It is symptomatic of those difficulties that Netto has pulled out of the UK and has sold its stores to Asda. The mainstream retailers have introduced their own low-price value for money generic brands to compete with the discounters, and furthermore, as the likes of Tesco start to expand into smaller store formats, they are starting to compete with the discounters for appropriate sites. Perhaps the most telling factor, however, is how each retail brand is perceived by the shopper. Mintel (2010b) found that while Tesco is not regarded as being 'fun' or 'inspiring', and is seen as profit-driven, it scores very highly on being 'accessible', 'friendly', efficient' and 'reliable'. Aldi, on the other hand is seen as relatively 'boring', 'unappealing' and 'disappointing' and scores lower than average on efficiency, friendliness and reliability (Leroux, 2011; Mintel, 2010a, 2010b).

**Intertype competition**. Intertype competition refers to competition at the same level in the channel but between different types of outlet. Thus, for example, the battle between the department stores, the High Street electrical retailers and large out-of-town warehouse operations to sell hi-fi equipment to the same customer base is a form of intertype competition. The manufacturer that has a choice may need to develop different approaches to handle each retailer type.

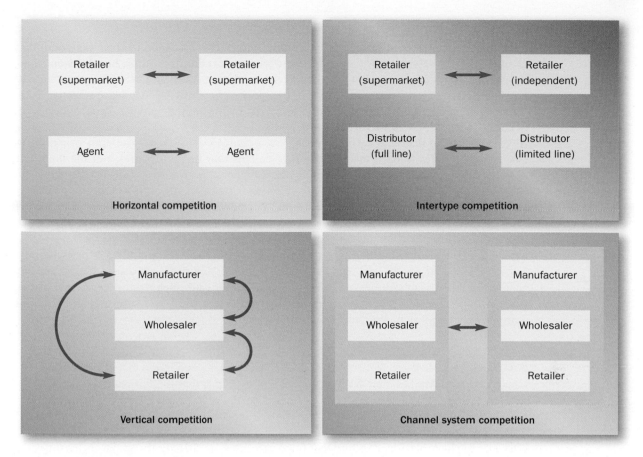

**Figure 8.5** Competition in channels

Of course, there are dangers if a manufacturer is seen to give unwarranted preference to one type over another, given the intense rivalries that can develop. This may start to lead to dysfunctional channel behaviour.

**Vertical competition**. Vertical competition can soon become a serious threat to the integrity and effectiveness of a channel. Here, the competition is between different levels in the channel, such as wholesaler and retailer, or even retailer and manufacturer. This type of competition can soon lead to internal rivalry, where the focus shifts from cooperative market penetration, focused outwards, to mutual cannibalism, focused inwards.

**Channel system competition**. The last form of channel competition is where a particular channel is in competition with different, parallel channels. The focus for the operator, therefore, is on ensuring that its system is more efficient and competitive than the others. The emphasis is on total channel efficiency, which may, however, involve some suboptimisation in the interests of a more effective chain.

*eg*
The car manufacturers operate through competing channel systems, especially where there are exclusive arrangements with dealers. Ford, therefore, wants to make sure that its channel system is functioning better than Renault's or Honda's to create extra value for existing and potential customers. This has implications for all aspects of marketing, including promotion, distribution, customer service, technical support and product development.

## Vertical marketing systems

To minimise the risks of internal competition within the channel and the risks of conflict, channel members, who wish to cooperate and gain the maximum possible benefits from channel membership, may form closely knit vertical marketing systems (VMS). These systems can become highly organised and dominated, to a point where the independence of some of the members disappears into a vertically integrated channel, with one member owning all or some of the other levels. There are three types of VMS.

**Corporate vertical marketing systems**. A corporate VMS exists where an organisation owns and operates other levels in the channel. This may be at any level, and the dominant organisation may be manufacturer, wholesaler or retailer. Forward integration means that the manufacturer owns and operates at the retail or wholesale level. A number of oil companies, for example, own their own petrol stations, while Firestone, the tyre manufacturer, owns its own tyre retailers. Backward integration occurs when the retailer owns and operates at a wholesale or manufacturing level. Retailers such as Zara operate in backwardly integrated markets.

**Contractual vertical marketing systems**. The most prevalent form of VMS is the contractual VMS. Members of the channel retain their independence, but negotiate contractual agreements that specify their rights, duties and obligations, covering issues such as stock levels and pricing policies, for example. This prevents unnecessary internal conflict and sub-optimal behaviour. Three types of contractual system are commonly found.

The corporate VMS has the advantage of creating a channel that is tailormade for the owner's product and marketing objectives. Furthermore, those objectives are shared throughout the channel. The owner also has ultimate control over the activities of the channel and its members. TUI, the German tour operator, operates a VMS so that it can tailor its holiday packages to client needs and ensure that these objectives are shared throughout the channel, as it has the ultimate control of its members' activities. The VMS includes travel agents selling the packages, airlines taking customers to holiday destinations, and the hotels looking after them, all packaged by owned, branded tour operators. In these situations, care must be taken to allay public fears that such close arrangements could restrict customer choice and result in biased advice from travel agents supporting one tour operator at the expense of others.

A retail cooperative exists where groups of retailers agree to work together and to combine and increase their purchasing power by supporting their own wholesaling operation. This sort of agreement helps the small independent retailers who are members of the cooperative with greater range, access to promotion and more competitive pricing.

A wholesaler voluntary chain is one where a wholesaler promotes a contractual relationship with independent retailers, whereby the latter agree to coordinated purchasing, inventory and merchandising programmes. The coordination enables some of the benefits of bulk buying and group promotion to be realised by smaller operators. Mace and the Independent Grocers' Alliance are UK examples.

Franchising is fast becoming a major model of contractual arrangement across Europe. Franchising is an ongoing contractual relationship between a franchisor who owns the product concept and a franchisee who is allowed to operate a business, within an agreed territory, in line with the methods, procedures and overall blueprint provided by the franchisor. Managerial support, training, merchandising and access to finance are effectively exchanged for conformity and a specified fee and/or royalties on sales.

**Administered vertical marketing systems**. Coordination and control are achieved in an administered VMS through the power of one of the channel members. It is, in reality, a conventional channel within which a dominant force has emerged. Therefore, although each member is autonomous, there is a willingness to agree to inter-organisational management by one of its members. Contracts may or may not be used to govern the parameters of behaviour.

Marks & Spencer uses an administered VMS to forge very close links with its suppliers, and to dominate decisions about what is supplied, how it is manufactured, quality levels and pricing. Suppliers accept this dominance because they regard M&S as a prestigious and trustworthy customer, and respect its experience of the market. Similarly, Ahold, the Dutch retailer, offers leadership within its distribution channels in terms of product development, manufacturing and purchasing.

The emergence of these integrated forms of channel system is increasingly questioning the traditional approach to channel management. They also provide a context within which behavioural aspects of channel relationships can be examined.

## Market coverage

One way of thinking about which types of channel are appropriate is to start at the end and work backwards. The sort of questions to ask relate not only to the identity of the end customer, but also to their expectations, demand patterns, frequency of ordering, degree of comparison shopping, degree of convenience and the associated services required. All of these elements influence the added value created by place, and the density and type of intermediaries to be used, whether at wholesaler or distributor or retail level. Market coverage, therefore, is about reaching the end customer as cost effectively and as efficiently as possible, while maximising customer satisfaction. To achieve this, three alternative models of distribution intensity can be adopted, as shown in Table 8.1, each of which reflects different product and customer requirements from place (Stern *et al.*, 1996). They are discussed below, in turn.

**Table 8.1** Alternative distribution intensities: general characteristics

|  | **Intensive** | **Selective** | **Exclusive** |
|---|---|---|---|
| Total number of outlets covered | Maximum | Possibly many | Relatively few |
| Number of outlets per region | As many as possible | A small number | One or very few |
| Distribution focus | Maximum availability | Some specialist retailer knowledge | Close retailer/ consumer relationship |
| Type of consumer product | Convenience | Shopping | Speciality |
| Number of potential purchasers | High | Medium | Low |
| Purchase frequency | Often | Occasionally | Seldom |
| Level of planned purchasing by consumers | Low | Medium | High |
| Typical price | Low | Medium | High |

### Intensive distribution

Intensive distribution occurs where the product or service is placed in as many outlets as possible, and no interested intermediary is barred from stocking the product. Typical products include bread, newspapers and confectionery, but more generally, most convenience goods (see p. 210) fall into this category. The advantage to the consumer is that convenience and availability may be just around the corner, and they can invest a minimum of time and effort in the purchasing process. Using this kind of market coverage also assumes that availability is more important than the type of store selling the product, hence, the growth of non-petrol products for sale in garages.

Intensive distribution usually involves a long chain of distribution (manufacturer–wholesaler–retailer–consumer). It is an efficient means of getting the product as widely available as possible, but total distribution costs may be high, especially where small retailers are concerned and unit orders are low.

## Selective distribution

As the term suggests, a more selective approach is designed to use a small number of carefully chosen outlets within a defined geographic area. These are often found with shopping products (again, see p. 210) where the consumer may be more willing to search for the most appropriate product and then to undertake a detailed comparison of alternatives. Unlike intensively distributed goods, which can virtually be put on a shop shelf to sell themselves, selectively distributed products might need a little more help from the intermediary, perhaps because they have a higher technical content that needs to be demonstrated, for instance. Manufacturers may also need to invest more in the distribution infrastructure, point-of-sale materials and after-sales service. It may thus pay to select a smaller number of intermediaries, where support such as training and joint promotions can be offered and controlled.

The major fine-fragrance manufacturers have long adopted a selective distribution strategy. Their rationale for this is that they are selling a luxury, upmarket product that needs to have an appropriate level of personal selling support and the right kind of retail ambience to reinforce and enhance the product's expensive image. In the early 1990s, they repeatedly refused to supply discount chemist chains, such as Superdrug in the UK, which wanted to undercut the prices charged by upmarket department stores and other existing fragrance retailers. Pressure from Superdrug and other discount retailers which obtained unofficial but perfectly legal supplies from third parties has thus led to a relaxation of the manufacturers' attitudes and to the wider availability of fragrances with a significant focus on price competition from all but the most upmarket retailers.

Selective distribution however, has, become more complex in the internet age. Luxury cosmetics producer Pierre Fabre Dermo-Cosmetique (PFDC) wanted to cultivate an exclusive image by only selling through retail stores and restricting online sales of its products. It argued that the online sales did not meet consumer expectations for dialogue with a pharmacist. However, an advocate-general to the European Court of Justice said that the refusal to allow French distributors to sell the products online was disproportionate and anti-competitive. The key to this is whether the involvement of a pharmacist is deemed essential to the sale of these products. EU regulations in general do not allow suppliers to restrict a distributor's ability to sell its products online, control online resale prices, or restrict the quantites they they are allowed to sell online. They can, however, select distributors or insist that they have one or more 'real' shops on the basis of certain quality standards as long as the intention is not to restrict online sales directly or indirectly. The luxury industry claims that widespread distribution of luxury products online would damage their exclusive image and encourage the market for fake products. Online retailers, however, including Amazon and eBay France, think (for obvious reasons!) that brands should no longer be allowed to insist that online distributors also have a store (Atligan, 2011; Diderich, 2010; Schneibel, 2011).

## Exclusive distribution

Exclusive distribution is the opposite of intensive distribution, and means that only one outlet covers a relatively large geographic area. This type of distribution may reflect very large infrastructure investments, a scattered low density of demand or infrequently purchased products. In B2B markets, the impact on the customer may not be particularly significant if a sales force and customer service network are in place. However, in consumer markets there may be some inconvenience to the customer, who may have to travel some distance to source the product and may effectively have no choice about who to purchase from.

Bang & Olufsen (B&O) has adopted a strategy of working closely with small retailers on a global scale. It has 400 B&O branded stores across the world operated by independent businesses. By adopting a branded store format, it is better able to control how these exclusive dealers display and demonstrate B&O audio-visual equipment. Keeping this level of exclusivity and control is essential, because if stock levels are not maintained and if demos are not available then multibrand hi-fi retailers are prone to 'switch selling', i.e. selling the customer an alternative brand which they *do* have in stock and which *does* have demos available.

B&O's dealers have to be highly motivated and dedicated to B&O. Getting customers to experience a demo is a critical part of the selling process, so the purpose of most of the marketing effort is to encourage potential customers to make an enquiry and become willing to visit a dealer. To this end, the current web strategy is to drive customers to dealers, not to encourage direct sales. The B&O website supports this effort, so that each dealer has a higher quality micro-site designed by B&O and potential customers can book a local demo through the main company website. One such local store, for example, is based in Oxford and its micro-site not only gives the expected information about store location and contact details and generic information about the ranges it stocks, but also shows a photograph of the store and gives profiles of its owner and his staff which gives it a much more friendly, intimate, small business feel. In further acknowledgement of the importance of the link between the consumer and the retailer, once the customer has established that Oxford is their local store, every time they log onto the B&O main website, a hyperlink direct to the Oxford store micro-site features on the homepage (www.bang-olufsen.com).

A Bang & Olufsen shop provides an appropriate ambience for its high-quality merchandise
*Source*: James Kirkikis/Photographers Direct

**Figure 8.6**
Factors
influencing
channel strategy

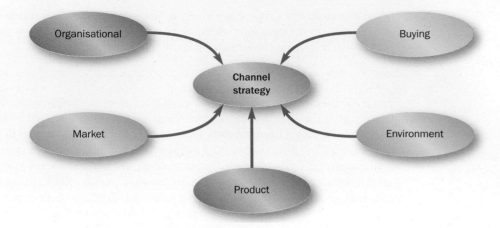

Such an exclusive approach may even fit in with the product's own exclusivity. It would also be appropriate where high degrees of cooperation in inventory management, service standards and selling effort are required between manufacturer and intermediary (Frazier and Lassar, 1996).

## Influences on channel strategy

There are several alternative channel design decisions facing the manufacturer who has a choice, but there are also several factors that may constrain these choices. These factors are outlined below, and are shown in Figure 8.6. While it may be desirable to adopt an optimal design in terms of marketing effectiveness and efficiency, rarely do organisations have the luxury of a clean sheet of paper. More often, they inherit the consequences of previous decisions, and the risks of changing design midstream need to be carefully considered before any planned improvement.

### Organisational objectives, capabilities and resources

The channel strategy selected needs to fit in with the organisation's objectives, capabilities and resources. If the objective is to generate mass appeal and rapid market penetration, then an intensive distribution approach would be necessary. This would have to be supported, however, with an equally intense investment in other marketing activities such as promotion. If the focus was on repositioning upmarket into a more exclusive niche, then a selective or even an exclusive distribution approach would be called for.

Objectives may change over time as environmental circumstances evolve. For example, demands for an improved delivery service or increased geographic coverage may require new distributors, more distributors or incorporating better service levels in the service structure of existing distributors.

Following on from the B&O example on p. 327, its competitor, Linn Hi-Fi, believes that the retailer must take the complexity out of the hi-fi buying decision for the consumer. The retailer has to be able to demonstrate, help design the best system, provide specialist listening facilities and be prepared to install a system. Some are even allowing home trials. But when the customer is potentially spending thousands on a sound system or home cinema set-up, everything has to be right.

## Market size, dispersion and remoteness

No channel strategy decision can ignore the impact of the market. If a manufacturer wishes to penetrate a market some distance from its base, it may lack the contacts, market knowledge or distribution infrastructure to deal directly. There may be little choice but to deal with intermediaries. Similarly, a small organisation might lack the resources necessary for building sales contacts and maintaining customer service, especially if resources are limited and there is a need to develop sales volume quickly.

When demand is more highly concentrated, or where there are a few, readily identifiable customers, it may be possible to build a direct operation, keep full control and eliminate intermediaries. Efficiency may be obtained in negotiation, delivery and support services. By way of contrast, a large, dispersed market, such as that for magazines, may require a well-structured, efficient chain of intermediaries.

## Buying complexity and behaviour

Understanding customer needs and buying criteria goes to the heart of effective marketing and has a major influence on channel selection (Butaney and Wortzel, 1988). Questions such as who buys, where they buy and how frequently they buy all indicate the kind of intermediary best suited to reach target customers. Matching the intermediary with customer needs, buyer expectations and product position is a challenging task. The move to out-of-town shopping, with its advantages of easy parking, convenience and large assortments under one roof, has meant a refocusing of effort by some manufacturers to ensure that they are well represented. Similarly, if a product occupies a specialist position, there is little point in dealing with a wholesaler that is primarily concerned with mass distribution.

## Product characteristics

Products that are complex to purchase, install or operate, products that are of high unit value and products that are customer specific tend to be distributed directly to the customer or through highly specialised intermediaries. This reflects the need for close dialogue during the pre- and post-sale situations that may be lost if additional parties are involved. By way of contrast, fairly standard, routinely purchased, low-unit-value products tend to be distributed intensively through intermediaries.

Other product factors may also have an impact. Highly perishable products need short distribution channels to maintain product quality or to assist in rapid turnover. Items that are

*eg*

McQuillan Engineering Industries (MEI) is a supplier of a wide assortment of components for aircraft interiors, such as overhead bins, galleys, sink units and even nuts and bolts. However, although considerable stocks are held, everything is manufactured to customer designs and specifications, and when demanded they can be assembled on site. Customers include Boeing, Saab and Airbus. With a specialism in batch or prototype production, the distribution and sales method is direct because of the complexity of individual customer orders. This contrasts with replacement parts for domestic electrical equipment, which are standardised by model and are widely stocked either in manufacturers' warehouses or through intermediaries such as repairers.

non-standard or difficult to handle or items that have the potential to create transport problems may be less attractive to intermediaries (Rosenbloom, 1987).

## Changing environment

The changing business environment, discussed in Chapter 2, creates new problems and opportunities for channel design. Three issues demonstrate the effect.

**Technology**. Technology offers the potential for closer integration between the manufacturer and the intermediary. Online systems may enable direct access to stock availability, electronic ordering and automated dispatch with the minimum of negotiation, if any. Electronic point-of-sale (EPOS) data can facilitate very rapid responses within the distribution system. Smaller organisations still relying on older technology, such as the telephone and manual checking, may soon become marginalised.

**Working patterns**. The growth in the number of women working has had a profound effect on some distribution channels, making some channels more difficult to operate, such as door-to-door selling during the daytime, while home shopping, online shopping and convenience shopping outside usual trading hours have become much more widely accepted.

**European Union regulations**. Generally speaking, manufacturers have the right to decide which intermediaries should or should not distribute their products. Both national and European regulatory bodies start to become interested, however, where exclusion of certain intermediaries might be seen as a deliberate attempt to distort competition or to achieve price fixing.

# Selecting a channel member

The final phase of the channel design strategy is the selection of specific intermediaries. The selection decision tends to become more critical as the intensity of distribution itself becomes more selective or exclusive. In mass distribution decisions, such as those concerning products like confectionery, any willing outlet will be considered. However, where a selective distribution approach is adopted, great care must be taken over the final selection of intermediary, as a poor decision may lead to strategic failure. For example, the selection of a wholesaler to allow entry into a new European market may be critical to the degree and speed of penetration achieved.

Klemm is part of the Bauer group and specialises in a range of German-built hydraulic rigs and drilling accessories for construction sites. Its channel approach is often to appoint sole distributors in target countries. Thus in the UK, Skelair handles all sales, while in the Netherlands, Dutch Drilling Consultants v.o.f. has exclusive rights. Klemm seeks to develop a close and effective relationship with its distributors. Although individual domestic markets may be relatively small, the selling task is complex in defining machines for applications, and good after-sales service is also crucial. This demands close technical support and a level of trust and confidence between manufacturer and distributor (www.klemm-bt.com).

In situations where organisations need to select intermediaries on a fairly frequent basis, it would be useful to select on the basis of predetermined criteria. Table 8.2 highlights a range of issues that should be examined as part of an appraisal process.

The relative importance of the various criteria will vary from sector to sector and indeed over time. Inevitably, there is still a need for management judgement and a trading off of pros and cons, as the 'ideal' distributor that is both willing and able to proceed will rarely be found. Remember too that intermediaries have the choice of whether or not they will sell the products offered. This luxury of choice is not restricted just to supermarkets and large multiple retailers.

Travel agents can stock only a limited number of holidays, and are very careful about offering new packages from smaller tour operators. In some industrial distribution channels, the intermediary can decide whether or not to stock ancillary products around the main products that it sells on a dealership basis.

**Table 8.2** Selection criteria for intermediaries

| Strategic | Operational |
| --- | --- |
| ■ Expansion plans | ■ Local market knowledge |
| ■ Resource building | ■ Adequate premises/equipment |
| ■ Management quality/competence | ■ Stockholding policy |
| ■ Market coverage | ■ Customer convenience |
| ■ Partnership willingness | ■ Product knowledge |
| ■ Loyalty/cooperation | ■ Realistic credit/payment terms |
| | ■ Sales force capability |
| | ■ Efficient customer service |

# Conflict and cooperation

Most of this chapter so far has concentrated largely on economic issues involved in channel decisions. However, all channel decisions are ultimately made between people in organisations. There is, therefore, always the potential for disagreement over the many decisions such as expected roles, allocation of effort, reward structures, product and marketing strategies that ensure the system operates effectively. A channel is an interorganisational social system comprising members who are tied together by a belief that by working together (for the time being at least), they can improve the individual benefits gained. A climate of cooperation is perhaps the most desirable within a channel system. It does not just happen, but needs to be worked on and cultivated.

Good communication, in terms of amount, direction, medium and content, is also essential for closer cooperation in a channel (Mohr and Nevin, 1990). In a study of computer dealers, Mohr *et al.* (1999) found that effective communication led to greater satisfaction, stronger commitment and better coordination. The development of electronic sharing of data and intelligence is strengthening many channel relationships as technology helps all members to make better decisions in times of market uncertainty as well as reducing selling and coordination costs (Huber, 1990).

Some view conflict and cooperation as being at opposite ends of a continuum, while others view them as distinct concepts. Whatever the view, strong cooperation can lead to a feeling of satisfaction and partnership, one of give and take. Cooperation may lead to strong personal and organisational ties that are difficult for outsiders to break. However, not all cooperation need be voluntary. A weaker channel member may think it best to cooperate and comply with the wishes of a more powerful member, rather than risk retribution.

Conflict is a natural part of any social system. Conflict may exist where, for example, one channel member feels that another member is not dealing fairly with it, or that the system is not working sufficiently in its favour. There are numerous possible causes of conflict, some arising from poor understanding, others from a fundamental difference of opinion that goes to the heart of the relationship.

Conflict needs to be spotted early and dealt with before it becomes too overt. This can be helped by regular meetings, frequent communication and ensuring that all parties emerge satisfied from negotiations. It is critical that each channel member should fully understand their role and what is expected of them, and that this is agreed in advance. If conflict does become overt, communication, formation of channel committees, a fast arbitration service and top management commitment to resolution are all essential to prevent an irrevocable breakdown of the channel.

With the development of their own websites, manufacturers in some sectors risk antagonising the retailers who also distribute their goods. If manufacturers develop online stores, the risk becomes greater as effectively it opens up another channel of distribution direct from the manufacturer to the end customer. This is a great source of channel conflict. Shopatron offers a partial solution with its 'Coex Freedom Order Exchange' service. It has around 1,000 brand manufacturers and 12,000 retail partners across 35 industries. Customers place orders via the manufacturer's website and then the Coex system assigns the order to one of the participating retailers, based on geographic proximity to the customer, and routes the order through to it. The buyer can then have same day pick-up of the goods or have them shipped by the retailer within 24 hours. This keeps both manufacturers and retailers happy. Shopatron's view is that this system 'allows brands to integrate eCommerce into their website, connecting directly to customers without taking sales away from retail and distribution partners' (www.ecommerce.shopatron.com).

The service started in the USA but has now expanded to Europe. In the UK, for example, the cycle company, Specialized, has adopted a 'click and collect' service facilitated by Shopatron so that shoppers can buy Specialized or Globe bicycles online and then collect them from regional Specialized Concept Stores. Also involving two-wheeled transport, albeit somewhat more powerful than the bicycle, Kawasaki Motors UK has also launched a Shopatron-based online store for selling Kawasaki branded clothing and merchandise. Again, orders will be placed and then fulfilled by Kawasaki dealerships. Kawasaki said, 'We wanted a way for our Kawasaki brand fans to easily find and purchase our products online while not losing the connection to their local dealer . . . The local dealer is an essential component in our superior customer experience, and this Shopatron initiative allows us to include them seamlessly in every sale – including offering a delivery or collection service to suit our customers' individual needs' (as quoted by *PR Newswire Europe*, 2011a). (Birchall, 2008; *PR Newswire Europe*, 2011a, 2011b; www.ecommerce.shopatron.com)

# Chapter summary

- The channel of distribution is the means through which products are moved from the manufacturer to the end consumer. The structure of channels can vary considerably depending on the type of market, the needs of the end customer and the type of product. Consumer goods might be supplied direct, but in mass markets for convenience goods this might not be feasible and longer channels might be used. B2B markets are far more likely to involve direct supply from manufacturer to B2B buyer. Some B2B purchases, however, particularly routine repurchases of non-critical items such as office stationery, might be distributed in ways that are similar to those used in consumer markets, with various intermediaries involved.

- Intermediaries play an important role in increasing efficiency and reducing costs, reduce the manufacturer's risk, gather, store, sort and transport a wide range of goods, and ease cash flow for manufacturers and for customers. These functions are not all necessarily performed by the same member of the distribution channel and the decision as to who does what may be made by consensus or by the use of power in the channel. Distributors, agents and wholesalers tend to act as intermediaries in B2B markets or as an interface between manufacturers and retailers. Retailers tend to serve the needs of individual consumers and can be classified according to a number of criteria: form of ownership (independents, corporate chains or contractual systems), level of service (full or limited), merchandise lines (breadth and depth) and operating methods (type of store, whether department store, supermarket, variety store or other). Non-store retailing, closely linked with direct marketing, has also become increasingly popular and widespread. It includes in-home selling, parties, mail-order operations, teleshopping and vending machines.

● Channel design will be influenced by a number of factors, including organisational objectives, capabilities and resources. Market size might also constrain the choice of channel, as might the buying complexity associated with the product and the buying behaviour of the target market. The changing environment can also influence the choice of channel. Selecting specific intermediaries to join a channel can be difficult but this choice can be a critical success factor since, for example, the speed of entry and the degree of penetration into a new market can depend on the right choice of intermediary. Sometimes, however, the intermediary has the power to reject a manufacturer or a specific product. Vertical marketing systems (VMS) have evolved to create a channel that is more efficient and effective for all parties, ideally working towards the common good in a long-term relationship. Clearly, voluntary cooperation is the best way of achieving an effective and efficient channel. However, conflict might arise and, if it is not dealt with promptly and sensitively, might lead, sooner or later, to the dissolution of that channel.

● Manufacturers are not restricted to using only one channel. There are three broad levels of intensity of distribution, each implying a different set of channels and different types of intermediary: intensive distribution, selective distribution and exclusive distribution.

# Questions for review and discussion

**8.1** What are the different types of *intermediary* that might be found in a distribution channel?

**8.2** What are the five factors influencing *channel strategy*?

**8.3** To what extent and why do you think that the creation of a VMS can improve the performance of a channel and its members?

**8.4** What kind of market coverage strategy might be appropriate for the following, and why:

(a) a bar of chocolate;

(b) a toothbrush;

(c) a home computer;

(d) a marketing textbook.

**8.5** Using Table 8.2 on p. 331 as a starting point, develop lists of criteria that a manufacturer might use in defining:

(a) 'good' retailers; and

(b) 'good' wholesalers to recruit for consumer market channels.

**8.6** In what ways and to what extent do you think that non-store retailing poses a threat to conventional retailers?

# STROLLING DOWN THE VIRTUAL AISLES

Not every shopper enjoys the 'fun' of shopping, especially when it involves a trip to the supermarket. It is this group (people who cannot or prefer not to visit the supermarket but who must buy) that is the target of online grocery-delivery services. It is a growing sector. According to the IGD (2011c), 3.2 per cent of all UK grocery shopping is online, and this is forecast to rise to 5.4 per cent by 2015. In 2010 we spent £4.8 billion online with grocery retailers (although that includes large non-grocery items sold through Tesco Direct, for example), and by 2015 that will be very close to £10 billion.

The reasons why home shopping should be popular are clear: increasingly busy lives with extended working hours; the increasing number of people at work, especially women; the feeling that people have better things to do with their free time such as 'real' leisure pursuits; and growing acceptance of home delivery in a range of sectors such as books, pizza, flowers, etc. All of this, combined with the increasing use of the internet, sets the scene for significant growth in home grocery shopping. The IGD's (2011b) research suggests that the people most likely to buy groceries online are typically younger, and the presence of children in a household has a lot to do with it; those families with younger infants or with kids at home during the school holidays are more likely to do online grocery shopping. Mintel's (2010b) research found that in 2009, just 7 per cent claim to be using online food retailers/supermarkets 'regularly' and a further 17 per cent use them 'occasionally'.

The competition doesn't just come from established grocery retail chains. In 2010, Amazon, already well-respected as an online retailer of non-food items, introduced grocery items into its mix. Grocery industry analysts and competitors weren't too impressed. One criticism is that it doesn't offer the same convenience and level of service as the mainstream online grocery retailers. As one analyst put it, 'In terms of food shopping, when you compare the website to other online offers, it is not functional at all. They are not offering a time slot for their deliveries, which is ridiculous as many consumers will not want to put up with that' (as quoted by *The Grocer*, 2010). In addition, some goods are supplied from Amazon, and others come directly

from suppliers, so potentially for one order, the shopper could be receiving a number of different deliveries on different days. This also raises the issue of delivery charges. The good news is that goods supplied from Amazon itself can qualify for free delivery, but those that come direct from the supplier carry the supplier's own delivery charge. This can lead to some bizarre anomalies. A bulk pack of 164 Pampers nappies can be delivered free, but 200 g of root ginger (retailing at 80p) costs £7.85 to deliver, while a 200g pack of Thai Kale (retailing at £3.99) costs £1.13 in delivery. Some savings could be made by buying multiple items from the same supplier, but looking at the page displaying all the choices within each category, it isn't always obvious who the supplier is, and on the whole, none of this is very customer-friendly. Where the Amazon grocery store might have more appeal is in the ranges of foreign brands and ingredients that are less easy to find in the UK.

By far the dominant force in online grocery retailing, however, is Tesco. Its annual online grocery sales are around £2 billion and in January 2011 alone, it generated nearly 7 million unique visitors, making it the fourth most visited retail website in the UK behind Amazon, Argos and Apple (ComScore, 2011). Overall, Tesco has more than three times as many unique users as Sainsbury's. It has 1.2 million online grocery shoppers and handles an average of 350,000 transactions per week. Sainsbury's, in contrast, handles around 130,000.

You don't have to have a major retail name to be a successful player in the online grocery market. Ocado, which began in 2002, entered early on into a partnership with Waitrose which at that time didn't have its own home delivery service. Since then, Ocado has become synonymous in many consumers' minds with Waitrose as they assume that it's 'the same thing' even though it's independent. Now, however, Waitrose is investing heavily in its own online service and a ten-year agreement not to compete with Ocado within the M25 area has come to an end. To help differentiate itself from Waitrose, Ocado has entered into an agreement with French supermarket chain Carrefour to distribute its Reflets de France range, and has increased its own brand range to 350 items.

Ocado is not without its problems, however. In fulfilling an average of 108,000 orders per week, it has been operating from an automated warehouse in Hertfordshire which is stretched to full capacity. The strain on this facility meant that Ocado's ability to fulfil orders accurately and to deliver on time slipped slightly, and constrained Ocado's ability to expand its customer base. Another problem with this degree of centralisation is that transport costs are high: Ocado is delivering to customers up to 150 miles away. This is mitigated to some extent by having delivery vans with detachable bodies. Customers orders can be made up and packed into a van body, and then batches of van bodies are delivered on a larger lorry to one of six regional hubs to be attached to a smaller delivery van just for the last leg of the journey. To reduce some of these operational costs and as a means of overcoming the capacity constraints in Hertfordshire, Ocado is extending and improving systems at Hertfordshire, and in addition to that, has opened/plans to open a number of other distribution warehouses, for example in Warwickshire, Wimbledon, Bristol and Oxford.

In contrast, Tesco's online shopping service has always fulfilled orders from normal stores within five to 10 miles of the customer ('store picking'). However, in areas where the sales volumes are high enough to justify it, Tesco has started to open 'dark stores' i.e. stores that are not open to the general public, but exist to fulfil online orders and will deliver to customers up to 50 miles away. By 2015, Tesco should have 15 of these stores and effectively, Tesco is moving slowly towards a warehouse model. As at 2011, Asda has two dark stores but otherwise, operates on a store picking model, as do Sainsbury's and Waitrose.

Shukri (2010) sees a lot of reasons why the future looks good for online grocery shopping. First, there's the improvements that the retailers have made in operations and customer service, with improved delivery coverage, tighter delivery slots and better processes for order fulfilment (Amazon take note!). This is important, as a survey undertaken by IGD (2009) suggests that reliable delivery, obtaining suitable delivery slots and ease of navigation and setting up orders is more important to online shoppers than price. The retailers are also giving the customer maximum flexibility by introducing 'click and collect' style services, whereby orders can be made online and then picked up from the store at the customer's convenience. Another interesting factor is the growth of *s-commerce*, i.e. the integration of social networking and interactive online magazines as a means of maintaining contact with customers and delivering promotions to them. Waitrose, for example, has invested in 'automated content personalisation' which means that each user gets a tailored version of the Waitrose online magazine and website content based on their previous behaviour. As an example of using social media, Tesco's Facebook fans are offered the opportunity to download and print money-off coupons for specific brands. Asda's view is that 'It's about finding new ways to talk to the customer and share our message . . . Digital is a great way of talking to all these customers and letting them talk to us, whether on Twitter or by composing a video on YouTube. Right to reply is really important' (as quoted by *New Media Age*, 2009).

Then there's *m-commerce*. The UK has the highest penetration of smartphones in Europe and the grocery multiples are exploring the potential. While some are experimenting with apps as a means of delivering promotions and information, Tesco became the first in 2010 to launch a transactional smartphone app. Tesco's view is that, 'We believe phones will be crucial to multichannel and we launched a few apps that include the scanning of products to add items to shopping lists and we've seen a significant number of transactions – between 30 per cent and 50 per cent – on our dotcom [home delivery service] that have been scanned' (as quoted by *Just-Food*, 2011a). Tesco has gone even further in Seoul, South Korea by creating virtual stores in subway stations. The walls of the station display pictures of products, presented as though on a supermarket shelf, with QR codes that can be scanned by a mobile phone. Shoppers can thus place an order while they are on their way to work and take delivery of them at home in the evening. This system was trialled for three months and according to Tesco, over that period the number of people registered for online shopping increased by 76 per cent and the number of transactions rose by 130 per cent.

Another big idea that Tesco is working on is 'visual searching'. Tesco's head of R&D, interviewed by Creasey (2011) said:

> . . . if your brain can identify objects in a scene when you look around, then so should a search engine. Point your phone's camera at a bunch of carrots and it should just 'know' it is looking at carrots. Point the camera at your kitchen sink and it might suggest Tesco products that could clean it! My quest is, in R&D, to make visual searching that can easily be used by Tesco shoppers.

So . . . wow . . . where does all this leave us? It seems to leave the shopper with nowhere to hide and no excuse for forgetting anything. As people increasingly start to manage their lives digitally and through their smartphones, they are going to be presented with more and more temptations to throw things into their virtual shopping baskets. We no longer have to remember that we have run out of toothpaste or write it down on a scrappy bit of paper that we lose long before we get to the store: we can just scan it with our phones and it's there in the basket, or its already on our virtual shopping list as a regular purchase. While it must be remembered that penetration of online shopping is still quite low, as its functionality improves and as it starts to integrate better with the whole range of digital media, it's surely going to encourage more of us to abandon the trolleys.

*Sources*: Baker (2011); ComScore (2011); Creasey (2011); Felsted (2011); *The Grocer* (2010); IGD (2009; 2011a; 2011b; 2011c); *Just-Food* (2011a; 2011b; 2011c); Mintel (2010b, 2011b); *New Media Age* (2009; 2011); Shukri (2010); Thompson (2011); www.amazon.co.uk.

## Questions

1 What are the advantages and disadvantages of store picking compared with an Ocado-style centralised distribution warehouse model for order fulfilment?

2 What do you think Tesco can gain from the development of dark stores?

3 Why do you think online shopping still accounts for such a relatively low proportion of total grocery sales? What role can m-commerce or s-commerce play in its further development?

4 Develop a short presentation to the senior management of Amazon analysing its current online grocery provision and making justified recommendations for improvement.

## References for chapter 8

Atligan, O. (2011) 'European Commission's New Vertical Restraints Block Exemption Regulation and Its Impacts on Internet Sales in the EU and Turkey', *Mondaq Business Briefing*, 11 January.

Baker, R. (2011) 'Ocado Partners with French Supermarket Carrefour', *Marketing Week*, 27 June.

Baksi, C. (2011) 'QualitySolicitors in WHSmith Tie-up', *Law Gazette*, 7 April.

Barker, M. (2009a) 'Capespan Cautious as it Delivers Best-ever Profits', *The Grocer*, 11 April.

Barker, M. (2009b) 'Purchase of Salads To Go Boosts Clout of Florette's Soleco UK', *The Grocer*, 16 May.

Barrett, C. (2011) 'Thorntons to Melt UK Estate', *Financial Times*, 29 June.

Bawden, T. (2011) 'Economy of Scales', *The Guardian*, 9 July.

Best, D. (2010) 'Carrefour to Enter Inner Mongolia', *Just-Food*, 22 January.

Birchall, J. (2008) 'How to Cut in the Middleman', *Financial Times*, 12 March.

*Birmingham Mail* (2011) 'Pets Firm Plea for Charities', *Birmingham Mail*, 4 August.

BMI Industry Insights (2011) 'Company News Alert – Emerging Markets Coming into Greater Focus for Tesco', *BMI Industry Insights – Food & Drink Asia*, 25 July.

Braithwaite, T. and Killgren, L. (2007) 'Argos Leads Home Retail Higher', *Financial Times*, 25 October.

Business Monitor International (2011) 'Market Overview – China – Q4 2011', *Business Monitor International Country Reports*, 28 July.

Butaney, G. and Wortzel, L. (1988) 'Distribution Power Versus Manufacturer Power: the Customer Role', *Journal of Marketing*, 52 (January), pp. 52–63.

Chesters, L. (2011) 'H&M to Bring New Labels to London', *Independent on Sunday*, 7 August.

Clark, A. (2011) 'Thorntons: Why the Chocolate-maker Has Gone into Meltdown', *The Observer*, 8 May.

ComScore (2011) 'Retail Websites Now Reach 75 Percent of European Internet Audience Each Month', press release issued by ComScore Inc., 21 March, accessed via http://www.comscore.com/Press_Events/ Press_Releases/2011/3/Retail_Websites_Now_Reach_75_ Percent_of_European_Internet_Audience_Each_Month.

Creasey, S. (2011) 'Untangling Tesco', *The Grocer*, 14 May.

Davidson, A. (2009) 'Young Master of the Flat-pack', *Sunday Times*, 1 November.

Diderich, J. (2010) 'Luxe Groups, E-tailers Approve of EU Rules', *Women's Wear Daily*, 21 April.

Economist Intelligence Unit (2011) 'Retail in China: All Eyes on Chinese Aisles', *Economist Intelligence Unit – Executive Briefing*, 26 May.

Felsted. A. (2011a) 'Concerns about Capacity Deliver Little to Celebrate', *Financial Times*, 28 June.

Felsted, A. (2011b) 'Waitrose Ready to Flex its Competitive Muscle', *Financial Times*, 2 July.

Frazier, G. (1999) 'Organizing and Managing Channels of Distribution', *Journal of the Academy of Marketing Science*, 27 (2), pp. 226–40.

Frazier, G. and Lassar, W. (1996) 'Determinants of Distribution Intensity', *Journal of Marketing*, 60 (October), pp. 39–51.

Goldfingle, G. (2011) 'Responsible Retailing – Why Fast Fashion Can Be Eco-fashion', *Retail Week*, 6 May.

Golding, A. (2009) 'The Lure of the Country', *Marketing*, 25 November.

Gray, L. (2010) 'Post Office Shift Online "Could Alienate Millions"', *Daily Telegraph*, 22 November.

*The Grocer* (2010) 'Amazon UK Grocery Debut is "Ridiculous"', *The Grocer*, 10 July.

*The Grocer* (2011) 'Sugro Angers Suppliers with New Website', *The Grocer*, 2 April.

Hall, J. (2011) 'Morrisons Opens Smaller Stores', *Daily Telegraph*, 9 July.

Hansegard, J. (2011) 'Early Frugal Nature Guides Today's IKEA Innovations', *Wall Street Journal Europe*, 4 July.

Harrison, N. (2011) 'WH Smith to Launch Funky Pigeon Stores', *Retail Week*, 21 April

Hogarth-Scott, S. and Parkinson, S. (1994) 'The New Food Discounters: Are They a Threat to the Major Multiples?', *International Journal of Retail and Distribution Management*, 22(1), pp. 20–8.

Howe, W. (1992) *Retailing Management*, Macmillan.

Huber, G. (1990) 'A Theory of the Effects of Advanced Information Technologies on Organizational Design, Intelligence, and Decision Making', *Academy of Management Review*, 15 (1), pp. 47–72.

IGD (2009) 'Online Shopping 2009', IGD, 11 December, accessed via www.igd.org.uk.

IGD (2010) 'Convenience Retailing Market Overview', IGD, 18 November, accessed via www.igd.org.uk.

IGD (2011a) 'Online Grocery Retailing', IGD, 8 March, accessed via www.igd.org.uk.

IGD (2011b) 'Online Grocery Shopping', IGD, 6 April, accessed via www.igd.org.uk.

IGD (2011c) 'Online and Private Label: Three Trends to Watch', IGD, 12 July, accessed via www.igd.org.uk.

IGD (2011d) *Convenience Retailing 2011: Forces Behind a Changing Landscape*, IGD, accessed via www.igd.org.uk.

*Industry Updates* (2011) 'Carrefour Likely to Close Another Two Outlets', *Industry Updates*, 16 February.

*Just-Food* (2011a) 'Online Food Retail – Innovation in Technology', *Just-Food*, 27 July.

*Just-Food* (2011b) 'Online Food Retail – the Key Operating Models', *Just-Food*, 27 July.

*Just-Food* (2011c) 'Online Food Retail – Case Studies from Tesco to Migros', *Just-Food*, 27 July.

Leng, S. (2011) 'Big Money: Is China's Hypermarket IPO Worth the Hype?', *The Edge Malaysia*, 18 July.

Leroux, M. (2011) 'Morrisons Gains Edge in Supermarket War' *The Times*, 19 July.

*Lloyd's List* (2007) 'A Fresh New Idea at Sheerness to Reduce Supply Chain Miles', *Lloyd's List*, 23 July.

*M2 Presswire* (2010) 'Pets at Home Extend Multi-channel Capability with the Addition of Click and Collect', *M2 Presswire*, 3 November.

MacDonald, G. (2010) 'Workplace Stores: Can Workers Provide a Big Break for WHSmith?', *Retail Week*, 29 October.

Marian, P. (2011) 'Talking Shop: Wal-Mart Bets on China's Online Growth with Yihaodian', *Just-Food*, 21 May.

*Marketing* (2011) 'H&M Enters Partnership with David Beckham', *Marketing*, 3 August.

Mintel (2009) 'Salad and Salad Dressings', *Mintel Market Intelligence*, August, accessed via http://academic.mintel.com/sinatra/oxygen_academic/search_results/show&/display/id=394588/display/id=475638?select_section=394588.

Mintel (2010a) 'Discounters UK', *Mintel Market Intelligence*, August, accessed via http://academic.mintel.com/sinatra/oxygen_academic/search_results/show&/display/id=479963/display/id=479963/display/id=479963/display/id=554918/display/id=541428&anchor=atom2?select_section=479823.

Mintel (2010b) 'Food Retailing', *Mintel Retail Intelligence*, November, accessed via http://academic.mintel.com/sinatra/oxygen_academic/search_results/show&/display/id=479963/display/id=554915?select_section=479963.

Mintel (2011a) 'Pet Food and Supplies', *Mintel Market Intelligence*, March, accessed via http://academic.mintel.com/sinatra/oxygen_academic/search_results/show&/display/id=545248/display/id=570704?select_section=545248.

Mintel (2011b) 'Digital Trends Summer', Mintel Retail Intelligence, July, accessed via http://academic.mintel.com/sinatra/oxygen_academic/search_results/show&/display/id=545146/display/id=586513?select_section=545146.

Mohr, J., Fisher, R. and Nevin, J. (1999) 'Communicating for Better Channel Relationships', *Marketing Management*, 8 (2), pp. 38–45.

Mohr, J. and Nevin, J. (1990) 'Communication Strategies in Marketing Channels: a Theoretical Perspective', *Journal of Marketing*, 54 (October), pp. 36–51.

*New Media Age* (2009) 'Delivering the Goods', *New Media Age*, 28 May.

*New Media Age* (2010) 'Pets at Home Appoints Web Agency AWA to Raise Customer Loyalty Online', *New Media Age*, 18 March.

*New Media Age* (2011) 'Waitrose Serves Personal Content', *New Media Age*, 2 June.

Paché, G. (1998) 'Logistics Outsourcing in Grocery Distribution: a European Perspective', *Logistics Information Management*, 11 (5), pp. 301–8.

Palamountain, J. (1955) *The Politics of Distribution*, Harvard University Press.

Phillips, B. (2010) 'Sugro Starts Buying Group to Support Smaller Wholesalers', *The Grocer*, 18 December.

Plunkett Foundation (2011) *Community-owned Village Shops: A Better Form of Business*, The Plunkett Foundation, January, accessed via www.plunkett.co.uk.

*PR Newswire Europe* (2011a) 'Kawasaki Motors Teams Up With Shopatron to Create Online Store in UK', *PR Newswire Europe*, 3 March.

*PR Newswire Europe* (2011b) 'Specialized Unveils Shopatron-Powered Click & Collect Service for Concept Stores', *PR Newswire Europe*, 11 May.

*Relaxnews International* (2011) 'Tesco Steps up Battle for Attention of Chinese Retail Consumers', *Relaxnews International*, 19 July.

Rosenbloom, B. (1987) *Marketing Channels: A Management View*, Dryden.

*Rural Retailer* (2011) 'Real Ales and Snoggable Garlic', *Rural Retailer*, Issue 13, Spring.

Schneibel, G. (2011) 'Brands May be Forced to Allow EU Online Sales', *Deutsche Welle*, 4 March.

*Shanghai Daily* (2011) 'Rush is on to Build Online Retail Empire', *Shanghai Daily*, 20 July.

Sharma, A. and Dominguez, L. (1992) 'Channel Evolution: a Framework for Analysis', *Journal of the Academy of Marketing Science*, 20 (Winter), pp. 1–16.

Shukri, D. (2010) 'The Rise of Online Grocery Retailing', IGD, 9 December, accessed via www.igd.org.uk.

Stephens, L. (2011) 'Local Shops for Local People', *The Independent*, 14 July.

Stern, L., El-Ansary, A. and Coughlan, A. (1996) *Marketing Channels*, 5th edn. Prentice Hall.

Stodell, H. (2011) Can Thorntons Perk Itself Up with a Shot of Caffé Culture?', *The Grocer*, 2 July.

*Thai News Service* (2011) 'China: Tesco, Gome Enter Strategic Cooperation', *Thai News Service*, 7 July.

Thomas, S. (2011) 'Value Farming', *Financial Mail*, 22 July.

Thompson, J. (2011) 'Ocado Still Delivers Food for Thought', *The Independent*, 26 July.

Thorntons (2011) 'Thorntons: Strategy Review Presentation', 28 June, accessed via http://investors.thorntons.co.uk/download/pdf/Strategy_Review_Final280611.pdf.

van Gass, C. (2008) 'Capespan Takes Top Honours', *All Africa*, 4 November.

Ward, A. (2011) 'H&M Brushes Off Performance Concerns to Look Long Term', *Financial Times*, 23 June.

Webster, F. (1979) *Industrial Marketing Strategy*, John Wiley & Sons.

Wembridge, M. (2011) 'Thorntons Sales Continue to Fall on High Street', *Financial Times*, 13 July.

# CHAPTER 9

# Promotion: integrated marketing communication

## LEARNING OBJECTIVES

This chapter will help you to:

- understand the importance of planned, integrated communication in a marketing context;
- appreciate the variety and scope of marketing communication objectives;
- explain the use of promotional tools in the communication process;
- identify the factors and constraints influencing the mix of communications tools that an organisation uses; and
- define the main methods by which communications budgets are set.

## INTRODUCTION

**THE PROMOTIONAL MIX IS** the direct way in which an organisation attempts to communicate with various target audiences. It consists of five main elements, as shown in Figure 9.1. Advertising represents non-personal, mass communication; personal selling is at the other extreme, covering face-to-face, personally tailored messages. Sales promotion involves tactical, short-term incentives that encourage a target audience to behave in a certain way. Public relations is about creating and maintaining good-quality relationships with many interested groups (for example, the media, shareholders and trade unions), not just with customers. Finally, direct marketing involves creating one-to-one relationships with individual customers, often in mass markets, and might involve mailings, telephone selling or digital marketing techniques such as e-mail, social media or viral marketing for instance. Some might classify direct marketing activities as forms of advertising, sales promotion or even personal selling, but this text treats direct and digital marketing as a separate element of the promotional mix while acknowledging that it 'borrows' from the other elements.

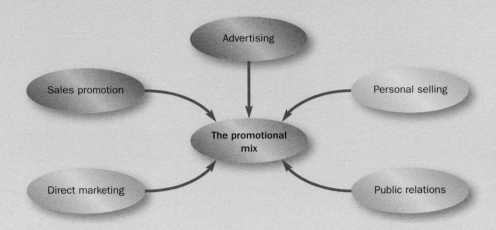

**Figure 9.1**
The elements of
the promotional
mix

Ideally, the marketer would like to invest extensively in every element of the mix. In a world of finite resources, however, choices have to be made about which activities are going to work together most cost-effectively with the maximum synergy to achieve the communications objectives of the organisation within a defined budget. Budgets obviously vary widely between different organisations, and depending on the type of product involved and the communications task in hand.

This chapter, along with the three that follow it, will aim to explain why such choices are made.

**eg** British Airways (BA) uses the full range of media to communicate with and build relationships with customers. Advertising; loyalty cards; direct mail; news letters; telephone and personal sales; public relations; and social media are all part of the promotional mix employed. It has also now added an online capability through its website which enables enquiries and bookings to be made, and this has also meant a thorough re-examination of hits to its own BA website and the click through from other sites. It has widened the boundaries of campaign integration and highlighted the need to ensure a close fit between all elements of the promotional mix to ensure sufficient leverage in the marketplace.

Bigmouthmedia handles the search engine account for BA to help it develop and maintain its digital marketing strategy. It worked on the content pages to create a lot of destination-specific information. Thus if you type in 'flights to Johannesburg', for example, you get a whole lot of information on the destination such as shopping trips, hotels and bars, not just flight information. This information can also be reached from BA banner advertising on other sites, not just direct clicks from search engine sites such as Google. It is important that many keywords link through to the BA site to help drive bookings. The pages through which the visitor enters the BA site are called landing pages.

If you type in 'flights to New York' on Google, the BA site comes high up on the results list, alongside other airlines and specialist flight agents. Destinations are categorised into one of three tiers according to their popularity and seat availability. If a route is likely to sell out it is automatically placed in the low-priority tier 3, which means that BA will appear in a lower position within the search results. Similarly, a search for a less popular, slow-selling destination will put BA higher up the results list. The campaign is thus driven strategically and tactically in real time using up-to-date reports, and has led to a 3 per cent increase in traffic to the BA website (www.ba.com; www.bigmouthmedia.com).

This chapter provides a general strategic overview by focusing on the integrated marketing communications planning process. Pickton and Broderick (2005, p. 26) define integrated marketing communication as:

> . . . a process which involves the management and organisation of all 'agents' in the analysis, planning, implementation and control of all marketing communications contacts, media, messages and promotional tools focused at selected target audiences in such a way as to derive the greatest enhancement and coherence of marketing communications effort in achieving predetermined product and corporate marketing communications objectives. In its simplest form, IMC can be defined as the management process of integrating all marketing communications activities across relevant audience points to achieve greater brand coherence.

This definition emphasises the need to plan and manage the integrated marketing communications function carefully and strategically within the market context and using the full range of communications tools effectively and efficiently. This chapter, therefore, looks at some of the influences that shape an appropriate blend within the promotional mix, allowing the marketer to allocate communication resources most effectively.

The main focus of the chapter is on developing a planning framework within which managerial decisions on communication activity can be made. Each stage in the planning flow is discussed in turn, with particular emphasis being given to relevant issues and the kind of integrated promotional mix that might subsequently be appropriate. It is becoming increasingly important for organisations to design and implement effective integrated marketing communications strategies as they expand their interests beyond their known domestic markets.

## Communications planning model

Figure 9.2, adapted from Rothschild's (1987) communications decision sequence framework, includes all the main elements of marketing communications decision-making. Given the complexity of communication and the immense possibilities for getting some element of it wrong, a thorough and systematic planning process is crucial for minimising the risks. No organisation can afford either the financial or the reputational damage caused by poorly planned or implemented communications campaigns.

Each element and its implications for the balancing of the promotional mix will now be defined and analysed in turn. The first element is the situation analysis, which has been split into three subsections: the target market, the product and the environment. Bear in mind, however, that in reality it is difficult to 'pigeon hole' things quite so neatly as this might imply, and there will, therefore, be a lot of cross-referencing.

**Figure 9.2**
The communications planning flow

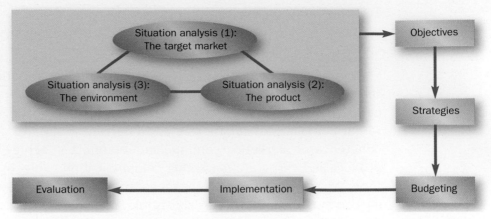

Source: Michael L. Rothschild, *Marketing Communications: from Fundamentals to Strategies*. Copyright © 1987 South-Western, a part of Cengage Learning, Inc., reproduced by permission, www.cengage.com/permissions

# Situation analysis (1): the target market

## B2B or consumer market

The target market decision most likely to have an impact on the balancing of the overall promotional mix is whether the market is a consumer market or a B2B market. Recalling the comparison made in Chapter 3 between consumer and B2B markets, Table 9.1 summarises the impact of the main distinguishing features on the choice of promotional mix. The picture that emerges from this is that B2B markets are very much more dependent on the personal selling element, with advertising and sales promotion playing a strong supporting role.

**Table 9.1** B2B vs consumer marketing communications: characteristics and implications

| B2B | Consumer |
|---|---|
| Fewer, often identifiable customers<br>■ *Personal and personalised communication feasible* | Usually mass, aggregated markets<br>■ *Mass communication, e.g. television advertising, most efficient and cost effective*<br>■ *Interactive media can add a degree of personalisation* |
| Complex products, often tailored to individual customer specification<br>■ *Need for lengthy buyer–seller dialogue via personal selling* | Standardised products with little scope for negotiation and customisation<br>■ *Impersonal channels of communication convey standard message* |
| High-value, high-risk, infrequent purchases<br>■ *Need for much information through literature and personal representation, with emphasis on product performance and financial criteria* | Low-value, low-risk, frequent purchases<br>■ *Less technical emphasis; status and other intangible benefits often stressed; incentives needed to build or break buying habits* |
| Rational decision-making process over time, with a buying centre taking responsibility<br>■ *Need to understand who plays what role and try to influence whole buying centre* | Short time scale, often impulse purchasing by an individual or family buying unit<br>■ *Need to understand who plays what role and to try to influence family* |

The converse is generally true in consumer markets. A large number of customers each making relatively low value, frequent purchases can be most efficiently contacted using mass media. Advertising, therefore, comes to the fore, with sales promotion a close second, while personal selling is almost redundant. Figure 9.3 shows this polarisation of B2B and consumer promotional mixes. This does, of course, represent sweeping generalisations about the nature of these markets, which need to be qualified. The product itself, for instance, will influence the shape of the mix, as will the nature of competitive and other environmental pressures. These will be addressed later (p. 348 *et seq.* and p. 352 *et seq.*).

**Figure 9.3**
B2B vs consumer
promotional mix

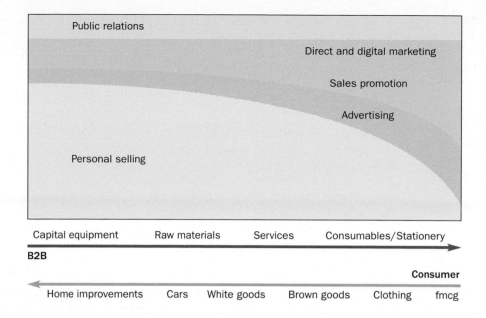

## Push or pull strategy

Remember, however, that even consumer goods marketers are likely to have to consider B2B markets in dealing with channels of distribution. Figure 9.4 offers two strategies, push and pull, which emphasise different lines of communication (Oliver and Farris, 1989). With a push strategy, the manufacturer chooses to concentrate communications activity on the member of the distribution channel immediately below. This means that the wholesaler, in this example, has a warehouse full of product and thus an incentive to use communication to make a special effort to sell it quickly on to the retailer, who in turn promotes it to the end consumer. The product is thereby pushed down the distribution channel, with communication flowing from member to member in parallel with the product. There is little or no communication between manufacturer and consumer in this case.

In contrast, the pull strategy requires the manufacturer to create demand for the product through direct communication with the consumer. The retailers will perceive this demand and, in the interests of serving their customers' needs, will demand the product from their wholesaler, who will demand it from the manufacturer. This bottom-up approach pulls the product

**Figure 9.4**
Push–pull strategy

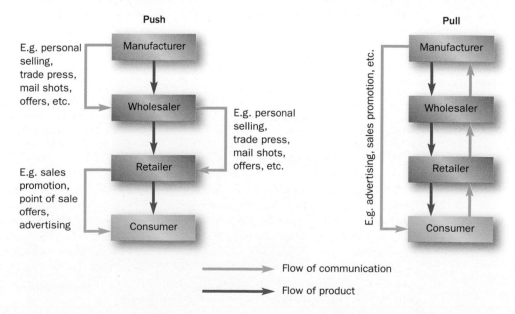

down the distribution channel, with communication flowing in the opposite direction from the product!

The reality is, of course, that manufacturers take a middle course, with some pull and some push to create more impetus for the product.

*eg* There are some markets which involve intermediaries – a middle link between the manufacturer and the consumer/end-user – where the end-user would feel highly uncomfortable if they thought the intermediary they were dealing with had been unduly influenced by the manufacturer's marketing initiatives. When we visit an Independent Financial Advisor for advice on financial products, we expect that the recommendations they make to us will be *independent*, i.e. based solely on our requirements, and taking into account what is on offer from the whole market, not from a brand provider that may have incentivised them in some way. Similarly, when we have a consultation with our doctor, we expect any drugs prescribed to be based on what is likely to cure our symptoms, and not be influenced by a Christmas gift from the drug rep. Markets such as these, where there are ethical considerations surrounding influence over the supply chain, are highly regulated. So while you may see a drug company's name on your GP's coffee mug, or the logo of a pension provider on the calendar on your IFA's desk, rest assured that any freebie they've received cannot cost more than £5. By the same token, brands may sponsor conferences and exhibitions in these markets, but the content must be judged to be educational, and any hospitality provided must be secondary to the educational purpose of the gathering. So if you want to be wined and dined, or do some wining and dining, steer clear of the pharmaceutical and investment markets (www.abpi.org.uk; www.mhra.gov.uk; www.unbiased.co.uk).

## Buyer readiness of the target market

In terms of message formulation, a further tempering influence on communication with consumers will be the buyer readiness stage of the target market. It is most unlikely that a target market is going to undergo an instant conversion from total ignorance of a product's existence to queuing up at the checkout to buy it. Particularly in consumer markets, it is more likely that people will pass through a number of stages *en route* from initial awareness to desire for the product. A number of models have been proposed – for example Strong's (1925) AIDA model, which put various labels on these stages, as shown in Figure 9.5 – but broadly speaking, they all amount to the same sequence.

**Figure 9.5**
Response hierarchy models

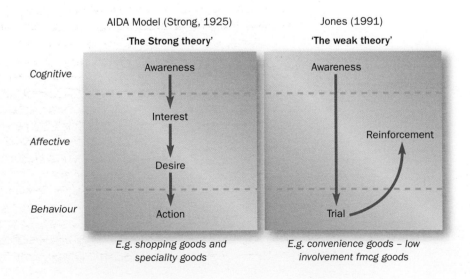

**Cognitive**. The cognitive stage involves sowing the seeds of a thought, i.e. catching the target market's attention and generating straightforward awareness of the product: 'Yes, I know this product exists.' As part of the launch of the Mini some years ago, for example, BMW used media advertising, PR, and hospitality events to get the updated brand known and understood as being something different and special. Now, digital media have started to play a big role, with dedicated websites, social networking sites, and search engine optimisation (i.e. ensuring that your company/brand appears early on in a search results list) all being used very effectively to spread the word on new developments

*eg*

The Oyster card is the preferred ticketing and revenue system of Transport for London (TfL). A credit-card-sized smartcard, it can store up to £90 of credit for passengers on London's Underground trains, buses, trams, Docklands Light Railway services and some overground train routes to use as a pay-as-you-travel alternative to paper tickets. Since its launch in 2003, take-up has been significant, with an estimated 80 per cent of all tube and bus fare payments in London being made with Oyster cards by the end of 2010, covering 2 million passenger journeys a week. Studies have shown that 40 passengers per minute can pass through entry and exit barriers at public transport stations using Oyster cards compared to only 15 passengers per minute with paper tickets. But imagine the frustration of running out of credit and holding the queue up, or finding that you're out of credit for the last bus home and that no top-up outlets are open.

Between December 2007 and March 2008, TfL ran a campaign to encourage Oyster card holders to register online for automatic top-ups once their balance fell below £5. Recognising that transport ticketing is a low-interest area for most people (until it goes wrong), the agency tasked with developing the promotion came up with the idea of linking the 'registering and topping-up online' mechanism, with the far more widespread and popular practice of downloading music onto iPods. As an incentive, TfL offered those registering to manage their Oyster top-ups online five free downloads from the iTunes store. The visuals for the press, poster and outdoor advertisements publicising this, and

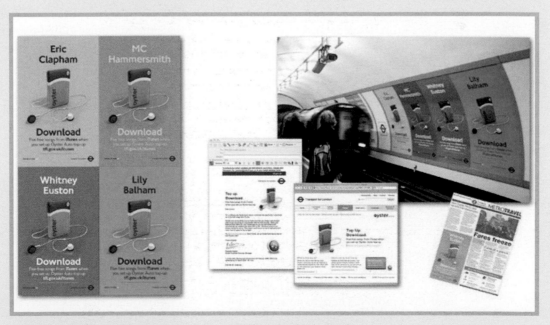

How about using One Direction to promote travel on the Circle Line?

*Source*: Transport for London

encouraging participation, showed the Oyster card as an iPod, and used plays on words with the names of famous London stations and well-known recording artists such as Whitney Euston, MC Hammersmith, Eric Clapham and Lily Balham. See if you can come up with any more for the series!

Of course, the London transport system is not only used by regular commuters; annually, there are 15 million tourists too. If they can be persuaded to use Oyster cards, it is easier for them to get around, as well as adding to the efficiency of passenger-throughput. Tourists are often unaware of, or not familiar with the Oyster system, and thus informative campaigns have been run. One initiative, for example, was run initially for Gatwick and Eurostar arrivals (www.kyp.com/Our-work/Clients/transport-for-london.aspx). They were handed a pocket-sized pack containing an Oyster card, a pull-out bus and tube map, and a cardboard device with information wheels, which line up to make the fare structure easy to understand. The pack also contained information on how to top up the Oyster card and where and how it could be used (Direct Marketing Association, 2008; Kemp, 2007; *Metro*, 2010; *UK Government News*, 2011; www.tfl.gov.uk).

An essential survival kit for tourists

*Source*: www.utalkmarketing.com and Transport for London

**Affective**. The affective stage involves creating or changing an attitude, i.e. giving the consumer sufficient information (whether factual or image-based) to pass judgement on the product and to develop positive feelings towards it: 'I understand what this product can do for me, and I like the idea of it'.

**Behaviour**. The behaviour stage involves precipitating action, i.e. where the strength of the positive attitudes generated in the affective stage leads the consumer to desire the product and to do something about acquiring it: 'I want this product and I'm going to go and buy it'. Many press advertisements incorporating a mail order facility are operating at this level and websites encourage a click through to a direct response.

The speed with which a target market passes through these stages depends on the kind of product, the target market involved and the marketing strategies adopted by the organisation. Nevertheless, each stage becomes increasingly more difficult to implement, since more is being asked of the consumer. Generating awareness, the first stage, is relatively easy as it involves little risk or commitment from the consumer, and may even operate unconsciously. The second stage needs some effort from consumers if it is to be successful, because they are being asked to assimilate information, process it and form an opinion. The third and final stage requires the most involvement – actually getting up and doing something, which is likely to involve paying out money!

The Strong (1925) theory of communication proposed these stages as forming a logical flow of events driven by marketing communication. Advertising, for example, creates the initial awareness, stimulates the interest and then the desire for the product, and only then does trial take place. In other words, the attitude and opinion are formed before the consumer ever gets near the product. There is, however, another school of thought that maintains that it does not always happen like that. The weak theory of communication (Jones, 1991) accepts that marketing communication can generate the awareness, but then the consumer might well try the product without having formed any particular attitude or opinion of it. Only then, after the purchase and product trial, does the marketing communication begin to contribute to attitude and opinion working alongside consumer experience of the product. Social media has a particular role to play here by helping to keep consumers informed and allowing them to share their experiences of using that product. With low-involvement products, the frequently purchased boring goods about which it is difficult to get emotional, such as detergents that's less likely to happen, but with higher involvement products, there are more opportunities.

Whatever the route through the response hierarchy, the unique characteristics of each stage imply that differing promotional mixes may be called for to maximise the creative benefits and cost-effectiveness of the different promotional tools. Figure 9.6, overleaf, suggests that advertising and search engine marketing is most appropriate at the earliest stage, given its capacity to reach large numbers of people relatively cheaply and quickly with a simple message. Sales promotions can also bring a product name to the fore and help in the affective stage: using a sample that has been delivered to the door certainly generates awareness and aids judgement and recognition of a product. Adding a coupon to the sample's packaging is also an incentive to move into the behaviour stage, that of buying a full-sized package.

*eg* A consumer might see a television advertisement for a new kitchen roll with improved absorbency, then forget about it until they are faced with it on the supermarket shelf during their next shopping trip. At that point they might think: 'I saw an ad for that – I'll give it a go' and buy a pack. Having tried it, if they've found that it performs well, they might pay more attention to the content of subsequent advertisements for that product as a way of legitimising and reinforcing their positive opinion.

Notice that in Figure 9.6 the role of advertising diminishes as the behaviour stage moves closer and personal selling or transactional digital media come to the fore. Advertising can only reiterate and reinforce what consumers already know about the product, and if this wasn't enough to stimulate action the last time they saw or heard it, it may not be so this time either. At this point, potential buyers may just need a last bit of persuasion to tip them over the edge into buying, and that last kick may be best delivered by a sales representative who can reiterate the product benefits, tailoring communication to suit the particular customer's needs and doubts in a two-way dialogue, or by a well-designed website, or comments on social networking sites. With many fmcg products sold in supermarkets, however, this is not a feasible option, and the manufacturer relies on the packaging and, to some extent, the sales promotions to do the selling at the point of sale without human intervention. Many fmcg products, therefore, strive for distinctively coloured packaging that stands out on the supermarket shelf, commanding attention. This issue will be readdressed in the following subsection.

*eg* The customer's progression through a relationship lifecycle can be managed through digital media. Thus the initial stage of finding a customer and establishing contact with them ('reach' and 'acquisition') can be influenced by managing search engine results so that the company or brand name appears in the top five results on Google, for example, leading them to the relevant website. Once they are there, the content needs to be sufficiently compelling and well managed to convince them to engage with the company or brand, enter into transactions and to keep coming back for more ('conversion' and 'retention'). 'Advocacy' means that the customers start to talk about their experiences (and you hope it's the good experiences they choose to talk about!), not only verbally but ▶

to a wider audience through positive comments on social media sites such as Twitter and Facebook, spreading the good word to other potential buyers. As customers increasingly use social media to rate their experience with the brand, it is a great opportunity to identify and develop relationships with brand followers. Coca-Cola already has 27 million followers and signs up 100,000 new friends each week (Choueke, 2011; www.leapfrogg.co.uk/how-we-do-it).

In reality, individuals within the target market may pass through the stages at different times or may take longer to pass from one stage to the next. This means that it may be necessary to develop an integrated promotional mix recognising that the various elements are appealing to subsegments at different readiness stages, with imagery and content tailored accordingly. The implementation of the various elements may be almost simultaneous, with some fine-tuning of the campaign over the longer term.

Knowledge of the target market is an important foundation stone for all of the communication decisions that you are going to make. The more you know about the people you want to talk to, the more likely you are to create successful communication. This means not only having a clear demographic profile of the target market, but also having as much detail as possible about their attitudes, beliefs and aspirations, and about their shopping, viewing and reading habits. In addition, it is important to understand their relationship with your product and their perceptions of it. This will be explained in relation to communication objectives at p. 358 *et seq.*

This is a good time for you to look back at Chapter 4 and revise some of the methods of segmenting markets, whether consumer or B2B, since the criteria by which the target market is defined (including product-oriented criteria) may well have a strong influence not only on the broad issue of balancing the promotional mix, but also on the finer detail of media choice and creative content.

## Situation analysis (2): the product

Inextricably linked with consideration of the target market is consideration of the *product* involved. This section will look again at the area of B2B and consumer products in the light of the influence of other product characteristics, and then explore the specific influence of the product lifecycle on the promotional mix.

**Figure 9.6**
Buyer-readiness stages and the promotional mix

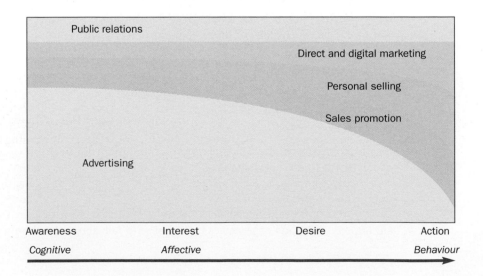

## B2B and consumer products

It is simplistic in the extreme to define a product either as a B2B purchase, personal selling being the best way to sell it, or as a consumer product, which must be advertised. Other product characteristics or the buying habits associated with the product may make such a distinction meaningless.

3M operates in the complex and fragmented office stationery market, its key products being Post-it Notes and Scotch Tape. Typically, communication in this market to those responsible for the purchase decision would be solely via product catalogues, product websites or in-store displays in specialist stationery supply retailers such as Staples. Historically, these focused on highly rational messages, and offered standard promotional incentives such as a percentage of the product free. Research showed that the stationery buyer in most office environments was female, aged 18–55, and with an interest in fashion. As a result, 3M felt the opportunity existed to use this insight into their audience to introduce a more persuasive *emotional* communication, engaging with them in their own language and their own media. This included digital marketing where a longer term platform for communication and relationship building was sought for 3M products in order to drive sales.

3M negotiated an exclusive deal with 20th Century Fox relating to their film adaptation of the best selling 'chick-lit' novel, *The Devil Wears Prada*. The story essentially takes place in the office environment of a leading fashion magazine in New York. Firstly, 3M used product placement – ensuring that all stationery supplies featured in the movie were from its range. The promotion was launched to the trade with key retail account personnel being invited to an exclusive premiere of the film five months before its official release in the UK. A media campaign was embarked upon with the objective of targeting stationery buyers during their lunch breaks using advertisements in *OK*, *Hello*, *Cosmopolitan* and *Grazia* magazines, and websites such as handbag.com and iVillage. These advertisements publicised the movie link, and drove traffic to the website where fashion and film related prizes could be won, and exclusive footage of the film could be viewed. To further promote interest via PR, 3M distributed findings to the media from its office worker survey showing that British women do more for their bosses than for their boyfriends. Incentive to purchase certain products was driven by a £5 fashion voucher redeemable at thousands of retailers, an offer that was unlimited to encourage repeat purchase. In combination, these initiatives saw 3M products standing out from the 'rational' competition, and gave a genuine sense of added value over own-label alternatives. During the campaign, response to promotion by 3M rose by 100 per cent compared with the previous year, and sales during the quarter in which the promotion ran increased by 27 per cent, contributing to an increase in annual sales of 16 per cent (Bowser, 2008).

At one end of the consumer product spectrum, a frequently purchased, low-involvement, low-unit-price bar of chocolate would not, of course, warrant an investment in personal selling to millions of end consumers, even if such an exercise were logistically possible. The marketing would be more likely to conform to the standard mix, emphasising mass communication through advertising whether through online or media. Increasingly, such purchases are being transferred to e-commerce rather than having any human intervention.

The example below serves as a warning that some B2B products behave more like consumer products and vice versa.

Another example chosen to illustrate the grey area between consumer and B2B markets is that of day-to-day consumable office supplies, such as pencils, pens and paperclips, for small businesses as we saw in the 3M example. This has more in common with the chocolate bar, although technically it is a B2B product, in that it is used to support the production of goods for resale. Compared with most B2B purchases, it is a routine re-buy, a low-priced, low-risk, low-involvement purchase, in the past delegated to an individual who goes out to the nearest stationer's or office supplies retailer at lunchtime with the contents of the petty cash tin but now, often set up for online ordering. It is simply not cost-effective to use personal selling of such a range of products to that buyer who belongs to a large and ill-defined target market (there are thousands of small businesses, in every kind of activity and market, and geographically widespread) and who makes such small-value purchases. At best, personal selling should be targeted at the stationer's or the office supplies retailer to set up the contract in the first place.

## The product lifecycle stage

One further product characteristic that may affect the approach to communication is the product lifecycle stage reached (see p. 234 *et seq.*). Since the overall marketing objectives tend to change as the product moves through each stage, it is likely that the specific communications objectives will also change. Different tasks need to be fulfilled and thus the balance of the promotional mix will alter.

**Introduction**. With the launch of a new consumer product, it is likely that there will be high initial expenditure on the promotional mix. Advertising and the use of digital media will ensure that the product name and benefits become known and spread quickly among the target market, while sales promotions, perhaps based on coupons and sampling, help to generate trial of the product. Sales promotions will also be used in conjunction with intense personal selling effort to gain retailer acceptance of the product.

**Growth**. Communications activity is likely to be a little less intense as the product begins to find its own impetus and both retailers and consumers make repeat purchases. There might also be less emphasis on awareness generation and information giving, and more on long-term image and loyalty building. As competitors launch similar products, it is important to ensure that differential advantage is maintained, and that customers know exactly why they should continue to buy the original product rather than switching over to a competitor. This could mean a shift towards advertising either online or through other media as a prime means of image creation that works over a longer period.

The sponsorship of television programmes can be very effective in either raising awareness of keeping a brand at the forefront of the consumer's mind, especially in combination with other media activities. Autoglass, the windscreen-repair organisation is typically dealing with a distress purchase, when spontaneous recall and an instant move towards a decision is often necessary. It spends £30 million on marketing in all forms and hopes to grow sales even further to combat increasing competition. This includes a move into social media to allow consumers to learn about the brand in practice through the ratings and review of other buyers and the introduction of an iPhone app and mobile website to allow customers to book an appointment. It also tried sports programme sponsorship by sponsoring *Afternoon Update* on Sky Sports for six months. All of this was designed to build brand presence, leading towards brand engagement.

Although it might be argued that chocolate can also be a distress purchase, it is certainly a frequently purchased product that can be subject to impulsive decisions at the point of sale. It is therefore important to keep the brand name at the front of the consumer's mind, and Cadbury's uses the full range of promotional media to help ot achieve this. As one of its marketing campaigns centred on its status as a sponsor of the London 2012 Olympics, Cadbury's launched a campaign called 'Keep Team GB Pumped' in the autumn of 2011. The campaign was multifaceted, including digital marketing, PR, mobile and on-pack promotions across the Cadbury Twirl, Cadbury Crunchie and Cadbury Dairy Milk brands, offering a chance to win cash prizes and music-related rewards. It also featured a viral marketing component with consumers encouraged to upload videos of themselves singing power training songs to motivate the Team GB athletes. The timing of the campaign also coincided with Cadbury's sponsorship of the television series *Minute to Win It* (*Marketing Week*, 2010b; 2011).

**Maturity**. The maturity stage is likely to be a defensive or holding operation, since competitors with younger products may be threatening to take custom away from the product. Most people know about the product; most people (apart from a few laggards) who are likely to try it have already done so. Thus the role of communication is reminding (about the brand image and values) and reassurance (about having chosen the right product), probably through mass advertising. In B2B markets, this stage is likely to be about further developing and consolidating relationships with customers in preparation for newer products in your portfolio.

Kuoni, the leading luxury travel and tour operator, has developed its promotional mix to ensure a steady flow of enquirers, followed up by a call to action. Heavy use is made of the travel brochure which specifies the full range of holidays so that potential consumers can window shop or seriously consider each option. The brochure request is a key trigger, followed by either a visit to a travel agent, a company-owned outlet or an online booking, although PR and advertising are important for getting the enquiry in the first place. However, Kuoni recognised that it needed to improve its exposure to the increasing number of would-be travellers buying or searching online in a marketplace which was mature and in an environment which was getting tougher with the economic recession.

Search-engine optimisation was based on a strategy that analysed the key search period for different destinations in order to maximise Kuoni's exposure during those periods. It also developed a Facebook link because social media are also important platforms for consumers sharing experiences as well as enabling Kuoni to embed videos to stimulate and retain interest. This formed part of an i-Travel guide where content and videos could be uploaded and linked to destination pages to boost the site's authoritativeness. The campaign achieved first page rankings on Google for over 90 per cent of relevant words (Bigmouthmedia, 2011).

**Decline**. Marketing communication is not going to rescue a product that is clearly on its way out; it can only stave off the inevitable for a while. The majority of consumers and, for that matter, distributors will have already moved on to other products, leaving only a few laggards. A certain level of reminder advertising, digital activity and sales promotion might keep them in the market for this product for a while, but eventually even they will drift off. There is little point in diverting resources that could be better used on the next new product.

The above analysis assumes that a product takes an unexceptional course through the classical stages of the lifecycle. Many consumer goods, however, are revamped at some time during the maturity stage to extend their lifecycle. In such a case, there is every reason to rethink the communications package and treat the process more like a new product launch. There is much to communicate both to the trade and to the consumer about the 'new improved' brand, the increased value for money, the enhanced performance, more stylish looks or whatever aspects are being emphasised. In a sense, this stage is even more difficult than the new product launch, as the marketer has to tread a fine line between overturning old preconceptions about the product, convincing the market that there is something new to consider and confusing and alienating existing users who might think that the familiar, comforting brand values have been thrown out.

The lifecycle concept, as discussed at p. 238 *et seq.*, does have its problems, and in the context of marketing communication, its unthinking, rigid application as a primary basis for communications planning is dangerous. If a product is assumed to be mature or declining, then the application of a communications package appropriate to that stage may well hasten its demise. There are other, more relevant factors, both internal and external, which should have a far greater bearing on the planning process. Some of the external factors will now be discussed.

## Situation analysis (3): the environment

Again, some revision of an earlier chapter might stand you in good stead here. Chapter 2 analysed the marketing environment in some detail. This section will, therefore, only look at ways in which environmental elements specifically affect communications.

*Social* and *cultural* aspects of the environment will mostly have an impact on the message element of communication. What is said about the product and the scenario within which it is depicted in advertisements will reflect what is socially acceptable and culturally familiar to the target market. There must be something that they can recognise, identify with and/or wish to aspire to, if they are going to remember the message, and particularly if they are expected to act on it. This reinforces what was said at p. 342 *et seq.* about the necessity of knowing the target market well.

Organisations are particularly keen to spot changes and shifts in social mores and then to capitalise on them, often creating a bandwagon effect. The 'green' issue is a good example of this. Many companies perceived that there was pressure on them to produce environmentally friendlier products, but rather than lose time in developing really new alternatives (and risk lagging behind their competitors), a few simply created new advertising messages and emphasised green-oriented product claims on their packaging to create the desired image. However, questionable approaches have been widely publicised, such as labelling washing-up liquid 'phosphate free' when that kind of product never contains phosphate anyway, and emphasising that packaging can be recycled when the recycling facilities do not exist, leading to confusion and suspicion in the consumer's mind about all green claims.

# MARKETING IN ACTION

## Invasion of the killer cucumbers

Poor old Spanish cucumbers. When the E. coli outbreak hit in June 2011 they were blamed for spreading the bacterium across Europe. E. coli is a gastrointestinal infection that in extreme cases can lead to kidney failure and death, and thus any outbreak is a serious threat to public health. In this outbreak, the Spanish cities of Almeria and Malaga were pinpointed as likely sources and sales of Spanish cucumbers collapsed, as nobody, from Russia, which banned imports, to Germany and the rest of Europe, was prepared to trust them. The Fruit and Vegetable Federation feared that the situation could cause demand for Spain's weekly agricultural exports worth €200 million to collapse completely. Spain refused to accept the blame, however, insisting that its cucumbers were safe and the Spanish Agriculture Minister said that, 'The image of Spain is being damaged, Spanish producers are being damaged and the Spanish government is not prepared to accept this situation' (as quoted by Abiven, 2011). Although news conferences were held nobody was listening, assuming that 'the Spanish would say that, wouldn't they?' Furthermore, the crisis didn't stop with cucumbers. As feared, many other vegetables and fruits from Spain were also shunned, and were left to rot, unsold in Spanish warehouses.

Cases of E. coli were reported in northern Germany along with Sweden, Denmark, the Netherlands and the UK. By 2 June, there had been 1,500 cases reported and 17 deaths. The infection was reported to have been traced back to Spain, and although the evidence wasn't conclusive, the damage had been done to Spanish exports. By 6 June, the death toll had reached 22 and 2,100 people were infected. Attention moved from cucumbers to bean sprouts (a prime suspect, given that they had been the cause of earlier outbreaks) but again, the results did not prove sufficiently conclusive. Further warnings were given in Germany not to eat tomatoes and lettuce until the source had been identified, coupled with horror stories in the press with quotes from experts such as 'One of the scary things about E. coli is that about 50 bacteria are enough to sicken and kill you . . . One hundred thousand of them would fit on the head of a pin' (as quoted by Marder and *PBS Newshour*, 2011). A distinguished professor said, 'if you don't kill them you make them stronger' (as quoted by Marder and *PBS Newshour*, 2011). That only made the panic worse and too many 'experts' were only too willing to give opinions to the media in the absence of scientific proof. It was not until two months later that the outbreak was considered to have been brought under control and ended. It had killed 50 people and affected a further 4,400. Although the scientists were not certain, in the end, fenugreek seeds imported from Egypt were believed to have been the likeliest source of the outbreak, not Spanish cucumbers, but it was too late – the losses to the industry were very large indeed.

So what's all this got to do with marketing communication? There are three phases in any crisis or negative news story. First, there is the initial 'breaking news' as the story of the crisis becomes generally known. The concern here is containment, and especially if the story is not true, the quicker the organisation's PR/crisis management team can act to show that it is a non-story, the easier it is to limit the damage and stop its spread. The second phase is about counteracting the negative stories about the organisation, with positive arguments supported by evidence. Finally, there is a phase of rebuilding confidence in the organisation or brand. The Spanish cucumber case concerns a whole sector and country in which individual producers are very small and relied on trade bodies and the Ministry of Agriculture to fight the battle for them. The story was too serious and escalated too quickly to be contained, and the complexity of the situation meant that there was ambiguous and contradictory scientific evidence emerging day by day, making it difficult to counter the story once and for all. News conferences and ministerial proclamations were simply not enough to counter the crisis that was building.

Once the E. coli outbreak was over, and it was generally accepted that Spanish produce was not the culprit, the rebuilding phase could begin by getting that message across to the trade and consumers. Initially, it started in Spain itself where a promotional campaign aimed to reassure Spanish consumers. The appeal was nationalistic with the slogan 'There are thousands of ways of supporting our vegetables - choose yours'. Public relations played a big part as did media advertising. To restore Spain's reputation down the ▶

Falsely accused – the work goes on to restore confidence in Spanish produce

*Source*: www.shutterstock.com/Ryan Rodrick Beiler

▶ international distribution channel, trade shows and taste festivals helped to re-establish confidence in Spanish produce among grocery buyers, especially in the UK and Germany. To reach consumers who live beyond Spain's borders, Spain called for a focused promotional campaign financed jointly by the EU and Germany (the country that suffered the most but also made many of the unfounded allegations). The EU responded by allocating €37 million for 26 co-financed marketing programmes across 13 member states, although that covered a wide range of food products. There's still a lot of work to be done, however, to understand how fundamentally this crisis has changed consumer attitudes towards fresh produce, especially from Spain. It could take years and a lot more than €37 million to restore confidence. After all, there are some who are still suspicious of British beef, years after the 'mad cow disease' problem was solved!

*Sources*: Abiven (2011); BBC (2011); Collen (2011); *The Economist* (2011); Marder and PBS *Newshour* (2011); Maxwell (2011a; 2011b; 2011c); Reuters (2011).

A more general criticism of advertisers' influence in the social and cultural area is about their alleged use and reinforcement of stereotypes. The advertisers argue that they simply reflect society as it is, and that it is not their business to change it – they *respond* to the customer's changing attitudes and lifestyle. Should there, however, be concern that if people see stereotypes being constantly presented through advertising as the norm, and even as states to be aspired to, then maybe the impetus to question their validity and to break them will be less urgent? This is a complex 'chicken and egg' debate that you may want to pursue for yourself outside these pages. There are no easy answers.

To be fair to the advertisers, the whole area of stereotypes does perhaps present one of the great insoluble dilemmas of mass communication. In moving away from one stereotype, it is too easy to replace it with another. Because the advertiser is trying to appeal to a relatively large number of individuals (even in a niche market), it is impossible to create an image that reflects every member of the target market in detail. What emerges, therefore, is a superficial sketch of the essential characteristics of that group and its aspirations, i.e. a stereotype! Thus the stereotypical housewife who lives in the kitchen and is fulfilled through the quality of her cooking has been usurped at the opposite extreme by the equally unrealistic stereotype of the 'woman who has it all'. It seems that the advertisers cannot win.

# MARKETING IN ACTION

## Hovis, born and bread

Despite the trend towards healthier eating, bread remains a firm favourite. Hovis has always had a good reputation for bread promotion. The 1973 'boy on a bike' commercial is an all-time advertising great, portraying a nostalgic view of an Edwardian working-class lifestyle. The brand was relaunched in 2008 with the strapline 'as good today as it's ever been', a clear reference to the brand's heritage, but bringing it into a contemporary context. The campaign featured a 122-second advertisement supported by extensive public relations showing a young boy running through iconic events of the twentieth century, to reinforce the brand's heritage but to show that it had been brought up to date. Sales increased in a declining sector in which competitors such as Warburton's are strong.

The Hovis brand name is an umbrella for a number of sub-brands with their own identities. 'Hovis Best of Both', a white, sliced bread containing wheatgerm, was launched in 2001. It was positioned as a 'healthy' alternative to traditional white loaves, which lack the nutritional goodness of wholemeal

The Hovis commercial in which a boy is seen to run through the iconic events of the twentieth century to the present day

*Source*: Image courtesy of The Advertising Archives

– hence, the name, 'Best of Both' (appearance and taste of white bread, but with healthy fibre content of brown). The brand was extremely successful, yet the brand's marketers were keen to grow it even further, believing that families still exist in which the mother would prefer to purchase the healthier option, but is resisted by children who will not eat anything other than white bread.

In May 2007, therefore, Premier Foods, the brand's owner, launched a £2 million marketing communications campaign aimed at persuading these willing mums of reluctant kids to give 'Best of Both' a try. Knowing that this represented a risky purchase for mum, and that it would be important to get kids on board too, a number of different elements of the promotional mix were used in combination to promote trial. The television commercials depicted a young boy, fussy about everything, being awkward about a variety of everyday activities from having his shirt tucked-in, to having to sit in a particular seat in the car, yet eating his Best of Both sandwich without complaint. This allowed the target audience for the communication to 'self-identify', and the acceptability of Best of Both to even the fussiest eaters was reinforced with the inclusion in the advertisements of taste test findings indicating that white bread buyers actually preferred the taste of Best of Both.

An on-pack promotion during the first two months of the campaign offered a money-back guarantee to anyone who bought but didn't prefer the taste of Best of Both – an initiative which lessened the risk for triallists, and this money-back promotion was also publicised using radio commercials. Leaflets about the promotion were distributed to households via door-drop, and a retail roadshow was mounted featuring BOB man, the Best of Both superhero. In supermarket car parks nationally, the BOB man van, with its superhero cartoon graphics, distributed samples for shoppers to try before entering the store, and masked BOB man himself, bedecked in blue tights and gold boots, pants and cape, challenged mums and kids alike to launch loaves of Best of Both at a hoarding of different-sized open mouths to score points and win prizes. Children up and down the country could be seen sporting BOB man masks around the supermarket alongside mums with Best of Both loaves in their trolleys.

The focus on families continued over the next few years through advertising and sales promotions, such as a door-drop of 1.2 million coupons targeting mums, emphasising that parents can buy Best of Both to give kids a healthier bread that they will enjoy. The promotional mix also included point of sale materials, press and radio advertising and PR. Best of Both also featured alongside other Hovis brands in a more generic £5 million television advertising campaign to promote the fact that Hovis products are all made from British wheat. This campaign was also supported by money-off offers, outdoor posters near supermarkets and PR. Thus in supporting the parent brand and its sub-brands, Hovis recognises that heritage and familiarity are not enough; it uses the full range of marketing communications techniques to keep the brand relevant to today's target audiences and their needs.

*Sources: Campaign* (2011); *Creativematch* (2007); IPM (2008); Lucas (2011); Nairn (2010); *Promotional Marketing* (2010); Quilter (2009).

No communications plan can be shaped without some reference to what *competitors* are doing or are likely to do, given the necessity of emphasising the differential advantage and positioning of the product in relation to theirs. This could affect every stage of the planning, from the definition of objectives, through the creative strategy, to the setting of budgets. These themes will be taken up under the appropriate headings later in this chapter, and will also feature in the chapters on the individual tools of the promotional mix.

Another important factor to take into account is the *legal/regulatory* environment, as discussed in Chapter 2. Some products are restricted as to where and when they can be advertised. In the UK, for instance, cigarette advertising is not permitted on television and alcohol advertising is highly regulated either legally or through codes of practice. Restrictions may also exist about what can or must be said or shown in relation to the product. Toy advertising cannot imply a social disadvantage through not owning a product, and must also indicate the price of the toy. More generally, advertising aimed at children cannot encourage them to pester their parents to purchase (not that they normally need encouragement). Some regulations are enshrined in law, while others are imposed and applied through monitoring watchdog bodies such as the Advertising Standards Authority. Professional bodies, such as the UK's Institute of Sales Promotion or the Direct Marketing Association, often develop codes of practice to which their members undertake to adhere. As yet, no unified codes have been developed that apply across Europe.

As we saw in Chapter 2 (see p. 67 *et seq.*), the Advertising Standards Authority (ASA) is the watchdog responsible for ensuring that the advertising and promotion industry complies with rules, regulations and codes of practice. When the public complain about a piece of marketing communication, the ASA investigates and adjudicates. For example, a Heineken press advertisement for beer showed a picture of Kronenbourg 1664 alongside the headline 'from the country that believes in the lunch (two and a half) hour'. The related text read:

**The French are famous for many things, hurrying isn't one of them. So naturally a beer from Strasbourg, eastern France is made rather slowly. From a patient approach to hop growing, to the delicate handling of the drying procedure, not one part of the brewing process is rushed. Make sure the drinking process is the same.**

What's wrong with that, you might ask. The problem was the beer was brewed in the UK not France. Heineken in its defence said that the beer did originate from Strasbourg and was brewed with hops that were unique to that region, and the nature of the beer meant it had to be brewed slowly. It was French lager, that consumers identified as being French but just happened to be brewed in the UK. The ASA disagreed, however, and the advertisement was deemed misleading as consumers naturally thought it was brewed in France. The complaint was thus upheld (www.asa.org.uk).

# MARKETING IN ACTION

## Advertising: driving you to drink?

Responsible promotion of alcohol has been a predominant issue for the drinks industry for many years. The advertising of alcohol has always been subject to stringent guidelines, but in line with the government's declared policy of reducing the harm caused by alcohol, tighter rules and codes of practice have been introduced in recent years with the specific objectives of protecting under-eighteens, preventing binge drinking and curbing anti-social behaviour as a result of drinking, The British Medical Association (BMA) is unequivocal, calling for a total ban on drinks advertising. It claims that there is a direct link between alcohol advertising, tobacco and fast-food consumption behaviour and, furthermore, that advertising encourages young people to drink alcohol sooner and in greater quantities and that's not good for them or society. It calls for an outright ban, shorter licensing hours, higher duty on alcohol and a special tax on the industry to fund alcohol abuse education. Alcohol abuse costs the NHS £3 billion per year.

Under existing guidelines, no alcohol advertisement should be likely to appeal to those under 18 years of age by reflecting or being associated with youth culture. Government guidelines state that no alcohol should be given to children under the age of 15, and between the ages of 15 and 17, it should only given under adult supervision. The reality is that 16 per cent of children aged 11 have had a drink and that rises to 81 per cent of 15-year-olds. The good (?) news, however, is that they are doing less illegal drinking in pubs, but a lot more drinking at home, at friends' homes and outdoors (Portman Group, 2010).

There is a move in some areas of parliament to ban alcohol advertising completely, as has been done for tobacco, but at present this is unlikely to succeed. The proposed ban would include sports sponsorship, but not cover print media aimed at adults, radio after 9 p.m. and films with an 18 certificate. Some promotion in pubs and similar licenced premises would be allowed, but the statements would have to be factual rather than having an emotional appeal, and all materials would have to carry an advisory message about responsible drinking. The rest would be banned, including television, social media and viral marketing. The bill is unlikely to become law because of the strength and influence of the alcohol lobby, reflecting a powerful industry, but it is an indication of how polarised the debate is becoming.

The industry prefers self-regulation through the ASA or the Portman Group codes of practice rather than legislation. A complaint about Kronenbourg 1664, for example, was upheld for breaching the Portman code. It featured banner advertisements on Spotify that directed viewers to Kronenbourg 1664's slowed down playlist as part of its 'slow the pace' campaign. The campaign centred on the idea of linking relaxed consumption with music that had been uncharacteristically slowed down from the original. The complaint was made about one of the tracks in the playlist, a cover of the Dead Kennedys' 'Too Drunk to Fuck' by Nouvelle Vague. Although the Portman Group ruling said that the theme did not encourage irresponsible drinking, the track name and lyrics associated the brand with immoderate consumption, and so the complaint was upheld. More generally, there should be no link between alcohol and sexual activity or success, nor any implication that alcohol can enhance attractiveness. Specifically on television, alcohol advertising must not show, imply or refer to 'daring', 'toughness', 'aggression' or 'unruly', 'irresponsible' or 'anti-social behaviour' or in any way glamorise yob culture. The challenge for the advertisers is how to adhere to that while creating entertaining and appealing advertising. Brands such as WKD show that it can be done!

The ASA regulates all kinds of media. One case it dealt with concerned a student poster for a night club in Leeds. Part of the poster stated '£1 drinks all night'. A complaint was made to the ASA that this was socially irresponsible. Voodoo Events, the organiser, said that the drinks market in Leeds was extremely competitive and that drinks priced at £1 or less were commonplace. It claimed to take irresponsible drinking seriously: its literature carried the 'drink aware' logo, and door staff at the club were instructed to refuse entry to anyone under the influence. It went on to say that in any case the only drinks for sale at £1 were shots of vodka and the rest of the drinks were £1.50 or more. It also defended itself on the issue of offering the deal all night on the basis that some promotions at some clubs only took place before a certain time. Although the ASA accepted some of the arguments, it ruled against the company and asked for the poster to be withdrawn on the basis that it suggested that the evening's main purpose was to consume cheap drinks all night and thus encouraged excessive consumption of alcohol. You have been warned!

According to the ASA, over 99 per cent of drinks advertisements do conform with the codes of practice, but of growing concern is the use of social media and there have been calls to include that in any ban. The 'Sponsored Stories' advertising format on Facebook, for instance, shows information about your friends who have interacted with a brand and could include images that would be in breach of

▶ the advertising code if they show people who are, or appear to be, under the age of 25. TBG Digital, an agency that deals with Facebook for a number of alcohol brands in the UK, has suspended use of sponsored stories for its brands while the ASA and the Portman Group consider the issue. Similarly, the use of smartphones has also opened the way for alcohol brands to interact with consumers in different ways, for example Stella Artois' Pub Quiz was a great success with 16,000 app downloads in one month, but again, such activities need to be designed and implemented with due regards for the codes.

The extent to which the drinks companies actually take their social responsibilities seriously could be debatable. Researchers at Stirling University examined internal documents including correspondence between advertising agencies and alcohol producers and found that a number of them used market research data from 15 to 18 years old to guide marketing campaigns, and that there was evidence to suggest that increasing consumption is a key promotional aim (Hastings *et al.*, 2010). If that is the case, then it is likely that calls for further tightening of codes or an outright ban on most forms of alcohol promotion will continue.

*Sources*: ASA (2009); Cooper (2009, 2011); Hastings *et al.* (2010); Hughes (2011); *Just-drinks* (2009); *Marketing Week* (2010a); McEleny (2011); *New Media Age* (2011); Portman Group (2010, 2011); Reuters (2010).

## Objectives

Now that the background is in place and there exists a detailed profile of the customer, the product and the environment, it is possible to define detailed objectives for the communications campaign.

Table 9.2, based on the work of DeLozier (1975), summarises and categorises possible communications objectives. The first group relates to awareness, information and attitude generation, while the second group is about affecting behaviour. The final group consists of corporate objectives, a timely reminder that marketing communications planning is not only about achieving the goals of brand managers or marketing managers, but also about the contribution of marketing activity to the wider strategic good of the organisation.

What Table 9.2 does not do is to distinguish between short-, medium- and long-term objectives. Obviously, the short-term activities are the most pressing and are going to demand more detailed planning, but there still needs to be an appreciation of what happens next. The nature and character of medium- and longer-term objectives will inevitably be shaped by short-term activity (and its degree of success), but it is also true that short-term activity can only be fully justified when it is put into the context of the wider picture.

Finally, Table 9.2 also stresses the importance of precision, practicality and measurability in setting objectives. Vague, open objectives such as 'to increase awareness of the product' are insufficient. Who do you want to become aware of the product: the retail trade, the general public, or a specific target segment? How much awareness are you aiming to generate within the defined group and within what time scale? A more useful objective, therefore, might be 'to generate 75 per cent awareness of the product within three months among A, B and C1 home-owners aged between 25 and 40 with incomes in excess of £40,000 per annum who are interested in opera and the environment'.

Until such precise definitions of objectives have been made, the rest of the planning process cannot really go ahead – how can decisions be made if you don't really know what it is you are aiming for? Precise objectives also provide the foundation for monitoring, feedback and assessment of the success of the communications mix. There is at least something against which to measure actual performance.

**Table 9.2** Possible communications objectives

| Area | Objective |
| --- | --- |
| Cognitive | Clarify customer needs |
| | Increase brand awareness |
| | Increase product knowledge |
| Affective | Improve brand image |
| | Improve company image |
| | Increase brand preference |
| Behaviour | Stimulate search behaviour |
| | Increase trial purchases |
| | Increase repurchase rate |
| | Increase word-of-mouth recommendation |
| Corporate | Improved financial position |
| | Increase flexibility of corporate image |
| | Increase cooperation from the trade |
| | Enhance reputation with key publics |
| | Build up management ego |

*Source*: DeLozier (1975). Copyright © 1975 The Estate of the late Professor M. Wayne DeLozier.

# Strategies

Having defined objectives, it is now necessary to devise strategies for achieving them. The analysis done so far may already have established the broad balance of the promotional mix, but there is still the task of developing the fine detail of what the actual message is to be, how best to frame it and what medium or media can be used to communicate it most efficiently and effectively.

Designing the message content, structure and format poses questions for managing any element of the promotional mix. Message content is about what the sender wants to say, while message structure is about how to say it in terms of propositions and arguments. The message format depends on the choice of media used for transmitting or transferring the message. This will determine whether sight, sound, colour or other stimuli can be used effectively. These are important themes, which will be further addressed in the context of each element of the promotional mix in the following three chapters. A money-off sales promotion, for example, is certainly appropriate for stimulating short-term sales of a product, but will it cheapen the product's quality image in the eyes of the target market? Is the target market likely to respond to a cash saving, or would they be more appreciative of a charity tie-in where a donation is made to a specific charity for every unit sold? The latter suggestion has the added benefit of enhancing corporate as well as brand image, and is also less easy for the competition to copy.

Doritos took advertising creativity to a whole new level when it came up with the 'King of Ads' campaign. Instead of the usual agency or in-house creativity, it harnessed user-generated content with the bonus of £200,000 in prize money. In 2008, the public were invited to enter a competition to have their advertisement broadcast in space! Does this mean that aliens get the munchies, we ask. The winning ad received £20,000 as well as the distinction of being the first advertisement broadcast extra-terrestrially. In 2010, another competition was run. Anyone was free to enter as long they had a creative idea and a camera with which to shoot a thirty-second advertisement.

At the start of it all, there was a comprehensive integrated marketing communications campaign designed to inform would-be creatives about the competition, and to stimulate and encourage their efforts. This included:

- direct mail to universities, colleges and film schools – packs included USB sticks with resources related to making advertisements;
- a university tour to promote the competition;
- partnership with the D&AD Student Pencil Award and the Youth Creativity Network;
- print ads in creative magazines and regional press titles;
- social media as a means of ongoing dialogue about the progress of entries;
- a dedicated website to act as a resource centre;
- using influential bloggers to talk about the competition.

The process of selecting the winner provided the entertainment and engagement for those who didn't enter the contest, through a format that enabled a presenter to tell stories about each entry and the people behind. It was all rather reminiscent of the kind of formula used by reality shows such as the *X Factor* or *Britain's Got Talent*. The addition of the talent show twist to the competition saw sales increase by 25 per cent on the previous year. It achieved 2,902 entries to the competition and 2.5 million video views. The number of entries was whittled down to a shortlist of just 15 which were presented to a panel of experts (in the style of *Dragon's Den*) and then the top three went to a public vote for the £200,000 prize. The winner was aspiring film-maker Craig Young with his advertisement 'Attack on Westminster' showing a giant Dorito hovering over London. It has been played extensively on TV and has been used virally.

All of this was achieved with a budget of just £1.8 million. The expenditure was largely £1 million on television and over £330,000 on online media. The competition also generated a lot of PR coverage which was estimated to have been worth the equivalent of £1 million in advertising (Cannes Creative Lions, 2011; Highfield, 2008; *Just-food*, 2008; *M2 Presswire*, 2010).

Doritos launched a competition for a creative ad made by the product's consumers

*Source*: Alamy Images/Lana Sundman

With advertising in particular, the organisation might use a character or a celebrity to communicate a message on its behalf to give it source credibility. The audience will see the spokesperson as the source of the message and thus might pay more attention to it or interpret it as having more credibility (Hirschman, 1987).

Whether the spokesperson, or presenter of the message, is a well-known celebrity or an invented character, it is important to link their characteristics with the communication objectives. The marketing manager might also have to decide whether or not to use personal or impersonal media. Table 9.3 compares the marketing advantages and disadvantages of a range of media, from informal word-of-mouth contact such as friends recommending products to each other through to a formal professional face-to-face pitch from a sales representative.

Whichever element of the communications mix is being used, the important consideration is to match the message and media with both the target audience and the defined objectives. These issues are covered in further detail for each element of the mix in the following chapters.

**Table 9.3** Comparison of personal and impersonal media for communications

| | Personal ← | | → Impersonal | |
| | Word of mouth/ social media | Sales representative | Digital media | Mass media advertising |
| --- | --- | --- | --- | --- |
| Accuracy and consistency of delivery | Questionable | Good | Excellent | Excellent |
| Likely completeness of message | Questionable | Good | Excellent | Excellent |
| Controllability of content | None | Good | Excellent | Excellent |
| Ability to convey complexity | Questionable | Excellent | Good | Relatively poor |
| Flexibility and tailoring of message | Good | Excellent | Good to fair | None |
| Ability to target | None | Excellent | Good | Relatively poor |
| Reach | Patchy | Relatively poor | Excellent | Excellent |
| Feedback | None | Excellent – immediate | Good | Difficult – costly and time consuming |

# Budgeting

Controlled communication is rarely free. The marketer has to develop campaigns within (often) tight budgets, or fight for a larger share of available resources. It is important, therefore, to develop a budgeting method that produces a realistic figure for the marketer to work with in order to achieve objectives.

Even in the same sector, the spend on advertising can vary considerably. In the fast food sector, for example, in 2010, McDonald's spent just over £50 million on advertising. Of that, just under £30 million (58 per cent of its total spend) went on television advertising; £14 million (28 per cent) on outdoor; and just £800,000 (less than 2 per cent) on the internet. Its main competitors, KFC and Burger King, spent only around £25 million and £12.5 million respectively. How they split their budgets between various media was quite different. KFC spent almost all its budget on television (62.3 per cent) and outdoor (37.5 per cent) whereas Burger King only spent 45.4 per cent on television and 31.3 per cent on outdoor. Unlike its competitors, Burger King also spent 7.6 per cent on cinema advertising, presumably seeking to influence the after-movie choices of hungry film-goers (Mintel, 2011).

There are six main methods of budget setting, some of which are better suited to predictable, static markets rather than dynamic, fast-changing situations.

## Judgemental budget setting

The first group of methods of determining budgets are called judgemental budget setting because they all involve some degree of guesswork.

**Arbitrary budgets**. Arbitrary budgets are based on what has always been spent in the past or, for a new product, on what is usually spent on that kind of thing.

**Affordable method**. The affordable budget, closely linked to the arbitrary budget, is one which, as its name implies, imposes a limit based either on what is left over after other more important expenses have been met or on what the company accountant feels to be the maximum allowable. Hooley and Lynch (1985) suggest that this method is used in product-led rather than in marketing-led organisations because it is not actually linked with what is to be achieved in the marketplace.

**Percentage of past sales method**. The percentage of past sales method is at least better, in that it acknowledges some link between communication and sales, even though the link is illogical. The chief assumptions here are that sales precede communication, and that future activities should be entirely dependent on past performance. Taken to its extreme, it is easy to imagine a situation in which a product has a bad year, therefore its communication budget is cut, causing it to perform even more poorly, continuing in a downward spiral until it dies completely. The judgemental element here is deciding what percentage to apply. There are industry norms for various markets; for example, in the pharmaceutical industry, 10 to 20 per cent is a typical advertising/sales ratio, but this drops to less than 1 per cent in clothing and footwear. For industrial equipment, the advertising/sales ratio is often lower than 1 per cent although the sales force cost/sales ratio is often considerably higher in such industries. However, this is only part of the picture. The industrial equipment manufacturer might well invest much more in its sales force. Such percentages might simply be the cumulative habits of many organisations and thus might be questionable when considered in the context of the organisation's own position and ambitions within the market.

**Percentage of future sales method**. None of the budgeting methods so far considered takes any account of the future needs of the product itself. However, the percentage of future sales method is an improvement, in that communication and sales are in the right order, but again there is the question of what percentage to apply. There is also an underlying assumption about there being a direct relationship between next year's expenditure and next year's sales.

## Data-based budget setting

None of the methods examined so far has taken account of communications objectives – a reminder/reinforcement operation is much cheaper than a major attitude change exercise – or indeed of the quality or cost-effectiveness of the communication activities undertaken. There is a grave risk that the money allocated will be insufficient to achieve any real progress, in which case it will have been wasted. This then paves the way for the second group of techniques, called data-based budget setting methods, which eliminate the worst of the judgemental aspects of budgeting.

**Competitive parity**. The competitive parity method involves discovering what the competition is spending and then matching or exceeding it. It has some logic, in that if you are shouting as loudly as someone else, then you have a better chance of being heard than if you are whispering. In marketing, however, it is not necessarily the volume of noise so much as the quality of noise that determines whether the message gets across and is acted on.

If it is to have any credibility at all, then the competitive parity method must take into account competitors' own communications objectives, how they compare with yours and how efficiently and effectively they are spending their money. For all you know, the competitors have set their budgets by looking at how much you spent last year, which takes you all back into a stalemate similar to that of the arbitrary budget method.

**Objective and task budgeting**. The final method of budgeting, arguably the best, is objective and task budgeting. This is naturally the most difficult to implement successfully. It does, however, solve many of the dilemmas posed so far and makes most commercial sense. It requires the organisation to work backwards. First define the communications objectives, then work out exactly what has to be done to achieve them. This can be costed to provide a budget that is directly linked to the product's needs and is neither more nor less than that required. A new product, for example, will need substantial investment in integrated marketing communication in order to gain acceptance within distribution channels, and then to generate awareness and trial among consumers. A mature product, in contrast, might need only 'maintenance' support, which will clearly cost much less. The only danger with objective and task budgeting, however, is that ambition overtakes common sense, leading to a budget that simply will not be accepted.

The art of making this technique work lies in refining the objectives and the ensuing budget in the light of what the organisation can bear. It may mean taking a little longer than you would like to establish the product, or finding cheaper, more creative ways of achieving objectives, but at least the problems to be faced will be known in advance and can be strategically managed.

De Pelsmacker *et al.* (2007) suggested that 40 per cent of companies use the objective and task method, while Mitchell (1993), as reported by Fill (2002), suggests that 27 per cent use a percentage of future sales, 8 per cent use a percentage of past sales, and 19 per cent use their own methods. Overall, across the whole promotional mix, organisations are likely to use some kind of composite method that includes elements of judgemental and data-based techniques (Fill, 2002).

Positioning the budgeting element so late in the planning flow does imply that the objective and task method is the preferred one. To reiterate, there is no point in throwing more money at the communication problem than is strictly necessary or justifiable in terms of future aims, and equally, spending too little to make an impact is just as wasteful.

eg

Waitrose operates in the highly competitive retail grocery sector which is dominated by Tesco, Sainsbury's and Asda. Although shoppers admired Waitrose's innovative products and its fair trading practices, it had a problem with the overall perception of value and tended to be regarded as a destination for selected purchases rather than the full family weekly shop. Although advertising was used, it was mainly to generate short-term increases in footfall with most of the growth driven by sales promotion. Waitrose decided to adopt a different approach and use television as the main part of its campaign. The advertising spend was doubled and shifted from a seasonal burst to weekly advertisements. In addition, two celebrity brand ambassadors were adopted: Delia Smith and Michelin-starred chef Heston Blumenthal. Their role was to demonstrate fresh cooking ideas based on good quality ingredients from Waitrose. Through the advertisements, the celebrities delivered a mini cookery show each week with a recipe, a tip and a special offer at Waitrose. The Christmas advertisement also included a QR code, allowing an app to be downloaded offering gift and recipe ideas.

Waitrose adopted celebrity chefs to demonstrate cooking ideas from ingredients sold by Waitrose

*Source*: Courtesy of Waitrose Ltd, www.waitrose.presscentre.com

The timing of the advertisements was normally between Thursday and Saturday when people were more likely to be thinking about the weekly shopping trip. There was also a regional weighting to take account of the fact that Waitrose stores tend to be more concentrated around London and the South-East. Waitrose also decided to sponsor food programming on Channel 4 as there was some overlap between the target audiences. Other promotions ran across print, online and outdoor media (www.thinkbox.tv/server/show/ConCaseStudy.1697).

## Implementation and evaluation

The aim of planning is *not* to create an impressive, aesthetically pleasing document that promptly gets locked in a filing cabinet for a year. It is too easy for the planning process to become an isolated activity, undertaken as an end in itself with too little thought about the realities of the world and the practical problems of making things happen as you want them to. Throughout the planning stages, there must be due consideration given to 'what if . . .' scenarios and due respect given to what is practicable and manageable. That is not to say that an organisation should be timid in what it aims to achieve, but rather that risks should be well calculated.

Planning also helps to establish priorities, allocate responsibilities and ensure a fully integrated, consistent approach, maximising the benefits gained from all elements of the communications mix. In reality, budgets are never big enough to do everything, and something has to be sacrificed. Inevitably, different activities will be championed by different managers and these tensions have to be resolved within the planning framework. For example, many organisations are reappraising the cost-effectiveness of personal selling in the light of developments in the field of direct marketing.

An equally important activity is collecting feedback. You have been communicating with a purpose and you need to know at least whether that purpose is being fulfilled. Monitoring during the campaign helps to assess early on whether or not the objectives are being met as expected. If it is really necessary, corrective action can thus be taken before too much time and money is wasted or, even worse, before too much damage is done to the product's image.

It is not enough, however, to say that the promotional mix was designed to generate sales and we have sold this much product and, therefore, it was a success. The analysis needs to be deeper than this – after all, a great deal of time and money has been invested in this communication programme. What aspects of the promotional mix worked best and most cost effectively? Was there sufficient synergy between them? Do we have the right balance within each element of the mix, for example choice of advertising media? Are consumers' attitudes and beliefs about our product the ones we expected and wanted them to develop? Have we generated the required long-term loyalty to the product?

It is only through persistent and painstaking research effort that these sorts of question are going to be answered. Such answers not only help to analyse how perceptive past planning efforts were, but also provide the basis for future planning activity. They begin to shape the nature and objectives of the continued communication task ahead and, through helping managers to learn from successes and mistakes, lead to a more efficient use of skills and resources. The following chapters will discuss some of the techniques and problems of collecting feedback on specific elements of the promotional mix, and Chapter 5 is also relevant in a more general sense.

## Communications planning model: review

Rothschild's (1987) model of the communications planning process (see Figure 9.2) is an invaluable framework, as it includes all the main issues to be considered in balancing the promotional mix. In reality, however, the process cannot be as clear cut or neatly divided as the model suggests. Planning has to be an iterative and dynamic process, producing plans that are sufficiently flexible and open to allow adaptation in the light of emerging experience, opportunities and threats.

It is also easy, when presented with a flow-chart type of model like this one, to make assumptions about cause and effect. There is a great deal of logic and sense in the sequencing of decisions indicated by this model – definition of target market defines objectives; objectives determine strategies; strategies determine budgets and so on – but in reality there have to be feedback loops between the later and earlier elements of the model. Budgets, for instance, are likely to become a limiting factor that may cause revision of strategies and/or objectives and/or target market detail. Objective and task is the preferred approach to budget setting, but it still has to be operated within the framework of the resources that the organisation can reasonably and justifiably be expected to marshal, as discussed earlier.

The concluding messages are, therefore, that the planning process:

1  is very important for achieving commercial objectives effectively and efficiently;
2  should not be viewed as a series of discrete steps in a rigid sequence;
3  should not be an end in itself, but should be regarded as only a beginning;
4  should produce plans that are open to review and revision as appropriate;
5  should be undertaken in the light of what is reasonably achievable and practicable for the organisation; and
6  should be assessed with the benefit of hindsight and feedback so that next year it will work even better.

Chapter 13 looks at marketing planning more generally, and will further discuss the techniques and problems of implementing plans within the organisational culture.

## Chapter summary

- An integrated approach to marketing communication planning is vital, given the importance of effective communication to the success of products and given the level of investment often required for integrated marketing communication activity. The main stages in the planning flow include analysing the situation, defining objectives, defining strategies, setting budgets, and implementation and evaluation.

- Communications objectives must be precise, practical and measurable. They can be cognitive (e.g. creating awareness and disseminating knowledge), affective (e.g. creating and manipulating brand images), behavioural (e.g. stimulating the consumer to purchase action) or corporate (e.g. building and enhancing corporate image).

- Different promotional tools are effective for different types of objective. While advertising might be more appropriate for cognitive objectives, personal selling and sales promotions could be better for behavioural objectives, for example. Direct marketing can be very useful in creating and enhancing longer-term relationships with customers.

- Communications budgets can be set in a number of ways. Judgemental methods involve a degree of guesswork, for example being set arbitrarily or on the basis of what can be afforded. They can also be set on the basis of expected future sales, or made dependent on historical sales figures. Data-based methods are more closely related to what is actually happening in the marketplace and include competitive parity and the objective and task method.

## Questions for review and discussion

**9.1** What are the five main elements of the promotional mix?

**9.2** What are the stages in the marketing communications planning flow?

**9.3** What are the three broad stages of buyer readiness, and how might the balance of the promotional mix vary between them?

**9.4** What are the main categories of marketing communication objectives?

**9.5** What are the main advantages and disadvantages of objective and task budget setting compared with the other methods?

**9.6** How and why might the balance of the promotional mix differ between:

(a) the sale of a car to a private individual; and

(b) the sale of a fleet of cars to an organisation for its sales representatives?

## CASE STUDY 9

# FLYING IN FROM RIO

In the same way that Scotland has a national spirit in whisky, and Russia in vodka, Brazil has *cachaca* (pronounced coshasa). The spirit, made from sugar cane, has been produced in Brazil for over 500 years, and the Brazilian population drink their way through 1.3 billion litres of it every year. But whereas Russia exports 50 per cent of the vodka it produces, less than 1 per cent of the cachaca produced in Brazil each year leaves the country. As with many national spirits, there is a variation in quality from the 'rough stuff' to the brands for aficionados. Brazil's premium quality cachaca brand is Sagatiba (pronounced sagachiba). The brand owners decided it was time for the rest of the world to experience Sagatiba, and thus embarked on a £20 million European launch campaign during 2005. The long-term objective was to make Sagatiba as well-known and popular as Bacardi, but starting from a zero awareness base, there was a long way to go.

The first stop was at advertising agency Saatchi and Saatchi, which was charged with developing press and poster advertising that could run in style magazines and on metropolitan billboards across Europe, in parallel with other brand awareness and image building initiatives that would 'spread the word'. Saatchi's produced an arresting campaign featuring a model who closely resembled the iconic 'Christ the Redeemer' statue that looks out across Rio de Janeiro. In each of four advertisements this young, stylised Brazilian was pictured in the midst of modern, hip, Brazilian life, adopting the same Christ-on-the-Cross pose, e.g. with arms wrapped around a pool cue in a bar, or with arms outstretched across the back of a taxi seat with the city in the background. Each execution carried the line 'Sagatiba – pure spirit of Brasil'. Creatives in the agency also worked on designs for strongly branded merchandise such as ash trays, bar seats and ice cube trays using the distinctive 'S' shape from the Sagatiba logo, with a view to their being placed in stylish bars in major cities. Viral initiatives such as a 'forward to your mates' e-mail quiz, which ended with directions on where to find a bar to sample Sagatiba, and a graffiti interpretation of the print campaign spray-painted on walls and buildings in fashionable parts of London's East End were also undertaken. The objection to this latter initiative by traditional graffiti artists, on the grounds that it was commercial interests hijacking their art form, only served to heighten interest in Sagatiba, and generate a curiosity amongst younger consumers who are often immune to conventional advertising.

When it was announced that Selfridges department store in London's Oxford Street was to hold a 'Brazilian Month', 1,600 bottles of Sagatiba were shipped to the store where the brand owners created a Brazilian beach bar in one of the shop windows. Here, models served and drank Sagatiba, danced to

By referring to an iconic Brazilian image, Sagatiba ads encourage drinkers to try something exotic and different
*Source*: Image courtesy of The Advertising Archives

Brazilian music, and invited shoppers to try the brand, which was then available in store for them to buy. In an attempt to drive listings in the right sorts of places, 12 of the top barmen from the UK's hippest venues were invited to a London bar where they were introduced to Sagatiba, and encouraged to experiment with the spirit. As an extension of this, Sagatiba sponsored the UK Bartender's Guild Cocktail Competition, where the challenge was to create a cocktail using a minimum of 35 ml of Sagatiba. Regional heats ran in major cities throughout the summer, and the winner bagged a luxury holiday in Brazil, and the right to represent the UK at the International Bar Association World Cocktail championships in Helsinki.

Sagatiba also ran a bar at the Taste of London event in Regent's Park where over four days gourmet food and drink from over 100 exhibitors was sampled and subsequently talked about, and written about in the press. Sagatiba's co-sponsors at the event included 40 of the capital's top restaurants serving signature dishes, the Wine and Spirit Educational Trust running a Wine and Spirit Academy, and Laurent Perrier champagne. Next steps include launching the brand in Rome, Amsterdam and other major European cities,

following the print advertising campaign with cinema and television, and depending on the impact the brand manages to have in Europe, achieving global brand awareness and trial of the product.

*Sources*: BBC (2005); *Design News* (2005); Malvern (2005); www.ukbg.co.uk; www.tasteoflondon.co.uk.

## Questions

1 Categorise the various communications activities mentioned in the case according to whether they represent push or pull tools.

2 Why do you think advertising alone was not considered sufficient for the brand launch?

3 What role do you think the specific venues and other brand names present there will have had on Sagatiba's brand image at the events it was associated with?

4 Why do you think viral or contagion mechanisms are often adopted by alcohol brands specifically?

# References for chapter 9

Abiven, K. (2011) 'Spain Hotly Denies Cucumber Blame', *Agence France Presse*, 30 May.

ASA (2009) 'ASA Adjudication on Voodoo Events Ltd', *ASA*, 15 July, accessed via www.asa.org.uk/ASA-action/ Adjudications/2009/7/Voodoo-Events-Ltd/TF_ ADJ_46555.aspx.

BBC (2005) 'Inside Saatchi & Saatchi', broadcast on BBC2, 15 February.

BBC (2011) 'E. coli Cucumber Scare: Cases "Likely to Increase"', *BBC News*, 31 May, accessed via www.bbc.co.uk/news/ world-europe-13597080.

Bigmouthmedia (2011) *Kuoni*, case study published by Bigmouthmedia, accessed via www.bigmouthmedia.com/ live/articles/seo-case-study--kuoni.asp.

Bowser, J. (2008) 'Inbox Scoops 3M's Digital Account', *Brand Republic*, 14 November.

*Campaign* (2011) 'Close-Up: The History of Advertising in Quite a Few Objects: 21 Gold Hill, Shaftesbury', *Campaign*, 5 August.

Cannes Creative Lions (2011) *Doritos: King of Ads*, case study published by Cannes Creative Lions accessed via http://www.warc.com/Content/ContentViewer. aspx?MasterContentRef=ee4886ad-3605-402e-b2b7- 21973e416ffe&q=doritos.

Choueke, M. (2011) 'Coca-Cola: Behind Closed Doors at the World's Most Famous Brand', *Marketing Week*, 26 May.

Collen, C. (2011) 'EC Approves Agri Marketing Programmes', Fruitnet.com, 7 July, accessed via www.fruitnet.com/ content.aspx?cid=11254&ttid=2.

Cooper, B. (2009) 'Focus – Alcohol Advertising Safe in Tory Hands', *Just-drinks*, 17 September.

Cooper, B. (2011) 'The Alcohol Debate: From the Other Side – Part II: The UK', *Just-drinks*, 27 February.

*Creativematch* (2007) 'Hovis 'Best of Both' Launch National £2m Campaign', *Creativematch*, 29 May, accessed via www.creativematch.com/news/ hovis-best-of-both-launch/94156/.

De Pelsmacker, P., Geuens, M. and van den Bergh, J. (2007) *Marketing Communications: A European Perspective*, 3rd edn. Harlow: Pearson Education UK.

DeLozier, M. (1975) *The Marketing Communications Process*, McGraw-Hill.

*Design News* (2005) 'Wallpaper Express, Salone', *Design News*, April, accessed via www.wallpaper.com.

Direct Marketing Association (2008) *Transport for London (TfL)*, case study published by the Direct Marketing Association, accessed via www.warc.com/Content/ContentViewer. aspx?MasterContentRef=d36d1f16-b247-4a7c-ac73- 6d95a094b0ff&q=oyster.

*The Economist* (2011) 'Don't Shoot the Cucumber', *The Economist*, 4 June.

Fill, C. (2002) *Marketing Communications: Contexts, Strategies and Applications*, 3rd edn. Financial Times Prentice Hall.

Hastings, G., Brooks, O., Stead, M., Angus, K., Anker, T. and Farrell, T. (2010) 'Alcohol Advertising: The Last Chance Saloon', *British Medical Journal*, January.

Highfield, R. (2008) 'UK Astronomers to Broadcast Adverts to Aliens', *Daily Telegraph*, 7 March.

Hirschman, E. (1987) 'People as Products: Analysis of a Complex Marketing Exchange', *Journal of Marketing*, 51 (1), pp. 98–108.

Hooley, G. and Lynch, J. (1985) 'How UK Advertisers Set Budgets', *International Journal of Advertising*, 3, pp. 223–31.

Hughes, D. (2011) 'TV Alcohol Advertising Ban Proposed', Press Association National Newswire, 30 March.

IPM (2008) *Best of Both Hovis*, case study published by accessed via www.theipm.org.uk/.

Jones, J. (1991) 'Over Promise and Under Delivery', *Marketing and Research Today*, 19 (November), pp. 195–203.

*Just-drinks* (2009) 'UK: Doctors Call for Hardline Stance on Alcohol', *Just-drinks*, 8 September.

*Just-food* (2008) 'UK: Doritos to Advertise in Space', *Just-food*, 10 March.

Kemp, E. (2007) 'TfL to Offer Oyster Users Free iTunes Songs', *Brand Republic*, 12 December.

Lucas, L. (2011) 'New Twists on Old Favourites', *Financial Times*, 17 February.

*M2 Presswire* (2010) 'Make an Ad, Make a Fortune; Make the Next Doritos Advert and Win up to GBP200k!', *M2 Presswire*, 16 February.

Malvern, J. (2005) 'Graffiti Artists Pour Scorn on Saatchi Street Art Campaign', *The Times*, 23 May, p. 26.

Marder, J. and *PBS Newshour* (2011) 'Sprouts? Cucumbers? Authorities Still Searching for Source of E. Coli', *Scientific American*, 6 June.

*Marketing Week* (2010a) 'MPs Divided Over Blanket Ban on Alcohol Advertising', *Marketing Week*, 14 January.

*Marketing Week* (2010b) 'Autoglass Ups Spend to Become a Superbrand', *Marketing Week*, 2 September.

*Marketing Week* (2011) 'Cadbury Uses the Power of Music to Help Team GB', *Marketing Week*, 1 September.

Maxwell, S. (2011a) 'Hortyfruta PR Drive for UK and Germany', Fruitnet.com, 17 June, accessed via www.fruitnet.com/ content.aspx?cid=11018&ttid=2.

Maxwell, S. (2011b) 'Proexport Calls for EU-wide PR Campaign', Fruitnet.com, 23 June, accessed via http://www.fruitnet. com/content.aspx?cid=11076&ttid=2.

Maxwell, S. (2011c) 'Spain Aims to Restore Consumer Confidence', Fruitnet.com, 28 June, accessed via www. fruitnet.com/content.aspx?cid=11127&ttid=2.

McEleny, C. (2011) 'Portman Group Urges Alcohol Brands to Await ASA Advice on Facebook Sponsored Stories Ads', *New Media Age*, 11 July.

*Metro* (2010) '£30m to Be Saved with Three-year Oyster Deal', *Metro*, 18 August.

Mintel (2011) 'Burger and Chicken Restaurants', *Mintel Retail Intelligence*, September, accessed via http://academic.mintel. com/sinatra/oxygen_academic/search_results/show&/ display/id=593794

Mitchell, L. (1993) 'An Examination of Methods of Setting Advertising Budgets: Practice and Literature', *European Journal of Advertising*, 27 (5), pp. 5–21.

Nairn, A. (2010) 'Hovis – As Good Today as it's Ever Been', case study published by Institute of Practitioners in Advertising, accessed via www.warc.com/Content/ContentViewer.aspx?MasterContentRef=9aadea4d-1d42-428d-928b-616a668b40ca&q=hovis.

*New Media Age* (2011) 'To the Good Times', *New Media Age*, 28 April.

Oliver, J. and Farris, P. (1989) 'Push and Pull: A One-Two Punch for Packaged Products', *Sloan Management Review*, 31 (Fall), pp. 53–61.

Pickton, D. and Broderick, A. (2005) *Integrated Marketing Communications*, 2nd edn. Financial Times Prentice Hall.

Portman Group (2010) 'Alcohol and Young People', fact sheet published by the Portman Group, accessed via www.portmangroup.org.uk/assets/documents/Fact%20Sheet%20-%20Alcohol%20and%20Young%20People.pdf.

Portman Group (2011) *Kronenbourg 1664 Spotify Promotion Breaches Portman Group Code*, Press release issues by the Portman Group, 4 July, accessed via http://www.portmangroup.org.uk/?pid=26&level=2&nid=367.

*Promotional Marketing* (2010) 'Hovis Launch Most Extensive TV Campaign Ever', *Promotional Marketing*, 15 February, accessed via www.promomarketing.info/hovis-launch-most-extensive-tv-campaign-ever/P003535/.

Promotional Marketing Council (2007) '3M – The Devil Wears Prada', case study published by the Promotional Marketing Council, accessed via www.warc.com/Content/ContentViewer.aspx?MasterContentRef=87f4082b-73ae-4717-8a97-3aa03b569be4&q=prada.

Quilter, J. (2009) 'Hovis Targets 1.2m Coupons in Best of Both Push', *Media Week*, 21 May.

Reuters (2010) 'Report Says UK Alcohol Advertising Code is Failing', *Reuters Health E-Line*, 21 January.

Reuters (2011) 'Germany Declares End to E. coli Outbreak', *Reuters Health E-Line*, 26 July.

Rothschild, M. (1987) *Marketing Communications: from Fundamentals to Strategies*, Heath.

Strong, E. (1925) *The Psychology of Selling*, McGraw-Hill.

*UK Government News* (2011) 'How Will Transport for London's Plans Change Public Transport Ticketing in London?', *UK Government News*, 5 September.

# CHAPTER 10

# Promotion: advertising and sales promotion

## LEARNING OBJECTIVES

This chapter will help you to:

- define advertising and its role within the promotional mix;
- appreciate the complexities of formulating advertising messages;
- differentiate between types of advertising media and understand their relative strengths and weaknesses;
- define sales promotion and appreciate its role in the communications mix through the objectives it can achieve and the various methods it uses in targeting consumers, retailers and B2B customers.

## INTRODUCTION

**THIS CHAPTER DISCUSSES ADVERTISING,** an indirect form of communication, largely designed to inform, remind and reinforce marketing communication messages, and sales promotion, a very direct way of prompting a potential buyer into action. Advertising is big business, a global industry worth $500 billion in 2010. Television advertising accounted for over 60 per cent of that total (Nielsen, 2011) but online is catching up fast on the second category – newspaper print media. This chapter thus examines the role of advertising in the promotional mix and the important aspects of message design and media selection in the development of successful campaigns. The stages in developing an advertising campaign are then presented, along with the main management decisions at each stage. Sometimes these decisions are made in conjunction with the support of an external advertising agency, while in other organisations the campaign process is controlled almost exclusively in-house. The decision to use an agency and the importance of the client–agency relationship are thus also considered within the chapter.

The second part of this chapter introduces sales promotion and its strategic role within the promotional mix. Traditionally the poor cousin of advertising, sales promotion actually covers a fascinating range of short-term tactical tools that can play a vital complementary role in long-term promotional strategy. Its aim is to add extra value to the product or service, over and above the normal product offering, thus creating an extra inducement to buy or try it. The chapter considers the various methods of sales promotion and what they can contribute to marketing communications objectives.

Caterpillar is a major player in the manufacture of construction and mining equipment. Although it is an American company, it has operations throughout the world and cannot assume that all its customers are able or willing to communicate in English. Currently, its website is offered in Chinese, Japanese, French, Spanish, Portuguese and German, as well as English. It also tends to put more emphasis on customers' partnerships with Caterpillar's local dealers than with Caterpillar itself, and thus advertising campaigns have to be developed on a regional basis. Caterpillar uses a network of advertising agencies that can contextualise the core corporate brand messages and materials for local markets. While awareness of Caterpillar generally is likely to be quite high among potential buyers, it is the detailed match between the customer's buying criteria and what is offered by the manufacturer and the local dealership that determines sales. That can be influenced by locally tailored press and trade advertising, brochures, factory tours, road shows and, increasingly, e-mail and online marketing communications in support of the personal selling effort (*PR Newswire*, 2010; Thinking Juice, 2011).

In an fmcg market, 'Brit Trips' was an on-pack sales promotion offered by Walkers Crisps. Packs carried codes which, once the customer had registered, could be turned into points to be saved and redeemed for discounts or special offers at a wide range of family-oriented leisure destinations. The promotion was supported by television advertising, PR, and online media. To allow customers to accumulate more points without purchasing any product, Walkers Crisps also developed the 'Brit Trips Mash Up' online game through which consumers could add to their Brit Trips account by spotting clues to mystery UK destinations. This was also linked with a weekly prize draw for the 50 customers who had accumulated the most points that week. The objective was to raise online awareness and increase purchase intent particularly among women (as the family's lead shopper). Exposure to the micro-site game increased the perception of Walkers as 'good value for money' by over 12 per cent, online awareness was raised by 15 per cent and purchase intent by 18 per cent (Microsoft, 2008; PepsiCo, 2008).

# The role of advertising

## Within the promotional mix

Advertising can be defined as any paid form of non-personal promotion transmitted through a mass medium. The sponsor should be clearly identified and the advertisement may relate to an organisation, a product or a service. The key difference, therefore, between advertising and other forms of promotion is that it is impersonal and communicates with large numbers of people through paid media channels. Although the term 'mass media' is often used, it has to be interpreted carefully. The proliferation of satellite and cable television channels, along with the increasing number of more tightly targeted special interest magazines and the use of the internet, means that on the one hand advertising audiences are generally smaller, but on the other the audiences are 'better quality'. This implies that they are far more likely to be interested in the subject matter of the advertising carried by their chosen medium.

Advertising normally conforms to one of two basic types: product oriented or institutional (Berkowitz *et al.*, 1992), as shown in Figure 10.1. A product-oriented advertisement focuses, as the term suggests, on the product or service being offered, whether for profit or not. Its prime task is to support the product in achieving its marketing goals.

Product-oriented advertising can itself take one of three alternative forms: pioneering, competitive, or reminder and reinforcement advertising.

## Pioneering advertising

Pioneering advertising is used in the early stages of the lifecycle when it is necessary to explain just what the product will do and the benefits it can offer. The more innovative, technically complex and expensive the product is, the more essential this explanation becomes. Depending on the product's newness, the prime emphasis might well be on stimulating basic generic demand rather than attempting to beat competition.

In these cases, the prime emphasis in the advertising, whatever media are used, is to provide enough information to allow potential buyers to see how this product might relate to them, and thus to stimulate enough interest to encourage further investigation and possibly trial.

## Competitive advertising

Competitive advertising is concerned with emphasising the special features of the product or brand as a means of outselling the competition. Usually the seller seeks to communicate the unique benefits, real or imaginary, that distinguish the product and give it its competitive edge. Given that most markets are mature and often crowded, this type of advertising is very common and very important.

This underlines one of the critical features of good and effective advertising: it must have truth at its core. Advertising simply cannot be used to create a false image, because as soon as consumers try the product or service for themselves, they will compare the reality against the advertising promises and pass judgement.

A form of competitive advertising that has grown in significance in recent years is comparative advertising. This means making a direct comparison between one product and another, showing the advertiser's product in a much more favourable light, of course (Muehling *et al.*, 1990). Alternatively, the comparison may be more subtle, referring to 'other leading brands' and leaving it up to the target audience to decide which rival product is intended. Initially, it was

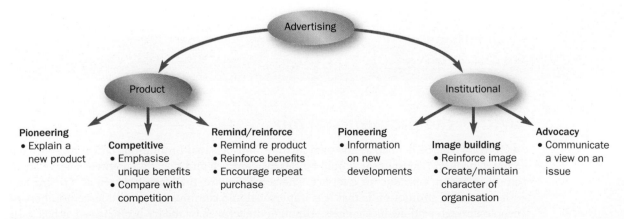

**Figure 10.1** Types of advertising

The online dating business is becoming more competitive, with many new entrants and an increasing tendency for singles to use social networking sites as a means of finding potential partners. There are currently over 1,400 dating websites and Mintel (2009) has forecast that the UK online dating industry will be worth £150 million by 2014. The barriers to entry are low although of course client satisfaction rates vary a lot across different sites. eHarmony is an online dating site for singles looking to find a new partner. It originated in the USA and then expanded internationally, and once it had been active in the UK for two years, it decided to look afresh at advertising as a means of further reinforcing its position as one of the top five dating sites in the UK. It set aside a budget of £8 million to create further awareness and stimulate brand preference.

The national advertising campaign featured real eHarmony members talking to the camera about why they joined and their experiences of the service, rather than simply promoting happy couples. This reflects the stage that eHarmony thought potential new members would have reached. Presumably, the idea is that the viewer can identify with the speakers and the reasons they are giving, and gain the confidence to investigate the site further. Although online searches are the main business driver, the advertising might help to attract people who hadn't thought seriously about online dating before to visit the site. Once they go online, the website content can reinforce that initial interest with further stories and encourage registration and subscription (Mintel, 2009; O'Reilly, 2011; Shearman, 2011a; Williams, 2011).

thought unwise to use a direct comparison approach as it gave a free mention to competitors and was likely to bring about a 'knocking copy' reaction. However, advertisers have now realised that in a competitive world, even if they do make a comparison with a market leader with already high awareness levels, the effect need not be negative.

## Reminder and reinforcement advertising

Reminder and reinforcement advertising tends to operate after purchase. It reminds customers that the product still exists and that it has certain positive properties and benefits. This increases the chances of repurchase and sometimes might even persuade consumers to buy larger quantities. The main emphasis is not on creating new knowledge or behaviour but on reinforcing previous purchasing behaviour, and reassuring consumers that they made the right choice in the first place.

This kind of advertising clearly relates to established products in the mature stage of the product lifecycle where the emphasis is on maintaining market share at a time of major competition.

## MARKETING IN ACTION

### It's Orlov or nothing

As we saw in Case study 7 (see p. 285 *et seq.*), the insurance price-comparison website business is now very competitive, and it is a marketplace in which 'accurate quotations' and 'lowest price' are the key drivers rather than brand loyalty. As all the main players sought to differentiate themselves through advertising, Comparethemarket.com was one that made a real breakthrough by recruiting Aleksandr Orlov, the Russian-speaking meerkat as its spokesanimal in what is undoubtedly one of

▶ the most successful advertising gimmicks of recent years. One word, 'simples', has come to evoke the entire brand and has quickly made it into the dictionaries!

The idea started as a small one in 2009 when an advertisement was made playing on the understandable confusion in people's minds between Comparethemeerkat.com and Comparethemarket.com, with Aleksandr explaining the difference ('Simples!'). However, Aleksandr's aristocratic charm and mangling of the English language made him a sensation and his popularity has continued to grow. It actually all started with a very pragmatic desire to lower search-engine optimisation costs: a click through from the search term 'compare' would cost as much as £12 per click, and 'market' would cost £5, whereas 'meerkat' cost just 5p per click, and thus a creative idea was born!

Comparethemarket.com now operates two websites. Comparethemeerkat.com tells us a lot more about Aleksandr's world, but that is just one click away from the Comparethemarket.com where the insurance business is transacted (and there are lots of opportunities to click through from one to the other). The advertisements focus on pleading with the viewer to stop visiting Comparethemeerkat.com expecting to find cheap car insurance as it disrupts the lives of the meerkats, rather than directly seeking to sell insurance price-comparison services. In that rather bizarre notion lies its entertainment value and its charm and effectiveness. As the popularity of the character began to take off, later advertisements started to feature Aleksandr's family history and a broader range of meerkat characters.

Aleksandr himself remains an inspiration for his many human followers. His autobiography was published in time for Christmas 2010 and outsold many other celebrity memoirs. The cover blurb on the book said, 'My story of struggles, successes and Sergei is the greatest, most thrillsy book ever written by a meerkat in the bath . . . With this book, I am hope to inspire the next generation of young businesskats. And with royalties I am hope to remarble roof on Orlov family mansion. Please enjoyment' (as quoted by Jones, 2010). He has nearly 750,000 Facebook fans, 46,000 followers on Twitter, and features widely on YouTube with over 1 million hits there. He has almost a cult following in his own right, quite unrelated to the insurance business (*The Guardian*, 2010). The expansion of the concept led to the launch of a digital meerkat village, Meerkovo, (www.meerkovo.com) in 2011 so that fans could meet new meerkats, explore

'I am pleased to be featuring in this book, *Essentials of Meerkats*, celebrating my business success'

*Source*: Image courtesy of The Advertising Archives

the village and explore buildings such as the Queasy Mongoose pub and Yakov's toy shop. All of this extends the interest in meerkats and keeps viewers wanting more, and again, there are many links to the price-comparison website. Aleksandr has even done some celebrity podcast interviews, starting with David Hasselhof and Piers Morgan.

This all helps to establish the brand name and drive consumers to the site, but the revenue is earned from click-throughs from the site to making a purchase from the insurers. To encourage consumers to take this action, and to build on the meerkats' popularity, a free stuffed toy of one of the meerkat characters was offered to those purchasing insurance through Comparethemarket.com. It was a fully integrated campaign and thus the promotion was supported by television advertisements featuring Aleksandr and his sidekick, Sergei, visiting bemused customers to deliver the toys. There is an additional business objective for this sales promotion. A Nielsen study found many consumers were fickle and only brand loyal while a particularly pleasing campaign was being run, and as soon as it finished, they were liable to switch allegiance. Encouraging people to collect the different meerkat toys could lead them to purchase other insurance products – you got a cute meerkat when you bought your car insurance through Comparethemarket.com, so why not buy your pet insurance or your home insurance too and get more?

In general, however, the price-comparison sites win or lose on the quality of their advertising, and thanks to the advertising war kicked off by Aleksandr, by 2009 the sector's total advertising spend was £85 million compared with only £35 million in 2006, and most of that spend was spread across just the top four competitors, all looking to win that precious click through.

*Sources: The Guardian* (2010); Jones (2010); *PR Newswire* (2011); Shearman (2011b); Sweney (2010a, 2010b).

## Institutional advertising

In contrast, institutional advertising is not product specific. It aims to build a sound reputation and image for the whole organisation to achieve a wide range of objectives with different target audiences. These could include the community, financial stakeholders, government and customers, to name but a few.

Institutional advertising may be undertaken for many reasons, as shown in Figure 10.1, for example, pioneering in the sense of presenting new developments within the organisation, image building, or advocacy in the sense of presenting the organisation's point of view on an issue. Some institutional advertising might be linked with presenting the organisation as a caring, responsible and progressive company. These advertisements are designed to inform or reinforce positive images with target audiences. Others may adopt an advocacy perspective, indicating the organisation's view on a particular issue for political, social responsibility or self-interest reasons.

## Within the marketing mix

The above categorisation of product and institutional advertising broadly describes the direct uses of advertising. Within the marketing mix, advertising also plays a less direct but equally important role in supporting other areas of marketing activity. In B2B markets, advertising often directly supports the selling efforts of the sales team by generating leads, providing information on new developments to a wider audience more quickly, and creating a generally more receptive climate prior to the sales visit.

Similarly, with sales promotion, a short-term incentive offer may be actively advertised to encourage increased traffic. For example, airlines offering 'two for one' deals or a free ticket competition frequently support their promotions with media advertising. Furniture stores also make frequent use of television and press advertising to inform the public of short-term promotional price cuts or low/no interest financing deals to stimulate interest in furnishing and to draw people into stores that they might not otherwise have thought of visiting at that particular time.

More strategically, advertising may be used to reposition a product for defensive or aggressive reasons in order to improve its competitive position. This may be achieved by demonstrating new uses for the product or to open up new segments, either geographically or benefit based.

In other situations, advertising may support other marketing mix activities to spread demand or to reduce sales fluctuations. The problems of seasonality are well known in the services field, whether in relation to holidays, restaurants or cinemas. Combined with pricing, advertising may seek to spread or even out demand patterns, saving the service provider from having to accept periods of marked under-utilisation of capacity. The various cross-channel ferry companies, for example, advertise low-priced deals to France during the winter to boost passenger numbers.

Overall, advertising's role within an organisation depends on a range of contexts, environments and competitive challenges, and may even change within the same organisation over time. The detailed role of advertising will be specified in the marketing plan, which will clearly specify objectives, resources, activities and results expected. These issues will be revisited at p. 391 *et seq.*, where the stages in developing an advertising campaign are considered.

eg Wyke Farms, in Somerset, was originally a small supplier of packaged cheese to Asda, but over the past few years it has expanded to cover all the major multiples in the UK and a number of continental European retailers too. The cheddar market in the UK is very competitive, dominated by Cathedral City and Seriously Strong, with brands such as Pilgrim's Choice and Wyke Farms challenging them. Investment in brand building through marketing communications activity is thus critical to gaining and retaining market share. For Wyke Farms, the brand positioning plays on the heritage of the farm where the family have owned and farmed the land and processed the cheese for over 150 years. The communications mix includes television, press and billboards. The 2011 campaign included 95 billboard locations to keep the brand in front of consumers along with advertising in nine national consumer titles such as *Good Housekeeping, Readers Digest* and *Hello*. It was thought that the campaign reached over 15 million consumers. Its advertising activity is supported by an active publicity department, social media presence and its own website. It also linked into a sampling campaign which reached over 1 million consumers at 30 consumer events such as Opera in the Park and the BBC Good Food Show. The trailer couldn't be missed at these events – it was the one with a 2.5 metre cow flying from the roof! (www.wykefarms.co.uk).

## Formulating the advertising message

The essence of communication, as outlined in the previous chapter, is to decide what to say, to whom, by what means and with what results. This section centres on the very demanding decision area of designing an appropriate message, with the emphasis on the message content, its tone and how it can then be presented for either print or broadcast communication.

### Message

Before producing an advertisement, you need to know who the target audience is and to give careful consideration to what you want to say to them. This requires a sound understanding of the targets, their interests, needs, motivations, lifestyles, etc. In addition, there needs to be an honest appraisal of the product or service to determine the differential characteristics or benefits that are worth highlighting to achieve the desired results.

Clearly, marketing and promotional objectives are at the heart of message formulation. If the prime objective is to generate awareness, then the message must offer clear information to alert the audience to what is on offer. If the objective is to stimulate enquiries, then the focus would need to be on moving the customer through to action, making sure that the response mechanism is clear and easy to use. There also needs to be consistency between the product positioning (see p. 242 *et seq.*) desired and the content and style of the advertisement.

The main aim in message design and execution is to prepare an informative and persuasive message in terms of words, symbols and illustrations that will not only attract attention but retain interest through its presentation so that the target audience responds as desired. Grabbing and holding attention may mean making someone watch an entire 30-second television advertisement, read a long, wordy print advertisement, or simply dwell long enough on a non-verbal graphic image to start thinking about what it means. Whatever the medium or the style of communication, it is therefore essential that the message is understandable and relevant to the audience.

Sometimes the message may be sent out through both broadcast and print media using the same theme. In other cases, a number of different messages may be communicated in different ways over the length of the campaign.

**eg** Wyke Farms, mentioned earlier in this chapter, adopts a simple theme throughout its advertising, packaging and brand positioning and that's 'farmhouse heritage' communicated through portraying the company as a family-run business from rural Somerset with a long tradition of working with cows.

A consistent message focused on history and heritage, albeit on a rather grander scale, is also communicated across different media by Warwick Castle. Its heritage dates back to before 1066, but the only battle it faces today is that of attracting visitors. In a very cost-effective campaign run over eight weeks, radio advertising was used, linked with a free-entry competition, alongside national and local press. Social media were used for a viral campaign, featuring two knights in full armour 'jousting' in unlikely situations – for example, they face each other on opposite sides of a pelican crossing and when the lights turn red they clash in the middle and one hits the other with a rolled-up newspaper. The campaign worked – revenue increased by 15 per cent over that summer period. The message was a consistent one: an exciting and informative day out with a chance to be in touch with history (RBH, 2008)

## Creative appeals

After the marketing issues of message content have been considered, the creative task can proceed. It is here that agencies can play a particularly major role in the conceptualisation and design of messages that appeal effectively.

**eg** The UK's number one tea brand, PG Tips, used live chimps, dressed as humans and provided with voices by a range of celebrities, to advertise the brand for 45 years. Originally inspired by the chimps' tea parties at London Zoo in the 1950s, despite being loved by many consumers for the anthropomorphic humour, by the late 1990s the campaign was being criticised by animal rights activists, and in any case was becoming tired. In 2002, the chimps were replaced by the T-birds. Tom the Irish owl, Maggie the London pigeon and Pete the Geordie starling were created by the award-winning animators, Aardman Animation (of *Wallace and Grommit* and *Creature Comforts* fame). However, these characters didn't really capture the public imagination and in 2007 the campaign was refreshed again with the introduction of Johnny Vegas and his rather sardonic sidekick, Monkey, having deep and meaningful conversations over a cuppa. Monkey is, in fact, a knitted doll dressed in a PG Tips tee-shirt. As well as 'slice of life' scenes in a domestic setting, memorable executions included Monkey in drag mimicking the Queen's speech to create a viral ad which won two gold BAFTA awards, and a somewhat risqué remake of THAT scene in *When Harry Met Sally*, stimulated by a cup of PG Tips, of course.

## Emotional appeals

Rational appeals centre on some kind of logical argument persuading the consumer to think or act in a certain way. However, often it is not just a case of *what* is said, but also *how* it is said. The bald logic in itself may not be enough to grab and hold the consumers' attention sufficiently to make the message stick. How it is said can introduce an emotional appeal into the advertisement to reinforce the underlying logic of the message. The concern here is not just with facts but also with the customer's feelings and emotions towards what is on offer. It is often the emotional element that gives the advertisement an extra appeal.

*eg* 'Experts' are often used in advertisements based on rational appeals. An expert might typically be a white-coated scientist demonstrating or affirming the germ-killing power of a loo cleaner, or the outstanding ability of a washing powder to turn your murky grey undies brilliant white. Negative emotions can be used very effectively in these contexts. To capitalise on fear, the toilet cleaner advertisement introduces elements that arouse fear of the health consequences of having a dirty toilet, while a shampoo advertisement subtly hints that having dandruff makes you a social embarrassment. Fear provides an ideal mechanism for advertisements wishing to show a 'problem and solution' or 'before and after' type of scenario. The fear is generated and then dispelled through using the product, and they all live happily ever after.

Positive emotions can be very effective in creating memorable and persuasive messages, which do not necessarily need any solid rational basis in order to be effective. Humour and sex are particularly powerful tools for the advertiser, particularly in appealing to people's needs for escapism and fantasy. It could be argued that television and video-based digital material is better at creating emotional appeals, as it is more lifelike, with sight, sound and motion to aid the presentation, whereas print is better for more rational, factually based appeals.

*eg* Music can add to the communications effectiveness of an advertisement and enhance purchase intent, brand attitude, recall, and response (Oakes, 2007). It is at the heart of advertising. Any emotional effect can be enhanced or reinforced by careful choice of music. Confused.com, a price-comparison website, has used the song 'YMCA' with rewritten lyrics as backing for its animated dance routine; Walkers Crisps used 'A Groovy Kind of Love', a sixties classic, in support of its Crinkles sub-brand; Talktalk has used 'Unchained Melody', and the VW cabriolet also went back to the sixties with 'Days' by the Kinks. Classical pieces have also been successfully used to create moods in advertisements. British Airways adopted the 'Flower Duet' from *Lakmé* as its theme, while in British minds, Dvořák's *New World Symphony* will for ever conjure up images of Hovis bread. Music can be very effective in creating or reinforcing the mood and style of the advertisement, making it more memorable for the viewer. The examples cited above have used tracks that are already familiar to the target audience but sometimes an advertisement can propel a relatively unknown artist or track into the limelight. 'Eliza's Aria' by Elena Kats-Chernin was virtually unknown but its exposure as the soundtrack to the Lloyds TSB 'for the journey' campaign captured the imagination of the general public. As a result, it topped the classical iTunes chart and as a spin off 10,000 ringtones were made available to Lloyds TSB customers. There was also a popular dance remix which made it into the charts. It is inconceivable now to have the advertisments without that music (Baldwin, 2008).

## Product-oriented appeals

Product-oriented appeals centre on product features or attributes and seek to emphasise their importance to the target audience. The appeals may be based on product specification (airbags or side impact protection bars in cars, for example), price (actual price level, payment terms or extras), service (availability) or any part of the offering that creates a potential competitive edge in the eyes of the target market.

With a product-oriented appeal, there are several options for specific message design strategy. These include, for example, showing the audience how the product provides the solution to a problem. The message could also centre on a 'slice of life', demonstrating how the product fits into a lifestyle that either approximates that of the target market or is one with which they can identify or to which they can aspire.

Getting closer to real life, news, facts and testimonials offer hard information about the product or proof through 'satisfied customers' that the product is all it is claimed to be. Magazine advertisements trying to sell goods that the target market might perceive to be more expensive, or goods that sound too good to be true, or goods that a customer would normally want to see or try before purchase, often use testimonials from satisfied customers. These might help to alleviate some of the doubt or risk and encourage the reader to respond to the advertisement.

In magazines and trade publications, news and fact-based approaches can also take the form of advertorials. These are designed to fit in with the style, tone and presentation of the publication so that the reader tends to think of them as extensions to the magazine rather than advertisements. The overall objective is that the reader's attention should be able to flow naturally from the magazine's normal editorial content into and through the advertorial and out the other side, maintaining interest and retention. This is particularly effective where the advertorial is short.

*eg*  Advertorials are a common form of advertising in magazines and other print media. Research by magazine publisher Emap has shown that advertorials work just as well as normal advertising in moving the reader through from awareness to interest, but are much better for getting information across and blending into the publication. Because of the association with the editorial style of the publication and the effectiveness of advertorials, media owners tend to charge more for the space, sometimes up to 20 per cent more than if exactly the same space in the same issue was used for ordinary advertising. Also, readers appear to understand the difference between advertorial and editorial copy and do not feel 'conned' into reading advertorials, perhaps because the content is so much more like journalism than advertising. In fact, readers trust advertorials more because of the implied link between them and the publication itself, and thus the credibility is high.

Even though advertorials must not look like journalism and must be clearly identified, there is a lot of scope for ambiguity. If it looks too much like advertising, it defeats the purpose of it in the first place but if it goes too far the other way, then it risks being referred to the ASA. The *Daily Express* ran into trouble over its advertorial coverage by publishing a page on which the top half appeared to be editorial copy and the bottom half an advertisement. The 'editorial' half was written by a journalist and then submitted to the relevant brand owner for factual checking only – the company had no right to change the copy otherwise. This is normal journalistic practice. The newspaper then offered to sell the advertising space on the bottom half of the page to that same company. The problem for the ASA was that the editorial half mirrored some of the information in the advertising half and furthermore, included product claims that would not have been allowed in an advertisement. The ASA decided that this was unacceptable, particularly because the same newspaper had published virtually the same page more than once, and concluded:

> **The routine publication of these pages and the nature of the articles strongly suggested a commercial arrangement existed between the newspaper and the advertiser and that the advertiser exerted a sufficient degree of control over the content of the articles to warrant the term 'Advertisement feature' or the like being placed above the articles. (ASA, 2009).**

The average reader would have assumed that the entire page was a single editorial feature on the product and thus the ASA's view was that the publisher and advertiser were intentionally misleading the reader (ASA, 2009; Barrett, 2009; Pandey, 2010).

## Customer-oriented appeals

Customer-oriented appeals are focused on what the consumer personally gains through using this product. Such appeals encourage the consumer by association to think about the benefits that may be realisable through the rational or emotional content of the advertisement. Typically, they include the following.

### Saving or making money

Bold 2-in-1, for example, could sell itself simply on the product-oriented appeal that it incorporates both a washing powder and a fabric conditioner in its formulation. In fact, its advertising takes the argument further into a customer-oriented appeal, demonstrating how this two-in-one product is cheaper than buying the two components separately, thus putting money back in the purchaser's pocket.

### Fear avoidance

The use of fear avoidance appeals is a powerful one in message generation and has been extensively used in public, non-profit-making promotions, for example AIDS prevention, anti-drinking and driving, anti-smoking and other health-awareness programmes. Getting the right level of fear is a challenge: too high and it will be regarded as too threatening and thus be screened out, too low and it will not be considered compelling enough to act on.

### Security enhancement

A wide range of insurance products aimed at the over-fifties are advertised not only on the rational basis that they are a sensible financial investment, but also on the emotional basis that they provide peace of mind. This is a customer-oriented appeal in that it works on self-interest and a craving for security. Stairlifts are also sold on the basis of security enhancement, with the implication that they make going up and down stairs easier for the elderly. The advertisements also suggest that with a stairlift, the elderly will be able to retain their independence and remain in their own homes longer, a great concern to many older people.

## Self-esteem and image

Sometimes, when it is difficult to differentiate between competing products on a functional basis, consumers may choose the one that they think will best improve their self-esteem or enhance their image among social or peer groups. Advertisers recognise this and can produce advertisements in which the product and its function play a very secondary role to the portrayal of these psychological and social benefits. Perfumes, cosmetics and toiletries clearly exploit this, but even an expensive technical product such as a car can focus on self-esteem and image.

## Usage benefits – time, effort, accuracy, etc.

An approach stressing usage benefits is very similar to a rational, product-oriented appeal, but shows how the consumer benefits from saving time, or gains the satisfaction of producing consistently good results through using this product. Such savings or satisfactions are often translated into emotional benefits such as spending more time with the family or winning other people's admiration.

Cosmetics advertising is about selling dreams and aspirations, and the use of beautiful and glamorous actresses and supermodels is a common way of showing a product at its very best. All is not as it might appear, however, and the ASA has become concerned with the extent to which such images are digitally altered post-production or 'airbrushed'. L'Oréal's brands Lancôme and Maybelline used Julia Roberts and Christy Turlington in their advertising, but the ASA felt that the photographic images used in the advertisements were overly airbrushed. L'Oréal admitted to using post-production techniques to enhance the images but claimed that the changes had not been substantial. The ASA, however, felt that the techniques used had exaggerated the product benefits to the extent of being misleading and should not be shown again in that form. It's not just airbrushing that the ASA is concerned about; there have also been examples of mascara advertising in which models are wearing false eyelashes to emphasise the effect of the product (longer, thicker, more luscious, individually defined, whatever) and advertising for hair products in which hair extensions are worn, which again could call into question whether the product's effects are being misleadingly exaggerated. (ASA, 2011a, 2011b; Sweney, 2011).

# Advertising media

Advertising media are called on to perform the task of delivering the message to the consumer. The advertiser needs, therefore, to select the medium or media most appropriate to the task in hand, given their relative effectiveness and the budget available. This section will look further at each advertising medium's relative merits, strengths and weaknesses, but first defines some of the terms commonly used in connection with advertising media.

## Some definitions

Before we proceed to examine the advertising media, several basic terms need to be defined, based on Fill (2002).

### Reach

Reach is the percentage of the target market that is exposed to the message at least once during the relevant period. If the advertisement is estimated to reach 65 per cent of the target market, then its reach would be classified as 65. Note that reach is not concerned with the entire population, but only with a clearly defined target audience. Reach can be measured by newspaper or magazine circulation figures, television viewing statistics or analysis of flows past advertising boarding sites, and is normally measured over a four-week period.

### Ratings

Ratings, otherwise known as TVRs, measure the percentage of all households owning a television that are viewing at a particular time. Ratings are a prime determinant of the fees charged for the various advertising slots on television. As the amount charged for an advertising slot is based on the number of people likely to be watching, it is the breaks in the most popular soap operas or reality shows, such as *Coronation Street* or *The X Factor*, that tend to be the most expensive.

Overall, the cost of most television advertising has fallen in recent years because of the influx of satellite channels and the fragmentation of audiences. The exact cost depends on a number of factors:

- **The time of year** – advertising can be very expensive in the run up to Christmas, but a lot less expensive in February or August.
- **The time of day** – weekdays during the day and the early hours of the morning are chepaest but if your target audience isn't viewing then there is not much point. The day is divided into 'dayparts', for example 'breakfast' (0600–0930) is a good daypart in which fmcg brands can reach housewives with kids, while 'peak' (1730–2300) is the most expensive as people are relaxing in front of the telly after work.
- **The channel** – terrestrial channels are effective for building brand awareness quickly as they reach a mass audience. The digital channels are a lot cheaper but need careful consideration of target audience profile.
- **The target audience** – this needs careful profiling to ensure the best match between the chosen channel and the viewing habits of the target audience.
- **Type of advertisement** – direct response advertising wants the viewer to take action immediately through calling a number or visiting a website and tends to work best during daytime television when home-based consumers are able and willing to respond.
- **Length of the advertisement** – the industry standard is 30 seconds but some are down to 10 seconds. In general, a ten-second advertisement will be approximately half the cost of a thirty-second one. Often a campaign can begin with longer advertisements and then once a certain level of OTS or reach has been achieved, shorter ten-second extracts will be used as reminders.
- **Regionality** – airtime can be purchased on a regional or national basis.

(*Marketing Minefield*, 2011; Thinkmedia, 2011)

## Frequency

Frequency is the average number of times that a member of the target audience will have been exposed to a media vehicle during the specified time period. Poster advertising space, for example, can be bought in packages that deliver specified reach and frequency objectives for a target audience.

## Opportunity to see

Opportunity to see (OTS) describes how many times a member of the target audience will have an opportunity to see the advertisement. Thus, for example, a magazine might be said to offer 75 per cent coverage with an average OTS of 3. This means that within a given time period, the magazine will reach 75 per cent of the target market, each of whom will have three opportunities to see the advertisement. According to White (1988), it is generally accepted that an OTS of 2½ to 3 is average for a television advertising campaign, whereas a press campaign needs 5 or more. As Fill (2002) points out, an OTS figure of 10 is probably a waste of money, as the extra OTSs are not likely to improve reach by very much and might even risk alienating the audience with overkill!

Ideally, advertisers set targets to be achieved on both reach and frequency. Sometimes, however, because of financial constraints, they have to compromise. They can either spend on achieving breadth of coverage, that is, have a high reach figure, or go for depth, that is, have a high level of frequency, but they cannot afford both. Whether reach or frequency is better depends entirely on what the advertisement's objectives are. Where awareness generation is the prime objective, then the focus may be on reach, getting a basic message to as many of the target market as possible at least once. If, however, the objective is to communicate complex information or to affect attitudes, then frequency may be more appropriate.

Of course, when measuring reach, the wider the range of media used, the greater the chances of overlap. If, for instance, a campaign uses both television and magazine advertising, some members of the target market will see neither, some will see only the television advertisement, some will see only the print advertisement, but some will see both. Although the overall reach is actually likely to be greater than if just one medium was used, the degree of overlap must enter into the calculation, since as a campaign develops the tendency is towards duplicated reach.

# Television

Television's impact can be high, as it not only intrudes into the consumer's home but also offers a combination of sound, colour, motion and entertainment that has a strong chance of grabbing attention and getting a message across. Television advertising presents a tremendous communication opportunity. Television enables a seller to communicate to a broad range of potentially large audiences. This means that television has a relatively low cost per thousand (the cost of reaching a thousand viewers) and that it has a high reach, but to largely undifferentiated audiences. Some differentiation is possible, depending on the audience profile of the programmes broadcast, and thus an advertiser can select spots to reach specific audiences, for example, during sports broadcasts, but the advertising is still far from being narrowly targeted.

The problem, therefore, with television is that its wide coverage means high wastage. The cost per thousand may be low, and the number of thousands reached may be very high, but the relevance and quality of those contacts must be questioned. Television advertising time can be very expensive, especially if the advertisement is networked nationally. Actual costs will vary according to such factors as the time of day, the predicted audience profile and size, the geographic area to be covered, the length of time and number of slots purchased and the timing of negotiation. All of this means that very large bills are soon incurred.

'Oh, yes' has now become a famous catchphrase because of an animated bulldog answering rather obvious questions about home and car insurance. Churchill (hence, the choice of a bulldog as the brand icon) advertises throughout the year as a key part of driving traffic to its website or telephone call centre. The animated dog placed into in real-life scenes was very successful in generating awareness and recognition but it also needed to generate enquiries through direct response mechanisms. It originally tried weekday daytime television slots which are thought to be the most effective for linking through to online response but research found that an equally good response later in the day and at weekends. By shifting to new slots, Churchill could advertise at times when competitors were not so vocal and gain even more cost effective responses (Thinkbox, 2011).

Quite apart from the cost involved, television is a low-involvement medium. This means that although the senders control the message content and broadcasting, they cannot check the receiver's level of attention and understanding, because the receiver is a passive participant in what is essentially one-way communication. There is no guarantee that the receiver is following the message, learning from it and remembering it positively. Retention rates tend to be low, and therefore repetition is needed, which in turn means high costs.

The impact of internationally broadcast cable and satellite television channels is changing the shape of television advertising by creating pan-European segment interest groups. MTV, for example, has opened up communication with a huge youth market linked by a common music culture.

## Radio

Radio has always provided an important means of broadcast communication for smaller companies operating within a restricted geographic area. It is now, however, beginning to emerge as a valuable national medium in the UK because of the growth in the number of local commercial radio stations and the creation of national commercial stations such as Classic FM, Virgin Radio and talkSPORT.

While still not as important as television and print, in general terms radio can play a valuable supportive role in extending reach and increasing frequency. Despite being restricted to sound only, radio still offers wide creative and imaginative advertising possibilities and, like television, can deliver to fairly specific target audiences. Narrow segments can be attractive for specialist products or services.

Churchill used radio to support its television advertising (see above). Research found that 49 per cent of those who had seen the television campaign planned to follow it up online. However, 62 per cent of people who had also been exposed to the radio advertising planned to follow it up (RAB, 2009). Radio can be very effective at working closely with television as the advertisements can be scheduled to coincide and follow linked themes. It is easier with Churchill as the dog's voice is very distinctive and the 'oh yes' catchphrase immediately ensures brand recognition and appeal, evoking the television ads.

Compared with television, radio normally offers a low cost per time slot. However, as a low-involvement medium, it is often not closely attended to, being used just as background rather than for detailed listening. More attention might be paid, however, to the car radio during the morning and evening journey to and from work. Nevertheless, learning often takes place only slowly, again requiring a high level of repetition, carrying with it the danger of counter-productive audience irritation at hearing the same advertisements again and again. Radio is, therefore, a high-frequency medium. Television for the same budget will provide more reach, but far less frequency. The choice between them depends on objectives, and brings us back to the earlier discussion of 'reach versus frequency'. Large advertisers, however, can use the two media in conjunction with each other, with radio as a means of reminding listeners of the television advertisements and reinforcing that message.

## Cinema

Cinema can be used to reach selected audiences, especially younger and male. In the UK, for example, nearly 80 per cent of cinema goers are in the 15–34 age group. The improvement in the quality of cinema facilities through the development and marketing of multiplexes has led to something of a resurgence in cinema audiences.

Cinema goers are a captive audience, sitting there with the intention of being entertained. Thus the advertiser has an increased chance of gaining the audience's attention. The quality and impact of cinema advertising can be much greater than that of television, because of the size of the screen and the quality of the sound system. Cinema is often used as a secondary medium rather than as a main medium in an advertising campaign. It can also screen advertisements, rated consistently with the film's classification, that would not necessarily be allowed on television.

## Magazines

The main advantage of a printed medium is that information can be presented and then examined selectively at the reader's leisure. A copy of a magazine tends to be passed around among a number of people and kept for quite a long time. Add to that the fact that magazines can be very closely targeted to a tightly defined audience, and the attraction of print media starts to become clear. Advertisers also have an enormous range of types and titles to choose from.

There exists an enormous number of special-interest magazines, each tailored to a specific segment. As well as broad segmentation, by sex (*Freundin* for women in Germany; *Playboy* for men anywhere), age (*Bliss* and *Mizz* for teenage girls; *The Oldie* for the over-fifties in the UK, described as the mature man's *Private Eye*!) and geography (*The Dalesman* for Yorkshire and its expatriates), there are many narrower criteria applied. These usually relate to lifestyle, hobbies and leisure pursuits, and enable a specialist advertiser to achieve a very high reach within those segments.

*Zoo* is a lifestyle magazine aimed at the younger man. It is light-hearted and covers what the publisher thinks most men are interested in: girls, beer, gadgets, football and sport, men's news and comedy. As the publisher puts it,

> The ZOO consumer is a young (16–24), single male, who sees himself as a bit of a Player. His life is dedicated to being the ultimate lad. He lives for the next party and the next girl. He certainly isn't worried about the future and debts can definitely wait until later. He is a young man relatively unencumbered by thoughts of credit crunches or falling house prices. (Bauer Media, 2011)

However, it would appear that the *Zoo* reader is something of an endangered species. Its circulation by June 2011 was just over 54,000 (although the actual readership is more like 590,000), a significant fall from the back end of 2009 when it was selling just over 100,000 copies. *Zoo* is not alone among so-called 'lads mags' in losing circulation – it seems that men are turning to health and well-being titles instead. Nevertheless, the *Zoo* readership is a well-defined target for certain types of advertiser. The readership is almost 90 per cent male, and 75 per cent are employed, yet with minimal financial commitments (so they've got lots of disposable income). More than half are aged between 15 and 24, and a further 26 per cent aged between 25 and 34.

To extend the readership and involvement with *Zoo*, there is a supporting website (zootoday.com) which is consistent with the main magazine but covers more depth and has movie trailers, clips and interviews along with music and games. All that, plus the showcase of girls' talents! There is also a viral component through which jokes and links can be forwarded to one's mates, and links to social networking sites where readers can also share pictures, videos, stories, links and opinions. It can also be accessed via mobile phone, with 90 per cent of the content automatically fed from the website (Banham, 2011; Bauer Media, 2011; Luft, 2011; Maden, 2011).

Trade and technical journals (whether published in print or online) are targeted at specific occupations, professions or industries. *Funeral Director Monthly*, *Semiconductor Science and Technology*, *The Grocer* and *Professional Security* each provide a very cost-effective means of communication with groups of people who have very little in common other than their jobs.

Magazines have other benefits. Some may have a long life, especially special-interest magazines that may be collected for many years, although the advertising may lose relevance. Normally, though, an edition usually lasts as long as the timing between issues. The regular publication and the stable readership can allow advertisers to build up a campaign with a series of sequential advertisements over time to reinforce the message. An advertiser may also choose to take the same slot – for example, the back page, which is a prime spot – to build familiarity. The advertiser may even buy several pages in the same issue, to gain a short burst of intense frequency to reinforce a message, or to present a more complex, detailed informational campaign that a single- or double-page spread could not achieve.

Trade magazines are under pressure as online plays a bigger role in our lives and publications such as *Accountancy Age* and *Computer Weekly* have abandoned their print format and gone online. In fact, *Media Week* managed to increase its users by 42 per cent by going online. Although the number of trade titles shrank from 5,108 in 2005 to 4,733 in 2010, the main emphasis for many of them has shifted to building an online community rather than a narrow subscription base. This is partially driven by a fall in advertising revenues for display advertising and recruitment advertising, which is increasingly going online. There is also a subtle shift to a diffferent kind of format where the cover price is raised, the articles get longer and are of higher quality, and the briefer news items are moved online. Thus the 166-year-old *British Journal of Photography*, for example raised its cover price from £1.75 to £6.99 to reflect these changes yet interestingly, circulation has increased (Dowell, 2011).

Magazines also have one potentially powerful advantage over broadcast media, which is that the mood of the reader is likely to be more receptive. People often save a magazine until they have time to look at it properly, and because they are inherently interested in the magazine's editorial content, they do pay attention and absorb what they read. This has a knock-on effect on the advertising content too. People also tend to keep magazines for reference purposes. Thus the advertising may not prompt immediate action, but if readers suddenly come back into the market, then they know where to look for suppliers.

The specific cost of a magazine advertising slot will vary according to a number of factors. These include its circulation and readership profile, the page chosen and the position on the page, the size of the advertisement, the number of agreed insertions, the use of colour and bleed (whether the colour runs to the edge of the page or not), and any other special requirements.

## Newspapers

The main role of newspapers for advertisers is to communicate quickly and flexibly to a large audience. National daily papers, national Sunday papers and local daily or weekly papers between them offer a wide range of advertising opportunities and audiences.

*Classified advertisements* are usually small, factual and often grouped under such headings as furniture, home and garden, lonely hearts, etc. This is the kind of advertising used by individuals selling their personal property, or by very small businesses (for example, a one-woman home-hairdressing service). Such advertisements are a major feature of local and regional newspapers. Display advertising has wider variations in size, shape and location within the newspaper, and uses a range of graphics, copy and photography.

*Display advertisements* may be grouped under special features and pages: for instance, if a local newspaper runs a weddings feature it brings together advertisers providing the various goods and services that the bride-to-be would be interested in. Such groupings offer the individual advertisers a degree of synergy.

Local newspapers are an important advertising medium, not only for small businesses, but for national chains of retailers supporting local stores and car manufacturers supporting local dealerships. In 2010, regional press had a 10 per cent share (worth £1.6 billion) of total UK advertising revenue, the same as national press and well behind television and online with 26 per cent each. This is a sign of the shift away from print media to more the more immediate, highly visual and personal communication possible through online and television media. We just have less time nowadays to read regional newspapers (Newspaper Society, 2010).

Advertising in the *Sunday Times* can be expensive: the back page of the main news section or the business section of the paper costs upwards of £98,000 (excluding VAT) for one insertion (http://nicommercial.com/assets/pdfs/timesdisplayratecard.pdf). It has a readership of 3.1 million and the *Sunday Times Magazine* is the undisputed market leader with those earning in excess of £50,000 per year. The average income of all *Sunday Times* readers is £37,000 so it is a very attractive advertising medium for upmarket and aspirationial brands.

The main problem with newspaper advertising is related to its cost-efficiency if an advertiser wants to be more selective in targeting. Wastage rates can be high, as newspapers can appeal to quite broad segments of the population. Furthermore, compared with magazines, newspapers have a much shorter lifespan and can have problems with the quality of reproduction possible.

## Advertising hoardings, ambient and outdoor media

The next group of advertising media includes posters and hoardings, ambient media (such as advertising on bus tickets, toilet walls and store floors) as well as transport-oriented advertising media (advertising in and on buses, taxis and trains and in stations). It can be very cost-effective in reaching a large number of people but the problem is whether such advertising is noticed and remembered.

Whatever the type of outdoor medium used, the purpose is generally the same: to provide quickly digestible messages to passers-by or to provide something for a bored passenger to look at. As with any medium, the advertising may be a one-off, or it may be part of a multimedia campaign. An advertisement at an airport for a nearby hotel would be a one-off but long-term campaign with a very focused purpose, whereas a hoarding advertising a car would probably be only one element tied into a campaign with a theme extending across television, print and direct marketing as well.

*Advertising posters* range from small home-made advertisements placed on a noticeboard to those for giant hoardings. This section concentrates on the latter group. Hoarding sites are normally sold by the fortnight. Being in a static location, they may easily be seen 10–20 times in a fortnight by people on their way to and from work or school, etc. In the UK, over one-third of poster sites are taken by car or drink advertisers. The reach may be small, but the frequency can be quite intense. They can, however, be affected by some unpredictable elements, out of the control of the advertiser. Bad weather means that people will spend less time out of doors, and are certainly not going to be positively receptive to outdoor advertising. Hoardings and posters are also vulnerable to the attentions of those who think they can improve on the existing message with some graffiti or fly posting.

Nevertheless, hoardings offer an exciting medium with a great deal of creative scope, capitalising on their size and location. Backlighting, for example, can give a clearer, sharper image, while the potential of digital hoardings to create moving, changing messages opens up many possibilities. It pays, however, to be careful in the location of such ultra-creative billboards, since to be the cause of multiple pile-ups by distracting drivers' attention is not desirable PR!

Size is one of the greatest assets of the advertising hoarding, creating impact. Over 80 per cent of hoarding space in the UK is taken by 4-, 6- or 48-sheet sites (a 48-sheet hoarding is 10 feet by 20 feet). Also, sites can be selected, if available, according to the match between traffic flows and target audience. However, in appealing to a mobile audience, the message needs to be simple and thus usually links with other elements of a wider campaign, either for generating initial awareness or on a reminder and reinforcement basis.

Finally, there are the *transport-oriented media*. These include advertisements in rail or bus stations, which capture and occupy the attention of waiting passengers who have nothing better to do for a while than read the advertisements. Similarly, advertising inside trains, taxis and buses has a captive audience for as long as the journey takes. Advertising on the outside of vehicles, perhaps even going so far as to repaint an entire bus with an advertisement, extends the reach of the advertisement to anyone who happens to be around the vehicle's route.

Advertising on the sides of buses was chosen as part of a campaign organised by the Ahmadiyya Muslim Association to tackle Islamophobia. The objective was to educate people about Islam and to overcome some of the prejudices and sterotypes of the faith. Almost 100 buses in London and 60 in Glasgow carried the poster for four to eight weeks, after which it was rolled out to buses in other major cities such as Birmingham, Bradford and Leicester, and coupled with a door-to-door leafleting campaign.

Research has shown that there are very deeply entrenched negative perceptions of the Islamic faith within mainstream British society, and the organisers of this campaign hope that it represents at least a small first step to making a difference. But there were critics, even within the Muslim community. Did the organisers really think that a bus advertisement would make any difference to entrenched beliefs (although it did generate a lot of secondary media coverage and debate), especially when negative stories from Pakistan, Afghanistan and other Islamic states flash across the news screens almost every night? Then there is the question of target audiences. Is it really people in the large cities with large Muslim populations that need to be addressed or does the problem really lie in 'middle

England'? Undoubtedly, the need to challenge the negativity and the stereotypes is very great, but it is a complex, difficult and long-term project (Talwar, 2011).

A poster on buses attempts to change negative perceptions of the Islamic faith
*Source*: E M Clements Photography

## Online advertising

Online advertising is a recognised medium for reaching target audiences, especially now that internet penetration is reaching 80 per cent across Europe. In the UK in 2010, online advertising was worth £4 billion and accounted for 25 per cent of advertising spend in the UK. To put this into context, £4.28 billion was spent on television advertising. It seems that many advertisers are starting to regard video-based display advertising on social media sites as an attractive medium, as expenditure on this doubled over the course of the year (*Daily Telegraph*, 2011). This is perhaps unsurprising given that users spend about 25 per cent of their online time on social networking sites, and watch an average of 4.1 hours of online video material per month. For the first half of 2011, it appears that the trend has continued, with expenditure on online advertising actually overtaking that of television (Fenton, 2011).

Internet advertising has many advantages, not least its potential to provide 'direct response' by clicking through to a website, its creative flexibility to use colour, sound and movement, and its capacity for targeting. This can work in the obvious way, for example an advertisement for an airline displayed on a travel website, to catch the attention of an interested audience. Advertisements running on sites with related content are 61 per cent more likely to be recalled than those shown on sites with unrelated content (McPheters & Co, 2009b). Internet advertising can also work in a more personalised way. If, for example, you have been browsing certain kinds of goods on a retailer's website, you might well find that advertisements for those goods start to appear on other websites that you are visiting. Clearly, you've shown interest by the initial act of browsing, and thus the advertising is inserted to try to convert that to action.

The internet is not a perfect advertising medium by any means. Pop-up blockers can prevent some advertising from being seen at all, and where advertisements are actually displayed, the viewer can ignore them or skip over them too quickly to take the message in. Research conducted by strategic branding agency McPheters and publisher Condé Nast (McPheters & Co, 2009a) suggested that 63 per cent of banner advertisements were not even seen by users of the web. The study showed that consumers' recall of magazine advertising is three times higher than that of internet banner advertising, and television ad recall is twice that of magazines.

*eg* Banner advertising appeared to work very well for Liam Gallagher and his band Beady Eye. During the first week of July 2011, the only advertising that was running for the band's album, *Different Gear, Still Speeding*, in the UK was in the form of expandable video banner advertising. These ads were placed in male-oriented lifestyle and sports websites. The ads were placed on a 'cost per engagement' basis, which means that the advertising space is only paid for when a viewer actively engages with it in a defined way for a specific length of time. It is not the same as 'pay per click' where the viewer clicks through to a different website. In Beady Eye's case, for example, the required engagement was a viewer rolling over the ad to expand it and set the video content going. By the end of the week, sales were 80 per cent higher than they had been at the start of the week, and overall the week's sales were 20 per cent higher than average weekly sales since the album's release. At first sight, it could be argued that the fact that the band were playing a number of gigs that week had helped sales, but analysis of the engagement data by the media companies involved suggested that the sales increase was attributable to the banner campaign (Brand-e.biz, 2011; Shearman, 2011c).

However, the limitations and disadvantages of online advertising are no more 'fatal' than those of any other medium, however, and simply emphasise the importance of incorporating the internet into a coherent integrated communications strategy. And as with any other medium, it is also important to understand the target market and its usage patterns in order to identify the most appropriate use of the medium. The message should be communicated in a way that will move the viewer through to further action, usually a click-through, whether that is to make an enquiry, place an order or just to get more detailed information.

*eg* It is increasingly difficult to think of campaigns in terms of only one communications medium these days. The ways in which consumers interact with various media and the resulting synergies between them mean that advertisers have to think 'integrated'. There is, for example, a natural synergy between television and online activity. Thinkbox has claimed that 60 per cent of viewers go online after watching television two or three times a week and 37 per cent claim to do it every day. Not all of that activity is directly linking brands' television advertising or sponsorship activity with the viewer's online behaviour. Some viewers may follow up something they've seen on television by visiting a brand's social media page even though the content of the two media isn't necessarily synchronised. What advertisers are interested in, however, is the relatively small proportion of viewers who are deeply involved in following up a direct link between something that was on television with related online content, such as we saw in the Churchill insurance examples earlier in the chapter. Domino's Pizza, for example, sponsored a new game show, *Red or Black?* on ITV, screened at a time on a Saturday night when people might well be thinking about having a pizza delivered! The campaign not only featured standard advertising in the ad breaks during the programme but also linked closely to online advertising, an online game and prompts within ITV's own *Red or Black?* play-along game on its own website. Everyone entering the game on itv.com got a coupon from Domino's, with the winners getting a different prize (Nutley, 2011).

## Developing an advertising campaign

It is almost impossible that one free-standing advertisement in the press or on television would be sufficient to achieve the results expected, in terms of the impact on the target audience. Normally, advertisers think about a campaign that involves a predetermined theme but is communicated through a series of messages placed in selected media chosen for their expected cumulative impact on the specified target audience.

Google with 86 per cent of the search market is still the first choice for most computer users but Microsoft launched a campaign in support of its own version, Bing in 2009. It used television advertisements across ITV, Channel 4 and Five, and on channels carried by Sky and Virgin over a three-month period with the objective of gaining awareness and use. It was supported by online and social network advertising. The strapline was 'Bing and Decide' and aimed to show consumers how it differed from other search engines in terms not only of its aesthetic appeal, but also of its more sophisticated approach to cutting the information overload that tends to face users of other providers by categorising the results. Microsoft realises that it is going to have to be patient in making headway against the might of Google – it might take 10 or 15 years. In June 2011, Bing had 4 per cent of the search market (Barnett, 2010; Shearman, 2011d).

There are a number of stages in the development of an advertising campaign. Although the emphasis will vary from situation to situation, each stage at least acknowledges a need for careful management assessment and decision-making. The stages are shown in Figure 10.2 and are discussed in turn below.

## Deciding on campaign responsibilities

This is an important question of organisational structure and 'ownership' of the campaign. If management is devolved on a product basis, then overall responsibility may rest with the brand or product manager. This certainly helps to ensure that the campaign integrates with sales promotion, selling, production planning, etc., since the brand manager is very well versed in all aspects of the product's life. If, however, management is devolved on a functional basis, then the responsibility for an advertising campaign will lie with the advertising and promotion manager. This means that the campaign benefits from depth of advertising expertise, but lacks the involvement with the product that a brand manager would supply. Whatever the arrangement, it is essential to define who is ultimately responsible for what tasks and what elements of the budget.

## Selecting the target audience

As discussed at p. 342 *et seq.*, knowing who you are talking to is the foundation of good communication. Based on segmentation strategy, the target audience represents the group at whom the communication is aimed within the market. In some cases, the segment and the target audience may be one and the same. Sometimes, however, the target audience may be a subdivision of the segment. If, for instance, an organisation served a particular hobby segment, different approaches to advertising would be taken depending on whether they wanted to talk to serious, casual, high spenders, low spenders, general-interest or specific-interest subgroups. This underlines the need to understand the market and the range of target audiences within it.

**Figure 10.2**
Stages in developing an advertising campaign

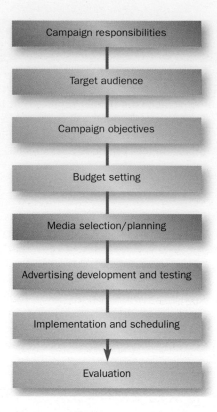

A profile of the target audience increases the chances of successful promotion and communication. Any details, such as location, media viewing (or listening or reading) habits, geodemographics, attitudes and values, can be used to shape the propositions contained within the campaign or to direct the creative approach and media choice.

Whatever the type of product, if the assessment of the target audience is incomplete or woolly, there may be problems in directing campaign efforts later.

## MARKETING IN ACTION

### Not in front of the children?

Sex sells. And undoubtedly there are many images in advertising featuring sexual themes from simply the presence of attractive models, through to mild flirtation or the more erotic executions that sometimes feature in perfume advertising, for example. While these advertisements are clearly targeting an adult audience, and while the media choices also reflect that (so that an advertisement that is acceptable when featured in a magazine with a very clearly defined adult target audience might not be allowed to feature on a billboard – see p. 68), the problem is that under-eighteens are also exposed to them, whether on television, print, posters or (increasingly) online. The fear is that exposure to sexual images featuring young, thin, pretty women can lead to poor self-esteem or even mental and physical problems for a younger viewer. Most adults may be able to rationalise the images they see in advertisements and have the confidence to be comfortable with the difference between the imagery in the advertisement and their own reality, but children could lack this (Holden, 2010). The Advertising Association's view is that there are robust rules and regulations in place to shield children from inappropriate content and that children should indeed be protected from things that are dangerous. It is also true to say, however, that there are many influences in society of which advertising is just one.

Is it realistic to try to prevent children from seeing more adult imagery? It could be argued that they need to be prepared for adult life and will be bombarded with sexual imagery when they reach 18. Currently, 25 per cent of 13–15-year-olds have received sexually explicit texts and 10 per cent of 10–12-year-olds and 25 per cent of 13–15-year-olds have seen explicit images on the internet as reported in the Family Lives survey (Belgutay, 2011). Some of the imagery featured in advertising is positively mild in comparison with the content of some of the more explicit music videos, especially on digital channels such as MTV which is targeted at 18–25-year-olds. Performances on prime-time Saturday evening ITV programmes such as *The X Factor* by artists such as Rihanna and Christina Aguilera before the 9 p.m. watershed have been judged to be very close to the margins of acceptability for a family audience. Then there's the internet. Inappropriate content and the internet can go hand in hand and all the parental controls in the world can't really stop it. Ofcom has found that only 37 per cent of children were constrained by parental controls on internet access, and 12–15-year-olds can spend over 15 hours per week online (Ofcom, 2011). Since 1 March 2011, however, the ASA has had its remit extended to cover online advertising, including pop-ups, banner ads and companies' own advertising on the web and on social networking sites. Advertisers in these media have to conform to the same standards as are applied elsewhere.

The Bailey Review, entitled *Letting Children Be Children* was commissioned by the UK government and published in 2011 (Bailey, 2011). One of the findings was the need for closer working relationships between businesses, broadcasters, advertisers and regulators to ensure continuity and consistency of approach. It included images in magazines and newspapers, parental restrictions on internet use and guidelines for retailers on the design, display and marketing of products for children (Malkani, 2011). It gave full backing to tighter controls on techniques that use children in advertising, and for advertising containing sexual images. The industry has been given 18 months to clean up its act before the government considers introducing legislation (Parsons, 2011). In response, the ASA has already tightened its approach to sexual imagery in outdoor advertising, not only in terms of content, but also in terms of placement (for example, on sites close to schools – see ASA, 2011c for a very detailed breakdown, with illustrations, of exactly what sort of images are, or are not deemed acceptable). It has also joined with other regulatory partners, such as Ofcom, the Press Complaints Commission and the BBC, among others, to launch a single website called ParentPort as a one-stop shop for parents to express concern or make complaints about advertising, products or programmes, etc. There is also a schools engagement programme designed to educate children and parents about advertising regulation, and ongoing market research in order to understand better society's views on what is harmful and offensive (ASA, 2011d).

The issue of what constitutes a sexual image is a subjective assessment of content, and that is why the ASA is so keen to take soundings on what society generally and parents in particular think. The ASA reflects the fact that we all share the responsibility for setting the boundaries of what our children should be exposed to, if they are to enter the adult world as happy, well grounded and balanced people (Shevlin, 2011).

*Sources*: ASA (2011c, 2011d); Bailey (2011), Belgutay (2011); Charlton (2011); Holden (2010); Malkani (2011); Ofcom (2011); Parsons (2011); Shevlin (2011).

## Campaign objectives

Communication objectives were considered at p. 358 *et seq.*, and provide a clear view of what the advertising should accomplish. These objectives need to be specific, measurable and time related. They must also indicate the level of change sought, defining a specific outcome from the advertising task. If there are no measurable objectives, how can achievements be recognised and success or failure judged?

Most advertising is focused on some stage of a response hierarchy model, such as those presented in Figure 9.5 (p. 344). These models highlight the stages in the process of consumer decision-making from initial exposure and awareness through to post-purchase review. Issues such as liking, awareness or knowledge, preference and conviction are important parts of that process, and advertising can aim to influence any one of them. These can thus be translated into advertising objectives with measurable targets for awareness generation, product trial and/or repurchase, attitude creation or shifts, or positioning or preferences in comparison with the competition.

These objectives should be driven by the agreed marketing strategy and plan. Note the difference between marketing and advertising objectives. Sales and market-share targets are legitimate marketing objectives as they represent the outcomes of a range of marketing-mix decisions. Advertising, however, is just one element contributing to that process, and is designed to achieve specific tasks, but not necessarily exclusively sales.

## Campaign budgets

Developing a communication budget was considered at p. 361 *et seq*. Look back to these pages to refresh your memory on the methods of budget setting. Remember that there is no one right or wrong sum to allocate to a campaign, and often a combination of the methods proposed earlier acts as a guide.

Often the setting of budgets is an iterative process, developing and being modified as the campaign takes shape. There is a direct link between budgets and objectives such that a modification in one area is almost certainly likely to have an impact in the other. Even if the underlying philosophy of the budget is the 'objective and task' approach, practicality still means that most budgets are constrained in some way by the cash available. This forces managers to plan carefully and to consider a range of options in order to be as cost-effective as possible in the achievement of the specified objectives.

The first job is to link marketing objectives with the tasks expected of advertising and promotion. Targets may be set, for example, in relation to awareness levels, trial and repeat purchases. Not all these targets would be achieved by advertising alone. Sales promotion, and of course product formulation, may play a big part in repeat purchase behaviour.

## Media selection and planning

The various media options were considered individually at p. 381 *et seq*. The large range of alternative media needs to be reduced down to manageable options and then scheduling (discussed at p. 395) planned to achieve the desired results. The resultant media plan must be detailed and specific. Actual media vehicles must be specified, as well as when, where, how much and how often. This means planning bookings by date, time and space. The plan is the means by which exposure and awareness levels can be achieved. The important aim is to ensure a reasonable fit between the media vehicles considered and the target audience so that sufficient reach and frequency are achieved to allow the real objectives of the advertising a fighting chance of success. This is becoming more difficult as audience profiles and markets change (Mueller-Heumann, 1992). The plan has an important role to play in integrating the campaign effort into the rest of the marketing plan and in communicating requirements clearly to any support agencies.

A number of considerations guide the selection of media. First, the media selected must ensure consistency with the overall *campaign objectives* in terms of awareness, reach, etc. The *target audience* is, however, critical to guiding the detailed media selection. As close a fit as possible is required between medium and audience. A consideration of the *competitive factors* includes examining what competitors have been doing, where they have been doing it, and with what outcomes. A decision may have to be made whether to use the same media as the competition or to innovate. The *geographic focus* might be relevant, depending on whether the target audience may be international, national or regional, and sometimes a selection of media or vehicles may have to be used to reach dispersed groups within the target audience. As discussed above, *budget constraints* mean that practicality and affordability usually enter into the planning at some stage. A proposal of 20 prime-time slots on television might well give the chief accountant apoplexy and have to be replaced with a more modest print campaign that makes its impact through stunning creativity. *Timing* too is an issue, as the plan needs to take into account any lead-in or build-up time, particularly if the product's sales have a strong element of seasonality. Perfumes and aftershaves, for example, look to Christmas as a strong selling period. Advertisers of these products use glossy magazine advertising all year round, but in the weeks up to Christmas, add intensive and expensive television campaigns (it's a good job we don't have smellyvision yet) to coincide with consumers' decision-making for gifts. Similarly, timing is important in launching a new product, to make sure that the right level of awareness, understanding and desire have been generated by the time the product is actually available.

As with any plan, it should provide the reader with a clear justification of the rationale behind the decisions, and should act as a guide as to how it integrates with other marketing activities.

## Advertising development and testing

At this stage, the advertisements themselves are designed and made, ready for broadcasting or printing. The creative issues involved have already been covered elsewhere within this chapter. As the advertisement evolves, pre-testing is often used to check that the content, message and impact are as expected. This is particularly important with television advertising, which is relatively expensive to produce and broadcast, and also would represent an extremely public embarrassment if it failed.

Tests are, therefore, built in at various stages of the advertisement's development. Initial concepts and storyboards can be discussed with a sample of members of the target audience to see if they can understand the message and relate to the scenario or images in the proposed advertisement. Slightly further on in the process, a rough video of the advertisement (not the full production – just enough to give a flavour of the finished piece) can also be tested. This allows final adjustments to be made before the finished advertisement is produced. Even then, further testing can reassure the agency and the client that the advertisement is absolutely ready for release. Print advertisements can similarly be tested at various stages of their development, using rough sketches, mock-ups and then the finished advertisement.

Pre-testing is a valuable exercise, but its outcomes should be approached with some caution. The testing conditions are rather artificial, by necessity, and audiences (assuming even that the testers can assemble a truly representative audience) who react in certain ways to seeing an advertisement in a theatre or church hall might respond very differently if they saw that same advertisement in their own homes under 'normal' viewing conditions.

## Implementation and scheduling

In the implementation phase, a number of professional experts may be needed to develop and deliver the advertising campaign. These will include graphic designers, photographers, commercial artists, copywriters, research specialists and, not least, media and production companies. The role of the advertising manager is to coordinate and select these professionals within a budget to achieve the planned objectives.

A key part of the implementation phase is the scheduling of the campaign. This describes the frequency and intensity of effort and guides all production decisions. There are many different scheduling patterns (Sissors and Bumba, 1989). Sometimes, advertising takes place in *bursts*, as shown in Figure 10.3. This means short-term, intense advertising activity, such as that often found with new product launches. Most organisations do not have the resources (or the inclination) to keep up such intense advertising activity indefinitely, and thus the bursts are few and far between. The alternative is to spread the advertising budget out more evenly, by advertising in *drips*, also shown in Figure 10.3. The advertising activity is less intense, but more persistent. Reminder advertising for a frequently purchased mature product might take place in drips rather than bursts.

A number of factors will help to determine the overall schedule. *Marketing factors* might influence the speed of the impact required. An organisation launching a new product or responding to a competitor's comparative advertising might want to make a quick impact, for example. If *turnover of customers* is high, then there is a need to advertise more frequently to keep the message available for new entrants into the market. Similarly, *purchase frequency*

**Figure 10.3**
Advertising
expenditure
strategies: 'bursts'
and 'drips'

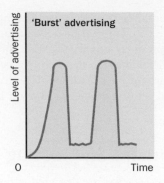
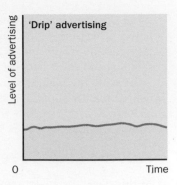

and *volatility* could be relevant factors. If demand is *highly seasonal* or *perishable*, then the scheduling might provide for a short period of high-frequency advertising. The peak time for advertising perfumes and toys, for example, is in the run up to Christmas. Similarly, various chocolate products peak at Easter or Mother's Day, for example. Alternatively, there may be a link with brand loyalty. Higher loyalty may need less frequency, provided that the product is not under competitive attack. This is, however, a dangerous assumption.

If the danger of forgetting is high, then the advertiser is likely to need a more active campaign implemented at regular intervals. Different groups learn and forget at different rates. Therefore, these *retention and attrition rates* of the target audience are yet another assessment that needs to be made. *Message factors* relate to the complexity of the message. A campaign for a new product may need more repetition than one for an established product, because of the newness of the message. More generally, simple messages or those that stand out from the crowd demand less repetition. Similarly, smaller advertisements or those placed in less noticeable spots within a print medium may need more frequency to make sure they are seen.

*Media factors* relate to the choice of media. The fewer media or advertising vehicles in the plan, the fewer OTSs are likely to be needed. This smaller limit may be important for a smaller business with a limited budget or for a major business seeking to dominate a particular medium by means of monopolising the best slots or positions. Such dominance increases the repetition to those in the target audience. The more congested the medium, the more OTSs there need to be, to cut through the background 'noise'.

None of this makes one media plan better than another. It depends on objectives and the particular market circumstances prevailing. If the product is new or seasonal, a more intensive effort may be appropriate. The scheduling plan may, of course, evolve over time. During the introduction stage of the product lifecycle an intensive burst of advertising will launch the product, and this may then be followed by a more spread-out campaign as the growth stage finishes. Creating awareness in the first place is expensive, but critical to a product's success.

## Campaign evaluation

The evaluation is perhaps the most critical part of the whole campaign process. This stage exists not only to assess the effectiveness of the campaign mounted, but also to provide valuable learning for the future.

There are two stages in evaluation. *Interim evaluation* enables a campaign to be revised and adjusted before completion to improve its effectiveness. It enables a closer match to be achieved between advertising objectives and the emerging campaign results. Alternatively or additionally, *exit evaluation* is undertaken at the end of the campaign. Post-testing can check whether the target audience has received, understood, interpreted and remembered the message as the advertiser wished, and whether they have acted upon it.

*eg*

Warburtons is a traditional, family-run baking business from the North-West of England that has now achieved national distribution. However, it needed to encourage more consumers in the South to become and remain brand loyal for their daily or weekly bread shopping. An interactive television advert encouraged viewers to 'press the red button' to participate in a competition to win a family holiday. The objective was to keep consumers on the site for a longer period of time to allow the branded messages to get through. Research showed that the average stay in the interactive area was four minutes, whereas the normal average time was just over two minutes. The campaign was very successful for awareness generation: the spontaneous recall of Warburtons as a bread brand rose from 35 per cent among those who had simply *seen* the ad to 63 per cent among those who had *interacted* with the ad. It was also found that the brand values of being a family-run, innovative yet traditional company were confirmed, and nearly half of those surveyed who had played the game said that they would choose Warburtons ahead of other brands (Sky Media, 2011).

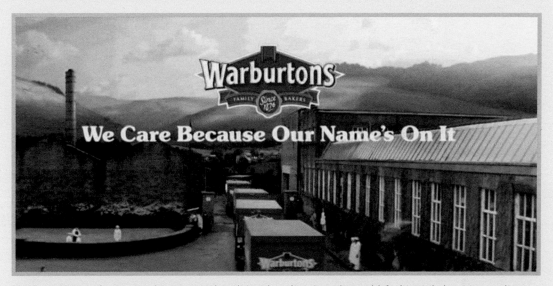

The brand image focuses on heritage and tradition, but there's nothing old-fashioned about its media choices!

*Source*: Image courtesy of The Advertising Archives

## Sales promotion

Traditionally the poor cousin of advertising, sales promotion actually covers a fascinating range of short-term tactical tools that can play a vital complementary role in long-term promotional strategy. Its aim is to add extra value to the product or service, over and above the normal product offering, thus creating an extra inducement to buy or try it. Although individual sales promotions are usually regarded as short-term tactical measures, sales promotion generally, as an element of the promotional mix, is increasingly being recognised as a valid strategic tool, working alongside and supporting other promotional elements. This section of the chapter will define more clearly what sales promotion is and what strategic role it can play within the promotional mix.

Vimto may not be a brand name that comes immediately to mind when you mention fizzy drinks. Despite it having been around for ever (so it seems), only a small percentage of consumers actually knew anything about the brand. Vimto thus turned to sales promotion to get the awareness levels up and to get a better understanding of its brand values. It partnered with Cluedo, the classic family board game, to create a fun and interactive experience for all the family, while communicating messages about Vimto. The game was adapted to the centenary-party preparations at the Vimto factory which included the mixing room, fruit-selection room and secret vault where the recipe is stored, mirroring the study, hall and ballroom, etc. that feature in the Cluedo game. Each room contained a puzzle game to solve against the clock, and there was an overall leader board and a free prize draw. In each room, the brand values of Vimto were highlighted, and the game was available to purchase at a reduced rate with redeemable coupons. The online game attracted 85,000 players and a substantial number of board games were sold, giving the customer a permanent reminder of the brand (www.vimtocluedo.com).

## Definition and role

According to the Institute of Sales Promotion, sales promotion is:

> **. . . a range of tactical marketing techniques designed within a strategic marketing framework to add value to a product or service in order to achieve specific sales and marketing objectives.**

The word 'tactical' implies a short, sharp burst of activity that is expected to be effective as soon as it is implemented. The fact that this activity is *designed within a strategic marketing framework* means, however, that it is not a panic measure, not just something to wheel out when you do not know what else to do. On the contrary, sales promotion should be planned into an integrated communications mix, to make the most of its ability to complement other areas such as advertising and its unique capacity to achieve certain objectives, mostly tactical but sometimes strategic (Davies, 1992).

The key element of this definition, however, is that the sales promotion should *add value to a product or service*. This is something over and above the normal product offering that might make buyers stop and think about whether to change their usual buying behaviour, or revise their buying criteria. As the rest of this chapter will show, this takes the form of something tangible that is of value to the buyer, whether it is extra product free, money, a gift or the opportunity to win a prize, that under normal circumstances they would not get.

Perhaps the main problem with the definition is that the area of sales promotion has almost developed beyond it. The idea of the short-term tactical shock to the market is very well established and understood, and will be seen to be at the heart of many of the specific techniques outlined in this chapter. With the development of relationship marketing, that is, the necessity for building long-term buyer–seller relationships, marketers have been looking for ways of developing the scope of traditional sales promotion to encourage long-term customer loyalty and repeat purchasing behaviour. Loyalty schemes, such as frequent flyer programmes, are sales promotions in the sense that they offer added value over and above the normal product offering, but they are certainly not short-term tactical measures – quite the opposite. Wilmshurst (1993) clearly states that creatively designed sales promotions can be just as effective as advertising in affecting consumers' attitudes to brands. This means, perhaps, that the definition of sales promotion needs to be revised to account for those strategic, franchise-building promotional techniques:

> **. . . a range of marketing techniques designed within a strategic marketing framework to add extra value to a product or service over and above the 'normal' offering in order to achieve specific sales and marketing objectives. This extra value may be of a short-term tactical nature or it may be part of a longer-term franchise-building programme.**

## Sales promotion objectives

### Overview

Sales promotion objectives all fall into three broad categories: communication, incentive and invitation.

Sales promotion has a capacity to communicate with the buyer in ways that advertising would find hard to emulate. Advertising can tell people that a product is 'new, improved', or that it offers certain features and benefits, but this is conceptual information, which people may not fully understand or accept. Sales promotion can, for instance, put product samples into people's hands so that they can judge for themselves whether the claims are true. Learning by one's own experience is so much more powerful and convincing than taking the advertiser's word for it. The incentive is usually the central pillar of a sales promotion campaign. The potential buyer has to be given encouragement to behave in certain ways, through an agreed bargain between seller and buyer: if you do this, then I will *reward* you with that.

Subway sandwiches has launched a loyalty scheme which is mobile based. Customers are able to collect points which can be redeemed through a 2D barcode on their mobile against further purchases in-store. The idea is to attract repeat purchases following an initial purchase in a market dominated by choice. It is a reward for loyalty as far as the customer is concerned, but for Subway, provides a foundation for more targeted, personalised marketing efforts (*Marketing Week*, 2010).

Through its incentives, the promoted product is saying 'Buy ME, and buy me NOW'. The promotion is, therefore, an invitation to consider this product, to think about your buying decision, and to do it quickly. The ephemeral nature of most sales promotions reinforces the urgency of taking up the invitation immediately. It prevents the buyer from putting off trial of the product, because the 'extra something' will not be around for long. For the consumer, in particular, the point of sale represents the crucial decision-making time. A product that is jumping up and down, shouting 'Hey, look at me!' through its sales promotion is offering the clearest possible invitation to do business. The rest of this section will focus on the objectives that sales promotion can achieve within the context of the relationship within which they are used.

### Manufacturer–intermediary (trade promotion)

The intermediary provides a vital service for the manufacturer in displaying goods to their best advantage and making them easily available to the consumer. Any individual intermediary, however, performs this function for a number of manufacturers, and so a manufacturer might wish to use sales promotion techniques to encourage the intermediary to take a particular interest in particular products for various purposes. However, depending on the balance of power between manufacturer and intermediary, the manufacturer might have little choice in the matter. Intermediaries might expect or insist on sales promotions before they will cooperate with what the manufacturer wants.

As shown in Figure 10.4, and discussed below, trade promotions revolve around gaining more product penetration, more display and more intermediary promotional effort. As Fill (2002) points out, however, this might cause conflict between the manufacturer and the intermediary, since the intermediary's prime objective is to increase store traffic. The level of incentive might thus have to be extremely attractive!

**Increase stock levels.** The more stock of a particular product that an intermediary holds, the more committed they will be to put effort into selling it quickly. Furthermore, intermediaries have limited stockholding space, so the more space that your product takes up, the less room there is for the competition. Money-based or extra-product-based incentives might encourage intermediaries to increase their orders, although the effect might be short lived and in the longer term might even reduce orders as intermediaries work through the extra stock they acquired during the promotion.

**Gain more and better shelf space.** There is intense competition between manufacturers to secure shelf space within retail outlets. Demand for shelf space far outstrips supply. Intermediaries, therefore, are willing to accept incentives to help them to allocate this scarce resource to particular products or manufacturers. Again, this may link with money- or product-based trade promotions, but could also be part of a joint promotion agreement or a point-of-sale promotion, for instance. The quality of the shelf space acquired is also important. If a product is to capture the consumer's attention, then it needs to be prominent. This means that it must be displayed either at the customer's eye level or at the end of the aisles in a supermarket where the customer is turning the corner and all the trolley traffic jams occur. There is keen competition for these highly desirable display sites, also called *golden zones*, and again, intermediary-oriented sales promotion may help a manufacturer to make its case more strongly.

**New product launch.** The launch period is a delicate time in any new product's life, and if the distribution aspects of the marketing strategy are weak, then it could be fatal. A new product needs to be accepted by the appropriate intermediaries so that it is available for all those consumers eager to try it. To the trade, however, a new product is a potential risk. What if it doesn't sell? Trade promotions (particularly with a push strategy – see p. 343 *et seq.*) can reduce some of that risk. Money-based promotions reduce the potential financial losses of a product failure, while 'sale or return' promotions remove the fear of being left with unsaleable stock. Sales force support, meanwhile, can reassure the intermediary that staff are ready, willing and able to sell the product and fully understand its features and benefits. This is particularly appropriate with more complex, infrequently purchased items, such as electrical goods.

**Figure 10.4**
Manufacturer–
intermediary
sales promotion
objectives

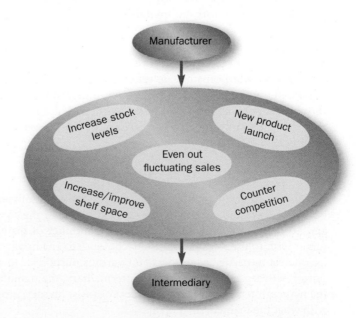

**Even out fluctuating sales.** Some products, such as lawnmowers, ice-cream and holidays, suffer from seasonality. While the design of the product offering or the pricing policies adopted can help to overcome these problems, sales promotion can also play a part. If manufacturers are able to encourage intermediaries to take on more stock or to push the product harder during the 'quieter' periods, sales can be spread a little more evenly throughout the year. This process can also be enhanced by a related consumer-oriented promotion, so that the manufacturer is gaining extra synergy through simultaneous push and pull activity.

**Counter the competition.** It has already been indicated that a manufacturer is competing with every other manufacturer for an intermediary's attention. Sales promotions, therefore, make very useful tactical weapons to spoil or dilute the effects of a competitor's actions. If, for instance, you are aware that the competition is about to launch a new product, you might use a trade sales promotion to load up a key intermediary with your related products, so that at best they will be reluctant to take on the competition's goods, or at worst, they will drive a much harder bargain with the competitor.

## Retailer–consumer (retailer promotions)

In the same way that manufacturers compete among themselves for the intermediary's attention, retailers compete for the consumer's patronage. Store-specific sales promotions, whether jointly prepared with a manufacturer or originating solely from the retailer, can help differentiate one store from another, and entice the public in. Retailers also try to use sales promotions in a longer-term strategic way to create store loyalty, for example through card schemes that allow the shopper to collect points over time that can be redeemed for gifts or money-off vouchers. Retailers use sales promotion for many reasons and these are summarised in Figure 10.5.

**Increase store traffic.** A prime objective for a retailer is to get the public in through the shop door. Any kind of retailer-specific sales promotion has a chance of doing that. Money-off coupons delivered from door to door or printed in the local newspaper, for example, might bring in people who do not usually shop in a particular store. Such promotions might also encourage retail substitution, giving shoppers an incentive to patronise one retailer rather than another. An electrical retailer might advertise a one-day sale with a few carefully chosen items offered on promotion at rock-bottom prices. This bait brings potential customers to the store, and even if the real bargains have gone early, they will still look at other goods.

**Increase frequency and amount of purchases.** Even if a customer already shops at one retailer's outlets, the retailer would prefer them to shop there more often and to spend more.

*eg*

Short-term promotions are often used by retailers to increase store traffic. Supermarkets, for instance, often use price-based offers to draw shoppers into their stores. By advertising rock-bottom bargains on a selected number of big-name brands in the local press and through door-to-door leafleting within a store's catchment area, shoppers are tempted to pay a visit. The range of offers changes week by week, thus keeping the shopper's interest fresh. The hope is that the shopper will keep returning every week and that once in the store, they will buy far more than just a limited range of discounted brands.

**Increase store loyalty.** Supermarkets in particular use sales promotion as a means of generating store loyalty. The kinds of activities outlined in relation to increasing the frequency and amount of purchases help towards this, as does a rolling programme of couponing and money-off offers. The problem with this type of promotion, however, is that it risks creating a 'deal-prone' promiscuous customer who will switch to whichever retailer is currently offering the best package of short-term promotions. To counteract this, some retailers have introduced loyalty schemes using swipe cards.

**Figure 10.5**
Retailer–
consumer sales
promotion
objectives

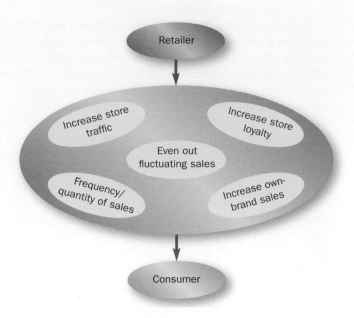

In the UK, Tesco was the first with its Clubcard, and Sainsbury's followed with its Reward card (which later became Nectar). Shoppers have an incentive to shop regularly at a particular retailer in order to accumulate points. Using the customer database, coupons and money-off vouchers can be regularly issued and delivered to the customer's own home, thus creating a stronger, more personal retailer–customer link. As well as promotions such as 'double points' linked with loyalty cards, the major supermarkets have run various aggressive promotions such as 'find it cheaper elsewhere and we'll refund double the difference' and other price matching promises in the battle to establish themselves as the best value provider. Most of them, however, have hitherto involved some effort on the consumer's part – visiting rival stores, buying the product, getting a receipt and then going back to the original store to prove that it could have been bought more cheaply elsewhere. Asda moved this on when it introduced online checking. The customer shops at Asda and then enters details from the till receipt at www.asdapriceguarantee.co.uk. The prices the customer paid at Asda are then compared with those of rival retailers and if the Asda total isn't more than 10 per cent cheaper, a voucher that can be used next time the customer shops at Asda is issued for the difference. Sainsbury's then went one better with its 'Brand Match' scheme, by checking the prices of branded goods at the checkout against competitors' prices. If a competitor's price is cheaper then a voucher is issued for the difference, again redeemable the next time the customer shops at Sainsbury's (Smithers, 2011).

**Increase own-brand sales.** Retailers are increasingly investing in their own-brand ranges. These are, therefore, legitimate subjects for a whole range of consumer-oriented promotions. These promotions do not have to be overtly price or product based.

In-store or online free recipe cards can help to promote the store's fresh foods or own-label products by giving the shopper meal ideas and encouraging them to buy the ingredients. This can be linked with other promotions so that, for instance, one of the own-label ingredients could feature a price reduction to encourage purchase further. Retailers' mailshots and websites can also promote own-label goods, again through recipes, through editorial copy explaining how products can be used and their benefits, or through the more obvious mechanism of extra money-off vouchers.

**Even out busy periods.** In the same way that manufacturers face seasonal demand for some products, retailers have to cope with fluctuations between the very busy periods of the week or year, and the very quiet times. Offering sales promotions that apply only on certain days or within certain trading hours might divert some customers away from the busier periods.

A one-day sale on a Wednesday or Thursday can be a good way for a retailer to divert shoppers away from the busier weekend, especially if it is well advertised in the local area. One DIY retailer also instituted Wednesday afternoon discounts for senior citizens, presumably because that is an easily defined group who can change their shopping day because they are not likely to be working. Tesco, in trying to get its new 'click and collect' shopping service established, offered to provide the service free on Tuesdays and Wednesdays in one store, as a means both of generating trial of it among customers and of diverting transactions onto quieter days of the week. There would normally be a charge of £2 to cover the costs of picking and packing the order ready for the customer to collect.

## Manufacturer–consumer (manufacturer promotion)

While it is obviously important for manufacturers to have the distribution channels working in their favour, there is still much work to be done with the consumer to help ensure continued product success. After all, if consumer demand for a product is buoyant, that in itself acts as an incentive to the retail trade to stock it, effectively acting as a pull strategy. There are many reasons for manufacturers to use sales promotions to woo the consumer, and some of these are outlined below and summarised in Figure 10.6.

**Encourage trial.** The rationale in encouraging trial is similar to that discussed earlier in relation to the intermediary and new product launches. New products face the problem of being unknown and, therefore, consumers may need incentives to encourage trial of the product. Samples help consumers to judge a product for themselves, while coupons, money off and gifts reduce the financial penalty of a 'wrong' purchase. Sales promotions thus play an important role in the early stages of a product's life.

**Expand usage.** Expanding usage involves using sales promotion to encourage people to find different ways of using more of the product so that, of course, they purchase more. Rice

**Figure 10.6**
Manufacturer–consumer sales promotion objectives

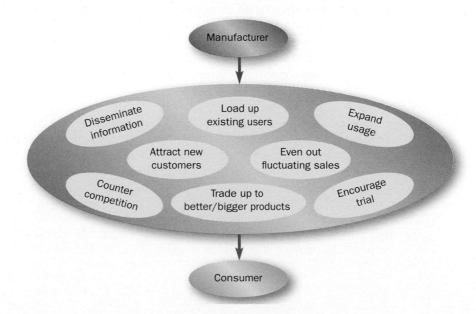

Krispies, for example, ran a promotion asking families to video themselves making recipes involving the product, with the best ones featuring in television advertising. This encouraged consumers to think creatively about how use the product in baking and of course the recipes featuring on television or on-pack give further inspiration.

**Disseminate information.** Sales promotions can be used effectively as a means of getting information across to consumers. Even a small sample pack distributed door to door, for example, not only lets the consumer experience the product, but also gives the manufacturer a chance to tell that consumer quite a lot about the product's features and benefits, where to buy it, and related products in the range. While advertising can do the same sort of information dissemination, it is easily ignored. If the consumer is tempted to try the sample, then they may take more notice of the information with it, and only then pay attention to the advertising.

**Attract new customers.** An established product may be striving to acquire new customers, either by converting non-users or by turning irregular customers or brand switchers into regular buyers. Advertising can only go so far in creating a positive image of the product, and sales promotion may be necessary to generate that first trial, or that repeat purchase. The kind of promotion that depends on collecting tokens over time to qualify for a mail-in offer might be sufficient, if it is backed up with strong advertising, to set up regular purchasing habits and brand preference.

**Trade up.** There are two facets to trading up. One is getting the consumer to trade up to a bigger size, and the other is to get them to trade up to the more expensive products further up the range. Trading up to bigger sizes is particularly useful where the manufacturer feels that the customer is vulnerable to aggressive competition. The bigger size will last longer and, therefore, that consumer is going to be exposed less frequently to competitive temptation at the point of sale. Any promotional effort that applies only to the bigger size rather than the smaller one might achieve that kind of trade-up objective. Persuading consumers to trade up to a product higher up the range benefits the manufacturer because such products are likely to earn higher margins. Car dealers and manufacturers often try to do this. Again, using promotions that are specific to one model or product in the range, or using increasingly valuable and attractive promotions as the range goes up, can help to focus the customer's mind on higher things. Price-based promotions are probably not a good idea in this case, because of the risk of cheapening the product's image.

**Load up.** Loading up is partly a defensive mechanism to protect your customers from the efforts of the competition. A customer who is collecting tokens or labels towards a mail-in offer with a tight deadline, or who finds a cut-price offer particularly seductive, might end up with far greater quantities of the product than can be used immediately. Effectively, that customer is now out of the market until those stocks are used up. This is a two-edged sword: the advantage is that they are less likely to listen to the competition; the disadvantage is that you will not be selling them any more for a while either, as you have effectively brought your sales to that customer forward. Of course, if that customer was originally a brand switcher, or a non-user, then you have gained considerably from loading them up.

In the household-cleaning market, sales promotion is seen as a major factor in influencing consumer choice at the point of sale. This increases the volume sold, but not necessarily the overall sales revenue level. Some of these promotions are held at retailer level such as Asda's 'Big Clean' events in January and September 2009 promoting the household cleaning category in its seasonal aisle. Asda ran three-week events offering deals such as two for £1 on Fairy washing-up liquid and Domestos and £1 for products such as Flash. Many point-of-sale promotions are done in conjunction with the manufacturers, as these events are seen as important in driving sales and encouraging more use (Barnes, 2010).

**Even out fluctuating sales.** Evening out fluctuating sales links with the comments made above in relation to manufacturer–intermediary sales promotions. If seasonality is a problem, then sales promotion aimed at the consumer could help to even out the peaks and troughs a little.

**Counter the competition.** Again, the concept of countering or spoiling competitors' activities was introduced in the discussion of manufacturer–intermediary sales promotions. Diverting the consumer's attention through your own promotion can dampen the effects of the competitors' efforts, particularly if what they are doing is not particularly creative in its own right. Also, a well-chosen, regionally based sales promotion can seriously distort or introduce an element of doubt into the results of a competitor's test marketing.

## Methods of sales promotion to consumers

### Money-based

Money-based sales promotions are a very popular group of techniques used by manufacturers or intermediaries. Sometimes they work on a 'cash-back' basis (collect a certain number of tokens then send away for a cash rebate), but more often they are immediate price reductions, implemented in various ways, designed as a short-term measure either to gain competitive advantage or to defend against competitive actions. Such price reductions must be seen to be temporary or else the consumer will not view them as incentives. Furthermore, if money-based methods are used too often, consumers will begin to think of the promotional price as being the real price. They will then think of the product as being cheaper than it really is, and adjust their perceptions of positioning and quality accordingly (Gupta and Cooper, 1992).

*eg*

The major supermarket chains are keen to give the impression that they offer better value for money than their competitors, and short-term reduced price promotions are one way of reinforcing this stance. All the major chains have their generic ranges (see p. 220 *et seq.*) at the bottom of the price range and occasionally these are used to make attention-grabbing price statements. Thus at various times shoppers have found washing-up liquid at 7p per bottle, tins of beans at 3p per can and other products selling at approximately 10 per cent of the price of their premium branded competitors. These are in addition to a day-to-day selection of less drastic short-term price cuts on other own-label and premium brands. The voluntary chains also need to develop their own price-cutting strategies in order to compete with the major multiples. Spar offers 50 'Real Deal' promotions every three weeks. These offers are based on comparisons with competitors and are heavily promoted at the point of sale to attract the customer's attention. In addition there are seasonal and special event promotions to keep the sense of value at the forefront of the customer's mind (www.spar.co.uk).

Supermarket chains vie with each other in offering price promotions to attract customers

*Source*: Spar, www.spar.co.uk

Coupons (printed vouchers that the consumer takes to a retail outlet and uses to claim a set amount of money off a product) are a form of money-based sales promotion that do not look like a price cut mainly because the price quoted on the shelf or on the product remains intact.

The coupon is also a little more selective, in that only those who collect a coupon and remember to redeem it qualify for the discount. However, to counter that, coupons are very common, and consumers are over-exposed to them. Unless a coupon carries a significant discount on the product, or applies to something intrinsically new and exciting, it is difficult as a consumer to be enthusiastic about them.

*eg* Stiletto Foods used a 50p coupon to drive trials and increase sales of its recently launched Mrs Crimbles gluten-free fresh bread. The bread is listed in Sainsbury's, Waitrose, Budgens, Nisa and Booths and has a recommended price of £1.99. The coupons were distributed through direct mail (Valassis Ltd, 2010).

Coupons are distributed using a variety of means. They are printed within advertisements, on leaflets delivered from door to door, on inserts within magazines and newspapers, through direct mail, at the point of sale and on packs. Increasingly coupons are distributed via the internet and mobile phones, adapting to fit with modern lifestyles. It's convenient for the customer, but there are also some advantages for the promoter, such as lower costs (no printing, postage or physical distribution costs); ability to use couponing with a younger audience; same-day distribution; and the ability to track individual coupons more easily. Electronically distributed coupons can also be targeted to individuals as part of a strategic relationship building campaign.

For manufacturers, coupons act as a kind of pull strategy, creating an upturn in consumer demand for the product, thus encouraging retailers to stock and prominently display the brand. By telling them what is available and by reducing the financial risks of purchase, coupons can help the consumer get round to trying a product, making a subsequent purchase, or trading up, either to larger sizes or to products further up the range. The main problem for manufacturers is misredemption. Some supermarkets, overtly or covertly, will accept any coupon at the checkout, regardless of whether the consumer has actually bought the coupon's product or not. Preventing this from happening is difficult.

A big drawback of money-based sales promotions is that because money-based sales promotions are so common among consumer goods, it is very difficult to raise much enthusiasm about them in the market. The main problem is the lack of creativity that usually accompanies these methods. It is also far too easy for a competitor to copy or match a money-based promotion, and thus any competitive advantage may be short lived.

# MARKETING IN ACTION

## Printing money

'The more you buy, the more you save with Lidl' is an attractive headline (*Daily Express*, 2010). Cut out the voucher in the newspaper to claim £5 off for every £30 spent. The usual sort of terms and conditions applied: 'one voucher per single transaction, copied, damaged or defaced coupons will not be accepted. Only original coupons are valid. This voucher has no cash value, is non-exchangeable and non-refundable. This voucher is valid in all UK stores.' At least this promotion isn't for a specific product; so as long as it is redeemed against shopping done in Lidl, it is being legitimately redeemed. Coupons against a specific brand can be harder to police, however. The brand owner relies on the retailer checking that the customer has actually bought the correct product and that the coupon is still valid. It doesn't always happen as it should. In the USA, a 25 cent coupon was printed in local newspapers for a new brand called 'Breen'. About 70,000 of the coupons were redeemed by retailers within a few weeks. The trouble was that there was no brand called Breen and it was an undercover operation by the Coupon Fraud Control centre!

This sort of misredemption may not seem like a big deal to the consumer who feels that they are getting just a few pence off their shopping or to the retailer who is just interested in keeping the checkout queue flowing, but effectively it is fraud. In essence, the brand owner is giving the customer money to which they are not entitled or as the ISP sees it, this is 'no different from allowing consumers to shoplift' (as quoted by Zuke, 2010a). Collectively, this sort of practice costs the brand owners £50 million, and it has been estimated that one in six of the 450 million coupons issued in the UK is redeemed against the wrong product, which undermines confidence in coupons. Up until October 2009, for example, Tesco allowed consumers to redeem coupons against any purchases and claimed the value back from the supplier. Pedigree Petfoods took a stand against this, however, and refused to reimburse Tesco. Tesco changed its policy and only redeems coupons against the relevant item. Barcode technology can help. Programming the checkout to check the expiry date and redeem a coupon only if the right product has been purchased is possible, but UK retailers are reluctant to do this, as they think that accepting any coupons regardless of what is purchased is popular with customers and gives a competitive edge. Tesco suppliers can pay £500 to have coupons checked electronically, or they can opt to have coupons manually checked by the checkout operator.

Although the retailers claim to have tackled misredemption, a mystery-shopping survey commissioned by the Institute of Promotional Marketing showed that it is still a problem in some chains. Half of the Waitrose stores visited misredeemed the coupon; 35 per cent of Tesco stores; 25 per cent of Asda stores; 24 per cent of Sainsbury's and only 15 per cent of Morrisons stores. Since the mystery shopper only purchased one item (that had nothing to do with the item for which the coupon was valid), it couldn't be dismissed as an oversight on the part of the checkout staff.

*Sources: Daily Express* (2010); Faulkner (2011); Smith (2009); Zuke (2010a).

It is also important to remember that money-based promotion can be an expensive way of putting money back in the pockets of people who would have bought the product anyway. If an organisation offers 10p off a product, then that costs the organisation 10p per unit sold in addition to the overhead costs of implementing the offer. In other words, in most cases money-based sales promotions cost the organisation their full cash value, unlike many of the merchandise offers, yet the long-term effect (especially if the technique is over-used) may be to cheapen the value of the product in the consumer's eyes (Jones, 1990).

In their favour, however, money-based promotions are relatively easy to implement, they can be developed and mobilised quickly, and they are readily understood by the consumer. They appeal to many consumers' basic instincts about saving money, and the value of 10p off a price, or £1 cash back, is easy for the consumer to assess. If the objective of the exercise is to attract price-sensitive brand switchers, or to make a quick and easy response to a competitor's recent or imminent actions, then this group of methods has a part to play.

*eg*

Price-based promotions are scrutinised very carefully by the OFT. It considers that such promotions have the potential to mislead consumers. At the heart of the concerns lie the question of what exactly is the price upon which the promotion is based? Is it a 'real' price or an artificially inflated price? If, for example, a price has been artificially raised in the run up to a promotion to make the discount look even better then that is misleading the consumer. The worst short-term pricing practices are described as being:

- drip pricing where an advertised promotional price is increased by supplementary hidden costs – this is often found in the travel and low cost airline sectors;
- time-limited offers which falsely claim that the offer is only available for a limited promotional period;
- 'baiting', where the reduced offer is only available on a limited quantity of stock;
- sales where a reduced offer ('was £100, now only £75') discourages shopping around.

Even with straightforward price-based promotions, there are reasons why brand manufacturers should be wary of using them excessively. Take frozen food, for example. Sales went up just 1.6 per cent in value during 2009, whereas the year before they had risen by nearly 7 per cent. This is not because of a fall in demand but because the big four retailers ran 1,000 more promotions in 2009 and one-third of frozen food was sold on promotion during that period. Promotions drive value out of a product category. The problem is that promotion, far from being a short-term stimulus to sales, becomes an entrenched part of the brand strategy on a long-term basis. The promotions may change, but there is always a promotion and consumers start to expect to see it (Bashford, 2010; Zuke, 2010a).

## Product-based

One of the risks of money-based promotions that was constantly reiterated in the previous section is the ease with which consumers can relate the promotion to price cutting, and thus the image of the product could, in their eyes, be cheapened. One way of overcoming that problem is to opt for a promotion centred on the product itself. The 'extra free' technique involves offers such as an own-label can of tomatoes with '20% extra free' or a pack of kitchen roll offering three rolls for the price of two, proclaiming 'ONE ROLL EXTRA FREE'.

A money-based promotion might put 20p back in the consumer's hand; a product-based promotion might give them 20p's worth of extra product free. To the manufacturer, either option rewards the buyer with 20p, but the buyer's perceptions of the two are very different. 20p in the hand is 'giving something back', whereas extra product free is clearly 'giving something in addition' and, in the consumer's mind, might be valued at a good deal more than 20p. These product-based promotions, therefore, break the link between promotion and price. This method may be especially attractive as a response to a competitor's price attack, as it can shape the value image of a product without a direct price war.

In contrast to offering extra free product within a single package, the BIGIF (*buy 1 get 1 free*) or the BOGOFF (*buy one get one for free*) offers centre on bigger rewards, and are aimed primarily at loading up the customer. Effectively, the offer is saying '100% EXTRA FREE'. Retailers are increasingly using a variation on this method, based around bulk purchasing, making the offer, 'Buy two and get a third one free' (B2G3F? – it doesn't quite have the same ring as BOGOFF, does it?).

*eg* BOGOFF offers may need shorter lead times than the '20 per cent extra free' type, because they do not involve significant changes to the packaging. The offer is made through notices at the shelf, and the checkout is programmed to make the discount automatically when the required number of items have been scanned through. The BOGOFF promotion is popular with marketers seeking to launch a brand or to load up customers. Dairy Crest, for example, has used BOGOFFs extensively to successfully encourage trial of its brands. However, the BOGOFF's days could be numbered if the OFT has its way. If promotional regulation is brought into line with that of other European countries, the BOGOFF as UK consumers know it could be threatened, as the use of the word 'free' is banned if there is any money involved. After all, a BOGOFF is not 'one free' it is 'two for the price of one'.

At retailer level, Tesco launched a variant of BOGOFF with its 'BOGOFF later deal' allowing consumers to pick up the 'free' product the following week to cut down on waste. This is a response to a major criticism of BOGOFFs and similar bulk buying promotions, particularly those involving food products, that they encourage consumers to take more than they actually need so that lots of food ends up being thrown away because the consumer didn't manage to use it all before it went off. Generally, however, BOGOFFs are becoming less popular as a competitive weapon. Asda set the tone, abandoning BOGOFFs in 2006 as it refined its 'Every Day Low Pricing' policy. Morrisons, Tesco and Somerfield responded by reducing the number of giveaways in favour of price cuts. In more recent recessionary times, there does appear to have been a resurgence in bulk buying deals; there are BOGOFFs around as well as bundled discount deals ('buy 2 for £5' where the items are £3 each, 'any 3 for £10' across a variety of goods within a category, or 'meal deals') that stop short of offering something for free.

So do BOGOFFs work? Well there is evidence that they can drive a trial; a survey by the IGD in 2007 showed that one-quarter of consumers had tried a new product because of a BOGOFF, compared with 16 per cent who had been lured by a 3 for 2, and 7 per cent by a free sample. They can also provide a short-term boost to sales but they need to be used sparingly to avoid longer-term problems with distorting consumers' price perceptions and sensitivity. And as mentioned earlier, there is the product type to consider: a BOGOFF might make more sense for products in 'expandable' categories such as biscuits, cake and sweets where an extra pack of product can easily be used by a household, but for meat and more perishable food products, or for health and beauty products where consumers don't end up using more as a result of a BOGOFF (they just stock up and then buy less frequently), it is more doubtful (*The Grocer*, 2008; *Just-food*, 2010; Zuke, 2010b).

## Gift, prize or merchandise-based

A wide range of activities depend on the offer of prizes, low-cost goods or free gifts to stimulate the consumer's buying behaviour. Holidays, brand-related cookery books, mugs or clothing featuring product logos and small plastic novelty toys are among the vast range of incentives used to complement the main product sale.

**Gifts or merchandise.** Self-liquidating offers invite the consumer to pay a small amount of money, and usually to submit specified proofs of purchase, in return for goods that are not necessarily directly related to the main product purchase. The money paid is usually just enough to cover the cost price of the goods and a contribution to postage and handling, and thus these promotions become self-financing if the expected number of customers takes them up. Often, such a promotion is used to reinforce the brand name and identity of the products featuring the scheme.

When Country Life Butter ran an advertising campaign it decided to run a family-oriented self-liquidating promotion at the same time. In return for three on-pack vouchers plus £1.99, a soft-toy forest animal could be acquired. The campaign was designed to encourage loyalty and to encourage consumers to select the Country Life brand at the point of sale. The offer was made on 12 million blocks of butter and thus the maximum number of soft toys required and the maximum cost could be calculated (*Promotions & Incentives*, 2006).

In the case of a free mail-in, the consumer can claim a gift, free of charge, in return for proofs of purchase and perhaps the actual cost of postage (but not handling charges or the cost of the gift itself). The free goods attract the consumer and encourage a higher response rate, and the responses potentially provide the organisation with direct marketing opportunities. Of course, the promotion is only free to the consumer. The promoter has to consider carefully the merchandise costs, postage, packing, processing and even VAT. All of this has to be put into the context of the likely response rate, so that the total cost of the promotion can be forecast and an appropriate quantity of merchandise can be ordered and available when the promotion begins.

Offering free gifts contained inside or banded on to the outside of the pack can make a big impact at the point of sale because the reward is instant, and the purchaser does not have to make any special effort to claim it. One-off gifts are designed to bring the consumer's attention to a product and to encourage them to try it. The offer might shake them out of a routine response purchase and make them think about trying a different brand.

*eg* Dreamworks was on the lookout for a brand to be a partner for on-pack promotions. It wanted a children's food brand as it was felt that there was synergy between children's food and films such as *Shrek*. The studio teamed up with McDonald's to promote *Bee Movie*, linking it with Happy Meals and followed that with a promotion linked with *Shrek the Third*. Dreamworks also created an on-pack competition with cereal brand Sugar Puffs (Buchanan, 2008).

'Free with product' is similar to an on-pack offer, except that the gift is not attached to the product but has to be claimed at the checkout. The consumer, for example, might be invited at the point of sale to buy a jar of coffee and claim a free packet of biscuits. The checkout can tell whether the conditions of the promotion have been met and automatically deducts the price of the biscuits from the final total.

**Customer-loyalty schemes.** Given the increasingly high cost of creating new customers, organisations have turned their attention to ways of retaining the loyalty of current customers. Major international airlines have their frequent flyer schemes, many different retail and service organisations give away air miles with purchases, and petrol stations and supermarkets issue swipe cards through which customers can accumulate points as mentioned earlier. All of these schemes are designed to encourage repeat buying, especially where switching is easy and generic brand loyalty is low.

Price promotions can be dangerous in that they encourage consumers to become price sensitive, and are easily copied by competitors. Tokens, points and stamps that can be traded in for other goods are all ways of adding value to a product, while avoiding costly price competition. They are thus known as alternative currencies.

One of the problems with loyalty schemes, however, is the sheer number of them. When every airline has a frequent-flyer scheme and when every supermarket has a loyalty club, then

*eg* Plumbing Trade Supplies (PTS) is a leading supplier of plumbing supplies with over 320 trade counters across the UK. It runs the Love2shop scheme through which its customers build up money towards a gift voucher for every purchase made from selected product ranges. The amount earned ranges from 25p (on a simple connector) to £100 (on a solar panel system). The gift vouchers are not for further plumbing supplies from PTS, but for high street retailers (PTS, 2011).

the competitive edge is lost. Furthermore, there is evidence that the loyalty generated by such schemes is questionable (MacDonald, 2010). Nevertheless, loyalty schemes are fast becoming an established part of the marketing scene.

Nectar is the most popular loyalty scheme in the UK with 16.8 million users followed by Boots (16.4 million) and Tesco (15 million). Loyalty cards enable the user to collect points in stores and then redeem them either for store-related discount vouchers or against other goods and services (for example, Tesco Clubcard vouchers can be used to buy discounted tickets for family days out).

Over 86 per cent of consumers regularly use a loyalty card but 93 per cent of shoppers would not stop visiting the store if it did not have a scheme (YouGov survey reported by MacDonald, 2010). Nevertheless, most major supermarkets have loyalty schemes, although Asda regards them as a gimmick and prefers to invest in offering lower prices at the point of sale. One reason suggested for Tesco outperforming Asda was the 'double points' scheme for its Clubcard holders which had proved highly successful.

Of course, loyalty schemes aren't really about sales promotion; they are about data collection and mining so that retailers can better understand consumer shopping behaviour and patterns as a foundation for targeted campaigns (see p. 173). Tesco has defined six broad segments among its customer base: upmarket shoppers, health-focused shoppers, traditional cookers, mainstream families, convenience shoppers and price-sensitive shoppers, and then there are a further 17 distinct customer groups within that, such as calorie counters, greens and promotion junkies. Promotions and information can thus be matched to the classification of a particular customer based on that individual's shopping history. It isn't just about targeting individual households with tailored offers, though. An analysis of customer data in a town showed that a large proportion of ethnic shoppers were not buying full meals, but staple items such as large bags or rice and loose herbs. Tesco decided to build a superstore in the area which offered 800 different foreign-food products, a Halal butcher, and newspapers in Urdu and Punjabi (Evans, 2010; Hayward, 2009; MacDonald, 2010).

**Contests and sweepstakes.** Gifts given free to all purchasers of a product necessarily are limited to relatively cheap and cheerful items. As Hoover found out, giving away expensive freebies to all purchasers is uneconomic. Contests and sweepstakes, therefore, allow organisations to offer very attractive and valuable incentives, such as cars, holidays and large amounts of cash, to very small numbers of purchasers who happen to be lucky enough to win. Such promotions might be seen as rather boring by consumers, unless there is something really special about them.

Contests have to involve a demonstration of knowledge, or of analytical or creative skills, to produce a winner. Setting a number of multiple-choice questions, or requiring the competitor to uncover three matching symbols on a scratch card, or asking them to create a slogan, are all legitimate contest activities.

With the 2010 World Cup in mind, Coca-Cola launched a 'Longest celebration' promotion for fans to win prizes including tickets to 2010 FIFA World Cup matches. Fans were invited to upload clips of their own goal celebrations with competitions to find the 'most African celebration' and the 'happiest celebration', for instance. Ten prizes were up for grabs, including three big screen televisions and seven experience packages to the World Cup, including flights, accommodation and match tickets. Lesser prizes included 4,500 copies of EA Sports 2010 World Cup South Africa videogame, and many MP3 downloads. Meanwhile, as a response to increased competition, Lucozade Energy ran an on-pack promotion to 'win an adventure every day' which offered such excitement as white water rafting and mountain biking for the lucky winners. This was a contest very much in keeping with the brand's positioning and designed to reinforce it (*Business Wire*, 2010; Julyan, 2010).

Sweepstakes do not involve skill, but offer every entrant an equal chance of winning through the luck of the draw. Additionally, they must ensure that entry is open to anyone, regardless of whether they have purchased a product or not. Thus *Reader's Digest* prize draws have to be equally open to those not taking up the organisation's kind offer of a subscription.

Such activities are popular with both consumers and organisations. The consumer gets the chance to win something really worthwhile, and the organisation can hope to generate many extra sales for a fixed outlay. With price or gift-based promotions, the more you sell, the more successful the promotion, the more it costs you because you have to pay out on every sale. With competitions and sweepstakes, the more successful the activity, the more entries it attracts, yet the prizes remain fixed. The only losers with a popular contest or sweepstake are the consumers, whose chances of winning become slimmer! However, at some stage consumers may become bored with such activities, especially if they do not think they have any reasonable chance of winning. At that point, a more immediate but less valuable incentive might be more appropriate.

### Store-based

This section looks more generally at what can be done within a retail outlet to stimulate consumer interest in products, leading perhaps to trial or purchase.

Sales promotion at the point of sale (POS) is critical in situations where the customer enters the store undecided or is prepared to switch brands fairly readily. Many different POS materials and methods can be used. These include posters, displays, dispensers, dump bins and other containers to display products, as well as video clips and message screens. Interactive POS systems can help customers to select the most appropriate offering for their needs, or can direct them to other promotional offers.

In-store demonstrations are a very powerful means of gaining interest and trial. Food product cooking demonstrations and tasters are used by retailer and manufacturer alike, especially if the product is a little unusual and would benefit from exposure (i.e. new cheeses, meats, drinks, etc.). Other demonstrations include cosmetic preparation and application, electrical appliances, especially if they are new and unusual, and cars. These demonstrations may take place within the retail environment, but the growth of shopping centre display areas provides a more flexible means for direct selling via a demonstration.

## Methods of promotion to the retail trade

Manufacturers of consumer goods are dependent on the retail trade to sell their product for them. Just as consumers sometimes need that extra incentive to try a product or to become committed to it, retailers too need encouragement to push a particular product into the distribution system and to facilitate its movement to the customer. Of course, many of the consumer-oriented activities considered in previous sections help that process through pull strategies. The main push promotions are variations on price promotions and direct assistance with selling to the final customer. These will now be looked at in turn.

## Allowances and discounts

Allowances and discounts aim to maintain or increase the volume of stock moving through the channel of distribution. The first priority is to get the stock into the retailer, and then to influence ordering patterns by the offer of a price advantage. All of the offers discussed here encourage retailers to increase the amount of stock held over a period, and thus might also encourage them to sell the product more aggressively. This may be especially important where there is severe competition between manufacturers' brands.

Retailers can thus be offered discounts on each case ordered or a bulk discount if they fulfil a condition relating to volume purchased. A version of BOGOFF (for example, buy 20 cases and get another two free) is also commonly used. A more complex technique is the discount over-rider, a longer-term, retrospective discount awarded on a quarterly or annual basis, depending on the achievement of agreed volumes or sales targets. These may be applicable to an industrial distributor selling components as a retail outlet. Although the additional discount may be low, perhaps 0.5 per cent, on a turnover of £500,000 this would still be an attractive £2,500.

Count and recount is also a retrospective method in that it offers a rebate for each case (or whatever the stock unit is) sold during a specified period. Thus on the first day of the period, all existing stock is counted and any inward shipments received during the period are added to that total. At the end of the period, all remaining unsold cases are deducted. The difference represents the amount of stock actually shifted, forming the basis on which a rebate is paid.

The theory is simple. Temporary cost-price reductions, retrospective discounts or advertising allowances are given by manufacturers to retailers to encourage them to increase their stocks and/or promote that brand, and this leads to improved sales for the manufacturer. But the reality is different, as bigger retailers take the promotional money on offer from suppliers and then use it generally to keep prices down across the whole store (Bagshaw, 2010). And the competition for shelf space is such that if one manufacturer doesn't play ball then there is another who will cooperate. Although some of the benefit of trade promotion is passed on to the consumer, whether that is reduced prices for one particular brand or across the store, that isn't always the case. It is estimated that 90 per cent of promotions are destined for retailer profit (Leyland and Ball, 2009). Nevertheless, to manufacturers the advantages of promotion are:

- increasing sales volume;
- building a closer relationship with retailers;
- attracting consumer interest, as a promotional price can bring a brand closer in price to the own-brand equivalent, enticing customers to trade up. There is a risk, though, that consumers only buy the brand when it is on promotion, thus leading to only short-term benefits;
- improving profit through volume sales.

The success of any promotion that is passed onto the consumer depends on the retailer, however. The retailer needs to ensure that the promotion is adequately signposted and that stock levels and shelf replenishment keep up with demand. The retailer also needs to ensure that they aren't running too many competing promotions at once within a particular product category, otherwise the impact will be diluted (Bagshaw, 2010; Leyland and Ball, 2009).

Price-based promotions aimed at the trade are less risky than those aimed at consumers, as the organisational buyer will view them as legitimate competitive tactics rather than using them judgementally to make emotive evaluations of the product. Price promotions appeal to the trade because they make a direct and measurable impact on the retailer's cost structure, and the retailer has the flexibility to choose whether to keep those cost savings or to pass them on to the end consumer. However, in common with price promotions offered to the consumer, trade-oriented price promotions do have the disadvantage of being quickly and easily copied by the competition, leading to the risk of mutually destructive price wars.

## Selling and marketing assistance

A number of manufacturer-supported sales and marketing activities assist the re-seller by means of promotion at both local and national level.

In cooperative advertising a manufacturer agrees to fund a percentage of a retailer's local advertising, as long as the manufacturer's products are featured in at least part of the advertisement. Cooperative advertising can be very costly, and thus the manufacturer needs to think very carefully before offering it, as it can potentially put far greater pressure on the manufacturer's own promotional budget than some of the methods previously discussed.

Although, in theory, manufacturer support may result in better advertising, attempts by re-sellers to crowd a print advertisement with products, often with price promotions, tend to undermine the position and value of some goods – fmcg brands in particular. Rather than leaving the control of the advertisement in the hands of an individual re-seller, therefore, some manufacturers prefer to develop dealer listings. These are advertisements, controlled by the manufacturer, which feature the product and then list those re-sellers from whom it can be purchased. These are particularly common with cars, higher value household appliances, and top of the range designer clothing, for example.

Using money to provide merchandising allowances rather than for funding advertising may have a more direct benefit to the manufacturer. Payment is made to the retailer for special promotional efforts in terms of displays and in-store promotions such as sampling or demonstrations. This is especially attractive if the product moves quickly and can sustain additional promotional costs.

A manufacturer may wish to offer training or support for a retailer's sales representatives who deal directly with the public. Such assistance is most likely to be found in connection with higher-priced products of some complexity, for which the purchaser needs considerable assistance at the point of sale. Cars, hi-fi equipment and bigger kitchen appliances are obvious examples of products with substantial technical qualities that need to be explained.

Various prizes, such as cash, goods or holidays, may be used in sales contests to raise the profile of a product and create a short-term incentive. Unfortunately, the prizes often need to be significant and clearly within the reach of all sales assistants if they are to make any real difference to the selling effort. This is especially true when other competitors may adopt similar methods.

Other more direct incentives than those already mentioned are also possible. Additional bonuses, i.e. premium money, may be made available to sales assistants who achieve targets. These are useful where personal selling effort may make all the difference to whether or not a sale is made. However, the manufacturer needs to be sure that the cost is outweighed by the additional sales revenues generated.

# Sales promotion to B2B markets

As the introduction to this chapter made clear, sales promotion in its strictest sense is inappropriate to many B2B markets. Discounts and incentives are applicable in situations where the buyer and seller are in direct contact and there is room for negotiation of supply conditions. Of course, where B2B marketing starts to resemble consumer marketing, for example in the case of a small business buying a range of standard supplies from a wholesaler, much of what has already been said about manufacturer–consumer or retailer–consumer sales promotions applies with a little adaptation.

# Chapter summary

- Advertising is a non-personal form of communication with an identified sponsor, using any form of mass media. Advertising can help to create awareness, build image and attitudes and then reinforce those attitudes through reminders. It is an invaluable support for other elements of the promotional mix, for example by creating awareness and positive attitudes towards an organisation in preparation for a sales team, or by communicating sales promotions. Advertising also has strategic uses within the wider marketing mix. It can contribute to product positioning, thus supporting a premium price, or it could help to even out seasonal fluctuations in demand.

- The advertising message is extremely important. It has to be informative, persuasive and attention grabbing. It has to be appropriate for the target audience and thus speak to them in terms to which they can relate. There are several types of creative appeal that advertisers can use: rational, emotional and product centred. Once the message and its appeal have been decided, the advertisement has to be prepared for print or broadcasting. In either case, the advertisement has to be relevant to the target audience, making a sufficient impact to get the desired message across and to get the audience to act on it.

- The advertiser has a wide choice of media. Television has a wide reach across the whole population, but it can be difficult to target a specific market segment precisely. Radio can deliver fairly specific target audiences, and is an attractive medium for smaller companies operating in a defined geographic area covered by a local radio station. Cinema is a relatively minor medium delivering captive, well-profiled audiences. It can make a big impact on the audience because of the quality of the sound and the size of the screen. Print media broadly consist of magazines and newspapers. Magazines tend to have well-defined readerships who are receptive to the content of advertisements relevant to the magazine's theme. Newspapers, on the other hand, have a very short life span and are often skimmed rather than read properly. A reader is unlikely to read through the same copy more than once. Outdoor media include advertising hoardings, posters, ambient and transport-related media. They can provide easily digested messages that attract the attention of bored passengers or passers-by. They can generate high frequency as people tend to pass the same sites regularly, but can be spoiled by the weather and the ambience of their location.

- Managing advertising within an organisation involves a number of stages. First, campaign responsibilities need to be decided so that the process and the budget are kept under proper control. Once the target market and their broad communication needs have been defined, specific campaign objectives can be developed. Next, the budget can be set in the light of the desired objectives. Media choices, based on the habits of the target audience, the requirements of the planned message and the desired reach and frequency, can then be made. Meanwhile, the advertisements themselves are developed. Testing can be built in at various stages of this development to ensure that the right message is getting across in the right kind of way with the right kind of effect. Once the advertising has been fully developed, it can be implemented. Both during and after the campaign, managers will assess the advertising's effectiveness, using aided or unaided recall, enquiry tests or sales tests, depending on the original objectives.

- Sales promotion is part of a planned integrated marketing communications strategy that is mainly used in a short-term tactical sense, but can also contribute something to longer-term strategic and image building objectives. Sales promotions offer something over and above the normal product offering that can act as an incentive to stimulate the target audience into behaving in a certain way. Manufacturers use promotions to stimulate intermediaries and their sales staff, both manufacturers and retailers use them to stimulate individual consumers, and manufacturers might use them to stimulate other manufacturers. The methods of sales promotion are many and varied. In consumer markets they can be classed as either money-based, product-based, or gift-, prize- or merchandise-based. Customer-loyalty schemes, in particular, have become increasingly popular in the retail trade and in service industries. Manufacturers stimulate retailers and other intermediaries by offering money back, discounts, free goods and 'sale or return' schemes, among other methods. They also offer sales-force incentives to encourage a more committed selling effort from the intermediary's staff.

# Questions for review and discussion

**10.1** In what ways can advertising support the other elements of the promotional mix?

**10.2** Find examples of advertising that uses:

(a) rational appeal

(b) a fear appeal.

Why do you think the advertisers have chosen these approaches?

**10.3** Find a current advertising campaign that uses both television and online media. Why do you think both media are being used? To what extent is each medium contributing something different to the overall message?

**10.4** Describe the stages in developing an advertising campaign.

**10.5** How do the objectives on retailer–consumer sales promotions differ from those of manufacturer-consumer sales promotions?

**10.6** Research a recent new product launch by a manufacturer in a consumer market. What role did sales promotion play in the launch?

# CASE STUDY 10

# CELEBRITY ENDORSEMENT: WE CAN'T SEE THE WOODS FOR THE TWEETS

A survey by Millward Brown (MB) estimated that one in five advertisements in the UK features the face, voice or testimony of a celebrity. It has been suggested that one in four of us buys a product simply because of the celebrity associated with it and 66 per cent of us believes that it makes the product stand out. David Beckham, despite no longer playing football for England or for a Premier League club is still the UK's most powerful celebrity, scoring highly on the MB index of celebrity power, including buzz, positive role model, marketability, familiarity and likeability. Interestingly, the most negative role models were seen as Amy Winehouse (this was the year before her death), Kate Moss and Ashley Cole.

Celebrity endorsement is an extension of reference group theory (see p. 105 *et seq.*). By linking with the celebrity, the consumer is achieving a small step in aspiring to be like them. There's more to successful celebrity endorsement than just popularity and aspiration, however. There needs to be some sort of congruity between the celebrity and the brand if it is to be believable, and celebrities need to ration their services to get the greatest impact: if one celebrity promotes too many brands, it can be counterproductive with the public either forgetting which brands they endorse or cynically assuming that the celebrity is 'only doing it for the money'.

Nevertheless, celebrity endorsement can be a cost-effective way to achieve image transfer and enhance brand attributes, but as in any relationship, things can turn sour if the chosen celebrity starts making the wrong kind of headlines. Tiger Woods had been the perfect celebrity endorser, a handsome, successful, clean-living role model until a minor car crash resulted in a cascade of revelations of personal transgressions and the breakdown of his marriage. It was a hot media topic for weeks and not surprisingly resulted in a loss of form on the golf course as well. His reputation was called into question by lurid allegations and thus his value as a role model suffered. Deals collapsed with Gillette, Accenture, Tag Heuer, and Gatorade and others leaving him with just three: his EA Sports video game, Kowa and Nike. Although Nike stood by him, it did penalise him for his indiscretions and it was estimated that his income from Nike alone fell by 60 per cent. Nike also did the unthinkable by launching a new range of golf clubs without his direct endorsement as Tiger Woods suspended his career. Nike and its retail partners were confident that the clubs would sell well even without his support, as it is worth remembering that two Nike-sponsored golfers won major tournaments in 2009 and neither of them was Tiger Woods.

In 2010, to try to meet the challenge head on and rehabilitate Tiger in the public mind by demonstrating his humility, Nike ran a thirty-second commercial featuring Tiger and his father's voice. In the advertisement, his father offered advice to Tiger and asked whether he had learnt anything (Sandomir, 2010). The viewer was meant to make a link between the words of advice and Tiger's troubles. His father however, had died in 2006, long before his son's fall from grace. The advertisement went viral with millions discussing what Woods, his father and Nike said. In less than four hours it had been viewed 2.2 million times and drew 670 comments. Nike sales continued to rise and the whole affair appeared to have done little harm to golf buyers. It appears that they were inclined to forgive him anyway, but more worrying for Nike was his loss of form. By 2011, he still had not won any major competition for three years.

Tiger Woods is not alone in causing problems with sponsors. Tennis players and athletes (apart from the odd performance-enhancing drugs scandal) are generally a safe bet, but footballers are the biggest risk and can be very unpredictable. Football is as much about celebrity as performance. Loss of form is bad enough – who wants to be associated with a losing side or an off-form player? – but bad behaviour on or off the pitch can have far greater implications, as we saw in the Tiger Woods example. When a Scottish Premier League player pleaded guilty to a charge of lewd and indecent behaviour with two underage girls, Sangs Ltd, which owns the brand MacB Water, cancelled its sponsorship deal with his club, Hearts, after it refused to sack the player. Public opinion supported the company, with 82 per cent saying that brands were right to drop misbehaving sports players. If the whole purpose of brand endorsement is to align the objectives of the brand image with the celebrity image and values then decisive action is needed if that relationship backfires, and it does the sponsor no harm to be seen to be taking a moral stand.

As in life, some celebrity/brand relationships end in divorce. In the same way that careful spouses with a lot to lose insist on a pre-nuptial agreement, advertisers can take out 'Death and Disgrace' insurance. This allows them to recoup some of the costs of pulling or recasting advertisements should their famous face die or do something else regrettable.

The emergence of social media has added a new dimension and a new intimacy to celebrity endorsement. What better way of convincing somebody of the value of a brand than a third-party endorsement, especially if it comes from a celebrity? Range Rover launched a Twitter campaign that featured celebrities tweeting about its new car, the Evoque 4 x 4. It had, for example, Sky Sports presenter Ben Shepherd saying nice things about the car. Where celebrities are paid for their tweets, it could be considered deceptive if they do not disclose that it is a paid-for endorsement. The Office of Fair Trading (OFT) is now investigating those celebrities who endorse products or companies without clearly stating their relationship with the brand. In the case of Range Rover a number of people with high profiles on Twitter were enlisted and they got a loan of the vehicle and could drive around in it, but under the terms of the deal they had to tweet about the car. In the USA the practice is more widespread but the tweet must contain the words 'ad' or 'spon' to show that the tweet reference has been paid for. The sums paid vary but could be anything up to $10,000 per tweet although $3,000 is closer to the norm. One company that arranges for the tweets is Ad.ly and it boasts a client list that includes Toyota, Microsoft and American airlines. Its celebrity list includes Mariah Carey who has nearly 5 million followers and Cristiano Ronaldo with just over 4 million. Ad.ly is quite upfront about the arrangements and claims to have secured 24,000 endorsements from 1,000 celebrities on behalf of 150 top brands.

It will be interesting to see what impact this emerging field of digital celebrity endorsement has, and whether regulatory moves to make it more transparently labelled as paid-for affect its effectiveness. Whether a brand is using digital or traditional media, if it is managed carefully and integrated into the rest of the promotional mix, celebrity endorsement can be very powerful as long as the persona of the celebrity doesn't overshadow the brand message.

*Sources: Asian News International* (2011a; 2011b); Brown (2010); Bustillo (2010); *Daily Record* (2011); MacDonald (2011); Mullman (2010); Oatts (2010); *PR Week* (2011); Roberts (2009); Sandomir (2010); Topping (2011); Verrinder (2010); Wright (2010).

## Questions

1 What are the advantages and disadvantages of using celebrities in advertising campaigns?

2 In what ways might the use of celebrities in social media, such as Twitter or Facebook overcome some of the disadvantages you have listed above? What additional benefits might this form of celebrity endorsement bring?

3 Find examples of what you consider to be 'good' and 'bad' celebrity advertising campaigns and discuss why you think they are good or bad.

4 Nike didn't drop Tiger Woods altogether, but MacB Water did withdraw its sponsorship from the errant Scottish footballer's club. Explain why you think the two companies' responses to their celebrity crises differed. Were they right to act as they did?

## References for chapter 10

ASA (2009) *ASA Adjudication on Express Newspapers*, adjudication by the ASA, 12 August, accessed via www.asa.org.uk/ASA-action/Adjudications/2009/8/Express-Newspapers/TF_ADJ_46700.aspx.

ASA (2011a) *ASA Adjudication on L'Oreal (UK) Ltd*, adjudication by the ASA, 27 July, accessed via www.asa.org.uk/ASA-action/Adjudications/2011/7/LOreal-(UK)-Ltd/SHP_ADJ_149640.aspx.

ASA (2011b) *ASA Lays Some Firm Foundations for Cosmetic Ads*, ASA, 15 September, accessed via www.asa.org.uk/Resource-Centre/Hot-Topics/Cosmetic.aspx.

ASA (2011c) *ASA Statement on Sexual Imagery in Outdoor Advertising*, press release issued by the ASA, 7 October, accessed via www.asa.org.uk/Media-Centre/2011/ASA-statement-on-sexual-imagery-in-outdoor-advertising.aspx.

ASA (2011d) *ASA at No 10 Summit*, press release issued by the ASA, 11 October, accessed via www.asa.org.uk/Media-Centre/2011/ASA-at-No-10-Summit.aspx.

*Asian News International* (2011a) 'Tiger Woods Income Falling', *Asian News International*, 16 July.

*Asian News International* (2011b) 'Nike to Slash Tiger Woods' Deal in Half If He Fails to Win US PGA Championship', *Asian News International*, 11 August.

Bagshaw, T. (2010) 'Price Cuts are Not the Only Promotional Route', *The Grocer*, 20 March.

Bailey, R. (2011) *Letting Children be Children – Report of an Independent Review of the Commercialisation and Sexualisation of Childhood*, Department for Education, June, accessed via www.education.gov.uk/publications/standard/publicationDetail/Page1/CM%208078.

Baldwin, N. (2008) 'Music Essays: So it's Uncool. So What?', *Campaign*, 30 May.

Banham, M. (2011) 'Bauer's Zoo Crashes 14% in Failing Lads' Sector', *Media Week*, 17 February.

Barnes, R. (2010) 'When Going Gets Tough, Tough Get Promoting', *The Grocer*, 6 February.

Barnett, E. (2010) 'Microsoft Launches First UK TV Advertising Campaign in Bid to Attract Google Users', *Daily Telegraph*, 8 March.

Barrett, L. (2009) 'Media: Supplementary income', *The Guardian*, 31 August.

Bashford, S. (2010) 'Promos Put a Freeze on Value', *The Grocer*, 19 June.

Bauer Media (2011) *Zoo*, accessed via www.bauermedia.co.uk/Brands/ZOO/.

Belgutay, J. (2011) 'Dressed to Oppress? The War Against the Sexualisation of Childhood', *Times Educational Supplement*, 5 August.

Berkowitz, E.N. *et al.* (1992) *Marketing*, Irwin.

Brand-e.biz (2011) *Different Gear, More Music Sales*, posted by Brand-e.biz, 5 August, accessed via http://brand-e.biz/different-gear-more-music-sales_15805.html.

Brown, R. (2010) 'Brands Take Out Celebrity Disgrace Insurance Cover', *The Grocer*, 13 November.

Buchanan, J. (2008) 'The Business: Pitch – Filmmaker DreamWorks in Search for Promo Agency', *Promotions and Incentives*, 8 July.

Business Wire (2010) 'Coca-Cola Invites Football Fans to Take Part in the Longest-Ever Goal Celebration', *Business Wire*, 3 May.

Bustillo, M. (2010) 'Nike Launches New Golf Clubs Without Tiger Woods', *Wall Street Journal*, 18 January.

Charlton, J. (2011) 'Advertising Industry "Not Sexualising Children"', *ePolitix.com*, 10 February, accessed via www. epolitix.com/latestnews/article-detail/newsarticle/ advertising-industry-not-sexualising-children/.

Daily Express (2010) 'The More You Buy the More You Save With Lidl', *Daily Express*, 29 July.

Daily Record (2011), 'Hearts Sponsor MacB Withdraws Backing in Wake of Craig Thomson Child Sex Scandal', *Daily Record*, 27 June.

Daily Telegraph (2011) 'Online Takes 25pc Slice of Advertising with Social Media Driving Demand', *Daily Telegraph*, 29 March.

Davies, M. (1992) 'Sales Promotion as a Competitive Strategy', *Management Decision*, 30 (7), pp. 5–10.

Dowell, B. (2011) 'Have Trade Magazines Got a Shelf Life?', *The Guardian*, 25 April.

Evans, T. (2010) 'Which is the Most Popular Loyalty Scheme?', *This is Money*, 23 February, accessed via www.thisismoney. co.uk/money/bills/article-1689767/Which-is-the-most-popular-loyalty-scheme.html#ixzz1XlUw2mop.

Faulkner, R (2011) 'Waitrose is the Worst for Coupon Misredemption', *The Grocer*, 15 January.

Fenton, B. (2011) 'Online Advertising Retakes Top Slot', *Financial Times*, 4 October.

Fill, C. (2002) *Marketing Communications: Contexts, Strategies and Applications*, 3rd edn. Financial Times Prentice Hall.

The Grocer (2008) 'Death of the Bogof?', *The Grocer*, 3 May.

The Guardian (2010) 'Meerkat Mission The Campaign that Broke the Ad Barrier', *The Guardian*, 22 February.

Gupta, S. and Cooper, L. (1992) 'The Discounting of Discount and Promotion Brands', *Journal of Consumer Research*, 19 (December), pp. 401–11.

Hayward, M. (2009) 'Loyalty Cards – The Two-way Street of Loyalty', *Retail Week*, 11 December.

Holden, M. (2010) 'Children Over-exposed to Sexual Imagery – UK Report', *Reuters News*, 26 February.

Jones, P. (1990) 'The Double Jeopardy of Sales Promotions', *Harvard Business Review*, September/October, pp. 141–52.

Jones, S. (2010) 'Compare the Memoir', *The Guardian*, 25 October.

Julyan, A-M. (2010) 'Lucozade in Ad and NPD Push to Hit Back at Rivals', *The Grocer*, 20 February.

Just-food (2010) 'Tesco Launches First "Bogof – Later" Promo', *Just-food*, 21 January.

Leyland, A. and Ball, J. (2009) 'Promote or BANG!', *The Grocer*, 4 April.

Luft, O. (2011) 'Big Annual Readership Falls for FHM, Zoo and Nuts', *Media Week*, 7 June.

MacDonald, G. (2010) 'Loyalty Cards: The Bedrock of Future Success?', *Retail Week*, 28 May.

MacDonald, J. (2011) 'Firm Pulls Out of Hearts Deal After Scandal', *Evening Express*, 28 June.

Maden, S. (2011) 'Lads' Mags Continue to Shed Readers', *Media Week*, 26 August.

Malkani, G. (2011) 'Why Sex Isn't Child's Play for Advertisers', *Financial Times*, 13 July.

Marketing Minefield (2011) 'The Cost of a TV Advertising Campaign', *Marketing Minefield*, accessed via www. marketingminefield.co.uk/television-advertising-cost/.

Marketing Week (2010) 'Subway Plots Mobile Phone Loyalty Points Programme', *Marketing Week*, 3 June.

McPheters & Co (2009a) 'TV and Magazine Ads More Effective Than Ads on Internet', McPheters & Co, 1 April, accessed via http://mcpheters.com/2009/04/01/. tv-and-magazine-ads-more-effective-than-ads-on-internet/.

McPheters & Co (2009b) 'Context is Key Factor in Internet Ad Effectiveness', McPheters & Co, 16 June, accessed via http://mcpheters.com/2009/06/16/ context-is-key-factor-in-internet-ad-effectiveness/.

Microsoft (2008) 'Walkers Brit Trips Go Extra Mile with Online Campaign', case study published by Microsoft, 1 November, accessed via http://advertising.microsoft.com/ uk/online-case-study-walkers.

Mintel (2009) 'Online Dating', *Mintel Leisure Intelligence*, April, accessed via http://academic.mintel.com/sinatra/oxygen_ academic/search_results/show&/display/id=395147/ display/id=455292?select_section=395147.

Muehling, D. et al. (1990) 'The Impact of Comparative Advertising on Levels of Message Involvement', *Journal of Advertising*, 19(4), pp. 41–50.

Mueller-Heumann, G. (1992) 'Markets and Technology Shifts in the 1990s: Market Fragmentation and Mass Customisation', *Journal of Marketing Management*, 8(4), pp. 303–14.

Mullman, J. (2010) 'For Nike, the Tiger Woods Brand was Too Big to Fail', *Advertising Age*, 12 April.

Nielsen (2011), *Global Advertising Rebounded 10.6% in 2010*, press release issued by Nielsen, 4 April, accessed via www.nielsen.com/us/en/insights/press-room/2011/ global-advertising-rebound-2010.html.

Newspaper Society (2010) *UK Media Advertising Expenditure 2010*, factsheet published by the Newspaper Society, accessed via www.newspapersoc.org.uk/sites/default/files/ PDF/UK_Adspend_2010.pdf.

Nutley, M. (2011) 'Double Your Impact with Two Screens', *Marketing Week*, 15 September.

Oakes, S. (2007) 'Evaluating Empirical Research into Music in Advertising: A Congruity Perspective', *Journal of Advertising Research*, 47 (1), pp. 38–50.

Oatts, J. (2010) 'Range Rover Recruits Stars for Twitter Campaign', *Marketing Week*, 25 October.

Ofcom (2011) *Half of Parents Say They Know Less about the Internet than their Children*, press release issued by Ofcom, 19 April, accessed via media.ofcom.org.uk/2011/04/19/ half-of-parents-say-they-know-less-about-the-internet-than-their-children/.

O'Reilly, L. (2011) 'Match and eHarmony Go Head-to-head to Attract Consumer Love', *Marketing Week*, 11 January.

Pandey, N. (2010) 'Increasing 'Commercial Features' in Newspapers – Edit-sanctity at Risk?', 1 December, Exchange4Media.com.

Parsons, R. (2011) 'Prime Minister Backs Curbs on Advertising', *Marketing Week*, 9 June.

PepsiCo (2008) *Walkers Brit Trips Campaign*, press release issued by PepsiCo, 8 February, accessed via www.pepsico. co.uk/our-company/trade-information/trade-media-centre/ trade-news/walkers-brit-trips-campaign.

*PR Newswire* (2010) 'New Caterpillar.com Designed to Elevate Enterprise Messages and Company Image', *PR Newswire*, 1 December.

*PR Newswire* (2011) 'Visitors Flock to New Meerkat Village', *PR Newswire*, 19 January.

*PR Week* (2011) 'Footballers Score Own Goal with Public', *PR Week*, 9 September.

*Promotions & Incentives* (2006) 'Self-liquidating Promotion: Country Life Gives Away Forest Animal Toys', *Promotions & Incentives*, 23 October.

PTS (2011) *The Original Big One 2011*, catalogue issued by PTS, October-December, accessed via www.ptsplumbing.co.uk/FlipCatalogues/The_Big_One_2011/index.html.

RAB (2009) *Churchill: Using Radio to Multiply the Effects of TV*, case study published by RAB, accessed via www.rab.co.uk/rab2009/showContent.aspx?id=9092.

RBH (2008) *Warwick Castle: Besieged by Visitors*, case study published by RBH, accessed via www.rbh.co.uk/ourwork/warwick-castle:-besieged-by-visitors/.

Roberts, J. (2009) 'Don't Just Reach for the Stars', *Marketing Week*, 17 December.

Sandomir, R. (2010) 'Voice from Past in a Nike Ad Featuring Woods', *New York Times*, 8 April.

Shearman, S. (2011a) 'eHarmony to Launch Campaign Featuring Real-life Singles', *Campaign*, 29 June.

Shearman, S. (2011b) 'Comparethemarket in Meerkat Toys Giveaway', *Marketing*, 1 July.

Shearman, S. (2011c) 'Video Banner Ad Campaign "Nearly Doubles" Liam Gallagher Sales', *Brand Republic*, 8 August.

Shearman, S. (2011d) 'Microsoft Reboots Marketing Approach', *Marketing*, 7 September.

Shevlin, I. (2011) 'She's Just a Kid . . .', *Sunday Tribune*, 7 August.

Sissors, J. and Bumba, L. (1989) *Advertising Media Planning*, 3rd edn. NTC Business Books.

Sky Media (2011) *Warburtons - Interactive Advertising Campaign*, Sky Media, accessed via www.skymedia.co.uk/Audience-Insight/Case-Studies/warburtons.aspx.

Smith, C. (2009) 'FMCG Companies Pay Price for Coupon Misredemption', *The Grocer*, 6 June.

Smithers, R. (2011) 'Sainsbury's Steps Up Supermarket Price War', *The Guardian*, 12 October.

Sweney, M. (2010a) 'How to Save the TV Advertising Industry? Simples! Send for Aleksandr the Meerkat', *The Guardian*, 16 January.

Sweney, M. (2010b) 'How Meerkat Aleksandr Orlov Helped Increase the Market for TV Ads', *The Guardian*, 1 July.

Sweney, M. (2011), 'L'Oréal's Julia Roberts and Christy Turlington Ad Campaigns Banned', *The Guardian*, 27 July.

Talwar, D. (2011) 'Bus Advertising Campaign Tackles Islamophobia', *BBC Asian Network*, 5 April, accessed via www.bbc.co.uk/news/uk-12956746.

Thinkbox (2011) *Churchill, is there a Robust Way to Link TV Spots to Web Response? 'Oh Yes . . .'*, case study published by Thinkbox, accessed via www.thinkbox.tv/server/show/ConCaseStudy.1604.

Thinking Juice (2011) *Caterpillar*, case study published by Thinking Juice, accessed via www.thinkingjuice.co.uk/our_work/case_studies/caterpillar-38.html.

Thinkmedia (2011) 'Television Media Buying', accessed via www.think-media.co.uk/media-buying/television-media-buying.

Topping, A. (2011) 'Twitter Endorsements Face OFT Clampdown', *The Guardian*, 9 January.

Valassis Ltd (2010) *Stiletto Foods Selects Valassis to Support Launch of Mrs Crimbles Gluten-Free Bread*, press release issued by Valassis Ltd, 11 January, accessed via www.marketinguk.co.uk/Promotions-Incentives/STILETTO-FOODS-SELECTS-VALASSIS-TO-SUPPORT-LAUNCH-OF-MRS-CRIMBLES-GLUTEN-FREE-BREAD.asp.

Verrinder, J. (2010) 'Millward Brown Adds Marketability Score to Celebrity Study', *Research Live*, 18 October, accessed via www.research-live.com/news/news-headlines/millward-brown-adds-marketability-score-to-celebrity-study/4003824.article.

White, R. (1988) *Advertising: What It Is and How To Do It*, McGraw-Hill.

Williams, M. (2011) 'eHarmony Kicks Off Pounds 8m UK Creative Pitch', *Campaign*, 22 July.

Wilmshurst, J. (1993) *Below-the-line Promotion*, Butterworth-Heinemann.

Wright, C. (2010) 'Sinners to Saints', *The Grocer*, 13 November.

Zuke, E. (2010a) 'Tesco Suppliers Angry at Coupon Destruction', *The Grocer*, 15 May.

Zuke, E. (2010b) 'Bogofs Threatened as the OFT Eyes "Misleading" Promotions', *The Grocer*, 5 June.

# CHAPTER 11

# Promotion: direct and digital marketing

## LEARNING OBJECTIVES

This chapter will help you to:

- understand what direct marketing is and appreciate its role in the communications mix through the objectives it can achieve and the various methods it employs;

- appreciate the importance of creating and maintaining a database of customers and understand the importance of using the database as a direct marketing tool;

- understand the range of tools and techniques involved in digital direct marketing;

- appreciate the role digital direct marketing plays in an integrated marketing-communications mix, as well as its potential for opening new channels through which relationships and transactions with customers can take place.

## INTRODUCTION

**THE DIRECT MARKETING SCENE** is rapidly changing as customers become more connected and increasingly expect 24/7 contact with all kinds of organisations from wherever in the world, and demand the facility to check on stock availability, to be offered quick collection or delivery, as well as easy access to detailed information. The retail store may be closed but in a multichannel world access is never denied and retailers must respond accordingly. Now, 44 per cent of transactions in the UK involve interaction with multiple channels of distribution and communication, including in-store, online, mail order and catalogue. The challenge is to integrate these into a package that attracts and retains customers. Physical stores are becoming showrooms, service locations and collection points. Store visits and online sales are interlinked, with each driving the other. The ease of price comparison, whether between physical store and online prices, or between competitors, encouraged by the growth of price comparison websites is changing the nature of price sensitivity among consumers, and making retailers think more carefully about their pricing and promotional strategies. Also expected to grow is the use of web-enabled mobile handsets, or smartphones, which make connectivity even easier (Deloitte Consumer Business Group, 2011). Even in the time that elapses between us writing this text and you reading it, doubtless direct marketing will have moved on significantly.

*eg* Unwanted gold? Whether you've got a ring, a necklace, a bracelet or even a dental crown, there are a number of companies that will offer to convert it into cash. All the postal gold buyers, such as Cash4Gold, CashMyGold and Postal Gold use mainstream media advertising, their websites and direct marketing extensively to generate awareness of their services and to prompt a response from the target customers. The concept is simple – the company provides an envelope which customers use to send in their gold item(s). A valuation is given and if the customer accepts it, he or she receives the cash amount agreed. Particularly because the transaction takes places at arm's length, via the mail, it is critically important for the customer to feel that doing business with these companies is worthy of their trust and that they provide a secure operation. However, many of these companies sprang up or arrived in the UK from the USA around 2008–9, at a time when people were really starting to feel the effects of the recession and were looking for ready cash, and because it was a new kind of concept in the UK it was unregulated. Many consumers were thus somewhat naive in their expectations and assumptions about what they would get.

Both the Office of Fair Trading (OFT) and consumer watchdog Which? started to investigate complaints. One practice, for example, was to send out the valuation in the form of a cheque. The customer was then given a very short period of time in which to return the cheque if they decided that they didn't like the valuation. Inevitably, some cheques got lost or delayed in the post or mislaid in administrative systems, and so some customers ended up with neither the cheque nor their gold item, or ended up having to accept a poor valuation because of the time limit. Valuations were often disappointing because they were based on the wholesale scrap metal value of the gold rather than the retail value of the gold or of the item as a piece of jewellery. As a result of its investigation, the OFT required these companies to clean up their acts by changing their operational practices. Cash4Gold, CashMyGold and Postal Gold all signed undertakings to change, for example, by explaining clearly to potential customers the basis upon which valuations are made and what other options the customer has for selling their item(s), as well as making the offer-acceptance-payment sequence more transparent and more realistic in terms of time scale. Two companies, CashYourGoldNow and Money4Gold, however, ceased trading in the UK after the OFT's intervention.

It's important for the OFT to monitor this and ensure that consumers' interests are protected. It's not just cashing in on unwanted gold – there's a lot of companies springing up turning the consumer into the seller by offering to buy old mobile phones, CDs, DVDs, computer games and even laptops, and there's concern that consumers are seduced by the promises in the glitzy ads and the convenience and ease of dealing with these buyers into accepting very poor valuations (rather than all the time and effort they would have to invest in posting the item on eBay, for example, then waiting for an appropriate buyer to come along, setting or negotiating a price and then getting a payment processed, etc.). The consumer as a distance seller still has a lot to learn (Hosea, 2009; King, 2011; Kumar, 2011; Serdarevic and Plimmer, 2011; White, 2009; www.oft.gov.uk; www.which.co.uk).

This chapter, therefore examines the interrelated areas of direct and digital marketing. Direct marketing is more than just 'junk mail'. It encompasses a wide range of commonly used techniques, not only direct mail but also telemarketing, direct-response mechanisms, and mail order, all of which are covered in the first part of the chapter. We then move on to the rapidly evolving area of digital direct marketing. There are various aspects of this that can be integrated with the more traditional tools and techniques of direct marketing with the aim of informing and persuading the customer, as well as creating and building closer relationships with them. The chapter looks at e-mail marketing, mobile marketing, viral marketing, and the use of social networking sites as a platform for brand community building and selling.

## Direct marketing

There are a number of reasons for the rapid growth of direct marketing, connected with the changing nature of the customer, the marketing environment and, in particular, technological development. Direct marketing is being used increasingly across a wide range of both consumer and B2B markets. Even in the relatively conservative financial services industry, there has been a marked increase in direct selling and direct marketing of a wide range of banking facilities and insurance. The next section of the chapter, therefore, looks more closely at what direct marketing is and how it is being used as an element of integrated marketing communications.

*eg* Renault UK was keen to get its new Clio CC into small and independent driving schools. Around 16,000 mailshots were sent out, each with a clipboard holding a personalised completed 'driving test form'. The form had been designed to show the car's features and benefits and, of course, the Clio appeared to have passed its 'driving test' on all criteria except price. The form showed that that 'failure' has been corrected by 'the examiner' crossing out the published price and writing in a new discounted figure. Behind the form was more information and instructions about how to book a test drive. The original target for the campaign was to sell 80 Clios. As it turned out, over 1,500 Clios were sold, representing business worth £17.7 million, with a sales conversion rate of 3.5 per cent (Publicis Dialog, 2011).

Renault 'passed the test' by targetting driving schools creatively
*Source:* Alamy Images/AMD Images

## Definition, role, aims and use

The US Direct Marketing Association has defined direct marketing as:

> **An interactive system of marketing which uses one or more advertising media to effect a measurable response at any location.**

This is quite a broad definition which does, however, capture some basic characteristics of direct marketing. Interactive implies two-way communication between buyer and seller, while *effect a measurable response* implies quantifiable objectives for the exercise. *At any location* implies the flexibility and pervasiveness of direct marketing, in that it is not inextricably linked with any one medium of communication, but can utilise anything (mail, phone, broadcast, print or electronic media) to reach anyone anywhere. What this definition does not do, however, is to emphasise the potential of direct marketing as a primary means of building and sustaining long-term buyer–seller relationships.

It is, therefore, proposed to extend this definition to form the basis of the content of the rest of this section:

> An interactive system of marketing which uses one or more advertising media to effect a measurable response at any location, forming a basis for creating and further developing an ongoing direct relationship between an organisation and its customers.

The key added value of this definition is the phrase *ongoing direct relationship*, which implies continuity and seems to contradict the impersonal approach traditionally offered by mass media advertising. Is it really possible to use mass media in a mass market to create a relationship with a single customer? Is it really possible to capitalise on the advantages of personal selling that arise from one-to-one dialogue to build and sustain that relationship without the need for face-to-face contact?

If the answer to those two questions is to be 'yes', then the problem becomes one of information gathering and management. To create and sustain *quality* relationships with hundreds, thousands or even millions of individual customers, an organisation needs to know as much as possible about each one, and needs to be able to access, manipulate and analyse that information. The database, therefore, is crucial to the process of building the relationship. We will look in some detail at the issues of creating, maintaining and exploiting the database at p. 434 *et seq*.

## Objectives

There are a number of tasks that direct marketing can perform, depending on whether it is used for direct selling or supporting product promotion. The tasks may be related to ongoing transactions and relationships with customers. At its most basic, therefore, direct marketing can fulfil the following objectives.

**Direct ordering**. Direct marketing aims to enable direct ordering, whether by telephone, by mail or, increasingly, online. The use of credit cards, passwords and specific account numbers makes this possible. All kinds of direct marketing techniques can be used to achieve this, but the examples of downloading music, software or e-books are particularly interesting because sellers can both take the order and deliver the product immediately.

**Information giving**. Direct marketing aims to open a channel of communication to enable potential customers to ask for further information. Information may be given verbally by a salesperson, or through printed or electronic literature.

A Virgin Media direct-mail campaign certainly grabbed attention, but perhaps not in the intended way. The ASA became aware of it and decided that it was misleading. The core message of the campaign sought to compare Virgin Media with BSkyB and featured the headline, 'Why Virgin TV is better than Sky TV by ex-Sky customers'. The mailshot was critical of the service offered by Sky and even Sky's picture quality. It also claimed that Virgin Media offered high-definition channels free while Sky charged £10 extra per month, and that the set-up was free from Virgin but cost £60 with Sky. But, of course, that message was highly selective. It did not take into account that Virgin Media offered fewer HD channels, and the price comparison was based on a special offer, not the standard charges. The ASA upheld BSkyB's complaint and Virgin Media had to change the mailing (Sweney, 2010; www.asa.org.uk).

**Visit generation**. Direct marketing aims to invite a potential customer to call in and visit a store, website, show or event with or without prior notification. Nissan, for example, used direct mailshots targeted at fleet buyers to encourage them to visit the Nissan stand at the UK Motor Show.

**Trial generation**. Direct marketing aims to enable a potential customer to request a demonstration or product trial in the home, office or factory.

*eg*

Bounty is a maternity-data specialist. Identifying expectant mothers and new babies is very useful for some organisations, such as Mothercare and suppliers of baby foods and toiletries. Bounty's maternity list covers 95 per cent of new and expectant mothers, all of whom are offered packs of sample products and the opportunity to sign up to an online community and to receive direct mail and other communication from various relevant companies. About 3.4 million Bounty packs are distributed every year. Many new mums are targeted in the maternity unit within hours of giving birth, and according to the National Childbirth Trust, companies such as Bounty are paying the NHS up to £5,000 for access, and then selling on contact details of mums to commercial companies for £1 each.

The sample pack is important for the companies that contribute to it. The samples in the Bounty packs are used by 95 per cent of new mums who receive them. Receiving a sample in advance is said to influence the actual purchase decision of 83 per cent of mums, and even if only a coupon rather than a sample is provided, around 70 per cent still said they were more likely to buy that product. Given the significance of a birth in terms of changing the family lifestyle, and the extent to which new or about-to-be mums lack the time and energy to shop around, it's a target audience that is likely to welcome information and advice. About 75 per cent of mums read mailings related to Bounty and 80 per cent of mums with children aged under four years old use the internet a lot. In short, she is a proactive consumer (Carter, 2011; Laurance, 2011; www.bounty.com/what-we-do/; www. starmedical.co.uk/profile-bounty-uk.php).

**Loyalty creation**. Direct marketing offers organisations the opportunity to create loyal customers. If customers have entered into dialogue with an organisation, and have had their needs and wants met through a series of tailored offerings, then it is going to be quite difficult for the competition to poach those customers. Furthermore, using techniques such as direct mail, an organisation can communicate at length and in-depth with its customers personally and privately (certainly when compared with advertising).

## How and when to use direct marketing

**Initiation**. An important decision in direct marketing is how best to use it at various stages of the relationship with the customer. The earliest stage, *initiation*, can be very difficult, as it involves creating the initial contact and making the first sale. A combination of appealing advertising and sales promotion techniques may be used, for example, to overcome the potential customer's initial apprehension and risk aversion. Thus in its introductory offer to new customers, an online store might reduce the customer's perceived risk by offering a discount on the first order, or a discount voucher code to someone who registers with the site. Alternatively, a sale on credit or even a free trial may ease the customer's initial fears, despite the high administration costs. Any of these methods makes it easier for customers to part with their cash on the first order, thus opening the opportunity for a longer-term relationship.

**Relationship building**. Most direct marketing is in fact aimed at the *relationship stage* customer. This is when the seller has started to build a buying profile, supported by more widely available non-purchase specific data. This enables a steady flow of offers to be made, whether by telephone, mailshot, e-mail or catalogue update. Customers are also likely to be more responsive at this stage, as they have established confidence in product quality and service performance.

**Combination selling**. Finally, combination selling results from using contacts gained from one medium, such as a trade exhibition, for regular contact by direct marketing means. This could be the mailing of special offers, price lists, catalogues or telephone calls to gain a face-to-face meeting, etc. The direct marketing activity is therefore used in combination with other methods.

The discussion so far has talked generally about the concept of direct marketing, with passing reference to specific areas such as direct mail and direct response, among others. The next section looks more closely at each of these areas and their individual characteristics. Figure 11.1 gives an overview of the range of direct marketing areas.

## Techniques

The scope of direct marketing is very wide. It utilises what might be called the more traditional means of marketing communication, such as print and broadcast advertising media, but it has also developed its own media, through mail, telecommunications and modem. Each of the main techniques in direct marketing will now be considered in turn.

### Direct mail

Direct mail is material distributed through the postal service to the recipients' home or business address to promote a product or service. What is mailed can vary from a simple letter introducing a company or product through to a comprehensive catalogue or sample. Many mailshots incorporate involvement devices to increase the chances of their being opened and read, through stimulating curiosity.

**Figure 11.1**
The range of direct marketing techniques

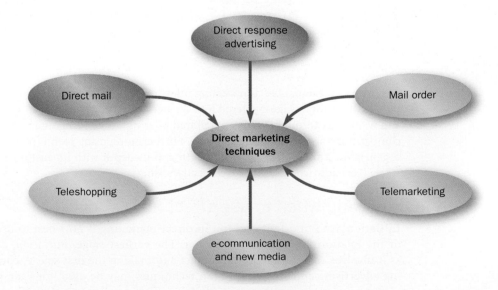

Most direct mail is unsolicited. Organisations compile or buy lists of names and addresses, and then send out the mailshot. The mailing list used may be cold, that is, where there has been no previous contact between the organisation and the addressee, or may reflect various selection criteria based on data held about previous or existing customers. The rise of opt-out services, however, such as the Mailing Preference Scheme, has gradually reduced the number of customers in the target pool for 'cold' lists and thus those who are still there are more likely to be receptive and to respond (Murphy, 2011a).

*eg*

Party Pieces offers all the essentials that you need for a children's birthday party on its website. There's nothing unusual about that, you might say, but the owner happens to be Carole Middleton, and the number of visitors to the website increased twenty-fold after her daughter Catherine became engaged to Prince William. The company rents out lists from its database of families with young children, and finance, travel and fashion companies have been keen to snap them up. A list of upmarket women with young families is particularly valuable for premium mail-order companies, and according to Schlesinger (2010), the lists are selling at about £120 per 1,000 names. The database has more than 230,000 names, and it's likely to be growing, assuming that Party Pieces is benefiting from the current trend among affluent families towards more traditional home-based children's parties. This selling-on of lists from a database is quite common among mail-order companies, and is well within the data-protection regulations as customers have to give consent for their details to be traded on, and there is an opt-out clause. A visitor to the site can find themselves on a list even if they just request a catalogue – details including the children's names and dates of birth must be given so that the latest catalogue can be sent out in good time. Although the company does not sell specific details about children, list buyers can tell the age range of children in each family on the list (Barrett, 2011; Kennedy and Ralph, 2010; Schlesinger, 2010).

Marketers are keen to benefit from the trend among affluent families towards home-based children's parties

*Source*: www.shutterstock.com/Morgan Lane Photography

Direct mail has the problem that it has suffered from bad PR. All of us as consumers can probably think of a couple of examples of direct mail we have received that have been completely inappropriate, and misconceptions about direct mail's effectiveness are often based on such personal experiences of receiving 'junk'. Historically, this has arisen partly from the lack of flexibility and detail within databases, and partly from poor marketing thinking. Increasingly, though, marketers are using the information at their disposal more intelligently, and mailing smaller groups of well-defined prospective customers, using better designed creative material. They are also keeping their databases more current, and so a household should not receive direct mail addressed to people who moved away or died over a year ago. In theory, then, individuals should be receiving less direct mail, but what they do receive should be of prime relevance and interest.

Although the information in Table 11.1 is heartening, it may not be enough. Think about the hierarchy of effects models shown in Figure 9.5, and how direct mail fits into those. Using the AIDA model as an example, opening the envelope begins the *awareness* stage, reading the content generates *interest* and *desire* and, finally, the mailshot clearly defines what subsequent *action* is expected. The main objective is to move the recipient quickly through all the stages from awareness to action. The key is not simply the opening of the envelope, but whether the content can pull the reader right through to the completion of action. As a consolation prize, if the recipient reads the content but chooses not to respond, there may still be an awareness or interest effect that may 'soften up' the customer for subsequent mailings or, in B2B markets, a sales visit.

**Table 11.1** Some facts about direct mail in the UK

- An average of 92 per cent of direct mail is opened.
- 49 per cent of people are more likely to open direct mail if they are intrigued by it.
- 41 per cent of people are more likely to open direct mail if it smells (and we assume that we are talking about pleasant smells!).
- 90 per cent of people read a catalogue received through the mail, and 70 per cent will follow it up online.
- 90 per cent of people open direct mail if they are already a customer of the company that sent it.
- 48 per cent of people have done something in response to direct mail that they have received, for example visiting a store, going online, keeping it for future reference, passing it on the someone else, buying something, etc.
- 76 per cent of people welcome direct mail that offers useful information.
- 75 per cent of people like receiving special offers or vouchers by direct mail.
- 48 per cent of people think that it's easier to take in information from direct mail than from an e-mail.
- 53 per cent think that direct mail gives a better impression of a company than e-mail.

*Source*: adapted from Bliss (2010).

# MARKETING IN ACTION

## Keeping direct mail exciting, but discreet

The sex industry has a particular problem when developing mailing lists as few people want unsolicited approaches for exotic sex aids! Any mailing list has to be sound and discreet. Adult catalogue operations can even have trouble in distribution, such as the time when a German sex shop chain, Beate Uhse, had the door-drop of its catalogue refused by UK postal workers in the Midlands even though great care was taken in the development of the mailing list. On a previous occasion, it ran into trouble when it delivered a catalogue mistakenly to a four-year-old girl in Lincolnshire. The envelopes are labelled 'for over 18s only' and carry a message 'please do not open if you are easily offended'.

Subscribers to men's magazines such as *Loaded* provide a useful list of potential targets for adult products, especially if the subscriber buys items by mail order off the page. Mail-order video buyers and users of x-rated chat-lines are a further source, and thus through a combination of methods a database can be built of people who may be generally reluctant to register their details. Such a list can be rented out to marketers of lifestyle products as well as those selling adult-related products. It can, however, be difficult to convince list buyers that those on it are interested in anything other than adult products!

Some companies, such as Ann Summers, only use direct marketing if it is highly targeted and is related to previous customers. They do not want to damage the brand by sending unwanted material to poorly defined target customers, thus causing offence. In 2011, Ann Summers ran a three-part campaign to promote its autumn/winter collection. First to arrive was a mysterious business card with a rabbit and a cat on one side directing the reader to pussyandrabbit.com, a microsite under the Ann Summers name which is linked with social media activity, PR and an online game all designed to re-inject some playfulness into the brand.

Then a few weeks later came a direct-mail flyer showing a lingerie model on one side and on the other side was an exclusive preview of the 2011 collection. Finally, there was an A5-sized booklet featuring the whole collection. The staged approach to the campaign was designed to whet the appetite and create a sense of anticipation. The mailing list comprises previous customers of Ann Summers and those signing up from the e-commerce site. This also enables buying patterns to be analysed and to move beyond the obvious cross-selling activities (bra and briefs; toy and lube) into complete packages focused in 'special nights in', similar to grocers' meal deal packages (see the Squeal Deal vignette on p. 216!). Despite the power of data mining and the potential effect on buying behaviour, the company does have a strong policy of never selling its customer lists to third parties, and it allows customers to opt-out at any time.

*Sources:* Baker (2011a); Goodman (2011); O'Reilly (2011); *Precision Marketing* (2004).

## Direct response advertising

Direct response advertising appears in the standard broadcast and print media. It differs from 'normal' advertising because it is designed to generate a direct response, whether an order, an enquiry for further information or a personal visit. The response mechanism may be a coupon to cut out in a print advertisement, or a phone number in any type of advertisement. This area has grown in popularity in recent years as advertisers seek to get their increasingly expensive advertising to work harder for them.

Slendertone UK became the market leader in the body-toning market within three years of its launch and much of this was attributed to its successful use of direct response media. Market share grew from 6 to 49 per cent. While sales went up sixteenfold, the cost per sale reduced by 40 per cent in just two years. How did they do it? After building a profile of target customers, the company was able to match it with the reader and viewer profiles of different media. The full range of direct response media were used, including television, press and radio as well as direct mail, catalogues and point-of-sale materials in selected retail outlets. Over 40 titles were used and each was tracked for the number and nature of responses. The campaigns were well integrated with the emphasis on creating impact. With the help of Coast Digital, online conversions increased by 50 per cent and online sales increased significantly. Potentially the world's largest bottom was featured on a billboard advertisement with the headline 'Does my bum look big on this?' at the junction of Oxford Street and Tottenham Court Road in London to announce the launch of the Slendertone Flex Bottom and Thigh System (www.coastdigital.co.uk; www.slendertone.com).

By using an eye-catching large bottom and making the viewer think of the common question 'Does my bum look big in this?', Slendertone managed to attract the attention of passers-by

*Source*: Slendertone, Biomedical Research Ltd

There is a range of types of direct response mechanisms that can be used in advertising. Advertisers can provide an address to write to, a coupon to fill in and send off for more information, telephone numbers or website addresses. The trend has been towards using the website as the main vehicle for response, although the telephone is still important particularly because of innovations in mobile marketing. Either the advertiser or the customer can pay for any postal or telephone charges. The ones who expect the consumer to pay for a phone call or postage, or who expect the consumer to compose a letter rather than filling in a coupon, are immediately putting up barriers to response. Why should consumers make any undue effort, or even pay directly, to give an organisation the privilege of trying to sell them something? In the light of that view, organisations either need to have incredibly compelling direct response advertising that makes any effort or cost worthwhile or, more realistically, they need to minimise the effort and cost to the potential customer. Schofield (1994) confirms that certainly in B2B markets, response should be as easy as possible. The easier the response, the greater the number of enquiries and the greater the conversion rate and revenue per enquiry.

*eg* QVC is a leading TV shopping channel operator that relies exclusively on direct response. Its sales in 2008 were around £360 million. It has around 1 million active customers generating 15 million calls and 13.9 million unit sales in the UK alone. Although the main mechanism for responding to the offers made on the television broadcasts is the telephone (including mobiles), there is also a website carrying the same broadcast online, and the customer can also respond and buy online. QVC mainly offers beauty, fashion, jewellery, craft and leisure, home electronics, garden and DIY products. Although sales have increased, profitability has not, however, as other television channels have entered the market, thus fragmenting the audience, and there has been aggressive price competition from store-based retailers. (http://www.qvcuk.com).

McAlevey (2001) identified a number of principles to follow to enable more effective direct response. Although generated in a North American cultural context, a number of them are relevant to European DR users seeking greater impact and higher response rates. The principles are as follows:

- The focus should always be on what sells.
- Don't always reinvent the wheel when designing campaigns.
- Make the 'offer' the central theme of the creative execution.
- Long copy can sell if the reader is engaged.
- Select creativity that sells, not that which just looks good.
- Always test and measure response.
- Select and retain media not on their ratings, but on their ability to sell for you.
- Always ask for the order or for further action. It must be loud, clear, easy to understand and easy to execute.

To McAlevey, success is 40 per cent the offer, 40 per cent the media/lists used and 20 per cent the message creativity. Perhaps that is why some of the hard-hitting, direct response television advertisements for double glazing (no names!) are such a turn-off.

## Telemarketing

While direct response advertising and direct mail both imply the use of an impersonal initial approach through some kind of written or visual material, telemarketing makes a direct personal, verbal approach to the potential customer. However, although this brings benefits from direct and interactive communication, it is seen by some as extremely intrusive. If the telephone rings, people feel obliged to answer it there and then, and tend to feel annoyed and disappointed if it turns out to be a sales pitch rather than a friend wanting a good gossip, and particularly if it turns out to be a recorded message.

Telemarketing, therefore, can be defined as any planned and controlled activity that creates and exploits a direct relationship between customer and seller, using the telephone.

Miele Professional uses telemarketing in the hospitality, health and catering industries. It uses an agency GasboxDMG to provide both inbound and outbound services. In particular, it uses inbound for handling sales enquiries, while outbound generates leads for the sales team to pursue. Although GasboxDMG is an external agency, its facilities and expertise in telemarketing coupled with the use of staff dedicated to the Miele contract and working closely with Miele's own staff puts it in a good position to get better conversion. Once leads have been generated and qualified, it uses e-mail and other digital means to give the prospect basic information so that when the sales representative calls on the prospect, some of the groundwork has already been done. The inbound service uses databases to track leads through to fruition and to control the information provided to potential clients prior to the sales process. It is important to Miele that the agency is consistent with Miele's own values and attitude to quality (www.callcentreclinic.com; www.hsm.co.uk/).

Miele is an example of outbound telemarketing, where the organisation contacts the potential customer. Inbound telemarketing, where the potential customer is encouraged to contact the organisation, is also popular. This is used not only in direct response advertising, but also for customer care lines, competitions and other sales promotions.

Telephone rental or ownership is high across Europe, averaging over 80 per cent of households, and thus if an appropriate role can be defined for telemarketing within the planned promotional mix, it represents a powerful communication tool. As with personal selling (see p. 457 *et seq.*), there is direct contact and so dialogue problems can be addressed. Similarly, the customer's state of readiness to commit themselves to a course of action can be assessed and improved through personal persuasion, and efforts made to move towards a positive outcome.

Nationwide has 1,500 call handlers based in the UK handling 1 million calls every month. They handle the full range of inbound services and rely on the call handler to build a rapport with the customers, something it thinks wouldn't happen so easily with overseas outsourcing. It has 13 million customers in the UK, spanning a wide range of ages and demographic profiles. Some still prefer to visit the branch, others use the phone more readily, while younger customers use the internet and ATMs. It is important that a range of contact points are offered (Abbott, 2008).

Outbound telemarketing is still not widely accepted by consumers and is often seen as intrusive and annoying, especially when the customer picks up the phone and is greeted by a recorded marketing message. Where customers have an existing relationship with an organisation, however, and where the purpose of the call is not hard selling, they are less suspicious. Customers generally don't mind, for example, receiving calls that check their satisfaction with the product or service or that simply thank them for their custom. If the outbound calls are badly handled, customers become annoyed and in this can damage the reputation and prospects for future business of that company.

Lea Valley Audi sells new and used cars and as the name implies, it specialises in Audi. When the Audi A3 was launched it had to get customers to come to the launch events and to book a test drive as quickly as possible afterwards, so it decided to use telemarketing. Confero was selected as the call centre. Part of the deal was the training on Audi products and visits to the showrooms so that when talking to customers, the agents would be fully informed of the product range. Phone calls were made to prospective customers especially at evenings and weekends when they would be more receptive. Over 408 hours of calls were made, and 497 people agreed to a test drive or attended the launch (www.confero.co.uk).

Outbound telemarketing involves the organisation contacting the potential customer. Inbound telemarketing means that the prospect or customer is encouraged to contact the organisation. Customer service and care lines are an important area within inbound telemarketing for handling orders, appointment or delivery booking, or bill payments. Many companies use specialist call centres and customer service centres.

Call centres often attract negative publicity for intrusive communication or for the exporting of jobs to other countries such as India. They have made a big impact, however, on customer service and relationship management. When successful, the effective use of a call centre can provide 24/7 customer service, but when handled badly, it can be time consuming and frustrating and can even generate anger. Some customer support lines take several minutes of customer detailing only to be told that all the agents are busy and someone will call back later (and then too often, the callback never happens). As service expectations continue to rise, so telemarketing inbound centres will need to progress to meet these expectations. Part of this can be resolved by training so that rather than a sterile scripted approach, more flexibility and empowerment can be given to call-handlers for customer interaction. Maintaining consistently high service standards can be a challenge, however, especially as costs are being forced downwards.

## Mail order

Mail order, as the name suggests, involves the purchase of products featured in advertising or selected from a catalogue. The goods are not examined before ordering, and thus the advertisement or the catalogue has to do a good sales job. Mail-order companies promote themselves

Scottish Power supplies electricity and gas to 5 million homes in the UK. It used an agency to handle its customer-service calls from clients with pre-payment meters. Usually inbound, the calls concerned either billing or supply issues, both of which required some training for the staff responsible for handling the calls. The complexity of the systems made it essential that the telephone agents were up to speed in handling the range of calls expected and techniques for handling angry and abusive callers. A key success factor in the operation was ensuring that the right staff were picked for the job. The agency handled 600 often difficult calls per day and offered a 98 per cent service level, which was better than Scottish Power's internal operation has achieved (PPT Solutions, no date).

through any media, and receive orders through the mail, by telephone or via an agent. Clearly, a lot of shopping that traditionally would have been done through mail-order catalogues is now shifting online. Mintel (2009) estimates that in 2008 sales via offline catalogues, television and direct response advertising amounted to about £4.6 billion, a 23 per cent share of the total home shopping market (compared with a 39 per cent share in 2005). In contrast, e-commerce's share rose from just over 50 per cent in 2005 to nearly 75 per cent in 2008.

Direct selling through one-off, product-specific advertisements has largely been covered at p. 429 *et seq.* under direct response advertising. This section therefore, will, concentrate on the mail-order-catalogue sector.

The home shopping market went through a period of rapid growth in the late 1990s, but now growth lies primarily in targeted direct catalogues rather than in the large agency-type catalogues such as those operated by GUS and Littlewoods. Society is changing, with the internet and e-mail also providing an alternative approach to retaining customers and generating repeat sales. The challenge for catalogues is to tailor offerings to the right target group, and developments in database building techniques, customer acquisition, promotion, fulfilment, postal services and logistics have all helped the shift towards speciality catalogue selling.

Lands' End is an international clothing retailer owned by Sears and Kmart. It has concessions in Sears stores in the USA but the bulk of its business is mail order and online selling. In the USA alone, it distributes over 270 million catalogues and has a fully integrated website to give its 7 million customers an alternative. It was the first clothing retailer to have an e-commerce enabled website, back in 1995.

The UK operation is quite small. Its core market is the over 50s and it has struggled to attract younger users. Several editions of the UK catalogue are released each year and smaller versions are also sent out for publicity purposes. Telephone ordering still takes place but online ordering is increasingly popular. It has also introduced Lands' End Live, a video chat feature so that a more personal approach can be adopted for online shoppers. The call centres, however, are staffed 24/7, 365 days a year to give expert advice to customers ordering by the telephone as well, and great emphasis is placed on answering the call at the first ring (Mintel, 2009; www.landsend.com).

This kind of catalogue is really a form of distribution channel, in that the operator performs the tasks of merchandise assembly, marketing and customer service. The important thing is to find the selection of merchandise appropriate to the market niche served, and to design an appealing kind of service package (in terms of ordering mechanisms, delivery, returns, etc.).

Table 11.2 shows the perceived advantages and disadvantages of mail order over retailing from the consumer's perspective.

**Table 11.2** Typical advantages and disadvantages of mail order compared with retail outlets

| Advantages of shops over mail order | Advantages of mail order over shops |
| --- | --- |
| Can see/touch goods | Delay payment |
| Can try on/test goods | Choose at leisure |
| No delay in acquiring purchases | Choose at convenience |
| Easy to return goods | Easy to return goods |
| Easy to compare prices | Saves time |
| Cheaper | No pestering |
| Shopping is enjoyable | Shopping is not enjoyable |
| Advice/service available | Home delivery of purchases |

## Database creation and management

Any organisation with a serious intention of utilising direct marketing, online or offline, needs to think very carefully about how best to store, analyse and use the data captured about its customers. This means developing a database with as detailed a profile as possible about each customer in terms of geodemographics, lifestyle, purchase frequency and spend patterns. In B2B markets, information might also be held about decision-makers and buying centres. Whatever the kind of market, the deeper the understanding of the customer, the easier it is to create effective messages and products. However, if database usage goes wrong, it can cause some unfortunate errors, for example, offering maternity wear or prams to pensioners. When the database works well, it can help to offer products that will appeal to the target audience and generate a response, enabling relationships to build and prosper.

This section looks at some of the issues connected with database creation and management, as summarised in Figure 11.2. Note that the end of the first cycle, customer recruitment and retention, is the start of a stronger second cycle, based on better, recorded information and subsequent targeting.

### Customer information

The customer and sales database is a most valuable source of information for relationship management and campaign planning. Having the software to edit, sort, filter and retrieve data is essential (Lewis, 1999). Typical information contained in a database describes customer profiles. Through analysis and model building, its predictive potential can be exploited.

**Figure 11.2**
Database creation
and management

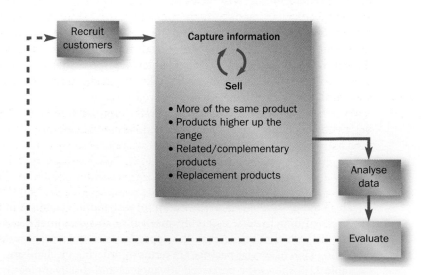

## Keeping customers and re-selling to them

As with any marketing effort, the continuation of exchanges will depend on how well needs have been satisfied, service provided and value offered. However, the real challenge for direct marketing is to continue to communicate actively with the customer and win further orders after the initial contact has been made. It is always more cost-effective to retain customers than to win new ones, so careful use of direct marketing can assist the overall promotional programme.

There are five stages in a retention and customer development programme. These are considered in turn.

1 *Welcome.* The obvious first stage applies shortly after the customer has become active. An early contact can be reassuring, and assists in engendering receptivity to further communication. When Next Directory called new customers to welcome them after receiving their first orders, a much higher proportion of new customers was retained and they spent 30 per cent more than 'non-welcomed' customers.

2 *Selling up.* Apart from normal repeat business, organisations should encourage the customer to trade-up to a better or higher-valued model. This approach would be appropriate for a wide range of products and services including cars, cameras and credit cards. American Express, for example, used direct mail to encourage green Amex cardholders to trade up to gold card status. The timing of contact will depend on the expected replacement period for the product.

3 *Selling across.* The selling across or cross-selling stage is where an organisation tries to sell a wider range of products than those in the area originally selected. A customer who purchases car insurance from a particular company might subsequently receive mailings about house insurance or private health cover, for example.

4 *Renewal.* With products that involve annual or regular renewal, such as motor insurance, the timing of appropriate and personalised communication around the renewal date can reinforce repeat purchases.

5 *Lapsed customers.* Customers may be temporarily dormant or permanently lost. A continuation of communication may be appropriate for a period of time so as not to lose contact, especially if reorder frequencies are high.

## Review and recycle

As implied above, once a database is up and running it should be monitored, reviewed and evaluated periodically to make sure that it is working well and achieving its full potential. This is not just about 'cleaning' the database (i.e. making sure that it is up to date and that any individuals who have disappeared without trace are deleted from it), but also about data analysis. As part of the strategic planning process, the organisation can look for opportunities to cross-sell to existing customers or to get them to trade up, for instance. Managers can also review whether the nature and frequency of contact are sufficient to achieve full customer potential. Perhaps more importantly, they can assess whether they have recruited the kind of customer expected and whether targets have been met.

All of this analysis can be used to plan the continuation of database building. Although the organisation will be trying primarily to hold on to the customers it already has, there will inevitably be some wastage as customers lose interest, or as their tastes and aspirations change, or as they move house without telling anybody. That wastage, as well as the organisation's own growth aspirations, means that new customers will have to be sought. Learning from the first implementation of the cycle, managers can assess whether the 'right' kind of media were used to attract the 'right' kind of desired customer. They can refine their profiling and targeting in order to improve response rates and perhaps attract even more lucrative customers. They can review which promotional offers or which kinds of approach were most successful and repeat those with new customers, or try similar activities again.

## Digital direct marketing

Digital direct marketing has moved beyond a series of discrete activities or a separate channel to becoming an integral part of the marketing communications landscape (Benjamin, 2011). It has evolved from direct mail through to telemarketing, into electronic channels using permission-based e-mail which provides a receptive and relevant audience. The latest evolution is mobile marketing, which again is permission-based with the consumer being able to opt-out at any time by texting the word 'stop' (Langdon, 2008). E-mail has slowly been superseded in digital communication but is still very popular, as marketers integrate it with social media, using e-mail as a means of driving interested consumers to Facebook and Twitter as a means of building a social community around a brand (Smith, 2010). The challenge is to get greater integration of e-mail, mobile and social media into campaigns with particular regard to getting a consistent message and a cumulative effect on the consumer. There is also the danger of information overload and clutter creating a crowded inbox and possibly reduced customer attention. What is for certain is that digital communication is changing rapidly how marketers communicate with their customers.

## E-mail marketing

More and more people use e-mail on a regular basis. In an office environment workers check their e-mails throughout the day and it has been estimated that 42 per cent of users check e-mails even while they are on holiday, and 53 per cent check e-mails constantly throughout the day (www.email-unlimited.com). However, the user has to contend with the risk of viruses, phishing and spam. Despite these difficulties, e-mail has emerged as a powerful means of communication that marketers are increasingly adopting as part of their promotional activity. We use e-mails primarily to keep in touch with friends, colleagues and contacts, and occasionally we use them to search for information or to place an online order. We may even welcome an incoming e-mail from a company that we have done business with previously or where we have declared an interest in what they are offering. What we do not want is to be bombarded with offers of cheap financing deals, special travel discounts, get-rich-quick schemes, no-questions-asked pharmaceuticals or pornography (and according to www.royal.pingdom.com, in 2010 over 89 per cent of all e-mail was spam). Many recipients are wary of receiving viruses via e-mails from unrecognised sources and, therefore, tend to delete 'cold calling' e-mails without opening them, just to be safe.

## MARKETING IN ACTION

### Cooking up your holiday

Thomas Cook has had to adapt over the past decade to take into account changes in the digital marketing environment. It now boasts sales of £8.9 billion from 22.5 million customers. It operates in six geographic segments in 21 countries, and is normally first or second in its core markets. It provides a range of holiday products, selling packages, flight-only or accommodation-only trips, and packaged holiday solutions.

The starting point in around 2000 was that Thomas Cook was a traditional high-street travel agent that sold heavily through the print brochures and used in-store agents to access the reservation system and make the booking on behalf of the customer. The main challenge was to drive consumers into the shops so that the personal selling process could begin. Thomas Cook ended the decade still with a high street presence, but backed up with strong digital support. Acquisition of new customers remained the focus, but now included highly targeted e-mails to keep in touch with the consumer and retain customer loyalty. This meant improving data collection and analysis to enable more personalised e-mail marketing campaigns that reflected the customer's interests. An increasing number of customers, however, decided to bypass the high-street stores altogether and book online, although some still were hesitant over online security fears and preferred the reassurance of direct contact. Thus 1,300 high-street stores remain as customer access points for brochures and to offer help with reservations.

Customers now have three options: they can make a store visit to collect a brochure, receive a hard copy of a printed brochure through the post, or access an electronic brochure either online or as an e-mailed attachment. The electronic option is particularly important as according to Mintel (2011), nearly half of consumers use the internet as a prime source of holiday information. For those customers wishing to make a booking there are customer service reps to guide them through the booking process, and there is also a telephone number so that customers can book direct.

Thomas Cook has had to integrate all its communications and develop a multichannel strategy to keep its competitive position in the marketplace. An interesting piece of research produced by Greenlight suggested that if the price was right, then the destination didn't matter so much! Over 60 per cent of holiday searches were not destination-specific and the most popular keywords were 'cheap holidays' and 'holidays' for online searching. This means that specific brands did not feature that highly in early stages of the search. Thomas Cook's was the third most visible website from a natural search after Thomson and Travel Supermarket, but it is the company's aim to become the UK's most visited travel agent online. Over half of holidaymakers surveyed by Mintel (2011) booked their holidays online, just over one-quarter did it all by phone, and only 13 per cent did it in person at a travel agent's. Ten years earlier, hardly anyone was booking online. Interestingly the use of mobile apps is now growing rapidly and now consumers are using that source too.

While accessing information online is relatively simple, it does require customer confidence to book online and some people needed to be guided through the process. However, as customers do gain more confidence, online sales will increase and it will be interesting to see in what ways the role of the bricks and mortar stores will evolve further. Thomas Cook does not want to be seen as a purely online operation, like Expedia or Google Travel.

*Sources: Business Wire* (2010); Eleftheriou-Smith (2011); Levy (2010); *M2 Presswire* (2010b); Mintel (2010, 2011); Shearman (2010); www.greenlightsearch.com.

Marketers are attracted to the potential of e-mail marketing as a communication tool that can target individuals rather than using mass media approaches. E-mail is such a cheap medium that it's tempting to send the same message to anyone and everyone, but research has shown that investment in segmentation, targeting and testing of different creative approaches leads to better responses. Campaign profitability can be increased eighteen-fold (Croft, 2008). Carefully designed e-mail marketing can help to create initial contact as well as helping to develop an online relationship once transactions have taken place. The aim from a marketing perspective is primarily to encourage the reader to look at a website and to obtain permission to send more information to the recipient or to a third party. Typical uses of an e-mail marketing campaign are shown in Figure 11.3.

*eg*

Happy Puzzle supplies a range of 400 puzzles, games and challenges to both the public and educational establishments to develop play and thinking skills. It operates through a catalogue, direct-response advertising in print media, and its website to generate sales but it also decided to supplement that with e-mail marketing. The database comprising people who had purchased within the last two years or who had elected to receive more marketing information provided a large list for e-mail. The campaign started in September 2010 and ran until January 2011. Over £100,000 worth of sales were generated (www.happypuzzle.co.uk; www.toinfinity.co.uk).

**Figure 11.3**

Typical uses of
e-mail marketing

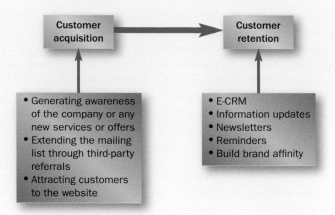

Some companies still operate on a free-for-all basis and are indiscriminate in sending out e-mails. This creates a perception of e-mail marketing as mostly 'junk' or 'spam' when e-mails for Viagra, porn or financial scams get included with the legitimate e-mails. In the EU, the legislation says that generally companies cannot send marketing e-mails unless they have the recipient's consent to do so (although consent is sometimes implied from the customer's failure to tick an opt-out box) or unless the recipient's details were collected 'in the course of a sale or negotiations for a sale'. Companies must also give recipients a clear and easy 'unsubscribe' option in each e-mail (www.ico.gov.uk). Concern has been prompted by the intrusive nature and sometimes dubious content of some spam e-mails, most of which originate from outside the EU and are sent from companies that pay no regard to the law whatsoever. As with any nefarious activity, as fast as the authorities close down one spamming operation, another one springs up, and while the online security firms claim to have stopped 98 per cent of spam from reaching the target the spammers continue to work hard to find more ingenious ways of breaching security (EIU, 2010).

Gaining consent or permission from the intended recipient is only the starting point, not the objective, of an e-mail campaign. The most effective campaigns work on the basis of precision or synaptic marketing (Langdon, 2008). This combines the power of e-mail with the power of IT to record and analyse responses to ensure even closer targeting and almost individual customer relationship management. In theory, each customer could receive different e-mail messages. Amazon, for instance, regularly e-mails its customers with suggestions or offers that are clearly based on their previous and buying behaviour and even their recent browsing activity (*see* Case study 8, as an illustration).

## Customer acquisition

Viral marketing is one way of building an e-mailing list (see p. 447) or a list can be purchased. Lists, whether they are purchased or rented, must be based on permission, a willingness to receive e-mails acknowledged by an opt-in mechanism. It is risky to use large, cheap lists of people to whom your communication may be most unwelcome. Some list owners are taking particular care about how their lists are used to avoid inappropriate or excessive use. Lifestyle data gatherers, such as Claritas, often record e-mail addresses as do online list builders, such as Bananalotto and MyOffers, which sell permission-based lists. Some website operators now offer lists as a sideline, gathered from the users of their sites, as we saw in the Party Pieces example on p. 427. Despite the attraction of such lists, the click-through rate may be low, however. The click-through rate is often 2 per cent or less from a rented list, rising to 6–10 per cent on a list that has been developed in-house (www.emailcenteruk.com/maxenews/archive/using_email_tracking_software.htm).

Online lists depend heavily on the sender's ability to track contacts from within its website. Sources can include online surveys, website registrations and responses to competitions and offers over the internet. Web forms vary in the degree of information required beyond the e-mail details. Some seek data to enable customer profiling to take place and better targeted messages to be sent before gathering the more specific information generated when or if clicks or orders are made. It is often advisable to seek only limited information at any one go, perhaps with three or four questions, rather than making the site visitor feel that they are being interrogated and delayed unnecessarily. If that happens, the visitor might lose patience or become uncomfortable about giving personal information away and fail to complete the registration process.

*eg* When Vodafone decided to adopt an e-mail marketing campaign to promote m-commerce in B2B markets, it established a list of existing and potential customers and then assessed them against predetermined qualifying criteria to ensure that they were appropriate decision-makers. At that stage Vodafone gathered the appropriate opt-in permission to enable it to e-mail only willing recipients confidently.

## Customer retention

One of the greatest benefits of e-mail marketing is its ability to create and build a relationship with a customer on an individual basis. The possibility of fostering a one-to-one relationship with a consumer is very powerful and attractive to the marketer (Hosea, 2011) and can, therefore, play an important part in any customer relationship (CRM) programme. This requires a list of opt-in respondents. Once the list has been developed or purchased, response mechanism tracking can develop usable and powerful customer profiles. E-mails can be tracked for opening, clicks and purchases, so quite a detailed history, far superior to anything direct mail can achieve, can soon be built up. The more powerful and carefully designed the database, the easier it is to define small, well-focused sub- or even micro-segments for targeting.

*eg* Although recording and analysing customer use of websites is a valuable tool for targeting offers and messages, some organisations also use e-mail newsletters to keep in touch with current and previous customers. These newsletters can play an important part of a more general CRM programme. Parker Harris uses e-mail to communicate with clients on projects. As a visual arts consultancy, it needs to keep in regular contact with those clients updating and querying projects. Each month it also sends an e-newsletter to 6,000 subscribers to keep them generally aware of what is going on. It is an easy and cost effective way of keeping in touch and Parker Harris even segments the subscriber base, sending different messages to different groups of individuals. By using e-mail Parker Harris can also monitor response rates from different groups to different messages and it can track click-throughs to other parts of its website. Although it is just one way of keeping customers informed, it makes a cost-effective contribution to maintaining relationships (www.parkerharris.co.uk; www.rubious.co.uk/email-marketing/).

Personalisation is the aim of most marketers in communications designed to build customer relationships. When successful, personalisation combines all the benefits of personal selling with the cost-effectiveness of technology-driven marketing. Personalisation can take many forms, depending on what is known about the recipient and their needs, preferences and interests, including content, offer proposition, frequency of contact, subjects of interest, spend, and/or purchasing history.

eg

The Fabulous Bakin' Boys in Witney, near Oxford, uses e-mail marketing. It created a database of jokes which could be downloaded from its website by registered users. The registration process asks basic questions such as gender, age, where you have seen the company's muffins for sale, and when you eat muffins. The prospect of some free samples is mentioned. It then introduced online games, and cheeky advertisements are regularly mailed out to previous website respondents (www.bakinboys.co.uk). The games are designed to attract repeat traffic and each can be 'mailed to a mate' as part of a viral campaign. Online ordering is possible and look out for the golf game and the retro games graveyard (www.bakinboys.co.uk/games_graveyard.php). Alternatively, you could send a retro postcard showing a couple in swimwear sitting on the beach with the caption 'Our muffins are better than sex' and 'Our muffins are moist and sticky, just like Fanny's'. Muffin munchin' will never be the same again.

The Fabulous Bakin' Boys website offers fun activities to reduce any possibility of grumpiness

*Source:* © The Fabulous Bakin' Boys, www.bakinboys.co.uk

As more organisations have become familiar with using the internet as more than just a brochure supplement, the use of e-mail linked website activity has also grown for smaller businesses. The fragmentation of high cost, national media and the availability of targeted media that are within the reach of small business marketing budgets mean that there has been much greater use of e-mail marketing.

## Response and review

One of the major advantages of e-mail campaigns is the speed of response. It has been estimated that between 50 and 80 per cent of responses are generated within 48 hours and 90 per cent within a week. (www.email-unlimited.com). This means that considerable care must be taken to have a system in place to handle the response traffic generated. In part, the technology infrastructure can help to handle 'bounced' e-mails, undeliverable e-mails and routine enquiries, but in some cases, it may be necessary to have an inbound e-mail answering service.

eg

In the Vodafone example mentioned earlier, a real-time reporting and tracking engine was employed that could list how many e-mails were sent, how many opened and how many clicked through. Normally, only 50 e-mails at a time were sent to allow for tracking, primarily over a six-hour period. Of the e-mails sent, over 50 per cent were opened and read and 21 per cent clicked through to the appropriate section of the website. Many of the latter were then converted into leads by the telemarketing team (www.inbox.co.uk).

After all the responses are in, the analysis of campaign effectiveness can begin. This often requires careful pre-planning to cross-check unsubscribers, to assign codes to different target segments or different message types and to record the type of response generated, including where clicking has taken place but no formal response has followed. Data measured by campaign, customer or product on the number of openings and clicks, unsubscription rates, and bouncing, as well as responses, can be collected. This is an invaluable aid to updating records and further campaign planning.

The channels for direct communication to consumers are expanding rapidly, giving consumers greater freedom to purchase what they want, when and how they want to. There is now *m-commerce* (mobile), *f-commerce* (Facebook) and *s-commerce* (social media) and *v-commerce* (viral marketing), all of which can fall under the umbrella of direct and digital marketing. Each is considered here in turn, but it is important to realise that the area is changing so rapidly that the data and concepts described here might well be outdated by the time you read this!

## Mobile marketing

When you are in an Asda store, it is possible to access the Asda price-comparison website by smartphone to check whether you're getting the best deal on your purchases. If you could have got that set of purchases cheaper from a competitor, the Asda site will print you a voucher for the difference plus one penny to use on your next store visit (Birchall, 2010). British Airways is seeking to reach a larger percentage of frequent flyers via SMS who don't engage with other forms of digital messaging, with the aim of getting a response to the advertisements (*New Media Age*, 2011b). Now you can book tickets for cinemas, theatres and concert venues, book flights and accommodation, go job hunting, gather news and enquire on websites, all using the mobile phone (*Afaqs!*, 2011). A study by Esendex found that nearly 50 per cent of respondents were prepared to pay the standard messaging charge to purchase travel tickets or to receive updates, and yet 62 per cent of UK businesses don't have the ability to use SMS as a communications tool (www.esendex.co.uk). Research by IAB showed that mobile users pick up their phones 18 times a day and 51 per cent of the UK population has engaged in m-commerce, either for information gathering or purchasing (Shearman, 2011a). Berg Insight has suggested that the total value of the global mobile marketing and advertising market will grow from €1.0 billion in 2008 to €8.7 billion by 2014 which will correspond to nearly 12 per cent of the digital advertising market (*M2 Presswire*, 2010a) as m-marketing or mobile marketing becomes more established as another major opportunity to target customers more closely, stimulated by advances in phone technology.

Argos, the multichannel retailer, has 130 million customers a year who visit the stores, driven by the catalogue and website offering the range of products. It added a mobile channel in 2004 to make it easier for customers to interact with the Argos brand. Customers can browse the Argos website or catalogue and text a catalogue number and their postcode to the company. Then they receive a text in return telling them the nearest store where it is in stock and giving them the option to reserve the product by text. The customer can also opt for notification when an out-of-stock product is back in their nearest store. Reservation confirmation messages are then sent to consumers who have reserved products via the website or over the phone, and if the item has not been collected within 24 hours, a text reminder is sent.

The mobile channel thus helps to set up the transaction, in terms of what will be purchased, where and when, but the final stage in the transaction, payment, still takes place in person at the counter. The system works: Argos claims that in 2009, this system generated over £60 million in incremental revenue. Over 250,000 customer-initiated messages per month were being handled (www.velti.com/customers/case-study-argos).

This system has been further developed to take advantage of the adoption of smartphones. The customer can download an Argos app that gives access not only to a 'check and reserve' service as described above, but also access to information on the latest price cuts, store opening hours and directions to get to stores, product reviews, and links to Argos on Facebook and Twitter. The Argos catalogue also now includes QR codes that can be scanned by a mobile and, again, gives instant access to more detailed information and up to date prices and offers (www.argos.co.uk).

M-marketing provides the means to carry voice messages, but is primarily used for sending text messages to targeted individuals at any time. Because of its intrusiveness and because different customers will be more receptive at different times of day, however, the m-marketer must fully appreciate consumer lifestyles and be careful in setting the right tone of the communication to avoid damaging any trust in the sender's brand. Consider, for example, your receptivity to a text message received as you dash for an important meeting compared with one received over a relaxing lunchtime meal.

As in e-mail marketing, compiling target lists and profiles is an essential starting point. Consumers must be able to choose whether or not they want to receive information and there is a responsibility to ensure that any information sent is relevant. Irritation will soon grow if a torrent of mortgage deal messages are sent to students struggling to find next month's rent. It also follows that it must be easy to opt-out from receiving messages. Again, therefore, as with e-mail marketing, content selection should be derived from customer profiling, but because of the nature of the medium, most text messages need to be short, alerting the individual to a special offer or promotion or engaging them with an interactive game that could direct them to a website.

## MARKETING IN ACTION

### Shopping by phone

Shoppers rely on three types of mobile content when making buying decisions: product details (including price), user reviews, and personalised recommendations. Each plays a role in the buying process and the mobile speeds up the information flow to the consumer. The third type of content, personalised recommendations, acknowledges the role that social media and friends play in helping with the buying decision by providing non-retailer generated assessment and recommendation, especially if the purchase is a high-involvement decision. The challenge for the retailer is to keep the consumer dedicated to that retail choice from the point of identifying that retailer as a potential supplier, through to product evaluation and final choice. It has, however, been estimated that 44 per cent actually switch to another retailer at that point. It seems, then, that retailers need to broaden their focus from prioritising 'the point of purchase', which reflects a bricks and mortar approach, to 'the point of decision' which happens online or via mobile. This means that the retailer can become better at nursing the consumer through the process.

A key issue though is whether the retailer's mobile-enabled site is purely for information or is transactional. Although around 80 per cent of retailers do have a mobile-enabled website, that often does not extend to making it transactional and further developments in consumers' willingness to use their mobiles to make purchases could leave some retailers even further behind. While 82 per cent of consumers participating in a Direct Marketing Association study wanted to make purchases via their mobiles, less than half the retailers in the study had a defined m-commerce strategy, and 14 per cent of them had no plans to develop one.

M&S was one of the early users of a fully operational mobile facility as part of its strategy for becoming a truly multichannel retailer. In the first year 5.5 million people used mobiles to access the website and generated 66,000 orders. A key early decision was to make access unrestricted, so that no special apps were needed, by using a mobile-optimised site that can be used with any reasonably modern phone. Perhaps surprisingly, M&S's mobile customers were not just the younger people targeted, but included mums and grandmas buying clothes and shoes from what they perceive as a trustworthy brand. Overall, the purpose of the site is to extend the M&S brand into mobiles, creating another direct communications channel with consumers and enabling them to access all product lines on the move.

Some retailers are investing in m-commerce, and food retailing is a sector that could benefit. Grocery shopping is a chore for many people so anything that makes it easier is welcome. Using the mobile means it can be done in parallel with other activities such as travelling on a train, watching television and even walking the dog! Grocery retailers have been slow to respond and innovate, however. Tesco introduced a transactional mobile phone application to enable shoppers to browse the brands on offer in order to create a shopping list and to make the purchase. Ocado, the home grocery shopping service saw mobile sales double from 6 to 12 per cent after it worked hard to introduce barcode scanning and voice ordering technology. Other retailers lag behind or are waiting for the technology to stabilise, however. Asda is launching a digital facility in 2011, but it does not extend to transactional and Sainsbury's has an app to locate a store but prefers to let the shopping take place on the premises. Casino in France has gone further with an app that makes personalised recommendations in the store, along with suggestions of cheaper alternatives or associated products. More generally, though, there is still much work to be done to ensure mobiles do add value as an alternative sales channel by factoring in aspects such as loyalty card data and lifestyle before the consumer can fully interact with the brand.

Even for smaller retailers for whom resources and expertise are limited, it is possible to engage in mobile shopping. For example, 24studio, a Manchester-based gift company, has launched a mobile-optimised website. It allows consumers to browse the full product range, and sales via mobile devices doubled in the year following introduction. Whether at home, work, having coffee or chatting to friends, using the mobile means the website is always at hand for browsing and sharing. Research by IAB suggests that 40 per cent of retailers planned to launch a transactional site within a year, but given that over three-quarters also said they needed more training before really understanding m-commerce, those plans could be aspirational. Overall, it is hard to see how sales in the UK via mobiles can reach the £13 billion predicted by 2021 unless there is a rapid and fundamental change in organisational attitudes to, and the priority given to m-shopping. In the UK, retailers only spend a small percentage of their marketing budgets on digital, and even Tesco, with all it has achieved in mobile shopping, only spends less than 2 per cent of its total marketing budget. As a comparison, in the USA, the average is around 15 per cent.

So, consumers are often disappointed with what is available, and m-commerce expectations are ahead of retailer provision. Some are responding, such as Tesco, M&S, Play.com, Amazon and House of Fraser, all of which have integrated a variety of new features into m-shopping in order to make the entire shopping process as seamless as possible. But the majority is hampered by slow loading pages and a lack of basic time saving features, and that's if any service is offered at all. Mobiles are an important part of lifestyles nowadays, but as technology moves on with 4G, the capabilities of what is on offer will improve too, so the potential may be considerable and the shopping experience transformed all from the palm of our hands. This process of transformation is now well underway in the United States but is hardly starting in the UK. That's why the Sales and Advertising Director of Google said, 'if you don't have a mobile strategy in place by the end of this year, you don't have a future strategy' (as quoted by Murphy, 2011b).

*Sources: Just-food* (2010); *Just-style* (2010); *M2 Presswire* (2010c); Marian (2011); Murphy (2011b); *New Media Age* (2010a; 2010b); Node (2011); Shearman (2011b); Shields (2010; 2011); Walmsley (2011).

Most text messaging is currently SMS (short messaging service) which, as the name implies, usually means short, sharp messages to remind or inform. SMS and MMS (multimedia messaging service) are now used frequently by Coca-Cola, Domino's, Burger King and Marks & Spencer but privacy issues stop it being a mass communication device (Shields and Joseph,

2011). Domino's doesn't use mobile marketing for branding but does use it to send reminders, especially on a Friday night, to buy pizza! Many campaigns, however, tend to consist of one-way communication, and fail to inspire or encourage interactivity, and there's always the marketer's background fear of their brand being associated with spam. Of course, mobiles are not used in isolation; they are part of an integrated campaign and the challenge is to ensure that m-marketing initiatives add value and fit within the overall digital strategy (Smith, 2010). Even for more infrequent, expensive purchases mobiles (especially smartphones) can play a role in the information search, but they could also be used after all the shopping around and store visits to place the order once a final decision has been made (Nutley, 2011).

One of the potential barriers to the development of text messaging is the continued bad practice of sending unsolicited text messages, along the lines of the earlier comments on e-mail spamming. One example that has become a classic was when an individual became alarmed at receiving a text message asking him to report to his local army recruitment centre after 11 September 2001, only to find that it was an advertisement for a computer war game. Some other activities are scams designed to encourage premium rate telephone calls. There are computer programs that will generate random mobile numbers and send out messages to all of them, whether there has been an opt-in or not, thus constant vigilance is needed from the service providers.

All of that must be measured, however, against those who would welcome reminders or updates on something of relevance. How many garages contact their customers to remind them that their car is due for its annual service? Text messaging enables low-cost reminders to be sent out along with a call for instant action to make a booking. Similarly, many dental practices have started to send text messages to remind patients of the date and time of their appointments.

The target market for m-marketing campaigns tends to be younger and more willing to try new ways of communicating. Mobile usage has become an important part of our lifestyles; witness the scenes in any high street or, more annoyingly, in a crowded commuter train. It has moved from being a status symbol to an essential communication device, and fits well with the rushed, high-pressure, last-minute lifestyles of many younger people who leave decisions to the last minute and often make them 'on the run'. That plays into the hands of the m-marketers.

Third-generation (3G) technology has done a lot to facilitate the development of m-marketing, but that was just the start. The next development is 4G, which will offer connection speeds faster than home broadband making faster downloading and clearer video a reality (Ashton, 2011). This will open up the opportunity for more marketing apps and allow new brands to use mobile marketing. The next phase of development is likely to witness integration between voice and text, games, images and sounds to better entertain and engage the recipient, but that depends on technological advances.

QR (quick response) codes are popping up all over the place: in advertisements, on product packaging, in shop windows, in brochures and mailshots, and anywhere else you can think of. The QR code is simply a small box comprising tiny black and white pixels that can be scanned by a mobile phone (once you've downloaded a QR reader) which then links you through to further content. Bosomworth (2011) outlined a number of things that QR codes could be useful for. As well as the obvious applications, such as linking you through to the company's or brand's 'normal' website, or offering coupons or special deals, there are some more interesting things QR codes can do. The exhibition industry and those who exhibit, for example, are interested in QR codes as a navigational aid. If you are lost in a huge exhibition hall, scanning a code can tell you exactly where you are or guide you towards the stand you want to visit. Once you are at the stand, QR codes on the exhibits can be used to link you to more information about that product and even trigger a message to alert a representative to you as a potential sales lead.

QR codes can also add richness to a brand's character. Imagine standing in the dairy aisle of the supermarket, or sitting down to your breakfast cereal and idly scanning a QR code on a bottle of organic milk. Immediately, you are watching a video telling you where that milk has come from and all about the farmers who produce it. At least, that's what Calon Wen, a Welsh dairy co-operative hope you will do. Another way of bringing food brands to life at the point of sale is to use QR codes to link through to recipes or serving ideas. Similarly, with non-foods, such as DIY products, there's an obvious link with 'how to' videos. This can also extend into after-sales service: you've got your flatpack bookcase home, unpacked all the pieces, and could do with a bit of extra detail on the assembly instructions . . . just scan the QR code on the packaging.

Organisations involved in travel and tourism have been quick to see the potential of QR codes. New York plans to put QR codes on historic buildings so that the tourist can instantly access detailed information about them. Travel agents can use QR codes to give travellers access to various services, such as shuttle buses, car hire or hotel check-in, and British Airways has an app that uses QR codes to turn your phone into a boarding card and, of course, the codes can also link with detailed information about your destination to help you plan your stay. The possibilities for e-ticketing via QR codes are endless (Blyth, 2011; Bosomworth, 2011; Cuddeford-Jones, 2011; Glotz, 2011).

An example from Amsterdam of a QR code for civil-protection alerts and information

*Source:* Alamy Images/© Stuwdamdorp

## F-commerce and s-commerce

Increasing numbers of companies are using Facebook and other social networking sites to bring e-commerce even closer to where decisions are made. This is moving beyond simple brand-building social interaction with fans/followers into functioning f-commerce capability, i.e. making it possible for consumers to buy from the Facebook page without leaving it. In 2011, for instance, e-tailer ASOS launched a fully integrated store on Facebook allowing its 425,000 followers to buy from the site without leaving the webpage. At the time of writing, Heineken and French Connection also intend to open transactional stores on Facebook (*New Media Age*, 2011a). It all stems from consumers taking recommendations on social networking sites to help them make online purchasing decisions, and the integration of social sites and e-commerce into f-commerce is the cutting edge of new development to make turning the thought into action even quicker and easier. More and more sites incorporate product reviews all of which can guide buyer decision making and third party endorsements are increasingly important in that process.

Simon Bird, Technical Director at dotCommerce offered some useful tips for retailers in using social media (as quoted by *Marketwire*, 2010):

- Publicise your social media presence.
- Find out where your customers are – not every network will be right for every brand.
- Quality content is key – social media success depends on creating great content that your followers or fans will want to share.
- Engage with your audience – most of the retailers using social media are just broadcasting information. Initiating conversations and engaging with your audience will help encourage loyalty and retention.
- Track your traffic – if you use a social channel to promote offers, make sure you use trackable tags in the links.

It is important, however, to understand the difference between commercial sites and social sites. The main reason people log on to social media is not to be sold to, but to share experiences. If they are pushed too hard by commercial sellers, it can be counter productive. The emphasis needs to be on listening, dialogue and understanding, even on the company's own social media page. Thus Kitbag, Europe's largest online sports retailer, for example, used social networking sites to steer people to the company's website where a sale could be made. The main topic on Kitbag's Facebook page was England's 2010 World Cup performance, and from there, visitors were guided subtly to the website. The Facebook content strategy included match reports for each World Cup game, and the blog saw the fan base grow from 800 to 20,000 in six months (*New Media Age*, 2011a).

Social media networking is a global phenomenon and the number of subscribers as well as the amount of time they spend on it is still increasing (*M2 Presswire*, 2010d). Facebook already has 600 million users globally, with 30 million in the UK and that's a lot of buying power if it can be harnessed (Fisher, 2011). Despite the popularity and number of social networking sites, transactional websites offering products are still not benefiting as much as they might. Social networking sites accounted for just 16 per cent of referrals to transactional websites in January 2011, compared with 33 per cent being directed from search engines (Portet, 2011).

The problem is how to incorporate social media in order to benefit the brand or organisation. A survey revealed that 53 per cent of retailers don't use social sharing tools as part of their marketing activity (Nutley, 2010). Yet a basic level of use could be used to inform customer service, just by noting what people are saying. This can be through passive observation, or through active dialogue if company representatives give a response. That can extend into becoming part of the customer service communications strategy, for example using social media to get non-selling messages out, such as information about flight delays and cancellations (Kirby, 2010). Harnessing that to create individual communication on a personalised basis is also possible using social media. Lufthansa, for example, created the My Sky Status tool that automatically sends informational messages out to users of Facebook and Twitter, thus helping to create loyalty and good relations. This example and others in the travel and leisure industry show that social media can improve engagement with customers (Hosea, 2010). From these beginnings, the use of social media can evolve into a more proactive attempt to influence 'fan' or 'follower' thinking and eventually lead to a transactional website. It is important to realise, however, that this is not just a cheap way to reaching customers at minimal cost but a real opportunity to target and design effective propositions to encourage further customer action (*Marketing Week*, 2011).

Coca-Cola used social media to reach a large audience, not for general brand building, but for the distribution of its 'Happiness' machine video. The video featured a vending machine that produces flowers, pizza and unlimited Coca-Cola and it was a highly successful viral campaign in the USA before being released in the UK. Coke followers posted an array of content including photos, song lyrics, stories and other videos, sometimes around interesting questions such as, 'What's the craziest place you've had a Coke?' The brand's Facebook page had to be moderated for inappropriate content, of course, and to ensure that the conversations were more meaningful both between consumers and with the company (*Marketing Week*, 2010).

There is some evidence from social media engagement that it works in influencing consumption. 'Followers' are regarded as ten times more likely to purchase than non-followers (Costa, 2011b). Even banks are trying to find ways of using social media to engage with customers, but it is difficult because of confidentiality considerations. The problem is the banks don't fully understand what followers want from them. Is it advice, financial services discussion, or access to new products? Clearly the customer would not wish to discuss investing £30,000 over social media but they might wish to seek information on a range of options before visiting the branch (Costa, 2011a) For other services, it is easier to engage with social media. LoveFilm, for example, enables users to express a liking for a film on its site and then automatically publishes the information to the customer's Facebook newsfeed. This service led to a 300 per cent increase in Facebook traffic over the course of a year (*New Media Age*, 2011a).

Retailers have been slow to exploit social media marketing into their mix. Around 42 per cent do have a social media presence but only 12 per cent are using more than one social site. Twitter is popular with 73 per cent using it for product updates, 62 per cent for marketing and 58 per cent to promote company news (*Marketwire*, 2010). There is a problem. A survey by ForeSee Results found that 20 per cent of those surveyed didn't want to hear at all from retailers when using the site and nearly two-thirds wanted promotional e-mails only rather than to be engaged in conversation (*PR Newswire Europe*, 2011).

Ritson (2010) takes a more provocative view by analysing the use of social media by top brands. Of the top 20 brands, five don't use social media at all, and those who do use it have relatively few followers – less than 1 per cent of the customer base. More people followed Peter Andre on Twitter than all the top 20 brands put together. In short, Ritson's suggestion is that social media represent a 'new and relatively insignificant communications tool that has limited potential for a very small proportion of brands', compared with more established marketing communications tools. The intriguing question is the extent to which the supposed benefit of social media as a marketing tool is either hype from those with a vested interest in the industry or a real opportunity to communicate in a different, more relevant way with consumers. Doubtless the answer will emerge over the next few years.

## Viral marketing

Viral marketing, or 'e-mail a friend', is word-of-mouth by e-mail. It is often deliberately stimulated by the marketer and is easy to achieve with use of a forwarding facility ('e-mail this page to a friend'). Alternatively, the customer could elect to provide details of friends who might like to receive information direct from the marketer. As considered in Chapter 10, word-of-mouth promotion and recommendation is often the most effective form of communication in terms of believability and trust.

Originally, viral marketing was associated with youth brands to create a bit of excitement. If the material or the attachment is different and enjoyable, then there is more chance that it will be passed on. Lastminute.com, Budweiser and Levi's have all used viral marketing. Viral campaigns are not just the preserve of younger people, however. Age Concern used a viral campaign when it devised an e-mail quiz to test general knowledge of historical events. The quiz was scored and players were prompted to forward it to a friend so that they could compare scores. With a fun theme, people were happy to comply.

*eg* Hi-Tec Sports specialises in sports shoes and claims to be the UK's number one. It now has 500 Hi-Tec sports styles sold in 80 countries worldwide, and covers many sports. It employs 500 people and has global sales of $250 million. It used viral marketing to develop the brand under the 'Liquid Mountaineering' campaign name. The purpose of the campaign was to create a buzz focused on a sense of adventure and pushing back the boundaries of physical challenge. Central to the campaign was a video that went onto YouTube in May 2010. The video was not initially linked with Hi-Tec; it purported to have been made by three men who had discovered that they could run on water, thanks to the water-repellent nature of their running shoes. The new sport of 'liquid mountaineering' was a sensation, and the video resulted in 2 million hits within two weeks as viewers scrutinised it to decide whether what they were seeing was real or fake. They e-mailed, Facebooked and tweeted their friends, and wrote blogs about the video. The whole debate also sparked off a lot of media coverage, until Hi-Tec admitted to being the brand behind the hoax in June, by which time the number of hits had risen to 4.5 million.

By November 2010, the video had attracted 7.5 million hits, had featured in a number of national newspapers, and had generated positive feedback from the trade. Hi-Tec estimated that the viral marketing campaign gave a return 10 times the original investment, and had helped to reposition the brand with prospective consumers. The key characteristics that Hi-Tec wanted to reinforce about the brand were 'proud', 'honest', 'fun' and 'hungry', all of which the company felt were successfully enhanced through the use of viral techniques. Almost a year later, the campaign was still running in the form of a game on Hi-Tec's website (see www.hi-tec.com/infinity-run) with a pair of Hi-Tec V-Lite Infinity shoes being given as a prize to the highest scorer every month (Allen-Mills, 2010; *Campaign*, 2010; *The Times 100*, 2011).

Hi-Tec's viral techniques have successfully raised awareness of the water-repellent running shoes
*Source*: Hi-Tec Sports, www.hi-tec.com

There are, however, risks in using this approach. If the message is too promotional, smacks of unsolicited mail and is being spammed, the marketer might risk losing a customer or the customer might risk losing a friend. This is prompting marketers to seek to add more value to their viral campaigns on the premise that it is becoming harder to get customers to listen, let alone act. The campaigns have to have sufficient appeal and relevance for recipients to be bothered to act. Handley (2010) argues that the more closely the viral campaign is connected to the brand values, the higher the pass-on rate.

There are two strands of viral marketing: the original strand aimed to get consumers to refer their friends to a website that then sought more details, but more recently, viral activity has focused more on generating interest and involvement through creativity, as we saw in the Hi-Tec 'liquid mountaineering' campaign above. Brands can also harness the consumer's own creativity. Vanclize, an online fashion brand in China, aims to allow shoppers to hack its own advertisements, use Photoshop to superimpose their own image, and then place the resulting fake advertisement on blogs (Moin, 2011). It has proved to be very successful. The more shocking, humorous or funny the viral campaign is, so the thinking goes, the more likely it is that it will catch on. The controversial iHobo launched by a youth homeless charity attracted many new supporters by showing the reality of homelessness to create controversy and make it go viral (Baker, 2011b).

# Chapter summary

- Direct marketing is a means of creating and sustaining one-to-one, personalised, good-quality relationships between organisations and customers. As well as direct ordering of goods, direct marketing can support the sales effort with information campaigns and after-sales customer care initiatives to help engender long-term loyalty. It can also pave the way towards sales by inviting potential customers to try out products or to make appointments to see sales representatives. Direct mail can be very effective in stimulating responses from tightly defined target audiences made up either of existing customers or of new ones.

- Direct response advertising uses broadcast and print media with the aim of stimulating some kind of response from the target audience. Telemarketing specifically covers the use of the telephone as a means of creating a direct link between organisation and customer. Mail order, e-communication and teleshopping similarly create selling opportunities and the means of building direct relationships.

- Organisations reap the best benefits from direct marketing when they use responses to build databases so that any one campaign or offer becomes just one of a series of relationship-building dialogues. It is important, however, to create and maintain a database that can cope with a detailed profile of each customer and their purchasing habits and history.

- Digital direct marketing uses electronic and online media to communicate with customers to build relationships and encourage a response. E-mail can be a relatively cheap way of communicating quickly with a large number of prospects or customers, but has to overcome public concerns about spam and security issues. Used in a strategic and creative way, however, it can deliver a targeted, personalised message to a customer, whether it is a straightforward reminder, information about matters of interest to the customer, or an invitation to click through to a website to take advantage of special offers.

- Mobile marketing includes the use of mobile phones and smartphones for two-way communication and transactions. Text messaging can be used in the same way as e-mail and faces the same issues of privacy and security concerns, and the risk of being perceived as intrusive 'junk'. The introduction of 4G and the development and adoption of smartphones, however, give the consumer the means to interact with an organisation whenever and wherever they want to, and to do anything by phone from accessing information from websites, or downloading video and apps, to completing transactions. Using QR codes, for instance, the smartphone can act as a direct gateway to much more detailed information and customer-service help from product packaging, advertising and direct mail materials of all kinds, or at the point of sale, as well as having the potential to play a role in service operations by turning the phone into an electronic ticket.

● F-marketing and s-marketing make use of social networking sites such as Facebook. F-marketing is an emerging trend, and involves making a brand's or company's Facebook page transactional so that it is even easier for the customer to act on friends' recommendations, third-party reviews and other stimuli by making a purchase. S-marketing utilises social media to build brand image and engage in two-way dialogue with customers and other interested parties. The real value and potential of f- and s-marketing are still being assessed, however, and some would question the extent to which they really add value over and above other more established marketing communications tools and techniques. Viral marketing is 'electronic word of mouth'. A piece of communication is sent out to certain recipients by any electronic means. This message intrigues or entertains the recipient so much that they pass it on to their own contacts.

# Questions for review and discussion

**11.1** Explain the role that direct marketing can play in both creating and retaining customers.

**11.2** Collect three pieces of direct mail and for each one assess:

(a) what you think it is trying to achieve;

(b) how that message has been communicated;

(c) what involvement devices have been used to encourage the recipient to read the mailshot; and

(d) how easy it is for the recipient to respond in the required way.

**11.3** Compile a checklist of criteria against which a fashion e-tail website might be assessed. Visit three websites e-tailing clothing to a similar target audience. Compare and contrast those sites in terms of their performance on those criteria. How could each of them improve its offering?

**11.4** Draw up a table listing the advantages and disadvantages of e-mail marketing compared with more traditional approaches to direct marketing. In what kind of situations do you think e-mail marketing might work best?

**11.5** Discuss Ritson's (2010) view that social media represent a 'new and relatively insignificant communications tool that has limited potential for a very small proportion of brands'.

**11.6** What is viral marketing and why is it so useful to the marketer?

# IF THE SHOE FITS . . .

ECCO is a Danish company that has been manufacturing and retailing well-designed, good-quality shoes since the 1960s. The brand is sold all over the world, mainly through ECCO's own outlets or franchises. ECCO Oxford, one of five franchisees in the UK, has been established in Oxford city centre for 22 years, and for the last 11 years, has also been selling ECCO shoes through a website (www.ecco-shoes.co.uk). ECCO Oxford has long recognised the value of customer data, whether those customers use the retail outlet or the website (or both), and has used the basic data to invite customers to in-store promotional events, but the company now feels that the philosophy has shifted towards customers expecting to take control of their own purchasing – they want to buy when they choose to and when they are ready, rather than just when they are invited to by a retailer. Thus the idea behind the Oxford store's integrated direct and digital-marketing strategy is to build an engaged community around the brand and to reassure customers that 'we are here when you need us'.

About 55 per cent of the company's business comes through the store and about 45 per cent through mail order/online. ECCO Oxford is happy to offer a multichannel service, with classic mail order, telephone, and online retailing in addition to the shop itself so that customers can use whatever channel or combination of channels suits them at the time they want to engage with the company. It is, however, the non-store media that appear to offer the best growth potential, if only because of their ability to increase the geographic reach of the store. Smartphones too are starting to play an important role. About 10 per cent of visitors to the website are currently arriving via smartphones, and the company is experimenting with QR codes as a means of making it even easier for prospective customers to access information.

The database is an important tool in developing the business. It contains details of about 39,000 customers, 24,000 of whom are very active in responding to direct marketing approaches, whether that means clicking through to the website from an e-mail or placing an order as a result of that e-mail or a direct mailing. Because of the nature of the product,

there can be quite long gaps between purchases, so patience is called for. Some fmcg companies might well delete someone from their database if there's been no response for a couple of years or bombard someone who has been quiet for six months with an intense flurry of non-specific communications. ECCO Oxford prefers a more focused but subtle approach – remind customers of the brand occasionally and they'll respond when they're ready. The company sends some generic e-mails to all customers, for example announcing an end of season sale, but generally prefers a targeted approach, sending e-mails to selected subsets of customers, based on their buying history or expressed interests. It's about sending the right thing to the right people at the right time.

If the online business is to grow, then acquisition of new customers and the cultivation of relationships with them is critical. To understand better the type of customer that is best suited to ECCO Oxford, a sample of data relating to typical customers was submitted to Reactivmedia for analysis by its 'Citizen' geodemographic profiling system. Citizen divides the UK population into six main segments (such as 'Baby Boomers' – high earners, big spenders, or 'Winding Down' – over 60, retired and traditional) each of which is then further divided into a number of subsegments according to its lifestyle and demographic characteristics. This exercise showed that almost half of ECCO Oxford's current customers tended to be clustered in the following subsegments:

- Baby Boomers: Big Cars (13.5 per cent of ECCO's sample)
- Baby Boomers: Super Suburbs (9.7 per cent)
- Winding Down: Gardening Grandparents (8.3 per cent)
- Generation X: Older Suburbs (6.2 per cent)
- Winding Down: Silver Sozzlers (5.6 per cent).

The analysis also showed where in the UK concentrations of those subsegments are located, allowing ECCO Oxford to focus its direct marketing activities into new geographic areas that are likely to deliver responsive prospects. One such region is being targeted through a matched mailing list that has been bought in. The company recognises that response might not be immediate and is looking to generate six or seven touchpoints between the company and those prospects over a period of six to nine months.

Another useful way of acquiring new prospective customers is search engine optimisation. In a Google search for ECCO shoes, the Oxford store comes up as the first or second result. The fact that the store's web address has a .co.uk domain name is seen as important for attracting customers. The company also uses AdWords (which produces the 'sponsored links' results to a search) which is more precisely targeted, so that if the customer enters 'ECCO sale' into a search, for example, the results will click them through to the sale page of the store's website rather than the general homepage. ECCO Oxford has also built a presence on social media, which generates a lot of interaction, and not just about shoes! The company's view is that it is very easy to automate everything, but then it becomes de-personalised and faceless. In the social media sphere, it's about a real person responding and interacting in real time with real customers and their concerns, giving the business a human face again. As well as Twitter and Facebook, the company has also posted material on YouTube: 'ECCO Shoes FAQs 1–10'.

The ECCO brand attracts a customer base that is very brand loyal – they like and want ECCO shoes, and certainly in terms of the online and mail order business, the Oxford franchise is in competition with other online suppliers, and thus it's important to be distinctive, to add value with high quality customer service and a more personal touch. One effect of the internet on consumer behaviour generally, in ECCO Oxford's view, is that customers don't have to 'do without' anything, however unusual their needs might be. If you want it, you can get it, albeit sometimes at a price. The challenge for retailers is to communicate that they have got it and can add value through service.

*Sources*: With grateful thanks to Hilary Fletcher: Director ECCO Oxford and Vicky Sparks: Communications Manager, ECCO Oxford.

## Questions

1 Outline the kind of information that would be useful to a shoe retailer such as ECCO Oxford in building a database for direct marketing.

2 How might ECCO Oxford's direct-marketing strategy and content differ between customers who visit the retail outlet and those who only buy by mail order?

3 ECCO Oxford bought a list of people in one region whose demographic profile matches that of its core customer groups. What are the advantages and disadvantages of buying lists? What other methods could be used to develop lists of prospective customers?

4 The company is experimenting with QR codes. In what ways could ECCO Oxford use QR codes and what are the advantages of using them?

## References for chapter 11

Abbott, R. (2008) 'Marketing League Table: Contact Centres – Contact Centre Leagues', *Marketing*, 7 May.

*Afaqs!* (2011) 'Rise of the Mobile Web', *Afaqs!*, 3 May.

Allen-Mills, T. (2010) 'It's All in the Shoes, Claim Water-walkers', *Sunday Times*, 16 May.

Ashton, J. (2011) 'Mobile Operators Use 4G Wave to Get up to Speed', *Sunday Times*, 16 January.

Baker, R. (2011a) 'Ann Summers Sexes Up Brand Strategy', *Marketing Week*, 20 May.

Baker, R. (2011b) 'Controversy Gets Consumers Talking About Brands', *Marketing Week*, 30 June.

Barrett, C. (2011) 'Budget Parties Hark Back to Bygone Era', *Financial Times*, 3 September.

Benjamin, K. (2011) 'Direct Marketing and Sales Promotion Leagues: Direct Power', *Marketing*, 30 March.

Birchall, J. (2010) 'Dialling in to See if the Price is Right', *Financial Times*, 3 June.

Bliss, J. (2010) *Key Reasons to Use Direct Mail*, document published by Mail Media Centre, October, accessed via www.linkmailing.co.uk/pictures/content26/key_reasons_rw_3.pdf.

Blyth, A. (2011) 'Quick Off the Mark', *Travel Trade Gazette*, 8 September.

Bosomworth, D. (2011) 'The Top Seven Applications of QR Codes for Marketing', *Mycustomer.com*, 8 September, accessed via www.mycustomer.com/topic/marketing/top-seven-applications-qr-codes-marketing/130269.

*Business Wire* (2010) 'Thomas Cook UK & Ireland Chooses e-Dialog as New Strategic Online and E-Mail Marketing Service Provider', *Business Wire*, 15 September.

*Campaign* (2010) 'Hi-Tec Behind Viral Hoax', *Campaign*, 4 June.

Carter, K. (2011) 'Cashing in on New Mums', *The Guardian*, 22 August.

Costa, M. (2011a) 'Banks Seek Admission to Social Media's Inner Circle', *Marketing Week*, 14 April.

Costa, M. (2011b) 'Sun, Sea, Sand and the Growing Status of Social Media', *Marketing Week*, 30 June.

Croft, M. (2008) 'Channelling DM Power', *Marketing Week*, 4 July.

Cuddeford-Jones, M. (2011) 'Control of All Event Traffic at Your Fingertips', *Marketing Week*, 15 September.

Deloitte Consumer Business Group (2011) 'Serving the Connected Consumer: the Multichannel Retail Opportunity', *Mondaq Business Briefing*, 14 April.

EIU (2010) 'The Changing Landscape of Online Fraud: Long Life Spam', *Economist Intelligence Unit Executive Briefing*, 26 November.

Eleftheriou-Smith, L. (2011) 'Travel's Online Challenge', *Marketing*, 20 July.

Fisher, L. (2011) 'Fools' Gold?', *Marketing Week*, 31 March.

Glotz, J. (2011) 'Calon Wen Turns to QR Codes to Tell its "Story"', *The Grocer*, 13 August.

Goodman, L. (2011) 'DM Campaign of the Week: Ann Summers', *DM Weekly*, 13 June.

Handley, L. (2010) 'Share Index is Measure of a Viral's Success', *Marketing Week*, 6 May.

Hosea, M. (2009) 'Worth its Weight in Gold', *Marketing Week*, 17 September.

Hosea, M. (2010) 'Brands Keep Their Finger on Impulsive Interaction', *Marketing Week*, 15 July.

Hosea, M. (2011) 'More Power to Your Inbox', *Marketing Week*, 24 March.

*Just-food* (2010) 'Tesco Develops Mobile Shopping App', *Just-food*, 5 August.

*Just-style* (2010) 'M&S Revamps Mobile Shopping Facility', *Just-style*, 12 May.

Kennedy, D. and Ralph, A. (2010) 'A Mail Order Bride?', *The Times*, 26 November.

King, M. (2011) 'All that Glitters is Far From Gold When You Look to Sell Online', *The Observer*, 16 January.

Kirby, M. (2010) 'Social Status', *Airline Business*, 26 March.

Kumar, N. (2011) 'Gold-buying Companies Told to Polish up their Act', *The Independent*, 15 February.

Langdon, B. (2008) 'Respecting Permission and Privacy – A Brave New World', *Financial Times*, 7 November.

Laurance, J. (2011) 'How Maternity Wards Cash in on Mothers', *The Independent*, 22 August.

Levy, K. (2010) 'Arena Beats Carat to Thomas Cook', *Campaign*, 26 November.

Lewis, M. (1999) 'Counting On It', *Database Marketing*, May, pp. 34–7.

*M2 Presswire* (2010a) 'Mobile Advertising and Marketing 3rd Edition Says Mobiles Will Account for 11.7 Percent of Digital Ad Spend in 2014', *M2 Presswire*, 19 February.

*M2 Presswire* (2010b) 'Greenlight Appointed to Manage Search Marketing for Thomas Cook UK & Ireland's Travel Portfolio', *M2 Presswire*, 30 March.

*M2 Presswire* (2010c) 'RichRelevance: Research Shows UK Shoppers Lack Brand Loyalty to Retailers', *M2 Presswire*, 10 November.

*M2 Presswire* (2010d) 'Social Media Marketing 2010 – Market Assessment', *M2 Presswire*, 7 December.

Marian, P. (2011) 'Retail Bytes: Food Retailers Going Mobile', *Just-Food*, 4 February.

*Marketwire* (2010) 'UK Retailers Failing to Make the Most of Social Media Marketing', *Marketwire*, 11 February.

*Marketing Week* (2010) 'When Engaging the Masses is Key', *Marketing Week*, 26 August.

*Marketing Week* (2011) 'Cut-price New Media is Making Us Lazy', *Marketing Week*, 14 April.

McAlevey, T. (2001) 'The Principles of Effective Direct Response', *Direct Marketing*, April, pp. 44–7.

Mintel (2009) 'Home Shopping', Mintel Retail Intelligence, March, accessed via http://academic.mintel.com/ sinatra/oxygen_academic/search_results/show&/ display/id=395647/display/id=395647/display/ id=447889?select_section=395647.

Mintel (2010) 'Travel Agents', *Mintel Leisure Intelligence*, December, accessed via http://academic.mintel.com/ sinatra/oxygen_academic/search_results/show&/display/ id=480970.

Mintel (2011) 'Holidays on the Internet', *Mintel Leisure Intelligence*, July, accessed via http://academic.mintel.com/ sinatra/oxygen_academic/search_results/show&/display/ id=545165.

Moin, D. (2011) 'The Speed of Change', *WWD*, 15 June.

Murphy, D. (2011a) 'This Time it's Personal', *Marketing*, 13 April.

Murphy, D. (2011b) 'Your Brand in Their Hands', *Marketing*, 22 June.

*New Media Age* (2010a) 'M&S Goes Down a Separate Path', *New Media Age*, 3 June.

*New Media Age* (2010b) 'Retailers Ready Transactional Mobile Sites but Admit They Need Training', *New Media Age*, 19 August.

*New Media Age* (2011a) 'Mates' Rates', *New Media Age*, 10 February.

*New Media Age* (2011b) 'BA Sends Offers Via SMS to Better Reach its Frequent Flyers', *New Media Age*, 7 April.

Node, W. (2011) 'Church-based Home Shopping Retailer 24studio.co.uk Has Launched its New Mobile', *Manchester Evening News*, 18 February.

Nutley, M. (2010) 'Social Media is Changing Everything', *Marketing Week*, 25 November.

Nutley, M. (2011) 'Sofa, So Good, For Mobile Marketing', *Marketing Week*, 14 April.

O'Reilly, L. (2011) 'Ann Summers Looks to Web to Drive In-store Promos', *Marketing Week*, 15 June.

Portet, S. (2011) *Facebook, Twitter: Social Networks Now UK's Top Online Destination*, 17 March, accessed via www.silicon. com/management/sales-and-marketing/2011/03/17/ facebook-twitter-social-networks-now-uks-top-online- destination-39747160/.

PPT Solutions (no date) *PPT Overcome Scottishpower Pre- Payments Call Challenge*, case study published by PPT Solutions, accessed via www.pptsolutions.co.uk/docs/ case-study-scottish-power.pdf.

*PR Newswire Europe* (2011) 'Report Shows Social Media Drives Just Three Percent of Retail Website Visits', *PR Newswire Europe*, 3 February.

*Precision Marketing* (2004) 'Is the Sex Industry Too Bashful to Go Direct?', *Precision Marketing*, 22 October, p. 11.

Publicis Dialog (2011) *Renault UK 'Renault Driving School' Direct Mail Campaign*, case study published by the Royal Mail Media Mail Centre, 8 March, accessed via www.mmc.co.uk/Knowledge-Centre/Case-Studies/ Renault-UK-Renault-Driving-School-direct-mail-campaign/.

Ritson, M. (2010) 'Social Media is for People, Not Brands', *Marketing Week*, 2 September.

Serdarevic, M. and Plimmer, G. (2011), 'OFT Action Reins in Online Buyers of Gold', *Financial Times*, 15 February.

Schlesinger, F. (2010) 'How Kate's Parents Are Making the Most of Their Party Pieces', *Daily Mail*, 27 November.

Schofield, A. (1994) 'Alternative Reply Vehicles in Direct Response Advertising', *Journal of Advertising Research*, 34(5), pp. 28–34.

Shearman, S. (2010) 'Thomas Cook Group to Boost Digital Strategy', *Marketing*, 10 November.

Shearman, S. (2011a) 'Brands Ramp Up Spend on Mobile Ad Platforms', *Marketing*, 23 March.

Shearman, S. (2011b) 'Asda Eyes M-commerce in Web Revamp', *Marketing*, 27 July.

Shields, R. (2010) 'Are You Making the Most From Mobile?', *Marketing Week*, 25 November.

Shields, R. (2011) 'Retailers Not Matching User Demand for Mobile Selling', *New Media Age*, 2 June.

Shields, R. and Joseph, S. (2011), 'FMCGs Regain Their Taste for Mobile Marketing', *New Media Age*, 30 March.

Smith, N. (2010) 'Digital Strategy: Revealed: the Changing Face of Email', *Marketing Week*, 25 November.

Sweney, M. (2010) 'Virgin Media's Anti-Sky Mailshot Banned', *The Guardian*, 16 September.

*The Times 100* (2011) *Using Promotion to Position a Brand*, case study from *The Times 100*, published on www.thetimes100.co.uk/case-study--using-promotion-to-position-a-brand--161-415-5.php.

Walmsley, A. (2011) 'Stores Must Buy into Mobile', *Marketing*, 10 August.

White, G. (2009) 'Postal Gold-buying Service Opens', *Sunday Telegraph*, 19 July.

# CHAPTER 12

## Promotion: personal selling, PR and sponsorship

### LEARNING OBJECTIVES

This chapter will help you to:

- appreciate the role that personal selling plays in the overall marketing effort of the organisation and define the tasks undertaken by sales representatives;

- analyse the stages involved in the personal selling process and appreciate the responsibilities involved in sales management;

- appreciate the contribution that trade shows and exhibitions can make to achieving B2B marketing objectives;

- define PR and understand its role in supporting the organisation's activities, and outline the techniques of PR and their appropriateness for different kinds of public;

- understand the role of sponsorship in the marketing communications mix and the benefits and problems of different types of sponsorship; and

- understand the nature of cause-related marketing and the benefits it offers to all parties involved.

## INTRODUCTION

**MANY ORGANISATIONS EMPLOY SALES** forces to help in the marketing communications and customer-relationship management processes. Whether that sales force takes a primary role in creating customers and then servicing their needs, or whether it simply receives orders at the point of sale, will vary according to the type of product, the type of customer and the type of organisation. As Chapter 9 suggested, personal selling will probably play a much bigger role in the promotional mix of a high-priced, infrequently purchased industrial good, for example, than in that of a routinely purchased consumer product. Nevertheless, personal selling is important in some consumer markets. Car manufacturers spend many millions on advertising, but the purchase decision is made and the final deal negotiated at the showroom. The sales assistants thus play a very important role, particularly in guiding, persuading and converting the wavering customer without being too pushy.

Regardless of whether the sales force is selling capital machinery into manufacturing businesses, fmcg products into the retail trade or financial services to individual consumers, the principles behind personal selling remain largely the same. This chapter will address those principles and show how they apply in different types of selling situation.

Trade shows and exhibitions are also a good means of generating sales leads, and thus these too are briefly considered, as a useful part of the B2B communications mix in particular. We examine their role and value to organisations, through their ability not only to generate qualified sales leads but also to reinforce the organisation's presence and image in the marketplace as a basis for future direct marketing campaigns.

A slightly different means of reinforcing presence and image in a marketplace, public relations (PR) is the area of marketing communications that specifically deals with the quality and nature of the relationship between an organisation and its publics, such as its financial backers, its employees and trades unions, its suppliers, the legal and regulatory bodies to which it is accountable, interested pressure groups, the media, and many other groups or 'publics' which have the ability to affect the way in which the organisation does business. Its prime concern is to generate a sound, effective and understandable flow of communication between the organisation and these groups so that shared understanding is possible. While publicity or press relations can make a significant contribution, PR utilises a much wider range of activities, which this chapter will cover.

The final sections of this chapter, which are also linked to the theme of reinforcing image and presence in a marketplace, consider sponsorship and cause-related marketing (CRM). Sponsorship of sport, television programmes and the arts will be discussed in terms of the benefits gained by both parties. CRM is loosely related to sponsorship, in that part of its remit is looking at how corporate donors or sponsors can help charities or other non-profit organisations. It also covers PR and sales promotion activities that link companies with non-profit organisations and examines the benefits gained by all those involved.

*eg*

Service delays are a prime source of frustration to weary travellers. Whether they are caused by strikes, weather, theft or even volcanic ash, how a company handles the situation can have a huge impact on its reputation.

The problems due to volcanic ash that closed airports and grounded flights across Europe in 2010 were either a PR disaster or an opportunity. The government said that volcanic-ash disruption was something we had to learn to live with, but travellers didn't want to hear that. Michael O'Leary of Ryanair, however, challenged the prevailing wisdom and hit out hard at the Met Office for blindly following bureaucratic procedure in response to the crisis. Ryanair even flew a test plane (without passengers) through the affected air space to show that it was indeed safe. It comes down to whether the public sympathises more with the aviation industry's claims that the regulations are too tight and were unnecessarily imposed on a blanket basis or with the government and its public safety agenda. It's about risk tolerance and management and, to some extent, about the balance between profit and risk. In the months following the ash crisis, however, the debate about what should have happened was overshadowed to some extent by emerging stories of how poorly passengers had been communicated with at the time, how shabbily some had been treated (and, of course, this was all far more interesting than the many examples of customer-service staff going above and beyond the call of duty to try to look after people), and then the frustration and difficulties faced by affected travellers in successfully claiming compensation and reimbursement from travel insurance companies and airlines.

Train operators also suffer reputational damage from circumstances that are not of their own making. Commuters are wearily familiar with the effects of leaves on the line, or 'the wrong kind of snow', but now there's a new kid on the block. The theft of copper cables causes delays due to faulty or unsafe signalling and other knock-on effects. The train-operating companies are entitled to compensation for those delays from Network Rail, the company responsible for track and infrastructure. One incident, in Newark in 2011, cost £620,758 in compensation after cable theft caused 34 cancellations and over 8,000 minutes of delays. Over 2010, incidents of theft increased by 67 per cent as metal prices rose sharply. It's not organised crime but often drug or alcohol abusers looking to make a quick buck. The train operators can't do much about it, but they do tend to bear the brunt of the passengers' displeasure, and overall, it does nothing positive for the reputation of travelling by rail (Bawden, 2011; Wilson, 2011).

## Personal selling: definition, role and tasks

According to Fill (2002, p. 16), personal selling can be defined as:

> An interpersonal communication tool which involves face to face activities undertaken by individuals, often representing an organisation, in order to inform, persuade or remind an individual or group to take appropriate action, as required by the sponsor's representative.

As a basic definition, this does capture the essence of personal selling. *Interpersonal communication* implies a live, two-way, interactive dialogue between buyer and seller (which none of the other promotional mix elements can achieve); *an individual or group* implies a small, select audience (again, more targeted than with the other elements); *to inform, persuade or remind . . . to take appropriate action* implies a planned activity with a specific purpose.

Note that the definition does not imply that personal selling is only about making sales. It may well ultimately be about making a sale, but that is not its only function. It can contribute considerably to the organisation both before and, indeed, after a sale has been made. As a means of making sales, personal selling is about finding, informing, persuading and at times servicing customers through the personal, two-way communication that is its strength. It means helping customers to articulate their needs, tailoring persuasive selling messages to answer those needs, and then handling customers' responses or concerns in order to arrive at a mutually valued exchange. As a background to that, personal selling is also a crucial element in ensuring customers' post-purchase satisfaction, and in building profitable long-term buyer–seller relationships built on trust and understanding (Miller and Heinman, 1991).

*eg*

Avon, the cosmetics company, has over 6 million sales representatives in 100 countries worldwide. It is the largest direct-sales operation in the world. Over 170,000 representatives are located in the UK, and all of them are self-employed, spending as much time selling Avon products as they choose. For some, it's just a casual, social activity, for others it's a serious income-earner. Either way, the representatives play a key role in providing advice, demonstrating products, allowing sampling, closing sales and relationship building on their territories. For those who are more serious about building an entrepreneurial business for themselves, Avon offers the opportunity to become a Sales Leader, so that they can take responsibility for recruiting, managing and motivating their own team of sales representatives. The Sales Leader then earns commission on their team's sales (www.avon.uk.com).

Avon has the largest direct selling operation in the world

*Source*: Alamy Images/© Jeff Morgan 14

Chapter 9 has already offered some insights into where personal selling fits best into the promotional mix. We discussed how personal selling is more appropriate in B2B than consumer markets at p. 342, while p. 349 *et seq.* looked at its advantages in promoting and selling high-cost, complex products. The discussion at p. 347 also notes that personal selling operates most effectively when customers are on the verge of making a final decision and committing themselves, but still need that last little bit of tailored persuasion.

## Advantages of personal selling

### Impact

If you do not like the look of a TV advertisement, you can turn it off, or ignore it. If a glance at a print advertisement fails to capture your further attention, you can turn the page. If an envelope on the doormat looks like a mailshot, you can put it in the bin unopened. If a sales representative appears on your doorstep or in your office, it is a little more difficult to switch off. A person has to be dealt with in some way, and since most of us subscribe to the common rules of politeness, we will at least listen to what the person wants before shepherding them out of the door. The sales representative, therefore, has a much greater chance of engaging your initial attention than an advertisement does.

It is also true, of course, that an advertisement has no means of knowing or caring that you have ignored it. Sales representatives, on the other hand, have the ability to respond to the situations in which they find themselves, and can take steps to prevent themselves from being shut off completely. This could be, for instance, by pressing for another appointment at a more convenient time, or by at least leaving sales literature for the potential customer to read and think about at their leisure. Overall, you are far more likely to remember a person you have met or spoken to (and to respond to what they said) than you are to remember an advertisement. In that respect, personal selling is very powerful indeed, particularly if it capitalises on the elements of precision and cultivation (see below) as well.

## Precision

Precision represents one of the great advantages of personal selling over any of the other promotional mix elements, and explains why it is so effective at the customer's point of decision-making. There are two facets of precision that should be acknowledged: targeting precision and message precision.

*Targeting precision* arises from the fact that personal selling is not a mass medium. Advertising can be targeted within broad parameters, but even so, there will still be many wasted contacts (people who are not even in the target market; people who are not currently interested in the product; people who have recently purchased already; people who cannot currently afford to purchase, etc.). Advertising hits those contacts anyway with its full message, and each of those wasted contacts costs money. Personal selling can weed out the inappropriate contacts early on, and concentrate its efforts on those who offer a real prospect of making a sale.

*Message precision* arises from the interactive two-way dialogue that personal selling encourages. An advertisement cannot tell what impact it is having on you. It cannot discern whether you are paying attention to it, whether you understand it or whether you think it is relevant to you. Furthermore, once the advertisement has been presented to you, that is it. It is a fixed, inflexible message, and if you did not understand it, or if you felt that it did not tell you what you wanted to know, then you have no opportunity to do anything about it other than wait for another advertisement to come along that might clarify these things. Because personal selling involves live interaction, however, these problems should not occur. The sales representative can tell, for example, that your attention is wandering, and therefore can change track, exploring other avenues until something seems to capture you again. The representative can also make sure that you understand what you are being told and go over it again from a different angle if you are having difficulty with the first approach. Similarly, the representative can see if something has particularly caught your imagination and tailor the message to emphasise that feature or benefit. Thus, by listening and watching, the sales representative should be able to create a unique approach that exactly matches the mood and the needs of each prospective customer. This too is a very potent capability.

## Cultivation

As Chapter 3 implied, the creation of long-term, mutually beneficial buyer–seller relationships is now recognised as extremely important to the health and profitability of organisations in many industries. The sales force has a crucial role to play in both creating and maintaining such relationships. Sales representatives are often the public face of an organisation, and their ability to carry the organisation's message professionally and confidently can affect judgement of that organisation and what it stands for. When Avon, the cosmetics company, decided to target the beauty business for teenagers and younger women, it realised that to build and maintain customer relationships it had to reconsider whether the direct sales force employed was suitable for the different customer group. The new sub-brand 'Mark' was launched in the USA in 2008, but instead of using an army of traditional 'Avon ladies', the company recruited 18–24-year-olds who are better placed to demonstrate and promote the products to that audience (Sweeney, 2010).

## Cost

All the advantages and benefits discussed above come at a very high cost, as personal selling is extremely labour intensive. In addition, costs of travel (and time spent travelling), accommodation and other expenses have to be accounted for. Generally, the salary paid is only around

50 per cent of the total cost of keeping a sales representative mobile and connected. The actual time spent selling to a customer can vary considerably. Alexander Proudfoot, an international consultancy group, found in an international study that on average, just 11 per cent of a sales rep's time is spent in active selling. A further 9 per cent is spent in prospecting, and 18 per cent in problem solving. The rest of the rep's time is spent in admin (31 per cent), travelling (15 per cent) and 'non-value-added time' (16 per cent) (Alexander Proudfoot, 2011). Some caution has to be exercised when interpreting these figures, however, as ultimately it is sales effectiveness that counts and relationship building and keeping in touch with customers both support the ongoing sales activity.

## Tasks of personal selling

There is a tendency to think of the sales representative in a one-off selling situation. What the discussion in the previous sections has shown is that, in reality, the representative is likely to be handling a relationship with any specific customer over a long period of time. The representative will be looking to build up close personal ties because much depends on repeat sales. In some cases, the representative might even be involved in helping to negotiate and handle joint product development. All of this suggests a range of tasks beyond the straight selling situation.

Figure 12.1 summarises the range of typical tasks of the sales representative, each of which is defined below.

### Prospecting

Prospecting is finding new potential customers who have the willingness and ability to purchase. For Rentokil Tropical Plants, for example, the role of the sales representative is to contact a range of potential clients including offices, hotels, shopping centres and restaurants to design and recommend individual displays of tropical plants on a supply and maintenance basis. Prospecting is an important task, particularly for organisations entering a new market segment or for those offering a new product line with no established customer base.

### Informing

Informing is giving prospective customers adequate, detailed and relevant information about products and services on offer. In B2B markets, once contact has been made with prospects, the sales representative needs to stimulate sufficient information exchange to ensure a technical and commercial match that is better than the competition.

**Figure 12.1**
Typical tasks of the sales representative

## Persuading

Persuading is helping the prospective customer to analyse the information provided, in the light of their needs, in order to come to the conclusion that the product being offered is the best solution to their problem. Sometimes, presenting the main product benefits is sufficient to convince the buyer of the wisdom of selecting that supplier. On other occasions, especially with purchases that are technically or commercially more complex, the persuasion might have to be very subtle and varied, according to the concerns of the different members of the buying team.

## Installing and demonstrating

Particularly with technical B2B purchases, the buyer may need considerable support and help to get the equipment installed and to train staff in its use. The sales representative may join a wider team of support personnel to ensure that all this takes place according to whatever was agreed and to the customer's satisfaction. The representative's continued presence acts as a link between pre- and post-purchase events, and implies that the representative has not stopped caring about the customer just because the sale has been made.

## Coordinating within their own organisation

The role of the sales representative is not just about forward communication with the buyer. It is also concerned with 'representing' the customer's interests within the selling organisation. Whether concerned with financial, technical or logistical issues, the sales representative must coordinate and sometimes organise internal activities on a project basis to ensure that the customer's needs are met. At Duracell, the UK market leader in batteries, a national account manager is responsible for all aspects of the relationship with the large grocery chains. This includes external roles of display, distribution and promotional planning as well as internal coordination of logistics and product category management.

## Maintaining relationships

Once an initial sale has been made, it might be the start of an ongoing relationship. In many cases, a single sale is just one of a stream of transactions and thus cannot be considered in isolation from the total relationship. An important role for the sales representative is to manage the relationship rather than just the specifics of a particular sale. This means that in many organisations, more substantial and critical relationships have a 'relationship manager' to handle the various facets of the buyer–seller evolution (Turnbull and Cunningham, 1981). In some cases, the sales representative might have only one relationship to manage, but in others, the representative might have to manage a network based in a particular sector.

The prime responsibility of an account manager at Colgate-Palmolive is to maintain and develop business relationships with major multiple retailer accounts. These relationships in some cases go back over many years. In order to achieve this, the emphasis is on cooperation and customer development through working together in such areas as category management, logistics and merchandising. There is a need to ensure a close fit between retail requirements and Colgate-Palmolive's brand strategies. This means that the account manager must be able to analyse brand and category information in order to develop plans that will help sales of Colgate's personal and household care products. Any account manager who sought short-term sales gains at the expense of customer trust and goodwill would not benefit Colgate-Palmolive's long-term plans for the account.

## Information and feedback gathering

The gathering of information and the provision of feedback emphasises the need for representatives to keep their eyes and ears open, and to indulge in two-way communication with the customers they deal with. 'Grapevine' gossip about what is happening in the industry might, for example, give valuable early warning about big planned purchases in the future, or about potential customers who are dissatisfied with their current supplier. Both of these situations would offer opportunities to the organisation that heard about them early enough to make strategic plans about how to capitalise on them. In terms of relationships with existing customers, sales representatives are more likely than anyone to hear about the things that the customer is unhappy about. This feedback role is even more important when developing business in export markets, where the base of accumulated knowledge might not be very strong. Personal contacts can help to add to that knowledge over time (Johanson and Vahlne, 1977).

## Monitoring competitor action

The representative works out in the field, meeting customers and, in all probability, competitors. As well as picking up snippets about what competitors are planning and who they are doing business with, the representative can provide valuable information about how his or her organisation's products compare with those of the competition in the eyes of the purchasers. During the course of sales presentations, prospective customers can be subtly probed to find out what they think are the relative strengths and weaknesses of competing products, what they consider to be the important features and benefits in that kind of product, and how the available offerings score relative to each other (Lambert *et al.*, 1990).

# The personal selling process

At the heart of the sales process is the sales representative's ability to build a relationship with the buyer that is sufficiently strong to achieve a deal that benefits both parties. In many situations the main decision relates to supplier choice rather than whether or not to buy. The sales representative's role is to highlight the attractions of the specification, support, service and commercial package on offer. Differences between products, markets, organisational philosophies and even individuals will all have a bearing on the style and effectiveness of the selling activity.

Although it has just been suggested that personal selling does not lend itself to a prescribed formula, it is possible to define a number of broad stages through which most selling episodes will pass (Russell *et al.*, 1977). Depending on the product, the market, the organisations and individuals involved, the length of time spent in any one of the stages will vary, as will the way in which each stage is implemented (Pedersen *et al.*, 1986). Nevertheless, the generalised analysis offered here provides a useful basis for beginning to understand what contributes to successful personal selling.

Figure 12.2 shows the flow of stages through a personal selling process.

# Prospecting

Before sales representatives can get down to the real job of selling something, they need to have someone to sell to. In some organisations, perhaps those selling an industrial product with a specific application to a relatively small number of easily defined B2B customers, this will be a highly structured activity, involving sales representatives and support staff, and will lead to the representative going out on a call knowing that the prospect is potentially fruitful. In contrast, double-glazing companies often employ canvassers to walk the streets knocking on doors to see if householders are likely prospects. This is not a particularly efficient use of the representatives'

**Figure 12.2**
The personal
selling process

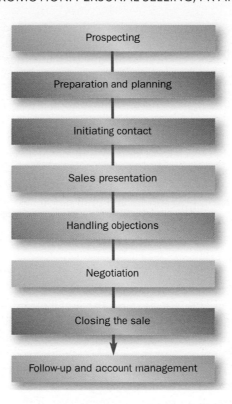

time, as most people will say that they are not interested, but in promoting an infrequently purchased, high-priced product, yet in a mass market, it is difficult to see what else in the way of
prospecting they can do.

In a B2B rather than a consumer market, the sales representative needs a prospect bank, a
pool of potential customers to be drawn on as appropriate. This bank could include potential
customers who have made online enquiries or responded to advertising, but not been followed
up already. Second, there are those who have already been approached in an exploratory way,
for example through telemarketing, and look promising enough to deserve further encouragement. Third, and most problematic, are the lists of names. These lists might be purchased from
a list broker or be compiled from a trade directory, from internet sources, or a list of organisations attending a particular trade exhibition. Sales representatives may have to develop
their own prospect banks, either from word of mouth, from contacts outside the organisation,
or from the telemarketing support staff discussed above. They can also compile lists from
directories, internet searches or from scanning the media for relevant company news that
might open up an opportunity. As with the telemarketers above, this might lead to a session
of preliminary cold calling (by phone, e-mail or in person) to establish whether this person or
organisation really is a viable prospect.

## Preparation and planning

Identifying a qualified prospect is only the beginning of the process. Before the real selling
begins, it is very important to obtain further information on the prospect in order to prepare
the best and most relevant sales approach and to plan tactics.

In selling to a B2B customer, this may mean scanning a number of company reports, assessing the norms for that industry in relation to likely buying criteria and needs. Analysing the
prospect's company report might promise indications of the strategic direction in which it is
moving, as well as revealing its financial situation. It is also necessary to think about the kind of
purchasing structures that the representative is going to have to work through, identifying the
most likely influencers and decision-makers. In addition, it is also useful to find out as much as

possible about the application of the product and the features and benefits required. This allows the representative to construct a sales presentation that will be relevant to the buyer and thus will have more chance of engaging their attention and being persuasive.

Sales representatives in B2B markets are fortunate that sufficient information exists about their buyers to allow them to prepare so well in advance. In consumer markets, it is more likely that representatives have to think on their feet, analysing customers while they are face to face with them.

Where it is possible, therefore, doing the homework is essential, and it often needs to be very thorough, especially in situations involving large, complex projects with stiff competition. Also, if the competition is already well entrenched in doing business with a prospect, it is even more important to find out as much as possible in advance, since getting that customer to switch supplier will probably be an uphill task unless you can find the right approach with the right people.

## Initiating contact

Making the first contact with the prospect is a delicate operation. There are two ways of approaching this stage. First, the initial means of contact that is used to qualify the prospect could also be used to solicit an appointment. Failure to achieve that means that the selling process cannot begin. The second approach is to use cold calling. This means turning up on the doorstep in the hope that someone will see you, as the double-glazing sales representative does. This can be very wasteful in terms of time and travel. There is no guarantee that the representative will get access to the key people, who probably would not in any case be able to spare time without a prior appointment. Even if the representative does get access, it is unlikely that a properly tailored sales presentation will have been prepared if there has not been preliminary contact with the prospect. Cold callers are often seen as time-wasters, and do not do themselves or their organisations any favours in the eyes of the prospects.

*eg* Whether it is double glazing, paved drives, kitchens, insurance or fresh fish, the cold calling, door-to-door sales representative is often seen as an unwelcome, intrusive time-waster. Although the door can always be slammed, elderly people, in particular, often become flustered and are vulnerable to predatory or persistent callers. The reputable sellers, however, obviously do not like having their image tainted by the activities of fly-by-night builders and con artists. The Direct Selling Association, therefore, developed its Consumer Code of Practice for legitimate sellers to sign up to. Although reputable companies, such as Kleeneze and Avon subscribe to, and follow the guidelines scrupulously, such as clear identification of sales staff and highlighting the cooling-off period during which any contract can be cancelled, it is a fight not to be tainted by the activities of fly-by-night builders and assorted con artists. Some local authorities have now even set up 'no cold calling' zones in their areas (www.dsa.org.uk/about-the-dsa/consumer-codes-of-practice/).

The message is clear: there's no 'Welcome' mat here

*Source:* Christian Short/Photographers Direct, photographersdirect.com

Otherwise, it is a case of 'buyer beware' as disreputable companies tend not to subscribe to trade associations and exploit legal loopholes that bypass the Office of Fair Trading rights and leave the consumer vulnerable to over-charging and poor quality and service.

Once an approach has been made and an appointment secured, the next stage is the initial call. This helps the representative to discover whether the initial assessment of the customer's likely need is borne out in practice. In these early meetings, it is important to build up rapport, mutual respect and trust between buyer and seller before the more serious business discussion gets under way. The time spent in establishing this relationship is well spent. It helps to build a solid foundation for the later stages of discussion.

## The sales presentation

At last, the representative has enough insight and information to allow the preparation of the sales presentation itself that lies at the heart of the selling process. The ease of its preparation and its effectiveness in practice owe a great deal to the thoroughness and quality of the work done in the earlier stages. The objective of the sales presentation is to show how the product offering and the customer's needs match. The presentation must not be product-oriented, but be concerned with what the product can do for that particular customer. In other words, do not sell the features, sell the benefits.

There may be some practicalities to be handled as part of the presentation. The representative may have to demonstrate the product, for example. The product or sample used must look right, and will need to be explained, not in technical terms, necessarily, but in terms of how it offers particular benefits and solutions. A demonstration is a powerful element of a sales presentation, because it gets the prospect involved and encourages conversation and questions. It provides a focus that can dispel any lingering awkwardness between buyer and seller. Also, in getting their hands on the product itself, or a sample, the prospect is brought very close to the reality of the product and can begin to see for themselves what it can do for them.

Back in 2007, the Office of Fair Trading (OFT) investigated complaints from the public against a company that was selling mobility products, specifically, therapy beds. The complaints centred around high-pressure selling techniques, which focused on vulnerable groups, such as the elderly and disabled. An undercover reporter who attended a training course for 'bed demonstrators' was told to prey on the fears of old people, and was also told that 'If you can't sell one of these beds to a diabetic, you should be put up against the wall and f***ing shot' (as quoted by Brown, 2008). The 'bed demonstrators' (or rather 'sales reps') were told that no potential customer was too poor to buy one of these £4,000 beds, and to make a sale, regardless of how many times the customer said 'no'. Their persistence was rewarded with commission of about £1,000 per sale. With that experience in mind, it's hardly surprising that the OFT investigation specifically required the company to undertake to stop:

- giving false or misleading information about the true purpose of their visit;
- discounting the price on condition that the consumer agrees to a sale the same day;
- claiming the [. . .] bed can alleviate the symptoms of a consumer's medical condition;
- dissuading consumers from having a third party present at the sales demonstration; and
- staying longer than two and half hours in a consumer's home when providing a sales demonstration. (OFT, 2007)

While that particular company now appears to have gone out of business, it was not alone in taking a rather cynical and exploitative view of its target customer, and concerns about this market more generally have triggered a wider ranging OFT study. By mid-2011, the research was still going on, but the interim findings suggest that a lot of buyers in this market do rely on home visits as their mobility problems make it difficult to get to retail outlets. Also, the more elderly customers, in particular, don't always have internet access, so shopping online can be a problem. Initial findings also suggest that getting pricing information can be problematic: some companies do not supply quotations up front, or insist on having personal contact details before they will consider giving a quote. This lack of price transparency might indicate that some companies at least could still be anxious to get 'a foot in the door' so that they can use pressure selling tactics to get a sale at an inflated price out of vulnerable customers who cannot easily shop around (Brown, 2008; OFT, 2007; 2011).

## Handling objections

It is indeed a rare and skilful sales representative who can complete an entire sales presentation without the prospect coming out with words to the effect of 'that's all very well, but . . .'. At any stage in the selling process that involves the customer, objections can and probably will be made. These may arise for various reasons: lack of understanding, lack of interest, misinformation, a need for reassurance or genuine concern. The sales representative must be prepared to overcome objections where possible, as otherwise the sale is likely to be lost completely. If the customer is concerned enough to raise an objection, the representative must have the courtesy to answer it in some way. Homespun wisdom among seasoned sales representatives argues that the real selling does not begin until the customer raises an objection.

Organisations that do not subscribe to the formula approach to selling often do train their sales staff to handle specific objections that commonly arise in their field in a set way. If a buyer says, for example, 'I think your product is not as good as product *x*', the sales representative should explore what is meant by the use of the word 'good'. This could cover a whole range of different areas in the competitive offering. The representative's response may therefore be designed to explore in more detail the underlying problem by asking 'In what way is it not as good?' Agreeing with the objection and countering it is often called the 'yes, but' technique. Where the objection is founded in fact, all the representative can legitimately do is agree with the substance of it, then find a compensating factor to outweigh it. Thus if the prospect argues that the product being sold is more expensive than the competition's, the representative can reply with 'Yes, I agree that value for money is important. Although our product is more expensive initially, you will find that the day-to-day running costs and the annual maintenance add up to a lot less . . .'. Such a technique avoids creating excessive tension and argument, because the customer feels that their objection has been acknowledged and satisfactorily answered.

All in all, handling objections requires a very careful response from representatives. They must not see objections as a call for them to say just anything to clinch the sale, since doing so will only lead to legal or relationship problems later. The representative must assess the situation, the type of objection and the mood of the customer and then choose the most appropriate style of response, without overstepping any ethical boundaries in terms of content. It is critical that winning the argument used to overcome the objection does not lead to a lost sale. Objections may interrupt the flow of the sales process either temporarily or permanently, and unless they are overcome, the final stages of the selling process cannot be achieved.

## Negotiation

Once the main body of the sales presentation is drawing to a close, with all the prospect's questions and objections answered for the time being, the selling process may move into a negotiation phase. Negotiation is a 'give and take' activity in which both parties try to shape a deal that satisfies both of them. Negotiation assumes a basic willingness to trade, but does not necessarily lead to a final deal. The danger for the sales representative, of course, is that a dead-locked or delayed negotiation phase may allow a competitor to enter the fray.

Despite the fact that deals are becoming more complex, sales staff are still expected to be able to negotiate. If they are going to be given the power to negotiate on behalf of the organisation, then they need clear guidelines on how far they are permitted to go in terms of concessions, and what the implications of those concessions would be. An extra month's credit, for example, could be quite expensive, particularly for an organisation with short-term cash flow problems, unless it is traded for another prized concession. This effectively means that the sales represent-ative needs financial as well as behavioural training in order to handle complex and sometimes lengthy negotiations.

As a final point, it must be said that negotiation need not be a separate and discrete stage of the selling process. Negotiation may emerge implicitly during the process of handling objec-tions, or may be an integral part of the next stage to be discussed, closing the sale.

## Closing the sale

The closing stage of the personal selling process is concerned with reaching the point where the customer agrees to purchase. In most cases, it is the sales representative's responsibility to close the sale, to ask for the order. Where the representative is less sure of the prospect's state of mind, or where the prospect still seems to have doubts, the timing of the closure and the way in which it is done could affect whether a sale is made. Try to close the sale too soon, and the buyer might be frightened off; leave it too long, and the buyer might become irritated by the prolonged process and all the good work done earlier in the sales presentation will start to dis-sipate. In a study of bluechip businesses, it was found that only one in five deals get closed, and that's a major waste of marketing and selling effort (Baker, 2007).

Watching the buyer's behaviour and listening to what they are saying might indicate that closure is near. The buyer's questions, for example, may become very trivial or the objections might dry up. The buyer might go quiet and start examining the product intently, waiting for the representative to make a move. The buyer's comments or questions might begin to relate to the post-purchase period, with a strong assumption that the deal has already been done.

A representative who thinks that the time to close is near, but is uncertain, might have to test the buyer's readiness to commit to a purchase. Also, if the prospect seems to be teetering on the edge of making a decision, then the representative might have to use a mechanism to give the buyer a gentle nudge in the direction of closure, for instance by offering the buyer a number of alternatives, each of which implies an agreement to purchase. The buyer's response gives an insight into how ready they are to commit themselves. Thus if the representative says, 'Would you like delivery to each of your stores or to the central distribution point?', there are two ways in which the buyer might respond. One way would be to choose one of the alternatives offered, in which case the sale must be very close, since the buyer is willing to get down to such fine detail. The other response would be something like 'Wait a minute, before we get down to that, what about . . .', showing that the buyer has not yet heard enough and may still have objections to be answered.

*eg* Most of the time, we are very happy with the puchases we make, and they turn out to be exactly what we thought they were. Sometimes, however, we get less than we bargained for, particularly at events like car boot sales where sellers can be pretty anonymous and untraceable after the event. Surrey Trading Standards officers are alert to this, and in 2010 seized 14,500 illegal items from markets and car boot sales including 800 items of fake Nike and Ralph Lauren merchandise. Pirated or fake DVDs, CDs, designer jewellery and ink cartridges are also common. Nevertheless, consumers come to buy these goods in the hope of getting a bargain, but too often clothing will wear out long before the real brands would, DVDs and CDs don't always work, designer jewellery and counterfeit make-up often contain chemicals that can cause skin irritation. 'Shoppers must remember these dishonest traders don't care about customer welfare and are only interested in making a quick profit' (Surrey Trading Standards Office, as quoted by Margrave, 2011).

At car boot sales the sellers may be anonymous and untraceable after the event

*Source*: Alamy Images/© David R. Frazier Photolibrary, Inc.

## Follow-up and account management

The sales representative's responsibility does not end once a sale has been agreed. As implied earlier at p. 461, the sales representative, as the customer's key contact point with the selling organisation, needs to ensure that the product is delivered on time and in good condition, that any installation or training promises are fulfilled and that the customer is absolutely satisfied with the purchase and is getting the best out of it.

At a more general level, the relationship with the customer still needs to be cultivated and managed. Where the sale has resulted in an ongoing supply situation, this may mean ensuring continued satisfaction with quality and service levels. Even with infrequently purchased items, ongoing positive contact helps to ensure that when new business develops, that supplier will be well placed. In the case of the consumer buying a car, the sales representative will make sure in the early stages that the customer is happy with the car, and work to resolve any problems quickly and efficiently. In the longer term, direct responsibility usually passes from the representative to a customer care manager who will ensure that the buyer is regularly sent product information and things like invitations to new product launches in the showrooms.

In the B2B market, an important role for the sales representative is to manage the customer's account internally within the selling organisation, ensuring that appropriate support is available as needed. Thus the representative is continuing to liaise between the customer and the accounts department, engineering, R&D, service and anyone else with whom the customer needs to deal.

## Sales management

The previous section concentrated on the mechanics of selling something to a prospective buyer. That is important, certainly, because if the selling process does not work well, then there will be no sales and no revenue. Equally important, however, is the management of the sales force. Whether in a multinational organisation or a small company, the selling effort needs to be planned and managed, and sales management provides an essential link between the organisation's strategic marketing plans and the achievement of sales objectives by the representatives in the field.

## Planning and strategy

The sales plan outlines the objectives for the selling effort and the details of how the plan should be implemented. This plan itself arises from, and must fit closely with, the marketing objectives set for products and market share, etc. These marketing objectives need to be translated into sales objectives, both for the sales force as a whole, and for individuals or groups within the sales force.

Setting sales objectives provides an essential yardstick against which to measure progress and to motivate and influence the selling effort. Normally, quantitative measures are used to specify exactly what is required. At the level of the total sales force, the targets will be in terms of sales value and/or volume. Setting objectives in sales and profit terms is often necessary either to avoid the dangers of chasing low profit sales or to lessen the temptation to reduce margins to generate more sales volume but less gross profit. Targets for individual sales representatives need not relate only to selling quantities of products. Performance targets might be agreed in terms of the number of sales calls, the number of new accounts recruited, the call frequency, call conversion rates (i.e. turning prospects into buyers) or selling expenses.

Assuming that the selling effort is to be managed internally, the sales manager also has to decide how the sales force will be organised: by geography (e.g. each sales representative is allocated a geographic region as their sales territory); by product (e.g. each sales representative is allocated a particular brand or family of product lines to sell); by customer type (e.g. each sales representative concentrates on a particular industry in which to sell); or by customer importance (e.g. the most important customers, perhaps in terms of sales, are identified and allocated their own sales representative or account team).

There is no one universally applicable and appropriate organisational structure. Sometimes a mixed structure may be best, combining geographic and major customer specialisation. Johnson & Johnson, for example, employs regionally based territory sales managers for its UK consumer products, but with specific responsibility for certain types of customer, such as independent pharmacies and wholesale cash and carries. This allows the organisation to benefit from the advantages of both types of allocation, while reducing the effect of their disadvantages. The chosen structure will be the right one as long as it reflects the objectives and marketing strategy of the firm.

A further decision has to be made on the ideal size of the sales force. A number of factors need to be considered, such as the calling frequency required for each customer, the number of calls possible each day, and the relative division of the representative's time between administration, selling and repeat calls (Cravens and LaForge, 1983). All these matters will have an impact on the ability of the sales force to achieve the expected sales results from the number of accounts served. For a smaller business, the issue may be further constrained by just how many representatives can be afforded!

# Recruitment and selection

As with any recruitment exercise, it is important to begin by developing a profile of who the organisation is looking for. A detailed analysis of the selling tasks should lead to a list of the ideal skills and characteristics of the representative to be recruited. Table 12.1 lists the attributes of sales representatives typically appreciated by buyers.

A common dilemma is whether previous experience is an essential requirement. Some organisations prefer to take on recruits new to selling, then train them in their own methods rather than recruit experienced representatives who come with bad habits and other organisations' weaknesses. Others, especially smaller organisations, may deliberately seek experienced staff, wishing to benefit from training programmes that they themselves could not afford to provide.

**Table 12.1** Sales representative attributes typically appreciated by buyers

Thoroughness and follow-up

Knowledge of seller's products

Representing the buyer's interests within the selling organisation

Market knowledge

Understanding the buyer's problems

Knowledge of the buyer's product and markets

Diplomacy and tact

Good preparation before sales calls

Regular sales calls

Technical education

The actual selection process needs to be designed to draw out evidence of the ability of each candidate to perform the specified tasks, so that an informed choice can be made. The cost of a poor selection can be very high, not just in terms of recruitment costs and salary, but also, and perhaps more seriously, in terms of lost sales opportunities or damage to the organisation's reputation. In view of the importance of making the right choice, in addition to normal interview and reference procedures, a number of firms employ psychological tests to assess personality and some will not confirm the appointment until the successful completion of the initial training period.

# Training

The recruitment process generally provides only the raw material. Although the new recruit might already have appropriate skills and a good attitudinal profile, training will help to sharpen both areas so that better performance within the sales philosophy of the employing organisation can be developed. Sales force training applies not just to new recruits, however. Both new and existing staff, even well-established staff, may need skills refinement and upgrading.

Training may be formal or informal. Some organisations invest in and develop their own high-quality training facilities and run a regular series of introductory and refresher courses in-house. This has the advantage of ensuring that the training is relevant to the organisation and its business, as well as signifying an ongoing commitment to staff development.

Other organisations adopt a more *ad hoc* approach, using outside specialists as required. This means that the organisation pays only for what it uses, but the approach carries two serious risks. The first problem is that the training may be too generalised and thus insufficiently tailored to the organisation's needs. The second problem is that it is too easy for the organisation to put off training or, even worse, to delete it altogether in times of financial stringency.

Finally, a third group uses informal or semi-formal 'sitting with Nelly', on-the-job coaching. This involves the trainee observing other representatives in the field, and then being observed

eg  Blue Banana specialises in a range of 'alternative' clothing to appeal to the late teens and early twenties, as well as providing tattooing and piercing services. It has a number of high-street stores throughout the UK, but felt that selling skills were lacking in many of the front-line staff and that sales opportunities were being wasted. MTD Sales Training was employed to offer a two-day programme to help staff acquire new skills. Although it is difficult to attribute cause and effect, there was subsequently a significant sales increase in some stores, up 25 per cent in one instance. Similarly, Porcelanosa Group, one of Europe's leading ceramic-tile manufacturers, had expanded its showroom and distribution capability and needed a training programme to promote and maintain high standards of professional showroom sales skills among both showroom managers and staff. Again, MTD was engaged to help sales staff to build strong and profitable customer relationships. A schedule was drawn up to roll out the training workshops to 160 staff spread over 26 locations. Again, although its is not easy to specify benefits, sales figures generally improved and conversions increased (www.mtdsalestraining.com/case_studies.html).

Blue Banana adopted a training programme to hone the sales skills of its front-line staff in its chain of UK shops

*Source*: Rosina Redwood Photography, Blue Banana shop, Exeter, © Rosina Redwood, Photographersdirect.com

themselves by experienced sales representatives and/or the sales manager. There is nothing quite like seeing the job being done, but with this approach the organisation needs to take great care to deal with a number of points. One concern is to ensure that such training is comprehensive, covering all aspects of the job. Another is to ensure that bad habits or questionable techniques are not passed on. The main problem with this kind of on-the-job training is that the training is not usually done by professional trainers. Therefore the quality can be variable, and there is no opportunity for fresh ideas to be introduced to the sales force.

## Motivation and compensation

An organisation will not only want to motivate new recruits to join its sales force, but also have an interest in making sure that they are sufficiently well rewarded for their achievements that they will not easily be poached by the competition (Cron *et al.*, 1988). There are many ways in which the sales team can be motivated to achieve outstanding results and rewarded, but they are not all financially based. Opportunities for self-development through training, well-defined career progression routes, and a feeling of being valued as an individual within a team can all increase job satisfaction.

Nevertheless, pay still remains a vital ingredient in attracting and retaining a committed sales force. Three main methods of compensation exist: straight salary, straight commission and a combination of salary and commission. Each method implies a number of advantages and disadvantages, listed in Table 12.2. The straight salary compensation plan is where a fixed amount is paid on a salary basis. The straight commission compensation plan means that earnings are directly related to the sales and profit generated. Finally, the most popular method is the combination plan, involving part salary and part commission. The selection of the most appropriate method will partly be determined by the nature of the selling tasks, and the degree of staff turnover that can be tolerated given the training and recruiting costs.

**Table 12.2** Comparison of compensation plans

|  | Commission only | Salary only | Part salary/ part commission |
|---|---|---|---|
| Motivation for rep. to generate sales | High | Low | Medium |
| Motivation for rep. to build customer relationship | Low | High | Medium |
| Motivation for rep. to participate in training | Low | High | Medium |
| Cost-effectiveness for organisation | High | Potentially low | Medium |
| Predictability of cost to organisation | Low | High | Medium |
| Predictability of income for rep. | Low | High | Medium |
| Ease of administration for organisation | Low | High | Low |
| Organisation's control over rep. | Low | High | Medium |
| Organisation's flexibility to push sales of particular products | High | Low | High |
| Overall, best where . . . | ■ Aggressive selling is needed<br>■ There are few non-selling tasks | ■ Training new reps<br>■ Difficult sales territories exist<br>■ Developing new territories<br>■ There are many non-selling tasks | ■ Organisation wants both incentive and control<br>■ Sales territories all have similar profiles |

# Performance evaluation

Given that many sales representatives work away from an office base, the monitoring and control of individual selling activity are vital functions in the sales management role. The sales representative's performance can be measured in both quantitative and qualitative terms. Quantitative assessments can be related to either input or output measures, usually with reference to targets and benchmarks (Good and Stone, 1991). Input measures assess activities such as the number of calls and account coverage. Output measures focus on the end rather than the means, and include measurement of sales volume, sales development, number of new accounts and specific product sales.

To create a rounded picture of the sales representative's performance, qualitative measures that tend to be informal and subjective are also used. These could include attitude, product knowledge, appearance and communication skills. Using them in conjunction with quantitative measures, the sales manager may be able to find explanations for any particularly good or bad performance underlying the quantitative evidence of the formal results achieved (Churchill *et al.*, 2000).

Either way, the assessment can form the basis of a deeper analysis to encourage a proactive rather than reactive approach to sales management. The analysis might indicate that action needs to be taken on call policy, training or motivation, or even that problems may lie not with the sales force, but with the product or its marketing strategies. The Alexander Proudfoot (2011) report mentioned earlier in the chapter asked companies what they felt they needed to do to improve their sales forces. Training existing staff was cited by 20 per cent of respondents, followed by better marketing (16 per cent), better sales management (also 16 per cent) and better sales support (14 per cent). Changing the incentive plan was only mentioned by 11 per cent of respondents, and more investment in technology by 9 per cent.

# MARKETING IN ACTION

## Cultivating the field-good factor!

Field marketing has grown in popularity as an effective substitute for client-owned sales forces, with an emphasis on the more routine tasks of order-taking, checking retailer compliance (for example, with in-store product displays or point of sale promotional materials), offering in-store demonstrations, and staffing other promotional events. Field-marketing services are provided by agencies acting on behalf of a client, for example an fmcg brand owner.

Some field marketing activity involves the use of contract sales staff, dealing with retailers, or in direct selling at shows and door to door, covering a wide range of products and services including cable television, utilities and financial services. Some clients might worry, however, that because field marketing staff, particularly those who are undertaking sales tasks, are not employed by them full time, there might be questions about their loyalty and motivation. Agencies are well aware of this and try to overcome it by setting up quality control systems to monitor the performance of their staff in the field, and ensuring that staff are fully and properly briefed at the start of an assignment. To try to engender 'loyalty' to the task in hand, the agency will also ensure that a member of staff is working for only one client in a particular product market at a time. Because of the amount of time contract staff spend in the field and because of the wide range of customers and product types they deal with, these agencies can amass a wealth of data about what is going on in the market that a company's own sales force would not have either the time or the resources to collect. Agencies can thus feed information back to clients, providing an additional benefit to their service.

Other field marketing activities are closer to being a cross between sales promotion and selling, with more of an emphasis on raising awareness and promoting brand image than doing a hard sell. E-Lites, for instance, are electronic cigarettes that deliver a nicotine 'hit' but not the tar and other harmful chemicals of a standard cigarette. There is also no threat of passive smoking from them and thus they can be legally 'smoked' indoors. Smokers are notoriously addicted to their habit, and getting them to switch to an alternative to cigarettes can be difficult. The company thinks that it is important for smokers to be able to try the product and see it demonstrated positively, and thus has used field marketing at busy commuter stations and at exhibitions such as the Gadget Show Live to complement its other marketing communications activities. To the company, 'It's a chance to meet with your customers, interact with them, present a human face and convey the company's values in a credible face-to-face environment' (as quoted by Cooper, 2011). Friendly and approachable field-marketing staff can show the product, allow a smoker to have a go with one, and answer any doubts or questions they might have. At least it raises awareness, but might also arouse sufficient interest for that smoker to seek further information or even to buy the product.

E-lites used social media as part of its field marketing campaign, and this type of integration is becoming very much the norm. Freeview has also benefited from an integrated campaign, using social media. Tapping into the public's interest in Prince William's wedding in 2011, Freeview asked the field-marketing agency, Gekko, to use the event as a focal point to demonstrate Freeview's HD service ▶

in the stores of major multiple retailers, and thus to make sales to new customers and encourage existing Freeview users to upgrade to HD. The in-store activity was supported by a Freeview royal wedding microsite and a YouTube page promoting the in-store activity, and there was also a related prize draw with a royal wedding hamper as a prize. Freeview's brand awareness rose as a result, and during the field marketing activity, 32 per cent of Freeview purchasers converted from a standard Freeview set-top box to HD DTVs (Benjamin, 2011).

The world of field marketing is still evolving. Some of the basic data collection tasks of field marketers, such as counting products on display in a store, checking that point-of-sale promotional material is being displayed correctly, photographing displays, and fact-checking are now being subcontracted out to members of the general public, thanks to the smartphone. Anyone can download an app, sign in and log their location and then be allocated tasks for which they are paid between £2 and £6. The company, Field Agent, has signed up over 7,600 people and undertakes work on behalf of a number of field marketing and mystery shopping agencies (Bashford, 2011; www.fieldagent.co.uk).

*Sources*: Bashford (2011); Benjamin (2011); Cooper (2011); www.fieldagent.co.uk.

## Trade shows and exhibitions

Both B2B and consumer sellers may introduce trade shows and exhibitions into their promotional mixes. Such events range from small-scale local involvement, for example, a specialist bookseller taking a stall at a model railway exhibition, to an annual national trade show serving a specific industry, such as the DIY and Home Improvement Show, or Pakex for the packaging industry. In either case, the exhibition may become an important element of the year's marketing activities, as this section will show. Even those who specialise in organising and supporting exhibitions have their own exhibitions!

Exhibitions and shows can be of particular importance to the smaller business that may not have the resources to fund an expensive marketing communications programme. The exhibition can be used as a cost-effective means of building more 'presence' and reputation with the trade, and to generate potential sales leads.

For any sized organisation, international exhibitions can be particularly valuable because they bring together participants from all over the world who might otherwise never meet, and can thus lead to export deals. The Nürnberg International Toy Fair (www.toyfair.de), for example, has been running for over 60 years. It represents an opportunity for the trade to present new products to retail buyers from across Europe. New product launches are often planned to coincide with the fair to maximise both the impact to visitors and the subsequent coverage in the trade and hobby press.

eg Some exhibitions are open to the public as well as the trade and provide a great opportunity for suppliers of goods and services to meet customers and potential customers face-to-face, and generate sales leads. The first London Pet Show, for example, took place at Olympia in May 2011, and attracted nearly 13,500 pet-lovers and over 110 companies and charities offering pet-related products and services. Such an event has to be well promoted, of course, to attract sufficient visitors to make it worthwhile for the exhibitors to attend, and the organisers of the London Pet Show claim that their five-month campaign in the

You can find everything you need to keep your 'small furry' happy at the London Pet Show

*Source:* © London Pet Show, www.londonpetshow.co.uk

run up to the show across a wide range of media generated 54 million OTS (opportunities to see – see p. 383). It is also important that as well as the exhibitors' stands, there are other attractions and focal points to keep the visitors occupied. Thus animal agility displays, and free information and advice through demonstrations and talks all add to the atmosphere and the experience that the visitors enjoy and remember, and directly or indirectly associate with the exhibitors (www.londonpetshow.co.uk/; e-mail from londonpetshow.co.uk, sent 27 July 2011).

For the manufacturer, attending exhibitions provides a formal opportunity to display the product range and to discuss applications and needs with prospective customers in a neutral environment. Depending on the type of show and the care that an organisation puts into planning its presence there, an exhibition provides a powerful and cost-effective way of getting the message across and making new contacts that may subsequently turn into sales.

Illy Coffee is a premium, aspirational brand of coffee working under the slogan 'One Brand, One Blend' in over 60 countries. It uses exhibitions both to meet with, and build better relationships with existing corporate clients, and to identify new leads with the potential for long-term business. It also helps to maintain visibility in the marketplace, and demonstrates success and leadership, especially when competitors are not so active and consistent in attending exhibitions. Occasionally, it will use an exhibition as a launch pad for a new product.

Illy deliberately selects niche shows to reflect the target market. Making the right exhibition decision is important. As Illy only attends a few events per year, it researches each potential exhibition thoroughly, looking at factors such as attendance figures and a breakdown of visitor profiles. It also checks what other premium brands are exhibiting – not just those selling coffee.

Once at an exhibition, because Illy is a very well established brand with not a lot of new things to talk about, it just makes sure it does simple things very well. Even the stand itself is low key, creating a relaxed coffee bar experience so that people feel at home there. However, Illy goes to great lengths to maximise the marketing benefit. It uses PR to raise awareness around key buying times, advertises in the trade press to let people know it is exhibiting, and uses the exhibition stand to maintain customer relationships. Any new leads made on the stand are followed up within six weeks (www.eventsindustryalliance.com/page.cfm/link=38).

## Public relations

## Definitions

Stanley (1982, p. 40) defined public relations as:

> **A management function that determines the attitudes and opinions of the organisation's publics, identifies its policies with the interests of its publics, and formulates and executes a programme of action to earn the understanding and goodwill of its publics.**

The Chartered Institute of Public Relations (CIPR) is rather more rounded in its definition:

> **Public relations is about reputation – the result of what you do, what you say and what others say about you. Public relations is the discipline which looks after reputation, with the aim of earning understanding and support and influencing opinion and behaviour. It is the planned and sustained effort to establish and maintain goodwill and mutual understanding between an organisation and its publics. (www.cipr.co.uk/content/careers-cpd/careers-pr/what-pr)**

The latter is, nevertheless, a more useful definition that gets close to the core concern of PR, which is *mutual understanding*. The implication is that the organisation needs to understand how it is perceived in the wider world, and then work hard to make sure, through PR, that those perceptions match its desired image. Two-way communication is essential to this process. Another interesting element of this definition is the specific use of the word *publics*. Advertising, in its commonest usage, is usually about talking to customers or potential customers. Public relations defines a much broader range of target audiences, some of whom have no direct trading relationship with the organisation, and thus PR encompasses a wide variety of communication needs and objectives not necessarily geared towards an eventual sale. Finally, the definition emphasises that PR is *planned and sustained*. This is important for two reasons. First, it implies that PR is just as much of a strategically thought-out, long-term commitment as any other marketing activity, and second, it counters any preconceptions about PR simply being the *ad hoc* seizing of any free publicity opportunity that happens to come along.

Jack Wills is not a name that automatically springs to mind (at least among the older generation) when thinking about clothing retailers, but it has certainly built up a reputation as a premium niche brand for younger people. It is well known in many red-brick universities, boarding schools and holiday resorts such as Salcombe (rather than Blackpool!), and promotes itself as 'University Outfitters'. The prices may shock some at £19 for a pair of socks or £69 for a hooded sweatshirt, but its style is a good quality, traditional English 'county' look, with a touch of tweed interpreted in a contemporary fashion. The company itself says: 'Jack Wills creates fabulously British goods for the university crowd. Drawing inspiration from Britain's rich history and culture, juxtaposed with a heavy dose of the hedonistic university lifestyle, we create authentic and relevant clothing for today' (www.jackwills.com). With the intention of offering a complete lifestyle, the brand has also diversified into toiletries/cosmetics and homeware (the kind of stuff you need to cheer up a room in halls or in a student house).

It doesn't advertise, but prefers to use PR events, word of mouth and viral communications focused largely on upmarket and aspirational university students and their leisure interests. During the spring term 2011, for example, it visited six university campuses and took over their coffee shops for 24 hours. During the afternoon, tea, T-shirt printing and other give-aways were offered, then in the evening, the all-night party began. Then, for those who were capable, breakfast was offered throughout the following morning. The Easter vacation 2011 saw Jack Wills, in conjunction with the British Universities Snowsports Council, running après ski and funicular parties at the resort of Tignes. During the summer terms and into the long vacation, Jack Wills can be found at summer balls, and it also sponsors the Varsity Polo Match, featuring Oxford vs Cambridge, Harvard vs Yale and Eton vs Harrow with, of course, the after-match party. Then there's the vintage horse box that goes round a number of smaller 'boutique' music festivals over the summer, bringing a variety of artistes with it. As well as these kinds of high-profile events, Jack Wills runs give-aways in university towns up and down the country offering items such as bespoke T-shirts, mugs and underpants!

As part of the commitment to word-of-mouth and viral communications, and in tune with the habits of its target market, Jack Wills uses social media a lot and claims that 220,000 Facebook and Twitter fans watch videos of its various events thus maximising the 'buzz' and the impact. There is even a team monitoring tweets and giving a fast response, thus engaging in direct dialogue with its target market. This is all part of a philosophy that allows target customers to 'discover' the brand for themselves or hear about it from their peers rather than feeling that it is being 'pushed' onto them (Greene and Pacheco, 2011; www.jackwills.com).

Jack Wills does not advertise to sell its upmarket clothing range to university students but relies instead on PR events, word of mouth and viral communications

*Source:* Boston Globe via Getty Images

A public is any group, with some common characteristic, with which an organisation needs to communicate. Each public poses a different communication problem, as each has different information needs and a different kind of relationship with the organisation, and may start with different perceptions of what the organisation stands for (Marston, 1979).

*eg* A university has to develop relationships with a wide range of publics. Obviously, there are the students and potential students and the schools and colleges that provide them, both nationally and internationally. The university also has to consider, however, its staff and the wider academic community. Then there are the sources of funding, such as local authorities, the government, the EU and research bodies. Industry might also be a potential source of research funds, as well as commissioning training courses and providing jobs for graduates. It is also important for a university to foster good press relations. Local media help to establish the university as a part of its immediate community, national media help to publicise its wider status, while specialist publications such as the *Times Higher Education Supplement* reach those with a specific interest and perhaps even the decision-makers within the sector.

A number of different publics, which relate generally to any kind of organisation, are shown in Figure 12.3. It is, however, important to remember that any individual may be a member of more than one public. This means that although the slant and emphasis of messages may differ from public to public, the essential content and philosophy should be consistent. Appropriate techniques within PR for communicating with a range of different publics will be looked at later (see p. 481 *et seq.*).

Not all publics will be regarded by an organisation as having equal importance. Some will be seen as critical, and be given priority in targeting PR activities, while others will just be left ticking over for the time being. As the organisation's situation changes, the priority given to each of the publics will have to be reassessed (Wilmshurst, 1993).

Even in the quietest and most stable of industries, the membership of each public will change over time, and their needs and priorities will also evolve. This process of change emphasises the need to monitor attitudes and opinions constantly, and thus to identify current and future pressure points early enough to be able to defuse or control them.

**Figure 12.3**
Publics

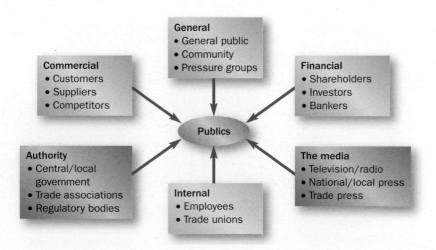

## Role of PR

As with any marketing activity, managers must be sure that PR integrates with the rest of the organisation's promotional efforts, and that it is clearly related to wider company objectives. Cutlip *et al.* (1985) distinguish between *marketing PR* and *corporate PR*. Although the two are not mutually exclusive, there may be differences in their scope and objectives.

### Marketing PR

Marketing PR may be used for long-term strategic image building, developing credibility and raising the organisation's profile, to enhance other marketing activities. When used in this way, it becomes a planned element of the wider promotional mix, working in synergy with the others. A new product launch, or the introduction of a big new innovative advertising campaign, for instance, might benefit from planned PR aimed at specific audiences through specific media to generate interest and awareness.

### Corporate PR

It is possible to use corporate PR as part of a long-term relationship-building strategy with various publics or as a short-term tactical response to an unforeseen crisis. By definition, short-term circumstances are somewhat unpredictable, and therefore any organisation needs to have contingency plans ready so that a well-rehearsed crisis management team can swing into action as soon as disaster strikes. This means, for example, that everyone should know who will be responsible for collating information and feeding it to the media, and that senior management will be properly briefed and trained to face media interrogation. Such measures result in the organisation being seen to handle the crisis capably and efficiently, and also reduce the chances of different spokespersons innocently contradicting each other, or of the media being kept short of information because everyone thinks that someone else is dealing with that aspect. Although the duration of the crisis may be short, and thus the actual implementation of PR activities is technically a short-term tactic to tide the organisation over the emergency, the contingency planning behind it involves long-term management thinking. Longer-term, corporate PR plays a useful role in generating goodwill and positive associations with key audiences, some of whom may one day be customers.

Given the many potential uses of corporate PR, it is important that there is clear thinking as to what is expected with different audiences and how best to approach each target group. Without such a rationale for action, it is difficult to assess what outcomes and achievements have been realised (Stone, 1991).

## MARKETING IN ACTION

### Pedals, pundits, pants, planes and PR

There is no such thing as bad publicity! That's what the old adage says but don't ask Toyota, Sky Sports, Abercrombie & Fitch, or United Airlines to comment!

Toyota had a outstanding reputation for quality until the defective accelerators debacle in 2009–2010. It had to recall 5.6 million vehicles for possible unintended acceleration that had allegedly caused some fatal accidents. This was caused by not installing a brake override system, a system which many other auto manufacturers had already installed. The focus was on recovery and stopping it happening again, rather than just reputational damage limitation. That's not surprising, given that Toyota faced

▶ around 30 lawsuits with 10 claiming death and injuries. Toyota accepted responsibility and even took out full page adverts in major Japanese newspapers to apologise for the recall, saying, 'We apologise from the bottom of our hearts for the great inconvenience and worries that we have caused you all'. The Toyota President also held a series of media briefings to give information about what Toyota was doing to overcome the crisis, and he even went in front of a US Congressional Committee to salvage the company's reputation in the critical US market. It seems to have worked, as market share improved during 2011 and a number of new models were introduced as the memory started to fade about the recalls.

Richard Keys and Andy Gray, presenters on Sky Sports, undertook routine coverage of the Liverpool vs Wolves soccer match in January 2011. The trouble started when they claimed that the assistant referee, who was a woman, would not be able to understand the offside rule. After all, soccer was designed by men for men! This was followed by footage (off-air, but recorded) of Gray asking a female colleague to tuck a microphone down the front of his trousers and Keys talking to a soccer pundit using inappropriate language about the ex-footballer's private life. Gray was sacked and Keys resigned, but it was definitely Sky Sports' problem as it brought the broadcaster's overall brand image into question. Needless to say, the comments had sparked public outrage, even from men, and even from the tabloid redtop newspapers which themselves have a somewhat questionable track record on sexism (*Schadenfreude?*). Sky Sports managed to overcome the damage to its reputation, but at the expense of losing Keys and Gray, who up to that point had been respected anchors of the broadcaster's football coverage.

Abercrombie & Fitch, the US-based clothing company, offered to pay Michael Sorrentino, a cast member in the series *Jersey Shore*, NOT to wear its clothes on what it considered to be a programme that was inappropriate to its brand image. In virtually every episode he wore something from Abercrombie & Fitch, including a tracksuit, sweaters and even underpants! The company said, 'We understand that the show is for entertainment purposes, but believe this association is contrary to the aspirational nature of our brand, and may be distressing to many of our fans' (as quoted by Goodwin, 2011). It's understandable that a company should want to maintain a degree of control over who is seen wearing its brand and in what context, but does 'paying off' this actor make this brand look too pretentious or is it an interesting PR stunt to underline the association and generate media coverage?

When United Airlines broke David Carroll's guitar while it was in transit and then added insult to injury by offering him a nightmare customer-service experience when he tried to get damages, he vented his frustration by recording a song 'United Breaks Guitars' about the experience and posted it on YouTube. It got three million views in the first week and currently has had nearly 11 million views, and has spawned a large number of related postings in response. United, meanwhile, took hasty steps to put things right with Mr Carroll and now uses the case as a customer-service training aid. All power to the aggrieved individual! This is, of course, just one incident that is not representative of the vast majority of service encounters that United's customers have, but it's a story that has spread round the world, and it's a story that people remember. Bad publicity like this, whether deserved or not, presents the service provider as uncaring, slowly erodes customer confidence, and gets spread around.

It has been argued that negative publicity is good for unknown firms, but bad for established ones (EIU, 2011). For smaller brands struggling to get recognition almost any publicity is beneficial as it gets the name known and consumers soon forget and even forgive minor transgressions. The *Borat* movie made Kazakhstan sound awful, yet there was a four-fold increase in enquiries to the national tourism authority. For bigger companies, in particular, how the company handles the crisis is critical. It needs to be fast, decisive in putting forward a counter-argument, and effective in calming down unrest. Sometimes, it means accepting the blame as in the Sky Sports and Toyota examples. Self-abasement and humility goes a long way, but sometimes, when the transgression is relatively minor, self-depreciating humour can do a good job too. When EA Sports released its Tiger Woods game in 2009, a programming glitch made it appear that the player was walking on water. Amusing, but irritating to gamers. The response from EA was to produce a video 'It's not a glitch. He's just that good', actually showing Tiger Woods walking on water and holing the ball from its position resting on a lily pad in deep water. It struck home, with over 3 million hits in its first year, and to date, over 6 million.

*Sources*: Ainsworth (2009); Barnes (2011); Colbin (2011); EIU (2011); *Financial Times* (2011); Goodwin (2011); Green and Cronin Fisk (2010); McCurry (2010); Shunk (2011); Whoriskey (2010).

# Techniques in public relations

## Publicity and press relations

Public relations and 'publicity' are often mistakenly used as interchangeable terms. Publicity is, however, simply one of the tools available for achieving the overall PR objective of creating and maintaining good relationships with various publics. Publicity is thus a subset of PR, focused on generating media coverage at minimal cost to the organisation. In other words, publicity happens when the media voluntarily decide to talk about the organisation and its commercial activities.

*eg*

Social media are taking an increasing role in public relations, and marketing managers ignore them at their peril. Like it or not, social media sites such as YouTube, Facebook and Twitter have an important role to play in giving online information, whether in writing or through video of news and events. They are powerful tools in reaching, teaching and influencing audiences to enhance brand and corporate reputation and image (Burrows, 2011). At the height of the BP oil-spill disaster in the Gulf of Mexico, Twitter had 175,000 followers on @BPGlobalPR (Hosea, 2010b).

Traditional PR relies on one-way dialogue from the organisation to the public, while social media offer two-way exchanges through channels which are not in the control of companies. These dialogues can take place not only vertically, between the organisation and its target public, but also horizontally between members of the public(s). This horizontal communication can be much more difficult to influence and this is where minor issues can escalate into major PR problems. Monitoring coverage on social media sites (as we saw in the Jack Wills example earlier), and engaging in the evolving dialogue is becoming an increasingly important means of trying to emphasise the good news and contain the potential damage from the bad news.

There is still room, however, for the good old-fashioned publicity stunt, even on social media. Legal and General, for example, published the *Digital Criminal Report 2010*. This report presented evidence to show how easily criminals can work out who you are, where you live, what you've got, when you're away from home, and how best to access your house by using postings on social media sites and other easy accessible online personal data that you probably don't even realise exists. The report also offers advice on how you can keep yourself and your property safe in the online environment. Within 24 hours, the report had become one of the highest trending topics on Twitter, doubtless helped by extensive national print and broadcast media coverage, and overall it was estimated that the campaign had reached more than 45 million people and had delivered the equivalent of £2.5 million of advertising (www.fishburn-hedges.co.uk). Perhaps the secret of its success was that it offered something of great value, importance and relevance to everyone but without a hard sell or gratuitous self-promotion. The report is not trying to sell insurance policies, and Legal and General emerge from this with an enhanced reputation as trying to safeguard the public.

Bloggers have also emerged as key influencers and opinion leaders in digital PR. Those who follow them see them as authoritative, knowledgeable, and independent, and thus they value their opinions. If a blogger can be persuaded to say something positive about a brand or company it can be very valuable, but of course, the risk is that bloggers can select what they want to use and interpret it as they choose. To harness the advantages of bloggers, Virgin has set up vtravelledblog (http://blog.vtravelled.com) on behalf of the various Virgin companies involved in travel and tourism, bringing together travel bloggers, established travel journalists, as well as Virgin-related editorial content. As with the Legal and General example, the purpose is not to make a hard sell, but to offer interesting information, travel tips, and inspiration (Hosea, 2010a). There is also a dedicated customer service representative on Twitter and Facebook so that it can provide an immediate response to developing issues (Burrows, 2011; Hosea, 2010a, 2010b; Legal and General, 2010; www. fishburn-hedges.co.uk; http://www.blog.vtravelled.com).

All areas of the mass media can be used for publicity purposes. Within the broadcast media, apart from news and current affairs programmes, a great deal of publicity is disseminated through chat shows (authors plugging their latest books, for instance), consumer shows (featuring dangerous products or publicising companies' questionable personal selling practices, for instance) and special interest programmes (motoring, books, clothing, etc.). Print and online media also offer wide scope for publicity. National and local newspapers cover general interest stories, but there are many special interest, trade and professional publications and websites that give extensive coverage to stories of specific interest to particular publics. It must also be remembered that sections of the media feed each other. National newspapers and television stations may pick up stories from local media or the specialist media and present them to a much greater mass audience.

Publicity may be unsought, as when the media get the smell of scandal or malpractice and decide to publicise matters which perhaps the organisation would rather not have publicised. To reduce the risk of bad publicity, however, most organisations cultivate good press relations, and try to feed the media's voracious appetite with 'good news' stories that will benefit the organisation. This can be done through written press releases or verbal press conferences or briefings.

The media are obviously very powerful, not only as a public in their own right, but also as a third-party channel of communication with other publics. It may be argued that advertising can do just as good a communication job, in spreading good news to mass audiences, but publicity has a few advantages. Advertising is paid for, and therefore publics have a certain cynicism about the bias within the message. Publicity, on the other hand, is seen as free, coming from a neutral third party, and therefore has more credibility. Also, a good PR story that captures the imagination so that it gets wide coverage across both print and broadcast media can achieve an incredible level of reach (see p. 382) at a fraction of the cost, and might even make an impact on sections of the audience who wouldn't normally see or absorb advertising.

These advantages do, however, need to be balanced against the big disadvantage, *uncontrollability*. Whereas advertising gives the advertiser complete control over what is said, when it is said, how it is said and where it is said, the control of publicity is in the hands of the media. The organisation can feed material to the media, but cannot guarantee that the media will adopt the story or influence how they will present it (Fill, 2002). The outcome of this might be, at worst, no coverage at all, or patchy coverage that might not reach the desired target publics. Another potential risk is distortion of the story.

It is not true to say that there is no such thing as bad publicity. The risks of negative coverage can, however, be minimised by the maintenance of ongoing, good press relations, and by setting up a crisis management plan so that if disaster strikes, the damage from bad publicity can be limited and even turned to advantage.

## Other external communication

Other forms of external communication are also used for PR. Advertising can be used as a tool of PR, although it is something of a grey area. The kind of advertising to which we are referring here is not the selling or promoting of a specific product or range of products, but the type that concentrates on the organisation's name and characteristics. As previously suggested, although this sort of advertising lacks the impartiality of publicity, it makes up for it in terms of controllability. As a means of helping to establish and reinforce corporate image, it is certainly effective, and as a mass medium will reach members of most publics.

An organisation can host or participate in various events for PR purposes. As well as press conferences, mentioned above, the organisation may host other social events. If it has just opened a new factory, for instance, it may hold a party on the premises for key shareholders, employees, customers and suppliers. Such one-off events will also, of course, create media interest.

An important public is the one with a financial interest in the organisation. The organisation's annual general meeting is an important forum for both shareholders and the financial media. Efficient administration and confident presentation can help to increase credibility (although none of that can disguise a poor financial position).

A well-presented annual report, distributed primarily to shareholders and the financial media, but often sent out to anyone who expresses an interest in the organisation, like the annual general meeting, is an opportunity to present the organisation in the best possible positive light and to make public statements about the organisation's achievements and its future directions.

Lobbying is a very specialised area, designed to develop and influence relationships with 'authority', particularly national and EU governmental bodies. Lobbying is a way of getting an organisation's views known to the decision-makers, and trying to influence the development and implementation of policy.

## Internal communication

Although employees and other internal publics are exposed to much of the PR that is directed to the external world, they do need their own dedicated communication so that they know what is going on in more detail, and they know it before it hits the wider media (Bailey, 1991). This emphasis on keeping people informed rather than in the dark reflects quite a major change in employers' attitudes towards their employees. It is important for motivation, as well as being a means of preparing people for change and strengthening corporate culture.

The two main types of communication are written (house journals, intranet pages or news-letters) and verbal (management briefings, for instance). Few people would want to read a long working paper written by the managing director on quality management or production targets, but most would at least glance at a well-illustrated, short, clearly written summary of the important points presented in journalistic style. Briefings provide a good mechanism for face-to-face contact between management and staff, and for increasing staff involvement and empowerment. Frequent, regular departmental or section meetings can be used to thrash out operational problems and to pass communication downwards through the organisation. Less frequently, once a year perhaps, more senior management can address staff, presenting results and strategic plans, and directly answering questions.

# Sponsorship

## Definition and role

Sponsorship is defined by BDS Sponsorship (www.sponsorship.co.uk) as:

> . . . a business relationship between a provider of funds, resources or services and an individual, event or organisation which offers in return some rights and association that may be used for commercial advantage.

While some sponsorship certainly does have altruistic motives behind it, its main purpose is to generate positive attitudes through associating the corporate name with sport, the arts, charitable enterprise or some other activity. That is why so many companies use sponsorship, including familiar names such as Coca-Cola, Ford, Heineken, Barclays, O2 and others.

Sponsorship grew in popularity during the 1980s, partly because of its attractiveness as a supporting element in the promotional mix, and partly because of the growing cost of media advertising compared with the potentially greater coverage of various sports and arts activities (Meenaghan, 1998). Sponsorship has also become more global and has fitted well with the increased trend towards brand globalisation (Grimes and Meenaghan, 1998). Its growth was also helped by the tobacco companies using it as a means of achieving exposure in spite of the ban on television advertising.

## Types of sponsorship

### Sport

With the widespread appeal of sport across all ages, areas and lifestyles, it is perhaps not surprising that sports sponsorship has grown in popularity. This is especially true when it is linked to the televising of the events. The mass audiences possible through television, even for some minority sports, enable the widespread showing of the sponsor's name.

*eg*

Flora sponsored the London marathon from the mid-1990s as part of its commitment to a healthier Britain. There was a clear link between the brand values and the nature of the event, and as a bonus, television viewing figures often exceeded 6 million and that, along with a website linking the event to Flora, led to an increase in spontaneous awareness of the brand by 50 per cent. The sponsorship came to an end in 2009 after 14 years, with 413,627 people having run in Flora marathons and £422 million having been raised for charity. The reason given was that Flora now wanted to challenge public perception in other ways.

The event was not left without a sponsor, however, as Virgin agreed a deal worth £17 million to be led, in the first instance by the Virgin Money sub-brand. The new sponsor claimed that it was the single biggest fundraising day in the world, and hoped to raise £250 million for charity over five years. To help encourage this effort, Virgin set up a fundraising website Virgin Money Giving, as 'the official fundraising website for the London Marathon' so that entrants could easily set up a means by which friends, family and others could make an online donation.

Virgin was very aware of the legacy left in people's minds by Flora's long association with the marathon, and this was anxious to make a big impact in its first marathon. It thus created Virgin Village as an improved facility for the runners, and to entertain the non-runners, set up entertainment hubs and hosted 'urban parties' at Tower Bridge and Canary Wharf, with live bands and music acts. All of this fits very nicely with Virgin's corporate brand image and creates direct and enjoyable interaction between the brand and the general public (Charles, 2007; *Marketing Week*, 2010; Sweney, 2008; Wiggins, 2010).

Many sports attract heavy television coverage and so although the typical sponsoring costs may be high, in comparison with the cost of direct television advertising, such sponsorship can actually be very cost effective. Sponsorship of sport has the added benefit that although people may ignore commercial breaks, they do pay attention when a 'real' programme is on and, therefore, may be more likely to absorb the sponsor's name.

Soccer has been one of the major sports to attract sponsorship because of its large-scale media coverage in all kinds of media. This has attracted sponsors at player, club, national league and international levels throughout the world; interested sponsors are not just the obvious sportswear brands such as Nike and Adidas, but also brands across all sectors, from cars to airlines, from mobile phones to electrical goods, from soft drinks to beer, from insurance companies to banks. Manchester United, for example, has its main shirt and equipment deal with Nike; Aon as the sponsor of the matchday shirts (£20 million per year); a training kit deal with DHL (£40 million across four years); a three-year partnership with Vietnamese mobile telecommunications company, Beeline, to distribute Manchester United content to fans in Vietnam, Cambodia and Laos; then there's sponsorship with Betfair, Audi, Thomas Cook, Turkish Airlines, Singha, Smirnoff, Epson . . . the list goes on of brands that see Man U as an attractive proposition due to its huge worldwide following. All are keen to be associated with the club through the website, live matches and so on (www.manutd.com). Not all clubs are quite so blessed and certainly in the lower leagues, clubs are more likely to link up with a number of smaller scale, local businesses for sponsorship. On a more modest basis than the multimillion-pound deals that the likes of Man U or Barça can command, companies can sponsor match programmes, balls or even the corner flags. Smaller or non-league clubs are appealing for local businesses who want to reinforce their role in the community, and even large organisations can value this.

All of this works well as long as the sport and the individual clubs continue to maintain a 'clean' image. A riot in the stands or a punch-up on the pitch generates the kind of publicity and media coverage of the type 'What kind of depths has the game sunk to?' that sponsors will not want to be associated with. Every time a player is sent off for violent conduct with the sponsor's name on his chest, an athlete becomes embroiled in a drugs allegation, an F1 vehicle breaks down, or a high-profile sportsperson becomes embroiled in a scandal in his or her personal life, there is a risk to the sponsoring organisation.

The UEFA Champions League is generates very large international television audiences (4 million live viewers reaching into 220 countries) and is a great opportunity for a brand to associate itself with the very best of European club soccer. Heineken sponsors the Champions League and has the right to exclusive content on social media platforms and to be the main partner for screening match highlights on UEFA's website. There are also opportunities for trade promotions, branded merchandise and PR spin-offs from the sponsorship. Heineken believes that it reinforces brand strengths across Europe and helps to build brand awareness and even loyalty in other parts of the world too. It is part of a strategy to make Heineken the most international beer brand, which includes a sponsorhip strategy that covers the Rugby World Cup in New Zealand and the London 2012 Olympic Games – all very high profile events (*Hugin Press Release*, 2011; O'Reilly, 2011).

Although this section on sports sponsorship has largely focused on soccer, as it is the number one spectator sport in many European countries, there are many other sports both large and small that receive, and indeed rely on sponsorship money. From curling and bowls through to tennis, golf, cricket, motor sport and athletics, the focus is on attracting and retaining sponsors. Each offers access to a defined target audience or offers access to spectators and viewers, either directly or through television and media coverage. What needs to happen in all cases is to manage the fit between the brand and the sport. The potential sponsor thus needs to assess how well the image and profile of the sport matches the brand's target market, and then what opportunities there might be for brand awareness and recognition; publicity and spin-off benefits.

Brit Insurance took over sponsorship of the England cricket team from Vodafone in 2010. Its aim was to improve its brand recognition in order to compete with Zurich and RSA in the B2B insurance market. This was Brit Insurance's third foray into cricket sponsorship, as it had previously sponsored Surrey Cricket Club (who, during the period of that sponsorship played at The Brit Oval) and the sponsorship of Sky's cricket broadcasts. As part of the England sponsorship, the Brit Insurance logo features on all the team's playing and

Brit Insurance sponsors the English cricket team as well as out-reach programmes for school children
*Source*: Brit Insurance

training kit. With the success of English cricket in the 2011 Ashes series and its subsequent rise to number one in the Test Match rankings, it was no bad time to become involved. In the build-up to the 2011 Ashes, Brit Insurance said, 'The branding on the kit achieves an excellent profile through print and broadcast in the build-up to matches and the series itself' (as quoted by Eleftheriou-Smith, 2010).

Brit Insurance's involvement with cricket extends to its internal marketing effort too. In partnership with the Cricket Foundation's 'Chance to Shine' programme, Brit Insurance employees volunteered to spend a day in schools, helping with cricket themed lessons across the curriculum as well as working on cricket skills with kids. Those employees were in good company: in one London school, England fast bowler Chris Tremlett took a PE class; the Minister for Sport took assembly; and the governor of the Bank of England (who also happens to be the president of Chance to Shine) taught a cricket-themed maths lesson (*Marketing Week*, 2009; *Post Magazine*, 2011).

## Broadcast sponsorship

Television sponsorship forms the largest part of broadcast sponsorship, but it still comprises a smaller proportion of a channel's commercial income compared with advertising revenue. In the UK, broadcast sponsorship was forecast by Mintel (2009) to be worth around £300 million in 2010, covering both radio and television. However, while 70 per cent of respondents could correctly match at least one television programme with the correct sponsor, only 10 per cent could do the same for radio. This could, however, be simply a reflection of our media consumption habits and the fragmentation of radio audiences. Nearly three-quarters of respondents in Mintel's survey claimed to pay no attention to the messages associated with sponsorship, just regarding them as another form of advertising, but it's also true to say that those who try to 'avoid' the advertisements in the programme breaks are far more likely to see the sponsor's 'idents' that come at the start and at the end of the break. Those who are watching the programme on playback on the Sky+ boxes or similar recording devices are likely to look out for the idents as a cue to stop fast forwarding through the ads!

Brylcreem decided to get involved with sponsoring entertainment as a means of improving its image and awareness among its core target market of 16–30-year-old males. It sponsored Soccer AM on Sky Sports, an irreverent Saturday morning mix of football, comedy and entertainment, thus associating the brand with something 'cool', humorous, and engaging. It worked: when asked which male hair products sponsored anything on television, 54 per cent of Soccer AM viewers mentioned Brylcreem compared with 9 per cent of non-viewers; 57 per cent of viewers said that they were likely to buy Brylcreem in the future. The perception of Brylcreem as a 'fashionable' brand also increased by 33 per cent. The sponsorship deal lasted for two years, during which time Brylcreem used the association with Soccer AM for various PR activities, and also launched a new range of products that were co-branded with Soccer AM (www.skymedia.co.uk/).

Television broadcasters are especially keen to exploit the potential of gaining sponsorship for major sports event coverage. The broadcasters gain much-needed additional revenue and the sponsors are clearly linked to the show in all screenings and associated promotional coverage and are exposed to very large audiences. Even within the current, fairly restrictive regulatory framework, broadcast sponsorship still has much to offer. As with advertising, of course, it is reaching potentially large audiences and creating product awareness. Further than that, however, it also has the potential to help enhance the product's image and message by association. Wink Bingo, for example, the online bingo and gaming brand, sponsored the second series of the raunchy ITV drama, *The Only Way Is Essex,* with a clear match of target audiences. To get the best out of broadcast sponsorship, however, it should be integrated into a wider package of marketing and promotional activities.

## The arts

Sponsorship money plays an important role in the funding of arts organisations. Such organisations derive only around 38 per cent of their income from their own earnings (e.g. ticket sales etc.), 47 per cent from public sources (for example, the Arts Council, local authorities and lottery funding, etc.), and 16 per cent from private investment, which includes business investment worth around £144 million per year (Mermiri and Tuchner, 2011). Over half of the money, however, went on projects in London, and over 70 per cent of it to major organisations, with an emphasis on museums, the visual arts and festivals. Companies in the financial sector and in the creative industries are the biggest donors.

To arts organisations, at a time of declining state funding, private sponsorship has become critical for survival. All over Europe, arts subsidies from government have been cut. In the UK, government subsidies for the arts are being cut by £100 million over a four-year period (Cooper, 2011), and arts organisations will have to look elsewhere to replace that funding. Theatres, opera houses, orchestras and galleries are not, however, able to sit back and wait for the sponsorship income to roll in. They have to be proactive and approach potential sponsors and donors for money, at a time when corporate donors themselves are facing economic hardship and cutting back on their philanthropic activities, or at least looking for a sound commercial payoff from it.

The important consideration for marketers in deciding whether to sponsor these events is understanding the link between the product and the music. To gain maximum value, it is necessary to ensure that the event features in all aspects of the communications mix, including packaging, advertising and sales promotion. This means exploiting the association before, during and after the music event.

*eg*

BP is one the the UK's most generous patrons of the arts, including sponsorship deals with the British Museum, Tate Galleries, the Royal Opera House, the National Portrait Gallery and other organisations thought to be worth more than £1 million per year. It can be a two-edged sword, however. While BP was winning acclaim by demonstrating its commitment across a broad arts portfolio, the oil spillage in the Gulf of Mexico was simultaneously attracting negative criticism and the attention of protestors. Protest groups themselves have become very adept in the art of PR and attention grabbing. The 'Greenwash Guerillas', dressed in white overalls and surgical face masks distributed leaflets outside the National Portrait Gallery during the BP Portrait Award ceremony, while the 'Don't Panic Collective' gatecrashed a related event and handed out wine glasses filled with thick black liquid to symbolise the oil spill. Then there was 'Liberate Tate', which, in a similar symbolic move, released dozens of black balloons with dead fish attached to them in the main hall of the Tate Modern.

Thus although BP had accepted responsibility for the disaster and was being pretty transparent in its response, it did not stop the protestors and the negative publicity. Groups such as 'Art Not Oil' even argued that to take BP's sponsorship money was as socially unacceptable as taking it from tobacco companies (Lawless, 2010). Greenpeace said, 'Organisations like the National Portrait Gallery help shape public attitudes towards the big issues of the day and if the gallery is serious about climate change then the sponsorship deal with BP has got to end' (as quoted by Vidal and Bowcott, 2010). The galleries and museums, however, collectively showed support for BP and said they would not re-examine the relationship, stating that, 'The income generated through corporate partnerships is vital to the mixed economy of successful arts organisations and enables each of us to deliver a rich and vibrant cultural programme' (as quoted by Vidal and Bowcott, 2010). But even a year later, the protests continued. The Tate Modern was again the venue for a protest by performance artist Reverend Billy and his Earthalujah gospel choir, who held a 'service' to exorcise the 'evil spirit' of BP from the Tate (Vidal, 2011).

With arts sponsorship there are a number of opportunities to present the sponsoring organisation, including on stage, in programmes, through associated merchandise including videos and CDs, around venues and even on tickets. There are also advantages in hosting key customers and suppliers at high-profile events, by offering the best seats and perhaps hosting a reception during the interval or after the show.

## MARKETING IN ACTION

### Let's party

Arts sponsorship isn't just about trying to reach an audience that is older, more affluent and more highly educated than the typical sports audience, through opera, ballet and fine-art exhibitions. A wider, if perhaps somewhat less discerning, younger audience can be reached through rock music and festivals.

There are many music festivals around the UK each year, over 650 (Warman, 2010). Some would say that's too many. At a time when fuel prices are rising and a lot of people are facing financial hardship, festival-goers are being more discerning about which events they go to, and are less willing to travel long distances to get to them. There is thus a lot of competition between the various festivals. It's also very difficult for the less well-established, smaller, or new festivals to succeed because there is a lot of up-front expense and investment required, such as securing the venue and facilities, obtaining the necessary licences, insurance, staffing and marketing, and additionally many artists require up-front payment (not to mention proof of an event's viability) before they will agree to perform. And all of this is paid out before a ticket has been sold, and with no guarantee of the weather (many festival-goers wait until the last minute to buy tickets, to be more certain of the likely weather). It's not surprising, therefore, that many festivals depend very heavily on sponsorship, and in a tough market environment, some have struggled to survive without it.

The Faenol Festival in Wales was founded in 2000 by the operatic bass-baritone Bryn Terfel and took place every year at the end of August. The 2010 festival was due to have Westlife as the headline act, and had a comedy night with Al Murray lined up. By the beginning of August, however, despite an appeal from Terfel in July to the people of Wales to buy their tickets early, and despite the offer of additional financial support from the Welsh Assembly, ticket sales had been so poor that it was decided to cancel the festival (Westlife, however, did do a gig in Llandudno instead, for which Faenol tickets were valid, you'll be pleased to hear). There was no festival in 2011, and at the time of writing it looked unlikely that the Faenol Festival would be revived in the near future. Faenol isn't the only casualty. In 2010, 34 festivals were cancelled, and up to August 2011, 31 had been wiped from that year's calendar.

Probably the biggest and best known British festival is Glastonbury. Tickets for the 2011 event sold out within two hours. It attracted over 170,000 visitors and featured a huge line-up of big names from a whole range of music genres, including Beyoncé, Paul Simon, Coldplay, U2, Tinie Tempah, Biffy Clyro, Wu-Tang Clan and many many others. The festival itself does not have an overarching sponsor but it does have commercial partners providing services at the event, for example, brewers are charged for the rights to put up beer pumps! Orange was the 'official communications partner' of the festival, and provided three Chill 'n' Charge tents on site. With a view to further establishing and capitalising on the profile of the Glastonbury brand, the 2011 festival had three media partners: the BBC, the *Guardian*, and *Q* magazine. The BBC's coverage, for example, was spread across a number of its television and radio channels, with the TV coverage reaching 18.6 million viewers in total, peaking with 2.6 million viewers for Beyoncé. The BBC was also able to sell highlights packages and coverage of headline performances across the world. The *Guardian*, as well as extensive coverage of the festival in its newspapers, also created a dedicated website which generated over 2 million page impressions over the weekend of the festival. Despite Glasto's success, there will be no 2012 event because of the London Olympics, and Michael Eavis the founder of Glasto, thinks that lack of demand, a crowded market, and even the rising costs of a university education could mean that even Glastonbury could only have three or four more viable festivals ahead of it.

The V Festival (Rihanna, Eminem, Arctic Monkeys, Jessie J, etc.), sponsored by Virgin Media, is also very popular. Not only does Virgin gain from exposure at the event, but it also gets extra coverage in specialist and national press as well as a Twitter feed. The sponsorship has been running for 16 years and enables Virgin to deliver on four criteria (as cited by www.bigfishevents.co.uk/virgin-media-v-festival):

- to reaffirm Virgin Media's position within music: the association means that Virgin is now closely attached to the V Festival, reinforcing the credibility of both the event and the Virgin Media brand;
- to communicate Virgin Media's services: a number of Virgin brands have featured in the sponsorship, Virgin Cola, Virgin Trains and Virgin Mobile have all had their turn, and since 2009, the headline sponsor has been Virgin Media. In 2010, the festival was used to highlight the benefits of Virgin Media's 50 meg broadband service by providing free 50 meg broadband access at the event and site-wide wi-fi access;
- to reward customers: Virgin Media customers who pre-registered were given exclusive access to 'The Hidden Garden' where they could chill out and enjoy posh loos, complimentary massages, and a bar with shorter queues than those found in the main areas, and customers can buy tickets to the festival before they go on open sale;
- to deliver profile and exposure throughout the year: the headline sponsorship benefits from the hype in the build-up to the announcement of the line-up and the sale of tickets, through the event itself and then the post-event reviews and analysis.

Overall, then, as with any form of sponsorship, success relies on a good match between the brand and the event in terms of target audience, and the ability of each to provide some sort of added-value to the other.

*Sources*: BBC (2010a, 2010b); Cable (2011); Cardew (2011); *ENP Newswire* (2011); Masson (2011a, 2011b); Michaels (2011); Tait and Bray (2010); Warman (2010); www.bigfishevents.co.uk.

## Cause-related marketing

Linkages between organisations and charities benefit both parties. If, for example, a company runs a sales promotion along the lines of 'We'll donate 10p to this charity for every pack you buy', the charity gains from the cash raised and from an increased public profile. Consumers feel that their purchase has greater significance than simple self-gratification and feel good about having 'given', while the company benefits from the increased sales generated by the promotion and from the extra goodwill created from associating its brands with a good cause. Murphy (1999) argued that companies are taking a longer-term view of cause-related marketing because of the positive image associated with a good and caring cause, and that still seems to be true now.

Archie is a powerful icon used to encourage people to raise money to provide goats for families living in poverty in developing countries. The idea is simple yet effective. 'Fighting Poverty, One Goat at a Time' was a joint campaign between Pizza Express and Oxfam that ran over the Christmas period. Customers in Oxfam shops were given a £5 discount voucher for Pizza Express, and Pizza Express donated a proportion of its sales revenue to Oxfam. Pizza Express customers who bought a main course were offered the opportunity to get another free of charge if they donated £1 to Oxfam. The proceeds of the campaign gave Oxfam the money to provide goats, which in turn provide milk and fertiliser for other crops to poorer communities. Balu in Nepal, for example, received nearly 100 goats so that the poorest farmers could help themselves in a sustainable way to make a long-lasting difference. The campaign also had extras such as wristbands and tee-shirts provided by Oxfam. The benefit to Pizza Express, apart from its contribution to Oxfam's work, was that 3 million customers were reached through the dedicated Oxfam/Pizza Express web-page, as well as 40,000 mailshots to businesses and an e-newsletter to 20,000 addresses that all reinforced the brand name and its association with a good cause. The partnership raised £285,000 for Oxfam and overall enabled the purchase of 11,400 goats (Cook, 2011; *Marketing*, 2011; www.oxfam.org.uk).

Not all cause-related marketing is linked with sales promotions, however. Many large organisations set up charitable foundations or donate cash directly to community or charitable causes. Others might pay for advertising space for charities, whether on television, radio, press or posters. This is important at a time when consumers are becoming more conscious of the ethical and 'corporate citizenship' records of the companies they patronise. Organisations clearly do not just take an altruistic view of their charity involvement, however. As with any other marketing activity, it should be planned with clear objectives and expected outcomes.

There are benefits in linking a brand to a good cause, especially if there is a direct synergy between values and aims, but if consumers feel it is just another means of gaining cash, it can backfire for both parties (Brennan, 2005). Cause-related marketing is now an established part of the marketing mix and when successful demonstrates brand values at a higher level than is possible in more traditional promotional marketing strategies. It is, therefore, important that care is taken before deciding the most appropriate charity, and lining up with a controversial social issue is often best avoided.

## Chapter summary

- Although personal selling can be an expensive and labour-intensive marketing communication activity, it has a number of advantages over other forms of communication. It makes an impact, because it involves face-to-face contact and is less likely to be ignored; it can deliver a precise and tailored message to a target customer who has already been checked out to ensure that they fit the right profile; and it helps in the cultivation of long-term buyer–seller relationships.

- The personal selling process can be a long and complicated marketing activity to implement. The process starts with the identification of prospective customers, and then the representative has to do as much background work on the prospect as possible in order to prepare an initial approach and a relevant sales presentation. Initial contact breaks the ice between buyer and seller, allowing an appointment to be made for the real selling to begin. The sales presentation will give the representative the opportunity to present the product in the best possible light, using a variety of samples and audio-visual aids, while allowing the customer to ask questions and to raise any objections they may have. Negotiating the fine details of the deal may lead naturally to closing the sale, and then all that remains is for the representative to ensure the customer's post-purchase satisfaction and work towards building a long-term relationship leading to repeat business and further purchases.

- Sales management is an important area of marketing, and involves a number of issues. Sales planning and strategy means making decisions about sales objectives, both for the organisation as a whole and for individual sales representatives or teams. Recruitment and training are also both important aspects of sales management. Apart from benefiting from training programmes, sales representatives have to be properly motivated and compensated for their efforts. A natural part of all this is performance evaluation. Sales managers need to ensure that representatives are achieving their targets and, if not, why not.

- Exhibitions and trade shows vary from small local events to major national or international shows. They bring together a wide range of key personnel in one place at one time, and can thus generate a great many potential sales leads cost effectively.

- Public relations is about the quality and nature of an organisation's relationships with various interested publics. Public relations performs an important supporting role, providing a platform of goodwill and credibility from which other marketing activities can develop and be enhanced. Public relations becomes particularly important in limiting the damage and repairing credibility when a crisis strikes an organisation. Publicity and press relations are important areas of PR. The media can be valuable in communicating messages to all kinds of publics and even in influencing opinion. There are, however, more controllable methods of PR. Advertising can be used to build corporate image and attitudes, and special events and publications can also target key publics.

- Sponsorship is used by many organisations as a means of generating PR and enhancing both their image and their other marketing communications activities. Sponsorship might mean involvement with sport, the arts, broadcast media or charities or other good causes. Both parties should gain. The sponsor benefits from the PR spin-offs from the activities and the public profile of the organisations and/or events it supports, while those receiving the sponsorship benefit from cash or benefits in kind. Sponsorship might be corporate or brand-specific, and the sponsor's involvement might be plainly obvious or quite discreet.

- CRM links PR, sponsorship and sales promotion activities with the aim of providing resources or publicity for charities and/or other non-profit organisations. This is important at a time when consumers are becoming more conscious of the ethical and 'corporate citizenship' records of the companies they patronise.

# Questions for review and discussion

**12.1** What are the stages in the personal selling process?

**12.2** Find 20 job advertisements for sales representatives and summarise the range of characteristics and skills sought. Which are the most commonly required and to what extent do you think that they are essential for a successful sales representative?

**12.3** What factors might contribute to successful exhibition attendance?

**12.4** What is PR and in what ways does it differ from other elements of the promotional mix?

**12.5** Find a corporate story that has made the news recently. It might be a 'crisis', a takeover battle, job losses or creation, new products or big contracts, for instance. Collect reports and press cuttings from a range of media on this story and compare the content. To what extent do you think that:

(a) the media have used material provided by the organisation itself?

(b) the story has developed beyond the control of the organisation?

(c) Imagine yourself to be the organisation's PR manager. Write a brief report to the managing director outlining what you feel to be the benefits and disadvantages of the coverage your organisation has received, and what you think should be done next regarding this story.

**12.6** Find out as much as you can about three different arts sponsorship projects. What role do you think the sponsorship plays in the sponsor's marketing strategy and what benefits do you think they derive from it?

# CASE STUDY 12

# TRUST: WINNING IT, EXPLOITING IT, LOSING IT

Misselling is a new word in the marketing lexicon popularised by some high-profile examples of the selling of financial services products. Misselling is a type of selling activity that is so focused on the needs of the seller that the best interests of the buyer are not considered. This has resulted in poor advice, dubious claims and downright lies at times in order to close the sale.

Misselling can be found in many situations, for instance, sales representatives persuading people to give up good occupational pension schemes to join inadequate private ones, selling endowment policies that were unlikely to cover the linked mortgage at maturity, selling overpriced insurance for loan repayments, and savings plans with hidden charges that

soon offset any gains. Sometimes it can be many years before the unwitting individual finds out that the financial product purchased does not live up to expectations. In an era of whistle blowing, regulation and media investigation, however, some cases of poor practice come to light sooner rather than later and can be dealt with. After the industry regulator became involved in the pensions misselling scandal, for example, it is thought to have cost companies £14 billion to pay the required compensation to the victims.

In some cases, the reason for misselling goes back to a basic rule of sales staff remuneration: the sales representative can make more money by selling than by not selling, i.e. the greater the sales, the greater the commission. For many years, field-sales staff in the financial-services sector were paid on a commission-only basis or were promised large bonuses for on-target performance. Now there are misselling accusations in other areas, especially for mobile phones and utilities contract sales with similar remuneration regimes. Phones 4U, the second largest independent mobile retailer, was found guilty by Ofcom of misselling in 2008. The retailer failed to provide refunds on faulty phones, made misleading sales promises about network coverage and phone plan details, made its check back offer difficult to redeem and had unfair terms in the returns policy. It also made cancellation terms vague. Phones 4U did, however, take action against sales staff who acted inappropriately (Minto, 2008).

More recently, the financial services industry has taken a big hit over the misselling of payment protection insurance (PPI). In April 2011, after the banks lost a court case against regulations that would make claims for misselling PPI easier, the floodgates opened on claims. Around 56,000 claims were made over the next three months, and that's only the start – it is estimated that about 16 million PPI policies were sold and millions of them are likely to have been missold, for example because the customer was never clearly told that they were signing up for this insurance when they took out a loan, or perhaps because the PPI included clauses that would have made it impossible for that customer ever to have made a claim on it. Compensation for PPI misselling is likely to cost the banking industry around £6 billion or more. Ironically, those who fell victim to PPI misselling are now also at risk of falling prey to aggressive claims-management companies that promise to manage your claim for you in return for a substantial fee which could be up to one-third of the compensation due to you. The Financial Ombudsman Service says, however, that making a PPI misselling claim is relatively simple, and particularly with the amount of support and advice available from consumer watchdogs such as *Which?*, there is no need to involve a claims management company. With unscrupulous claims-management companies cold-calling by phone, text and e-mail, however, it is easy to see why some worried consumers might give in to them. The Ministry of Justice closed down 350 such firms in 2010–11.

Staff selling utilities packages have also come under criticism. The *Sunday Times* reported how some energy sales staff lied to householders in order to close the sale (Swinford and Gardner, 2008). Npower called in all its 1,000 door-to-door sales staff for retraining, and suspended a team of 17 staff over the allegations. The journalists found that promises were made that money would be saved by switching to Npower when many consumers would actually be worse off. Tactics included exploiting people who spoke poor English, making customers sign forms without revealing they were contracts, and lying about standing charges. With the doorstep sales reps of some companies relying on commission for more than 50 per cent of their income, it's probably not surprising that they were prepared to push the boundaries somewhat.

In an attempt, perhaps, to regain a degree of control over the situation, some companies, such as British Gas and Southern Electric have ended (or at least suspended) their door-to-door, cold-calling sales efforts. British Gas has said 'Our customers have told us they don't like that knock on the door during East Enders, they have told us they think it is outdated' (as quoted by Lea, 2011). This is confirmed by *Which?* – it found that 93 per cent of householders wouldn't let an energy salesperson in, and one-third wouldn't even open the door. British Gas's face-to-face sales effort will now be focused on energy advisers located within supermarkets and contact through community groups, such as the Women's Institute.

For Southern Electric, ending doorstep sales means the loss of 900 jobs, but given that it had already been found guilty of deliberately misleading householders in 2008/9, and that along with EDF Energy, Npower and ScottishPower it is currently (2011) again under investigation for misselling by industry regulator Ofgem, it's probably the best course of action. The reputational damage that has been done to the utilities companies over the years by the misselling scandals (Ofgem has been trying to sort this issue out for over ten years) has, it could be argued, made them a soft target for politicians looking to gain public approval. Thus everything they do is subject to very public scrutiny, and the big energy companies are more unpopular than the banks! Although the energy companies are under pressure now to voluntarily offer compensation to the victims of misselling, by mid-2011 the emphasis is starting to shift from misselling to pricing strategies, and as one industry analyst said, 'Political pressure is increasing, and that's a function of the general fact that domestic consumers are stretched by inflation, a lack of pay increases, the recession and a series of energy bill increases' (as quoted by Blair, 2011c), and this is leading to the threat of legislative changes that would completely restructure the whole industry.

And the next likely focus for misselling claims? According to *Which?*, it could be packaged bank accounts. With a packaged bank account, the customer pays an annual fee of up to £500 and in return gets the bank account plus other products such as travel insurance. The number of complaints about these accounts is rising, as the banks are starting to push them quite hard. Consumers are starting to complain, however, that they are poor value for money in that the insurance policies within them are being sold at above-market rates and contain clauses that make them inappropriate.

All of this is confusing for the consumer and it is an even bigger challenge for the majority of honest sellers that remain. For example, the public now would rather believe friends, family and neutral advisers than banks and insurance companies. Those selling financial services or utilities packages now rank alongside other such 'popular' careers as estate agents, traffic wardens and used-car salespeople! However, it is often the motivation and compensation packages being offered that are the prime cause of the problem, human nature being what it is. In some cases, if sales targets are not achieved then a sacking may not be far behind, and thus the temptation to pressurise potential customers and to missell can be very real.

Although real attempts have been made to counter misselling, the damage has been done. While sales representatives must always give the best advice to customers if they want long-term business, the pressure to meet challenging targets in one-off sales situations means that *caveat emptor* must continue to be the watchword for consumers. And let's not forget that consumers can protect themselves from misselling by following simple advice provided by BT: ask for, check and keep a record of individual identification and company details; log any calls or visits you receive and make notes on conversations; never give out your bank details as a means of identification; ask questions, particularly about price and if in doubt, ask for information in writing; and remember that it's your decision – take as long as you need.

*Sources*: Atherton (2008); Blair (2011a, 2011b, 2011c); Bradshaw (2008); *Daily Mail* (2011); *ENP Newswire* (2009); Foggo and Newell (2008); Gammell (2011); Lea (2011); Minto (2008); *Money Marketing* (2011); Moore (2011); Parker (2008); Simon (2011); Swinford and Gardner (2008); Webb (2011).

## Questions

1 What factors led to accusations of misselling in the financial services and energy industries?

2 What could the various companies involved have done to avoid this situation?

3 The boss of Npower said, 'I'm sick and tired of the energy industry transforming itself into a faceless machine. I've had enough . . . The easiest thing to do is to keep your mouth shut and your head down. I would rather die trying than not try at all . . . The industry has not done enough in the past to position ourselves in the right kind of context. We have allowed ourselves to become a machine, which gets shouted at every time we make a profit' (as quoted by Webb, 2011).

(a) To what extent do you think his view is justified?

(b) Thinking about PR, define an energy company's publics and consider what that company should do to improve its relationships with those publics.

## References for chapter 12

Ainsworth, J. (2009) *Bad Publicity – Your Examples Please*, 1 June, accessed via www.marketingdonut.co.uk/node/1688.

Alexander Proudfoot (2011) *Sales Effectiveness: An International Study of Sales Force Performance*, report published by Alexander Proudfoot, accessed via www.alexanderproudfoot.com/uploadedFiles/Pages/Case_Studies/Content/Sales%20Effectiveness%20Productivity%20Report%20Brochure.pdf.

Atherton, M. (2008) 'Customers Blow a Gasket over Billing Flaw', *The Times*, 24 May.

Bailey, J. N. (1991) 'Employee Publications' in P. Lesly (ed.), *The Handbook of Public Relations and Communication* (4th edn), McGraw-Hill.

Baker, N. (2007) 'Death of a Salesman', *Director*, January.

Barnes, R. (2011) 'Sky Sports', *Marketing*, 9 February.

Bashford, S. (2011) 'Brands Go Back to the Shop Floor', *Marketing*, 8 June.

Bawden, T. (2011) 'Network Rail Pays High Price for Copper Theft', *The Guardian*, 7 June.

BBC (2010a) 'Faenol Festival Near Bangor Off After Low Ticket Sales', *BBC News*, 5 August, accessed via www.bbc.co.uk/news/uk-wales-north-west-wales-10872370.

BBC (2010b) 'Bryn Terfel Rules Out Faenol Plan for Time Being', *BBC News*, 21 October, accessed via www.bbc.co.uk/news/uk-wales-north-west-wales-11595518.

Benjamin, K. (2011) 'The World at Their Feet', *Marketing*, 10 August.

Blair, D. (2011a) 'MPs Turn on Utilities Over Misselling', *Financial Times*, 12 May.

Blair, D. (2011b) 'MPs Call on Utilities to End 'Del Boy' Tactics', *Financial Times*, 25 July.

Blair, D. (2011c) 'Political Climate Turns Against "Big Six" Utilities', *Financial Times*, 18 August.

Bradshaw, T. (2008) 'Phones 4U Faces Ofcom Misselling Investigation', *Financial Times*, 15 May.

Brennan, J. (2005) 'Marketers Learn the Laws of Good Cause and Effect', *Sunday Times*, 3 April, p. 10.

Brown, A. (2008) 'Ruthless Beds Company that preyed on Elderly Goes Bust', *Scottish Daily Record*, 25 February.

Burrows, D. (2011) 'PR: Why Blogs and Tweets Give PR Machine Bite', *Marketing Week*, 24 March.

Cable, S. (2011) 'So Glastonbury Fans are Getting Older . . .', *Daily Mail*, 24 June.

Cardew, B. (2011) 'Glastonbury: The Glasto Factor', *Music Week*, 9 July.

Charles, G. (2007) 'Flora Ends London Marathon Sponsorship', *Marketing*, 5 December.

Churchill, G., Ford, N., Walker, O., Johnston, M. and Tanner, J. (2000) *Sales Force Management* (6th edn), Richard D. Irwin Inc.

Colbin, K. (2011) 'Online Spin: No Such Thing As Bad Publicity? We'll See . . .', *MediaPost*, 22 April.

Cook, B. (2011) 'The Business Charity Awards 2011: Cause-related Marketing – PizzaExpress and Oxfam', *Third Sector*, 17 May.

Cooper, L. (2011) 'Human Face of Brands Receives an E-makeover', *Marketing Week*, 9 June.

Cravens, D. and LaForge, R. (1983) 'Salesforce Deployment Analysis', *Industrial Marketing Management*, July, pp. 179–92.

Cron, W., Dubinsky, A. and Michaels, R. (1988) 'The Influence of Career Stages on Components of Salesperson Motivation', *Journal of Marketing*, 52 (July), pp. 179–92.

Cutlip, S., Center, A. and Broom, G. (1985) *Effective Public Relations*, Prentice Hall.

*Daily Mail* (2011) 'Fury Over Missold Insurance', *Daily Mail*, 3 August.

EIU (2011) 'Bad Publicity: Better to be Reviled than Ignored', *EIU Executive Briefing*, 1 March.

Eleftheriou-Smith, L. (2010) 'Brylcreem Embarks on Ashes Marketing Drive', *Marketing*, 10 November.

*ENP Newswire* (2009) 'New Campaign Slams the Slammers', *ENP Newswire*, 29 September.

*ENP Newswire* (2011) 'Orange – Smartphones Headline Glastonbury in 2011', *ENP Newswire*, 4 July.

Fill, C. (2002) *Marketing Communications: Contexts, Strategies and Applications*, 3rd edn, Financial Times Prentice Hall.

*Financial Times* (2011) 'Abercrombie Hitch', *Financial Times*, 20 August.

Foggo, D. and Newell, C. (2008) 'Energy Firm Sacks Staff as Probe into Misselling Begins', *Sunday Times*, 27 April.

Gammell, K. (2011) 'If They Breach the Rules, They Will be Closed Down', *Daily Telegraph*, 6 August.

Good, D. and Stone, R. (1991) 'How Sales Quotas are Developed', *Industrial Marketing Management*, 20 (1), pp. 51–6.

Goodwin, D. (2011) 'The Edgy Label's Z-list Nightmare', *Sunday Times*, 21 August.

Green, J. and Cronin Fisk, M. (2010) 'Toyota Pedal Recall May Spur US to Require New Brake Systems', *Bloomberg BusinessWeek*, 4 February.

Greene, L. and Pacheco, F. (2011) 'Pretty, Posh and Profitable', *Financial Times*, 14 May.

Grimes, E. and Meenaghan, T. (1998) 'Focusing Commercial Sponsorship on the Internal Corporate Audience', *International Journal of Advertising*, 17 (1), pp. 51–74.

Hosea, M. (2010a) 'Brands Keep Their Finger on Impulsive Interaction', *Marketing Week*, 15 July.

Hosea, M. (2010b) 'Stick with Glue that Holds Diverse Industry Together', *Marketing Week*, 29 July.

*Hugin Press Release* (2011) 'Heineken International Renews UEFA Champions League Sponsorship', *Hugin Press Release*, 27 May.

Johanson, J. and Vahlne, J. (1977) 'The Internationalisation Process of the Firm: a Model of Knowledge Development and Increasing Foreign Market Commitment', *Journal of International Business Studies*, 8 (1), pp. 23–32.

Lambert, D., Marmorstein, H. and Sharma, A. (1990) 'Industrial Salespeople as a Source of Market Information', *Industrial Marketing Management*, 19, pp. 141–5.

Lawless, J. (2010) 'Environmentalists Protest Outside BP-sponsored Arts Award Ceremony in London', *The Canadian Press*, 22 June.

Lea, R. (2011) 'British Gas Closes Door on "Field Sales"', *The Times*, 12 August.

Legal and General (2010) *Digital Criminal Report 2010*, report published by Legal and General, accessed via www.legalandgeneral.com/_resources/pdfs/insurance/digital-criminal-2.pdf.

Margrave, L. (2011) *Summer Surrey Matters – Bargain Hunters Beware*, Surrey County Council, 7 July, accessed via www.surreycc.gov.uk/sccwebsite/sccwspages.nsf/LookupWebPagesByTITLE_RTF/Summer+Surrey+Matters+-+Bargain+hunters+beware? opendocument.

*Marketing* (2011) 'Marketing Society Awards for Excellence 2011: Cause-related Marketing', *Marketing*, 1 June.

*Marketing Week* (2009) 'Insurer Takes on England Cricket Team Sponsorship', *Marketing Week*, 30 July.

*Marketing Week* (2010) 'Virgin Money to Leverage Marathon Sponsorship', *Marketing Week*, 8 April.

*Marketing Week* (2011) 'Culture Club Courting Mass-market Brands', *Marketing Week*, 26 May.

Marston, J. (1979) *Modern Public Relations*, McGraw-Hill.

Masson, G. (2011a) 'It's Sink or Swim for Newbie Festivals', *Music Week*, 2 July.

Masson, G. (2011b) 'Record Numbers of UK Festivals Being Dissolved', *Music Week*, 6 August.

McCurry, J. (2010) 'Toyota to Fit Brake-override System in All Future Models', *Guardian Unlimited*, 18 February.

Meenaghan, T. (1998) 'Current Developments and Future Directions in Sponsorship', *International Journal of Advertising*, 17(1), pp. 3–28.

Mermiri, T. and Tuchner, J. (2011) *Private Investment in Culture 2009/2010*, report published by Arts & Business, accessed via http://artsandbusiness.org.uk/media%20library/Files/Research/pics-0910/artsandbusiness-PICS0910-3-1.pdf.

Michaels, S. (2011) 'Michael Eavis: "Glastonbury is on the Way Out"', *Guardian Unlimited*, 12 July.

Miller, R. and Heinman, S. (1991) *Successful Large Account Management*, Holt.

Mintel (2009) 'Mintel Broadcast Sponsorship', *Mintel Market Intelligence*, October, accessed via *store.mintel.com/broadcast-sponsorship-uk-october-2009.html*.

Minto, R. (2008) 'Phones 4U Guilty of Misselling', *Financial Times*, 10 November.

*Money Marketing* (2011) 'FSA's Cole Hammers Banks for Hard-sell Tactics', *Money Marketing*, 30 June.

Moore, E. (2011) 'Banks Sell Insurance "Like PPI"', *Financial Times*, 21 May.

Murphy, C. (1999) 'Brand Values Can Build on Charity Ties', *Marketing*, 25 March, p. 41.

OFT (2007) *Scottish Mobility Products Company Undertakes to Provide Higher Standards of Consumer Protection*, press release issued by the OFT, 19 November, accessed via http://www.oft.gov.uk/news-and-updates/press/2007/158-07.

OFT (2011) *Mobility Aids: An OFT Market Study Progress Update: Emerging Key Findings and Invitation to Contribute*, report published by the OFT, 26 May, accessed via http://www.oft.gov.uk/shared_oft/market-studies/mobilty-aids-findings.pdf.

O'Reilly, L. (2011) 'Heineken Extends UEFA Champions League Sponsorship', *Marketing Week*, 27 May.

Parker, A. (2008) 'Ofcom to Step Up Action on Mobiles' Misselling', *Financial Times*, 19 March.

Pedersen, C., Wright, M. and Weitz, B. (1986) *Selling: Principles and Methods*, Irwin.

*Post Magazine* (2011) 'National Cricket Day Bowls School Over', *Post Magazine*, 7 July.

Russell, F., Beach, F. and Buskirk, R. (1977) *Textbook of Salesmanship*, 10th edn. McGraw-Hill.

Shunk, C. (2011) *Toyota Sees Increased U.S. Market Share in 2011*, 6 January, accessed via www.autoblog.com/2011/01/06/report-toyota-sees-increased-u-s-market-share-in-2011/

Simon, E. (2011) It's Time to Make Your PPI Claim as Banks Wave the White Flag', *Daily Telegraph*, 14 May.

Stanley, R. (1982) *Promotion: Advertising, Publicity, Personal Selling, Sales Promotion*, Prentice Hall.

Stone, N. (1991) *How to Manage Public Relations*, McGraw-Hill.

Sweeney, C. (2010) 'Avon's Little Sister is Calling', *New York Times*, 13 January.

Sweney, M. (2008) 'Virgin Succeeds Flora as Marathon Sponsor', *The Guardian*, 16 May.

Swinford, S. and Gardner, J. (2008) 'Lying Salespeople Reined in after Undercover Exposé', *Sunday Times*, 13 April.

Tait, S. and Bray, E. (2010) 'Festivals Begin to Feel the Pinch', *The Independent*, 23 July.

Turnbull, P. and Cunningham, M. (1981) *International Marketing and Purchasing: A Survey Among Marketing and Purchasing Executives in Five European Countries*, Macmillan.

Vidal, J. (2011) 'Reverend Billy Leads Exorcism of BP's "Evil Spirit" From Tate Modern', *Guardian Unlimited*, 20 July.

Vidal, J. and Bowcott, O. (2010) 'Galleries and Museums Face Summer of Protest Over BP Arts Sponsorship', *Guardian Unlimited*, 24 June.

Warman, J. (2010) 'How Music Festivals are Singing the Changes', *The Guardian*, 27 August.

Webb, T. (2011) 'I'm Sick of the Energy Industry Being Transformed into a Faceless Machine', *The Times*, 2 August.

Whoriskey, P. (2010) 'Toyota Did Not Install Brake Override Systems Despite Complaints', *Washington Post*, 29 January.

Wiggins, K. (2010) 'Virgin Site Nets Half as Many Pages as Rival JustGiving', *Third Sector*, 4 May.

Wilmshurst, J. (1993) *Below-the-line Promotion*, Butterworth-Heinemann.

Wilson, B. (2011) 'Why Ash isn't Just "Something to Live With"', *Daily Telegraph*, 26 May.

# CHAPTER 13

# Marketing strategy and planning

## LEARNING OBJECTIVES

This chapter will help you to:

- define marketing planning and the internal and external influences affecting it;
- understand the different types of plan found within organisations and the importance of formal planning processes;
- define the stages in the marketing planning process and their contribution to sound, integrated plans;
- outline alternative ways of structuring a marketing department and their advantages and disadvantages; and
- understand the need for evaluation and control of marketing plans and their implementation, and the ways in which this can be achieved.

## INTRODUCTION

**SO FAR, THIS BOOK** has looked at the practical aspects of marketing, from identifying consumer needs and wants through to designing and delivering a product package that aims to meet those needs and wants, and maintains customer loyalty despite the efforts of the competition. The tools that make up the marketing mix are, of course, critical for implementing the marketing concept, but so far, the focus on the marketing mix elements has largely been operational and oriented to the short term. Managers must, however, think of their operational marketing mixes in the context of wider, more strategic questions, such as:

- Which markets should we be in?
- What does our organisation have that will give it a competitive edge? (This need not necessarily come directly from marketing.)
- Do we have the resources, skills and assets within the organisation to enable planned objectives to be achieved?
- Where do we want to be in five or even 25 years' time?

- What will our competitors be doing in three or five years' time?
- Can we assume that our current modus operandi will be good enough for the future?

These concerns are strategic, not operational, in that they affect the whole organisation and provide a framework for subsequent operational decisions. The focus is on the future, aligning the whole organisation to new opportunities and challenges within the changing marketing environment, as discussed in Chapter 2. The questions suggested above seem deceptively simple, but finding answers to them is, in fact, a highly skilled and demanding task. The future welfare of the whole organisation depends on finding the 'right' answers.

*eg*

Moshi Monsters began life as an online game but has also gone offline to boost brand awareness and to expand merchandising opportunities. It has now become the biggest selling children's magazine in six months with around 150,000 copies sold in the UK. The online operation is still the core of the business, as it has 50 million online players in 150 countries. The brand is expected to earn $100 million from online subscriptions and toy, book and trading-card sales in 2011. In 2012, it is likely that there will be nearly 80 million members across 200 countries making it truly global in scale. It has become the world's fastest growing toy brand and is advertised on television in more than 20 countries, and yet it wasn't launched until 2007. The formula is simple: fun and entertainment for 7 to 14-year-olds. They can create their own pet monster which they can nurture, house and feed and send on adventures in which they can interact with other monsters and their owners. It is a form of social media for those who are just a bit too young for Facebook.

Moshi Monsters carries no advertising and can be accessed for free, although the really interesting stuff requires a subscription. So why go offline? The answer lies in the vision for the business. It regards itself as an entertainment brand that creates a social network opportunity that starts with the online game and extends into the magazine. Magazines engage with children in a different way and over different time-scales from the internet, and might also be better for promoting related merchandise. This merchandise is important for 'lifting' the brand from the two-dimensional screen or page into the child's real world. As the CEO of Mind Candy, the owner of the Moshi Monsters brand, said, 'Moshimonsters.com is the heartbeat of the brand, but we're looking forward to developing many new physical products that connect back to the virtual world and enhance the experience for our players' (as quoted by *License! Global Weekly E-news*, 2010).

Moshi Monsters has become the world's fastest growing toy brand

*Source*: Rex Features/Alex Lentati/Evening Standard

Strategic partners have been selected to develop the physical merchandise, and thus Moshi Monsters has teamed up with Vivid Imaginations for character merchandising under licence; Scholastic (for books in the USA); Penguin (for books in the rest of the world); and Topps (for global trading cards) to exploit the opportunity further. So Mind Candy can see a synergistic relationship between online and offline activity. Not only does the offline activity fit with the style and content of the online brand, but also enables mutual support between the channels. If online activity is dropping off for any reason, the offline content can pull players back to the website. The offline content includes keys which unlock further online content and that is a guaranteed way of keeping a child's interest, thus there is a clear incentive for the child to engage with both media.

Further strategic expansion is possible, as both the game and the magazine are currently only available in English which leaves the opportunity open for expansion into China, Japan, South America and Russia to enable Moshi to become a truly monster global brand. But that's another story (Barnett, 2011b; Bradshaw, 2011; Hall, 2011; *License! Global Weekly E-news*, 2010; *M2 Presswire*, 2010; *New Media Age*, 2011).

This chapter first introduces strategic marketing issues by defining some of the commonly used terms and showing how they fit together. It examines some of the issues associated with designing a planning system for marketing and how it fits into the organisational planning process. Then, the various stages of the marketing planning process are discussed in detail. Although the implementation of the planning process may vary from situation to situation, the outline given here at least demonstrates the interrelated nature of many planning decisions.

The chapter then moves on to examine other managerial issues associated with managing marketing. Making sure that the organisational structure of the marketing function is appropriate, for example, is essential to the achievement of the tasks specified in the plans. Issues of marketing control and analysis are also considered because without adequate and timely control systems, even the best laid plans may be blown off course without managers realising the seriousness of the situation until it is too late to do anything about it.

## The role and importance of marketing planning and strategy

Planning can be defined as a systematic process of forecasting the future business environment, and then deciding on the most appropriate goals, objectives and positions for best exploiting that environment. All organisations need to plan, otherwise both strategic and operational activities would at best be uncoordinated, badly focused and poorly executed. At worst, the organisation would muddle through from crisis to crisis with little sense of purpose, until eventually competition would gain such an advantage and demand reach such a low level that continuation would just not be viable. The marketing plan provides a clear and unambiguous statement concerning which strategies and actions will be implemented, by whom, when and with what outcomes.

Marketing strategy cannot be formulated in isolation. It has to reflect the objectives of the organisation and be compatible with the strategies pursued elsewhere in the organisation. This means that marketers must refer back to corporate goals and objectives before formulating their own strategy, to ensure consistency, coherence and relevance. The two-way process between marketing and corporate strategy is shown in Figure 13.1.

To help to clarify the two-way interaction, the rest of this section is divided into two. First, we provide an overview of some of the different, and often overlapping, internal strategic perspectives, both corporate and marketing specific, that marketers have to consider in their strategic thinking. We then examine some of the broader factors that affect the formulation of marketing strategy in practice.

**Figure 13.1**

The two-way interaction between marketing and corporate strategy

## Definitions

This subsection outlines some of the strategic perspectives of the organisation, starting with the broad picture required by corporate strategy, then gradually focusing down towards the very specific detail of marketing programmes.

### Corporate strategy

Corporate strategy concerns the allocation of resources within the organisation to achieve the business direction and scope specified within corporate objectives. Although the marketing department is primarily responsible for responding to perceived marketing opportunities and favourable competitive environments, it cannot act without the involvement of all other areas of the organisation too. Corporate strategy, therefore, helps to control and coordinate the different areas of the organisation – finance, marketing, production, R&D, etc. – to ensure that they are all working towards the same objectives, and that those objectives are consistent with the desired direction of the business as a whole. Typical issues of concern to corporate planners might thus be market expansion, product development priorities, acquisition, divestment, diversification and maintaining a competitive edge.

To help to make the corporate planning process more manageable, larger organisations often divide their activities into strategic business units (SBUs). An SBU is a part of the organisation that has become sufficiently significant to allow it to develop its own strategies and plans, although still within the context of the overall corporate picture. SBUs can be based on products, markets or operating divisions that are profit centres in their own right.

# MARKETING IN ACTION

## A sound strategy

Linn Products is a Scottish manufacturer of high-quality hi-fi equipment that targets the high-performance, top end of the European market. It made its mark with its first product in 1972, the Linn Sondek LP12, a transcription turntable that became the benchmark against which all the others were judged. The company applied the same standards and positioning to Linn speakers and the first solid state pitch accurate amplifiers. It became a world leader in sound technology, innovative design and precision engineering. However, profitability was declining in 2006 due to a combination of poor exchange rates and rising costs. It thus decided to innovate further and to renew itself strategically from being a manufacturer of CD players, tuners and amplifiers, etc. Linn ceased offering CD players in 2009 and instead concentrated on digital-streaming download equipment. This was something of a leap of faith, as over 90 per cent of users still played music on CDs. Now, however, digital-streaming players account for over 30 per cent of Linn's sales.

Multiroom systems and digital streaming are at the heart of the business and Linn is well placed at the head of the technological curve. It operates a policy of continuous improvement to ensure that it stays at the cutting edge of its niche. In 2010, it spent £1.53 million of its £17 million turnover on R&D. Linn's mission is 'to thrill customers who want the most out of life from music, information and entertainment systems that benefit from quality sound by working together to supply them what they want when they want it'. Systems find their way into the homes of the rich and famous including Hollywood film stars. Each product has the signature of the product builder. One product builder is responsible for the assembly, testing and packaging of an item. An old-fashioned attention to detail does not mean old-fashioned inefficient production processes, however, as Linn has a highly automated manufacturing plant and uses only the best components. Within that, 'real-time' manufacturing is practised, meaning that each day's production is made to order for specific customers. The product designers too are close to the customer and are committed to continuous improvement. Such is the commitment to quality that because of problems sourcing the best components for the multi-award winning Sondek CD12 CD player, Linn announced its premature withdrawal rather than compromise on its performance specification.

Linn's customer care philosophy extends from the manufacturing process through to the distribution channel. The company is selective about appointing dealers because it sees the key to selling its products as the expertise and product demonstration offered by the retailer. Linn is looking for those retailers who are the best in their area and have a quality reputation that fits with Linn's own. It is international in its reach with the USA, Germany and Japan as important markets, and Asia as the focus of attention for growth. Asia currently accounts for 15 per cent of sales. But whether Linn is selling in Houston or

Linn speakers are quality products sold to customers by knowledgeable retailers with time to discuss individual needs

*Source:* © Linn Products Limited, www.linn.co.uk

▶ Singapore, the criteria for retailers are the same: it wants retailers who want to sell quality products and are prepared to spend time with customers demonstrating and installing them. Retailers should be able to:

- work with customers to discover what kind of musical expectations and sound needs they have;
- appreciate the cost–value relationship inherent in Linn systems, if necessary comparing them with the competition;
- show customers how best to use and accommodate equipment; and
- help customers consider system expandability.

Linn is very reluctant to supply retailers who are not trained or are unable or unwilling to stock the range for demonstration purposes. Selling a multiroom system and digital streaming equipment implies a high degree of user knowledge and experience. Although entry prices may be as low as £3,000, a typical digital streaming system can cost £50,000 for a complete system. Some systems can run to £1 million. These systems don't just stream from the internet but also allow conventional CDs to be played. To reinforce that, Linn even has its own record label, focused on top quality music downloads.

Linn Products operates in a highly competitive market, occupying a niche for high quality products. Despite the challenges it faces, Linn is an excellent example of how the corporate vision and values can be translated into a competitive marketing strategy. While the technology and the products have evolved, the fundamental strategic focus has not changed. Linn is still providing 'exceptional music entertainment performance to discriminating customers' and that aim will continue to drive the innovation and the competitive strategy for the years ahead.

*Sources*: Bolger (2010); Rogerson (2005); Smith (2010); Vass (2010); www.linn.co.uk.

## Competitive strategy

Competitive strategy determines how an organisation chooses to compete within a market, with particular regard to the relative positioning of competitors. Unless an organisation can create and maintain a competitive advantage, it is unlikely to achieve a strong market position. In any market, there tend to be those who dominate or lead, followed by a number of progressively smaller players, some of whom might be close enough to mount a serious challenge. Others, however, are content to follow or niche themselves (i.e. dominate a small, specialist corner of the market).

## Marketing strategy

The marketing strategy defines target markets, what direction needs to be taken and what needs to be done in broad terms to create a defensible competitive position compatible with overall corporate strategy within those markets. Marketing mix programmes can then be designed to best match organisational capabilities with target market opportunities.

## Marketing plan

It is in the marketing plan that the operational detail, turning strategies into implementable actions, is developed. The marketing plan is a detailed, written statement specifying target markets, marketing programmes, responsibilities, time scales and resources to be used, within defined budgets. Most marketing plans are annual, but their number and focus will vary with the type of organisation. The plan might be geographically based, product based, business unit based, or oriented towards specific segments. An overall corporate marketing plan in a large organisation might, therefore, bring together and integrate a number of plans specific to individual SBUs. Planning at SBU level and then consolidating all the plans ensures that the corporate picture has enough detail, and allows overall implementation and control to be managed.

## Marketing programmes

Marketing programmes are actions, often of a tactical nature, involving the use of the marketing mix variables to gain an advantage within the target market. These programmes are normally detailed in the annual marketing plan, and are the means of implementing the chosen marketing strategy. Programmes provide clear guidelines, schedules and budgets for the range of actions proposed for achieving the overall objectives. These are determined within the framework of the overall marketing plan to ensure that activities are properly integrated and that appropriate resources are allocated to them.

# Influences on planning and strategy

These are various influences on an organisation's marketing strategy, each of which is now discussed in turn.

## Organisational objectives and resources

Marketing strategists need to be guided by what the organisation as a whole is striving for – what its objectives are and what resources it has to implement them. Some organisations might have very ambitious growth plans, while others might be content with fairly steady growth or even no growth at all, that is, consolidation. Clearly, each of these alternatives implies different approaches to marketing.

Resources are not only financial. They also include skills and expertise, in other words, any area of the organisation that can help to add value and give a competitive edge. The exploitation, through marketing, of things that the organisation does well, such as manufacturing, technical innovation, product development or customer service, might help to create non-financial assets such as reputation and image, which are difficult for competitors to copy.

The Swiss company, Holcim, is one of the world's largest suppliers of cement, aggregates and concrete with sales of CHF21 billion in 2010. For any company of this nature to survive, there have to be economies of scale in production, consistent supplies of raw material and low transport costs. Consequently, Holcim has established three fundamental strategic principles to guide its competitive position: cost leadership in its many overseas markets, market leadership to achieve volume sales, and strong vision and firm control over central strategy while still allowing local autonomy.

When operating margins are down to around 25 per cent and price competition for a relatively undifferentiated product is severe, a focus on efficiency and keeping costs down is essential for survival. To achieve cost leadership, Holcim invests heavily in technology to reduce unit costs and often locates plants either near to raw materials or near to customers. Cement is manufactured through large-scale production facilities and their upgrade is essential for sustaining competitiveness, so capital expenditure is high as Holcim strives to maintain that efficiency. Through a process of acquisition and new plant openings, it now has interests in cement plants in 70 countries, giving the company over 150 cement and grinding plants and over 1,450 ready-mix concrete plants, many of which operate under different names. Wherever Holcim decides to expand, largely driven by construction opportunities because of demographic development or infrastructure renewal, the formula is the same: large volumes, efficient operations and local service.

The strategic risk is spread by its involvement in many different markets, each at different stages of growth, decline and maturity, and this allows it to concentrate on its core business, to the point of divesting more marginal activities.

The priorities are different depending on the state of the market. In emerging markets the focus is on building up and expanding cement production. In maturing economies, vertical integration is important as Holcim aims to establish ready-mix concrete facilites in major urban facilities. Finally, in developed markets, the product range is diversified to include aggregates and the key to success is securing access to high-grade raw-material reserves. This categorisation guides investment and acquisition decisions. Holcim is geographically diverse, with 33 per cent of its sales coming from Europe and nearly 30 per cent from the Asia-Pacific region. It is not, however, quite so strong in North America which generates just 16 per cent of its sales.

Although Europe is still its strongest market, it is also one of the toughest as Holcim vies with France's Lafarge for leadership. It is in emerging markets that the most severe competition is experienced, however. Asia and Latin America are especially important for future growth. Holcim has a mix of strategic decisions. The local management can decide on market development, cost efficiencies and nurturing community relations, but the major decisions about which markets to develop and the corporate portfolio are made at HQ to enable global leadership (www.holcim.com).

As the case of Holcim shows, marketing strategies do need to be compatible with corporate objectives and to capitalise on available resources.

## Attitude to change and risk

The corporate view on change and risk often depends on the approach of top management. Risk tolerance varies widely from individual to individual, and from management team to management team. Managers will also, of course, be guided by the nature of the organisation and their interpretation of its business environment. The managing director of a small business may not want to take on high risk projects, feeling that the firm's size makes it more vulnerable to failure through its lack of resources. A larger firm might be able to absorb any losses, and therefore feel that the risk is worth taking.

The biotechnology industry is a good example of the difficulties of managing risk and innovation in scientific fields. It was British scientists working in British universities who provided the intellectual foundation of the industry, but it has been US groups, such as Amgen and Genentech, that have been at the forefront of innovation and commercialisation rather than invention. The academic culture in many British science universities favours spin-offs from the laboratory, but it is then that the strategic problems start.

The biotechnology sector in the UK has no shortage of innovative ideas, indeed, there has been a steady stream of technological breakthroughs, many coming from smaller companies. Being a smaller organisation can help to create a culture that encourages flexibility and inventiveness as long as there is sufficient capital to see it through the leaner start-up period. Venture capitalists do absorb some of the early risk on the promise of future returns but that source of funds has become more difficult in recent years and many firms have gone into liquidation such as Cambridge BioStability, York Pharma, Alizyme and Intercytex after running out of cash. Then there is always the risk of product failure late in clinical trials, for example Renovo's scar-reduction medicine, Juvista. There are about 345 biotech firms in the UK at present but most have to survive hand-to-mouth until product sales take off, unless they have a basket of products at different stages of development, but many don't have that luxury.

Even if a company survives the early years, all too often in the UK, as soon as the product looks promising it is the large, well-financed organisations such as Amgen that move in to acquire the smaller companies, as happened with AstraZeneca's purchase of CAT in 2006. This was also the case when Celltech, one of the UK's greatest hopes for market leadership to rival the Americans, was bought out by a US company, as it lacked the ability to build a sustainable long-term biotechnology business that could compete globally. Now China and India are also attracting investment to commercialise products developed by British R&D.

A critical factor in the life of a biotechnology company is its ability to manage risk. The early period of development is concerned with the risk of sustaining the business at a time when the product has not been launched. Then there are risks associated with commercialisation, especially in a global industry, as not only does it drain resources further, but given the lead time for new product development, it often means that funds need to be diverted to the next generation of products. That is often too much for under-resourced smaller organisations when the shareholders may be prepared to take a risk, but institutional investors prefer to give in to the temptation of an early return when a buy-out offer comes along.

BTG is one of the best known British companies to have survived to become an international healthcare specialist with acquisition of Biocompatibles and Protherics, and partnership arrangements with other companies to develop and market a more balanced portfolio of products in different stages of development. The returns are great for products that have been successfully launched. For some firms, strategic alliances rather than acquisitions are preferable, so that the risk on projects can be shared, especially where there is a large upfront investment needed. InhibOx, the Oxford and Princeton computer-aided, drug-discovery company (CADD), survived the early years and has built a strong reputation. It is in a complex market and has entered into partnership with a number of organisations, such as CCDC, Intelligensys and COSMIC Discoveries of Hyderabad so that it can deliver cutting-edge computational drug discovery and development.

In an industry characterised by high risks, long-term projects and sometimes spectacular failures, it is not surprising that an appetite for risk is an important prerequisite for any strategic marketing plan. It's all about trading the risks of product development and the costs against the rewards of a successful and sustainable market entry. It sounds easy enough, but for many smaller biotechnology companies it is even easier to cooperate when the giants show an interest in acquisition.

Often, the large pharmaceutical companies could learn from the enterprise and drive of the smaller biotech companies, while the smaller companies could learn from the expertise of the big manufacturers in achieving success in getting ideas to the marketplace. Many of these larger organisations actively seek out smaller biotechnology companies for purchase. All this suggests a 'feeding chain' in which universities invent, smaller firms launch, larger biotech firms commercialise, and then larger pharmaceutical firms capitalise through alliances and mergers. At each stage, however, the culture must be ambitious and risk-accepting if success is to be achieved (Aldridge, 2011; www.biocompatibles.com/; www.inhibox.com/).

## Competitor strategies

The competitive structure in different product markets will vary to create conditions of strong or weak competition. In markets such as computer chips, the dominant competitor has a major influence over the level and nature of competition. Challenges can still arise, but nevertheless, within constraints set by governmental competition policy and public pressure, a dominant competitor is effectively able to decide when and how to compete. The dominant competitor is likely to be confident that it has sufficient strength through its market position, its volume sales, and thus perhaps its cost base to fight any serious challenger successfully.

Mothercare (www.mothercare.com) is a retailer of specialist accessories and clothing for babies and children up to eight years old, with 945 stores in the UK and internationally generating a turnover of £794 million in 2010. In the UK, it is claimed that over 90 per cent of pregnant women visit one of its stores in the UK before giving birth. From its launch in 1961, Mothercare has worked hard to establish a reputation for quality, own-label brands, an attractive retail environment and a comprehensive range including maternity wear. Since 1984, export sales have been developed through direct retail outlets and franchises, resulting in operations in over 56 countries including 70 stores in Russia. It also has franchises in Columbia, Chile, Morocco and Iraq and has joint ventures in China and India.

Despite its strong market presence, in recent years its UK performance has not lived up to expectations and market share has been lost. Globally the brand is stronger than it is domestically. Particular difficulties have been experienced in the 4–8-year-old age group because children are developing fashion consciousness from an earlier age, but even apart from that, Mothercare has been under attack in all segments. Pregnancy is no longer an excuse for the removal of fashion clothing from the wardrobe, and Mothercare has had some difficulty in providing an acceptable variety of fashionable maternity clothing compared with more fashion-oriented stores. The trendier end of the children's clothing market has been driven by the likes of Baby Gap and Jigsaw Junior, Boots has moved aggressively into the babywear, while the value end of the market has been hit hard by Asda, Tesco and H&M.

Then there is the shift away from bricks and mortar towards online shopping (see p. 319). Mothercare has responded to this, and now its transactional website provides 20 per cent of its UK sales and Gurgle.com is the new social networking arm of Mothercare.

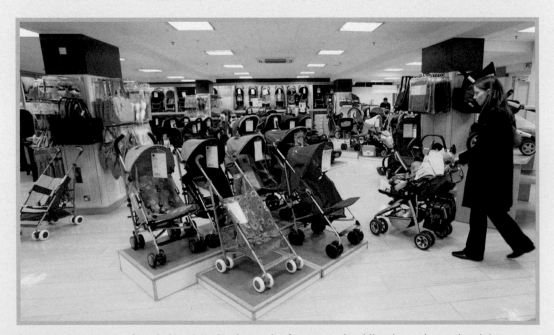

Since Mothercare was founded in 1961, the demands of mums and toddlers have changed and the competitive landscape has evolved accordingly

*Source*: Getty Images/Bloomberg

To reflect the shift in buying patterns to online and out of town shopping, over 110 stores of its 300 stores in the UK will have been closed by the end of 2013. Mothercare had also acquired the Early Learning Centre (ELC) in 2007 and this is still being absorbed. There is still work to do in ELC's store rationalisation, new formats and digital capability. The challenge, therefore, is for Mothercare to plot its future corporate and marketing strategy. Should it concentrate on pregnancy and babies and toddlers, where margins tend to be higher and there is still a strong awareness and market penetration, and move away from the 4–8-year-old segment? Mothercare is still a respected and valued brand, but some of its clothes have failed to make an impact in a society where children have become a fashion statement. The aim is still to make the Mothercare group the world's leading specialist retailer of parenting and children's products (Barrett, 2011; Lee, 2010; Wearden, 2011; www.mothercareplc.com).

## Types of plan

It is important to distinguish between *plans*, the outcomes of the planning process, and *planning*, the process from which plans are derived. While the process of planning is fairly standard and can be transferred across functions and organisations, there are often wide variations in the actual use of plans to guide strategy and operations. This is partly because there are several different types of plan that can emerge from a planning process. Plans may be differentiated in terms of a number of features. These are as follows.

### Organisational level

Managers are involved with planning at all levels of an organisation. The concerns of managers, however, change at higher levels of the organisation, and the complexities affecting planning also change. The more senior the manager, the more long-term and strategic becomes the focus. At the highest level, the concern is for the whole organisation and how to allocate resources across its various functions or units. At lower levels, the focus is on implementation within a shorter-term horizon, and on operating within clearly specified parameters. The marketing director may thus have a particular concern with developing new innovative products and opening new segments, while the sales representative may have to focus on sales territory planning to achieve predetermined sales and call objectives.

### Timescale

Plans may be short-, medium- or long-term in focus. *Short-term* normally means the shortest period of time appropriate to the operations of the organisation. Normally this is one year, or in some industries, such as fashion, one season. *Medium-term plans* are more likely to cover a one- to three-year period. The focus is not so much on day-to-day operations and detailed tactical achievement as on renewal. This could include the opening up of a new market, a new product innovation, or a strategic alliance to improve market position, for example. *Long-term* plans can be anything from three to 20 years, with the timescale often dictated by capital investment periods. Long-term plans are nearly always strategic in focus and concerned with resource allocation and return.

### Regularity

Most longer-term plans have annual reviews to monitor progress. Shorter-term plans are often part of a hierarchy linking strategy with operations. Some plans, however, are not produced regularly as part of an annual cycle, but are campaign-, project- or situation-specific. A *campaign plan*, for example for a specific advertising campaign, might have a limited duration to achieve defined objectives. *Project plans* are specific to particular activities, perhaps a new product launch, a change in distribution channels, or a new packaging innovation. These activities are of fixed duration and are not necessarily repeated.

## Focus

Plans will vary in their focus across the organisation. *Corporate plans* refer to the longer-term plans of the organisation, specifying the type of business scope desired and the strategies for achieving it across all areas of the business. The focus is on the technology, products, markets and resources that define the framework within which the individual parts of the organisation can develop more detailed strategies and plans. *Functional or operational plans*, therefore, are developed within the context of the organisational corporate plan but focus on the implementation of day-to-day or annual activities within the various parts of the organisation.

## Organisational focus

Plans will vary according to the nature of the organisation itself. A number of alternative ways of organising marketing are considered later (see p. 541 *et seq.*). If the organisational focus is on products, then plans will also take that focus, while if markets or functional areas are emphasised, plans will reflect that structure. For example, a functional organisational marketing plan will have distinct elements of pricing, advertising, distribution, etc. If SBUs are formed, then there is immediately a requirement for a two-tier planning structure: (a) considering the portfolio of SBUs at a corporate level, and (b) for each SBU, looking at the more detailed organisational design. Similarly divisional, regional, branch or company plans may all be used in different circumstances.

There are several benefits to be gained from taking a more organised approach to planning marketing activity. In summary, the benefits can be classified as relating to the development, coordination or control of marketing activity, as shown in Figure 13.2.

Despite the obvious benefits, we cannot assume that all organisations practise planning, and even those that do might not achieve all the results they expect. Planning in itself does not guarantee success. Much depends on the quality of the planning, its acceptance as a fundamental

**Figure 13.2**
Benefits of
planning

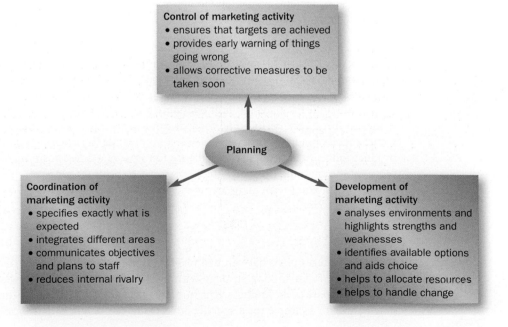

driving force within the organisation, and the perceived relevance of the resulting plans.

There is no room for a weak link in the chain, since the plans are only as good as the process that generated them, and the process is pointless if it does not result in acceptable, implementable plans.

## The marketing planning process

The purpose of marketing planning has been defined as:

> to find a systematic way of identifying a range of options, to choose one or more of them, then to schedule and cost out what has to be done to achieve the objectives.
> (McDonald, 1989, p. 13)

Although the structure of a marketing plan will vary according to the complexity and variability of the organisation, and the emphasis may vary according to the turbulence in the environment and the resultant challenges facing the organisation, a number of broad phases in the planning process are likely to operate in any case. The main stages in the planning process are shown in Figure 13.3 and each stage is considered in turn.

**Figure 13.3**
Stages in the planning process

 Heinz has many leading brands in its portfolio, such as Heinz Tomato Ketchup, Heinz Beans, Heinz Salad Cream, Heinz Cream of Tomato Soup and Heinz Spaghetti Hoops. The marketing plan seeks to identify the strategy and detail the actions that will be taken to keep each brand first or second in its marketplace. Heinz's top 15 global brands account for two-thirds of its global sales so they get the priority, although increasingly it's a category management approach that's taken. The idea is that by focusing on creating growth within the category, the marketer is more likely to concentrate on the customer, understanding their needs, and finding new ways to segment the market. Focusing only on market share tends to put more emphasis on the competition than the customer.

Creating growth in a category isn't that easy, even if you are the category leader. Consumers are being more careful in their spending, commodity costs are rising, and the grocery retailers are pressurising suppliers on price and deals. Currently, around 40 per cent of grocery sales are made on promotions such as BOGOFFs, and that can undermine category value. Heinz considers that the grocery sector is also changing with the hard discounters at one end and the likes of Waitrose at the premium end, stretching price ranges and opening up opportunities at both ends.

There are three main strategic thrusts in the plans for growth: renovation, innovation and consumption. This means defining new benefit, usage or 'occasions' segments, which might increase the spend of existing customers or attract new customers. This can be done through brand extensions, such as organic or low sugar/salt variants, or innovation in pack design, such as microwavable snap-pots or the fridge jar for beans, or promoting the use of Heinz products such as ketchup or soups as cooking ingredients. This is all about keeping the marketing offering relevant to the needs of consumers and works in conjunction with innovation in product and packaging development.

As well as the products, the marketing plans need to cover price points, trade discounts, price promotions and of course the promotional activity. Digital media now account for 20 per cent of the marketing budget including the use of Facebook and Twitter, but in Heinz's view, it is traditional media that create the strongest emotional connection with consumers and generate real brand preference, convincing consumers that indeed 'It has to be Heinz' (Alarcon, 2009; Barnett, 2011a; Humphries, 2010; *New Media Age*, 2010).

## Corporate objectives and values

Corporate objectives are at the heart of the planning process, since they describe the direction, priorities and relative position of the organisation in its market(s). Some objectives, such as market share (by value), sales, profit and ROI, are quantitative, while others, such as the philosophies reflected in mission and values statements, are more qualitative in nature.

Philosophical targets, often called vision and values statements, have grown in popularity in recent years as a more enduring and all-embracing perspective of where an organisation seeks to journey and how it intends to conduct itself on the way. McDonald's has the vision of providing the world's best quick-service restaurant experience, and to achieve that it seeks to provide a level of quality, good service, cleanliness and value that makes every customer in a restaurant smile. In contrast, Vivendi, the entertainment company, has the vision of being the world's preferred creator and provider of entertainment, education and personalised service to consumers anywhere, at any time and across all distribution platforms.

Qualitative targets also include items such as service levels, innovation and scope. Increasingly, corporate social responsibility objectives are being incorporated into both quantitative and qualitative objectives. This can be seen in the Marks & Spencer case study at the end of the chapter. Over 170 environmental and social targets are specified in its Plan A, and progress towards their achievement can be measured for all of them. The link between business strategy and social and environmental issues, however, remains tenuous in many organisations. It is now the fashionable thing to say and detail CSR strategy in the company report but the link between CSR and business is still evolving.

Whether quantitative or qualitative, these objectives help to create guidelines for marketing plans, since the output of the corporate planning process acts as an input into the marketing planning process. All objectives must be realistic, achievable within a specific time scale, and cited in order of priority. This will lead to a hierarchy of interlinking objectives.

## The marketing audit

The marketing audit systematically takes stock of an organisation's marketing health, as the formal definition implies:

> [The audit] is the means by which a company can understand how it relates to the environment in which it operates. It is the means by which a company can identify its own strengths and weaknesses as they relate to external opportunities and threats. It is thus a way of helping management to select a position in that environment based on known factors. (McDonald, 1989, p. 21)

It is really the launching pad for the marketing plan, as it encourages management to reflect systematically on the environment and the organisation's ability to respond, given its actual and planned capabilities. The marketing audit is first and foremost about developing a shared, agreed and objective understanding of the organisation. Table 13.1 summarises the issues that a marketing audit should consider.

**Table 13.1** Marketing audit issues

- Macro environment: STEEPLE factors (see Chapter 2)
- Task environment: *competition, channels, customers* (see Chapters 3 and 4)
- Markets (see Chapter 13)
- Strategic issues: *segmentation, positioning, competitive advantage* (see Chapters 4 and 13)
- Marketing mix (see Chapters 6–12)
- Marketing organisational structure and organisation (see later in this chapter)

The audit should be undertaken as part of the planning cycle, usually on an annual basis, rather than as a desperate response to a problem. To help the audit process, it is critical to have a sound marketing information system covering the marketing environment, customers, competitors, etc., as well as detail on all areas of the internal organisational marketing effort. In order to complete an audit, managers thus have to look at both operational variables (i.e. an internal audit) and environmental variables (i.e. an external audit).

## Internal audit

The internal audit focuses on many of the decision areas discussed in Chapters 3–12 and their effectiveness in achieving their specified objectives. It is not just, however, a post-mortem on the 4Ps. Auditors will also be interested in how smoothly and synergistically the 4Ps fit together, and whether the marketing actions, organisation and allocated resources are appropriate to the environmental opportunities and constraints.

**Portfolio analysis.** In assessing the marketing health of the organisation, it is not enough to look simply at the performance of individual products. Although products may be managed as individual entities on an operational basis, strategically they should be viewed as a product portfolio, that is, a set of products, each of which makes a unique contribution to the corporate picture. The strategist needs to look at that corporate picture and decide whether, for example, there are enough strong products to support the weak ones, whether the weak ones have development potential or whether there are appropriate new products in development to take over from declining ones. The various portfolio models outlined below can be applied either to SBUs or to individual products, and thus the use of the word 'product' throughout the discussion should be taken to mean either.

**The BCG matrix.** Sometimes referred to as the Boston Box, or the BCG matrix, the Boston Consulting Group (BCG) market growth–relative market share model, shown in Figure 13.4, assesses products on two dimensions. The first dimension looks at the general level of growth in the product's market, while the second measures the product's market share relative to the largest competitor in the industry. This type of analysis provides a useful insight into the likely opportunities and problems associated with a particular product.

Market growth reflects opportunities and buoyancy in different markets. It also indicates the likely competitive atmosphere, because in high growth markets there is plenty of room for expansion and all players can make gains, while in low growth markets competition will be more intense, since growth can only be achieved by taking share away from the competition.

Market share position is measured on a logarithmic scale against the product's largest competitor. Thus a relative share figure of 0.2 means that the product achieves only 20 per cent of the market leader's sales volume, a potentially weak competitive position. Similarly, a share figure of 2 would mean that the product has twice the market share of its nearest rival. A share figure of 1 means roughly equal shares, and therefore joint leadership.

Figure 13.4(a) gives an example of the resultant matrix after all the products of an organisation have been thus analysed. The next stage is to plot the products within a simpler four-cell matrix that reflects the differing competitive positions, as shown in Figure 13.4(b). Each cell offers different types of business opportunities and imposes different resource demands. The general labelling of the cells as 'high' and 'low' gives an instant and sufficient feel for each product's situation, and the circle that represents each SBU's contribution to the organisation's total sales volume provides a further indication of the relative importance of different products. In Figure 13.4(b), for example, Product 2 can be seen to be the biggest contributor to overall sales volume, whereas Product 1 contributes very little. The 'ideal' model is one where the portfolio is reasonably balanced between existing strength and emerging opportunity. We now look in turn at each cell of the matrix.

*Dog (low share, low growth).* A dog holds a weak market share in a low growth market, and is likely to be making a loss, or a low profit at best. It is unlikely that its share can be increased at a reasonable cost, because of the low market growth. A dog can be a drain on management time and resources.

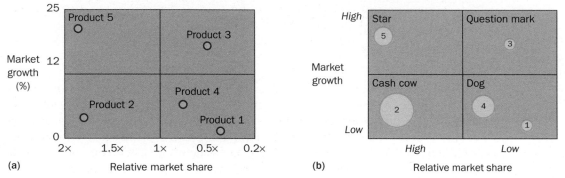

Plotting each product's position within the matrix

**Figure 13.4** The BCG matrix

Iced versions of hot drinks are a problem for brand owners. What sells in the rest of Europe, is a major challenge in the UK. Liptonice, a cold, fizzy, canned lemon tea, and other products like it have proved successful in continental Europe but not in the UK. What they had not taken into account was the nature of the British consumer's love affair with tea and the perception of it among younger consumers. In the British mind, tea should be drunk hot and milky – even drinking it hot and black with lemon is considered a bit risqué. The ritual of making tea 'properly' is also deeply culturally ingrained. Add to that the young person's view that tea is for grannies, and the prospects for canned, cold, fizzy-lemon tea start to look less promising. A £6 million product launch and later a £4 million relaunch failed between them to achieve the product's target of £20 million sales per year and the product quietly disappeared from UK stores. The initial failure did not, however, deter further attempts, even with hard-hitting messages such as 'Don't knock it until you've tried it', but we still didn't try it in suffecnt volume for the brand to be successful.

Now the battle with attitudes has moved on to coffee, and the early signs are more encouraging, in part due to the influence of the coffee houses such as Starbucks which have featured iced coffee without the need to commit to a brand. Illy launched a premium iced coffee which was successfully launched in 17 countries before it hit the UK shops in 2011. It's a £35 million global brand, with forecast sales of £1 million for its first year in the UK.

A pioneering brand in this sector in the UK was Emmi's Caffè Latte brand, launched in 2004 and now worth about £3.3 million. Emmi was looking to further establish its position in the UK market with a £900,000 celebrity-backed PR campaign, outdoor advertising and sampling campaign to launch a new variant, Caffè Latte Extra Strong. Perhaps the increasing penetration of iced coffee will provide the stimulation that tea needs to lift it out of the doghouse! (Gardner, 2004; *The Grocer*, 2011b; Riley, 2011).

The question, therefore, is whether or not to shoot the dog, that is, withdraw the product. Much depends on the strategic role that the dog is fulfilling and its future prospects. It may, for example, be blocking a competitor (a guard dog?), or it may be complementing the company's own activities, for example creating customers at the bottom of the range who will then trade up to one of the organisation's better products (a guide dog, or a sheep dog?).

*Star (**high share, high growth**).* A star product is a market leader in a growth market. It needs a great deal of cash to retain its position, to support further growth and to maintain its lead. It does, however, also generate cash, because of its strength, and so it is likely to be self-sufficient. Stars could be the cash cows of the future.

Amazon launched the Kindle in the USA in 2007 and didn't realise that it would start a revolution in how we read books (see Case study 1). In just four years digital e-books have outperformed published books in USA sales and Kindle sales in 2011 were three times more than in 2010 (Edgecliffe-Johnson, 2011). The Kindle has gained a market share of 67 per cent in the US, with its nearest rival Nook now standing at 22 per cent. But the Kindle is a star under threat. Barnes and Noble, a national bricks-and-mortar bookstore chain which owns Nook, is investing heavily in its strategy for the e-reader to improve its market share relative to the Kindle, using bricks and mortar outlets to its advantage. It is trying to establish the Nook among college students through campus bookstores and by offering free software to make the reading and annotation of textbooks easier. It has also set up areas within the best performing stores to demonstrate Nook and sell accessories. By the end of 2011, there will also be a colour Nook which will give Barnes and Noble a significant advantage in very visual media, such as children's titles, cookbooks and magazines.

As we saw in Case study 1, one response by Amazon is to work on lowering its prices. The Kindle was launched at $399 but that has progressively fallen to just over $100. Then there is the cut-price Kindle which carries advertising. Although Amazon's roots are in physical books, the shift to electronic versions is now well underway, and Amazon appears to be willing to take a loss on e-books to gain market share for Kindle, even doing a deal with public libraries to make e-books more widely available.

In China, however, piracy, copycat producers and a lack of support from domestic producers is likely to delay progress on the Kindle. Local companies have already launched e-readers in China, backed by domestic content providers, that come in at a lower prices than Kindle. It has been estimated that sales of e-readers in the Chinese market will grow to 3 million units or 20 per cent of global sales in 2011. Amazon has so far held back from entering this market, but at the end of October 2011, it was rumoured that Amazon was negotiating with the Chinese government about launching Kindle products there. If this is true, it will be interesting to see whether the Kindle can move from question mark to star status, and how long it takes (Alva, 2010; Edgecliffe-Johnson, 2011; Horn, 2011; Jopson and Gelles, 2011; Limin, 2010; Townsend, 2011; *Warren's Washington Internet Daily*, 2011; Williams, 2011).

*Question mark (low share, high growth).* The high market growth of a question mark is good news, but the low share is worrying. Why is relative market share so low? What is the organisation doing wrong, or what is the competition doing right? It may simply be that the question mark (also sometimes called a problem child or a wild cat) is a relatively new product that is still in the process of establishing its position in the market. If it is not a new product, then it might just need far more investment in plant, equipment and marketing to keep up with the market growth rate. There is also a risk, however, that a question mark with problems might absorb a great deal of cash just to retain its position.

MMA, the French insurance company that owns UK broker Swinton, wanted to enter the price comparison market because this is growing much faster than the conventional insurance market. The decision was made to take on the dominant players such as Comparethemarket.com, Confused.com, Moneysupermarket.com and Gocompare.com (see Case study 7). It will be tough job to shift from question mark to star status, even though MMA intends to surpass the £20 million promotional budgets that the bigger players spend with a £30 million launch. At the time of writing, it is unclear whether or not the MMA's new price comparison site will carry the Swinton branding. Either way, as we saw earlier, each of 'the big four' has had time to establish a strong brand image and level of awareness to a greater or lesser extent and it is going to take some marketing skill, even with a £30 million budget, for a new entrant to make an impact (Brownsell, 2011; *Marketing*, 2011).

Some of the alternatives for question marks, such as dropping or repositioning, are the same as for the dogs, but there are some more creative options. If the product is felt to have potential, then management might commit significant investment towards building market share, as mentioned above. Alternatively, if the organisation is cash rich, it might seek to take over competitors to strengthen its market position, effectively buying market share.

*Cash cow (high share, low growth).* As market growth starts to tail off, stars can become cash cows. These products no longer need the same level of support as before since there are no new customers to be had, and there is less competitive pressure. Cash cows enjoy a dominant position generated from economies of scale, given their relative market share.

Wrigley's has a dominant position in the global chewing gum market with annual sales of over $22 billion with sales in 180 countries. Although there are competitors such as Cadbury's with its Trident brand, in the UK as in many other countries, Wrigleys is still the market leader with over 80 per cent as we saw in Case study 2. Wrigley's works hard to protect its position through strong branding and advertising and promotion, with a wide appeal. Because of its market leadership position, it is able to out-promote and out-distribute its rivals, and furthermore because of the sheer volume of product that it sells, its costs per pack sold are actually much lower than those of its competitors, making it even more difficult for them to rival Wrigley's. It generates a lot of cash, which has been estimated at 14–15 per cent of sales,

Wrigley's global success is generating the funds for developing a presence in the emerging Chinese market

*Source:* Alamy Images/Art Directors & Trip

which in part is used to refresh the product range and innovate within it. It was this that made Wrigley's attractive to Mars which purchased the company in 2009, releasing funds for developing a presence in the potentially lucrative Chinese market (www.wikinvest. com/stock/Wm._Wrigley_Jr._Company_(WWY); www.wrigleys.com).

The management focus here is on retention and maintenance, rather than on seeking growth. Management might be looking to keep price leadership, and any investment will be geared towards lowering costs rather than increasing volumes. Any excess cash can be diverted to new areas needing support, perhaps helping to develop dogs and question marks into stars.

Once the BCG matrix has been developed for an organisation, it can be used to assess the strength of the company and its product portfolio. Ideally, a strong mix of cash cows and stars is desirable, although there may be embryonic stars among the dogs and question marks. The situation and the portfolio become unbalanced where there are too many dogs and question marks and not enough cash cows to fund new developments to allow them to break out of those cells. There is also a risk dimension to all this. The organisation as a whole is vulnerable if there are too many products with an uncertain future (question marks).

Abell and Hammond (1979), however, identified a number of weaknesses in the BCG model and its assumptions, for instance that cash flow and cash richness are influenced by far more than market share and industry growth, and that return on investment (ROI) is a more widely used yardstick of investment attractiveness than cash flow. Although it is conceptually neat, the BCG matrix does not adequately assess alternative investment opportunities when there is competition for funds, as for example when it is necessary to decide whether it is better to support a star or a question mark.

**Market attractiveness model: the GE matrix**. Developed first by General Electric (GE), the market attractiveness–business position portfolio assessment model was designed to overcome some of the problems of models such as the BCG matrix.

The GE matrix adds more variables to aid investment decision appraisal. It uses two principal dimensions, as seen in Figure 13.5: *industry attractiveness* (the vertical axis) and *business strengths* (the horizontal axis). Within the matrix, the circle size represents the size of the market and the shaded part the share of the market held by the SBU.

The first dimension, industry attractiveness, is a composite index determined by market size, rate of growth, degree of competition, pace of technological change, new legislation and profit margins achieved, among others. The second dimension, business position, is another composite index, comprising a range of factors that help to build stronger relative market share, such as relative product quality and performance, brand image, distribution strength, price competition, loyalty, production efficiency, etc. Both dimensions need to work positively together, since there is little point in having a strong position in an unattractive market, or a weak position in a strong market.

**Figure 13.5**
The GE matrix

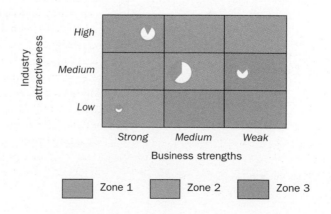

Within the matrix, there are three zones, each implying a different marketing and management strategy:

1 *Zone 1 (high attractiveness, strong position)*. The strategy here should be investment for further growth.
2 *Zone 2 (medium attractiveness)*. Because there is a weakness on one dimension, the strategy here should be one of selective investment, without over-committing.
3 *Zone 3 (least attractive)*. Either make short-term gains or proceed to pull out.

The main areas of concern with this model are linked to methodology and the lack of clear guidelines for implementing strategies.

**Shell's directional policy matrix**. Shown in Figure 13.6, the Shell directional policy matrix has two dimensions: competitive capabilities and prospects for sector profitability. The nine cells of the matrix offer different opportunities and challenges, so that placing each product in an appropriate cell provides a guide to its strategic development.

**Review of portfolio models**. Portfolio models have been criticised, but they have, nevertheless, been useful in forcing managers, especially in large complex organisations, to think more strategically. Their great advantage is that they force managers to reflect on current and projected performance, and to ask important questions about the continued viability of products, their strategic role and the potential for performance improvement. These models do not, however, give solutions about what strategies should be adopted, and they need to be supported by clear action plans. Their main problem is the rather simplistic use of variables that contribute to the axes and the decision rules sought from the models. The preoccupation with market share is of particular concern, since it might be just as valid to consolidate and perform better as to pursue high-growth, high-share business. The models also fail to consider the synergies between businesses, where one may support another.

In some situations, it might be more appropriate to focus on a small number of areas and perform really well in these than to over-extend in the pursuit of market share or market growth. In many markets, a set of businesses survive with little reference to market share as niche operators. They might, therefore, develop attractive returns without necessarily seeking market share for its own sake or incurring the costs and risks associated with the pursuit of relative sales volume. This is also true in situations where technological change and obsolescence can quickly erode any significant advantage gained.

Although these models are commonly described in textbooks, they are not so widely used in practice. They are conceptually easy to design, but very difficult to implement effectively. They require considerable management skill and judgement, because of their focus on the identification of variables, weighting decisions and future changes, rather than just on present, tangible, measurable factors.

**Figure 13.6**
Shell directional
policy matrix

| Competitive capabilities | Weak | Disinvest? | Gradual withdrawal? | Take a risk? |
| | Average | Gradual withdrawal? | Maintain or look for growth? | Try harder! |
| | Strong | Cash generator! | Look for growth? | Maintain leadership! |
| | | Unattractive | Average | Attractive |

Prospects for sector profitability

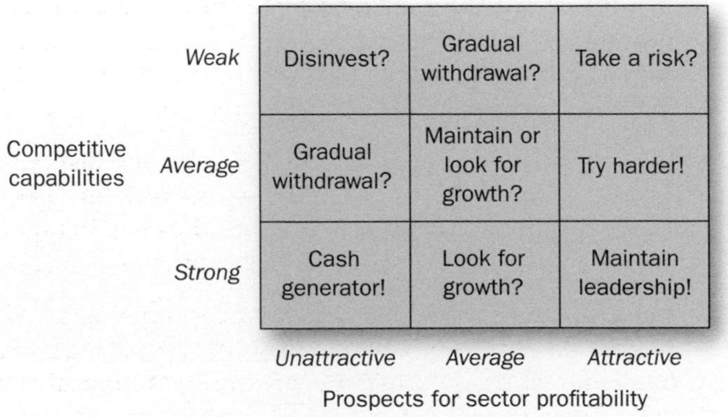

# External audit

The external audit systematically looks at the kinds of issues covered extensively in Chapter 2 as the STEEPLE factors. Sociocultural changes, such as in the demographic make-up of a market or in public concerns or attitudes, may well influence the future strategic direction of an organisation. The early identification of technological change might also change strategic direction, as the organisation plans ways of exploiting it to make cheaper, better or different products ahead of the competition. Economic and competitive factors are both, of course, very important. Low disposable incomes among target customers may force the organisation towards more rigorous cost control or into changing its product mix, while high interest rates on organisational borrowing might delay diversification or other expansion plans. Finally, the external audit should note what is happening in terms of the political and regulatory frameworks, whether national or European, that bind the organisation.

**Competitor analysis**. As part of the external audit, competition also has to be analysed very carefully on all aspects of its marketing activities, including its response to STEEPLE factors and its choice of target markets. Competitors are an important factor that will influence the eventual success or failure of a business in any market. Ignore competition, and the likelihood of being taken by surprise or of being caught out by a strong new product or a major attack on a loyal customer base is very great and can create severe problems.

At the macro level, Porter (1979) in his Five Forces Model defined the competitive forces that operate in an industry. They are:

- the bargaining power of suppliers
- the bargaining power of customers
- the threat of new entrants
- the threat of substitute products and services
- the rivalry among current competitors.

Porter's five forces form a useful starting point for undertaking a competitive analysis, in particular because they encourage a very wide definition of competition. Competition is not just about established, direct competitors at end-product level, but also about indirect and future competitors and about competition for suppliers. Before the development of the Channel Tunnel, the cross-channel ferry companies felt little need to compete aggressively with each other. Once the concept of the tunnel became a reality, however, they were shaken into action because of the perceived competitive threat.

The Porter model gives a sound foundation, but there are still several areas that should be analysed, if there is to be a full appreciation of competitors.

*Competitor identification.* As the Porter model implies, the identification of competitors is often broader than it first appears. The exercise should look at potential competitors, focus on the extent to which market needs are being satisfied and look at the needs that are emerging, as well as evaluating the activities and capabilities of the obvious competition. Latent or new competitors can take a market by surprise. Any organisation should take a wide view of who it is competing with. Small local shops discovered the hard way that they were competing with the supermarket multiples.

In a large market, it might be possible to group them into clusters, depending on their focus and strategy. This can provide a useful framework for identifying opportunities, but remember that in order to implement the technique, the organisation needs detailed competitor information, not just on financial performance but also on segments served, marketing strategies, etc.

*Competitive strengths and weaknesses.* Examining a competitor's strengths and weaknesses provides a valuable insight into its strategic thinking and actions. A full range of areas should be examined, for example manufacturing, technical and financial strengths, relationships with suppliers and customers, and markets and segments served, as well as the usual gamut of marketing activity. It is particularly worth undertaking a detailed review of the product range, identifying where volume, profits and cash come from, where the competitor is the market leader, where it is weak and where it seems to be heading.

India has developed a competitive strength in call centres due to its pool of relatively low-cost, English-speaking labour, combined with a relatively sophisticated communications technology infrastructure. The sector now employs 350,000 people and the main centres are in Bangalore, Delhi and Mumbai, but each now suffers from the same problem that shifted call centre operations away from Europe in the first place: the high turnover rate of staff, sometimes as high as 50 per cent per year. The difference is, however, that there is a large pool of willing replacements in a nation in which approximately 2.5 million young people graduate each year. Around 80 per cent of employees in call centres are in the 20–25-year-old age range but few consider it a long-term career option. Some staff in India sometimes have even gone to great lengths to appear British, they check the local weather, keep up with soap-opera story lines and have adopted English names but problems still exist with communication made worse by the high turnover.

There are signs that a reversal back to UK-based operations is now taking place. Santander has been one of the early companies to move call centres back. This reflected increasingly negative customer feedback, ranging from frustration to dissatisfaction through to cancelled accounts, all of which badly affected Santander's customer-service rankings. BT and Powergen have also returned to the UK, although Barclays has adopted a different approach based on the account potential. If the customer has cash, he or she is dealt with in a UK call centre, but if the account is stretched, the call goes to India!

However, it's not all about communication as the technology for providing customer service is also changing. The telephone is still used, but so too is the internet. The volume of calls has thus diminished but those customers relying on the telephone now tend to have more complex issues to resolve. In addition, customer service expectations have increased and service has become a point of differentiation. Outstanding service, not just 'service', is the aim and that favours British-based and trained staff. Now there's a choice between e-mail, website, automated voice services and a telephone call.

Call centres in India are still growing but the market is changing

*Source*: Corbis/Jagadeesh/Reuters

This does not necessarily mean the end of the competitive strength of Indian call centres and they are still experiencing growth but the market is changing, the basis of their competitive strength is changing, and to add to the pressure, there are more new entrants to the market from South Africa, Kenya and the Philippines (Arnott 2011; Best, 2011; *DNA Sunday*, 2010).

*Competitors' objectives and strategies.* It is important to understand what drives competitors, what makes them act as they do. Most firms have multiple objectives beyond the simple notion of profit. Objectives could relate to cash generation, market share, technological leadership, quality recognition or a host of other things. Sometimes developing an understanding of a competitor's product portfolio provides a valuable insight into likely competitive objectives. Once you understand their objectives, you have strong clues about how their strategy is likely to unfold in terms of their positioning, marketing mix and vulnerable points for attack, or your best means of defence.

*eg*

Duracell leads the battery power category but it has a main rival, Energizer. Between them, they account for 77 per cent of the market and 98 per cent of advertising expenditure. It is not a growth market, but a stable one, worth around £315 million in the UK. It is a market in which brand switching predominates, depending on sales promotions.

Duracell is still experiencing strong value growth, but sales of Energizer are down. In the 12 months to May 2011, sales of Energizer fell by over 27 per cent, own label sales were static and Duracell sales rose by over 13 per cent. To try to counter this, Energizer is innovating in the category with its new Energizer High Tech product which (it is claimed) lasts up to 40 per cent longer than existing Energizer batteries.

But the big problem is sales promotion. Such is the level of promotion that consumers are getting up to 50 per cent discount (for instance through BOGOFF offers) and at any one time around half of batteries are on offer. Energizer has tended not to follow that, instead limiting the discount to about 30 per cent, but the price of not following competitors has meant a loss of share. One way of encouraging growth is to have numerous locations in the store where batteries can be purchased rather than a fixed aisle. This is important as nearly half of purchases are made on impulse, so a purchase can be triggered by point of sale displays. Another is to ensure that the consumer buys the right battery for the right product, which requires education at the point of sale and on the packaging. The growth area is rechargeable batteries but this sector is following a similar pattern to that of the disposable batteries.

Energizer has also come up with a charitable link as a promotion to divert attention away from price. Its 'Be a Hero' campaign makes a donation to the charity Help for Heroes for each pack sold, and the promotion is integrated with advertising and in-store support. It's not easy being number two in the market and it is important to find ways of competing that allow the brand to differentiate itself from the leader (Bamford, 2011; *Convenience Store*, 2011).

*Competitive reaction.* It is very important to be able to assess competitors' responses to general changes in the marketing environment and to moves in major battles within the market. These responses could range from matching a price cut or an increase in promotional spend, through to ignoring events or shifting the ground completely. An organisation can learn from experience how competitors are likely to behave. Some will always react swiftly and decisively to what is seen as a threat; others may be more selective depending on the perceived magnitude of the threat.

# MARKETING IN ACTION

## Adding flavour to competition

There is a battle going on in the UK market between Premier Foods, Heinz and Unilever for domination of a number of grocery categories and smaller companies have become embroiled. Heinz has traditionally been a dominant player in the categories in which it competes. In the bottled-sauces sector, for example, seven out of the top 10 products belong to Heinz. From that leadership position it has a better chance of influencing distribution, sales promotion and pricing and has a better chance of getting new products on the supermarket shelves.

In recent years, things have been hotting up in the UK bottled-sauces market, as competitors try to move into the space occupied by the others as part of a product-led growth strategy. Thus Heinz is actively marketing its mayonnaise range, Hellmann's (Unilever) has launched its own ketchup directly against Heinz, and Branston is aiming to improve its presence in ketchup, mayonnaise and relishes. And that's just the tip of the iceberg as retailers have also been busy launching more premium own-label products into all of the above subcategories. Sales growth of almost 26 per cent took place in the bottled sauce market over five years, largely due to innovation in flavours and pack sizes. There aren't many new customers out there, as 99 per cent of households have at least one table sauce choice in their cupboard, and often between six and 10 choices, and thus expansion has had to be achieved through brand diversification (to put yet another bottle of sauce into the consumer's cupboard) or taking share away from competitor brands.

In the ketchup sector, Heinz had also been dominant for a long time, with a market share of around 60 per cent, with own label taking the bulk of the remainder. Nevertheless, Hellmann's decided to launch a product in that sector, competing head on with Heinz. Hellmann's thought that the values associated with its trusted brand name established in the mayonnaise sector could be transferred and would encourage consumer trial of its ketchup. It even offered some unique benefits, as the product contained 22 per cent fewer calories, 27 per cent less sugar and 40 per cent less salt than Heinz. Hellmann's also included some flavoured varieties rather than just relying on plain old tomato ketchup. Heinz retaliated with its HP Sauces of the World, which included spicier flavours, particularly to appeal to younger audiences, and different pack sizes to open up new segments. In 2009, Heinz introduced 'Big Pack Great Value' labels on its 1.2 kg bottles of tomato ketchup and 850 g bottles of HP Sauce, and at the other end of the spectrum, Heinz's Squeeze Me! variety pack caters for snacking and lunchboxes. Heinz also increased its advertising spend to defend ketchup sales. The battle continues.

Mayonnaise is another battleground in the UK market. In this sector, it's Hellmann's that is finding its dominant position under threat from both Heinz and Branston. In 2010, Hellmann's accounted for 75 per cent of the mayonnaise

Branston is seeking to increase its presence in the UK market for products such as mayonnaise, relishes and ketchup

*Source*: with kind permission from Premier Foods Plc solely as the UK brand owner market which was growing as consumers found new uses for the sauce. This was attractive to Branston, and it expanded into flavoured mayonnaise through its 'Mayo with a Twist' range with five varieties, such as sweet chilli, peri-peri, and lemon and roast garlic. The twist range was highly successful with sales up 71 per cent in 2010. It appealed to a younger audience than the Hellmann's core target market of 35–45-year-old housewives with children. Heinz mayonnaise, meanwhile, by 2011 only held a 5 per cent share of the market, although it was growing faster than most with some help from a packaging redesign to give it a stronger association with the Heinz family to encourage trial. The brand has also been heavily supported by sales promotion, also to encourage trial. Not to be outdone, Hellmann's also launched two flavoured additions to its mayonnaise range, lemon and chilli and has retained its market leader position.

In the salad-cream sector, the leading brand is Heinz again, with a 77 per cent share. The sector is worth around £11 million and Branston decided to challenge Heinz. Branston is proving to be an aggressive competitor, and launched the Salad Cream with a Twist range, including salad cream with garlic and herb, and salad cream with caramelised onion. Heinz defended its position by offering its first ever flavoured salad cream in order to tempt customers away from the mayonnaise category. It launched limited edition flavours such as lemon and black pepper, backed by a £1 million campaign which included radio advertising. Research has suggested that the new flavours do not cannibalise sales of the standard product; instead it puts another bottle into the cupboard (or possibly the fridge).

The big branded manufacturers are not only slugging it out with each other, but retailers are also innovating, especially Tesco and Asda. Although they are not gaining much share with own label products, they do appeal to the more price sensitive segment, even while offering premium own brands. The ultimate winners in these battles is the consumer who can enjoy the benefits and convenience of more variety in flavours, pack sizes, and price range among the products available on the supermarket shelves.

*Sources*: Bainbridge (2011); Branston (2011); Creasey (2010); *Food and Drink Innovation Network* (2011); *The Grocer* (2010b; 2011a); Mintel (2010).

*Competitive information system.* The above discussion of competitor analysis demonstrates the need for a well-organised and comprehensive competitor information system. This would be part of the MIS discussed in Chapter 5. Often, data need to be deliberately sourced on an ongoing basis, collated, analysed, disseminated and discussed. Then, management at all levels can learn what is happening. They may dispute the findings or the data may provide a basis for seeking further insights.

## Market potential and sales forecasting

The extent to which plans can be successfully implemented depends not only on managers' abilities in setting and implementing strategies, but more fundamentally on their ability to predict the market accurately. This means two things: first, assessing the market potential, that is, working out how big the total cake is; and second, forecasting sales, that is, calculating how big a slice of that cake our organisation can get for itself. The following subsections will look at both of these areas.

**Market and sales potential**. The concept of market potential is very simple, but in practice it is very difficult to estimate. Market potential is the maximum level of demand available within the total market over a given period, assuming a certain level of competitive marketing activity and certain conditions and trends in the marketing environment. This definition immediately raises problems in calculating a figure for market potential, as it involves many assumptions about competitors and the environment, needs a precise definition of 'the market' and requires methods of quantifying the variables concerned.

Having a clear idea of market and sales potential provides a useful input to the marketing planning process. It is especially important for planning selling efforts and allocating resources. The allocation of sales force effort, and the establishment of distribution points and service support centres, for example, can reflect sales potential rather than actual sales, thus allowing scope for expansion. Similarly, sales potential can also be used to plan sales territories, quotas, sales force compensation and targets for prospecting.

Smoking in China is both big business and an unhealthy business. It has been estimated that there are 300 million smokers in China (*2011 China Tobacco Control Report*) with more than half of all Chinese men smoking. Add to that the passive smokers, including the effect on 182 million children and the figure rises to over one billion. Unsurprisingly, the medical, lost labour and social costs are extremely high. Over one million people die from smoking related illnesses each year and this figure will increase rather than decrease over time, with one estimate putting the figure at 3.5 million per year by 2030.

Despite legislation introduced in 2011 banning smoking in public places such as schools and hospitals, the practice is rife. Although smoking is officially banned in the workplace, it is still not uncommon to be offered a cigarette in an office and in a survey it showed that over 40 per cent of smokers light up at work, despite smoke-free policies. The cynics say that the government says one thing and does another. Certainly the domestic tobacco industry in China is very powerful, as it is worth $93 billion and contributes to the Chinese economy through employment and taxes. If there was a serious attempt to reduce smoking, the economic costs through its effect on the tobacco industry would be a lot more than would be saved by reducing medical costs of treating smoking-related disease. It is even suggested that such is the power of the state owned monopoly that it can impede anti-smoking measures, and it is certainly true that the government still has not raised taxes on cigarettes, as Western countries have done, to make cigarettes less affordable.

So, what is the market potential for smoking cessation products? At a simplistic level, there is a potential market of 300 million smokers, but they vary by intensity of smoking, receptivity to anti-smoking messages and a range of social criteria such as education, family lifestyle, and environment. It would appear that the causal link between smoking and health isn't widely understood or accepted as a reason to quit. Research could help to identify the size and breakdown of the market potential, and maybe it's the better educated urban dweller that could form the initial target market. But even in Beijing, the nation's capital, only 1,000 people come forward each year seeking help from the nation's first smoking cessation clinic.

There are signs, however, that some smokers are heeding the health message, especially now that smoking is banned in many public places (but not often enforced!). Research in the West has shown that smoking bans have reduced consumption by 20 per cent, accompanied by a rise in sales of smoking-cessation aids. Nicotine patches are the most popular, but so too are electronic cigarettes with 56,000 e-cigarettes having been sold through the site taobao.com. There are also Chinese medicines to aid cessation, but some of these are not approved by the government. Western companies such as Johnson & Johnson, Pfizer and Novartis make a lot of money in international markets, but can they also succeed in the largest market in the world? Although individual strategy may well determine the sales potential of each company, especially investment in trade promotion and consumer advertising, they are still going to have to work against the inertia and even hostility that exists in this market. The situation isn't helped by the fact that it can cost 2,000 yuan (£150) for a full round of treatment which leaves some thinking about how many cigarettes they could buy with that money!

It's a tough challenge. Even in schools, there are now some anti-smoking messages, but then the school might well be named after the tobacco company, and benefit from numerous college sponsorships funded by the tobacco industry. It could be a long time before Western companies selling cessation aids start to see a return on the market potential as they strive to compete against each other and against Chinese brands (*New Scientist*, 2011; Wan, 2011; Wang, 2011; *Xinhua News Agency*, 2011).

# Estimating market and sales potential

The methods used for estimating sales and market potential will vary, depending on just how new or innovative the product or service is, and how mature the market is. The two main groups of methods discussed here are *breakdown*, that is, working from the aggregate level of the whole market down to the segment of interest, and *build-up*, that is, starting with individual customers then aggregating up to industry or market totals.

## Breakdown methods

Breakdown methods fall into two main groups: those based on total market measurement and those based on statistical series analysis.

**Total market measurement.** The total market measurement method begins with any total industry or market data that may be available from secondary research, and then breaks that information down to market segment level and thence to the organisation's own sales potential. This method relies heavily on the availability of a long series of data on industry sales volume and consumption by segments within that market, but rarely are such complete and detailed data available. Potential is thus often estimated from what data are available and then adjusted to take account of the current marketing environment. Once market and segment potentials have been established, sales potential can be derived by estimating competitors' relative market shares and then calculating how those might change as a result of expected actions, for example, a new product launch.

**Statistical series analysis.** Statistical series analysis is a means of calculating potential for market segments. It is based on developing a statistical relationship, correlating sales and key factors influencing them. The success of this method depends on identifying the right factor or combination of factors (i.e. statistical series) to use in the analysis. The calculation might be further influenced by weightings reflecting managerial judgements on the relative importance of segments and the likely effect of other environmental factors on the future development of those segments.

## Build-up methods

There are three main methods for aggregating data to produce reliable market and sales potential figures: census, survey and secondary data.

**Census.** The census method is based on a detailed consideration of every buyer and potential buyer in a market. This may be difficult, if not impossible, in mass consumer markets, but is more feasible in industrial situations, where demand might be concentrated and orders infrequent but of high value. The market potential is effectively the sum of all the potentials estimated for individual purchasers.

**Survey.** The survey method is more widely used in consumer markets where a representative sample (look back at Chapter 5) of consumers are asked about their purchase intentions. This information can then be used as a basis for calculating total market or sales potential. The main problem, however, is that respondents might lie about their intentions, or fail to follow them through in the future. Even more problematic is establishing intent to purchase a particular brand. A consumer might genuinely intend to replace their car with a Ford, but if at the time of the actual purchase Renault or Volvo are running a particularly attractive promotion, then . . . who knows?

**Secondary data.** Finally, secondary data can be used to establish sales and market potential. Internal sales records can be used to predict individual customers' purchasing on the basis of past behaviour. In this approach, the sales potentials are produced first and the market potential is then derived from those figures.

# Market and sales forecasting

## Sales forecasting

Marketing often plays a central role in preparing and disseminating forecasts. This is perhaps one of its most important functions, as the sales and market forecasts provided are the basis of all subsequent planning and decision-making within most areas of the organisation. Whether the organisation is a car manufacturer forecasting the demand for each model, a tour operator forecasting demand for specific destinations, or a university forecasting numbers of full-time, part-time and overseas students by programme area, the forecast is the starting point for all subsequent decisions. Get it wrong and the whole organisation can be caught out by major capacity or cash flow problems. In fashion markets, for example, it can be very difficult to forecast what styles are going to sell in what quantities, hence the popularity of 'end of season' sales as retailers try to sell off surplus stock. Holiday companies also find forecasting difficult, and again find themselves selling off surplus holidays at a discount right up to departure dates.

Forecasting and planning are, however, different functions. Forecasting attempts to indicate what will happen in a given environmental situation if a specific set of decisions and actions is implemented with no subsequent changes. Planning assumes that the environmental situation, especially that relating to the competitive arena, can be influenced, or at least better dealt with, by changing management decisions and actions. The focus of planning is, therefore, on alternatives and outcomes. Of course, there needs to be interaction between planning and forecasting, so that forecasts can be revised to take account of the new conditions likely to be created by the implementation of proposed plans.

There is no such thing as a rigid or absolute forecast. Different forecasters using different forecasting methods are almost certain to come up with different results. Forecasts should:

- be based on historical information from which a projection can be made;
- look forward over a specific, clearly defined time period; and
- make clearly specified assumptions, since uncertainty characterises the future.

But many companies still get it horribly wrong!

# SWOT analysis

The marketing audit is a major exercise which ranges widely over all the internal and external factors influencing an organisation's marketing activity. It generates, therefore, a huge amount of material that has to be analysed and summarised to sift out the critical issues that will drive the marketing plan forward. The commonest mechanism for structuring audit information to provide a critical analysis is the SWOT analysis (strengths, weaknesses, opportunities, threats).

## Strengths and weaknesses

Strengths and weaknesses tend to focus on the present and past, and on internally controlled factors, such as the 4Ps and the overall marketing package (including customer service) offered to the target market. The external environment is not totally ignored, however, and many strengths and weaknesses can be defined as such only in a competitive context. Thus, for example, our low prices may be seen as a strength if we are pricing well below our nearest competitor in a price-sensitive market. Low prices, however, may be a weakness if we have been forced into them by a price war and cannot really sustain them, or if the market is less price sensitive and our price is associated with inferior quality when compared with higher-priced competitors in the minds of the target market.

*eg*  Teuscher (www.teuscher.com) truffle shops claim to offer a fairytale experience to all their visitors. Top quality chocolate presented in over 25 elaborately designed stores worldwide helps Teuscher to stand out from the crowd. The designs are deliberately themed and changed simultaneously in all shops four or five times per year. Examples have included autumn pheasants, pink flamingoes and bears, to name but a few, all set amid plants and flowers. Attention to detail also extends to the products themselves. The raw material is carefully selected couverture that has been specially tempered and has a high cocoa content and low melting point. Such delights as champagne truffles, chewy florentines, candied orange slices, hearts and fish shapes, golf balls, trains and pianos are all offered – in chocolate, of course. This attention to detail, a high level of creativity and an emphasis on first class products, service and retail ambience make Teuscher shops very special places.

If it's real quality and taste you're after, these chocolates should hit the spot

*Source:* © Teuscher Chocolates of Switzerland, www.teuscher.com

## Opportunities and threats

Opportunities and threats tend to focus on the present and the future, taking a more outward-looking, strategic view of likely developments and options. Thus the organisation that is the price leader in a price-sensitive market might see the opportunity to get its costs down even further as a means of maintaining its position and pressurising any challengers. The challenger's SWOT analysis would define that same scenario as a threat, but might see an opportunity in opening up a new, non-price-sensitive segment. Many opportunities and threats emerge from the marketing environment, when shifts in demographic and cultural factors are taken into account; when developments in emerging markets, such as China, are analysed; when, in fact, the implications of anything included in Chapter 2's STEEPLE factors are considered.

## Understanding the SWOT analysis

The SWOT analysis, therefore, helps to sort information systematically and to classify it, but still needs further creative analysis to make sense of it. The magnitude of opportunities and threats, and the feasibility of the potential courses of action implied by them, can only really be understood in terms of the organisation's strengths and weaknesses. If strengths and weaknesses represent 'where we are now' and opportunities and threats represent 'where we want (or don't want) to be' or 'where we could be', then the gap, representing 'what we have to do to get there', has to be filled by managerial imagination, as justified and formalised in the body of the marketing plan.

Management consultancy Deloitte summarised what it considers to be the significant changes affecting the UK retail sector and how those changes might affect retailers' business models. Some of the issues are described below:

- A fall in disposable income as a result of high consumer debt and rising unemployment has led to a situation where consumers need to buy less but have to spend more, as prices are rising. Value and customer service, can therefore, can be important strategies to retain share.
- Consumers' expectations of how they want to interact with organisations are changing. Consumers of all ages are online and increasingly mobile so what is needed is a full range of direct and digital channels to be utilised, whether for transactions or just communications purposes.
- For a number of years, the amount of retail floor space has been expanding. Now, it is contracting and some of it is moving out of town. Online shopping has increased, taking some business away from stores and changing the cost pressures. This can endanger poorly performing stores.
- Recent years have seen a growth in global sourcing, rather than relying on the UK or Europe. This is at a time of exchange rate devaluation which makes imports more expensive. Combined with higher VAT and other increasing costs, this is putting even more pressure on supply chains and stronger retailers are demanding more support from manufacturers.
- Retailers need to reduce operating costs to seek to retain profitability. This means cutting store costs, cutting inventory levels and renegotiating supply and payment terms.
- At the same time, many retailers need to go multichannel to enhance capability and in some cases just to remain competitive.
- Retailers need to expand overseas operations to reduce their dependence on the UK market.

Overall, any retailer needs to undertake a rapid assessment of its strengths and weaknesses in the context of the opportunities and threats that it faces in order to determine what strategy is best: defensive or aggressive or simply surviving. Benchmarking can be an important part of this assessment, comparing retailer performance with the sector as a whole (Geddes, 2011).

## Marketing objectives

Objectives are essential for clearly defining what must be achieved through the marketing strategies implemented, and also to provide a benchmark against which to measure the extent of their success. Marketing objectives do, however, have to be wide ranging as well as precise, as they have to link closely with corporate objectives on a higher level but also descend to the fine detail of products, segments, etc. They must, therefore, be *consistent* with each other and with corporate goals, *attainable* in that they can be achieved in practice and their progress can be measured, and *compatible* with both the internal and external environments in which they are to be implemented. These criteria are generally applicable, despite the fact that marketing objectives can vary over time and between organisations.

Whatever the basis of the objectives, they cannot be left at such a descriptive level. It is not enough to say that our objective is to increase our market share. It is essential to quantify and make explicit precisely what is intended. Even when those questions have been answered, the objective is still quite general, and a number of detailed sub-objectives, which will perhaps relate to constraints or parameters within which the main objective is to be achieved, should also be defined. The main objective of increasing market share, for example, may have sub-objectives relating to pricing. Thus the marketing manager might have to find a way of increasing market share without compromising the organisation's premium price position.

## Marketing strategies

A marketing strategy is the means by which an organisation sets out to achieve its marketing objectives. In reality, an organisation will be presented with a range of strategic options, relating to its defined objectives. Some will be related to increasing volume, while others relate to improving profitability and holding on to what the organisation already has (reducing costs, increasing prices, changing the product mix, streamlining operations, etc.).

This section examines a number of different strategies that organisations might adopt if their priority is growth. It is important to remember, however, that growth is not always a priority. In many small firms, for example, survival or sustaining the *status quo* might be the main objective. In other situations, standing still might be the right strategy if the market is starting to tighten up. The preoccupation with growth, therefore, should not be assumed to be relevant to all organisations all the time.

### The Ansoff matrix

The product–market matrix proposed by Ansoff (1957) provides a useful framework for considering the relationship between strategic direction and marketing strategy. The four-cell matrix shown in Figure 13.7 considers various combinations of product–market options. Each cell in the Ansoff matrix presents distinct opportunities, threats, resource requirements, returns and risks, and will be discussed below.

**Figure 13.7**
Ansoff's growth matrix

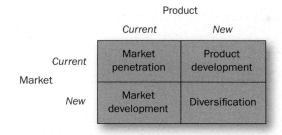

## MARKETING IN ACTION

### Flying out of formation

Bmi was caught in strategic no man's land. As the UK's second biggest scheduled airline it had to fight on two fronts. On the one hand it had to compete with British Airways (BA), a full service provider for the scheduled UK and European market, and on the other hand it had the low-cost airlines, such as Ryanair and easyJet, which were taking an increasing share of the value end of the market. This is a dangerous territory as Bmi could claim to be neither one nor the other. It was a poor second best as a market challenger to BA as it had only a fraction of the resources and therefore had to redefine its service offering and pricing structure to complement BA rather than competing head on.

Bmi tried to look both ways and offer full service but with competitive fares. It thus offered a one-class model with three fare types for business class travel: Tiny, Standard and Premium, based on the ticket flexibility required and the service level desired, such as access to airport business lounges.

▶ Other changes included lower catering costs, online check-in systems and fewer staff on flights, saving Bmi around £30 million a year, assuming that passenger numbers held up. But passenger numbers did not hold up. Due to the recession, business travellers were harder to come by, even with reduced fares, as some were forced to fly economy or not at all, and Bmi did not have the low operating costs to compete directly on price with the low-cost airlines. It still had slots at Heathrow rather than Luton or Stansted, offered a full service booking system and on-board services, and it couldn't match the 20–30 minute turnaround time for a landing aircraft that the low-cost airlines could achieve. Even its low-cost subsidiary, Bmi Baby, struggled against the other low-cost airlines. As a result of this, passenger numbers and profitability declined between 2006 and 2008, and by 2009 losses were approaching £200 million.

Such losses could not continue and in 2009 the airline was purchased by Lufthansa. There were redundancies, aircraft were returned to leasing companies and some services were curtailed including the London–Brussels route which was under pressure from Eurostar competition. The fleet size was reduced from 39 to 30 planes. One of the early decisions was to axe business class services on all of Bmi's domestic flights, despite its earlier and unsuccessful claims of being primarily a business carrier. Even the strapline 'Better for Business' disappeared as aircraft cabins were completely converted to economy class, although 'Flexible economy' was introduced to offer business lounges, guaranteed seating at the front of the plane and complimentary food and drink – in short, it was business class by another name.

What, therefore, is the main proposition now offered by Bmi and how does that relate to the market? The incoming management thought that the recovery was about new routes, strategy and good fortune. They thought that Bmi had lost its way over the previous 10 years in the customer's perception and that it was now time to get that back with more clarity. It would start by being transparent in pricing at a time when value airlines were increasingly hiding the true costs of advertised flights. It doesn't hide baggage, seat selection and online check-in costs, but offers a fully inclusive price. It was thought that this would add value. Lufthansa's investment included new cabin interiors, a new fleet and offered new routes for short haul and medium haul. But internationally, it became more selective in its desire to grow by market development. It focused on destinations such as Marrakech and Casablanca rather than Madrid and Cologne which are highly competitive. These African markets were growth areas for tourist traffic while others such as Bergen and Stavanger were chosen for their appeal to tourists and those business flyers in the oil and gas exploration industry. It is all about establishing the right network and offering the right service product to meet the demand but you also need a bit of luck.

However, Bmi's losses continued to mount, and as well as cost cutting, Lufthansa planned to sell six daily take-off and landing slots at Heathrow to BA. Bmi owns about 11 per cent of the landing slots at Heathrow and this is considered its greatest asset, worth around £700 million as there is real pressure on slots at one of the world's busiest airports. This sale concerned Virgin Atlantic which accused Lufthansa of 'salami slicing' Bmi by selling the most profitable assets – the landing slots.

Even this was not enough and by late 2011, it was estimated that Lufthansa had lost £1 billion on Bmi (taking into account acquisition costs, losses and emergency funding). Lufthansa decided that it had exhausted its possibilities for Bmi, particularly in the current economic climate, and started to negotiate a £300 million sale of BMI . . . to BA. BA would be happy to take on Bmi, partly because it would draw a line under Lufthansa's (and its 26 other partner airlines in the Star Alliance) attempt to challenge BA's dominance of Heathrow, and partly because BA wants Bmi's Heathrow slots. Heathrow cannot expand any further in the foreseeable future and the number of slots is finite. One analyst said, 'The availability of Bmi represents a valuable opportunity to secure an improved share of Heathrow slots, which should facilitate BA's future long-term growth into the developing markets of India and China' (as quoted by West, 2011).

At the time of writing, the deal has not been concluded. Virgin Atlantic is said to have made a bid, again, partly to increase its presence at Heathrow through Bmi's slots, but also because there is an obvious synergy between the long-haul based Virgin Atlantic and Bmi's domestic and short-haul focus. This would create an airline with a full range of market coverage where long-haul and short-haul can be integrated with connecting flights and joint marketing. The industry analysts seem to think that the BA bid is more likely to succeed, but Virgin is pinning its hopes on the possibility that the competition authorities will take exception to the prospect of BA having an even greater stranglehold on Heathrow. BA's answer to that is to point out that even after adding Bmi's slots, BA would only have 53 per cent share of the landing slots at Heathrow, while Lufthansa has 63 per cent at Frankfurt, Air France has 55 per cent at Charles de Gaulle, and KLM has 51 per cent at Schiphol. Thus BA would be no more dominant at Heathrow than its major European rivals are in their own national airport hubs. Furthermore, if BA were to agree to sell off a few slots and perhaps guarantee to protect some domestic routes, it might appease any competition concerns. Virgin Atlantic's Chief Executive's response to this, however, is that

Rich pickings for flight slots after the demise of Bmi
*Source*: Alamy Images/Tristar Photos

'British Airways on its own has more capacity and market share across the North Atlantic, which is still the world's biggest market, than the whole of Skyteam [Air France and allied airlines] in Paris or the Star [Alliance] team in Germany so they're just comparing apples and pears' (as quoted by Cave, 2011).

If Bmi is sold to BA, Virgin Atlantic will possibly have to look across the Atlantic for allies (such as United or Delta) to help it challenge BA on its home turf.

*Sources*: Brownsell (2010); *Business and Finance* (2011); Cave (2011); Lyons (2009); O'Connell (2011); Robertson (2009); Rothwell (2011); West (2011).

## Intensive growth

Three cells of the Ansoff matrix offer opportunity for sustained growth, although each one has different potential according to the market situation.

**Market penetration**. The aim of market penetration is to increase sales volume in current markets, usually by more aggressive marketing. This means using the full range of the marketing mix to achieve greater leverage.

*eg*

United Parcel Service (UPS) is a leading distribution and delivery company operating on a global scale. The statistics are staggering: 15.6 million packages a day delivered in the USA and 2.3 million internationally. The European fleet alone has 8,800 vehicles, and runs 156 intra-European flights per day and 136 intercontinental flights from Europe. It has acquired a large portfolio of customers and has developed a transportation and systems infrastructure to provide reliable and consistent service to customers worldwide. It seeks to maximise its competitive strengths by selling existing and new services to its current customer base, emphasising the technology-driven operation which all but the largest competitors find hard to emulate. It seeks to integrate its technical solutions into its customers' business processes, thereby providing timely information on parcel movements.

UPS does not rule out other growth routes, and is developing a domestic service in China attracted by the growing middle class in the main cities. The Chinese market currently moves 5 million parcels per day and is expected to grow in value to $9 billion by 2016. There is a large number of carriers in China (Amazon alone uses 500 of them), but many are small and inefficient and thus foreign companies have tended to focus on international trade rather than domestic. If UPS succeeds in China, it will help UPS to reinforce its strategy of building market position internationally (Lemer, 2010; Maddox, 2010; www.ups.com).

**Market development**. Market development means selling more of the existing product to new markets, which could be based on new geographic segments or could be created by opening up other new segments (based, for example, on age, product usage, lifestyle or any other segmentation variable). Danish firms control nearly half of the world's market for wind turbines. Companies such as Vestas Wind Systems depend heavily on achieving growth by developing new markets.

Vestas Wind Systems (www.vestas.com) is the world's leading manufacturer of wind turbines. It has installed 43,000 wind turbines in 66 countries on six continents. The world market for wind-turbine systems is expected to continue growing over the next 10 years due to greater energy consumption, more environmental awareness and greater efficiency as technology continues to lower unit costs. From its origins in Scandinavia, Vestas now leads the world's market for wind power with a 12.5 per cent share but this is significantly down on the 23 per cent that it held in 2007. European markets have been opened up, especially in Germany and Poland and Spain, but these are now considered mature and the focus for growth prospects is particularly on the USA and China. By opening up new markets, Vestas is able to retain and build its global position. In China it won a contract with the China Datang Corporation Renewable Power Co. Ltd, for the design and delivery of the Dayuanshan wind farm in North China with 90 per cent of the components for the wind turbines being produced in China. Latin America is also a priority market for development despite Vestas having been there for 20 years. Vestas has delivered 590 mw of power for projects across Latin America and it now has another 472 mw signed in 2011, indicating the benefits of taking a long haul perspective to market development.

Part of the market development strategy is to establish local production facilities through acquisition or direct investment to aid government approval. In addition to factories in Denmark, Vestas also has facilities in Germany, Spain, China as mentioned above and in the USA. Sales offices have also been opened to support progress in markets such as South America, as it could take some time to achieve regulatory approval and to negotiate with power providers. Despite the international coverage, the success of Vestas has been built on the platform of product development, quality, pre- and post-sales service, efficient production and competitive pricing. Although still primarily a wind turbine producer, Vestas' sales grew to €6.9 billion in 2010 in a market in which long-term growth prospects are excellent with the drive towards renewable energy sources. Vestas still aims to hold on to its position as the world's leading wind energy provider. The market has, however, become more competitive with GE Energy and Siemens now big players, the latter with orders in the UK (in which market it has a 90 per cent share), Germany and Turkey. Vestas, as essentially a 'one product' company, could find it difficult to hold on to share (*China Energy*, 2011; *Renewable Energy Focus* (2009); Reuters (2010); Woodhead, 2009).

**Product development**. Product development means selling completely new or improved products in existing markets.

Vestas entered into an agreement with the Portuguese utility company, EDP, to undertake an R&D project to develop a full-scale, semi-submersible, floating wind turbine. This would open up new markets for offshore projects for countries with long and deep coastlines. Similar projects have already been launched by competitors, however, which means that the race to market is on. Making use of a floating platform, the key requirement is the integration of that platform with the turbine and then the accumulation of the electricity generated. The first system is planned for the Portuguese coast and the results of this project will determine the long-term potential (Price, 2011).

Vestas has entered into an agreement with EDP, a Portuguese utility company, to develop a floating wind turbine

*Source*: Getty Images/Bloomberg

## Diversification

Diversification, the final cell in the Ansoff matrix, happens when an organisation decides to move beyond its current boundaries to exploit new opportunities. It means entering unfamiliar territory in both product and market terms. One of the main attractions of this option is that it spreads risk, moving the organisation away from being too reliant on one product or one market. It also allows expertise and resources to be allocated synergistically, for example theme parks diversifying into hotel accommodation, or airlines diversifying into tour packages. The danger is, of course, that the organisation spreads its effort too widely into areas of low expertise, and tries to position itself against more specialist providers.

There are two main types of growth through diversification, as follows.

**Concentric diversification**. Concentric diversification happens where there is a link, either technological or commercial, between the old and the new sets of activities. The benefit is, therefore, gained from a synergy with current activities. An organisation could, for example, add new, unrelated product lines to its portfolio, but still use the same sales and distribution network.

When Amazon purchased Lovefilm.com it projected it into a new product area associated with film rental, whether on a DVD delivered by mail, or increasingly streamed online. At first glance it may appear to be an unrelated acquisition, as it is a new product category for Amazon, but when the operational and logistics systems are considered, it still utilises the strengths that Amazon has built up in database management and home delivery through selling books and DVDs. Customers can choose from 70,000 movie titles and it has 1.7 million customers across the UK, Germany, Sweden, Denmark and Norway. This is another step in the development of Amazon as a diversified online retailer (www.lovefilm.com).

**Conglomerate diversification**. The conglomerate diversification route is taken when an organisation undertakes new activities in markets that are also new. This involves risks in both the product development area and gaining acceptance in the marketplace.

American Express decided to become a multiproduct business, building on its image and its experience with certain lifestyle segments gained through its credit cards. Online banking was developed initially but more recently, mobile phone services, travel insurance and private health care insurance have all been launched. The mobile phone service interests reflect a desire to challenge rivals such as Visa and Google with mobile transaction services. Payments using mobile phones are expected to grow from $240 billion in 2011 to $670 billion by 2015, a market too large to ignore (Kharif, 2011). But the common thread for the expansion and diversification has been the use of the Amex name and lifestyle segments that it targets.

## 'No growth' options

Not all strategies have to be growth-oriented. *Harvesting* is a deliberate strategy of not seeking growth, but looking for the best returns from the product, even if the action taken may actually speed up any decline or reinforce the no-growth situation. The objective is, however, to make short-term profit while it is possible. Typically, products subjected to harvesting are likely to be cash cows in the mature stage of their lifecycles (see p. 237 *et seq.*), in a market that is stable or declining, as considered at p. 511 *et seq.* Harvesting strategies could involve minimal promotional expenditure, premium pricing strategies where possible, reducing product variability and controlling costs rigidly. Implementing such strategies helps to ensure that maximum returns are made over a short period, despite the potential loss of longer-term future sales. Effectively, the company is relying on the short-term loyalty of customers to cushion the effect of declining sales.

In more extreme cases, where prospects really are poor or bleak, *entrenchment* or *withdrawal* might be the only option. A timetable for withdrawal or closure would be developed and every effort made to maximise returns on the remaining output, in the full knowledge that harm will be done to sales volume in the short term. Some care should, however, be exercised when considering withdrawal, as highlighted in our discussion of 'dogs' (see pp. 512–13). Although the profit potential may be poor and the costs of turnaround prohibitive, the loss of a product in a range may affect other parts of the range adversely. Thus entrenchment, protecting the product's position as best you can without wasting too many resources on it, might be the most appropriate course of action.

## Growth through internationalisation

Market development, the taking of existing or similar products into new international markets, demands a lot from the marketing function in terms of strategy and operational contribution, even if effectively all it is doing is replicating what has been tried before. For some organisations, an international orientation is so deeply ingrained into their strategy and operations that the domestic market in which the corporate headquarters are located is regarded as a relatively minor part of the total trading picture. Others, however, take a much more *ad hoc* approach, simply responding to any export enquiries that might drift in but with no special commitment to developing new markets. In between are those who proactively want to expand by developing an international strand to their businesses. Organisations that are looking to expand their customer base internationally, however, face challenges that might be very different from those encountered in domestic markets. Decisions have to be made about the most attractive markets to pursue and develop, the best methods of entering new markets, and how much adaptation of the marketing package is necessary to achieve the desired positioning in the context of local needs and buyer expectations. These decisions are not, of course, too different from those required for domestic markets, and many of the key concepts presented in this book are just as applicable when dealing with Americans, Japanese or Danes. What are different, however, are the practice and implementation of marketing in order to take into account local customs, trading contexts, competition and other special factors that might inhibit or encourage free trade. Some organisations, such as McDonald's and Coca-Cola, choose to ignore any differences and market in the same way internationally, but the majority have to modify their marketing carefully to suit local conditions.

Forever 21 is an American fast fashion retailer with big ambitions in the UK of opening 100 stores across the country. It currently has 500 stores worldwide and considers international expansion as central to its growth strategy. As well as expanding in various European countries, it is continuing to expand in Asia with stores in India, South Korea and the Philippines, while its revenues in the last 10 years have blossomed from $200 million (£127.6 million) to $3.5 billion (£2.23 billion).

It is still primarily a US and Asian operator that thinks it can replicate its retail format elsewhere in the world. In Europe, it needs to adapt and reflect local tastes within its overall brand position. It is trendy and yet low priced, despite its origins in Beverly Hills, and shoppers around the world are buying into the American young-woman lifestyle. Normally, large stocks are not held and there are deliveries every day to keep the range fresh and customers interested. It's a strategy based on speed – the product is here today but gone tomorrow, so buy it today.

It has just two stores in the UK and, if it wants to grow, it will have to be at the expense of competitors such as New Look, Primark and H&M, as the fashion market overall is not growing. Whether it is offering something sufficiently differentiated to win market share remains to be seen. According to Thomson (2011), it is not easy to trade overseas successfully. Many are keen to exploit online opportunities and international expansion but unless research has been done to establish that the brand will fit in, the target markets appraised carefully, and the entry methods thoroughly assessed, internationalisation can be fraught with problems. The value proposition might well be the same globally but the implementation will vary. Nobody wants to repeat the mistake that M&S made in Shanghai: it ran out of smaller sizes! (Costa, 2011; Goldfingle, 2011; Thomson, 2011; Wiseman, 2011).

As an organisation intensifies its international activity so its approach to international market development evolves. An organisation might, for example, acquire or set up a manufacturing company to serve the market in a foreign country. That company is part of an international group, but at a local level it does not market across national boundaries but concentrates on its own domestic market. The parent organisation might get involved to a greater or lesser extent in critical issues such as strategic direction, resource allocation or product strategies, but otherwise the manufacturer is largely autonomous (for example, *see* Holcim, pp. 503–4). Truly global organisations such as Shell, Rank Xerox and McDonald's, therefore, are likely to have production, distribution and/or marketing organisations to serve different nations or regions.

*eg*

The Subway restaurant chain provides an excellent example of the pace of international market development possible through a franchised system (where the owner of a product, trade mark, process or service licenses another person or organisation to use, buy, sell or operate it in exchange for some form of payment). Subway was started in 1965 in the USA by a 17-year-old high-school graduate wanting to pay his way through college. The franchise concept is simple: the provision of high-quality hot and cold sandwiches, deli style, with salad and hot and cold drinks, offering value and speed of service. The average store is between 50 and 150 m$^2$ in extent, with a take-away and small eating-in area. Since starting to use franchising in the 1970s, the chain has opened over 35,000 units in 98 countries. Sales figures are not published but are thought to be in excess of $15 billion with $10 billion coming from its 24,000 US outlets.

Penetration has been more difficult in the UK, Germany and France given the different traditions of sandwich making and it could be argued that Subway is still trying to find the best proposition for those markets. As with McDonald's, the menu stays the same around the world other than catering for minor cultural and religious variations. The start-up costs are around $15,000 for the franchise fee but the restaurant set-up costs can vary between $70,000 and $200,000 depending upon the location. If the company had tried to own this number of outlets, it would have stretched its resources to the limit and would have probably been impossible (Jargon, 2011; www.financeinvestments.com/annual-report/subway-restaurant-annual-report.html; www.subway.com).

International marketing is, therefore, far more complex and less easy to define than the simple trading across frontiers. Its complexity arises not only from operational considerations, but also from the attitude of organisations towards it. International marketing could be an integral part of the corporate culture or it could be viewed as an add-on extra of less importance than domestic marketing.

Thus international marketing means different things to different organisations. To small organisations and companies still primarily operating from one main manufacturing base, most marketing involves product movement across national boundaries and the design of a marketing mix for each market. For other organisations, the scale of international operation has become so great that product movement across national boundaries is minimal or part of a carefully planned strategy. To such multinational or transnational organisations, the distinction between international and domestic marketing becomes very artificial from a strategic-marketing perspective.

*eg*

Selling yachts to the Chinese would have been unthinkable 20 years ago but now the very rich make a viable target for international yacht builders. They are the ultimate statement of wealth along with a Ferrari or Maserati! The British motor-yacht builder, Sunseeker, sold four boats at the Cannes boat show in 2011, all destined for China. It would appear, however, that the aspiration to sail is ahead of the ability to do so. There is a poor infrastructure in terms of marinas, service or repair facilities and personnel, and there is also restrictive regulation in terms of where boat owners can actually sail. Because of all this, the yacht companies are largely responding to enquires from China rather than proactively seeking business there. There are better pickings in the Middle East, Brazil and North America for European boat builders, and that's where marketing effort is being applied (Giuffrida, 2011).

While expanding across a range of different international markets requires more investment of resources and effort, the broader the range of markets served, the less likely it is that failure in any one market will cause terminal corporate decline. Germany may be mature but China is in high growth. Different markets are at different stages of development and competitive intensity, and make different resource demands. If, therefore, the organisation has a well-spread portfolio, resources can be shifted for further development, for combating short-term difficulties, or even to allow withdrawal. Russia and the Far East are currently regarded as markets that need investment if a long-term presence is to be built, whereas many western European markets are generally regarded as mature, with any growth arising from aggressive techniques for stealing share from competitors.

## Competitive positions and postures

A final stage in the determination of a competitive strategy is to decide how to compete, given the market realities, and how to either defend or disturb that position. This means that the organisation has to consider its own behaviour in the context of how competitors are behaving, and select the most appropriate strategy that will enable overall objectives to be achieved. Two aspects need to be considered: competitive position and competitive posture. *Competitive position* refers to the impact of the organisation's market position on marketing strategies, whereas competitive postures are the strategies implemented by organisations in different positions who want to disturb the status quo.

**Competitive positions**. An organisation's competitive position usually falls into one of four categories, according to its relative market share. The four categories, and the kinds of marketing strategies that go with them, are shown in Figure 13.8 and are now considered in turn.

*Market leader.* In many industries, one organisation is recognised as being ahead of the rest in terms of market share. Its share might only be 20–25 per cent, but that could still give it a dominant position. The market leader tends to determine the pace and ways of competing in the market. It sets the price standard, the promotional intensity, the rate of product change and the quality and quantity of the distribution effort. Effectively, the market leader provides a benchmark for others to follow or emulate, and market leadership can be at company, product group or brand level.

**Figure 13.8**
Competitive position and strategy

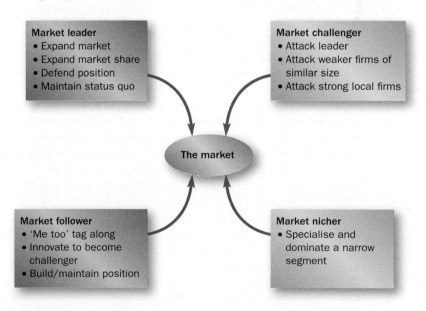

Bombardier is a leading global supplier of specialist and innovative transport solutions. Bombardier Transportation specialises in rail technology for mass transportation systems. It won a contract to supply a complex signalling system for Line 5 of the Sao Paulo metro in Brazil. The contract was worth €70 million and allowed the maximum capacity for the line to be achieved with just 75 seconds between trains. The system offered gives the buyer improved safety, greater capacity and reliability, shorter headways between trains, and reduced maintenance costs. This also means that savings can be made elsewhere, such as needing a smaller fleet to carry the same capacity. The contract price is only one variable to be considered, alongside system reliability, total cost benefits, state of the art technology and the likelihood of realising the full benefits.

The key to market leadership is Bombardier Transportation's proven track record in rail technology around the world, most recently in London and Madrid, so that the buyer can proceed with confidence. That's what makes it a market leader which is difficult to emulate (*Market News Publishing*, 2011).

*Market challengers.* Market challengers are organisations with a smaller market share, but who are close enough to pose a serious threat to the leader. However, an aggressive strategy can be costly, if the challenger is thinking of attacking where there is uncertainty over winning. Before making a concerted effort to steal share, therefore, the challenger needs to ask itself whether market share really matters so much, or whether there would be greater benefit from working on getting a good ROI from existing share.

In the early 2000s, there was a fight between the dominant market leader Intel and the challenger AMD in the PC chip market. Price battles took place between the two as AMD challenged Intel's supremacy. Despite the challenge, Intel came in with around 80 per cent of the market and AMD with 20 per cent. However, that particular battle started to subside as the decade progressed because technology moved on and consumers started to buy fewer PCs and more tablets and smartphones.

Originally, the system builders such as HP, IBM and Dell predominated and AMD was simply an alternative to Intel. Now, with the expansion of the smartphone and tablet computer markets, there are more players in the arena – it's not just about the traditional system builders any more – and the ability of chips to support high definition video and 3D games now matters more than simple processor power. This has meant a rethink by AMD as to where its technology can best build sustainable competitive advantage and it has decided to focus on processors for tablets rather than smartphones as that gives more scope for graphics and longer life applications. The tablet market is expected to grow from about 70 million units in 2011 to 294 million by 2015, so it is an attractive market and one where the boundaries are not so evident as with PCs (*eWeek*, 2011; Pimentel, 2011; Tan, 2011; Yeraswork, 2011).

Assuming that the decision is made to attack, there are two key questions: where to attack, and what the likely reaction will be. It is never easy to attack leaders, who tend to retaliate through cutting prices or by investing in heavy promotion, etc. It is, therefore, a high-risk but high-return route. The challenger needs a clear competitive advantage to exploit to be able to neutralise the leader.

*Market followers.* Given the resources needed, the threat of retaliation and the uncertainty of winning, many organisations favour a far less aggressive stance, acting as market followers. There are two types of follower. First, there are those who lack the resources to mount a serious challenge and prefer to remain innovative and forward thinking, without disturbing the overall competitive structure in the market by encouraging open warfare. Often, any lead from the market leader is willingly followed. This might mean adopting a 'me too' strategy, thus avoiding direct confrontation and competition (see Bmi vignette, p. 527 *et seq.*)

The second type of follower is the organisation that is simply not capable of challenging and is content just to survive, offering little competitive advantage. Often, smaller car rental firms operate in this category by being prepared to offer a lower price, but not offering the same standard of rental vehicle or even peace of mind should things go wrong. A recession can easily eliminate the weaker members of this category.

*Market nichers.* Some organisations, often small, specialise in areas of the market that are too small, too costly or too vulnerable for the larger organisation to contemplate. Niching is not exclusively a small organisation strategy, as some larger firms may have divisions that specialise. The key to niching is the close matching between the needs of the market and the capabilities and strengths of the company. The specialisation offered can relate to product type, customer group, geographic area or any aspect of product/service differentiation.

*eg* Are iPads a niche-market product? Britton (2011) thinks so despite it being counterintuitive. He quotes research by YouGov which found that only 2 per cent of UK adults owns a tablet compared with 75 per cent of the population being online and 35 per cent owning a smartphone. Like 3D TV, tablets are still niche products. The research showed that the owners tend to be more affluent, aged over 45 with an average household income of £109,000. For tablets to move into the mainstream, a lower price point is the key and Apple doesn't like doing that until it needs to respond to an increasing number of competitors. For Apple, the iPad is just one niche product in a bigger portfolio, but sometimes, the whole company can be niche. Take, for example, Brompton, which is known for its folding bike. It produces 28,000 bikes a year and has grown by 25 per cent over the past six years, but still supplies less than 1 per cent of the UK market for bikes. Most are exported overseas as the home market is small. In the Netherlands, for example, 40–50 per cent of all journeys under three miles are by bike but in the UK it is just 2 per cent (Nielsen, 2010). All the remaining British bike manufacturers need to export to survive and are niche operators either by product, such as Brompton, or by brand reputation such as Raleigh.

The key to niche marketing is to match closely the needs of the market and the strengths of the company

*Source:* Alamy Images/MBI

**Competitive postures**. The previous subsection considered the underlying rationale for defending, attacking or ignoring what is going on in the market from the point of view of an organisation's relative market position. This section examines *how to attack* or *how to defend* a position and the possibilities of alliances with competitors.

*Aggressive strategies.* Aggressive strategies are implemented when one or more players in a market decide to challenge the status quo. Again, the question of who to attack, when to attack and where to attack all need to be answered carefully in the context of the resources needed, the competitive reaction and the returns to be gained at what cost. Even in warfare, head-on assaults can be costly and do not always succeed.

eg

Asda and Tesco are in a battle to win a bigger share of supermarket customers' spend and have embroiled Sainsbury's and Morrison's in the process. Although the price war has been running ever since Walmart took over Asda, there have been periods of intense activity. In 2010 Asda launched a 'price guarantee' scheme by which if Asda customers found they could purchase a basket of eight or more comparable products at the other big three retailers, Asda would give them a money-off voucher for the difference plus a penny to be redeemed on the next visit to Asda. In January 2011, Asda went further by offering to refund the difference if customers found that it wasn't 10 per cent cheaper than rivals. In short, the claim that Asda will not be beaten on price was given teeth! A year later, Asda was confirmed as the UK's cheapest supermarket but more importantly for Tesco, Asda managed to take Tesco's crown as the UK's favourite supermarket too.

The problem is, however, that the price comparison approach is easily matched. Sainsbury's launched a trial at 18 of its stores, effectively guaranteeing to match its rivals on 12,000 branded products. Tesco decided that its would redeem the vouchers that were issued to Sainsbury's customers reclaiming the difference, and Asda then installed internet booths at some of its stores near Sainsbury's supermarkets to test the price guarantee. Thus the impact of the price promotion was diluted.

Price competition between the retailers has become more aggressive and it is initially the one who initiates it gets all the credit and publicity, but the real long term advantages are negligible as others copy or retaliate in other ways. Perhaps too all these price matching schemes are getting too confusing and complicated for the shopper, as they are based on savings on a total shopping basket rather than hard brand by brand comparisons. It's all about creating perceptions of value for money, and the general impression seems to be that Tesco may not be cheapest but offers good value and includes the loyalty card benefits, unlike Asda.

If you want to start a price war, it is important that you be capable of seeing it through to victory. Tesco and Asda both believe that they can win (Craven, 2011; Halliwell, 2011; Thompson, 2010b; Wallop, 2011; Wood, 2011).

*Defensive strategies.* Defensive strategies might be adopted by a market leader under attack, or by a market follower or nicher put under pressure by competitive activity. Even a challenger needs to reflect on likely competitive retaliation before committing itself to aggressive acts. One option is to sit tight and defend the current position. This can be risky, in that such defences might then be bypassed rather than attacked directly.

Selective withdrawal, to delay or even offset the attacking force, is also a form of defence. In commercial terms, that could mean withdrawing from marginal segments and areas where the presence is small and cannot be defended. This might mean that in areas where strengths do exist a better, more concentrated fight can take place.

The phrase 'the best form of defence is to attack' is now a recognised business strategy. If an organisation feels that it might soon be under attack, rather than wait for that to happen it

eg

Zurich Insurance specialises in the middle of the corporate insurance market where other companies have not been that active, compared with the more exclusive top end of the market and the cheaper price comparison end of the market. All segments of the market have competition of course, but a recent increase in competitive activity from Axa and Aviva threatens Zurich's market share and thus it decided to take defensive action. It revamped its insurance product range to offer better value and introduced new products such as product recall insurance with a standard cover of £100,000 (*Post Magazine*, 2010). This was all part of a defensive strategy to protect its share before the main assault by much bigger competitors.

takes deliberate aggressive actions. This might mean a particular marketing mix emphasis, for example advertising, dealer loaders or new products. Alternatively, signals can be sent that any attack would be vigorously defended.

*Cooperation.* It would be incorrect to assume that all competitive behaviour is challenging and confrontational. Many situations are characterised by peaceful coexistence and at times by cooperative alliances between competitors. Strategic alliances occur when organisations seek to work together on projects, pooling expertise and resources. This could include R&D, joint ventures or licensing arrangements, sometimes on a worldwide scale. Many large construction projects demand that different firms work together to provide a turnkey package. The alliance can be general, on many fronts or specific to a certain project (Gulati, 1998).

eg

Telefonica from Spain and China Unicom formed a strategic alliance for cooperation in a number of areas, including procurement, marketing, roaming technology and mobile service platforms. This reflected Telefonica's objective of having a global presence. Through the alliance it now has a customer base of 590 million or approximately 10 per cent of the world's population, which gives a lot of scope for new product launches. The link with China followed acquisitions in Brazil and the UK. In China, acquisition was not an option, however, so an alliance was formed. China Unicom has 187 million mobile subscribers, 96.6 million local access subscribers and 47 million broadband subscribers, and thus it is a major player. It would have taken Telefonica a lot of time and resources to establish even a fraction of that market (*ENP Newswire* 2011; Perez, 2010).

Finally, *collusion* is where firms come to an 'understanding' about how to compete in the market. Legislation prevents this from extending to deliberate price fixing: neither retailers nor manufacturers can openly collude to set retail or supply prices between them, although they can, of course, watch each other's pricing policies carefully and choose to match them if they wish.

eg

Virgin and Cathay Pacific were accused of collusion in price fixing on passenger fares on the Hong Kong to London route. A series of meetings that took place over the years could have resulted in the coordinating of respective pricing strategies through the exchange of commercially sensitive information, which is against the spirit of the free market. An OFT ruling is awaited, but Cathay Pacific has been granted immunity for whistle-blowing (Arnott, 2010).

Although collusion is the unacceptable side of cooperation, the scale of investment and rate of change in technology, accompanied by increasingly global markets, are likely to generate more alliances and ventures in future.

# Marketing programmes

Whereas the previous stage was about designing marketing strategies, this one is about their detailed implementation. The marketing programme will precisely specify actions, responsibilities and time scales. It is the detailed statement that managers have to follow if strategies are to be put into operation, as it outlines required actions by market segment, product and functional area. Within the marketing programme, each mix element is considered individually. This is in contrast to the marketing strategy itself, which stresses the interdependency between elements of the mix for achieving the best synergy between them. Now, the individual strands that make up that strategy can be picked out, and for each functional area, such as pricing, managers can go through planning processes, audits, objectives, strategies, programmes and controls.

On the basis of the overall marketing strategy, managers can emphasise those areas of comparative strength where a competitive edge can be gained, strengthen those areas where the organisation is comparable with its competition, and work to develop further or overcome those where the organisation is more vulnerable. The key challenge at the end of it all, however, is to ensure that the marketing mix is affordable, implementable and appropriate for the target segment. With that in mind, and given the dynamic nature of most markets, managers will also have to review the mix on a regular basis to make sure that it is still fresh and still serving the purposes intended.

# Marketing budgets

The marketing plan must specify and schedule all financial and other resource requirements, otherwise managers might not be able to accomplish the tasks set. This is partly about costs, such as those of the sales force which include their associated expenditures, advertising campaigns, dealer support, market research, etc., and partly about forecasting expected revenues from products and markets. In determining budgets, managers need to balance precision against flexibility. A budget should be precise and detailed enough to justify the resources requested and to permit detailed control and evaluation of the cost effectiveness of various marketing activities, yet it also needs the flexibility to cope with changing circumstances.

We discussed budget setting, and some of the issues surrounding it, in Chapter 9 in a marketing communications context (see p. 361 *et seq.*). Many of the points made there are more widely applicable, particularly the relative strengths and weaknesses of objective and task budgeting compared with methods based on historical performance (for example, basing this year's budget on last year's with an arbitrary 5 per cent added on).

# Marketing controls and evaluation

Control and evaluation are both essential if managers are to ensure that the plans are being implemented properly and that the outcomes are those expected. Although the defined marketing objectives provide the ultimate goals against which performance and success can be measured, waiting until the end of the planning period to assess whether they have been achieved is risky. Instead, managers should evaluate progress regularly throughout the period against a series of benchmarks reflecting expected performance to date. At that point, managers can then decide whether their strategies appear to be well on target for achieving objectives as planned or whether the deviation from expected performance is so great that alternative actions are called for.

Control and evaluation can take either a short- or a longer-term perspective. In the short term, control can be monitored on a daily basis through reviewing orders received, sales, stock-turn or cash flow, for example. Longer-term strategic control focuses on monitoring wider issues, such as the emergence of trends and ambiguities in the marketing environment. This has strong links with the marketing audit, assessing the extent to which the organisation has matched its capabilities with the environment and indeed the extent to which it has correctly 'read' the environment.

This whole area of control and evaluation will be considered in greater detail at p. 543 *et seq.*

# Organising marketing activities

Effective marketing management does not happen by itself. It has to have the right kind of infrastructure and place within the organisation in order to develop and work efficiently and effectively. Central to the marketing philosophy is a focus on customer needs, and by understanding markets, customers' needs and wants and the ways in which they are changing and why, the marketer is providing essential information for planning corporate direction and the activities of other functions within the organisation.

It is important, however, to distinguish between a functional marketing department and marketing orientation as a management philosophy. Any organisation can have a marketing department, yet not be truly marketing-oriented. If that marketing department is isolated from other functional areas, if it is just there to 'do advertising', then its potential is wasted. Marketing orientation permeates the whole organisation and *requires* marketing's involvement in all areas of the organisation.

Whether or not there is a marketing department, and how it is structured, depends on a number of factors. These might include the size of the organisation, the size and complexity of the markets served, the product and process technology and the rate of change in the marketing environment. There are several ways of incorporating and structuring marketing within the organisation, and these are discussed below.

## Organisational alternatives

There are four main choices for structuring marketing management within a department, focusing on function, products, regions or segments. The marketing department might also choose to develop a matrix structure, allowing an equal focus on both function and products, for example. These are all shown in Figure 13.9. The organisation might, of course, choose not to have a formal marketing department at all. Each of these choices is discussed below.

### Functional organisation

A functional department is structured along the lines of specific marketing activities. This means there are very specialised roles and responsibilities, and that individual managers have to build expertise. Such a department might have, for example, a market research manager, an advertising and promotions manager and a new product development manager, each of whom will report to the organisation's marketing director.

This system works well in organisations where the various business functions are centralised, but problems can arise where they are decentralised. Then, functional marketing tasks have to be coordinated across diverse areas, with greater or lesser degrees of cooperation and acceptance.

### Product organisation

Giving managers responsibility for specific products, brands or categories of product might suit a larger company with major brands or with diverse and very different product interests. The manager, reporting to a product group manager or a marketing director, builds expertise around the product, and is responsible for all aspects of its development, its strategic

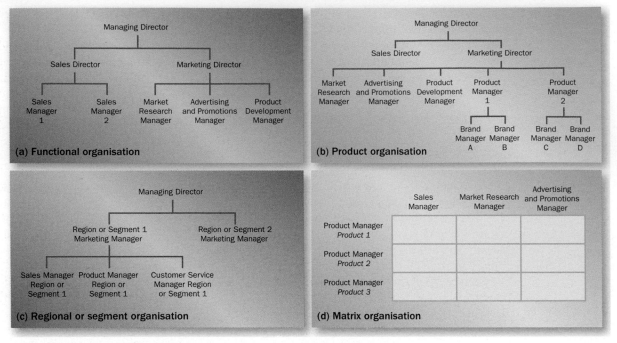

**Figure 13.9** Forms of marketing organisation

and marketing mix planning and its day-to-day welfare. Other specialist staff, such as market researchers, might be involved as necessary to help the product manager.

The product, brand or category management approach is very popular in fmcg markets. It gives clear lines of management responsibility, but there is still a need for a central function to coordinate the overall portfolio. The main problem with product organisation is working with other functions, such as production, finance, etc., to get the resources, attention and effort that the product needs. There is also the risk that too many management layers will be introduced, hence the move towards category management (i.e. responsibility for a group of brands) rather than individual brand management.

## Regional organisation

An organisation with its activities spread over a wide geographic area, or one operating in markets with distinct regional differences, might find regionally based marketing responsibility attractive. The regional marketing manager, along with a support team, will make all marketing decisions relevant to planning and operations in that territory. There will then be some mechanism for coordinating regional efforts at a national or international level to ensure consistency and strategic fit. As larger organisations become more international, this approach is becoming more common. The main benefit is that local managers develop the knowledge and expertise to know what is best for their region. They can then develop the most appropriate, fully integrated marketing mix package, as well as contributing intelligently to the organisation's overall strategic planning for that region.

Regionally based marketing departments are particularly attractive to organisations with a great emphasis on selling in the field, where close coordination and control are necessary. They are also appropriate for service industries, such as hospitality, where local conditions may differ and where, again, close control and coordination of service delivery are required.

## Segmental organisation

An organisation that serves diverse groups of customers with very different needs might choose to develop marketing teams dedicated to each of those groups. This is because the marketing decision-making and the marketing mixes have to be tailored to the individual needs of segments in which the competitive threats may be very different.

A brewery, for example, will market to the licensed trade (for instance pubs and clubs) and the retail trade (for instance, supermarkets and off-licences) very differently; a manufacturer of wound dressings will market differently to the hospital sector and to the pharmacist; a car dealer will market differently to the family motorist and to a fleet buyer. The volume purchased by individual customers within the same segment might create differences that are reflected in the marketing effort. An fmcg manufacturer will create a different kind of marketing mix and customer relationship with the top six multiple supermarket chains than with the many thousands of small independent grocers.

The marketing manager for a particular segment or customer group will have a range of specialist support staff and will report to a senior marketing manager or director with overall responsibility for all segments.

## Matrix organisation

A matrix approach allows the marketing department to get the best of more than one of the previous methods of organisation. It can be particularly useful in large diverse organisations or where specialists and project teams have to work on major cross-functional activities, for example PR, new product development or marketing research programmes.

## No department

Of course, another option is not to have a department at all. Small organisations might not be able to afford specialist marketing staff and thus perhaps the owner finds himself or herself performing a multifunctional role as sales representative, promotional decision-maker and strategist rolled into one. If a small organisation does decide to invest in marketing staff, the recruit might be put into an office-based administrative support role or into a sales role.

## Sales-driven organisations

Some organisations are still driven by sales. They might have a few very large customers and be selling a complex technology. In such a case, the role of marketing is relegated to a support role that is largely concerned with PR and low-key promotional activity. Other organisations, particularly those currently or previously in the public sector, are still in the process of developing marketing departments. Universities, for example, are reappraising the role of marketing. Although they might have marketing departments, many of the key variables are beyond the control of their marketing managers. For example, academics, with or without the benefit of market research, develop and validate new courses; in another area, domestic full-time student fees and student numbers are agreed with the government. Often, universities see the marketing department's role as purely functional, handling student recruitment fairs, prospectuses, schools liaison and advertising. In short, there is no guarantee that having a department means that there will be a marketing orientation in the organisation.

# Controlling marketing activities

Control is a vital aspect of implementing marketing plans, whether strategic or operational. It helps to ensure that activities happen as planned, with proper management. It also provides important feedback that enables managers to determine whether or not their decisions, actions and strategies are working appropriately in practice.

# The marketing control process

The marketing control phase, shown in Figure 13.10, is not an afterthought to be bolted on to the end of the planning process, but should be designed as an important part of that process. In setting marketing objectives, it is important to define them in terms of detailed time-specific goals against which performance can be measured. This makes the task of control more manageable, since those areas where serious deviation is occurring can then be easily diagnosed. Management effort can thus be focused on areas of greatest need rather than being spread too thinly.

As soon as the control mechanism shows that a gap is opening between proposed targets and actual achievement, managers can start to look for reasons for this happening. Sometimes the reasons might be obvious, for example, a stockout in a particular region or the loss of a major customer. In other situations, however, further research might have to be commissioned to support deeper analysis of the underlying causes. If, for example, a brand's market share continues to decline despite increased marketing effort, managers might start asking serious questions about customer responsiveness and the brand's competitive positioning. Failure to achieve targets does not, however, mean automatic condemnation of the marketing plan and its manager. It could be that targets were hopelessly optimistic, in the light of the emerging market conditions. Alternatively, other departments within the organisation, such as production or logistics, may have failed to achieve their targets.

**Figure 13.10**
Marketing control

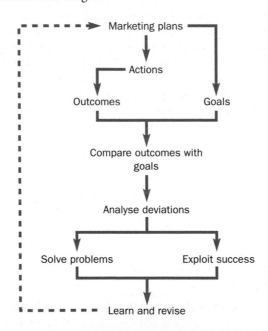

## Chapter summary

- Marketing planning is about developing the objectives, strategies and marketing mixes that best exploit the opportunities available to the organisation. Planning should itself be a planned and managed process. This process helps organisations to analyse themselves and their marketing environments more systematically and honestly. It also helps organisations to coordinate and control their marketing activities more effectively. Planning should be a flexible, dynamic activity that is fed with accurate, reliable and timely information, and is not divorced from the managers who have the day-to-day responsibility for implementing the plans. Marketing plans can be strategic or operational. The plans help to integrate activities, schedule resources, specify responsibilities and provide benchmarks for measuring progress.

- There are eight main stages in the planning process: corporate objectives, the marketing audit, marketing analysis, setting marketing objectives, marketing strategies, marketing programmes, controls and evaluation, and budgeting. Techniques such as product portfolio analysis and competitor analysis can be used to help compile the marketing audit, the key points of which can then be summarised in the SWOT analysis, a snapshot of 'where are we now?' On the basis of the SWOT, objectives can be set and strategies defined with the help of tools such as the Ansoff matrix ('where do we want to be?' and 'how do we want to compete?'). These strategies are operationalised through marketing programmes ('how do we get there?'). Controls and evaluation help to monitor progress towards achieving objectives.

- In order to fulfil its function properly, the marketing department should have a central role within the organisation, with senior management of equal status to those in other functional areas. It is also important, however, that the marketing philosophy pervades the whole enterprise, regardless of the size or formality of the marketing department. There are several approaches to structuring the marketing department itself. These are the functional, product-based, regional, segmental or matrix approaches.

- As marketing plans are being implemented, they have to be monitored and controlled. Strategic control concerns the longer-term direction of marketing strategy, whereas operational control assesses the day-to-day success of marketing activities. Using information gathered in the monitoring process, the actual achievements of marketing strategies can be compared with planned or expected outcomes. Managers can then analyse gaps and decide whether they are significant enough to warrant corrective action. Although this can be a quantitative analysis, it should still be looked at in the context of more qualitative issues concerning customer needs and synergies between customers, markets or products.

# Questions for review and discussion

**13.1** Define the main factors influencing organisations' *marketing strategies*.

**13.2** Define the stages in the *marketing planning process*.

**13.3** What is a *product portfolio* and what are the problems of implementing portfolio models in practice?

**13.4** Using whatever information you can find, develop a SWOT analysis for the organisation of your choice. What are the implications of your analysis for the organisation's short- and long-term priorities?

**13.5** For each cell of the Ansoff matrix, find and discuss an example of an organisation that seems

to have implemented that particular growth strategy.

**13.6** What kind of marketing organisational structure would be appropriate for each of the following situations and why?

(a) a small single product engineering company;

(b) a large fmcg manufacturer selling a wide range of products into several different European markets;

(c) a pharmaceutical company manufacturing both prescription and 'over the counter' medicines.

# RETAILING A SUSTAINABLE STRATEGY

Marks & Spencer (M&S) has always upheld high standards of business behaviour and now its policies are enshrined in a statement of their approach to corporate social responsibility (CSR) that is available to customers, employees, shareholders, suppliers, media, government and the public. M&S has brought together the various strands of CSR into its Plan A (there is no Plan B!) to enable clearer communication with all those publics and to set identifiable and measurable targets as milestones. Plan A is an action plan focused on CSR that shows real ambitious commitment to operational change in areas such as climate change, waste management, sustainable raw materials, fair partnership with suppliers, and health. It covers the operating period up until 2015. When it was launched in 2007, it listed 100 commitments, and a further 80 were added in 2011. Over 95 of them have already been achieved, and all but seven are on target.

There is, however, also a business dimension as around £70 million was added back to M&S's profitability as a result of the various initiatives under Plan A but, of course, that needs to be put into the context of M&S's £9.5 billion sales revenue. M&S is a large operation with 600 stores in the UK alone, with 21 million people visiting a store each week and the objective is that 95 per cent of the UK population should live within a thirty-minute drive of a store. Online retailing has made an impact, but still represents less than 10 per cent of sales and thus M&S is still largely a bricks and mortar operation. It has positioned itself as a high-quality but good-value clothing and homeware store, with 2,000 suppliers globally. The brand name is its greatest asset. Over the 100 years or more of M&S's existence, the brand has come to represent quality, fair dealing and good service. CSR policies need to work within that framework. To M&S, CSR means:

## Protecting the environment

There is a clear recognition of the effects of global warming due to greenhouse gases, and a fundamental part of M&S's commitment is a reduction in its carbon footprint. M&S has contributed to the Carbon Trust's standard for measuring the carbon footprint of products but as yet, does not envisage going further by introducing carbon labels on its products. The M&S supply chain is also affected by efforts to reduce greenhouse emissions, and targets have been set to guide suppliers, although these are not yet rigidly enforced. With food suppliers, M&S is working on a sustainability award framework with farmers and growers. The 'greener living' shop concentrates on Fairtrade, organic and recycled products. It even has carbon neutral lingerie from the first carbon neutral manufacturing plant in Sri Lanka which produces 30 per cent less carbon emissions. The Autograph Leaves Lingerie range includes six bras, three briefs and one suspender, all of which are carbon neutral. M&S has calculated the emissions right through from raw material harvesting to manufacturing, shipping, distribution and final use and disposal.

Packaging is a major contributor to landfill sites so efforts are being made to reduce that by improving sustainability and increasing recyclability. That includes improving the range and quality of packaging, at the same time recognising that virtually all of it is destroyed after purchase. Food waste is a problem for food retailers. M&S think it is good business and good for the environment if prices are reduced by up to 30 per cent before the sell by date to encourage customers to buy and use something. Any remaining food is then sold to employees or donated to local charities. To date, food waste has been cut by 29 per cent with nearly all the rest of the unsold food used for fertiliser and biofuels. M&S is also encouraging its customers to reduce waste at home, by helping them to plan their shopping better. Consumers throw away 5 million tonnes of usable food each year. It's not just food that gets wasted: the carrier bags in which it is taken home are a problem. Thus, since, 2008 M&S has charged 5p for a plastic carrier bag and this has succeeded in reducing usage by 80 per cent. M&S has extended recycling to Christmas cards, batteries, small electrical products and even clothes hangers.

Clothing is a core product for M&S. It works with Oxfam to re-use and recycle unwanted clothes and works with its suppliers to ensure that environmental damage in harvesting raw materials and the production of garments is kept to a minimum.

Sustainably-sourced materials are at the heart of its buying and many of the issues identified in this book have already been tackled by M&S. All wood comes from FSC certified sources (see p. 71), and six items have been targeted for special consideration in reducing the damage to rainforests: palm oil, soya, cocoa, coffee, leather and some woods. None of these items will be used by M&S if they contribute to further deforestation. Animals and fish are also covered. It doesn't sell any fish that is on the Marine Conservation Society 'blacklist' (see pp. 42 and 583), only uses free range eggs, and it never tests beauty and household products on animals.

M&S has been praised for its comprehensive approach to the environment which it treats holistically, and it encompasses its suppliers and customers as well. M&S certainly promotes the environmental agenda and some initiatives, such as the charge for carrier bags, have been pioneering and outstanding successes.

## Code of ethics

Upholding high ethical standards is seen as important for guiding how the organisation values its staff, suppliers and customers. The code covers bribery both home and overseas (see p. 21), employment policy, diversity and equality and sets benchmarks that guide local decision making. M&S does not undertake collective bargaining but prefers to communicate through Business Involvement Groups and Works Councils. It is not a signatory to the UN Global Compact or International Labour Organisation Conventions. Bribery is commonplace for getting things done overseas, especially with government officials and public bodies, but M&S takes a firm stand on that.

M&S is largely a UK employer but its international business from franchised and part-owned operations accounts for 5 per cent of its turnover. It offers similar conditions and frameworks to overseas employees as it does to domestic ones. It recruits mainly people from the local community and seeks to cap the proportion of expatriate managers at 20 per cent.

## Dealing with the community

M&S recognises the valuable role that businesses can play in the community, not just from a trading perspective but also in the broadest sense as good citizens. M&S invested over £13 million in community projects in 2009. It was a founder member of Business in the Community and it supports charities with donations of clothing, food and unwanted equipment and that has helped organisations such

as Oxfam and Shelter. In addition, M&S makes cash donations to a wide range of good causes including Breakthrough Breast Cancer (£2.1 million), Macmillan, The Prostate Cancer Charity, Shelter and WWF at a national level as well as running an annual Charity Challenge. At the other end of the scale, it supports some schools and hospitals with small donations. Through clothes hanger recycling it aims to donate £650,000 to UNICEF per year for three years to support work with vulnerable children and families. Interestingly, M&S does not support religious bodies or political parties. It responds to major disasters with some circumspection, and a factor is whether the disaster has occurred in a region of the world where it has an interest through its stores or suppliers.

## Supplier policy

M&S has always taken a rigorous approach to developing suppliers and expects a high degree of conformity in its supply chains. It reaches out to 70 countries with 2,000 suppliers and has local buying offices and, more importantly, regional compliance staff in Turkey, India, Bangladesh, Vietnam, Sri Lanka and China. It insists on compliance with all relevant local and national laws, particularly on working hours and conditions, health and safety, rates of pay, terms of employment and minimum age of employment. If breaches are serious or repeated then the supplier is dropped. This is monitored by M&S, a third party, or self-audits as the last thing M&S wants is to be accused of buying from a supplier that is in breach of human rights by employing children, for example.

In Sri Lanka, M&S continues to work with 25 suppliers including groups such as Brandix and Hirdramani, despite the country having lost its favoured EU status for labour abuses. These abuses did not affect M&S suppliers, and so M&S continued to work with them within its own policy framework, giving employment to 75,000 people. It has been estimated that 21 per cent of the clothing sold in M&S comes from Sri Lanka. Only China supplies more.

Closer to home, M&S pledged in 2010 that it would not stock any food brands that did not fit with environmental and ethical concerns. That pledge covers 30,000 lines. By 2015, over 50 per cent of its own-brand products will carry a sustainability or ethical quality mark and that process will be complete by 2020. However, 350 fmcg brands will not be required to sign up to the initiative, although they are expected to live up to the standards. There is a limit to the power of the retailer in insisting that other brands comply. By 2012, all M&S farmers who supply meat, dairy produce and flowers will have had to sign up to the scheme however. This stance has been questioned, as potentially making M&S less flexible in changing supply sources and is bound to put even more pressure on suppliers, for example in ensuring traceability, at a time when prices are not moving much. This is especially problematic when the sources are overseas. Is it wise to place so much emphasis on sustainability over other differentiating factors? Eco-factories and better employment conditions sound good in theory but do they add to labour's welfare overseas or make a business more competitive, unless all suppliers do it?

## Healthy consumers

Finally , a section of its CSR statement is devoted to consumer health. M&S as a food retailer wants us to have a better diet and to live healthier lifestyles. Salt levels in food have been reduced considerably and there are now no artificial colours or flavourings in food. But the bigger challenge is obesity, which is a societal problem (see p. 95). M&S insists on adequate labelling to inform consumers of guideline daily amounts (GDA) on labels, in line with the Food Standards Agency's recommendations. It has also replaced hydrogenated fats and oils in its products to make them healthier. All of this is detailed in information booklets for consumers, although, of course, those in greatest need don't necessarily read them!

Organic foods are important for the green agenda, and by some are thought to contribute to a healthier diet, but this is an issue that shows how conflict can exist between what M&S thinks is right and what consumers demand. Sales of organic food are actually lower than 2005/6, despite M&S wanting to treble sales. Now, consumers think it is just another claim alongside Fairtade, free range and certified. Although consumers value organic foods, it does not mean that they will pay a premium for them (see Chapter 2, p. 61).

Consumer health is also a concern that informs M&S's approach to alcohol, except this time it has the backing of government. Alcohol intake and all drink products are labelled with guidance on consumption limits, for those who bother reading them. It also supports the 'Think 25' campaign which requires proof of age from anyone who appears to be under 25 to deter underage drinking (see p. 356). Its aim is not to stop drinking, but to encourage responsible consumption.

So M&S takes its CSR responsibilities very seriously and has enshrined them within Plan A. But it's not just hype or good public relations. Managerially, M&S has appointed a Director of Plan A, CSR and Sustainable Business who coordinates activities and reports to the Chief Executive on progress. Managers responsible for parts of Plan A discuss and report progress monthly so that there is a chain of command and an information flow. This makes Plan A a programme that affects all areas of the business, including stores as well as suppliers. Some parts of it require investment, such as with the supply chain and Fairtrade, others lead to new product ranges with the potential for good sales, such as Autograph Leaves, but overall is hoped that the benefits gained outweigh any costs so that the net cost to the consumer is zero.

Customers are becoming increasingly involved through social networking sites such as Facebook and Twitter, as the various initiatives and campaigns lend themselves to chat and the passing of information. These include, for example, Oxfam putting 3 million unwanted garments to use, raising over £3 million in the process; the fact that 90 per cent of the wild fish sold were from sustainable sources compared with 62 per cent the previous year; and under the 'ethical model factory' scheme, three factories in India were added to 12 in Bangladesh as examples of good practice.

But is the approach flawed? What is the point in claiming to be the most sustainable retailer in the world if there are no agreed benchmark criteria to measure against? It must be more than a series of excellent and well intentioned actions. Other major retailers also make strong claims in this area. Sainsbury's, for example, claims to be a leader in addressing environmental and ethical issues. If there is no agreed definition of sustainability, any actions could be said to contribute towards it. Even an M&S spokesperson is quoted as saying, 'there is no current benchmarking system for retailers on sustainability' (as quoted by *The Guardian*, 2010).

What is beyond doubt is that M&S has a deep and ongoing commitment to CSR that is backed up with positive action. The question remains, however, is it enough and does it really make a difference?

*Sources*: Clews (2011); *Greenwire News Agency* (2010); *The Grocer* (2010a); *The Guardian* (2010; 2011); *Lanka Business Online* (2010); *Management Today* (2010); *Marketing Week* (2010; 2011); Phillips (2011); Pickard (2011); *Sunday Observer* (2011); Thompson (2010a); http://plana.marksandspencer.com/media/pdf/how_we-do_business_report_2011.pdf.

# Questions

1 What do you think might be the particular problems that M&S might face in implementing the kind of Plan A initiatives described in the case?

2 Does a sustainability and CSR agenda offer sufficient grounds for a viable competitive positioning strategy in the retail sector?

3 According to an IGD survey, 68 per cent of shoppers agree strongly, or tend to agree that 'food and grocery companies should just get on with doing the right thing for the environment rather than telling me about it' and 83 per cent agree strongly or tend to agree that 'I expect food and grocery companies to be constantly checking that their suppliers are acting responsibly towards the environment' (Pickard, 2011). What are the implications of these findings for Plan A and M&S's management of the interface between Plan A and the general public?

4 M&S found a certain amount of consumer reluctance to 'buy into' its provision of organic foods. How could M&S overcome that? To what extent should a retailer be expected to tell its customers 'what's good for them'? Should it simply respond to consumer demands?

## References for chapter 13

Abell, D. and Hammond, J. (1979) *Strategic Market Planning*, Prentice Hall.

Alarcon, C. (2009) 'Heinz Unveils £5m Brand Push to Strengthen "Emotional Ties"', *Marketing Week*, 22 October.

Aldridge, S. (2011) 'British Biotech Rebuilding Momentum', *InPharm*, 26 May, accessed via www.inpharm.com/news/156274/british-biotech-rebuilding-momentum.

Alva, M. (2010) 'Amazon's New Kindle Off to Fast Start', *Investor's Business Daily*, 27 August.

Ansoff, H.I. (1957) 'Strategies for Diversification', *Harvard Business Review*, 25 (5), pp. 113–25.

Arnott, S. (2011) 'UK Firms Decide It's Time to Hang Up on Indian Call Centres', *The Independent*, 9 July.

Arnott, S. (2010) 'Virgin in Price-fixing Inquiry as Cathay Turns Whistle-blower', *The Independent*, 23 April.

Bainbridge, J. (2011) 'All Shook Up', *Marketing*, 2 March.

Bamford, V. (2011) 'Losing Power', *The Grocer*, 3 September.

Barnett, M. (2011a) 'Heinzmeanzbusiness', *Marketing Week*, 25 August.

Barnett, M. (2011b) 'Online Brands Set Off on New Marketing Journey', *Marketing Week*, 15 September.

Barrett, C. (2011) 'Mothercare Undergoes Midlife Crisis', *Financial Times*, 19 September.

Best, J. (2011), 'Santander Hangs Up on Indian Call Centres', Silicon.com, 8 July.

Bolger, A. (2010) 'Linn Products Benefits from Digital Switch', *Financial Times*, 23 November.

Bradshaw, T. (2011) 'Moshi Monsters Maker Valued at $200m', *Financial Times*, 24 June.

Branston (2011) 'Salad Cream with a Twist – from Branston', *Talking Retail*, 8 March, accessed via www.talkingretail.com/products/product-news/salad-cream-with-a-twist-from-branston.

Britton, T. (2011) 'The YouGov Take: iPad – the Mass Market Niche Product', *Marketing Week*, 18 May.

Brownsell, A. (2010) 'Bmi Scraps Business Class on Domestic Flights', *Brand Republic*, 25 January.

Brownsell, A. (2011) 'Swinton Owner Eyes UK Launch', *Marketing*, 20 July.

*Business and Finance* (2011) 'New Routes to Success', *Business and Finance*, 25 February.

Cave, A. (2011) 'Virgin: Regulator Must Look at BA Bid', *Sunday Telegraph*, 6 November.

*China Energy* (2011) 'Vestas Inks Wind Turbine Deal with China Datang Renewable', *China Energy*, 20 June.

Clews, M. (2011) 'M&S Reduces its Plan A Organic Produce Targets', *Marketing Week*, 9 June.

*Convenience Store* (2011) 'Batteries – Power Selling', *Convenience Store*, 18 September, accessed via www.thegrocer.co.uk/articles.aspx?page=independentarticle&ID=221079.

Costa, M. (2011) 'Forever 21 Brings "Speed Retailing" to the UK', *Marketing Week*, 29 September.

Craven, N. (2011) 'Supermarkets Set for New Price War', *Mail on Sunday*, 11 September.

Creasey, S. (2010) 'Sauces Raise Their Game', *The Grocer*, 18 September.

*DNA Sunday* (2010) 'Indian Call Centres for the Poorer Customers Only', *DNA Sunday*, 14 March.

Edgecliffe-Johnson, A. (2011) 'Kindle E-book Sales Soar for Amazon', *Financial Times*, 19 May.

*ENP Newswire* (2011) 'Telefonica and China Unicom Strengthen their Strategic Alliance and Agree a New Mutual Investment', *ENP Newswire*, 25 January.

*eWeek* (2011) 'AMD Choosing Tablets Over Smartphones Reports', *eWeek*, 9 August.

*Food and Drink Innovation Network* (2011) 'Heinz Mayo to Become Heinz Mayonnaise with New Packaging Design', *Food and Drink Innovation Network*, 2 June, accessed via www.fdin.org.uk/2011/06/.heinz-mayo-to-become-heinz-mayonnaise-with-new-packaging-design/.

Gardner, R. (2004) 'Lipton Continues "Don't Knock It" Idea', *Campaign*, 18 June, p. 10.

Geddes, I. (2011) 'UK Retailing at the Turning Point – Your Game Plan for Success', *Mondaq Business Briefing*, 18 April.

Giuffrida, A. (2011) 'Can a Toy for the Rich Find Home Port in China?', *International Herald Tribune*, 22 September.

Goldfingle, G. (2011) 'Forever 21 Boss Spells Out Strategy for UK Offensive', *Retail Week*, 29 July.

*Greenwire News Agency* (2010), 'Marks & Spencer Aims to Become World's Greenest Retailer by 2015', *Greenwire News Agency*, 14 June.

*The Grocer* (2010a) 'Brands Must Meet M&S's Plan A Ideals', *The Grocer*, 6 March.

*The Grocer* (2010b) 'Sauces: Table', *The Grocer*, 18 December.

*The Grocer* (2011a) 'Branston to Take on Heinz in Salad Cream', *The Grocer*, 5 March.

*The Grocer* (2011b) 'Emmi to Spend Big on its Summer Push', *The Grocer*, 25 June.

*The Guardian* (2010) 'Marks & Spencer Sustainability Pledge is Flawed', *The Guardian*, 15 March.

*The Guardian* (2011) 'Marks & Spencer – an Ambitious Commitment to Tackling Waste', *The Guardian*, 24 May.

Gulati, R. (1998) 'Alliances and Networks', *Strategic Management Journal*, 19 (4), pp. 293–317.

Hall, E. (2011) 'Mind Candy's Moshi Monsters Sets Out to be the "Facebook for Kids"', *Advertising Age*, 13 June.

Halliwell, J. (2011) 'Always Cheapest. But Now it's the Favourite', *The Grocer*, 18 June.

Horn, L. (2011) 'Will Amazon Introduce Kindle Devices in China?', *PC Magazine*, 28 October.

Humphries, K. (2010) 'On the Money: Heinz Sees Increased Trade Marketing Spend', *Just-Food*, 27 February.

Jargon, J. (2011) 'Subway Runs Past McDonald's Chain', *Wall Street Journal*, 8 March.

Jopson, B. and Gelles, D. (2011) 'Amazon to Launch Library Service for Kindle', *Financial Times*, 20 April.

Kharif, O. (2011) 'American Express Seeks Acquisitions to Expand in Online, Mobile', *Bloomberg*, 14 September, accessed via www.bloomberg.com/news/2011-09-14/american-express-seeks-acquisitions-to-expand-e-commerce-mobile-payments.html.

*Lanka Business Online* (2010) 'Eco Apparels: Sri Lanka Eco-friendly Apparel Making Gives Edge: Marks & Spencer', *Lanka Business Online*, 1 October.

Lee, J. (2010) 'Mothercare', *Marketing*, 28 April.

Lemer, J. (2010) 'UPS to Tap China's Booming Domestic Market', *Financial Times*, 27 September.

*License! Global Weekly E-news* (2010) 'Moshi Monsters Forecasts $100 m Merch Revenue in 2011', *License! Global Weekly E-news*, 3 November, accessed via www.licensemag.com/licensemag/Toys+%26+Video+Games/Moshi-Monsters-Forecasts-100M-Merch-Revenue-in-201/ArticleStandard/Article/detail/693581.

Limin, C. (2010) 'Rival Warns Kindle Will Fail in China', *China Daily*, 27 October.

Lyons, R. (2009) 'BMI's Future up in the Air as Firms Balk at Asking Price', *The Scotsman*, 3 November.

*M2 Presswire* (2010) 'Moshi Monsters Ready to Invade Toy Shops', *M2 Presswire*, 24 June.

Maddox, K. (2010) 'Brand Experts Mixed on New UPS Campaign', *B to B*, 11 October.

*Management Today* (2010) 'Green Business Awards 2010: Green Business of the Year - Winner Marks and Spencer', *Management Today*, 1 November.

*Market News Publishing* (2011) 'Bombardier Inc Wins Third Mass Transit Complete Signalling System In Brazil', *Market News Publishing*, 21 September.

*Marketing* (2011) 'Insurance Site Hires Corfield', *Marketing*, 5 October.

*Marketing Week* (2010) 'M&S "Risks Shackling Itself" Through Extension of Plan A', *Marketing Week*, 4 March.

*Marketing Week* (2011) 'Case study: Marks & Spencer', *Marketing Week*, 13 April.

McDonald, M. (1989) *Marketing Plans*, Butterworth Heinemann.

Mintel (2010) 'Bottled Sauces', *Mintel Market Intelligence*, November accessed via http://academic.mintel.com/sinatra/oxygen_academic/search_results/show&/display/id=479955.

Nielsen, T. (2010) 'Wheels on Fire', *Director*, 1 November.

*New Media Age* (2010) 'Heinz Works with Supermarkets on Digital Campaign', *New Media Age*, 14 October.

*New Media Age* (2011) 'Case Study: Moshi Monsters Add Fun to Learning', *New Media Age*, 30 June.

*New Scientist* (2011) 'China Tries Again to Stop Smoking', *New Scientist*, 2 April.

O'Connell (2011) 'BA's Win-win on Slots', *Sunday Times*, 6 November.

Perez, S. (2010) 'Interview – Cesar Alierta', *Wall Street Journal Europe*, 1 November.

Phillips, B. (2011) 'M&S Plan A "Behind Plan" for Organic Food', *The Grocer*, 18 June.

Pickard, T. (2011) 'Why Sustainability is a Smart Strategy', *IGD Newsletter*, 10 November.

Pimentel, B. (2011) 'AMD "Becoming Irrelevant" as Intel Alternative', *MarketWatch*, 11 July.

Porter, M. (1979) 'How Competitive Forces Shape Strategy', *Harvard Business Review*, 57 (2), pp. 137–45.

*Post Magazine* (2010) 'Zurich Moves to Keep Pace with Mid-market', *Post Magazine*, 30 September.

Price, T. (2011) 'Vestas to Deploy Its First Floating Wind Turbine', *Renewable Energy Magazine*, 11 March.

*Renewable Energy Focus* (2009) 'Vestas to Scale Back Production Facilities in Europe', *Renewable Energy Focus*, 29 April, accessed via www.renewableenergyfocus.com/view/1602/vestas-to-scale-back-production-facilities-in-europe/.

Reuters (2010) 'Vestas Will Not Chase Market Share at Any Price', *Reuters*, 1 September, accessed via www.reuters.com/article/2010/09/01/us-vestas-idUSTRE6807MA20100901.

Riley, L. (2011) 'Illy Iced Coffee Set to Keep "Cold Hot" Drink Category on the Boil', *The Grocer*, 14 May.

Robertson, D. (2009) 'Bmi's Fight for Survival Brings Job Cuts and Closed Routes', *The Times*, 26 November.

Rogerson, P. (2005) 'Linn Sales Volume Is Turned Down as Income Falls 8 Per Cent', *The Herald*, 3 September, p. 20.

Rothwell, S. (2011) 'Branson Seeks Halt to BA "Salami Slicing" of Lufthansa's BMI', *Bloomberg*, 26 September, accessed via www.bloomberg.com/news/2011-09-26/

branson-seeks-halt-to-ba-s-salami-slicing-of-lufthansa-s-bmi.html.

Smith, M. (2010) 'Music Sounds Better as Linn Turn to Downloads', *The Herald*, 24 November.

*Sunday Observer* (2011) 'M&S Intimates, Marks & Spencer Launch Autograph Leaves', *Sunday Observer*, 22 May.

Tan, A. (2011) 'Battle of the Chips', *Digital Life*, 22 June.

Thompson, J. (2010a) 'Marks & Spencer Sets Out Its Sustainable Stall', *The Independent*, 2 March.

Thompson, J. (2010b) 'Asda Vows to End "Phoney Price Wars" with Guarantee', *The Independent*, 28 April.

Thomson, R. (2011) 'New Markets – Making the Right Moves', *Retail Week*, 20 May.

Townsend, M. (2011) 'Barnes & Noble Sinks Most Since June After Halting Dividend', *Bloomberg*, 22 February, accessed via www.bloomberg.com/news/2011-02-22/barnes-noble-falls-after-dividend-halt-same-store-sales-rise.html.

Vass, S. (2010) 'How Close were we to Going Bust? One Hates to Speculate. Really Close . . .', *Sunday Herald*, 18 July.

Wallop, H. (2011) 'Tesco Cuts Prices as Fight Taken to its Rivals', *Daily Telegraph*, 22 September.

Wan, W. (2011) 'In China, Battling State-owned Big Tobacco', *Washington Post*, 27 June.

Wang, F. (2011) 'China Smoking Deaths Could Triple by 2030, Report Warns', *Agence France Presse*, 7 January.

*Warren's Washington Internet Daily* (2011) 'Apple, Publishers Fixed Ebook Prices to Halt Amazon's $9.99 "Anchor", Suit Alleges', *Warren's Washington Interet Daily*, 11 August.

Wearden, G. (2011) 'Mothercare to Close Nearly a Third of UK Stores', *The Guardian*, 19 May.

West, K. (2011) 'Germans Retreat from Heathrow', *Sunday Times*, 6 November.

Williams, C. (2011) 'Water Plans E-reader to Challenge Amazon Kindle', *Daily Telegraph*, 9 September.

Wiseman, E. (2011) 'The Gospel According to Forever 21', *The Observer*, 17 July.

Wood, Z. (2011) 'Tesco's Price War Threat Sends Supermarket Shares Plunging', *The Guardian*, 22 September.

Woodhead, M. (2009) 'How Germany Won the War for the Renewable Energy Sector', *Sunday Times*, 29 October.

*Xinhua News Agency* (2011) 'China Sees Huge Market Potential in Smoking Cessation', *Xinhua News Agency*, 27 May.

Yeraswork, Z. (2011) 'Intel, AMD Ramp Up Chip Game', *CRNTech*, 1 March.

# CHAPTER 14

# Services and non-profit marketing

## LEARNING OBJECTIVES

This chapter will help you to:

- define the characteristics that differentiate services from other products and outline their impact on marketing;
- develop an extended marketing mix of 7Ps that takes the characteristics of services into account and allows comprehensive marketing strategies to be developed for services;
- understand the importance and impact of service quality and productivity issues; and
- understand the special characteristics of non-profit organisations within the service sector, and the implications for their marketing activities.

## INTRODUCTION

**THE FOCUS OF THIS** chapter is on the marketing of services, whether sold for profit or not. Service products cover a wide range of applications. In the profit-making sector, services marketing includes travel and tourism, banking and insurance, and personal and professional services ranging from accountancy, legal services and business consultancy through to hairdressing and garden planning and design. In the non-profit-making sector, services marketing applications include education, medicine and charities through to various aspects of government activity that need to be 'sold' to the public.

Marketing these kinds of services is somewhat different from marketing physical products. The major marketing principles discussed in this book – segmenting the market, the need for research, sensible design of the marketing mix and the need for creativity, strategic thinking and innovation – are, of course, universally applicable, regardless of the type of product involved. Where the difference arises is in the detailed design and implementation of the marketing mix. There are several special factors that provide additional challenges for the services marketer.

This chapter, therefore, will examine in detail the special aspects of services that differentiate them from physical products. It will then look at the issues involved in designing the services marketing mix and the marketing management challenges arising from its implementation. Finally, the whole area of marketing services in the non-profit sector will be considered.

eg
Whether it's the fun fairs of Rhyl, the wide open beaches of Porthmadog, the cultural heritage of Caernarfon Castle, the wild beauty of Snowdonia or the bustling city of Cardiff, Wales has much to offer tourists, from England, the rest of Europe, and increasingly the world. But what is the product? It's the sum of all the experiences, memories, and fun that go to make up a short break, or a longer holiday. The job of Visit Wales is to provide the marketing expertise to sell the promise of those holidays on behalf of the Welsh Government.

It launched a new 'visit Wales' campaign in the spring of 2010. It featured a real UK family which had previously had a disappointing holiday abroad and filmed them having a 'proper' holiday in Wales, emphasising the authentic, memorable and different experiences that characterise the country. The target for the campaign was to generate 80,000 quality enquiries, 50 per cent of which had to be from people who had not visited Wales within the previous three years. It aimed to get at least 40 per cent conversion, defined in terms of actually taking a holiday or break in Wales. The budget was £1.26 million and that was mainly spent on television, inserts in appropriate print media, database marketing and online advertising. The promotion of Wales as a destination is just one part of the services marketing mix, however.

Visit Wales works with the travel trade to ensure that Wales is kept at the forefront of people's minds. These include tour operators, travel agents and coach tour operators, all of whom work with tourists before they arrive in Wales. Then there are also the accommodation providers, ranging from campsites through to the five-star hotels. Although they are all independent businesses in their own right, the experience that the tourist has when staying

Visit Wales works with the travel trade to keep Wales at the forefront of people's minds

*Source:* © Crown copyright (2011) Visit Wales, http://brochures.visitwales.co.uk

with them can be crucial to the overall satisfaction levels with the country as a destination generally. Visit Wales thus works with these providers to ensure effective grading of establishments to ensure comparable quality at fair prices so that the tourist doesn't develop unrealistic expectations. Visit Wales also works with accredited attractions, activities, sightseeing locations and events of interest to help them make the most of any opportunity for an enhanced customer experience. Some of these are non-financial, such as ensuring that a beauty spot has adequate toilet facilities and that information and interpretation of the site is available. Other venues, such as restaurants and night clubs, may not be central to the holiday service package but they can provide important ancillary experiences (new.wales. gov.uk/topics/tourism/marketing/properhols/?lang=en; www.visitwales.co.uk).

# Perspectives on service markets

Services are not a homogeneous group of products. There is wide variety within the services category, in terms of both the degree of service involved and the type of service product offered. Nevertheless, there are some general characteristics, common to many service products, that differentiate them as a genre from physical goods. This section, therefore, explores the criteria by which service products can be classified, and then goes on to look at the special characteristics of services and their implications for marketing.

## Classifying services

There are few pure services. In reality, many product 'packages' involve a greater or lesser level of service. Products can be placed along a spectrum, with virtually pure personal service involving few, if any, props at one end, and pure product that involves little or no service at the other. Most products do have some combination of physical good and service, as shown in Figure 14.1. The purchase of a chocolate bar, for example, involves little or no service other than the involvement of a checkout or till operator. The purchase of a gas appliance will involve professional fitting, and thus is a combination of physical and service product. A new office computer system could similarly involve installation and initial training. A visit to a theme park or theatre could involve some limited support products, such as guides and gifts, while the main product purchased is the experience itself. Finally, a visit to a psychiatrist or a hairdresser may involve a couch, a chair and some minor allied props such as an interview checklist or a hair-dryer. The

**Figure 14.1**
The product
spectrum

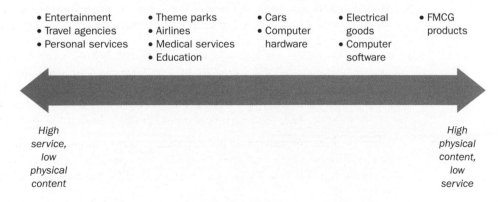

real product purchased here, however, is the personal service manufactured by the service deliverer, the psychiatrist or the hairdresser.

# Special characteristics of service markets

Five main characteristics have been identified as being unique to service markets (see, e.g. Sasser *et al.*, 1978; Cowell, 1984).

## Lack of ownership

Perhaps the most obvious aspect of a service product is that no goods change hands, as such, and therefore there is no transfer of ownership of anything. A legal transaction does still take place; an insurance company agrees to provide certain benefits as long as the premiums are paid and the terms and conditions of the policy are met. A car-rental company allows the customer full use of a vehicle for an agreed length of time, subject to some restraints on named drivers and type of usage, but the ownership of the vehicle remains with the rental company. A train seat can be reserved for a journey, but it is not owned. A subscription to the National Trust provides rights of access free of charge but no actual share in the ownership of its properties. The access, use or experience of the service is, therefore, often time-specific, usage-specific and subject to contractual terms and conditions.

The lack of ownership raises the issue of the transient nature of the purchase. Most service products involve some kind of 'experience' for the customer. This might be surrounded by props, for example a stage, lighting and sound systems, a lecture theatre, an insurance policy, a vehicle or a room, but these only serve to enhance or degrade the experience of the service. The faulty fuel gauge which means that the car hirer runs out of petrol in the most remote location, the hotel room next to the building site, the ineffective microphone at a concert all spoil the memory of the service consumed.

## Intangibility

A visit to a retail store reveals an inviting display of products to purchase. These products can be examined, touched, tried on, sampled, smelt or listened to. All this can help the customer to examine what is on offer and to make choices between competing brands. The consumer regularly uses the whole range of senses to assist decision-making. This is especially important before the purchase is made, but even after the sale the product can be assessed in terms of its use, its durability and whether it lives up to general expectations. If there is a fault with a physical product, it can be returned or exchanged.

With service products, it is far more difficult to use the senses in the same way as a means of making a purchase decision because the actual service experience can only take place after that decision has been made. The heart of a service is the experience created for the customer, whether individually as with a personal service such as dentistry or hairdressing, or as a group experience, such as a lecture, a show or a flight. In many cases, once the purchase decision has been made, all the customer will receive is a ticket, a confirmation of booking or some promise of future benefit. The service experience itself is intangible, and is only delivered after the customer is committed to the purchase.

Despite the problem of intangibility, the potential customer can make some kind of prior assessment of the service product. Using available tangible cues, the customer can assess whether a particular service provider is likely to deliver what is wanted. The actual cues used and the priority given to them will vary according to the customer's particular needs at the time. In choosing a hotel, for example, a customer might look at the following:

1 *Location.* If the customer is on holiday, then perhaps a hotel near to the beach or other tourist attraction would be preferred, or one in a very peaceful scenic setting. A business traveller, in contrast, might look for one that is convenient for the airport or close to the client being visited.

2 *Appearance.* A customer's expectations about a hotel are likely to be affected by its appearance. Does it look shabby or well kept? Is it too big or too small? Does it look welcoming? What is the decor like, both internally and externally? Do the rooms seem spacious enough and well-appointed?

3 *Additional services.* The customer might be concerned about the peripheral aspects of the service on offer. The tourist who will be spending two weeks in a hotel might be interested in the variety of bars and restaurants provided, hairdressing, laundry or crèche facilities, shopping and postal services, or the nightlife. The business traveller might be more concerned about car parking, shuttle buses to the airport, or fax and telephone provision.

4 *Customer handling.* If the potential customer contacts the hotel for further information or to make a reservation, the quality of the handling they receive might affect the purchase decision. Courtesy and friendliness will make a good impression, as will a prompt and accurate response to the query. This kind of efficiency implies a commitment to staff training and good operating systems to assist easy access to relevant information and the speedy processing of bookings.

# MARKETING IN ACTION

## A fighting fit market?

'Fitness' is a facility-driven industry, but one in which the product consumed by the user is essentially intangible, achieving personal targets in fitness by having access to the equipment, routines and perhaps expert personnel of the facility. Prices for the privilege vary considerably, depending upon the gym's facilities and location. Many of the private gym clubs operate on membership contracts of up to a year at a time, although local authority gyms can operate on a 'pay as you go' basis.

A fitness-oriented society coupled with rising levels of obesity was a major factor behind the rapid growth of the health and fitness sector through to 2008, although growth has slowed considerably since then. Much of the recent growth has been due to the local authorities improving and refurbishing public facilities rather than through the private-sector fitness clubs. Disposable incomes fell during the recession, and that, coupled with a general feeling that many people weren't actually using their fitness clubs often enough to get value for money from their subscriptions, meant that 'pay as you go' schemes became more attractive. Nevertheless, contract subscription fees overall stood at £2,482 million in 2010.

Within a static market, consolidation has been evident and some repositioning of fitness clubs has taken place to portray them as social clubs allied to a fitness theme. Many now offer, for example, dance and aerobic classes, and the bar and social areas are seen as important facilities for increasing the frequency of visits and the amount of time spent at the local fitness centre.

In 2010, the majority of health and fitness clubs were located in the South of England, accounting for 37 per cent of clubs in the UK. This reflects the high population density and the relative affluence of the population. The market for subscriptions is expected to pick up between 2011 and 2015, reflecting the spin off benefits from the 2012 London Olympics and the 2014 Glasgow Commonwealth Games. And, of course, the problems of obesity and the desire to look good are still there in the population. An increasing number of kids are also being targeted, as concern about child obesity also grows. At David Lloyd Leisure, around 266,000 children each month enjoy activities and facilities especially for the under-fives. Smaller children being active in swimming, tennis, and other healthy activities are ensuring the longer term membership of the clubs. For the 6–11 age group, having a wide range of sporting activities under one roof is a great benefit, but many are not given much encouragement other than money from parents! When asked how they would like to see kids spend their leisure time, the most popular answer was doing more sport, followed by doing more homework, and playing a musical instrument. Meanwhile, the parents are undoubtedly watching more telly!

The market leaders are Fitness First and David Lloyd Leisure. The latter, with 78 clubs, has invested heavily in varied facilities such as swimming pools and indoor tennis courts, but its main means of growth has been in opening new facilities rather than increasing usage at existing premises. Now, members can take a swim, attend classes, relax and unwind in the sauna, or make use of on-site hair salons or bars, as well as working out in the gym.

Virgin is also involved, with 70 Virgin Active sites in the UK, along with 35 fitness centres and 20 racket clubs purchased from Esporta. Sir Stelios Haji-Ioannou, founder of easyJet, plans to expand the number of easyGyms, a no-frills gym concept. This will all help bring subscription prices down and expand the market still further, with lower entry costs for the consumer.

*Sources*: Bridge (2011); *Estates Gazette* (2011); Jacobs (2011); *Marketing and Business Development* (2010); http://www.davidlloyd.co.uk.

In a wider sense, marketing and brand building are also important, of course. These help to raise awareness of a hotel chain's existence and positioning, and differentiate it from the competition. These communicate the key benefits on offer and thus help the customer to decide whether this is the kind of hotel they are looking for, developing their expectations. Advertising, glossy brochures and other marketing communications techniques can help to create and reinforce the potential customer's perception of location, appearance, additional services and customer handling, as well as the brand imagery. Strong marketing and branding also help to link a chain of hotels that might be spread worldwide, giving the customer some reassurance of consistency and familiarity. Business travellers in a strange city can seek out a known hotel name, such as Novotel, Holiday Inn, Sheraton, Campanile or Formule 1, and be fairly certain about what they are purchasing.

Pizza Hut's menu, decor, servers, order processing, equipment, cooking procedures, etc. are all standardised (or allow minor variations and adaptations for local conditions), creating a consistent and familiar experience for the customer all over the world. Customers thus have a strong tangible impression of the character of Pizza Hut, what to expect of it, and what it delivers.

One of the greatest problems of intangibility is that it is difficult to assess quality both during and after the service has been experienced. Customers will use a combination of criteria, both objective and subjective, to judge their level of satisfaction, although it is often based on impressions, memories and expectations. Different customers attach significance to different things. The frequent business traveller might be extremely annoyed by check-in delays or the noise from the Friday night jazz cabaret, while the holidaymaker might grumble about the beach being 20 minutes' walk away rather than the five minutes promised in the brochure. Memories fade over time, but some bad ones, such as a major service breakdown or a confrontation with service staff, will remain.

## Perishability

Services are manufactured at the same time as they are consumed. A lecturer paces the lecture theatre, creating a service experience that is immediately either consumed or slept through by the students. Manchester United, Barcelona or Inter Milan manufacture sporting entertainment that either thrills, bores or frustrates their fans as they watch the match live. Similarly, audiences at Covent Garden or La Scala absorb live opera as it unfolds before them. With both sport and entertainment, it is likely that the customer's enjoyment of the 'product' is heightened by the unpredictability of live performance and the audience's own emotional involvement in what is going on. This highlights another peculiarity of service products: customers are often directly involved in the production process and the synergy between them and the service provider affects the quality of the experience. A friend might tell you, 'Yes, it was a brilliant concert. The band were on top form and the atmosphere was great!' To create such a complete experience, the band and their equipment do have to perform to the expected standard, the lighting and sound crews have to get it right on the night, and the venue has to have adequate facilities and efficient customer handling processes. The atmosphere, however, is created by the interaction between performer and audience and can inspire the performer to deliver a better experience. Customers, therefore, have to be prepared to give as well as take, and make their own contribution to the quality of the service product.

Perishability thus means that a service cannot be manufactured and stored either before or after the experience. Manufacture and consumption are simultaneous. A hotel is, of course, a permanent structure with full-time staff, and exists regardless of whether it has customers or not on a particular night. The hotel's service product, however, is only being delivered when there is a customer present to purchase and receive it. The product is perishable in the sense that if a room is not taken on a particular night, then it is a completely lost opportunity. The same is true of most service products, such as airline seats, theatre tickets, management consultancy or dental appointments. If a dentist cannot fill the appointment book for a particular day, then that revenue-earning opportunity is lost for ever. In situations where demand is reasonably steady, it is relatively easy to plan capacity and adapt the organisation to meet the expected demand pattern.

Even where demand does fluctuate, as long as it is fairly predictable managers can plan to raise or reduce service capacity accordingly. A larger plane or an additional performance might be provided to cater for short-term demand increases. It can be more difficult, however, if there are very marked fluctuations in demand that might result in facilities lying idle for a long time or in severe overcapacity. The profitability of companies servicing peak-hour transport demands can be severely affected because vehicles and rolling stock are unused for the rest of the day. Airlines too face seasonal fluctuations in demand.

Most airlines oversell seats on planes to allow for cancellations and 'no shows'. If too many booked passengers do the unthinkable, and actually turn up for their flight, then some passengers might by offered free air miles for taking a later flight instead. All of that is designed to avoid loss of revenue from empty seats. Mongolian Airlines, however, took the practice to a whole new level by taking reservations on ghost flights! In order to sell extra tickets on its Seoul to Ulan Batar service, it increased the number of advertised flights from six to nine, and took bookings on all nine flights. The trouble was that it did not have permission to fly more than six flights a week. Customers who bought tickets for the three ghost flights were forced to wait for empty seats on authorised flights. According to most customers, the airline failed to disclose the information (and let's face it, if you were told that the flight you were booking didn't actually exist, would you complete the transaction?!) and it meant that about 750 customers a week were left stranded due to no capacity (Lee, 2011).

The concept of perishability means that a range of marketing strategies is needed to try to even out demand and bring capacity handling into line with it. These strategies might include pricing or product development to increase demand during quieter periods or to divert it from busier ones, or better scheduling and forecasting through the booking and reservation system. Similarly, the capacity and service delivery system can be adapted to meet peaks or troughs in demand through such strategies as part-time workers, increased mechanisation or cooperation with other service providers. These will be considered in more detail later (see p. 575 *et seq.*).

eg

Overcapacity plagues many service providers, whether they are airlines, hospitality providers or rail operators. In Dublin, for example, hotel occupancy rates rose around 5 per cent in 2011 to just under 67 per cent, but the average daily rate for each room sold fell by €6 to €79 (Madden, 2011). There is little an individual hotel manager can do to influence weather and consumer demand, but they can manipulate the marketing mix to make some difference, hence, the drop in the average daily rate. The number of travellers coming to Dublin airport fell by 10 per cent in 2010, so it's an uphill struggle for hoteliers. It's the same in other European cities, for example, in Copenhagen room numbers expanded with new hotels opening but at the same time the number of bookings decreased, resulting in room rate falls of 10–35 per cent (*Esmerk*, 2010).

In Ireland, too, there was a huge expansion in the number of hotels during the boom years of the 'Celtic Tiger' economy, when finance was easy to come by, tourism projects attracted tax incentives, and bankers didn't look too closely at business plans. By 2011, however, in more sober times, it was realised that Ireland as a whole had up to 15,000 hotel beds too many, and because 80 per cent of tourists to Ireland only visit 20 per cent of the country, a lot of hotels are in the 'wrong place' and in some hotspots the extent of oversupply is huge. Hoteliers in both Sligo and Limerick, for instance, face a much more difficult situation than those in Dublin as in both those cities, it is estimated that there are twice as many hotel beds as the market needs. For struggling hoteliers, things were made a lot worse because 82 hotels that had been repossessed by the banks were then taken over by the government-owned National Asset Management Agency (NAMA – set up as part of the bail-out of the Irish banking sector) which subsequently continued to run them as 'zombie' hotels, charging ridiculously low, non-commercial room rates just to claw something back and keep the staff in employment. Great for the traveller, but impossible to compete with. The (kind of) good news is that in 2011, NAMA decided to close and mothball at least some of these hotels which should take a little bit of excess capacity out of the marketplace (O'Carroll, 2011; *Sligo Weekender*, 2010).

Zombie hotels that have made life even more difficult for commercial hoteliers are starting to be killed off

*Source*: Alamy Images/© Manor Photography

## Inseparability

Many physical products are produced well in advance of purchase and consumption, and production staff rarely come into direct contact with the customer. Often, production and consumption are distanced in both space and time, connected only by the physical distribution system. Sales forecasts provide important guidelines for production schedules. If demand rises unexpectedly, opportunities might well exist to increase production or to reduce stockholding to meet customer needs.

As has already been said, with service products, however, the involvement of the customer in the service experience means that there can be no prior production and no storage and that consumption takes place simultaneously with production. The service delivery, therefore, cannot be separated from the service providers and thus the fourth characteristic of service products is inseparability. This means that the customer often comes into direct contact with the service provider(s), either individually, as with a doctor, or as part of a team of providers, as with air travel. The team includes reservations clerks, check-in staff, aircrew and perhaps transfer staff. In an airline, the staff team has a dual purpose.

_eg_ As part of the opening of the border between Taiwan and China, TransAsia Airways was anxious to recruit cabin crew who spoke Chinese dialects rather than English and Japanese. This is to meet the demand of the independent Chinese traveller who is not part of a tour. Current restrictions mean that only 4,000 tourists per day can travel from China to Taiwan and only then as part of a tour group, but those restrictions are about to be relaxed to permit independent travel, so the airlines need to be ready for it. However, there is still a long way to go before Taiwanese carriers match Emirates whose cabin crew comprise 131 nationalities speaking more than 80 different languages (_ENP Newswire_, 2011; Hsin-Yin, 2011).

Clearly, they have to deliver their aspect of the service efficiently, but they also have to interact with the customer in the delivery of the service. An uncooperative check-in clerk might not provide the customer's desired seat, but in contrast, friendly and empathic cabin staff can alleviate the fear of a first-time flyer. The service provider can thus affect the quality of the service delivered and the manner in which it is delivered.

_eg_ Behaviour of the cabin crew can play an important part in the enjoyment of a flight experience. Virgin Atlantic pays particular attention to the training of staff in that regard, so you can imagine the horror when it all went horribly wrong on one of its flights. In the premium economy cabin, passengers were roused by the early morning greeting on their personal televisions: 'Get up you c***s'. As a wake up call, it certainly had the desired effect but, understandably, caused outrage. Of course, it was a mistake, as the message was meant only for the eyes of fellow crew members who were taking a break in empty passenger seats. Oops. It could cost two or three crew members their jobs for insulting passengers, and some offended travellers are seeking compensation (Boulton and Miller, 2011).

While the delivery of a personal service can be controlled, since there are fewer opportunities for outside interference, the situation becomes more complex when other customers are experiencing service at the same time. The 'mass service experience' means that other customers can potentially affect the perceived quality of that experience, positively or negatively.

As mentioned earlier, the enjoyment of the atmosphere at a sporting event or a concert, for example, depends on the emotional charge generated by a large number of like-minded individuals. In other situations, however, the presence of many other customers can negatively affect aspects of the service experience. If the facility or the staff do not have the capacity or the ability to handle larger numbers than forecast, queues, overcrowding and dissatisfaction can soon result. Although reservation or prebooking can reduce the risk, service providers can still be caught out. Airlines routinely overbook flights deliberately, on the basis that not all booked passengers will actually turn up. Sometimes, however, they miscalculate and end up with more passengers than the flight can actually accommodate and have to offer free air miles, cash or other benefits to encourage some passengers to switch to a later flight.

What the other customers are like also affects the quality of the experience. This reflects the segmentation policy of the service provider. If a relatively undifferentiated approach is offered, there are all sorts of potential conflicts (or benefits) from mixing customers who are perhaps looking for different benefits. A hotel, for example, might have problems if families with young children are mixed with guests on an over-50s holiday. Where possible, therefore, the marketer should carefully target segments to match the service product being offered.

Other people, whether they are fellow guests, passengers or simply other customers, can impact upon enjoyment of the service experience. Late-night revellers can ruin a night's sleep at a hotel; abusive or rioting soccer fans can set a very bad example to those in the family enclosure, and that customer ahead of you in the Post Office queue with six parcels to weigh and post and a car-tax application to process can cause excessive frustration. Sometimes customer patience can wear a bit thin. On a Middle East Airlines flight to Beirut, for example, passengers mutinied collectively at the way they were being treated. Delays in London due to thunderstorms, heavy rain and high winds caused many flights to be delayed or cancelled but the experience of the Middle East Airlines passengers was something else. They were held for seven hours on the runway at Heathrow and they didn't like it at all. Some became hysterical, others raided the galley for food, and confrontations with the cabin crew became common place. Even the crew gave up apologising and explaining after four hours, and calm was only restored when police boarded the plane. The captain was alleged to have said in response to abuse that the passengers should fly the plane (Gray, 2011).

It's unlikely that passengers on Hong Kong Airlines would behave similarly, if they had any sense. Hong Kong Airlines has started training its staff (both male and female) in martial arts to combat drunken violence on the China to Hong Kong route, and passengers are shown a video highlighting the crew's new found expertise! This was in response to incidents that were occurring up to three times a week on flights (Lewis, 2011).

Finally, the behaviour of other customers can be positive, leading to new friends, comradeship and enjoyable social interaction, or it can be negative if it is rowdy, disruptive or even threatening. Marketers prefer, of course, to try to develop the positive aspects. Social evenings for new package holiday arrivals, name badges on coach tours, and warm-up acts to build atmosphere at live shows all help to break the ice. To prevent disruptive behaviour, the service package might have to include security measures and clearly defined and enforced 'house rules' such as those found at soccer matches.

The implications of inseparability for marketing strategy will be considered at p. 571 *et seq.*

## Heterogeneity

With simultaneous production and consumption and the involvement of service staff and other customers, it can be difficult to standardise the service experience as planned. Heterogeneity means that each service experience is likely to be different, depending on the interaction between the customer and other customers, service staff, and other factors such as time, location and the operating procedures. The problems of standardising the desired service experience are greater when there is finite capacity and the service provided is especially labour intensive. The maxim 'when the heat is on the service is gone' reflects the risk of service breakdown when demand puts the system under pressure, especially if it is unexpected. This might mean no seats available on the train, delays in serving meals on a short-haul flight, or a queue in the bank on a Friday afternoon.

*eg*

Most of us experience smooth travelling but most of us can remember vividly the rare occasions when it all goes wrong. Rail passengers are especially vulnerable to delays and cancellation, whether that's due to rolling stock breakdown, signalling problems or adverse weather conditions. The heavy snowfall in the UK in December 2010 caused such widespread disruption to railways and airports that a Parliamentary Transport Select Committee was set up to look into the problems. The delays are estimated to have cost the economy £280 million per day, and airports and train operators south of the Thames were particularly badly hit. Recommendations arising from the Committee's investigations included 'snow plans' for airports and railways, new equipment, better passenger welfare assistance information on service disruption, and even replacing the third electric rail with overhead cables on the railways. That, however, is evidently not a complete cure, as passengers on the East Coast main line found in December 2010 when overhead power cables came down in bad weather causing suspension of services between London Kings Cross and Peterborough (*M2 Presswire*, 2010; Odell, 2011).

Heavy snow adversely affects the rail network with a high cost to the economy
*Source*: Press Association Images

Some of the heterogeneity in the service cannot be planned for or avoided, but quality assurance procedures can minimise the worst excesses of service breakdown. This can be done by designing in 'failsafes', creating mechanisms to spot problems quickly and to resolve them early before they cause a major service breakdown. Universities, for example, have numerous quality-assurance procedures to cover academic programmes, staffing and support procedures that involve self-assessment, student evaluation and external subject and quality assessment.

# MARKETING IN ACTION

## Where there's a will . . . there's a mystery shopper

Mystery shoppers are widely used to monitor service levels and the service experience provided. They eat at restaurants to check food, service and facilities, stay in hotels, drink in pubs, travel on planes, and visit shops, cinemas, health clubs and garages. The lucky ones even get to go on expensive foreign holidays. The feedback provides front-line commentary and often shows companies the difference between the service promise and the reality of what is delivered. Most of the time, the focus is on the overall experience rather than individual performance, although at times staff are also the focus of attention. Normally, the mystery shopper is given a checklist of points to watch out for, and they have to be skilled in classifying and memorising elements of the delivered service.

The staff's view of mystery shoppers doesn't have to be that they are some sort of head-office 'spy' looking for 'failure', of course; mystery shopping can be used as part of a very positive incentive scheme to uphold and improve customer service. Every UK branch of the sandwich chain Pret A Manger is visited by a mystery shopper every week, who rates the outlet on criteria such as the speed of service, product availability and cleanliness, and also rates the 'engagement level' of the staff member who served them in terms of eye contact, smiling and conversation. The store gets its results on a Thursday and if it scores a 'pass' level of at least 43 points out of 50, every member of staff gets an extra £1 for every hour worked that week, and any staff member cited as having provided outstanding service gets an additional £50. The payout rises to £100 if the branch scored top marks. According to the CEO, 8 per cent of outlets miss out on the bonus every week, which is sufficiently low to make employees and store managers believe that the pass level is actually achievable, but not so low as to make them complacent and think of the bonus as a 'right'.

Mystery shoppers can be used to test out any sort of service encounter. The Legal Services Consumer Panel decided to look into the will-writing industry. Anyone can draw up a legal will, and a lot of small will-writing companies have sprung up scenting a money-making opportunity. Qualified solicitors had complained that these companies are unregulated, there is no guarantee of the quality of the work that they do, and thus the public would be better off going to a 'proper' solicitor. So the mystery shoppers were brought in to test the services offered by both will-writing companies and solicitors. The resulting wills were examined by experts who found that around 25 per cent of them 'failed' and, perhaps surprisingly, the wills drawn up by solicitors were just as likely to fail as those produced by will-writers. The best and most reputable will-writing firms were found to be just as good as the competent solicitors.

The problem with the will-writers is that they sometimes use heavy selling tactics, and when firms go out of business, the wills tend to disappear with them. However, they do tend to be cheaper than solicitors and offer flexible service, for example, visiting the customer at home (and given that too many people don't bother with making a will at all, anything that makes it easier is to be commended). However, the lack of regulation is a concern – at least with solicitors there is recourse to a well established set of frameworks for complaint and redress. While this was a small-scale exercise, the indicative evidence is sufficient to start a debate about whether and how will-writing should be regulated, raising questions not only about the training and competence of the specialist will-writers, but also about the training and competence of solicitors themselves in this area.

*Sources*: Cuddeford-Jones (2011); Goodman (2011); Rose (2011); Shoffman (2011).

Management, therefore, has to develop ways of reducing the impact of heterogeneity. To help in that process, they need to focus on operating systems, procedures and staff training in order to ensure consistency. New lecturers, for example, might be required to undertake a special induction programme to help them learn teaching skills, preparing materials and handling some of the difficulties associated with disruptive students. Managers have to indicate clearly what they expect of staff in terms of the desired level of service. This must cover not only compliance with procedures in accordance with training, but also staff attitudes and the manner in which they deal with customers.

The next section looks in more detail at the impact of the particular characteristics of service products on the design and implementation of the marketing programme.

# Services marketing management

So far, this chapter has looked at the characteristics of service products in a very general way. This section looks further at the implications of those characteristics for marketers in terms of formulating strategy, developing and measuring quality in the service product and issues of training and productivity.

## Services marketing strategy

The traditional marketing mix, consisting of the 4Ps, forms the basis of the structure of this book. For service products, however, additional elements of the marketing mix are necessary to reflect the special characteristics of services marketing. Shown in Figure 14.2, these are as follows:

- *people*: whether service providers or customers who participate in the production and delivery of the service experience;
- *physical evidence*: the tangible cues that support the main service product. These include facilities, the infrastructure and the products used to deliver the service;
- *processes*: the operating processes that take the customer through from ordering to the manufacture and delivery of the service.

Any of these extra marketing mix elements can enhance or detract from the customer's overall experience when consuming the service. However, despite the special considerations, the purpose of designing an effective marketing mix remains the same whether for services or physical products. The marketer is still trying to create a differentiated, attractive proposition for customers, ensuring that whatever is offered meets their needs and expectations.

All seven of the elements in the services marketing mix will now be considered in turn.

## Product

From a supplier's perspective, many services can be treated like any other physical product in a number of ways. The supplier develops a range of products, each of which represents profit-earning opportunities. A hotel company might treat each of its hotels as a separate product with its own unique product management requirements arising from its location, the state of the building and its facilities, local competition and its strengths and weaknesses compared with others in the area. These products might, of course, be grouped into product lines and SBUs based on similarities and differences between them, just as physical products can be.

Many of the product concepts and the decisions concerning them that were discussed in Chapter 6 apply equally to services and physical products. Positioning, branding, developing a mix, designing new services and managing the product lifecycle are all relevant.

**Figure 14.2**
The services
marketing mix

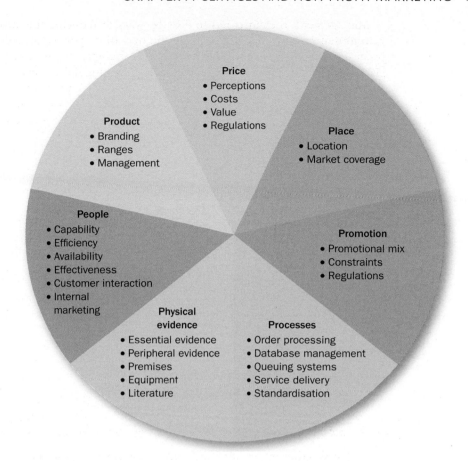

 Many financial service products cannot be tested in the same way as physical goods through limited launches, but test marketing concepts can nevertheless still be applied. A new financial services product can be launched on a regional basis, for example. Banks can also use in-house innovation labs. Here, ideas can be tested in the relative security of lab conditions prior to launch on regional or even a single branch basis. Websites can also be used to present soon-to-be-released services for feedback, so that the concept can be refined if necessary before commercialisation (Epper Hoffman, 2010).

**Product development**. Product development in some service situations can be complex as it involves 'packaging' otherwise separate elements into a service product. Therefore, a holiday company may need to work with airlines, hotels and local tour companies to blend a package for the target segment. From a consumer perspective, any failure in any part of the system will be regarded as a criticism of the holiday company, even though air-traffic delays or faulty plumbing may not be directly under the company's control. At a regional and national level, government and private companies may work together to develop new attractions and infrastructure for tourists.

Hong Kong has adopted Mickey, Minnie, Donald, Stitch and Buzz Lightyear at the Disney theme-park resort in an effort to boost tourism. Although the smallest of the Disney theme-parks, the Hong Kong Disneyland park still has 1,000 beds on site and has attracted over 20 million visitors since its 2005 opening, over one-third of whom come from mainland China. An investment of that size and risk was only possible through a joint venture between Disney and the Hong Kong government. The park includes four main attaction areas such as Adventureland, with others in the pipeline, two large themed hotels and a wide variety of restaurants. It is a big employer as well, with a 5,000 strong cast of staff in the park and hotels. The Hong Kong authorities are highly supportive of the park as it makes Hong Kong a premier international tourist destination and has spin-off benefits for the whole economy, in terms of investment in infrastructure and employment in transportation, hospitality, catering and other related industries. This is particularly true of tourism on Lantau island, where the park is located, and efforts are being made to draw visitors to other attractions on the island as it is only 30 minutes from central Hong Kong. Access to the resort is by a special train, based on a Mickey Mouse theme, of course! (http://hkcorporate.hongkongdisneyland.com/).

## Price

Because services are intangible, their pricing can be very difficult to set and to justify. The customer is not receiving anything that can be touched or otherwise physically experienced, so it can be hard for them to appreciate the benefits they have gained in return for their expenditure.

A solicitor's bill or the labour charges added to a repair bill can seem to be incredibly high to customers, because they do not stop to think about the training that has gone into developing professional skills nor of the peace of mind gained by having the job done 'properly'. As with any product, therefore, the customer's perception is central to assessing value for money.

The prices of some services are controlled by bodies other than the service provider. The amount that dentists charge for work under the National Health Service or that pharmacists charge to dispense a prescription is imposed by central government. Similarly, the BBC is funded by licence fees determined by government and charged to television owners. Other services price on a commission basis. An estate agent, for example, might charge the vendor a fee of 2 per cent of the selling price of the house, plus any expenses such as advertising.

Other service providers are completely free to decide their own prices, with due respect to competition and the needs, wants and perceptions of customers. In setting prices, however, service providers can find it very difficult to determine the true cost of provision, perhaps because of the difficulty of costing professional or specialist skills, or because the time and effort required to deliver a service vary widely between different customers, yet a standard price is needed. Perishability might also affect the pricing of professional services. A training provider, for example, who has little work on at the moment might agree to charge less than the normal daily rate, just to generate some income rather than none.

In service situations, price can play an important role in managing demand. By varying the price, depending on the time at which the service is delivered, service providers can try to discourage customers from purchasing at the busiest periods. Customers can also use price as a weapon. Passengers purchasing airline tickets shortly before the flight or visitors looking for a hotel room for the night might be able to negotiate a much lower price than that advertised.

This is a result of the perishability of services: the airline would rather have a seat occupied and get something for it than let the flight take off with an empty one and, similarly, the hotel would rather have a room occupied than not.

The rail pricing system has changed considerably in the UK in recent years. Traditionally, the passenger bought a ticket, walked onto the train and found a seat. Few bothered to pay the additional charge for a seat reservation. The emphasis is now on encouraging advance booking so that capacity can be better planned. Buying a ticket from London to Scotland three months ahead of travelling, for example, can cost as little as £19, and the better you plan, the better the price. The ticket cannot be changed once it has been booked, however, by day or by time of train. Turn up the day to buy a ticket, or seek to change the date of travel, and it can suddenly become very expensive (Brignall, 2009).

Over the years, the system has become very complex, and difficult for both passengers and ticket office staff to understand. In 2011, however, at a time when rail fares generally were rising steeply, Chiltern Railways decided that it was time to buck the trend. Chiltern announced a simple pricing structure with just three price points for its London–Birmingham mainline service which represented a reduction in peak-time fares and shorter peak-time periods. All these fares are available on the day of travel – no advance booking is necessary. Chiltern's view was that 'We believe that customers shouldn't be held to ransom by extortionate walk-up fares or held captive in stations with an endless wait until the ever-extending peak is over. Our new fares are a commitment to customers to avoid unnecessary complexity and make it easier for them to travel' (as quoted by Smithers, 2011). There is, of course, also a strategic objective of increasing market share on that route both by getting people out of their cars, and taking passengers away from competing services.

## Place

According to Cowell (1984), services are often supplied direct from the provider to the customer because production and consumption are simultaneous. Direct supply allows the provider to control what is going on, to differentiate through personal service, and to get direct feedback and interaction with the customer. Direct supply can take place from business premises, such as a hairdresser's salon, a solicitor's office or a university campus. Some services can also be supplied by telephone, such as insurance and banking services. Others are supplied by the service provider visiting the customer's home or premises, such as cleaning, repair of large appliances, equipment installation and servicing, or home hairdressing services.

Direct supply can cause problems for the service provider. It limits the number of customers that can be dealt with and the geographic coverage of the service. For sole traders or small businesses that particularly value the rapport and personal relationships built up with regular clients, this might be perfectly acceptable. Businesses that want to expand might find that direct supply involving the original proprietor of the business is no longer feasible. Professional service businesses, such as accountants or solicitors, might employ additional qualified staff to expand the customer base or to expand geographic coverage.

Other service businesses such as fast food outlets, domestic cleaners or debt collection agencies might opt to expand by franchising, while others will decide to move towards indirect supply through intermediaries paid on a commission basis. Thus the local pharmacist might act as an agent for a company that develops photographic film, a village shop might collect dry cleaning, insurance brokers distribute policies, travel agencies distribute holidays and business travel, and tourist information offices deal with hotel and guest house bookings. In some of these cases, the main benefit of using an intermediary is convenience for the customer and spreading the coverage of the service. In others, such as the travel agency and the insurance broker, the service provider gains the added benefit of having its product sold by a specialist alongside the competition.

## Promotion

Marketing communication objectives, implementation and management for services are largely the same as for any other product. There are a few specific issues to point out, however. As with pricing, some professional services are ethically constrained in what marketing communication they are allowed to do. Solicitors in the UK, for example, are allowed to use print advertising, but only if it is restrained and factual. An advertisement can tell the reader what areas of the law the practice specialises in, but it cannot make emotive promises about winning vast amounts of compensation for you, for example.

Service products face a particularly difficult communications task because of the intangibility of the product. They cannot show you pretty pack shots, they cannot whet your appetite with promises of strawberry and chocolate-flavoured variants, they cannot show you how much of this amazing product you are getting for your money. They can, however, show the physical evidence, they can show people like you apparently enjoying the service, they can emphasise the benefits of purchasing this service. Testimonials from satisfied customers can be an extremely effective tool, because they reassure the potential customer that the service works and that the outcomes will be positive. Linked with this, word-of-mouth communication is incredibly important, especially for the smaller business working in a limited geographic area.

Finally, it must be remembered that many service providers are small businesses that could not afford to invest in glossy advertising campaigns even if they could see the point of it. Many can generate enough work to keep them going through word-of-mouth recommendation, websites and advertisements in the *Yellow Pages*. Much depends on the level of competition and demand in the local market for the kind of service being offered. If the town's high street supports four different restaurants, then perhaps a more concerted effort might be justified, including, for example, advertising in local newspapers, door-to-door leaflet drops and price promotions.

According to a review in *Time Out*, whatever the organisers promised, the Edinburgh International Film Festival was a bit of a damp squib in 2011. The films were slated by some critics as weak; visiting talent was largely absent; films were screened that people didn't want to see, and the ticket prices were considered expensive. The net result was rows of empty seats – lost revenue for ever. There were no multiticket buys and no catalogue offering a critical appraisal of the films, so unsurprisingly attendance figures declined (Johnston, 2011). This is the reviewer's opinion, but as the judgement of an experienced reviewer in a well-respected publication, it's likely to be an opinion that film-lovers take seriously and it might well put them off the 2012 event.

It is important to remember, however, that customers are likely to use marketing communication messages to build their expectations of what the service is likely to deliver. This is true of any product but, as will be discussed at p. 571 *et seq.*, because of intangibility, the judgement of service quality is much more subjective. It is based on a comparison of prior expectations with actual perceived outcomes. The wilder or more unrealistic the communication claims, therefore, the greater the chances of a mismatch that will lead to a dissatisfied customer in the end. The service provider does, of course, need to create a sufficiently alluring image to entice the customer, but not to the point where the customer undergoing the service experience begins to wonder if this is actually the same establishment as that advertised.

*eg* 'There's nothing like Australia.' Tourism Australia makes heavy use of imagery to portray the unique natural and cultural delights of Australia to European audiences. Whether it is kangaroos, Uluru, the Great Barrier Reef or the Sydney Opera House, the visual message is the same: Australia is vibrant, exciting and surprising, reflecting the brand proposition: 'On holiday in Australia you don't switch off you switch on. The unique experiences you have and the people you meet will make you feel uplifted and full of life.' The website, media advertisements and PR usually reinforce these themes, making full use of holiday programmes and travel shows as well as supporting Australia-themed national supplements in some of the daily newspapers. 'Brand Australia' campaigns, however, are targeted to attract different audiences and a number of campaigns are run simultaneously in different geographic markets.

Tourism Australia is targeting what it has defined as a key segment: 'experience seekers', which describes 30–50 per cent of the visitors to Australia. The experience seeker is not defined by age or nationality, but does tend to have higher than average income; is very well educated; is an opinion leader; and is open minded and interested in world affairs. The experience seeker is also a seasoned international traveller who is active, sociable and looking for authentic experiences that are different from his or her normal life.

Because of their characteristics, this is a very sophisticated audience that doesn't like being patronised by marketers, and is very selective in its media consumption. In terms of broadcast media, they are attracted to news and current affairs, and documentary-type programmes and thus channels such as National Geographic and Discovery are ideal media. It is also a digitally literate audience that actively seeks information in making holiday choices, thus communication through websites (see www.australia.com and www.nothinglikeaustralia.com) and online advertising is very important. A key foundation for the digital campaign was the involvement of Australians themselves. They were asked to submit photos and stories to explain why they thought tourists should visit their area, and the 30,000 submissions received were all uploaded on to an interactive, searchable map to help the potential visitor discover for themselves where they would like to go and what they would like to see, through content that has the authentic voice of 'the locals' rather than the stamp of a polished marketing sales pitch. Once you've found a location that takes your fancy, you can click through to further information about the area, such as accommodation, transport, other things to see and do etc. (www.tourism.australia.com/en-au/marketing/default.aspx).

Tourism Australia targets a particular group: people not defined by age or nationality but instead by their above average income, education, open-mindedness, interest in world affairs and their desire to have experiences outside those of their daily routine

*Source:* www.tourism.australia.com. Image used courtesy of The Advertising Archives

## People

Services depend on people and interaction between people, including the service provider's staff, the customer and other customers. As the customer is often a participant in the creation and delivery of the service product, there are implications for service product quality, productivity and staff training. The ability of staff to cope with customers, to deliver the service reliably to the required standard and to present an image consistent with what the organisation would want is of vital concern to the service provider. This is known as *internal marketing*, and will be discussed later at p. 573 *et seq*. The role of the customer in the service is known as *interactive marketing*, and will be discussed at p. 571 *et seq*.

*eg* The Holiday Inn is renowned for excellent personal service, and this service culture is a fundamental part of its staff training. It was taken to a new level, however, when the hotel experimented with human bed-warmers to act like a giant water bottle so that your bed would be nice and warm when you got into it. The idea is that it's easier to get to sleep in a warm bed, so the guest gets a better night's sleep overall. Before your imagination starts running riot, however, it must be stressed that it's all done in the best possible taste: the bed-warmers are dressed in all-in-one sleeper suits and only stay in the bed for five minutes (*Belfast Telegraph*, 2010).

## Physical evidence

Physical evidence comprises the tangible elements that support the service delivery, and offer clues about the positioning of the service product or give the customer something solid to take away with them to symbolise the intangible benefits they have received. Shostack (1977) differentiates between *essential evidence* and *peripheral evidence*. Essential evidence is central to the service and is an important contributor to the customer's purchase decision. Examples of this might be the type and newness of aircraft operated by an airline or of the car fleet belonging to a car hire firm, the layout and facilities offered by a supermarket or a university's lecture theatres and their equipment as well as IT and library provision. Peripheral evidence is less central to the service delivery and is likely to consist of items that the customer can have to keep or use.

## Processes

Because the creation and consumption of a service are usually simultaneous, the production of the service is an important part of its marketing as the customer either witnesses it or is directly involved in it. The service provider needs smooth, efficient customer-friendly procedures. Some processes work behind the scenes, for example administrative and data processing systems, processing paperwork and information relating to the service delivery and keeping track of customers.

Systems that allow the service provider to send a postcard to remind customers that the next dental check-up or car service is due certainly help to generate repeat business, but also help in a small way to strengthen the relationship with the customer. Other processes are also 'invisible' to the customer, but form an essential part of the service package. The organisation of the kitchens in a fast food outlet, for example, ensures a steady supply of freshly cooked burgers available for counter staff to draw on as customers order. Well-designed processes are also needed as the service is delivered to ensure that the customer gets through with minimum fuss and delay and that all elements of the service are properly delivered. This might involve, for example, the design of forms and the information requested, payment procedures, queuing systems or even task allocation. At a hairdressing salon, for instance, a junior might wash your hair while the stylist finishes off the previous customer, and the receptionist will handle the payment at the end.

Smartcards are revolutionising service-delivery processes by cutting out human interaction, which can be slow, inconsistent and unreliable. Smartcards which are similar in size to a credit card have an embedded microprocessor and a memory that can be activated by either a reader or a signal-emitting device. The cards are especially popular with transport providers as a means of reducing queues at ticket offices and for travel authentication. The cards are not bound by travel zones and time restrictions, as are normal season tickets and travel cards. The card reader at a station will automatically account for the journey time and distance, and the fare can be deducted from the previously topped-up card.

When the new tram operator for Nottingham takes over the franchise, it will be using smartcards that are valid on all modes of transport in the city. At present, passengers must use combined tickets for trams and buses but these will be phased out by 2014 when the multi-use smartcard comes into effect. The fare that is deducted from the card goes back to the company one is travelling with. In Bristol, use of the card will entitle users to a saving of around 15 per cent on travel, reflecting reduced operating costs. These schemes are based on the London Oyster Card, which pioneered smartcards in the UK and is widely used on the world's metro systems.

In Hong Kong, the equivalent of the Oyster was launched in 1997, and it is now used by 95 per cent of the population, not only for fares but for everything from buying a cup of coffee to paying parking fees, and even as a key card for apartments – a long way from simply being an electronic bus ticket. The next phase in the UK is the integration of the technology so that the smartcard can be used wherever you travel. Stagecoach has already become the first major bus operator using smartcard technology nationwide. It handles 53 million transactions every year, and the smartcard makes the ticketing process easier and quicker for the passenger and cheaper and more effective for the transport operator once the initial investment has been made. There's still a lot of work to do to integrate the systems of different providers, let alone extending smartcard use along the lines of the Hong Kong model, but in terms of a service experience it beats getting stuck in a ticket queue behind the bloke who is fumbling through his pockets for change. (Jeory, 2010; Lowbridge, 2011; Rkaina, 2011).

## Interactive marketing: service quality

Central to the delivery of any service product is the *service encounter* between the provider and the customer. This is also known as interactive marketing. This aspect of services is an important determinant of quality because it brings together all the elements of the services marketing mix and is the point at which the product itself is created and delivered. The challenge for the service marketer is to bring quality, customer service and marketing together to build and maintain customer satisfaction (Christopher *et al.*, 1994). Quality issues are just as important for service products as they are for a physical product, but service quality is much more difficult to define and to control. Authors such as Lovelock *et al.* (1999), Devlin and Dong (1994) and Zeithaml *et al.* (1990), for example, stress the importance of customer perceptions and use them as the basis for frameworks for measuring service quality.

Home delivery of pizzas is usually associated with supplier guarantees of free pizzas if delivered outside a certain period. This helps emphasise the speed of delivery and reinforces the convenience of home ordering services. A number of chains, such as Domino's, have added online ordering, with a central call centre directing orders to the nearest retail stores. The customer is then free to browse the menu at leisure and the site can be frequently updated with offers, etc. It has also gone further in ensuring improved service through the introduction of the Domino's 'Heat Wave' hot bags with a patented electrically warmed heating mechanism. Once unplugged, it keeps the pizza hot during normal delivery times (www.dominos.co.uk).

## Measuring service quality

Some aspects of the service product can, of course, be measured more objectively than others. Where tangible elements are involved, such as physical evidence and processes, quality can be defined and assessed more easily. In a fast-food restaurant, for example, the cleanliness of the premises, the length of the queues, the consistency of the size of portions and their cooking, and the implementation and effectiveness of stock control systems can all be 'seen' and measured. Whether the customer *actually* enjoyed the burger, whether they *felt* that they had had to wait too long, or whether they *felt* that the premises were too busy, crowded or noisy are much more personal matters and thus far more difficult for managers to assess.

A particular group of researchers, Berry, Parasuraman and Zeithaml, have developed criteria for assessing service quality and a survey mechanism called SERVQUAL for collecting data relating to customer perceptions (see, e.g., Parasuraman *et al.*, 1985, 1988; Zeithaml *et al.*, 1990). They cite 10 main criteria that, between them, cover the whole service experience from the customer's point of view:

1 *Access.* How easy is it for the customer to gain access to the service? Is there an outlet for the service close to the customer? Is there 24-hour access by telephone to a helpline?

2 *Reliability.* Are all the elements of the service performed and are they delivered to the expected standard? Does the repair engineer clean up after himself after mending the washing machine and does the machine then work properly? Does the supermarket that promises to open another checkout when the queues get too long actually do so?

3 *Credibility.* Is the service provider trustworthy and believable? Is the service provider a member of a reputable trade association? Does it give guarantees with its work? Does it seem to treat the customer fairly?

4 *Security.* Is the customer protected from risk or doubt? Is the customer safe while visiting and using a theme park? Does an insurance policy cover all eventualities? Will the bank respect the customer's confidentiality? Can the cellular telephone network provider prevent hackers from hijacking a customer's mobile phone number?

5 *Understanding the customer.* Does the service provider make an effort to understand and adapt to the customer's needs and wants? Will a repair engineer give a definite time of arrival? Will a financial adviser take the time to understand the customer's financial situation and needs and then plan a complete package? Do front-line service staff develop good relationships with regular customers?

These first five criteria influence the quality of the *outcome* of the service experience. The next five influence the quality of the *inputs* to the process to provide a solid foundation for the outputs.

6 *Responsiveness.* Is the service provider quick to respond to the customer and willing to help? Can a repair engineer visit within 24 hours? Will a bank manager explain in detail what the small print in a loan agreement means? Are customers' problems dealt with quickly and efficiently?

7 *Courtesy.* Are service staff polite, friendly and considerate? Do they smile and greet customers? Are they pleasant? Do they show good manners? Do service staff who have to visit a customer's home treat it with proper respect and minimise the sense of intrusion?

8 *Competence.* Are service staff suitably trained and able to deliver the service properly? Does a financial adviser have extensive knowledge of available financial products and their appropriateness for the customer? Does a librarian know how to access and use information databases? Do theme park staff know where the nearest toilets are, what to do in a medical emergency or what to do about a lost child?

9 *Communication.* Do service staff listen to customers and take time to explain things to them understandably? Do staff seem sympathetic to customer problems and try to suggest appropriate solutions? Do medical, legal, financial or other professional staff explain things in plain language?

10 *Tangibles.* Are the tangible and visible aspects of the service suitably impressive or otherwise appropriate to the situation? Does the appearance of staff inspire confidence in the customer? Are hotel rooms clean, tidy and well appointed? Do lecture theatres have good acoustics and lighting, a full range of audiovisual equipment and good visibility from every seat? Does the repair engineer have all the appropriate equipment available to do the job quickly and properly? Are contracts and invoices easy to read and understand?

It is easy to appreciate just how difficult it is to create and maintain quality in all ten of these areas, integrating them into a coherent service package. In summary, Figure 14.3 shows the service experience and the factors that affect consumers' expectations of what they will receive. The criteria that influence their perception of what they actually did receive are also shown, as well as the reasons why there might be a mismatch between expectations and perceptions. This can have an important impact on the customer's perception of value and willingness to repeat purchase (Caruana *et al.*, 2000).

## Internal marketing: training and productivity

Because of the interaction between customers and staff in the creation and delivery of a service, it is particularly important to focus on developing staff to deliver high levels of functional and service quality. The pay and rewards system employed can also help to boost staff morale and encourage them to take a positive approach to service delivery. Heskett *et al.* (1997) highlighted the connection between employee and customer satisfaction within services. The 'satisfaction mirror' can actually enhance the customer's experience if the service personnel are approaching service delivery in a positive way. They suggested that employees feeling enthusiastic about their job communicate this to customers both verbally and non-verbally and are also more eager to

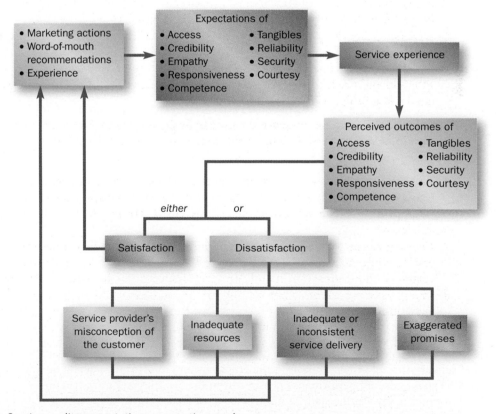

**Figure 14.3** Service quality: expectations, perceptions and gaps

serve the customer. Similarly, employees who remain in the job longer reach higher capability levels and often a better understanding of customers, which again can enhance customers' feelings of satisfaction. Defining the ideal profile and right remuneration package for staff is not easy.

*eg* It's not just the commercial service industries that have to train the right attitudes into staff. The NHS has suffered from its fair share of criticism. Patients have complained of being dehumanised, humiliated and embarrassed by the very doctors and nurses that are supposed to care for them. A survey of 12,000 patients found that staff were often rude, arrogant and lazy and treated patients like numbers, not human beings. One-third was satisfied with the staff service and attitude, but two-thirds were unhappy with some aspect of their treatment, for example standards of hygiene, waiting times and staff attitudes. The research was conducted by Patient Opinion (www.patientopinion.org.uk) a website aimed at sharing opinions and experiences of dealing with the NHS. Of course, the respondents to the site are self-selecting and may not be representative of other people's experience of the NHS and, indeed, if you search for your local hospital on the site, you will probably find that for every person who thinks it's a 'disgrace to the NHS' there will be another who experienced 'amazing care and compassion'. Nevertheless, it is still a reminder to NHS employees that they are providing a service and care to people, and not just concerned with the treatment of patients (Borland, 2011).

While Patient Opinion is independent of the NHS, the Care Quality Commission (CQC) is the independent regulator in England for health and social care, licensing and monitoring services. Among many other activities, it carries out its own inspections of facilities and practice, and carries out regular large scale patient surveys and staff surveys. The 2010 staff survey, for example, included 165,000 respondents and asked them about their views of their own experiences as NHS employees, as well as their opinions of the quality of care offered to patients. There are several patient surveys, each focusing on a different aspect of the NHS, so there's a survey about patients' experience of ambulance services, one for out-patient services, one for in-patient services, another for maternity services, etc. The Emergency Department (A&E) survey uncovered a wide range of issues from its 50,000 respondents, from what might appear to be minor detail, such as the difficulty of finding a parking spot for the 50 per cent of patients who arrive at A&E by car, to more serious issues such as the quality of care given in A&E and the extent and accuracy of the advice and information given on discharge from A&E. All of this information helps the NHS to share good practice, to make recommendations for improvement, and to focus resources (www.cqc.org.uk).

## Staff training

Many service failures actually do stem from staffing problems. As Table 14.1 shows, some staff have direct or indirect involvement in the creation of the service product, and some staff are visible, whereas others are invisible to customers.

Staff who have direct involvement are those who come into contact with a customer as a key part of service delivery. In an airline, these might be cabin staff, check-in staff, and those at the enquiries desk. Indirect involvement covers all staff who enable the service to be delivered, but do not normally come into contact with the customer. They affect the quality of the service delivery through their impact on the efficiency and effectiveness of the operating system and the standards and performance possible from the facilities and infrastructure. In cafés and restaurants, many waiting staff are not trained to operate to their full potential: they need technical skills, product knowledge and interpersonal skills. These can be taught. In addition, the contribution of waiting staff to customer satisfaction must be emphasised (Pratten, 2004).

**Table 14.1** Staff in the service function

|  | Visible to the customer | Invisible to the customer |
|---|---|---|
| Direct involvement | <ul><li>Airline cabin crew</li><li>Cashiers</li><li>Sales assistants</li><li>Medical staff</li><li>Receptionists</li></ul> | Telephone/internet-based services:<ul><li>order takers</li><li>customer helplines</li><li>telephone/online banking</li></ul> |
| Indirect involvement | <ul><li>Hotel chambermaids</li><li>Supermarket shelf fillers</li></ul> | <ul><li>Office cleaners</li><li>Airline caterers</li><li>Administrative staff</li><li>Website technicians</li></ul> |

Ramada Jarvis Hotels places special emphasis on its staff training in its promotional material. Entitled 'Summit Quality Signature', its brochure outlines the various dimensions of training and the phased approach to awarding the quality signature to all members of staff. The first stage concentrates on core values and considers such issues as service delivery, clear merchandising, first impressions, introductions, cleanliness, freshness and how to encourage extra sales. The second stage is concerned with consistency. Quality standards are set for each core value and both self-checking and regular external 'flight tests' are organised to ensure that standards are being maintained and that, where necessary, corrective action is being taken (Ramada Jarvis Hotels corporate literature).

Visible staff (both those with direct involvement and those with indirect involvement with the customer) are in the front line of service delivery. Not only are they concerned with the practical aspects of service delivery to the required standards, but their appearance, interpersonal behaviour and mannerisms will also make an impression on the customer. Airlines, for example, will pay particular attention to a cabin attendant's personal grooming and dress standardisation to ensure a consistent visual impact. Dress is often used to help the customer identify visible staff, both those directly involved in the service, such as aircraft cabin crew, and those who are indirectly involved, such as stewards at football matches or security staff.

Indirect visible staff also include people such as the cleaners at McDonald's, chambermaids in hotels, or staff supporting the cashiers in banks. Invisible staff might or might not have direct contact with customers. Staff who take telephone bookings or those who deal with customer queries on the telephone are heard, but not seen. In some cases, these staff might be the only major point of contact for the customer, and thus although their visibility is limited, their ability to interact well with customers is still extremely important.

The organisation's strategy for internal marketing will vary, depending on the different categories of staff employed. Staff who are in the front line of service delivery, with a high level of customer contact, will have to be trained to deliver the standards expected. Staff who do not have direct contact still have to be motivated to perform their tasks effectively and efficiently. They have to understand that what they do affects the quality of the service delivered and the ability of the front-line staff to perform to expected standards. All of this strongly implies, however, that the different groups of staff have to work closely and efficiently together, and deliver a quality service to each other, which in turn will affect the quality of service delivered to the end customer (Mathews and Clark, 1996).

## Staff productivity

Staff productivity within services is also a difficult issue for managers. According to Cowell (1984), there are several reasons for service productivity being difficult to measure. The main reason is that services are 'performed', not 'produced', and there are too many external factors influencing this live creation of a product. The service production process simply cannot be controlled and replicated as reliably and consistently as a mechanised factory line. Service productivity particularly suffers from the involvement of the customer. If customers do not fill forms in properly, if they are not familiar with procedures or they do not really know what they want, if they turn up late for appointments, if they want to spend time in idle chatter rather than getting on with the business in hand, then it will take service staff much longer to deliver the product. Where productivity is measured in terms of the number of transactions handled, the amount of revenue generated, or the number of customers processed, such delays essentially caused by the customer can reflect unfairly on service staff. This raises the whole question, however, of what constitutes appropriate and fair measures of service productivity. A customer who is given a great deal of individual help or who feels that service staff have taken time for a friendly chat with them might well feel that they have received a much better quality service and appreciate not being treated with cold, bureaucratic efficiency. It might be worth tolerating a slightly longer queue if you feel that you will be treated with care, respect and humanity when you get to the front of it. Definitions and measures of productivity therefore need to be flexible and sympathetic, striking a fine balance between the customer's needs and the business's need to work efficiently.

None of this absolves managers from looking at ways in which service productivity can be improved. There are several possibilities for delivering services more efficiently without necessarily detracting too much from their quality.

**Staff**. Through improved recruitment and training, staff can be given better skills and knowledge for dealing with customers. A clerk in a travel agency, for example, can develop a better knowledge of which tour operators offer which resorts so that the key brochures can be immediately pulled out in response to a customer query. Library staff can be fully trained in the use and potential of databases and online search mechanisms so that customers can have their problems solved immediately without having to wait for a 'specialist' to return from a lunch break. Improving the staff profile might also allow more delegation or empowerment of frontline service staff. A customer does not want to be told 'I can't do that without checking with my supervisor' and then have to wait while this happens. Staff should be given the responsibility and flexibility to deal with the real needs of customers as they arise.

**Systems and technology**. The design of the service process and the introduction of more advanced technology can both help to improve service productivity and the service experience for the customer (Bitner *et al.*, 2000).

Technology combined with well-designed systems can be very powerful in creating market transactions where no interpersonal contact is required between buyer and seller (Rayport and Sviokla, 1994). Libraries, for example, have used technology to improve their productivity. Laser scanning of barcodes in books makes it far quicker to issue or receive returned items than with the old manual-ticketing systems. This has also allowed them to improve the quality of their service. The librarian can immediately tell you, for instance, which books you have on loan, whether or not another reader has reserved a book you have, and which other reader has borrowed the book you want. Some technology means that the service provider need not provide human interaction at all. In the financial sector, 'hole in the wall' cash machines, for instance, give customers 24-hour, seven-day-a-week access to their bank accounts, usually without long queues, and because of the way these machines are networked they provide hundreds of convenient access points.

**Reduce service levels**. Reducing service levels to increase productivity can be dangerous if it leads to a perception of reduced quality in the customer's mind, especially if customers have become used to high levels of service. Reducing the number of staff available to deliver the service might lead to longer queues or undue pressure on the customer to move through the system more quickly.

Reducing service levels also opens up opportunities for competitors to create a new differential advantage. Discount supermarkets, such as Aldi and Lidl, keep their prices low partly

If a busy doctor's surgery introduces a system that schedules appointments at five-minute intervals, one of two things might happen. A doctor who wants to maintain the schedule might hurry patients through consultations without listening to them properly or allowing them time to relax enough to be able to say what is really worrying them. Patients might then feel that they have not got what they came for and that the doctor does not actually care about them. Alternatively, the doctor may put the patient first, and regardless of the five-minute rule take as long as is needed to sort out the individual patient. The patient emerges satisfied, but those still in the waiting room whose appointments are up to half-an-hour late might not feel quite so happy.

through minimising service. Thus there are few checkout operators, no enquiries desk and nobody to help customers pack their bags. The more mainstream supermarkets have been able to use this as a way of emphasising the quality of their service, and have deliberately invested in higher levels of service to differentiate themselves further. Thus Tesco, for example, promised its customers that if there were more than three people in a checkout queue, another checkout would be opened if possible. Tesco also announced that it was taking on extra staff in most of its branches, simply to help customers. These staff might help to unload your trolley on to the conveyor belt or pack your bags, or if you get to the checkout and realise that you have forgotten the milk, they will go and get it for you.

**Customer interaction**. Productivity might be improved by changing the way the customer interacts with the service provider and its staff. It might also mean developing or changing the role of the customer in the service delivery itself. The role of technology in assisting self-service through cash machines has already been mentioned. The whole philosophy of the supermarket is based on the idea of increasing the customer's involvement in the shopping process through self-service.

Customers might also have to get used to dealing with a range of different staff members, depending on their needs or the pressures on the service provider. Medical practices now commonly operate on a group basis, for example, and a patient might be asked to see any one of three or four doctors. If the patient only wants a repeat prescription, the receptionist might be able to handle it, or if a routine procedure is necessary, such as a blood test or a cervical smear, the practice nurse might do it.

If any measures are taken that relate to the nature of customer involvement and interaction, the service provider might have a problem convincing customers that these are for their benefit and that they should cooperate. Careful use of marketing communications is needed, through both personal and non-personal media, to inform customers of the benefits, to persuade them of the value of what is being done and to reassure them that their cooperation will not make too many heavy demands on them.

**Reduce mismatch between supply and demand**. Sometimes demand exceeds supply. Productivity might well then be high, but it could be higher still if the excess demand could be accommodated. Some customers will not want to wait and might decide either to take their business to an alternative service provider or not to purchase at all. At other times, supply will exceed demand and productivity will be low because resources are lying idle. If the service provider can even out some of these fluctuations, then perhaps overall productivity can be improved.

The service provider might be able to control aspects of supply and demand through fairly simple measures. Pricing, for example, might help to divert demand away from busy periods or to create extra demand at quiet times. An appointment booking system might also help to ensure a steady trickle of customers at intervals that suit the service provider. The danger is, though, that if the customer cannot get the appointment slot that they want, they might not bother at all. Finding alternative uses for staff and facilities during quiet times can also create more demand and increase productivity. Universities, for instance, have long had the problem of facilities lying idle at weekends and during vacations. They have solved this by turning halls of residence into conference accommodation or cheap and cheerful holiday lets in the vacations, or hiring out their more attractive and historic buildings for weddings and other functions at weekends, with catering provided.

If the service provider cannot or does not wish to divert demand away from busy times, the ability to supply the service to the maximum number of customers will have to be examined. If the peaks in demand are fairly predictable, many service providers will bring in part-time staff to increase available supply. There might be limits to their ability to do so, however, which are imposed by constraints of physical space and facilities. A supermarket has only so many check-outs, a bank has only so many tills, a barber's shop has only so many chairs, a restaurant has only so many tables. Nevertheless, part-time staff can still be useful behind the scenes, easing the burden on front-line staff and speeding up the throughput of customers.

# Cause-related marketing

The main focus of this section is the charities aspect of non-profit marketing, reflecting the growth of cause-related marketing (CRM) and the radical changes in the ways in which charities generate revenue, their attitudes to their 'businesses' and their increasingly professional approaches to marketing. Cause-related organisations form an important part of the non-profit sector. According to the Charity Commission, at the end of June 2011, there were nearly 162,000 charities in the UK generating almost £56 billion in income (www.charity-commission.gov. uk). A lot of those charities are quite small: 75 per cent of those charities account for less than 4 per cent of that income between them. It is increasingly important for charities to become brands with attributes, emotive appeals and value statements that are designed to appeal to the population of interest, as they are fighting for a share of consumers' disposable income. British consumers are generous to charities, but there's more they could do, particularly the more affluent ones. According to Brinsden (2011), the top 10 per cent of households by income donated just 1.1 per cent of their spending to charities, while the bottom 10 per cent donated 3.6 per cent of income. Furthermore, the economic recession meant something like a £700 million drop in donations as consumers cut back on what they regarded as non-essential spending. In other words, fewer people are giving and they are giving less, and thus the charities are going to have to work a lot harder and a lot smarter to maintain their donation income. There are many more charities competing for attention and donations, and the attitudes of both individual and corporate donors have changed. Thus all sorts of organisations that have not traditionally seen themselves as 'being in business' have had to become more businesslike, fighting for and justifying resources and funding.

This section, therefore, discusses the characteristics that differentiate non-profit from profit-making organisations. Then, the implications for marketing will be explored.

*eg*

Missing People was first registered as a charity in the UK in 1993 (as the National Missing Person's Helpline). It was set up because at any one time there are up to 250,000 people 'missing' in the UK, yet at that time there was no central body to offer advice and support to missing persons' families, to coordinate information on missing people, or for missing people to contact for help. Although many people do 'go missing' on purpose and do not wish to be found, others disappear because they are distressed, ill or confused and need help and reassurance to solve their problems. A few are the victims of abduction.

Missing People, therefore, offers a number of services, including:

- a national 24-hour helpline for families of missing people;
- a confidential 'Message Home' service so that missing people who do not want to be 'found' can at least leave a message to reassure their families that they are all right;
- a confidential 'Runaway' helpline for young people who need help and counselling, available by phone, text or e-mail;
- a national database of missing people;
- searching for missing people, using contacts among the homeless population, advertising and publicity, and social media;
- image-enhancing 'age progression' software that can create a photograph of what someone who has been missing for several years might look like now.

The charity's 'customers' are not just missing people and their families. The police find Missing People and its database invaluable in assisting with identifying corpses and helping with missing persons cases generally. Missing People also works in conjunction with similar organisations internationally. It is one of 23 non-governmental bodies that form Missing Children Europe which works across the EU to help missing or sexually exploited children.

In marketing terms, Missing People's main problem is generating a steady and reliable flow of income. It generated £1.9 million in 2010, and spent £1.7 million. It relies very heavily on volunteers, and does not charge commercial rates for its services, even to the police. It hopes, of course, that those who have benefited from the service will make a donation, but this is unlikely to cover the full cost. It thus relies heavily on cash donations, corporate donations of goods and services, fundraising and promotional events. The higher the profile of the event, the greater the opportunity to raise awareness and cash. When the UK's largest choir, Rock Choir, got together at Wembley Arena, 10,000 posters of missing children were displayed to raise awareness of International Missing Children's Day as part of a partnership with the charity. This event was given coverage in a wide range of media, including an ITV documentary about the choir, further raising the profile of Missing People (www.missingpeople.org.uk).

## Classifying non-profit organisations

As suggested above, non-profit organisations can exist in either the public or the private sector, although the distinction between them is rather blurred in some cases. A hospital that treats both National Health patients and private patients, for example, is involved in both sectors.

## Characteristics of non-profit organisations

Clearly, all non-profit organisations operate in different types of market and face different challenges, but they do have a number of characteristics in common that differentiate them from ordinary commercial businesses (Lovelock and Weinberg, 1984; Kotler, 1982). These are as follows.

**Multiple publics**. Most profit-making organisations focus their attention on their target market. Although they do depend on shareholders to provide capital, most day-to-day cash flow is generated from sales revenue. Effectively, therefore, the recipient of the product or service and the source of income are one and the same. Non-profit organisations, however, have to divide their attention much more equally between two important groups, as shown in Figure 14.4. First, there are the customers or clients who receive the product or service. They do not necessarily pay the full cost of it. A charity, for example, might offer advice or help free to those in need, whereas a museum might charge a nominal entry fee that is heavily subsidised from other sources. Thus clients or customers concern the non-profit organisation largely from a *resource allocation* point of view. The second important group is the funders, those who provide the income to allow the organisation to do its work. A charity, for example, might depend

**Figure 14.4**
Non-profit
organisations:
multiple publics

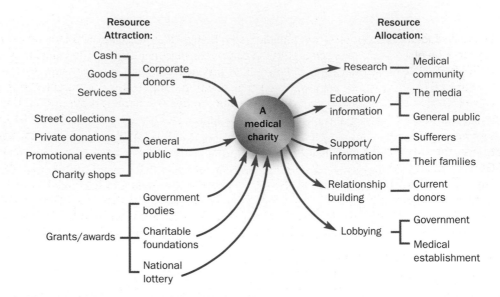

mainly on individuals making donations and corporate sponsors, a medical practice on government funding and a museum on government grants, lottery cash, individual donations and corporate sponsorship as well as entrance fees. Thus funders concern the organisation from a *resource attraction* point of view.

## MARKETING IN ACTION

### Oh my GOSH! . . . there's so many ways to love ya

Great Ormond Street Children's Hospital (GOSH) has the widest range of paediatric specialists in the UK, and welcomes over 192,000 patient visits every year, 44 per cent of whom are aged under four years. In order to provide better care, to maintain its position at the frontier of medical research and to enhance its reputation for pioneering surgery, it needs to supplement the income it gets from the government via the National Health Service. Great Ormond Street Hospital Children's Charity (GOSHCC) aims to raise £50 million a year from individuals and organisations to fund pioneering research into childhood diseases, buy vital new medical equipment and offer improved support services to families.

Fundraising is playing an important role in the re-building of the hospital site to ensure that more children can benefit from the world class care that the hospital provides. The hospital still needs to raise £75 million to complete Phase 2 of the redevelopment, including the construction of a new clinical building due to open in 2016.

The hospital, therefore, must interact with a number of publics if it is to achieve its targets. Its core activities mean that it is working with patients, parents and medical professionals. Each group has an interest in the paediatric care work of the hospital. The government and the NHS also have an interest in the hospital, not only because of the public funds that are committed to it, but also because of its role and profile as a specialist, pioneering unit. Nevertheless, the various groups of donors are critical to the future of GOSH and thus the hospital has an active fund-raising programme through GOSHCC. Schemes include sponsorship, private donations, payroll covenants and legacies.

A sustained partnership with a specific organisation can be very valuable. Arsenal Football Club raised over £800,000 in a season for the Arsenal Lung Function Unit in the hospital, due to open in 2012.

Events included contributions from a dedicated match against Chelsea, 300 fans raised £50,000 from a run, and the players and fans celebrated the end of the season in style at the Gunners' World Ball, raising £450,000, while 60 journalists raised £6,000 at the Media Five-a-Side Tournament.

Meanwhile Disney, as part of 70 years of ongoing support for the hospital, has partnered with GOSHCC to raise £10 million towards the hospital's redevelopment. It is supporting the construction of a new café and a Disney Interactive area for the patients. Disney supports GOSH by employee volunteering, joint events, cause-related licensing, awareness films and even arranging for Disney characters to visit the kids in hospital. Fundraising doesn't always have to be on such a grand scale, however. The GOSH website offers lots of ideas and advice for individuals wanting to raise funds. It also targets employers and employees with ideas for fundraising that can be run within a workplace.

All of these events and programmes mean that GOSHCC has to plan its activities and communications carefully to maintain good relations with individuals and organisations to attract resources, and in return to ensure that the gratitude and goodwill from the well-being of its patients is fed back to the supporters.

*Source*: http://www.gosh.org.uk.

Great Ormond Street Children's Hospital supplements the income it receives from the National Health Service with donations from individuals and organisations

*Source*: by permission of Great Ormond Street Hospital Children's Charity, www.gosh.org.uk

**Multiple objectives**. One definition of marketing offered earlier in this book is to create and hold a customer at a profit. As we have seen, there are many different ways of achieving this and many possible sub-objectives on the way, but in the end for most organisations it is all about profit. As a result, success criteria can be fairly easily defined and measured. In the non-profit sector, however, there might be multiple objectives, some of which could be difficult to define and quantify. They might concern fund raising, publicity generation, contacting customers or clients (or getting them to visit you), dispensing advice, increasing geographic coverage or giving grants to needy clients.

**Service rather than physical goods orientation**. Most non-profit organisations are delivering a service product of some sort rather than manufacturing and selling a physical product. Many of the services marketing concepts already covered in this chapter therefore apply to them. In some non-profit bodies, the emphasis is on generating awareness about a cause, perhaps to generate funds, and giving information to allow people to help themselves solve a problem. Particularly where charities are concerned in generating funds, donors as a target audience are not directly benefiting from their participation in the production of this service, other than from the warm glow of satisfying their social conscience. This contrasts with the more commercial sector, where the customer who pays gets a specific service performed for their benefit (a haircut, a washing machine repaired, a bank account managed for them, etc.).

eg

Oxfam International is delivering not only a service product, but one that is often directed at beneficiaries many thousands of kilometres away. Its many programmes vary from very high-profile activities such as dealing with humanitarian crises in East Africa or the Pakistan floods of 2010. It is also involved in long-term projects such as the one in Mindanao in the Philippines, where years of conflict between government troops and Muslim rebels have left 120,000 people dead and scores more homeless. The Oxfam effort is aimed at promoting peace and unity through children. Meanwhile the River Basin project in Bangladesh aims to prepare people for disaster so that they know how to minimise the damage and can save lives with Oxfam rescue boats at times of flooding.

Oxfam needs high-profile media coverage to communicate more clearly just how much people are suffering, and how even small donations can make a difference to it. With natural disasters, much of the media coverage is done for Oxfam and the focus is on channelling goodwill and sympathy and making donating easy. In other cases, more subtle lobbying and influence are required to achieve the mission of 'saving lives and restoring hope'. Reports can be used to help inform decision-makers and try to influence policy. *Growing a Better Future*, for example, highlights how the global food distribution system only works for some of us, and just how many exist with insufficient food. It is particularly hard-hitting about the role of government, stating that 'the failure of the system flows from failures of government – failures to regulate, to correct, to protect, to resist, to invest – which mean that companies, interest groups, and elites are able to plunder resources and to redirect flows of finance, knowledge, and food' (Oxfam, 2011). In short, the demand for food is outstripping supply and the distribution system is inequitable.

Central to Oxfam's campaign are informing consumers about trade-related causes of poverty, promoting a consumer movement in favour of fair and ethical trade, and lobbying for change in world trading systems where these cause poverty. The greater the publicity, the more tangible the problems and the more powerful the call for help. Oxfam has to be cautious in how it goes about managing its advertising and publicity and is keen not to be seen to be incurring excessive costs. Some charities are perhaps a little less professional and controlled in their approach. The charity Millennium Foundation aimed to support patients in the developing world by raising money from airline travellers. In reality, it raised only a few thousand for the cause but spent millions in operating costs including marketing. In 2009, it raised only $150,000 while spending $11 million given to it by governments on salaries, advertising and legal expenses! (Baker, 2011; Jack, 2010, Oxfam, 2011; www.oxfam.org.uk)

**Public scrutiny and accountability**. Where public money is concerned or where organisations rely on donations, there is greater public interest in the activities and efficiency of the organisation. To maintain the flow of donations, a charity has to be seen to be transparently honest and trustworthy and to be producing 'results'. The public wants to know how much money is going into administrative costs and how much into furthering the real work of the charity.

*eg* Greenpeace relies exclusively on support from individuals and foundations. It makes a deliberate point in its publicity of stating that it does not seek funds from governments, corporations or political parties and will not take individual donations if they compromise its independence of action. It is proud to state that it has no permanent allies or enemies. Such a principled stand means that Greenpeace must be entirely transparent if it is to avoid criticism from parties who have suffered from its direct action, or even the wider publics that support its cause.

To achieve a policy of openness, Greenpeace must make public its campaigns, its governance arrangements and its financial affairs. The annual reports reveal detailed information in all areas. The campaigns in climate, toxins, nuclear, oceans, forests, ocean dumping and genetic engineering are all specified and details provided of the main achievements in each area. An important part of retaining public support is highlighting successes.

In 2011, a number of campaigns were being run in parallel as part of a broad agenda including issues relating to climate, forests, oceans, agriculture, toxic waste and nuclear energy. One campaign aimed to clean up tinned tuna which resulted in John West shifting to sustainable tuna to protect marine reserves. The nets used meant that other sea life was swept up in them including threatened sharks, turtles and juvenile tuna, enough to fill 1 billion cans per year. Also some tuna stocks, are at risk of extinction from needlessly

## Tuna league table 2011

**Update: 26 July 2011:** At last, John West has announced it will change its policies, making its tinned tuna 100 per cent Fad-free and pole and line by 2016. All the companies listed on our league table have now agreed to end the use of Fads (fish aggregation devices) which are responsible for indiscriminate catches including sharks, rays and other fish. Read more >>

**Update, 12 April 2011:** Now Morrisons supermarkets have joined the rest of the UK's stores to commit to Fad-free tuna in all it's own-brand products for 2013. Fantastic news, this leaves just one brand using destructive tuna fishing methods: John West. Find out more here >>

**Update, 9 March 2011:** both Princes and Asda have committed to removing tuna caught using fish aggregating devices in combination with purse seine nets from their supply chains by 2014. Read more >>

Fishing practices used by the global tinned tuna industry are responsible for the death of marine animals including sharks and rays, and even rare and endangered sea turtles. Tuna stocks are also in trouble because of overfishing and widespread fishing methods that catch juvenile tuna.

With the UK being the second largest consumer of tinned tuna in the world, Britons have a lot of influence over the fish industry and we can put pressure on them to change. We surveyed major tinned tuna brands and retailers to see how their fishing practices stacked up. All have taken steps to improve their environmental performance in the

**Spread it**
Help get the word out by sharing the table using the buttons below or by emailing your contacts

331 tweets    **3296** Share

**Take Action**
You're not just getting tuna when you buy John West. Tell them to change their tuna
Email now

**Fish guide**
We've produced a free guide to help you

The campaign by Greenpeace, an independent, international organisation for environmental protection, has been successful in persuading some to change the type of nets used to catch tuna, which had been sweeping up young tuna and other forms of sea creatures – some endangered species – in the same net

*Source*: Greenpeace UK, www.greenpeace.org.uk

destructive fishing methods and overfishing. Princes also changed its sourcing methods after receiving 80,000 emails from Greenpeace supporters and agreed to state species information on its tins and stop the use of FADs (fish aggregation devices) which are harmful to other ocean wildlife. Other campaigns were aimed to protecting the Indonesian rain forests, and a nuclear-safety campaign was given added impetus by the Japanese tsunami and earthquake in 2011 and concerns over the safety of the Fukushima Daiichi nuclear plant.

The financial breakdown and uses and sources of funds are all detailed in the Greenpeace annual reports and reassuringly demonstrate that around half of any donation goes into front-line activity. All of this is designed to retain the support of the 2.8 million members spread over 41 countries and to demonstrate Greenpeace's credibility to external groups (Clydesdale, 2011; www.greenpeace.org.uk).

## Marketing implications

In general terms, the same principles of marketing apply equally to non-profit organisations as to any purely commercial concern (Sargeant, 1999). There are, however, a few specific points to note. A non-profit organisation might have quite a wide-ranging product portfolio, if the needs of both funders and customers or clients are taken into account. Their products might, for instance, vary from information, reassurance and advice to medical research and other practical help such as cash grants or equipment. Donors might be 'purchasing' association with a high-profile good cause or the knowledge that they have done a good deed by giving. Because the products vary so much, from the extremely intangible to the extremely tangible, and because there are so many different publics to serve, a strong corporate image and good marketing communication are particularly important to pull the whole organisation together.

If dispensing information and advice or increasing the profile of a cause are central objectives of the non-profit organisation, then marketing communication is an essential tool. This might mean using conventional advertising media, although that can be expensive for organisations such as smaller charities unless advertising agencies and media owners can be persuaded to offer their services cheap or free as a donation in kind.

*Publicity* can also be an invaluable tool for the non-profit organisation, not only because of its cost-effectiveness, but also because of its ability to reach a wide range of audiences. Publicity might encourage fund raising, help to educate people or generate clients or customers. Association with high-profile commercial sponsors can similarly help to spread the message, through publicity, sponsored fund-raising events or joint or sponsored promotions.

In sectors where a non-profit organisation offers a more clearly defined product to a specific target segment within a competitive market, then a more standard approach to marketing communication might be used. A university, for example, is offering degree courses to potential students. As discussed elsewhere in this book, it might use advertising media to tell potential students why this is the best place to study; printed material such as the prospectus, brochures and leaflets to give more detail about the institution, its location and the courses on offer; visits to schools and education fairs to meet potential recruits face to face; and publicity to increase awareness and improve its corporate image.

*Pricing* is applied somewhat differently in the non-profit sector than in the commercial world. As mentioned earlier, those providing income might be totally different from those receiving the product. It is accepted in most areas of the non-profit sector that the recipient might not have to bear the full cost of the service or product provided. In other words, the recipient's need comes first rather than the ability to pay. In the profit-making sector it is more likely to be the other way around: if you can pay for it, you can have it. Non-profit pricing, therefore, might be very flexible and varied. Some customers will not be asked to pay at all, others will be asked to make whatever donation they can afford for the service they have received, while others still will be charged a full market price.

Issues of distribution, process and physical evidence, where applicable, are similar for non-profit organisations to those of other types of organisation. The organisation has to ensure that the product or service is available when and where the customer or client can conveniently access it. This might or might not involve physical premises. Clearly, non-profit institutions such as universities, hospitals, museums and the like do operate from premises. They face the same issues as any other service provider of making sure that those premises are sufficiently well equipped to allow a service to be delivered and to deal with likely demand. They also have to realise that the premises are part of the marketing effort and contribute to the customer's or client's perception of quality. Prospective students visiting a university on an open day might not be able to judge the quality of the courses very well, but they can certainly tell whether the campus would be a good place for them to live and work, whether the teaching rooms are pleasant and well equipped, and how well-resourced the library and IT facilities seem to be.

Some non-profit organisations that focus mainly on giving information and advice by mail or by telephone do not, of course, need to invest in smart premises. Their priority is to ensure that customers or clients are aware of how to access the service and that enquiries are dealt with quickly, sympathetically and effectively.

_eg_

The Samaritans service exists to provide confidential counselling to those in a desperate emotional state and those who are contemplating suicide. The service is offered 24 hours a day from 198 branches staffed by volunteers who answer the telephones and raise local donations. There is no move towards developing a central call centre as it would undermine the whole structure of the service. Volunteers are carefully selected and trained locally, and give of their time for no charge.

In 2010, there were over 15,000 active listening volunteers, normally giving no more than 180 hours per year each. Although the caller may not care where the Samaritan is located, the organisation insists that its volunteers should not have to travel more than 60 miles to an office. There were 5 million calls in 2010 in the UK and Ireland and the operation has to be able to cope with that demand, especially during the recognised peaks between 10 p.m. and 2 a.m. Although 85 per cent are phone calls, an increasing number are now coming through e-mail and text. Each volunteer takes over 250 calls per year, and some calls can last for a long time, depending on the needs of the caller. It costs over £10 million per year to run the Samaritans. Each branch runs as an autonomous operation, generating its own funds to cover the c. £17,000 cost per phone line and office expenses (www.samaritans.org.uk).

Marketing in non-profit-making areas is rapidly evolving and the techniques used in commercial situations are being transferred, tested and evolved to cope better with the complexity of causes, ideas and attitude change in a wide range of situations. Marketing thinking is being applied to encouraging more 'users' and 'customers' to come forward to benefit from supportive contact for people or children at risk, such as that provided by the Samaritans and the NSPCC. It is also being applied backwards to attract resources into charitable organisations that often rely on voluntary staff and generous donations from individuals and corporations.

In addition, corporate sponsorship and affiliated programmes have been fast developing, as association with a number of the causes listed above does little harm to a corporate reputation. For example Tesco, Green Flag and Lindt all work with the RSPCA for their mutual benefit. Whether they take the form of joint promotions, supported advertising, or sponsored programmes and campaigns, the opportunities for cooperation are considerable.

# Chapter summary

- Although the variety of service products is very wide, all of them share some common characteristics that differentiate them from other types of product. With service products, for instance, there is often no transfer of ownership of anything, because a service is intangible. Services are also perishable, because they are generally performed at a particular time and are consumed as they are produced. This means that they cannot be stored in advance of demand, nor can they be kept in stock until a customer comes along. The customer is often directly involved in the production of the service product and thus the manufacture and delivery of the product cannot be separated. It also means that there is extensive interaction between the customer and the service provider's staff. Finally, because of the 'live' nature of the service experience and the central role of human interaction, it is very difficult to standardise the service experience.

- The normal model of a marketing mix consisting of the 4Ps is useful but insufficient for describing services, and an additional 3Ps – people, processes and physical evidence – have been added to deal with the extra dimensions peculiar to services. *People* takes account of the human interactions involved in the service product; *physical evidence* looks at the tangible elements that contribute either directly or indirectly to the creation, delivery, quality or positioning of the service; and *processes* defines the systems that allow the service to be created and delivered efficiently, reliably and cost-effectively.

- Service quality is hard to define and measure. Judgement of quality arises largely from customers' comparisons of what they expected from various facets of the service with what they think they actually received. Management can ensure that the service product is designed with the customer's real needs and wants in mind, that it is adequately resourced, that it is delivered properly, and that they try not to raise unrealistic expectations in the mind of the customer, but in the end, quality is a subjective issue. Staff are an important element of service and its delivery and must be fully qualified and trained to deal with customers and their needs, and to deliver the service reliably and consistently. The emphasis that is put on this will vary depending on whether staff have direct or indirect involvement with customers, and whether they are visible to customers or not. Like quality, productivity is a difficult management issue because of the live nature of services and the involvement of the customer in the process. Managers have to think and plan carefully in terms of staff recruitment and training, systems and technology, the service levels offered and the way in which customers interact with the service, to try to maintain control and efficiency in the service delivery system. Trying to manage supply and demand can also help to streamline productivity.

- Non-profit organisations, which might be in the public or private sector, form a specialist area of services marketing. They differ because they are likely to serve multiple publics; they have multiple objectives that can often be difficult to quantify; they offer services, but the funder of the service is likely to be different from the recipient of it; and finally, they are subject to closer scrutiny and tighter accountability than many other organisations. It is also possible that where non-profit organisations are in receipt of government funding or where their existence or operation is subject to regulation, there will be limits placed on their freedom to use the marketing mix as they wish. Pricing or promotion, for example, might be prescribed or set within narrow constraints.

# Questions for review and discussion

**14.1** What are the main characteristics that distinguish services from physical products?

**14.2** What are the ten criteria that affect customers' perceptions of service quality?

**14.3** Design a short questionnaire for assessing the quality of service offered by a local dental practice.

**14.4** In what ways might the following service organisations define and improve their productivity:

(a) a theme park;

(b) a university;

(c) a fast food outlet?

**14.5** In what ways do non-profit organisations differ from other types of business?

**14.6** What do you think might be the main sources of revenue for the following types of non-profit organisation and what revenue generation problems do you think each faces:

(a) a small local charity;

(b) a National Health Service hospital;

(c) a public museum?

## CASE STUDY 14

# FAST FOOD: FEEDING THE HUNGRY TRAVELLER

Ever fancied cooking eggs or serving soup without spilling it at 100 mph? That's the challenge facing onboard rail caterers every day. Serving meals on trains began in 1879 when a dining room carriage was added to a London to Leeds train, and that had grown to nearly a 1,000 dining cars a day by the 1970s. Isambard Kingdom Brunel was being prophetic, if slightly conservative, when he said in 1831, 'The time is not far off, when we shall be able to take our coffee and write whilst going noiselessly and smoothly at 45 mph' (as quoted by Webster, 2009). Things really started to change, some say for the worse, when the rail network was privatised in the 1990s and full catering services began to be withdrawn in favour of snack trolleys which now account for most onboard catering. Mintel's (2010) finding that only 7 per cent of rail travellers felt that eating/drinking onboard is part of the train travel experience shows just how far the tradition and culture of the dining car has been forgotten. The fact is that the space taken up by the preparation and serving of meals can be more

profitably used for seats and luggage storage. Arriva even removed the more compact food shops from its trains. It seems that snack trolleys take up less space and passengers are more likely to buy food and drink if it is brought to their seats, rather than them having to wander off down the train to find it, facing the dilemma of whether to risk leaving their luggage unattended at their seat or take it all with them.

Train operators have also found that the demand for catering has changed with modern lifestyles. Many people are used to either skipping lunch or having something on the run. Certainly, the demand for full meals is no longer what it used to be. Although breakfast and evening-meal demand is still there, lunchtime is much less clear-cut, given the alternatives and passengers' lifestyles. Instead snacking is more popular and the trend towards station catering at the larger stations has reflected this trend. There is now a wide array of food franchises at stations, burgers, pasties, sandwiches, pizza and so on. When the new Eurostar terminal opened in 2007 at St Pancras, it had more alternative places to eat than most large shopping centres and also had a range of pubs offering snacks and bar meals. Most of these undercut onboard catering in terms of price. Mintel (2010) found that half of people who said they had been on a train in the last two years had eaten/drunk onboard and over 40 per cent of them felt that onboard catering was too expensive, while one-third brought their own food and drink aboard. It's so easy, especially if you have time to kill in the station before departure, to grab something that's appropriately packaged for carrying around and eating on the go, and that is sufficient for most journeys in the UK other than the longest distances. The station offerings are also well researched by the professional fast food outlets with a view to variety and the usage situation, and this all makes the onboard snack trolley look outdated and limited. Nearly one-quarter of those who had eaten/drunk on a train said that the choices were too limited.

So, the onboard catering has gravitated towards the snacks trolley which can be pushed through the carriages, and so as long as you are not seated towards the end of its run, there is some choice! Actually, the operators claim 98.5 per cent availability for trolley food (Walmsley 2011) but, of course, the key issue for passengers is the breadth and depth of choice, rather than the availability of what is actually stocked. That said, not even a trolley service is offered on the fast routes, such as Newbury to Paddington or short-haul commuter routes. There has been some experimentation with new catering formats. Virgin Trains' North of England service has introduced new facilities such as Virgin Shops which occupy some carriage space and offer food and drink and a few travellers' requirements, such as magazines. On First Great Western, Express Cafés provide coffee and warm panini, along with a fully refrigerated display space for a loss of just 20 seats. Another innovation is pre-purchased buffet vouchers which give the traveller a discount on goods purchased from onboard buffet bars or trolleys.

However, it's the full-service catering that has seen the greatest decline in use. In some cases, this is due to the need to sacrifice food for speed. On the London to Bristol route, for example, the reduction in some trains from 8 to 7 carriages means faster journey times, but the loss of dining facilities (*Modern Railways*, 2010). Now it's only the very long-distance trains that also operate restaurant cars and/or at-seat service of meals. In part that's due to overcrowding, so there is a premium for extra seats that could take fare-paying passengers, and thus catering investment has suffered. Also, the development of high speed commuter networks, such as Bournemouth to Waterloo, or Euston to Milton Keynes, means that journey times are now too short, and the demand for higher density seating too great to justify restaurant cars (*Modern Railways*, 2007).

Much depends on the train operator's attitude towards onboard catering; is it a profit centre that must pay its way or is it a means of providing added-value to the service, forming the basis of differentiation for the overall travel experience (Canizal Villarino et al., 2008)? Is it part of an overall package that includes car parking provision, ticket services and station facilities or free standing?

There has been a trend towards bundling meals in with ticket prices on higher margin first class tickets (such as the £350 first class return fare between London and Manchester). Breakfast time offers the greatest opportunity for onboard meal service, because later in the day there are more options for consumers who are perhaps looking forward to a full business lunch or a meal when they arrive home. The scale of the breakfast requirements across all trains is staggering, with current average weekly requirements amounting to 16,200 sausages, 15,000 rashers of bacon, and 40,000 eggs (Canizal Villarino et al., 2008). Apart from breakfast, some trials were given to chef-led menus on longer routes but they never really took off. On First Great Western, Pullman dining is down to just two trains in each direction from London to Plymouth, offering three-course meals freshly cooked by an onboard chef. Passengers can chose between two starters and three main courses with vegetarian options. Excluding wine, that costs over £27, and is available to all ticket holders. Meanwhile, the Travelling Chef menu is offered on ten services, offering a range of baguettes, breakfast platters, light meals and deli sandwiches (*Modern Railways*, 2010).

Overall, however, high level provision although possible, has a low take-up from customers and it adds to the cost base of the operator which has to be clawed back through higher fares, regardless of whether they are used or not (*Modern Railways*, 2010).

In most European countries except Germany, train catering is outsourced. In Germany, onboard catering has undergone a revolution. Instead of closing down onboard restaurants in 2002 after years of dismal performance, DBB, the train operator, has given them a quality and marketing overhaul. Although only 5 per cent of passengers dine in the onboard restaurant, many more enjoy onboard catering and it has proved a good selling point against other modes of transport. The emphasis has been on quality, not cheapness as it can't compete on price with the catering provision found at stations. About two-thirds of consumers using onboard restaurants are first class passengers and they are offered an in-seat service. DBB also uses promotion a lot, for example using famous chefs and featuring promotions on fine wines. The spin-off benefits are great, with a typical pasta promotion selling 18,000 portions.

In France, the emphasis is on assessing customer needs and providing them what they want. In first class the price of a ticket includes a gourmet boxed meal, reflecting the need for rapid service. The trend is away from the sandwich to cooked dishes and 80 per cent of passengers think that the bar is a good feature of rail travel and gives it the edge over other modes. Train operator SNCF contributes to the higher service costs of onboard catering, to assist in profitability. With limited carrying capacity, the TGV (high speed service on longer haul routes) bars have some 50 different items and the range of hot food offered is changed at regular intervals to remain fresh in consumers' minds. There are also regional promotions and promotions surrounding special events.

In Russia, there is vast rail network, with trains mostly offering substandard catering, but on the St Petersburg to Moscow high-speed link there is a modern food-service facility. For passengers in business class there is breakfast or dinner included in the ticket, and the passenger can indicate special preferences when booking the ticket. The meal is delivered to the seat, often with a chinaware service. For economy class passengers, the bistro car seats 40 and places can be reserved when buying a ticket. For €10, there is a substantial breakfast available until 12 noon (Matveeva, 2011).

It is, therefore, possible to take a narrow view of onboard catering as practised by UK train operators or a more market orientated view, as part of the overall travel experience. The demand for food will depend upon the class of travel, time and length of journey, different eating habits and whether an inclusive meal or needs based service solution is appropriate. Either way, onboard catering should be fresh, competitively priced, and easy to consume. It is the choice between the airline model with food for all passengers which is included in the ticket price, thus achieving economies of scale, or the needs based model, assuming, of course, that the passenger is actually given the option (Canizal Villarino *et al.*, 2008).

*Sources*: Canizal Villarino *et al.* (2008); Matveeva (2011); Mintel (2010); *Modern Railways* (2007, 2010); Walmsley (2011); Webster (2009).

## Questions

1  How might consumer attitudes and buying behaviour differ between eating on a train and eating out in their home town?

2  In terms of service quality, what could go wrong with onboard train catering? How could these risks be minimised?

3  DBB in Germany operates its own onboard catering services, whereas other train operators in Europe contract them out. What are the advantages and disadvantages of these alternative operating models?

4  To what extent do you think the UK train operators are making the most of opportunities for onboard catering? What more could they do?

## References for chapter 14

Baker, R. (2011) 'Oxfam Highlights Global Food Crisis', *Marketing Week*, 1 June.

*Belfast Telegraph* (2010) 'Hotel Starts Human Bed-warmer Trials', *Belfast Telegraph*, 18 January.

Bitner, M., Brown, S. and Meuter, M. (2000) 'Technology Infusion in Service Encounters', *Journal of the Academy of Marketing Science*, 28 (1), pp. 138–49.

Borland, S. (2011) 'Rude, Arrogant, Lazy', *Daily Mail*, 23 February.

Boulton, J. and Miller, H. (2011) 'We Hope You've Had a Good Sleep on Your Flight, Now it's Time to . . .', *People*, 19 June.

Bridge, M. (2011) 'Don't Lose Too Many Pounds with Your Gym Membership', *The Times*, 15 January.

Brignall, M. (2009) 'But Follow Our Top Money-Saving Tips and You Might Yet Beat the System', *The Guardian*, 12 September.

Brinsden, J. (2011) 'Charities Bulletin, July 2011', *Mondaq Business Briefing*, 4 August.

Canizal Villarino, M., Fresia, F., Wachholz, M., Freeling, C., Navolokova, D., Mecke, B. and Whitehall, B. (2008) 'F&B in Trains: Driven by Logistics', *Food Service Europe & Middle East*, 12 February.

Caruana, A., Money, A. and Berthon, P. (2000) 'Service Quality and Satisfaction – the Moderating Role of Value', *European Journal of Marketing*, 34 (11/12), pp. 1338–53.

Christopher, M., Payne, A. and Ballantyne, D. (1994) *Relationship Marketing: Bringing Quality, Customer Service and Marketing Together*, 2nd edn. Butterworth-Heinemann.

Clydesdale, S. (2011) 'Same Fish, New Business Model', Blogpost, 17 August, accessed via www.greenpeace.org.uk/blog/oceans/same-fish-new-business-model-20110817.

Cowell, D. (1984) *The Marketing of Services*, Butterworth-Heinemann.

Cuddeford-Jones, M. (2011) 'Mystery Shopping', *Marketing Week*, 10 March.

Devlin, S. and Dong, H. (1994) 'Service Quality from the Customers' Perspective', *Marketing Research*, 6 (1), pp. 5–13.

ENP Newswire (2010) 'Stagecoach First Major UK Bus Operator with Smartcard Ready Fleet', *ENP Newswire*, 27 October.

ENP Newswire (2011) 'Emirates Cabin Crew Numbers Cruise over 12,000', *ENP Newswire*, 14 March.

Epper Hoffman, K. (2010) 'More Banks Try to Seed Innovation Through Labs', *American Banker*, 5 February.

*Esmerk* (2010) 'Denmark: New Hotels Put Pressure on Copenhagen Market', *Esmerk*, 2 September.

*Estates Gazette* (2011) 'Virgin Active is Doubling in Size in the UK with the Takeover of Rival Gym', *Estates Gazette*, 30 April.

Goodman, M. (2011) 'The Secret Ingredient for Success', *Sunday Times*, 6 March.

Gray, S. (2011) 'Passengers 'Mutiny' on Flight Delayed Seven Hours at Heathrow', *The Times*, 28 May.

*Guardian Unlimited* (2010) 'Really Getting Somewhere', *Guardian Unlimited*, 17 November.

Heskett, J., Sasser, W. and Schlesinger, L. (1997) *The Service Profit Chain*, The Free Press.

Hsin-Yin, L. (2011) 'Ability to Speak Chinese Dialects Valued by Taiwanese Carriers', *Central News Agency*, 12 March.

Jack, A. (2010) 'Charity that Targets Air Passengers Spent Millions to Raise Only Thousands', *Financial Times*, 7 July.

Jacobs, R. (2011) 'Virgin Buys Rival Gym Business', *Financial Times*, 27 April.

Jeory, T. (2010) 'Smartcard Revolution in UK Travel', *Express on Sunday*, 5 September.

Johnston, T. (2011) 'The Death of the Edinburgh International Film Festival?', *Time Out*, 25 June.

Kotler, P. (1982) *Marketing for Non-Profit Organisations* (2nd edn), Prentice Hall.

Lee, R. (2011) 'Mongolian Airlines Sells Tickets for "Ghost" Flights', *Korea Herald*, 6 July.

Lewis, L. (2011) 'The Captain Speaking: Rowdy Travellers May Face a Heavy Landing', *The Times*, 20 April.

Lovelock, C. and Weinberg, C. (1984) *Marketing for Public and Non-Profit Managers*, John Wiley and Sons.

Lovelock, C., Vandermerwe, S. and Lewis, B. (1999) *Services Marketing*, Financial Times, Prentice Hall.

Lowbridge, C. (2011) '22 New Trams, Smartcard Ticketing Are Lined Up for City's Extended Network', *Nottingham Evening Post*, 30 March.

*M2 Presswire* (2010) 'East Coast Service Disruption Update at 14.15hrs', *M2 Presswire*, 21 December.

Madden, C. (2011) 'Dublin Hotels Increase Occupancy but Rates Fall', *Irish Times*, 23 February.

*Marketing and Business Development* (2010) 'UK Health & Fitness Clubs Market', *Marketing and Business Development*, 28 July.

Mathews, B. and Clark, M. (1996) 'Comparability of Quality Determinants in Internal and External Service Encounters', in *Proceedings: Workshop on Quality Management in Services VI*, Universidad Carlos III de Madrid, 15–16 April.

Matveeva, J. (2011) 'New Era for Russian Train Catering', *Food Service Europe & Middle East*, 19 April.

Mintel (2010) 'Onboard Catering', *Mintel Leisure Intelligence*, May, accessed via http://academic.mintel.com/sinatra/oxygen_academic/search_results/show&/display/id=480776.

*Modern Railways* (2007) 'Is Commuterisation Affecting the Intercity Catering Product?', *Modern Railways*, September.

*Modern Railways* (2010) 'FGW Catering Keeps Pace with the Times', *Modern Railways*, June.

O'Carroll, L. (2011) 'Ireland's "Ghost Hotels" to be Boarded Up', *The Guardian*, 1 February.

Odell, M. (2011) 'MPs Call for Shake-up After Travel Chaos', *Financial Times*, 12 May.

Oxfam (2011) *Growing a Better Future*, report produced by Oxfam, updated 20 June, accessed via www.oxfam.org.uk/resources/papers/growing-better-future.html.

Parasuraman, A., Zeithaml, V. and Berry, L. (1985) 'A Conceptual Model of Service Quality and Its Implications for Future Research', *Journal of Marketing*, 49 (Fall), pp. 41–50.

Parasuraman, A., Zeithaml, V. and Berry, L. (1988) 'SERVQUAL: A Multiple Item Scale for Measuring Consumer Perceptions of Service Quality', *Journal of Retailing*, 64 (1), pp. 13–37.

Pratten, J. (2004) 'Customer Satisfaction and Waiting Staff', *International Journal of Contemporary Hospitality Management*, 16 (6), p. 385 *et seq.*

Rayport, J. and Sviokla, J. (1994) 'Managing in the Marketspace', *Harvard Business Review*, 72 (November/December), pp. 2–11.

Rkaina, S. (2011) 'Getting Smart is the Way to Travel in Discount Style', *Bristol Evening Post*, 21 January.

Rose, N. (2011) 'Where There's a Will Should There Be Regulation?', *Guardian Unlimited*, 16 July.

Sargeant, A. (1999) *Marketing Management for Nonprofit Organizations*, Oxford University Press.

Sasser, W., Olsen, R. and Wyckoff, D. *et al.* (1978) *Management of Service Operations: Text, Cases and Readings*, Allyn & Bacon.

Shoffman, M. (2011) 'Mystery Shopping Reveals "Shocking" Quality of Wills', *Financial Adviser*, 21 July.

Shostack, L. (1977) 'Breaking Free from Product Marketing', *Journal of Marketing*, 41 (April), pp. 73–80.

*Sligo Weekender* (2010) 'Sligo Has Largest Oversupply of Hotel Beds in the Country', *Sligo Weekender*, 28 September.

Smithers, R. (2011) 'Chiltern Railways Frees Passengers From "Ransom" of Extortionate Walk-up Fares', *Guardian Unlimited*, 28 July.

Walmsley, I. (2011) 'Meals on Wheels', *Modern Railways*, June.

Webster, B. (2009) 'A Leisurely Meal Gives Way to Fast Food as Last Dining Cars Are Dumped for Extra Seats', *The Times*, 7 March.

Zeithaml, V., Parasuraman, A. and Berry, L. (1990) *Delivering Quality Service: Balancing Customer Perceptions and Expectations*, The Free Press.

# Index

# Index of company names